.

FREEDOM'S ANCHOR:
AN INTRODUCTION TO NATURAL LAW JURISPRIDENCE IN AMERICAN CONSTITUTIONAL HISTORY

by

Andrew P. Napolitano

FREEDOM'S ANCHOR:
AN INTRODUCTION TO NATURAL LAW JURISPRIDENCE IN AMERICAN CONSTITUTIONAL HISTORY

by

Andrew P. Napolitano

ACADEMICA PRESS
WASHINGTON~LONDON

Library of Congress Cataloging-in-Publication Data

Names: Napolitano, Andrew P. (author)
Title: Freedom's anchor : an introduction to natural law jurisprudence in american constitutional history | Andrew P. Napolitano
Description: Washington : Academica Press, 2023. | Includes references.
Identifiers: LCCN 2022949446 | ISBN 9781680537079 (hardcover) | 9781680537086 (paperback) | 9781680537093 (e-book)

I see the liberty of the individual not only as a great moral good in itself (or, with Lord Acton, as the highest political good), but also as the necessary condition for the flowering of all other goods that mankind cherishes: moral virtue, civilization, the arts and sciences, economic prosperity. Out of liberty, then, stem the glories of civilized life. But liberty has always been threatened by the encroachments of power, power which seeks to suppress, control, cripple, tax, and exploit the fruits of liberty and production.*

– Murray Rothbard (1926-1995)

***

ALSO BY ANDREW P. NAPOLITANO

Constitutional Chaos: What Happens When
Government Breaks its Own Laws.

The Constitution in Exile: How the Federal Government Has
Seized Power by Rewriting the Supreme Law of the Land

A Nation of Sheep

Dred Scott's Revenge: A Legal History of Race and Freedom in America

Lies the Government Told You: Myth, Power,
and Deception in American History

It is Dangerous to Be Right When the Government
Is Wrong: The Case of Personal Freedom

The Freedom Answer Book

Theodore and Woodrow: How Two American
Presidents Destroyed Constitutional Freedom

Suicide Pact: The Radical Expansion of Presidential Powers
and the Lethal Threat to American Liberty

DEDICATION

This work is dedicated to the memory
And to the intellectual offspring of
Walter F. Murphy
Late McCormick Professor of Jurisprudence at
Princeton University
And to
Charles E. Rice
Late Professor of Law at the
University of Notre Dame Law School,
Whose joint understanding of the laws of nature
Happily stirred the author's thinking in ways
That can never be fully repaid.

CONTENTS

ACKNOWLEDGEMENTS

No work of this magnitude is the result of one person's ideas or labors. Though the concept for this book has been teasing my brain since my undergraduate and law student days, the work itself – which took four years to research and write – did not begin to coalesce as a realistic project until I was a Visiting Professor of Law at Brooklyn Law School. There I met the three colleagues without whose labors this book would not have come about.

Randal John Meyer and Mark Potkewitz were my students when we first met. They were attracted to the idea of this book and I was attracted to their thought processes and work habits. Randal is now a sought after lawyer and lobbyist in Washington, DC and Mark is Co-Director at the Ulster Centre for Legal Innovation in Belfast, Ireland. They worked long and hard hours in tandem, each adding a different strength to the work.

Kimberly Sialiano Catala has been my Research Fellow at Fox News Channel for seven years and for most of my time at Brooklyn Law School. She not only worked tirelessly on this book, but also was the glue that kept it together and the energy that moved it forward. In those years, she found time to get married and bring two beautiful babies into the world. She has been my right hand throughout this work. Without her, the book simply would not have come to pass.

I am also deeply grateful to David Gordon, Ph.D., who generously read the manuscript of this book and offered many helpful improvements.

Whatever merits, if any, this book offers are the result of the diligence and prudence of my three youthful lawyer colleagues and Dr. Gordon. Whatever weaknesses may be found here are mine and mine alone.

Andrew P. Napolitano
Hampton Township, New Jersey
January 2023

INTRODUCTION

Natural law should be like an uncompromising demon breathing down the neck of all the legislators of the world.[1]

– Leszek Kołakowski (1927-2009)

What is the Natural Law Tradition? Is the natural law related to the medieval church and the nature of man as a divine creation? Or is it a philosophical methodology linked to Enlightenment ideas of personhood? Perhaps it is a legal rule with specific form and content incorporated by the Ninth Amendment to the U.S. Constitution? The truth is that the natural law is often confounded among many of these questions, and as such, we must look backwards throughout history to discern its complete meaning if we are to look forward and see how we may use it to achieve the best form of government.

The Natural Law Tradition (NLT) teaches us that there are certain universal rights *intrinsic* to human nature and discoverable through reason. But first, let us start at the beginning. What is a right? A right is an indefeasible claim that stems from our humanity, from within — not from the government, despite what many would have us believe — and our humanity is a gift from our Creator. As such, we exercise our inalienable rights on a daily basis without giving a second thought to the fact that they are innate. Thinkers from St. Thomas Aquinas, to Thomas Jefferson, to the Rev. Dr. Martin Luther King, Jr. have all argued that our rights are a natural part of our humanity. We own our bodies, therefore we own the gifts that emanate from our bodies. So, under the Natural Law Tradition our right to life, our right to develop our personalities, our right to think as we wish, to say what we think, to publish what we say, our right to worship or not worship, our right to defend ourselves, to use our own property as we see fit, to travel, our right to due process – fairness – from the government, and our right to be left alone, are all rights with which we are born, and – in the case of life – conceived. More specifically, such rights are claims made against others, including the government, to protect our freedoms.

Even those who question or reject the existence of a Creator can embrace the concept of natural rights, for they can accept that our exercise of human reason leads us to discern right from wrong, and in turn, discover truth. An atheist will agree that there are certain basic values acknowledged everywhere, in all times and circumstances. After all, even a person deprived of senses has the ability to reason.

Take, for example, a list of truisms, innate knowledge that all humans possess and no one can seriously challenge, such as at some point I did not exist, now I am alive, I want to stay alive, I can think and hope, things change (hot coffee left alone cools, tree leaves fall, spring turns into summer etc.). Implied in these truisms are opportunities to do what you recognize to be right and to avoid what you conclude is wrong. How do we know these things? Because we can reason. And reason has taught us that the freedoms of thought, speech, association, religion, self-defense, privacy, consensual personal intimacy, property ownership and use, travel, and fair treatment from the government, to name a few, are worth protecting.

Moreover, Thomas Jefferson – who wrote the Declaration of Independence – and James Madison – the scrivener at the Constitutional Convention and the author of the Bill of Rights – were clear in their articulations that the premise of America at its birth was that our rights are personal and natural because they come from our humanity, not from the government. When Jefferson wrote that we are endowed by our Creator with certain inalienable rights, he was marrying the nation at its birth to the ancient principles of the natural law that have animated the Judeo-Christian tradition: Aristotle (knowledge), Saint Augustine (revelation), and Saint Thomas Aquinas (reason). Those principles have operated as a break on all governments that recognize them by enunciating the concept of natural rights. As such, not only do our inherent rights exist in the absence of government, but they are immune from government interference. Natural rights cannot be abrogated by the popular will, the stroke of a legislator's pen, nor a chief executive's order. It is the choice of every individual whether to give them up. Neither our neighbors nor the government can make those choices for us, because we are without the moral or legal authority to interfere with another's natural rights. You may consent to the curtailment of your own rights, but not the curtailment of mine.

To assure that no government would infringe upon the natural rights of anyone in our fledgling country, the Founders incorporated Jefferson's thesis underlying the Declaration into the Constitution, and shortly thereafter Madison drafted the Ninth Amendment to cement the government's obligation to recognize and protect the existence and exercise of these unarticulated natural rights residing within all of us. Undoubtedly, the prominence of the natural rights discourse from thinkers in the colonial era, as well the common folks played a crucial role in guiding the creation and development of the American Republic.

For these reasons, the recognition of a right as natural or fundamental or pre-political is not merely an academic exercise, but one that has real-life consequences. For when the government seeks to curtail rights under the guise of the common safety or refuses to acknowledge new, unnamed but innate rights, a person harmed thereby has a right to challenge the government.

Through an extensive review of saints, philosophers, revolutionaries, scholars, and jurists, this book aims to demonstrate the prevalence of natural rights and natural law in the rhetoric and understanding of Americans during the early days of our country's founding, the Framers' acceptance of such, and ultimately, the government's duty to protect natural rights.

The book examines philosophers and theologians from around the globe who influenced the American Framers. In order to understand the intellectual context surrounding the imperial crisis between Great Britain and the colonies, we must appreciate the omnipresent influence of natural law philosophy in early-modern Europe and America and explore its underlying premises.

Western Philosophy begins with the Greeks, and so much attention is given to Aristotle, who was deeply concerned about the moral and legal status of the individual within the community. He recognized that there are universal, common laws, which are unwritten, eternal, and cannot be changed. Aristotle, a Greek, St. Augustine, an African, and St. Thomas Aquinas, a European, each strengthened natural law theory by answering contrary arguments, such as, how there may be a universal natural law when the laws and customs amongst peoples differ. Aristotle taught that universal laws are knowable through our senses. Augustine's argument was that right and wrong can be discerned universally through revelation; and belief in God's goodness impelled understanding natural rights. Aquinas argued that reason is the sole guide to morality because we can discover such with or without divine revelation, and therefore, all of humanity has access to universal norms.

In discussing the secular influence of Hugo Grotius in the 1600s, one can see the neutral aspects that underlie the natural law. Many would take issue with giving the force of "law" to religious interpretations; after all, "the law can no longer rely on doctrines in which citizens are entitled to disbelieve."[2] Grotius, well-known for his contributions to the doctrine of individual natural rights, contemplated how people behaved in society and developed an approach conducive to the prevailing scientific principles of his time. Grotius looked to Aquinas, but also noted that human nature contains not just reason, but passion as well.

Any review of early philosophers would be incomplete without delving into Thomas Hobbes' and John Locke's ideas about the purpose of government. Hobbes rejected Aristotle's belief that man's nature is teleological (i.e., ordered toward a particular end or purpose). Whereas Aquinas had argued that the human person is directed to one ultimate end, namely God, Hobbes believed man had no particular end, and as such, a government could not exist for the sake of instructing man in virtue.

Instead, for thinkers such as Hobbes and Locke, the exclusive task of a government was protecting an individual's natural rights, foremost among these being the right to self-preservation. Each saint, philosopher, scholar, and jurist, working upon the foundations of his predecessors, and applying his own reason and analysis, advanced and refined natural law concepts. Their works would, in turn, influence generations of lawyers and judges who would enshrine in their arguments and opinions enduring natural law principles that would influence the leaders behind the American Revolution.

Locke, whose ideas greatly influenced Jefferson and Madison, believed in the separation of Church and State, and that one's greater obligations were to secure eternal salvation over secular freedom. Thus, to Locke, the divine law – the laws of nature – were superior to written laws. The commands of a properly formed conscience are to take precedence over human law.

The NLT passed to early English lawyers and judges through official court reports and exhaustive treatises written by giants such as Sir Edward Coke and Sir William Blackstone. By looking at the common law, Coke believed one could trace the refinement of natural law principles through the refractory lens of reason. He emphasized the need to understand the purpose of a law in his landmark opinion in *Calvin's Case* (1608); and in *Dr. Bonham's case* (1610), he recognized that the natural law can, *sua sponte*, void an act of Parliament that runs contrary to it. Blackstone published an equally important work entitled *Commentaries of the Laws of England*, which embraced the common law and presented jurists and lawyers with a methodological framework for arguing and deciding cases.

Blackstone's treatise contains numerous references to the natural law and indeed, characterized it as "superior" to all other "human," positive law.[3] However, Blackstone, a champion of parliamentary supremacy, did not share Coke's view that judges could legitimately disregard legislation that they considered inconsistent with reason or with the law of nature.[4] Blackstone allows for a legislature to abridge or destroy the natural rights only when the owner of such rights engages in behavior tantamount to a forfeiture of those rights. If Parliament were to defy the law of nature (a prospect that Blackstone thought almost inconceivable), the only remedy would lie in the streets rather than in the courts. Blackstone, though clearly establishing the existence of the natural law as a superior legal rule, gave a degree of deference to parliamentary action broader than what was accepted by most of the public mind in America at the time of the ratification.[5] This stood in stark contrast, as Jefferson would later argue, to "a universal and almost uncontroverted position in the several states," that "the purposes of society do not require us to surrender all of our [natural] rights to our ordinary governors."[6]

Colonial revolutionaries invoked and used the principles of Coke and Blackstone, not only in early American tribunals, but also in the streets and in the press, as they relied on natural law philosophy for ideological support of the American Revolution when rallying against the grievous affronts to their liberties, such as the Intolerable Acts, the Stamp Act, and Coercive Acts to name a few. The numerous revolutionary pamphlets and broadsides that survive today provide us with a first-hand, comprehensive account of the views of the wider American population at the time of the Revolution, many of whom were calling for some form of action – any action – to respond to the debilitating taxation inflicted upon them by the English crown.

For example, in a widely circulated pamphlet entitled *Rights of British Colonies Asserted and Proved (1763)*, the famous lawyer James Otis insisted that without colonial representation in Parliament, that body had no right to tax the colonies, for "if a shilling in the pound may be taken from me against my will, why may not twenty shillings; and if so, why may not my liberty and my life?"[7] Invoking natural law as a limit on Parliament, Otis makes clear that the colonists need not look back to the old *Magna Charta* to discern from where all human rights originate for they are rooted in the law of nature. Similarly, Thomas Jefferson's *A Summary View of the Rights of British America* (1774) was yet another pamphlet widely read that was grounded on legal, historical claims, and ultimately, the Lockean natural rights of man. Jefferson "rejected all parliamentary authority whatever over the colonies" while still acknowledging that allegiance was owed only to the king.[8] After all, the First Continental Congress was not originally set upon the notion of breaking allegiance to the Crown. It did establish a committee on colonial "Rights, Grievances and Means of Redress," and the committee pondered whether the colonists should use natural law reasoning as the basis of its condemnation of the behavior of the English Parliament. The prevailing wisdom sought not to displace the natural law with the positive law of constitutions, charters, and compacts; it sought to run them as parallel or complementary.

And so it was Jefferson and Madison, who during the revolutionary era note the heavy influence of natural law reasoning. They understood and embraced it in their legal arguments, their polemic pamphlets, and their private writings. A concern for natural rights inspired their indignation and nurtured their outrage. It was through the natural law that the thinking, writing, and arguing colonists viewed the legacy of the common law they inherited from their English forbearers and cultivated through their communities and institutions. The Declaration of Independence, for example, echoes Aquinas in proclaiming truths to be *self-evident* and rights to be *unalienable*.

The caselaw argued by the leading lawyers of the American colonial era reveals that many colonists were not only familiar with the idea of the natural law, they employed such reasoning in their understanding of their inherent rights even while suffering under an oppressive rule of the King. In *Paxton's case* (1761), Otis illustrates to a colonial jury how the broad authority granted to British officials by general warrants had been abused – a practice he believed was incompatible with English liberties. According to Otis, the almost absolute and unlimited discretion granted to officials and their informers to search the colonists' homes interfered with the colonists' rights to privacy; and, he asked what is the origin of that right to privacy?

They looked to the Natural Law Tradition. In *Hancock's Case (1768)*, the future president John Adams defended a wealthy merchant who was charged with smuggling in violation of the Sugar Act by questioning the validity of the legislation under which the case was tried since it denied his client the right of a jury trial (it was heard before an admiralty court). Moreover, Adams and Josiah Quincy II later defended British soldiers accused of killing innocent colonial civilians, on the grounds that self defense is an innate right for all – quoting Blackstone – "founded in principles that are permanent, uniform and universal, always comfortable to the feelings of humanity and the indelible rights of mankind."[9] Through these various cases, we see the colonial position gradually shift from opposition to specific parliamentary efforts to tax the colonies to an eventual appeal for full independence. Natural law philosophy and discourse provided Americans with legitimate recourse to counter British claims of parliamentary sovereignty. The American Revolution having been won, the Constitutional Convention can be seen as a quest to reformulate the founding document and amend the Articles of Confederation either so as to structure better the government of the burgeoning nation, and facilitate commercial intercourse, or to enshrine a class of bankers and merchants with regulatory control over that commercial intercourse. It would take four months of collaboration, debate, and revision between the delegates to produce the text of the Constitution of the United States, which was then passed on to the governments of the several states for their ratifications. The Convention was marked by alliances, factions, and coalitions; particularly, a division between the Federalists (including Madison, Alexander Hamilton, John Jay, George Washington, and Benjamin Franklin), who pushed for a stronger central government, and the Anti-Federalists (Patrick Henry, George Mason, George Clinton, and Sam Adams), who feared a strong central government would threaten personal liberties and state sovereignty.

Madison's Notes provide contemporary readers with the most complete account of the proceedings of the Convention. These notes shed light on the substantive issues raised at the Convention, and demonstrate the numerous references to natural law made by the delegates. Delegates spent hours laboring over particular language and clauses. Through their discussions, it became clear that the Anti-Federalists would not be satisfied with merely a Constitution, but also would need an instrument of equal power and validity – a Bill of Rights – to restrain the new government.

The ratification debates within and amongst the states, would focus primarily on the main point of contention: the absence or insertion of a Bill of Rights as a condition for approving the Constitution. The Federalists saw a Bill of Rights as a danger to liberties since it could be understood by some as protection for only those rights expressly enumerated. The Anti-Federalists, however, wary of a strong central government, felt the absence of a Bill of Rights would render individual rights vulnerable to abrogation by a federal government untethered by any meaningful negative constraints. Though the Federalists began with a tremendous lead, securing ratification victories in Delaware, Pennsylvania, New Jersey, Georgia, and Connecticut, the Anti-Federalists, won a key victory in Massachusetts, and impressed upon enough state conventions their desire for a Bill of Rights to secure more firmly fundamental liberties and freedoms – natural rights – against what they viewed as a federal leviathan that would surely, they feared, develop.

What is gained from this examination of the ratification and the Massachusetts Compromise, in a general sense, is the understanding that the *sine qua non* to the passage of the Constitution by nine or more states was the express eventual written recognition of pre-political, natural rights into the document: "The necessity of amendments is universally admitted. It is a word which is reechoed from every part of the continent," remarked Virginia's Patrick Henry.[10] Even Madison agreed to this. "[I]t may not be thought necessary to provide [enumerated constitutional] limits for the legislative power in [England], yet a different opinion prevails in the United States."[11] Thus, the Constitution, so exhaustively debated with compromise, would need to be amended in its infancy.

Under the guidance, supervision, and editorial control of Madison, his Constitution was amended. Once assembled, the First Congress was the venue for Madison systematically to lay out all his proposed amendments. In doing so, Madison restated all the popular arguments for and against the Bill of Rights; after all, he needed to manage two competing arguments: the disingenuous argument of Hamilton, that any enumeration of rights "could be used to justify any unwarranted expansion of federal power" as the government is of enumerated powers, and to enumerate rights implies areas of rights the government can reach into beyond those enumerated; and, the Madisonian argument that "any right excluded from enumeration would be jeopardized."[12] Madison's solution was an amendment to be included that would make explicit that the Bill of Rights did not contain an exhaustive list of rights. This would allow Madison to put a capstone upon the Anti-Federalist-required enumeration of rights to assuage any concerns that he, and his Federalist colleagues harbored, that the simple act of giving voice to certain rights could lead future congresses, executives, jurists, and generations to believe themselves only to be possessed of – or restrained from tampering with – the rights explicitly listed in the federal constitution.

Thus, through what we now know as the Ninth Amendment, "[t]he enumeration in the Constitution, of certain rights, shall not be construed to deny or disparage others *retained* by the people,"[13] Madison incorporated the natural law "principle that constitutions are not made to create rights in the people, but in recognition of, and in order to preserve them, and if any are specifically numerated and specially guarded, it is only because they are peculiarly important or peculiarly exposed to invasion."[14]

Congressman Madison began to sound more like his most famous constituent, Secretary of State Jefferson, and less like his old Federalist self. We learn, importantly, that the Bill of Rights was a creature of ruthless congressional compromise that is emphatically not a complete statement of the higher natural and civil liberties of the people. However, it contains the assurances of the Ninth Amendment, crafted to protect the unenumerated natural rights of all persons, and essential unenumerated civil liberties against government encroachment. Beyond the Ninth Amendment, many of the other rights protected from federal encroachment by the Bill of Rights were in fact fundamental rights in and of themselves, and thus morally mandated; or were man-made mechanisms for enforcing fundamental rights.

With the framework set to begin self-governance, we see the interplay between the three branches of government, the states, and the people as each began to test the strength of the boundaries of the structures erected by the Constitution. In particular, the new Supreme Court, receptive to natural law arguments in its earliest days, began interpreting the new Constitution, the new amendments, and the new laws. The highest court of the land slowly began to decide such questions as jurisdiction, separation of powers, and the boundaries of individual rights, and government powers. With time, the Supreme Court came to recognize that its opinions reached far beyond the pages of the Supreme Court reporter and judicial chambers to the desks of legislators and arguments of the public. Consequently, justices began to preach from the bench the virtues of republican government, lend support to the efforts of the Congress, and bolster their federalist allies. The approach of this early Supreme Court represents the pinnacle of juridical and jurisprudential thought contemporary to the founding generation. Though many justices subscribed to natural law principles, others began to decamp to the emerging side of positivism. Such a move marked the commencement of a gradual shift in jurisprudential approaches, with occasional returns to the natural law, that would impact nearly a century-and-a-half of Supreme Court jurisprudence.

Soon, historical forces – foreign and domestic – would assault the natural law in the American Republic's infancy. While the embroiled federal government of the 1790s struggled to manage international relations, disagreements over the separation of powers depleted somewhat the Federalist ranks in the new government. Helmed by Thomas Jefferson and James Madison, the Democratic-Republicans pushed back against Alexander Hamilton and the administration of John Adams. They feared the Federalists had begun to adopt monarchical tendencies at the cost of the republican ideals and natural law principles, ubiquitous in the Founding Era and baked into the Constitution. The Federalists in government took actions, like passing the Alien and Sedition Acts of 1798, that angered many people who, and states which, in turn, engaged in behavior aimed to oppose, embarrass, and disrupt. People rebelled, and states adopted resolutions condemning actions by the Federalists who seemed to abandon protection of

natural rights in favor of expanding federal power. The Democratic-Republicans
– basically, the Anti-Federalists plus their newest and most important convert and
member, James Madison – embraced the natural law principles of the American
founding and presented a powerful alternative to the quickly corrupted Federalists
who sought to aggrandize federal power at the expense of the powers of the states
and the liberties of the people. They responded to the concerns of the people and
states that ousted the Federalists in the election of 1800.

It is in this historical context of growing discontent with the Federalists, that
this book examines early American legal arguments offered by lawyers in jury
trials in order to provide insight into the mind of the public in the early American
Republic. For instance, the line of reasoning presented in *Henfield's Case* (1793),
a case that questioned what role our fledgling nation should have in the conflict
between Great Britain and Revolutionary France, is rife with natural law
references. After France had declared war on Great Britain, President George
Washington, issued a proclamation of Neutrality in April 1793; shortly thereafter,
Gideon Henfield, an American mercenary soldier/sailor serving aboard a French
privateer, was indicted for violating the Neutrality Proclamation. Henfield did not
dispute the fact that he had signed on as a crew member on the French privateer
Citizen Genêt, but instead argued that he had "exercised his 'natural right of
expatriation,' one of the inalienable and universal rights of mankind,"[15] and
ultimately a jury found him not guilty.

In 1794, the Jay Treaty, created a special relationship between Britain and the
United States with respect to maritime channels of commerce and rules of trade,
but drew ire from the French who perceived the treaty as an American betrayal.
Eventually, however, discord between the United States and France came to a
head, and a diplomatic mission meant to smooth things over, ended in disaster
when the American delegation took offense to demands from their French
counterparts, identified with the pseudonyms X, Y, and Z, who solicited bribes
and large loans for France. News of the XYZ affair erupted in the United States
creating uproar and calls for war, ultimately leading to the passage of the Alien
and Sedition Acts under a Federalist Congress and signed by President John
Adams. These acts were a low point in our history, in that they represent the
criminalization of making false, malicious, or scandalous statements, about the
President or that criticized the federal government's bromides against France. As
they had during the Revolution, factions formed and printed newspapers and
pamphlets decrying the Alien and Sedition Acts and asserting that "the right of
states and individuals to disobey unconstitutional laws"[16] was a natural right.
Their writings demonstrate the anger and fury prompted by any government
encroachments upon their inalienable rights such as freedom of speech and
assembly.

Legislators rallied in Virginia and Kentucky and passed and issued a series
of statements that became known as the Virginia and Kentucky Resolutions in a

blatant act of defiance of the federal government. Although written anonymously, it is now widely understood that the Kentucky Resolution was authored by Jefferson and the Virginia Resolution was authored by Madison. In particular the Kentucky Resolution provided a clear argument in favor of a natural law interpretation and states' rights view of the Constitution, which it referred to as a compact. The Virginia Resolution condemned the actions of the federal government in passing the Alien and Sedition Acts as outside the scope of the authorities granted to it by the Constitution.

Did the great Chief Justice embrace Natural Law Tradition? Did Chief Justice John Marshall in his tenure at the helm of the Supreme Court defend the natural law or succumb to the rising tide of Positivism? Marshall took major steps to weave the natural law into the fabric of American jurisprudence despite the occasional divergences like *McCulloch v. Maryland.* Influenced by Scottish Enlightenment ideals, Marshall set the founding Court on the path to becoming the rarified institution as we know it today, beginning with his appointment as Chief Justice in 1801 until his death in 1835. He sought ways to bolster the Court's legitimacy in the eyes of the people, and as the available corpus of law from Congress grew as well as the available volumes of case reporters, the Supreme Court had little choice but to utilize these tools available to it. By examining the decisions of the Supreme Court in the early nineteenth century one can see not only the Court's employment of Natural Law theory, but also the influence of new modes of thought that sought to overcome the Natural Law theory in favor of dogmatic reliance on statutory law.

Under Marshall's stewardship, Supreme Court justices took strides to solidify the Natural Law Tradition into their decisions. In a series of opinions, Marshall and his brethren, including Justice Joseph Story, considered a range of issues through a natural law lens as if to send a message to future generations of judges and lawyers about the importance of the natural law. Ultimately, in perhaps his most significant ruling, *Marbury v. Madison,* Chief Justice Marshall left the judiciary a powerful tool, and the natural law, a powerful protection in establishing judicial review as a check on legislative excess.

But Natural Law Tradition had competition from academic minds such as Jeremy Bentham, who espoused a "scientific" approach to jurisprudence that sought to eradicate from its roots the moral component of the law and replace it with adherence to process and words of the statutes themselves. Legal positivism, though Bentham never referred to it by such a name, became the chief antagonist to natural law thought and theory, and its influence had far-reaching implications for legal thought throughout the nineteenth and twentieth centuries. Legal positivism seeks to examine law as one might a science by relying only on concrete observation, usually only the observation of the text of a statute and the process by which it became law. Bentham, however, erred by ignoring the forces that contribute to human behavior that Aquinas and Grotius had recognized centuries earlier; reasoning to right and wrong and accounting for human nature.

It is in this context, the emergence of Bentham's positivism, we see in Chief Justice Marshall's opinion in *McCulloch v. Maryland* (1819), the court addressing the power of Congress to engage in legislative behavior outside the boundaries delimited by the Constitution and a decision that would allow the federal government to brandish the Necessary and Proper Clause to pass a wide range of far-reaching, and never-contemplated-by-the Framers intrusive legislation.

In interpreting that clause, Marshall concluded, *necessary* did not mean *absolutely necessary* but rather some other, vaguer abstraction of necessity since "[i]t would have been an unwise attempt to provide, by immutable [positive] rules, for exigencies which, if foreseen at all, must have been seen dimly, and which can be best provided for as they occur."[17] It was a perverse use of inverse positivism (an interpretation of the law based on an *unwritten* word) that not even Jeremy Bentham would have ascribed to, because Madison did not use "absolutely" to modify necessary, the word necessary somehow came to mean needful or helpful.

We then follow the regrettable tradition of legal positivism that persisted and allowed for the emergence of governments with legitimate authority, through a legitimate process, to adopt and promulgate laws so egregious and offensive as to shock the conscience. For instance, in *Dred Scott v. Sandford* (1857) the Supreme Court, following positivist principles, held that a former slave now free, who descended from African slaves who had been kidnapped and brought in chains to the United States, could not become a U.S. citizen, was not among those referenced as "men" in the Declaration of Independence, or a "person" as the Constitution used that word, and therefore, was not entitled to protection under the U.S. Constitution.[18]

Positivism again reared its head in the Supreme Court's decision in *Plessy v. Ferguson* (1896), in which the majority upheld forced segregation. This case gave us the lamentable standard of "separate, but equal" and turned to positivism to avoid deciding a case based on principles well known to the Framers – right and wrong. We can, however, look to Justice Harlan's dissent to shed light on the civil and natural violations. *Lochner v. New York* (1905) is an anomaly in this era – a glimmer of NLT hope during the reign of Positivism – in which the court found in favor of the natural right to economic liberty over the power of a state legislature.

However, subsequent cases led to further invasion of natural rights; like *Wickard v. Filburn* (1942) during the New Deal Era, in which paternalism reigned supreme. The holding in *Wickard* represents the most far reaching example of Congress' authority to regulate under the Commerce Clause, as the Supreme Court adopted an aggregation theory and ruled that immeasurable economic behavior, when combined with other personal producers of immeasurable impact, the effect could, in the aggregate, be substantial enough to make the activity subject to congressional regulation. Likewise, following the attack on Pearl Harbor on December 7, 1941, the United States, swept up in a frenzied and xenophobic fear of invasion, branded all persons in the country with Japanese heritage as potential saboteurs. In *Korematsu v. United States* (1944), the Court ignored *Marbury v. Madison* and its progeny, and failed to conclude that the rules targeting those of Japanese descent solely for their ancestry run contrary to the principles of the natural law and, indeed, the Constitution itself.

Not until the end of World War II, when legal scholars struggled to find philosophical grounding for prosecution of the Nazis did legal positivism fail to supply sufficient legal justification and fall out of favor. Renewed interest in Natural Law theory inspired a natural law renaissance which gave birth to a new generation of legal philosophers and critics who modernized our understanding of Natural Law theory and its role in contemporary jurisprudence. This new generation of mid twentieth century scholars, beginning with Edwin S. Corwin and Leo Strauss, examined Aquinas and labored to update Natural Law theories to fit a contemporary understanding of legal and moral philosophy responding to the first half of the twentieth century. Each added to and refined the theories of those who came before and established a modern foundation for the later twentieth century scholars who would follow.

Following Corwin and Strauss, scholars and theorists, such as H.L.A. Hart and Lon Fuller, began to explore the role of competing schools of jurisprudence in the modern age and how we could apply such principles and ideas in a world that had survived the horrors of two world wars, and was facing the rise of Communism, the Korean War, and the changes to society along gender and racial lines following the end of World War II.

While legal positivism dominated the field of jurisprudence, two of Bentham's disciples distinguished themselves and made their own significant contributions to the field. John Austin built upon Bentham's approach to laws and morals and John Stuart Mill explored Bentham's ideas of Utilitarianism. While Aquinas had advocated for reliance on human reason to derive a rational set of rules aimed at doing good and avoiding evil, Mill adopted a more secular approach arguing that humanity functioned at its best when it sought to achieve the maximum amount of happiness for the largest number of people. Moreover, the Millian Harm Principle states that "the only purpose for which power can be rightfully exercised over any member of a civilized community, against his will, is to prevent harm to others."[19] This idea speaks to the principles of limited powers of government, and reflects the prohibition of interference in the liberty of a man or woman unless he or she acts in a manner to interfere with the liberty of others.

H.L.A. Hart carried Austin's torch and elevated modern notions of legal positivism, while Lon Fuller became the standard bearer in modern Natural Law theory in which he incorporated some of the Millian Harm Principle. To many, Hart represented the academic successor to Bentham and the largest positivist lighting rod worthy of the most serious and thorough criticism. Through debate with Hart and his new positivism the early modern Natural Law theorists, such as Lord Patrick Devlin, strengthened and clarified their arguments and developed modern approaches to natural law more consistent with contemporary sensibilities.

The important social and political changes in the latter half of the twentieth century affecting the makeup of national institutions and attitudes, including the Civil Rights Movement, were not bereft of Natural Law Tradition. A series of court cases and public incidents pushed forward this new era, and the Supreme Court began to render decisions that radically expanded notions of civil rights that often overlapped with natural law principles of fairness, due process, and inalienable, pre governmental rights. That is not to say that the Supreme Court adopted a doctrinal approach that examined matters before it with strong deference to natural law and natural rights, but rather that liberal and conservative courts alike ruled on matters in such a fashion as to incorporate into *stare decisis* certain natural law principles.

In *Shelley v. Kramer* (1948) the Supreme Court confronted restrictive land covenants that prevented landowners in an area of St. Louis from selling their property to "any person not of the Caucasian race."[20] While the Supreme Court elected to preserve the rights of contract in the private action of private individuals, it did recognize that certain actions, such as private contracts between private individuals covering private matters cease to remain private when one or more of the parties involved invokes the courts for their enforcement. While preserving natural rights of contract, the Supreme Court simultaneously struck a serious blow against the use of government institutions to advance racist ends, a movement the Supreme Court boldly catapulted to the forefront of the American psyche in a series of cases captioned *Brown v. Board of Education.* After all, the natural law is – thankfully – color-blind. A ruling in the *Brown* cases by the Warren Court, certainly consistent with the Fourteenth Amendment, also happened to coincide with natural law principles of ascertaining right and wrong by the exercise of reason. In its discussion of the matter, the Warren Court seems to have *avoided* discussion of natural law and natural rights favoring instead the language of civil rights. Yet, even the language of civil rights invoked NLT. In Dr. Martin Luther King Jr.'s iconic *Letter from a Birmingham City Jail*, defending civil disobedience, he asserted that one has a moral responsibility to disobey unjust law by citing to Augustine — "an unjust law is no law at all" — and Aquinas who defined an unjust law as "a human law that is not rooted in eternal law and natural law."

The Warren and Burger courts provide us with an additional collection of caselaw in which natural law principles align with contemporary progressive ideals. Beginning with *Griswold v. Connecticut* (1965), the Supreme Court struck down Connecticut's anti-contraceptive law on the basis of the "right to privacy" not expressly stated in the Constitution.[21] Justice William O. Douglas delivered the opinion of the Court and appeared to bend over backwards to avoid mentioning Natural Law theories and principles, opting instead to use the peculiar language of penumbras and emanations of rights. Justice Arthur Goldberg, joined with Chief Justice Warren, and Justice William J. Brennan, placed more reliance on the Ninth Amendment than did Douglas. Goldberg and his colleagues agreed "that the concept of liberty protects those personal rights that are fundamental, and is not confined to the specific terms of the Bill of Rights." He concluded "that the concept of liberty is not so restricted that it embraces the right of marital privacy though that right is not mentioned explicitly in the Constitution" and such a view finds support both in numerous decisions by the Court "and by the language and history of the Ninth Amendment."[22]

Channeling Madison, Goldberg spoke directly to the principles of natural law shared by the Founders but opted instead to use the more contemporary, secular term *fundamental* rather than the more traditional and familiar term *natural* which remains vulnerable to criticism because of its historical association with religious moralism. Yet again, in *Loving v. Virginia* (1967), when discussing one's freedom to marry the Court seems to embrace natural law principles without declaring them so and instead resorts to vague allusions to natural law watchwords such as "personal rights essential to the orderly pursuit of happiness." In *Bowers v. Hardwick* (1986), the Burger Court upheld Georgia's anti-sodomy law and asserted that it was not "inclined to take a more expansive view of our authority to discover new fundamental rights imbedded in the Due Process Clause."[23] Not until *Lawrence v. Texas* (2003) would the Supreme Court reject its prior holding in *Bowers*, and recognize the substantive due process right – another secular phrase for natural right – to choose a sexual partner of the same gender free from government interference.

Present day theorists and philosophers have sought to update the ideas of their predecessors to accommodate Natural Law theory to changes in contemporary society. John Rawls argued for government to prioritize justice to help the less advantaged, while Robert Nozick argued that the government lacks the moral authority to transfer wealth, even for justice's sake. Joseph Raz buttressed Hartian Legal Positivism, and Randy Barnett argued for a return to first principles in a modified minimalist version of Originalism. These formulations inspired new debates and deeper exploration into the roles and goals of government and challenged long-held conceptions of the limitations of the state vis-à-vis individual liberty.

Is there a common ground between the antagonists legal positivism and Natural law theory – a modified form of legal positivism that reflects and respects the commands of the Ninth Amendment? We may be able to find such a compromise by visiting the opinions of Justice Antonin Scalia, one of the foremost proponents of a version of positivism known as "Originalism," who brought to the Supreme Court a conservative doctrinal approach that called for the narrow interpretation of statutes and constitutional provisions consistent with the original public understanding of the words in question at the time they were ratified or enacted. Far from using Originalism as a restriction, Justice Scalia advocated for a considered approach to interpretation that looked to the original public understanding of the words of the text but allowed for the occasional divergence from obsolete sensibilities in favor of a reasonable, contemporary outlook. His approach, along with Professor Randy Barnett's emphasis on the power of the Ninth Amendment allows for an originalist approach to jurisprudence that also firmly incorporates Natural Law theories through the Ninth Amendment. Borrowing then from Professor Murray Rothbard, perhaps the twentieth-century's most prominent libertarian theorist who promulgated the Non-Aggression Principle, a successor to Mill's Harm Principle, and working within the framework of a united natural law and positivist methodology, but not its jurisprudence, we can formulate a new series of principles designed to minimize government overreach and maximize individual freedom. Rothbard, born and raised as a Jew, became a champion of Aquinas, but not uncritically. Rothbard challenged Aquinas' conflation of "society" with "the State" and argued that even though humans are social animals, we can enjoy natural rights to the fullest in the absence of the state.

Despite its universal beginnings, we have seen that Natural Law theory has ebbed and flowed; while it yielded ground to legal positivism during the waning days of the Marshall Court, it was never truly abandoned in American jurisprudence. An exhaustive account of all Supreme Court cases, in which the justices have turned to Natural Law theory or expressly rejected it when contemplating fundamental rights and the limits of state action is a useful tool for understanding the movement of NLT through American history.

Following the Supreme Court's decision in *Lochner v. New York*, several justices used the Due Process clauses of the Fifth and Fourteenth Amendments as well as the Privileges and Immunities Clause of the Fourteenth as avenues through which they could enshrine natural law principles into the common law. Various cases provided opportunities for the Court to recognize more expansive views of property rights and further develop principles of due process as understood through reason, common sense, and fairness. The Court recognized that, as society changes, new circumstances emerge that require due consideration of how our understanding of natural law and natural rights extend to these evolving facets within society. Changes, the Court found, provide new opportunities to discover new areas of natural law theory. This holds true today.

Beyond Positivists, there have been other prominent jurists and thinkers throughout the twentieth and twenty first centuries who have opposed the Natural Law Tradition in favor of doctrinal offshoots and successors to legal positivism and utilitarianism. Justice Oliver Wendell Holmes was an outspoken detractor of the natural law and a significant figure in the legal realism movement. Princeton's Robert P. George's artful refutation of Holmes's critiques are an instructive debate. Moreover, Justice Scalia's opinions that are unfavorable to the natural law are peppered with deferential reliance to federal or state legislatures and he voices opposition to rulings that veered too far from the well-trodden path of tradition – whether in the common law or *stare decisis*. Both Holmes and Scalia endorsed an approach that remained internally consistent, but which rarely aligned, with the Natural Law theory so long as they considered its principles to be articulated directly within parts of the Constitution.

The goal of this book is to lay out a convincing case for why a natural law perspective is the appropriate interpretation of the text, is itself a theory of both flexibility and restraint, and is a viable alternative to less-textually principled forms of living constitutionalism. After all, the Constitution, properly interpreted, defers to the legal doctrine known in the Eighteenth and Nineteenth Centuries as the natural law, on questions of the supremacy of individual liberty over government action. Today, however, the Jeffersonian and Madisonian ideals of personal natural rights and governmental legitimacy conditioned upon the individual consent of the governed have themselves become myths. Most people in government reject natural rights and personal sovereignty, but instead believe that the exercise of one's rights is subject to the will of those in the government. Today, most in government believe that they can write any law and regulate any behavior, without being subject to the natural law, the sovereignty of individuals, or cognizant of history's tyrants.

Yet this is emphatically not so; government's only lawful role in a free society is to enforce natural rights. The whole theory of natural rights is that each individual is sovereign, each individual has human liberty, and everything the government does, is a negation of that liberty. The only legitimate negation of that liberty occurs when the government prevents or punishes one person from interfering with the natural rights of another.

That is Rothbard's Non-Aggression Principle. Utilize the guiding principles of natural law to ensure that government enforces natural rights and does no more.

John Stuart Mill captured the essence of the Natural Law tradition when he wrote:

> If all mankind minus one, were of one opinion, and only one person were of the contrary opinion, mankind would be no more justified in silencing that one person, than he, if he had the power, would be justified in silencing mankind.[24]

Just look at what Mill has written. If the freedom of speech is a natural right, then it – and its companion rights – cannot be taken away by an army or a dictator, or a legislature, or all the world but one.

CHAPTER 1

HISTORY OF THE NATURAL LAW: PHILOSOPHICAL ORIGINS AND UNDERPINNINGS

The Argument

The natural law approach to jurisprudence essentially is the belief that certain universal rights and rules intrinsic to human nature and discoverable through reason, exist and persist as integral to human nature and as one of the most influential and enduring approaches to law.

Under the natural law, immutable and ubiquitous principles flow from humans that, when properly contemplated by human reason, reveal a cascading hierarchy of natural rights aimed at maximizing objective good. Once we meet the criterion of life, we can follow by striving to lead a virtuous life.

Several ancient minds explored the Natural Law theories first chronicled in antiquity by Aristotle. Each saint, philosopher, scholar, and jurist, working upon the foundations of his predecessors, and applying his own reason and analysis, advanced and refined natural law concepts. The most enduring of these is St. Thomas Aquinas.

Their works would, in turn, influence generations of lawyers and judges who would enshrine in their arguments and opinions enduring natural law principles that would influence the leaders behind the American Revolution.

***

If men were angels, no government would be necessary.[1]

– James Madison (1751-1836)

EARLY HISTORY OF THE
NATURAL LAW BY GEOGRAPHY

The Natural Law, once the prevailing theory in western jurisprudence, has fallen in and out of favor for centuries.[2] It addresses and reconciles the relationship between the law and human nature.[3] Philosophies, unlike wars, migrations, or dynasties do not begin at one particular point in time so that we can say "here marks the beginning of the natural law tradition." We cannot pinpoint its origins like we do with World War I or the Holy Roman Empire; there is no Gavrilo Princip or Archduke Ferdinand, and no Napoleon. However, we can look to a particular place and time, a unique moment shared by a group of extraordinary thinkers and leaders, who changed the course of history through their bravery, wisdom, and temperament. We can identify that group of people at that particular place in that particular era and work our way backwards to see what they knew, examine what they read, and try better to understand the role of history and its heroes in this tremendous undertaking. Through our exploration of the influences of the founding fathers and early American patriots, we can better grasp the meanings behind their declarations, the ambitions behind their rhetoric, and the meaning of our nation's crucial governmental documents.

Greco-Roman Influences on the Natural Law:
Aristotle and Saint Augustine of Hippo

No exploration into the philosophies and rhythm of thought that impacted America's founding would be complete without a trip to the Aegean, or, perhaps, the Adriatic. Though not the focus on this journey, the importance and impact that classical Greek (and Roman) thought had on the common law tradition in England and America cannot be overstated. Western Philosophy truly begins with the Greeks, and so we begin with Aristotle. The great philosopher Aristotle, (384-322 B.C.), wrote during the golden age of Athenian democracy. Many theorists and thinkers who followed Aristotle subsumed his teachings, including an insistence upon the rule of law. For millennia, philosophers, thinkers, jurists, and even the Founders continued to admire the writings of Aristotle.[4] The philosopher observed that man is a political animal.[5] "Political actors as different as Niccolò Machiavelli and David Hume, John Locke and John Adams, Sir Mathew Hale and Thomas Jefferson, to name a few, shared a conviction that the existence of [the political animal] was demanded by nature and was, as such, endowed with a self generating legitimacy."[6]

The trouble with Aristotle, however, arises when it comes to his articulation—though not his recognition—of natural rights. Professor Fred Miller has written "[a]lthough there are undeniably deep differences between Aristotle and modern natural rights theorists such as John Locke and Robert Nozick, the claim that 'there are no rights in Aristotle' is an oversimplification which misrepresents [Aristotle's] views."[7] The confusion arises in that "no single word in classical Greek is a precise counterpart of the modern English [...] noun 'right,' this is not a decisive reason for holding that Aristotle and other Greeks did not have a concept of rights."[8] And, although Aristotle rarely used the term *natural law*, Professor John Kroger noted that he incorporated into his several works "concepts of natural justice into his social and political theories" when "he [spoke] of a justice and law that is *kata physin*, 'based on' or 'in accordance with' nature."[9]

Aristotle, like many philosophers, was "concerned about the moral and legal status of the individual within the community, and he express[ed] this concern in terms of political justice."[10] Through observation and analysis, Aristotle studied the governments of the Greek city-states and attempted to deduce an objective standard of law. We now identify his efforts as some of the earliest written articulations of natural law. In particular, his ideas about ethics and politics "start[ed] by observing what people d[id] and then reasoning dialectically about it" in a search for "standards [regarding] human behavior or belief...as they are known to mankind."[11]

In *On Rhetoric*, Aristotle crafted a "handbook in the art of persuasion,"[12] and, at its outset, made an important distinction between the two types of laws that are just: specific and common. On one hand, *specific* laws may be written (i.e., laws against theft, mayhem and adultery) or unwritten (i.e., decisions of equity made by judges to compensate for the indeterminateness of legislative enactments) and are promulgated by each separate *polis* or community to regulate its own affairs. Since they differ from state to state, these laws are changeable and frequently altered.[13] On the other hand, Aristotle recognized that there are universal, common laws, which are unwritten, eternal, and cannot be changed or altered: I regard law as either particular or universal, meaning by "particular" the law ordained by a particular people for

> their own purposes, and capable of subdivision into written and unwritten law, and by "universal" the law of Nature. For there exists, as all men divine more or less, a natural and universal principle of right and wrong, independent of any mutual intercourse of compact.[14]

Aristotle endorsed and propounded the notion that some universal laws or rules existed that governed human conduct. He even encouraged advocates to employ arguments based in the Natural Law Tradition when facing written law unfavorable to their position: It is clear that, if the written law is unfavourable to our case, we must appeal to the universal law and to the principles of equity as expressing justice of a higher order. *We must contend* that the formula "according to the best of my judgment" implies that the juror is not absolutely bound by the letter of the law. We must urge that, while equity and universal law, as being conformable to Nature, are perpetual and invariable, written laws are liable to frequent change. [...] Again, *we must argue* that justice is something which is genuine and beneficent, but that the sham justice *which consists in a rigorous interpretation of the law* is quite the contrary; hence the written law is neither genuine nor beneficent, as it does not discharge the proper function of law. Or that a judge is like an assayer of coin, whose business it is to distinguish base justice from genuine. Or that a higher virtue is displayed in loyalty and obedience to unwritten than to written laws."[15]

Many have noted, however, that while Aristotle may have believed in the existence of natural law, here he is not citing it "to argue for the existence or the validity of natural law, but rather as advice to a... lawyer on how to win his case."[16] Nevertheless, according to the renowned Professor Edwin S. Corwin, "[w]hile this advice scarcely reveals any deep devotion on Aristotle's part to the Natural Law concept, it does evidence the short step, which even at that date existed in men's minds, between the concept and the idea of a *juridical* recourse to it."[17]

In his seminal work, *Politics*, which in part discusses the relationship between the individual and the citystate,[18] Aristotle argued as an empirical fact, that we "can determine whether institutions or practices, be they legal or nonlegal in character, are natural or not by examining if the institution or practice is common to all."[19] Specifically, Aristotle noted, if we wish to discern whether a human institution or practice (i.e., slavery) is natural or not, we can "learn it from what actually happens."[20] The deduction, then, can be made that "if law comes in only two types, (1) laws specific to a particular polis and (2) laws that are universal [as we saw in *On Rhetoric*], and universal laws are natural in origin, then any universal, nonspecific human legal practice must be natural."[21] Beyond his discussion of natural justice, Aristotle embraced many ideals in *Politics* such as individualism, the protection of freedom (both positive and negative liberty as we know it today) and the significance of happiness,[22] all of which are later echoed by Jefferson in the Declaration of Independence.

St. Augustine of Hippo (354-430), an early Christian philosopher perhaps best remembered for his thirteen books of "confessions" which collected his life's experiences and documented his conversion to Christianity, deeply influenced the next thousand years of jurisprudential thought.[23] Longtime Notre Dame philosopher and professor of law, Anton-Hermann Chroust (1907-1982), under whom your author happily studied as a law student, explained "St. Augustine's philosophic and jurisprudential thought may indeed be called the crossroads of ancient and medieval intellectual history and possibly the decisive instance in the transition from pagan to Christian intellectualism."[24] In many ways, St. Augustine Christianized the philosophical contributions of the Greek stoics on *lex aeterna* (eternal law) and *lex naturalis* (natural law).[25] Professor Chroust further explained "Perhaps St. Augustine's most far-reaching and most significant contribution to the issue of the *lex aeterna* is his awareness of the grave dangers inherent in any effort to equate the cosmic orderliness or *lex aeterna* with God Himself, as the

Stoics had done."[26] Rather, Chroust explained, St. Augustine believed "the cosmic *logos* or *lex aeterna* [is] a 'deliberate' act of God—without a doubt a most radical alteration of the Stoic tradition—which presupposes a personalist and theistic conception of God, insisting that 'the Divine Wisdom is the universal law.'"[27]

Moreover, in the course of his text, *On Free Choice of the Will*, St. Augustine encountered a number of challenging questions and issues. In the first book of this work, Augustine and his interlocutor, Evodius, discussed the origin of evil in the world, and more particular, why man "does" evil (adultery, murder, sacrilege, etc.). Augustine ultimately reasoned that God should not be blamed for the presence of evil, but rather the fault should lay with man, who abuses his God-given free will and does wrong. In reaching such conclusions, Augustine engaged in an interesting discussion which concludes with perhaps his most famous line:

> Evodius: If murder is killing a human being, it can sometimes happen without sin. For instance, a soldier kills an enemy; a judge or his agent executes a convicted criminal; someone throws his weapon by chance imprudently and against his will. They do not seem to me to be sinning when they kill someone.

> Augustine: I agree. But they are not usually called murderers, either. So tell me: Do you hold that someone who kills his master, at whose hands he fears brutal torture, should be counted among those who kill someone but do not merit the name of murderer?

> Evodius: I see that this case is quite different. In the earlier cases, the people were acting according to the laws – or at least not against the laws – whereas no law sanctions the crime of this slave.

> Augustine: Once again you are calling me back to authority. You must remember that we have now undertaken to understand what we believe. We do indeed believe the laws; hence we should try, if we somehow can, to grasp whether it is not an error for the law to punish the slave's deed.

> …

> Augustine: Then, although the master is slain by the slave on account of his desire, he is not slain on account of a blameworthy desire. Consequently, we have not yet found out why this deed is evil. For we agreed that all evildoings are evil precisely because they come about from lust, that is, from a blameworthy desire.

> Evodius: It seems to me now that the slave was condemned unjustly. Yet I would not dream of saying so if I had another reply to offer

> …

Augustine: Therefore, the law is unjust which grants permission (a) to a traveler to kill a highway robber, so as not to be killed himself; (b) to any man or woman to slay a rapist in his onslaught, if possible, before enduring rape. Indeed, the law bids a soldier to kill the enemy, and if he holds back from this bloodshed he pays the penalties from his commander.

Surely we will not dream of calling these laws unjust – or rather, not to call them "laws" at all, for a law that is not just does not seem to me to be a law.[28]

St. Augustine's works remained preeminent in the fields of law and jurisprudence until they were, in many ways, interrogated and abrogated by subsequent thinkers and philosophers.

Early English Influence on the Natural Law: Henry de Bracton

In England, the natural law goes back at least to the days of Henry de Bracton in the Thirteenth Century, who included in his work *De Legibus et Consuetudinibus Angliae* (*On the Laws and Customs of England*), in a section entitled *Quid sit ius naturale*, or "What the Natural Law is."[29] *De Legibus et Consuetudeinibus Angliae* cemented Bracton as a towering figure in history, analysis, and development of English law. Bracton's significance persists not as a primary source but rather as an oft-cited authority by those English commentators who followed him, such as Sir Edward Coke, Sir William Blackstone, Pollock and Maitland, as well as many others.

Bracton's work served to record the laws and customs of England rather than to provide extensive commentaries and analysis. Instead of posing philosophical questions and exploring the relationship of possible answers to the human condition, Bracton adopted a clinical and straightforward approach to his writing. He observed that "Natural Law is defined in many ways[,]" but that "[i]t may first be said to denote a certain instinctive impulse arising out of animate nature by which individual living things are led to act in certain ways."[30]

To Bracton, natural law related to some intrinsic, atavistic impulse written into the DNA of all living things. Declaring "Natural Law is that which nature, that is, God himself, taught all living things," Bracton emphasizes the theistic roots of the Natural Law.[31] He also suggests that "Natural Law is that [which is] taught all livings things by nature, that is, by natural instinct."[32] However, as we will see, other scholars and theorists favored reason over will, impulse, or instinct, and Bracton's recorded definition of natural law gave way to its evolution under the studied and methodical approach of other thinkers like Thomas Aquinas.

Italian Influence on the Natural Law: Saint Thomas Aquinas

St. Thomas Aquinas (1225-1274),[33] steeped in the works of Aristotle and Cicero, built upon the foundation begun by Albertus Magnus (~1200-1280) in developing Natural Law theory.[34] According to Aquinas, "God himself was Natural Law's source."[35] Aquinas believed "[t]he Natural Law is promulgated by the very fact that God has instilled it in the minds of [all persons] so as to be known to them naturally."[36]

As Notre Dame Professor Emeritus, Michael Zuckert noted, "[t]here were, to be sure, natural-law doctrines prior to Thomas Aquinas, but none so elaborate, so detailed, or so philosophically successful."[37] Zuckert continued, "[f]or at least four hundred years, Aquinas's version of natural law served as the backdrop for most political thinking in Europe, and even today, advocates of natural law for the most part look back to Aquinas and develop theories more or less of his type."[38]

Aquinas, of course, spoke not always literally, but often metaphorically. The natural law does not spring forth fully formed from our minds like Athena from the head of Zeus. Rather, Aquinas believed God the Father endowed humanity with reason,[39] and, that by using reason, and free will, individuals could discover and embrace the universal laws and thus ascertain truth.[40] To Aquinas, reason is the tool, freedom is the fuel, and truth is the goal. Aquinas had enormous respect for Aristotle to whom he referred in numerous writings simply as *the philosopher*; to Aquinas, an ancient thinker without peer.[41]

We can reduce the Thomistic natural law scheme into three main precepts. First, Aquinas believed the natural law to be universally valid and therefore it applies to all human beings.[42] Second, the natural law maintains its universality because it relates to the "protection and promotion of interests that are based on the very nature of [all] human beings[, ... and] its requirements are not imposed on humans from sources outside their own essential natures[.]"[43] Finally, the natural law has been discovered and is discoverable through reason.[44]

Reason, then should dictate the goals and functions of the law, and the law, in turn, serves as "rules or measures of acts whereby people are induced to act or restrained from acting."[45] Aquinas considered the goals and functions of law as "directed toward the common good of humankind."[46] He also adopted an interesting premodern populist view regarding the role of the individual in understanding the natural law. Aquinas believed everyone is capable of using reason to discover universal laws.[47]

Determining what to pursue and what to avoid, "one must examine our natural tendencies, our propensities, and inclinations" so that "a series of self-evident... primary principles of the Natural Law emerge."[48] To begin, it requires a belief in an objective "good that is to be done and promoted, and evil [that] is to be avoided."[49] Once we satisfy the criterion of life, we can then expand our development into improving the quality and purpose of that life by striving to achieve some objective common good.[50] Aquinas, the quintessential Catholic philosopher, whom the Roman Catholic Church calls a Doctor of the Church, in Aquinas' case, "The Angelic Doctor," may have seen the ultimate good as leading a virtuous life,[51] or, rather, "to do good and avoid evil[,]" and thereby end up in Heaven.[52]

Defining "law" as, "an ordinance of reason made for the common good by the public personage who has charge of the community, and promulgated[,]" Aquinas hints at several major elements which take leading roles in his following four-paragraph definition of law.[53] He begins, "law is a defined measure or rule by which we are led to act or withheld from acting."[54] By declaring reason to drive proper human behavior, "[t]he rule and measure of human activity is the reason, the first principle of human activity whose function it is to direct means to ends," Aquinas emphasizes the principle that *reason* retains primacy in the pantheon of human motivations.[55] Therefore, "[i]n every class [of human activity,] the first principle is the rule and measure of all else."[56] Reason, too, necessarily should "regulate" the "impulse of the will" in order to "[endow]" "the willing of what is commanded [...] with the strength of law."[57] Here, Aquinas intimates that commands bereft of the spark of reason fall short of the command of law. Aquinas, too, places *reason* above *will* in the hierarchy of human behavior since will can err, but to Aquinas reason cannot.[58]

Aquinas identifies reason as "the first principle of human acts" and calls for this principle to "[work] as the principle to [other principles]" to which the "chief and main interest" of law "must be referred."[59] In other words, law must refer to, or, rather, derive from reason. And, "[t]he first principle of the practical reason is our ultimate end, or happiness" so the "law is chiefly concerned with planning for this [ultimate end; happiness]."[60] "[L]aw is engaged mainly with the scheme of common happiness."[61] Every law is ordered to the common good, and a precept has the force of law only when it serves this community benefit.[62] But who announces the law aimed at shepherding the common good?

Aquinas declares, "the whole of the people or [...] its viceregent" possesses the authority "[t]o direct affairs for the common good."[63] Consequently, any institution that serves as "guardian of the community" has the power to enact laws.[64] Aquinas also emphasizes the need to promulgate laws,[65] and the link between knowledge of the law as a result of its promulgation and the obligation to adhere to its restrictions.[66] In the Thomistic scheme, natural law , an accessible derivation of the distillation of eternal law passed through the filter of divine law, is universal and can be discovered by all persons through the exercise of reason.[67] Once discovered, that natural law, reason-based and designed to promote life and human happiness, essentially encourages persons to do good and avoid evil.[68] To that end, human law, adhering to practical natural law principles, can be established and promulgated by a legitimate authority charged with safeguarding the community.[69] Essential to the power of human law to induce or restrict human action is that the regulations be known to those whose behavior they are intended to bind.[70]

Spanish Influence on Natural Law: Francisco Suarez

Francisco Suarez S.J. (1548-1617) set out to resolve questions concerning "the origin and nature of natural rights, and their relation to natural law, civil law, virtue, and the common good."[71] In his massive work, *Tractatus de legibus ac Deo Legislatore* [A Treatise on Laws and God the Lawgiver](1612), Suarez "provides an understanding of and justification for a natural right as a moral power or faculty pertaining to the individual subject rooted in selfgovernance."[72] Specifically, Suarez begins by describing the meaning of right (*ius*) as:

> properly being called a certain moral faculty which anyone has either over a thing or to a thing due him. For in this way, an owner of a thing is said to have right in a thing (*ius in re*), and the worker is said to have a right to a wage (*ius ad stipendum*), by reason of which he is called worthy of hire. [73]

Steven Brust looks deeper into Suarez's explanation of *ius*, later defined as a man's "power in himself and in the use of his faculties and members of his body,"[74] and Suarez's belief that man has an "intrinsic right of liberty" [75]: This explanation of ius as a moral power over oneself is in accord with, and appears to be, the essence of the grounding for man's dignity and being in the image of God, and hence the grounding for one being sui iuris. Thus, one can conclude that man is sui iuris – of his own right– because he possesses a subjective moral power or faculty to be master of himself or, to express it another way, that he is a person with the capacity for selfgovernance.[76]

Suarez tempers such liberty, however, when he states: "natural liberty is the faculty to do whatever one pleases that is not prohibited by law."[77] Brust believes that for Suarez, "subjective rights exist only within a framework of communities, laws, and the respective powers which make those civil, canonical, natural, and divine laws, and this framework helps define the very concrete nature of the rights."[78] As a result, "any natural, divine, civil, or canonical rights of the person are also conditioned by civil (and canon) laws prohibiting vices and prescribing virtues, as well as by natural and divine law, for the sake of man's natural (and supernatural) happiness."[79] In discussing this hierarchy between natural rights and man made law, Brust aptly summarizes Suarez's belief:

> [M]an is given wide "civil latitude" to exercise his natural rights. It is here where there exists a "zone of free choice" whereby one can de facto, and legally, choose evil. With regard to this (legal) right to immunity from civil punishment (and non-interference), it is essential to understand that an individual's actions are never separable from a law

superior to civil law. This means that, first, one cannot have a legal or natural right or faculty to do injury to another, and second, the divine and natural law are still binding on everyone—they do not permit evil actions and no evil actions are left unpunished. Understood from this perspective, a legal right not to be interfered with in many of one's actions does not necessarily promote a loss in virtue or selfishness, or lack of commitment to the temporal (and eternal) happiness of the person and the common good.[80]

In other words, Suarez believed that legal rights "presuppose an understanding of the moral good shared by all based on man's common spiritual and moral nature."[81] Moreover, Suarez believed that the natural law discerned by reason "indicated what was intrinsically good or evil and also commanded the one and forbade the other. But, in discerning natural law, reason also discerned the will of God for humankind. Since God chose to create humans as creatures endowed with reason, we can know that he intended them to act in accord with the dictates of their rational nature."[82]

Professor Tierney explains, "in considering the relationship between rulers and subjects, the right that Suarez insisted on most explicitly and emphatically was the right of self-sense. For Suarez, this was 'the greatest of rights,' a natural inalienable right that inhered in individuals and communities, a right that could be exercised by subjects against a tyrannical ruler."[83] Moreover, it was through this power "from its inherent right of self-defense and because the original compact that instituted a king always assumed that he would rule 'politically not tyrannically'" that the community had the power to judge and depose a tyrannical ruler.[84] Professor Tierney correctly concludes that:

> In various ways – through his definition of a right as a moral faculty, and through his arguments that political societies were formed by the volition of free individuals, and that a right of self-defense persisted after a government was instituted – the Spanish master [i.e., Suarez] helped to establish the substructure on which later theories of rights would be built.[85]

Dutch Influence on the Natural Law: Hugo Grotius

While Aquinas focused on the role of reason in developing law, and the role of law in society, his work heavily influenced the Sixteenth and early Seventeenth Century Dutch philosopher, Hugo Grotius (1583-1645), who "is widely acknowledged to have made important contributions to an influential doctrine of individual natural rights."[86] Until the rediscovery of Aquinas, legal theorists and jurists often looked to Grotius as the "starting point of one of the best marked eras in the history of jurisprudence."[87] Roscoe Pound (1870-1964), Dean of Harvard Law School, believed that Grotius thrived in a time perfect to receive him; the

Reformation preceding the Scientific Revolution.[88] Grotius lived and wrote in a time when the great intellectual minds of Europe sought to apply scientific principles, as they understood them, to all aspects of humanity and society.

Grotius contemplated human nature and its relationship to how people behaved in society and developed an approach conducive to the prevailing scientific principles of the time. "The importance was methodological: It provided a rational, and what the Seventeenth Century regarded as scientific, method for arriving at a body of propositions underlying legal arrangements and the provisions of the positive law."[89] In developing his theories, Grotius looked to Aquinas,[90] but also noted that human nature contains more than reason; it also contains passion.[91]

In addition to incorporating the impact of human passion into the understanding of the natural law, Grotius also decoupled theology from natural law.[92] In the *Prolegomena* to his 1625 work *De Jure Belli ac Pacis* [On The Law of War and Peace], Grotius indulged in some rather radical speculation often referred to as the Grotian Hypothesis or the *etiamsi daremus* passage (roughly translated to "even if we should concede") in which he wrote:

> What we have been saying (viz., about the Natural Law) would have a degree of validity even if we should concede that which cannot be conceded without the utmost wickedness, that there is no God, or that the affairs of men are of no concern to him.[93]

While many look to the Grotian Hypothesis as the Dutch philosopher's attempt to sever the link between religious moralism and the natural law,[94] others question whether the passage was mere rhetorical flourish.[95] The answer to whether Grotius intended the *etiamsi daremus* passage to cleave religious moralism from the natural law in favor of some form of secular moralism died twenty years later with Grotius in August 1645. However, those who followed Grotius read such intent into his *Prolegomena*, and this prevailing notion elevated the idea from what might have been an historical palimpsest to one of the most significant developments in the natural law since Aquinas took quill to parchment.[96]

Whereas Aquinas focused on the relationship between eternal law, divine law, natural law, and human law,[97] Grotius was more concerned with how natural law limited civil government in order to preserve individual liberty.[98] He taught that liberty was integral to all persons and crucial to all social and political life.[99] According to Grotius, the individual was governed and liberated by natural law, but also existed in a society organized by an "order which transcends the individual."[100] He extrapolated his theories on individuals and their roles in society under the natural law to encompass the roles of societies as they relate to one another on the international stage.[101]

Grotius based nearly all of his contributions to the field of law on his natural law framework.[102] While Grotius relied on "good faith" as a concept rooted in natural law, he also "made it a non-religious concept ... since he clearly recognized the binding force of treaties between Christians and non-Christians."[103] Just as Aquinas before him distinguished between will and reason, Grotius contributed to the further separation between principles of natural law and religious moralism.[104]

For Grotius, the primary role of the law, developed in accordance with human intelligence, is to maintain social order.[105] Grotius succinctly outlines the necessity of refraining from infringing on the property of others, the need to restore another's property in the event of an intrusion, "the obligation to fulfil promises, the making good of a loss incurred through our fault, and the inflicting of penalties upon men according to their just desserts."[106] Grotius also believed that the natural law obliges men to "abide by pacts" and, in a proto social-contract theory, that men consent (or impliedly consent) to the majoritarian rule of the societies with which they have associated themselves.[107] While the nature of man "is the mother of law and nature[,]" the "mother of municipal law is the obligation which arises from mutual consent; and since this obligation derives its force from the law of nature, nature may be considered, so to say, the great-grand-mother of municipal law."[108] Unmistakably, Grotius viewed the natural law as consistent with the notion of consent to subject oneself to the rules and customs of a society rooted in the Natural Law Tradition.[109] In this way, the views of Grotius on consent to participate in society are similar to those of English philosopher Thomas Hobbes (1588-1679).

A Return to English Influence: Thomas Hobbes, Algernon Sidney, and John Locke

Thomas Hobbes' more nuanced view of the law accepted natural law as arrived at by reason, and as placing human life at the pinnacle of the hierarchy of rights.[110] Hobbes (1588-1697) also viewed liberty—in a foretaste to the revolutionary Austrian economist Ludwig von Mises—as the "absence of external impediments"[111] which he noted often "take away part of man's power to do what he would."[112] Cautioning that impediments, however, "cannot hinder [a man] from using the power left [to] him, according as his judgment, and reason [would] dictate to him," Hobbes emphasized the continuing role of personal judgment and reason in man's self-regulating societal behavior.[113]

Hobbes lived during "a time of great political and intellectual transformation [... when] changing political structure [combined] with the emergence of states as the foremost political entities in the international arena [... and] the divine right of kings to rule began to be questioned and rudimentary ideas of representation as the basis for political legitimacy emerged."[114] So, Hobbes imagined the harshest and most dangerous state of nature: A state of anarchy in which one's life was "solitary, poore [*sic*], nasty, brutish, and short."[115] As Psychology Professor Steven Pinker explains,

> The title of his masterwork identified a way to escape [stateless anarchy]: the Leviathan, a monarchy or other government authority that embodies the will of the people and has a monopoly on the use of force. By inflicting penalties on aggressors, the Leviathan can eliminate their incentive for aggression, in turn defusing general anxieties about preemptive attack and obviating everyone's need to maintain a hair trigger for retaliation to prove their resolve. And because the Leviathan is a disinterested third party, it is not biased by the chauvinism that makes each side think its opponent has a heart of darkness while it is as pure as the driven snow.[116]

In this context, Hobbes examined the relationship between law and right, and the relationship between obligation and liberty. To Hobbes, *right* pertained to the "liberty to do or to forebear,"[117] whereas *law* determined and "[bound] to [the right to do or to forebear]."[118] In other words, law attaches to, hinders, and regulates one's rights.[119] In *Leviathan* (1651), he remarked, "[a]nd first it is manifest, that law in general, is not counsel, but command; nor a command of any man to any man; but only of him, whose command is addressed to one formerly obliged to obey him."[120] Essential to Hobbes's formulation is the notion that a preexisting obligation must be present in order to bind one to the laws of another, i.e., actual consent. Accordingly, "[f]or Hobbes, [...] command, sanction, and obligation are three independent and severable concepts."[121] In other words, command (orders), sanction (punishment), and obligation (duty), maintain their own independent character. "For Hobbes, all obligations, including political obligation to obey the sovereign, arise from voluntary choice."[122]

The *Discourses Concerning Government* by Algernon

Sidney (1623-1683), first published posthumously in England in 1698, came to be widely reprinted throughout the 18th century and helped fan the fire of rebellion against tyranny in the colonies.[123] Sidney's defense of republican government, preserved the heart of the political teaching of the ancients, and was written in response to Sir Robert Filmer's *Patriarcha* (1680), an ode to the divine right of kings and their absolute power. Filmer's argument, summarized by Sidney, is that God "caused some to be born with crowns upon their heads, and all others with saddles upon their backs,"[124] and as such, it is God's will that the king, even a tyrannical one, remain free to rule without constraint.

Sidney fervently disputed this premise, and instead argued that "man must be naturally free," equal liberty being "the gift of God and nature."[125] Taking issue with the idea that birth determined men's rightful rulers, Sidney argued that free choice was the only legitimate source of a ruler's power.

Man cannot continue in the ... liberty that God hath given him. The liberty of one is thwarted by that of another; and whilst they are all equal, none will yield to any, otherwise than by a general consent. This is the ground of all just government.[126]

He further discussed the purpose of government, which "discovered by reason, is to protect the people in their natural liberty as far as that is prudent,"[127] and otherwise, leave individuals free to make their own decisions on issues concerning their "lands, goods, lives, and liberties."[128] The society in which I live cannot subsist unless by rule; the equality in which men are born is so perfect, that no man will suffer his natural liberty to be abridged, except others do the like:

> I cannot reasonably expect to be defended from wrong, unless I oblige myself to do none; or to suffer the punishment prescribed by the law, if I perform not my engagement. But without prejudice to the society into which I enter, I may and do retain to myself the liberty of doing what I please in all things relating peculiarly to myself, or in which I am to seek my own convenience.[129]

The idea of a government deriving its powers from the consent of the governed limited by that consent and the natural law, is thus, the linchpin of a just government. Should a governing body not have such limitations, Sidney argued, the people have a right to overthrow their rulers. Beyond this right of revolution,[130] Sidney echoed Aquinas, "[t]hat which is not just is not law, and that which is not law ought not to be obeyed."[131] Sidney believed that law should be

> ...void of desire and fear, lust and anger. Tis *mens sine affectu* [mind without passion], written reason, retaining some measure of the divine perfection. It does not enjoin that which pleases a weak, frail man, but without any regard to persons commands that which is good, and punishes evil in all, whether rich or poor, high or low.[132]

Sidney's arguments are echoed by many who followed, as we will see with John Locke, and were revered by "radicals" in Revolutionary America.

John Locke (1632-1704) believed the sovereignty of the individual is the source of political authority,[133] but also supported the idea that man must choose whether to enter into society. "Locke argued that a political society came into existence when a group of people 'incorporated' and formed themselves into '*one Body Politick*.'"[134] This incorporation required the actual consent of the individuals in the group, and, following this incorporation, the group "could act by the consent of the majority to institute a government for themselves."[135]

However, unlike Aquinas, who viewed the creation of law as a *natural* extension of human reason, Locke appeared to "[reject] the central doctrine of Aristotelian and Thomist[ic] political philosophy, the naturalness of political life, and envisaged instead a state of nature where a political community had to be created by human artifice."[136] Brian Tierney, a Cornell University philosopher, suggests the apparent divide between Aquinas and Locke derives from "a misunderstanding of medieval thought about natural law and human nature."[137] According to Professor Tierney, "the Natural Law that medieval jurists and philosophers knew [suggested that] humans were by nature free and equal."[138] Accordingly, government does not develop spontaneously, but rather is created by man.[139] This is an expression of the link between Aquinas and Locke.

Locke begins the substantive part of his exegesis, the *Second Treatise on Government*, with an explanation of the state of nature. As "a state of perfect freedom to order [one's own] actions, and dispose of [one's own] possessions and [person] as [one] think[s] fit" so long as it remains in the bounds "of the law of Nature," Locke's state of nature describes not nihilistic anarchy but rather a permissionless condition in which man freely exercises his natural rights according to the dictates of his own reason and in harmony with the natural rights of others and intending for man to go to Heaven after death.[140]

"The state of Nature[,]" of course, "has a law of Nature to govern it, which obliges every one, and reason, which is that law, teaches all mankind who will but consult it, that being all equal and independent, no one ought to harm another in his life, health, liberty, or possessions."[141] In modifying the formula of those natural law scholars that came before him, Locke reflects the strong dispositions of his time to the importance of one's personal choices, personal possessions, and acquisition of real property.[142]

Later in his *Second Treatise*, Locke revisited the natural rights and powers with respect to man's relationship with others. In this famous passage, Locke records his well-known axiom that later serves as a battle cry of the American Republic, *life, liberty,* and *estate*: "Man being born, as has been proved, with a title to perfect freedom and an uncontrolled enjoyment of all the rights and privileges of the law of Nature, equally with any other man, or number of men in the world, hath by nature a power not only to preserve his property—that is, his life, liberty, and estate against the injuries and attempts of other men, but to judge of and punish the breaches of that law in others, as he is persuaded the offence deserves, even with death itself, in crimes where the heinousness of the fact, in his opinion, requires it."[143]

However, when man enters into a compact to form a society, he entrusts certain powers and rights to that society to act as safeguard of his rights and person.[144] Once man joins society, he necessarily demonstrates a willingness to refrain from exercising certain rights and allow "the community [...] to be umpire."[145] The community then, "understanding indifferent rules" comes to "authorize" men to execute the rules and "[decide] all the differences that may happen between any members of that society concerning a matter of right, and [punish] those offences which any member hath committed against the society" with the established penalties.[146]

Locke proclaimed those in such a collective to be members of a "civil society," and those living outside such an arrangement to exist in a "state of nature."[147] To exit the state of nature, man must "[agree] with other men, to join and unite into a community for their comfortable, safe, and peaceable living, [...] in secure enjoyment of their properties, and a greater security against any that are not" within it.[148] The purpose of government then becomes to provide man with the security to enjoy his property and liberty,[149] such that men then permit government to make, promulgate, and enforce those laws to that end.[150]

Locke's ideas about the purpose of government eventually found their way into the Declaration of Independence in the oft-quoted passage where Jefferson wrote:

> We hold these truths to be self-evident, that all men are created equal, that they are endowed by their creator with certain inalienable Rights, that among these are Life, Liberty and the Pursuit of Happiness-that to secure these Rights, Governments are instituted among Men, deriving their just powers from the consent of the governed.[151]

These thinkers and philosophers explored and developed Natural Law theories and ideas that would, in turn, inform those who followed. Each, building upon the works promulgated by his predecessors, refined and advanced the human understanding of the natural law.

Aristotle laid a foundation. Aquinas provided a framework. Grotius recognized its universality and secularized the natural law by divorcing it from religious moralism. Hobbes explained how the natural law relates to choice, and man-made law to voluntary self-imposed obligation to obey. Locke explored the requirements man must accept in order to enter into society, and how certain rights must necessarily be individually and voluntarily entrusted to a controlling body or organ granted the power to ensure the safety and happiness of the community. And he stressed the natural principle that governments exist *only* to protect the liberty and property of individuals.

The ideas discussed by these iconic thinkers had lasting and far-reaching impact on those who followed. These ideas peak out from the leaves of parchment and velum upon which future jurists and scholars penned opinions and treatises. As judges and lawyers confronted necessary issues resulting from the changing legal and political landscape brought on by tumbling and emerging monarchical dynasties, they turned to the only set of rules or guidelines that they found universally applicable, and generally immutable: the Natural Law Tradition. We turn now to an examination of the reverence shown to natural law by the highest jurists in England.

CHAPTER 2

THE NATURAL LAW:
FROM THE DESK TO THE BENCH

The Argument

The writings and ideas of the natural law thinkers and philosophers were widely taught throughout Europe and the West, and influenced lawyers, legal scholars, and appellate jurists.

The practitioners of law on both sides of the bench relied upon the arguments and rationale espoused by the natural law trailblazers and enshrined their principles into the common law and legal psyche through legal opinions and treatises, which were then studied throughout the courts and the academy.

Canonizing these natural law principles through official reports and exhaustive, dispositive treatises, lawyers and judges like Coke and Blackstone secured for posterity the role of the natural law in western jurisprudence.

While the natural law philosophers would provide many of the ideological underpinnings of the American Revolution, it was the natural law lawyers and judges who provided the evidence argued by the colonial patriots in tribunals.

It was on this confluence of philosophy and common law reality that the American patriots would rely for much of the ideological support for the American Revolution.

***

Judges wear legal professionalism and precedent as a mantel that secures legitimacy for their decisions. It's how they distinguish themselves from politicians or administrative agencies, while wielding power that is sometimes much greater than those democratically accountable actors.[1]

– **Yochai Benkler (b. 1964)**

Sir Edward Coke: Dr. Bonham's Case and Calvin's Case

While Aquinas, Grotius, Hobbes, and Locke contributed immensely to social, political, and judicial thought, none of them sat on the bench like their philosophical descendant, Sir Edward Coke (1552-1634). Coke's *First Institutes of the Laws of England*, first published in 1628, is peppered with natural law arguments. Explaining that, "[r]eason is the life of the law," Coke invokes a now familiar natural law axiom: *Reason drives the law*.[2] Qualifying that "the common law itself is nothing else but reason[,]" Coke signals the importance of reason in the path of the law.[3] The common law, "an artificial perfection of reason, gotten by long study, observation, and experience," does not come from "every man's natural reason[,]" since, as Coke slyly remarks, "*Nemo nascitur artifex*[:]" no one is born an artist.[4] He concludes the paragraph with another Latin quip, "*Neminem oportet esse sapientiorem legibus*: no man (out of his own private reason) ought to be wiser than *the law, which is the perfection of reason*."[5] With this simple phrase—law is the perfection of reason—Coke showed himself as both descendant and pupil to his natural law progenitors.

As indicated by its full title,[6] Coke's First Institute was written as a commentary on Thomas de Littleton's treatise on land tenure.[7] Though recognized as a seminal work on the history of the development and analysis of the common law in England, Coke's First Institute, as well as his subsequent works, suffered greatly from deficiencies in organization so widespread and consistent as to render it, "in a manner[,] lost to the [legal] profession" for a time.[8] Noting the importance of Coke's Institutes while simultaneously lamenting its organization, an iconic Coke scholar noted, "although [Coke's Institutes] loses much of its value by its chaotic form, it may still [1814] [sic] be considered as the fundamental code of English Law"[9] Thomas Jefferson himself underscored Coke's impact on legal thought.[10]

> [Lord] Coke has given us the first view of the whole body of law worthy now of being studied: for so much of the admirable work of Bracton is now obsolete that the student should turn to it occasionally only, when tracing the history of particular portions of the law. *Coke's Institutes are a perfect Digest of the law as it stood in his day.* after this, new laws were added by the legislature, and new developements [sic] of the old laws by the Judges, until they had become so voluminous as to require a new Digest.[11]

In the common law, Coke believed, one could trace the refinement of natural law principles through the refractory lens of reason. He also emphasized the need to understand the purpose of a law,[12] and further elaborates on this in his discussion in *Calvin's Case*.[13]

In the landmark 1608 opinion in *Calvin's Case*, Lord Coke delivered a robust defense of the natural law in finding that a child born in Scotland five years after the Union of the Crowns in 1603, in which James the VI of Scotland ascended to the thrones of England and Ireland, was an English subject and therefore could legally inherit land in England.[14] *Calvin's Case* was decided on natural law principles, and Coke relied heavily on the "laws of nature" in his argument.[15] Declaring without the need for further justification that the "law of nature is a part of the laws of England," Coke demonstrated the popular and widespread acceptance of the natural law as a jurisprudential reality.[16] Coke also recorded "[t]hat the law of nature was before any judicial or municipal law in the world[,]" and that "the law of nature is immutable, and cannot be changed."[17]

Coke announced more than his intent to ground his decision within the bounds of the natural law. Surely, a jurist as prominent as Coke would not bind a decision in gossamer wisps of ethereal speculation and medieval superstition. The prominent place he accepted for natural law in English law demonstrated his view of its importance and acceptance. However, Coke felt the need to clarify its exact role. He showed the need for explicit delineation of, what he deemed to be, the static and immutable laws of nature and how they should run concurrently with the laws of man. This seemingly minor inclusion in *Calvin's Case*, the reliance on the natural law, signaled perhaps a larger understanding that where the laws of the state did not automatically agree with the natural law, since the natural law is immutable, the laws of the state must defer to it. Coke saw the issues in *Calvin's Case* as obscured by the trappings of politics and custom, causing "doubt [that] grew from some violent passion, and not from any reason grounded upon the law of nature."[18] Clearly, he favored the natural law as the polestar guiding his judgment. In *Calvin's Case*, Coke gave a robust definition and discussion of the nature of the natural law:

> The law of nature is that which God at the time of creation of the nature of man infused into his heart, for his preservation and direction; and this *lex æterna*, the moral law, called also the law of nature. And by this law, written with the finger of God in the heart of man, were the people of God a long time governed, before the law was written by Moses, who was the first reporter or writer of law in the world. [...] And the reason hereof is, for that God and nature is one to all, and therefore the law of God and nature is one to all.[19]

Coke's words mirrored Aquinas' precisely, that the "[t]he Natural Law is promulgated by the very fact that God has instilled it in the minds of men so as to be known to them naturally."[20] In upholding Robert Calvin's property rights notwithstanding who was the British King at the time of Calvin's birth, Coke echoed the Grotian idea of the universality of natural law principles while simultaneously stretching the boundaries of natural law in an attempt to address the expansive force of government, and the recognition of inalienable individual rights which government is bound to recognize.

Coke would later note in his *Institutes*, in an exhaustive list of the divers[e] laws within the realm of England, Natural Law in the third of many below "the law of the crown[,]" the elusive (and perhaps inconsistent[21]) laws and customs of parliament, and above "the common law of England" and "statute law[s] [...] established by the authority of parliament."[22] Coke's list contained fifteen types of law that would be taught to law students throughout the English-speaking world. Etched into the minds of law students, this list even passed through the quill of a twenty-three-year-old John Adams.[23]

A structuralist approach, one that considers the organization of the agencies and instrumentalities of government, might suggest that Coke put the rules of the Crown and laws and customs of Parliament above the natural law for pragmatic, not formal reasons. A structuralist approach might also call for placing the Second Amendment in the U.S. Constitution above the Fourth, and, perhaps, the Eighteenth Amendment above the Twenty-First. However, any structuralist argument aimed to attribute to Coke the boorish belief that Britain's Crown could claim, parallel to parliament, some sort of superimposed supremacy over the natural law famously fails when filtered through Coke's judicial opinions where Coke did not wilt at the prospect of defying the Crown or Parliament. He decided cases like the *Case of Proclamations*, in which Coke, along with other judges, found that the King could only make laws through Parliament[24]—imposing significant and unprecedented limits on the arbitrary powers of the Crown—and *Dr. Bonham's Case*, in which Coke would opine on conditions which could render a law invalid.

A couple years after *Calvin's Case*, Coke would rely on the natural law in *Dr. Bonham's Case*, a dispute in which a physician, Thomas Bonham, was fined and imprisoned by the College of Physicians on the grounds that he was not licensed to practice by the College.[25] Bonham sued for false imprisonment, and Coke found the penalties unjust since the Act of Parliament seemed to enfranchise the college's Censors to serve as judge, jury, and enforcer: "The Censors, cannot be Judges, Ministers, and parties; Judges, to give sentence or judgment; Ministers to make summons; and Parties, to have the moyety [moiety] of the forfeiture, [...] and one cannot be Judge and Attorney for any of the parties."[26] Such a ruling would later serve as reasoning expanded upon in the American concept of due process. Coke continued, announcing that:

> And it appeareth in our Books, that in many Cases, the Common Law doth control Acts of Parliament, and sometimes shall adjudge them to be void: for when an Act of Parliament is against *Common right and reason*, or repugnant, or impossible to be performed, the Common Law will control it, and adjudge such Act to be void.[27]

Here, Coke composed a common refrain which would later be quoted by American Revolutionary pamphleteers, lawyers, and jurists, that the natural law, sometimes referred to as the Common Right and Reason by Coke and his peers, can void an act of Parliament that runs contrary to reason, is repugnant to it, or is otherwise impossible to be performed. In other words, Coke recognized that the natural law can, *sua sponte*, void an act of Parliament that runs contrary to it.

John Milton's Aeropagitica

Other natural law arguments appeared frequently in the historical record. In 1644, the poet and essayist John Milton (1608-1674) delivered a polemic opposing a licensing and censorship order from Parliament issued one year prior. Known as *Aeropagitica*, the text is often hailed as one of the most eloquent and enduring encomia of free speech. Central to Milton's argument against censorship is the natural law.

> For those actions which enter into a man, rather than issue out of him, and therefore defile not, GOD uses not to captivate under perpetual childhood of prescription, but trusts him with the gift of Reason to be his own chooser; there were but little work left for preaching, if law and compulsion should grow so fast upon those things which heretofore were governed only by exhortation.[28]

Milton argued that reason, a gift to all humans from God, should prevail over the encroachment of hastily-issued laws and decrees running contrary to the exercise of natural reason, which, to Milton, numbered among the powers endowed by our natural faculties.

Milton was not the first to rely on the natural law to appeal to the minds of Parliament. Nor was he the last. As R. H. Helmholz noted in 2005, "the list of common law jurists who wrote positively on the Natural Law in England" is indeed a lengthy list.[29] It even includes a saint, Thomas More.

Sir William Blackstone's
Commentaries of the Laws of England

Numbering amongst the luminaries developing the natural law was the English justice, Sir William Blackstone (1723-1780).[30] Blackstone published his *Commentaries of the Laws of England* between 1765 and 1769. The future Chief Justice of the United States Supreme Court, John Marshall, devoured the first American edition of Blackstone's commentaries when it was first published in 1772 when Marshall was 16 or 17.[31] Revolutionary demigods like "George Wythe, [Chancellor of William and Mary], John Jay, James Wilson, Roger Sherman, John Adams, and virtually every leading member of the legal profession" in the Revolutionary Era subscribed to the treatise's first American publication.[32] Blackstone's embrace of the common-law presented jurists and lawyers with a methodological framework for arguing and deciding cases.

Biographer Jean Edward Smith explains that "the British method" of training lawyers involved them "apprenticing themselves to an established practitioner and 'reading law' under his supervision."[33] This approach required reading "the decisions of King's Bench and the High Court of Chancery and whatever colonial reports might be available."[34] Smith notes that even John Adams, who studied law in the British fashion, referred to it as "[a] dreary ramble."[35]

The issues endemic to this approach of learning law resulted from the fact "that the cases upon which the profession relied were sometimes capricious, occasionally perverse, and often obscure."[36] In addition, "[t]here were few laws on the statute books to apply, and those that did exist were rarely collected into a single volume, much less codified in usable form."[37] While a few significant legal treatises did exist, such as *Coke's Institutes*, these treatises often recounted and analyzed cases rather than expounding upon methods and principles.[38] Noting that "[s]ince only the most established and successful lawyers might be fortunate enough to own a copy of one of these works," Smith concluded that "the novice attorney was consigned to a relentless process of reading cases and memorizing the decisions."[39]

As a result, "[t]he consequence was a legal profession trained to know every precedent in excruciating detail but largely lacking a fundamental understanding of the law."[40] Concluding, "[t]he typical lawyer of the day simply could not see the forest for the trees," Smith underscored how most practitioners of the legal profession adopted a narrow approach to the law and recounted mostly well-known and well-worn judge-made precedent, or the common law, rather than steadfast reliance on statutes. Blackstone managed to take the first significant step to change the way that law was learned, taught, and practiced by the organization and focus of his *Commentaries*.

Blackstone's treatise contains numerous references to the natural law and indeed, placed it "superior" to all other law, "human," positive or otherwise, yet subject to human error in discovery.[41] Organizationally, it is the first source of law discussed in his treatise. In Chapter 1, "Of the Absolute Rights of Individuals," Blackstone explains: Persons ... are divided by the law into either natural persons, or artificial. Natural persons are such as the God of nature formed us; artificial are such as created and devised by human laws ... which are called corporations or bodies politic...

> The rights of persons considered in their natural capacities are also of two sorts, absolute and relative. .... By the absolute *rights* of individuals, we mean those which are so in their primary and strictest sense; such as would belong to their persons merely in a state of nature, and which every man is entitled to enjoy, whether out of society or in it...

> For the principal aim of society is to protect individuals in the enjoyment of those absolute rights which were vested in them by the immutable

laws of nature, but which could not be preserved in peace without that mutual assistance and intercourse which is gained by the institution of friendly and social communities. Hence it follows that the first and primary end of human laws is to maintain and regulate these absolute rights of individuals.[42]

Blackstone proceeds by examining how far law should, and how far the laws of England do, "take notice of these absolute rights, and provide for their lasting security."[43] He delineates the rights of the people of England into three primary categories, "the right of personal security, the right of personal liberty, and the right of private property: because . . . the preservation of these, inviolate, may justly be said to include the preservation of our civil immunities in their largest and most extensive sense."[44]

However, Blackstone, a champion of parliamentary supremacy, did not share Coke's view that judges could legitimately disregard legislation that they considered inconsistent with reason or with the law of nature.[45] Blackstone wrote:

> With regard to the first of these [several parts of the law—declaratory, directory, remedial, and vindicatory—], the declaratory part of the municipal law, this depends not so much upon the law of revelation or of nature, as upon the wisdom and will of the legislator. This doctrine, which before was slightly touched, deserves a more particular explication. Those rights then which God and nature have established, and are therefore called natural rights, such as are life and liberty, need not the aid of human laws to be more effectually invested in every man than they are; neither do they receive any additional strength when declared by the municipal laws to be inviolable. On the contrary, *no human legislature has power to abridge or destroy them, unless the owner shall himself commit some act that amounts to a forfeiture.*[46]

In other words, Blackstone allows for a legislature to abridge or destroy the natural rights only when the owner of such rights engages in behavior tantamount to a forfeiture of those rights. If Parliament were to defy the law of nature (a prospect that Blackstone thought almost inconceivable), the only remedy would lie in the streets rather than in the courts.

Like others before him, Blackstone viewed the natural law as instilled in man by God, and thus discoverable through reason.[47] Noting that since God possesses "infinite *wisdom*," and God "laid down" only the laws related to justice that existed before "any positive precept[;]" before the laws of man, Blackstone signaled his firm recognition that the natural law predates and preempts positive human law.[48] He also believed these laws of nature "[were] the eternal immutable laws of good and evil, to which the Creator himself, in all his dispensations, conforms; and which he has enabled human reason to discover, so far as they are necessary for the conduct of human actions."[49] Included in such a belief rests the notion of a fatalistic predeterminism regarding the natural law — that it is *static*, *eternal*, and *immutable*, as Coke stated in *Calvin's Case*, and thus cannot be ignored, changed or preempted.

However, Blackstone cleverly asserted that God has enabled human reason to discover these natural laws, but only "so far as they are necessary for the conduct of human actions," which allowed for a flexible approach to the natural law and hinted at Blackstone's understanding that future discoveries would need to be made in response to future human conduct and needs.[50]

Like others before him, Blackstone began his natural law analysis flowing from the "one paternal precept."[51] Whereas Aquinas began with human life striving to live virtuously and avoid evil, Blackstone, quoting Justinian, believed "that man should pursue his own true and substantial happiness."[52] To Blackstone, this precept served as the "foundation of what we call ethics, or Natural Law."[53] Blackstone's assertion, that natural law, "[t]his law of nature, […] is […] superior in obligation to any other" and "is binding over all the globe in all countries, and at all times," indicates a prevailing Grotian belief in the universality of the natural law.[54] Further asserting, "no human laws are of any validity, if contrary to [the natural law], and such of them as are valid derive all their force and their authority, mediately or immediately, from this original," Blackstone echoed Coke in holding that natural law serves as the foundation for objectively good laws.[55]

Blackstone demurs, however, maintaining that all human laws depend on the "law of nature and the law of revelation" so that "no human laws should be suffered to contradict these."[56] Instead of declaring any human law that contradicts the natural law to be invalid, Blackstone's use of the modal verb *should* suggests a weaker assertion than *shall* or *must*. Perhaps he merely recognized the tertiary position of the judiciary in a government of Crown and Parliament. At any rate, Blackstone proposed a preference rather than a command. He clarified his position:

> There are, it is true, a great number of indifferent points in which both the divine law and the natural leave a man at his own liberty, but which are found necessary, for the benefit of society, to be restrained within certain limits. And herein it is that human laws have their greatest force and efficacy; for, with regard to such points as are not indifferent, human laws are only declaratory of, and act in subordination to, the former.[57]

For the benefit of society, Blackstone argued, certain liberties afforded man by divine law and natural law, may be necessarily restrained.[58] Blackstone did not object when only those indifferent or insignificant or inconsequential liberties are restrained. Indeed, he argued that human law was most effective when *only* restraining those indifferent liberties.

Such restraints, however, only became necessary when man entered into a society.[59] Reasoning that "[I]f man were to live in a state of nature, unconnected with other individuals, there would be no occasion for any other laws than the law of nature, and the law of God," Blackstone made clear his belief that the man-made laws may only become justified for a greater benefit when man organized into a society.[60]

And, as observed by Locke, when man organizes into society, the need for municipal law arises.[61] Blackstone harkened back to classical antiquity invoking Justinian's *Institutes* in his definition of municipal law. He declared "[m]unicipal law, thus understood, is properly defined to be 'a rule of civil conduct prescribed by the supreme power in a state, commanding what is right and prohibiting what is wrong.'"[62] Blackstone engaged in a rhetorical analysis of the expression, distinguishing a rule from a compact or agreement,[63] municipal law (as a written and ratified rule of civil conduct) from "natural" or "revealed" law,[64] and noted the need for promulgation.[65] Finally, Blackstone, quoting Justinian again, discussed the source of municipal law, "the supreme power in a state."[66] But only natural reason could determine what is right and what is wrong. According to Blackstone, the legislature "is the greatest act of superiority that can be exercised by one being over another."[67] Blackstone conceded the necessity of some legislative body. "For when civil society is once formed, government at the same time results of course, as necessary to preserve and to keep that society in order."[68] Blackstone viewed government as a natural result, or requirement, of the formation of society. Without government, "some superior [...] whose commands and decisions all the members [of the society] are bound to obey, [the members of the society] would still remain in a state of nature, without any judge upon earth to define their several rights, and redress their several wrongs."[69] According to Blackstone, those possessed of "wisdom, of goodness, and of power" should comprise this superior since these are "the attributes of Him who is emphatically styled the Supreme Being."[70] Clearly, this is his anti-Grotius side as religious moralism still featured prominently in his notion of law and society.

Blackstone, though clearly establishing the existence of the natural law as a legal rule that is "of course, superior in obligation to any other [...] binding over all the globe in all countries," gave a degree of deference to parliamentary action broader than what was ascribed to by most of the public mind in America at the time of the ratification of the U.S. Constitution.[71] This stood in stark contrast, as Thomas Jefferson would later argue, to "a universal and almost uncontroverted position in the several states," that "the purposes of society do not require us to surrender all of our [natural] rights to our ordinary governors."[72] Indeed, Blackstone observed in his *Commentaries* that a legislature or the judiciary may recognize an abridgement or destruction of natural rights only when the owner of such rights engages in behavior tantamount to a forfeiture of those rights.[73]

St. George Tucker (1752-1827), an American professor and judge, said in his *Notes on Blackstone's Commentaries*, that this notion of legislative supremacy was abrogated based on the doctrine of delegated powers, arguing that this applies to societies where power has been transferred to "usurpers of their natural rights," not where a free compact has been made with express delegation.[74] Indeed, James Wilson, a signer of the Declaration of Independence and Pennsylvania delegate to the Constitutional Convention, would later note, "[t]o every suggestion concerning a bill of rights, the citizens of the United States may always say, WE reserve the right to do what we please."[75] The application of Blackstone's view of the balance of legislative powers and the people's natural liberty—a balance to be regulated by Parliament—is based on a more complex history of conquest and vestment of all sovereignty in parliament, inapplicable to a delegated powers approach with an underlying natural law base wherein the people individually and collectively retain ultimate sovereignty and liberty.[76] Stated differently, supremacy in America, as we shall soon see, would never emerge in the federal government because of the Framers' understanding and respect for the natural law.

The writings of Coke and Blackstone served as scripture to the students kneeling at the altar of the common law. While the works of natural law philosophers informed social and political thought, the works of jurists like Coke and Blackstone transmitted ideas and tenets into rules and precedent. Colonial lawyers and judges relied upon the precedents set by the great jurists whose cases they read and whose treatises they devoured as students. Patriots whose names grace American towns and streets, and whose luminous portraits peer at visitors from walls of the National Portrait gallery, quoted philosophers in their polemics and cases but cited to Coke in briefs, oral arguments, and decisions.

How effectively did those arguments migrate into early American jurisprudence – even early American passion? It is to that fascinating subject to which we now turn.

CHAPTER 3

THE NATURAL LAW
EMIGRATES TO THE NEW WORLD

The Argument

Natural Law theories, foundational in the development of western jurisprudence, travelled across the Atlantic in the rich, common law tradition of England. The great minds of the colonies read the great minds of Europe and were inspired. The colonial agitators of the eighteenth century, who were not always lawyers, were nevertheless well versed in the important writings of the time – as well as the works of classical antiquity.

The numerous pamphlets and broadsides that survive provide a comprehensive account of the views of the wider American population at the time of the Revolution, calling for some form of action – any action – to respond to what they believed represented a grievous affront to their rights as Englishmen and a dangerous encroachment on their personal liberties. Through a thorough review of these materials we see the natural law principles which were continuously invoked as a justification for rebellion.

Ultimately, the First Continental Congress assembled to explore options for expressing grievances to King George III, and the Second Continental Congress adopted the Declaration of Independence – a document packed with natural law arguments – and began a war with Great Britain.

***

As to the history of the Revolution, my Ideas may be peculiar, perhaps Singular. What do We mean by the Revolution? The War? That was no part of the Revolution. It was only an Effect and Consequence of it. The Revolution was in the Minds of the People, and this was effected, from 1760 to 1775, in the course of fifteen Years before a drop of blood was drawn at Lexington.[1]

– John Adams (1735-1826)

Until now, our substantive exploration has focused on important philosophical developments in Natural Law theory rather than empirical history or biography. In other words, the focus of this work thus far has been on principles and ideas rather than personalities and incidents. However, as we approach our discussion of the American Revolution, and endeavor to uncover the understanding of the law held by America's founders, we must take into account the surrounding circumstances, recent historiography, and unfolding events to contextualize the positions taken and decisions made impacting our founding and the rule of law in the early days of the American Republic.

Historians have quibbled for two centuries over the direct and indirect causes of the American Revolution. Revolutions are seldom born from a singular cause or on the back of a singular individual. The American Revolution happened, and, undoubtedly, different leaders within the ranks of the rebels had different motivations for taking up arms against the British. This work addresses events and persons involved in the Revolution to the extent that such discussions further the endeavor in which we find ourselves. Naturally, some historical figures will be absent from this tableaux, and issues deserving of prominence in a chronicle of history will, unavoidably, not receive the type of billing some may feel they deserve. On the canvas on which this chapter is painted are drawn public events, the course of which were influenced by the principles of natural law.

The understanding of rights during "the revolutionary era arose primarily out of the traditional English conception of fundamental law [...] superior to all organs of government [...] [that were] renewed and fortified [...] by the political and legal theories of the Enlightenment."[2] Writers such as "Pufendorf, Burlamaqui[,] and Vattel" informed this understanding since they "stressed limitations upon legislative power imposed by both general Natural Law and by the particular provisions of each nation's constitution."[3] These writers, as well as Thomas Rutherforth, "stressed the importance of Natural Law and natural rights."[4] However, "unlike Locke [...]—and more seriously than Blackstone— they claimed *legally binding* force for the law of nature. They insisted that legislative power could not lawfully infringe the first principles of morality and politics."[5] It was largely these Enlightenment thinkers who "reinforced and partly reformulated the idea of a fixed and binding constitution placing legal limitations on legislative power in addition to those imposed by Natural Law."[6]

A. HISTORICAL CONTEXT: 18TH CENTURY BRITISH AFFRONTS TO AMERICAN LIBERTIES

A series of acts by Parliament, starting in the 1760s as an attempt by England to raise revenue to cover the costs of the expensive French and Indian War, began to tax the patience, as well as the pockets, of the colonists. Although the French and Indian War (also known as the Seven Years' War) ended on February 10, 1763 with the Peace of Paris, and gave Britain "undisputed dominance over the eastern half of North America,"[7] the war nearly doubled Great Britain's national debt,[8] and "British officials found themselves having to make long-postponed decisions concerning the colonies that would set in motion a chain of events that ultimately shattered the empire."[9]

In addition to the growing debt, new peace-time expenses included maintaining a standing army of 10,000 troops in America at a cost of 220,000 pounds per year;[10] after all, "until the Englishmen outnumbered the hostile French and Indian population, there would be a constant danger of repossession by France in a future war."[11] As a result, the British Crown sought sources of revenue from the colonists to pay a share of the mounting debt, and began to impose "legislative or administrative action based upon a British theory that the colonies were subject in every respect to the sovereignty of the King, Lords and Commons of Great Britain in Parliament assembled."[12] As many historians have noted, however, this sovereignty was one in which the colonists had "no voice or vote."[13]

The Sugar Act of 1764

In April 1764, Parliament passed the Sugar Act, in which the House of Commons alarmingly proclaimed in the preamble: "it is just and necessary, that a revenue be raised in America for defraying the expenses of defending, protecting, and securing" the colonies.[14] Although there had been some prior legislation, such as the Molasses Act of 1733 "which, if properly enforced, would have made it possible to collect additional revenue...[specifically,] six pence per gallon tax on the importation of foreign molasses into the colonies,"[15] "the affairs of the British Empire were so poorly run in the American Colonies that it was costing the British eight thousand pounds per year to collect two thousand pounds in custom duties."[16]

As a result, the Sugar Act taxed commodities such as sugar, wines directly imported from their point of origin, foreign coffee, indigo, and foreign silks. In addition to the six sections of the Act dealing with taxation, in order to ensure that its provisions were enforceable, the Sugar Act "was devoted to a revision of the customs and commerce regulations which amounted to a constitutional revolution in the relation of the colonies to the home country."[17] According to then Governor Francis Bernard of Massachusetts, notice of the enforcement of this tax "caused a greater alarm in America than had the French capture of Fort William Henry six years before," resulting in "not only the merchants but the rest of the public ... denounce[ing] customs officers for restricting the natural rights and liberties of the people."[18]

Response from the Colonial Assemblies to Sugar Act

This concern regarding the natural right to use and enjoy private property was voiced officially, and in September 1764 the New York Assembly appointed a committee to draft a protest insisting on the right to be taxed only by consent, with "absolutely no concessions to a supposed expediency."[19] According to historian Bernhard Knollenberg, the New York Assembly's protests (one each to the Houses of Commons and Lords, and one to the king) were "among the great state papers of the prerevolutionary period."[20] The Assembly argued that the exemption from nonconsensual taxation was not simply a privilege but a "natural right of mankind ... a Right ... inseparable from the very idea of property, for who can call that his own which can be taken away at the pleasure of another?"[21]

The Stamp Act of 1765

The following Spring, on March 22, 1765, Parliament passed the Stamp Act, which required a broad range of printed materials to be produced on paper bearing the stamp of the tax collector in order to prove that its duties had been paid, including, for example, documents used in court proceedings, college diplomas, appointments to public office, bonds, grants and deeds for land, mortgages, indentures, leases, contracts, bills of sale, playing cards, dice, pamphlets, newspapers (and advertisements in them), and almanacs.[22] Thomas Whatley, a British member of Parliament, who served as Secretary to the Treasury, had been tasked with preparing the Stamp Act, yet was unsure how such restrictions would be received in the colonies. Jared Ingersoll, later appointed as Stamp Master for the colony of Connecticut, warned Whatley:

> the minds of the people 'are filled with the most dreadful apprehensions from such a Step's taking place, from whence I leave you to guess how easily a tax of that kind would be Collected' tis difficult to say how many ways could be invented to avoid the payment of a tax laid upon a Country without the Consent of the Legislature of the Country and in the opinion of most of the people *Contrary to the foundation principles of their natural and Constitutional rights and Liberties*.[23]

Ingersoll, of course, was correct. The colonists felt that they were being taxed unfairly without the opportunity for adequate representation to speak on their behalf. Objections were voiced based "upon colonial charters, upon the British constitution and common law which they insisted had emigrated with them from England, and, finally... upon 'the Law of Nature and of Nature's God.'"[24]

Response from the Colonial Assemblies and Local Meetings to The Stamp Act: Pennsylvania, Massachusetts and Connecticut Take a Stance

In June 1765, the Massachusetts Assembly took its first steps to counter the Stamp Act. An invitation was written by members of the Assembly, including James Otis, and sent to the legislatures of the several colonies for all to convene and consult together on their present circumstances and to consider a "general and united, dutiful, loyal and humble representation of their condition to his majesty and to the parliament, and to implore relief."[25] These infringements, and the use of writs to enforce taxation mandated by the British crown, spurred the first gathering of colonial representatives, known as The Stamp Act Congress in New York in October 1765, to which nine of the thirteen colonies sent a total of twenty seven delegates. Although not yet interested in independence from Great Britain (delegates were sure to profess their loyalty to the Crown), the Stamp Act Congress emphasized the point that the colonists possessed all the "inherent rights and privileges of Englishmen," and became one of the first organized and coordinated political actions of the American Revolution.[26] There was, however, a struggle in the Congress regarding a declaration of principles.

The first draft composed by Pennsylvania's John Dickinson, pledged colonial obligation to "all acts of Parliament not inconsistent with the rights and liberties of the colonists,"[27] however Christopher Gadsden of South Carolina, insisted on taking a stand on "the broad and common ground of those natural and inherent rights" that all Americans possessed, not only as Englishmen but as *men*. A final version committed Americans to a more limited "all due subordination" to Parliament, which, according to Professor Rothbard, "conceded nothing to England since the word 'due' remained undefined."[28] Privately, Christopher Gadsden later wrote: "I have ever been of opinion, that we should all endeavor to stand upon the broad and common ground of those natural and inherent rights that we all feel and know, as men and as descendants of Englishmen, we have a right to, and have always thought this bottom amply sufficient for our future importance...There ought to be no New England men, no New Yorker, &c., known on the Continent, but all of us Americans; a confirmation of our essential and common rights as Englishmen may be pleaded from the Charters safely enough, but any further dependence on them may be fatal."[29]

Several colonial resolves soon followed, and the assemblies of Pennsylvania, Massachusetts, and Connecticut included explicit references to colonists' natural rights. On September 21, 1765, the Pennsylvania Colonial Assembly had proclaimed that the inhabitants of colonies were: entitled to all the Liberties, Rights and Privileges of his Majesty's Subjects in Great

> Britain or elsewhere, and that the Constitution of Government in this Province is founded on the natural Rights of Mankind and the noble Principles of English Liberty and therefore is, or ought to be, perfectly free. ... That it is the inherent Birthright and indubitable Privilege of every British Subject to be taxed only by his own Consent or that of his legal Representatives, in Conjunction with his Majesty or his Substitutes.

> ... That the vesting and Authority in the Courts of Admiralty to decide in Suits relating to the Stamp Duty, and other Matters foreign to their proper Jurisdiction, is highly dangerous to the Liberties of his Majesty's American Subjects, contrary to Magna Charta, the great Charter and

Fountain of English Liberty, and destructive of one of their most darling and acknowledged Rights, that of Trials by Juries.[30]

On October 29, 1765, the Massachusetts Colonial Assembly echoed with similar language, asserting "there are certain essential rights of the British constitution of government which are *founded in the law of God and nature*, and are the common rights of mankind."[31] The members in Massachusetts further resolved: ... That the inhabitants of this province are *unalienably* entitled to those essential rights in common with all men: and that no law of society can, consistent with the law of God and nature, divest them of those rights. ... That no man can justly take the property of another without his consent; and that upon this original principle the right of representation in the same body, which exercises the power of making laws for levying taxes, which is one of the main pillars of the British constitution, is evidently founded. ...That this inherent right, together with all other essential rights, liberties, privileges,

> and immunities of the people of Great Britain, have been fully confirmed to them by Magna Charta, and by former and later acts of Parliament.

> ...That his majesty's subjects in America are, in reason and common sense, entitled to the same extent of liberty with his majesty's subjects in Britain.

> ...That by the declaration of the royal charter of this province, the inhabitants are entitled to all the rights, liberties, and immunities of free and natural subjects of Great Britain, to all intents, purposes, and constructions whatever.[32]

Perhaps even more representative than the colonial assemblies in New England, or even of the Stamp Act Congress itself, were the local town meetings, which had been "busily adopting resolutions supporting the boycott proposals and demanding the repeal of all obnoxious laws."[33] For example, on December 10, 1765, "a large assembly of the respectable populace" of New London was held, and "proclaimed an uncompromisingly revolutionary natural-rights position,"[34] namely:

> ...That every form of government rightfully founded, originates from the consent of the people.

> ... That the boundaries set by the people in all constitutions are the only limits within which any officer can lawfully exercise authority. ... That whenever those bounds are exceeded, the people have a right to reassume the exercise of that authority which *by nature* they had before they delegated it to individuals.

... That every tax imposed upon English subjects without consent is against the *natural rights* and the bounds prescribed by the English constitution.

... That the Stamp Act in special, is a tax imposed on the colonies without their consent. ... That it is the duty of every person in the colonies to oppose by every lawful means the execution of those acts imposed on them, and if they can in no other way be relieved, *to reassume their natural rights* and the authority the *laws of nature and of God* have vested them with.[35]

The meeting concluded that it is the duty of every colonist to oppose execution of these invalid acts, and if necessary "to reassume their natural rights, and the authority the laws of nature and of God have vested them with."[36] Ultimately, after months of widespread protest in the colonies, the British Parliament voted to repeal the Stamp Act in March 1766.

The Townshend Acts of 1767 and Colonial Response

On June 29, 1767, Parliament passed the Townshend Acts, which were "designed to bring in forty thousand pounds annually... [,] imposed new import duties on glass, lead, paint, paper and tea,"[37] and served to clarify British authority to issue writs of assistance – general search warrants – in the colonies to enforce custom regulations, which were being met with universal disdain by the colonists, as we will soon see.[38] Such infringements as the colonists saw this Act, reignited the flame and passion against British oppression, and opposition began both formally and in the streets as it had in the case of the Stamp Act.

Some of the loudest voices came from Samuel Adams and James Otis, who drafted the Massachusetts Circular Letter (intended for widespread distribution among the colonists) on February 11, 1768, which the Massachusetts House of Representatives then issued to the other colonial legislatures, denouncing the Townshend duties as unconstitutional violations of the principle of no taxation without representation. The Massachusetts Circular Letter represented the House of Representative stance as follows:

the Acts made there, imposing duties on the people of this province, with the sole and express purpose of raising revenue, are infringements of their *natural* and constitutional rights;[39]

In effect, Adams and Otis believed the doctrine of consent to taxation was an "unalterable right in nature ingathered into the British constitution."[40] After receiving this letter, according to historian Gordon S. Wood, the secretary of state of the newly created American Department, Lord Hillsborough, "ordered the Massachusetts House to revoke its circular letter[, and w]hen the House defied this order by a majority of 92 to 17 [...], Governor Francis Bernard dissolved the

Massachusetts assembly."[41]

As a result, with the only "legal means for dealing with grievances silenced, mobs and other unauthorized groups in the colony broke out in violence."[42] Boston, which was rapidly becoming a symbol of colonial resistance, "ordered its inhabitants to arm and called for a convention of town delegates.... [and as a result], customs officials in Boston found it impossible to enforce the navigation regulations and pleaded for military help."[43] In turn, Governor Bernard made clear that British soldiers were indeed coming to Massachusetts, and shortly thereafter a petition to hold a town meeting quickly circulated, where Adams, Otis, and others reportedly prepared resolves for adoption.[44] The Boston Town Meeting took place on September 12, 1768 and again stressed that "taxation without their representation violated the British constitution and *natural law*; and sending an occupying army to enforce such unconstitutional acts was all the more unconstitutional."[45]

The Resolutions of the Boston Town Meeting, read as follows:

> Voted, as the opinion of this town, that the levying money within this province for the use and service of the Crown in other manner than the same is granted by the Great and General Court or assembly of this province is in violation of the said royal charter; and the same is also in violation of the undoubted *natural rights* of subjects, declared in the aforesaid Act of Parliament, freely to give and grant their own money for the service of the Crown, with their own consent, in person, or by representatives of their own free election.

When troops began arriving in Boston a few weeks later on October 1, 1768, their appearance "marked a crucial turning point in the escalating controversy: For the first time the British government had sent a substantial number of soldiers to enforce British authority in the colonies [, and b]y 1769 there were nearly 4,000 armed redcoats in the crowded seaport of 15,000 inhabitants."[46]

The Boston Massacre

Relations between colonists and soldiers deteriorated until, finally, on March 5, 1770, several Bostonians harassed British soldiers, prompting them to fire on a threatening crowd and kill five civilians. The Boston Massacre, as this event became known, "aroused American passions and inspired some of the most sensational rhetoric heard in the Revolutionary era."[47] On an almost daily basis, colonial newspapers "denounced Britain's authority, and mobs were becoming increasingly common in the countryside as well as in city streets, [while] customs officials, under continual intimidation, quarreled with merchants, naval officers, and royal governors...[making] enforcement of the trade acts impossible[, or atleast] arbitrary and discriminatory."[48]

In April 1770, "Parliament repealed the Townshend Duties, save for a duty on tea meant to maintain Parliament's right to tax colonists,"[49] "as a mark of the supremacy of Parliament, and an efficient declaration of their right to govern the colonies."[50] This withdrawal was a response to colonial boycotts which had increased to the point of reducing "British exports to the colonies [...] from £2.5 million in 1768 to £1.6 million in 1769."[51] Ultimately, the financial cost to implement the customs reforms outweighed the returns, as "by 1770 less than £21,000 had been collected from the Townshend duties, while the loss to British business because of American nonimportation movements during the previous year was put at £700,000."[52]

Following the repeal of the Townshend Duties, for the next two years, Rothbard notes, "the colonies had settled into an uneasy stability with regard to Great Britain,"[53] otherwise referred to by Samuel Adams as a period of "sullen silence."[54] The silence, however, was broken when, in the fall of 1772, under Samuel Adams's leadership, Massachusetts towns once again began organizing committees of correspondence. On November 20, 1772, Adams presented, from one such committee to the Boston Town Meeting, a document he called the Boston Resolves and State of the Rights of the Colonists, in which he boldly asserted colonists' natural rights:

> Among the *natural rights* of the colonies are these: First, a right to *life;* secondly to *liberty;* thirdly to *property;* together with the right to support and defend them in the best manner they can-Those are evident branches of, rather than deductions from the duty of self preservation, commonly called the first law of nature;

> All men have a right to remain in a state of nature as long as they please: And in case of intolerable oppression, civil or religious, to leave the society they belong to, and enter into another.

> *Every natural right not explicitly given up or from the nature of a social compact necessarily ceded remains.*[55]

The document was "sent to the 260 towns of Massachusetts, and more than half responded positively in the greatest outpouring of ordinary local opinion the resistance movement had yet seen."[56]

The Tea Act and Colonial Response

When Parliament passed the Tea Act on May 10, 1773, a measure of corporate welfare to aid the floundering British East India Company, "it angered colonial merchants, who stood to lose their profitable business in smuggled tea"[57] and set off the final series of explosions between the colonists and Great Britain. "The act not only allowed colonial radicals to draw attention once again to the unconstitutionality of the existing tax on tea, but it also permitted the company to grant monopolies for selling tea to favored colonial merchants"—a provision that infuriated American traders who had been excluded from this favorable arrangement.[58] As an act of imperial hubris, "the East India Company sent seven ships laden with taxed tea bound for four colonial ports: Boston, New York, Philadelphia, and Charles Town."[59] In turn, "New York, Philadelphia, and Charleston either turned away East India ships or impounded their tea."[60] On December 16, 1773, Bostonians, disguised as Native Americans, under cover of darkness, boarded several cargo ships in Boston Harbor and destroyed "90,000 pounds of tea"[61] by dumping "340 chests [...] into the harbor"[62] in an operation known colloquially, festively, and of course historically as the Boston Tea Party. The young lawyer John Adams proclaimed, "this is the most magnificent movement of all...This destruction of the tea is so bold, so daring, so firm, intrepid, and inflexible, and it must have so important consequences, and so lasting, that I can't but consider it an epocha in history."[63]

The following Spring of 1774, Parliament passed a series of Acts that were largely a punitive response to the Boston Tea Party.[64] These acts closed the port of Boston until reparations were made for the tea (allowing only shipments of food and fuel), reformed the charter of government of Massachusetts to consolidate power in the royal governor, transferred trials from Massachusetts to Britain or any other colony, and, permitted any military commander to compel homeowners to quarter troops.[65] The colonists called these *The Intolerable Acts*, for they "punished the whole citizenry of Massachusetts for the acts of the few participants in the Boston Tea Party."[66] To the colonists, "Parliament could not have provided a better example of the despotic control which the policy of the 1766 Declaratory Act made possible...aimed at one colony which had been a hotbed of resistance to the London government."[67]

REBELLION IN THE STREETS: A REVIEW OF POPULAR ACTION IN THE PRESS THROUGH PAMPHLETS AND BROADSIDES

Scholars continue to debate the extent to which the Founders relied on the natural law as their collective *raison d'être*.[68] While we know that many Founders were familiar with the writings of Locke and Francis Bacon,[69] we need to look to the language and the actions of the broader American public as strong indicators reinforcing the importance of natural law principles as a significant leitmotif in the tapestry of the American Revolution.

Though Bradburn notes "[a] recent trend in the literature of law and rights in the American Revolution has rejected the importance of 'natural rights' to the imperial crisis[,]" he dismisses "[s]uch an argument [as reflecting] an old trend—as old as the Revolution itself—and has enough truth in it to be [only] *occasionally* convincing."[70] In other words, Bradburn criticizes the resurgent *au courant* sidelining of natural rights arguments to the margins of American Revolution historiography. Surely several philosophies and beliefs contributed to the popular groundswell that resulted in rebellion. While we cannot point to *one* particular line of philosophical thought as the sole impetus behind the American Revolution, we can focus on one of several that featured prominently in the thinking of the time.

Accordingly, it becomes important to reinforce the specific original texts discussed earlier against the background of popular action and inaction—"this is the difference between a mere constitutional debate and a revolution, and between what could have happened and what did happen."[71] In the end, after an examination of the relevant events, one comes to the conclusion that "[i]t is [...] absolutely untenable [...] to suggest that Natural Law was not important to the making of the American Revolution."[72] As the heralded historian Gordon S. Wood, observed, "the American Revolution has always seemed to be an unusually intellectual and conservative affair—carried out not to create new liberties, but to preserve old ones."[73] Wood recognizes the importance of such "old" liberties, liberties under the natural law, that needed preservation.

The influential Harvard Professor Bernard Bailyn, a teacher of Gordon S. Wood and Pauline Maier, in his seminal work, The Ideological Origins of The American Revolution, explores the massive pamphletting culture surrounding the American founding.[74] It was through pamphlets, Bailyn argues, "that much of the most important and characteristic writing of the American Revolution appeared."[75] Speculating that "[f]or the Revolutionary generation, [...] the pamphlet had peculiar virtues as a medium for communication[,]" since pamphlets "allowed one to do things that were not possible in any other form" and were amenable for use in "publishing short squibs and sharp, quick rebuttals" and "much longer, more serious and permanent writing as well."[76]

Because pamphlets, which were "booklets consisting of a few printer's sheets, folded in various ways to so as to make various sizes and numbers of pages" were so inexpensive, "usually [sold for just] a shilling or two[,]" they gained tremendous popularity as a medium for expression.[77] "Highly flexible, easy to manufacture, and cheap, pamphlets were printed in the American colonies where there were printing presses, intellectual ambitions, and political concerns."[78] Accordingly, "pamphlets appeared year after year and month after month in the crisis of the 1760s and 1770s."[79] Noting "[m]ore than 400 [pamphlets] bearing on the Anglo-American controversy were published between 1750 and 1776 [and] over 1,500 appeared by 1783[,]" Bailyn underscored the widespread use and political significance of pamphlet culture.[80]

He noted that "[m]ost commonly the thought of the Revolution has been seen simply as an expression of the natural rights philosophy: the ideas of the social contract, inalienable rights, Natural Law, and the voluntary contractual basis of government."[81] In light of the importance of natural rights arguments in case law and popular public expression like pamphlets during the founding era, "[i]t is impossible to deny the crucial importance of Natural Law and 'inalienable natural rights' to the ultimate meaning of American citizenship in the Founding Era."[82]

James Otis' Rights of British Colonies Asserted and Proved

In a widely circulated pamphlet entitled *Rights of British Colonies Asserted and Proved (1763)*, James Otis insisted that without colonial representation in Parliament, that body had no right to tax the colonies, for "if a shilling in the pound may be taken from me against my will, why may not twenty shillings; and if so, why may not my liberty and my life?"[83] Invoking natural law as a limit on Parliament, Otis continued: To say the parliament is absolute and arbitrary, is a contradiction. The parliament cannot make 2 and 2, 5; Omnipotency cannot do it. The supreme power in a state, is *jus dicere* [law declared] only;—*jus dare* [law made], strictly speaking, belongs alone to God. Parliaments are in all cases to *declare* what is parliament that makes it so: There must be in every instance, a higher authority, viz. GOD. Should an act of parliament be against any of *his* natural laws, which are *immutably* true, their declaration would be contrary to eternal truth, equity and justice, and consequently void: and so it would be adjudged by the parliament itself, when convinced of their mistake.[84]

Moreover, Otis continued, "every British subject born on the continent of America, or in any other of the British dominions, is by the law of God and nature, by the common law, and by act of parliament, (exclusive of all charters from the Crown) entitled to all the natural, essential, inherent and inseparable rights of our fellow subjects in Great Britain."[85] Otis makes clear that the colonists need not look back to the "old *Magna Charta*" to discern from where all the rights of men and citizens spring, but that they are rooted in the law of nature. He then proceeded to list several rights which "no man or body of men, not excepting the parliament, justly equitably and consistently with their own rights and the constitution, can take away,"[86] and laid out the boundaries of Parliament's permissible role, "which by God and nature are fixed, hitherto have they a right to come, and no further."[87] Otis discusses "the first principles of law and justice, and the great barriers of a free state, and of the British constitution in particular," and concluded that the legislature may only engage in the following:

1. To govern by stated laws.
2. Those laws should have no other end ultimately, but the good of the people.
3. Taxes are not to be laid on the people, but by their consent in person, or by deputation.
4. Their whole power is not transferable.[88]

Otis highlights how such principles can be reconciled with the "fundamental maxims of the British constitution, as well as the natural and civil rights, which by the laws of their country, all British subjects are intitled [sic] to, as their best inheritance and birth-right," and ultimately urged that the colonies, who were without one representative in the House of Commons, should not be taxed by the British parliament.[89] As free born British subjects, the colonists were entitled to all the essential civil rights of such, and they could not have "ever dreamt, surely, that these liberties were confined to the realm."[90] The imposition of taxes, "whether on trade, or on land, or houses, or ships, on real or personal, fixed or floating property, in the colonies,"[91] was utterly "irreconcilable with the rights of the Colonists, as British subjects, and as men. I say men, for in a state of nature, no man can take my property from me, without my consent: If he does, he deprives me of my liberty, and makes me a slave."[92] Therefore, Otis concluded, where a proceeding breaches the law of nature, "no law of society can make it just."[93]

Thomas Jefferson's *A Summary View of the Rights of British America*

Thomas Jefferson's *A Summary View of the Rights of British America* (1774) was yet another pamphlet read far and wide that "proposed instructions for the Virginia delegates to First Continental Congress, and rejected all parliamentary authority whatever over the colonies," while still acknowledging that allegiance was owed only to the king.[94] Jefferson grounded his case on legal claims, historical claims, and ultimately, the Lockean natural rights of man.

He began by offering a reminder to the king that, "our ancestors, before their emigration to America, were the free inhabitants of the British dominions in Europe, and possessed a right which nature has given to all men, of departing from the country in which chance, not choice, has placed them, of going in quest of new habitations, and of there establishing new societies, under such laws and regulations as to them shall seem most likely to promote public happiness."[95] In particular he noted, that the natural rights of the colonists included "the exercise of free trade with all parts of the world,"[96] and this right could not be invalidated by even parliamentary attempts to regulate American trade. Jefferson reminded the king that "... kings are the servants, not the proprietors of the people. Open your breast, sire, to liberal and expanded thought. Let not the name of George III be a blot on the page of history."[97] He then concluded, "these are our grievances which we have thus laid before his majesty, with that freedom of language and sentiment which becomes a free people claiming their rights, as derived from the laws of nature, and not as the gift of their chief magistrate."[98]

James Wilson's *Considerations on the Nature and Extent of the Legislative Authority of the British Parliament*

Shortly after the publication of Jefferson's pamphlet, James Wilson, a rising young Pennsylvania lawyer, issued an updated version of an unpublished paper he had authored six years before, entitled *Considerations on the Nature and Extent of the Legislative Authority of the British Parliament.* Following in Jefferson's footsteps, Wilson argued that Parliament had no authority to pass legislation regulating the colonies' internal or external affairs. Championing independence of parliamentary authority, Wilson believed that legislatures must themselves be regulated by natural law. He proclaimed: All men are, by nature, equal and free: no one has a right to any authority over another without his consent: all lawful government is founded on the consent of those who are subject to it: such consent was given with a view to ensure and to increase the happiness of the governed, above what they could enjoy in an independent and unconnected state of nature. The consequence is, that the happiness of the society is the first law of every government.

> This rule is founded on the *law of nature*: it must control every political maxim: it must regulate the legislature itself.[99]

Moreover, Wilson argued that any invasions of this principle were illegitimate acts of government. He questioned, from what source does the "mighty... uncontrolled authority of the house of commons flow?" Further exploring his own inquiry, he proclaimed: Have they a natural right to make laws, by which we may be deprived of our properties, of our liberties, of our lives? By what title do they claim to be our masters? What act of ours has rendered us subject to those, to whom

> we were formerly equal? Is British freedom denominated from the soil, or from the people of Britain? If from the latter, do they lose it by quitting the soil? Do those, who embark, freemen, in Great Britain, disembark, slaves, in America? Are those, who fled from the oppression of regal and ministerial tyranny, now reduced to a state of vassalage to those, who, then, equally felt the same oppression? Whence proceeds this fatal change?[100]

Daniel Leonard and John Adams' Dueling Pamphlets

Many of these pamphlets often prompted a back and forth scholarly debate regarding the proper relationship between the colonies and mother country. For example, the leading champion of the Tory case was written in a series of letters by Daniel Leonard, under the *nom de plume* "Massachusettensis," in the *Massachusetts Gazette and Boston Post-Boy*, between December 12, 1774 and April 3, 1775.[101] Among the themes highlighted by Leonard, who condemned what he saw as anarchy in the colonies, were "the practical dangers in the course the whigs were pursuing; the reciprocal relations of protection and subordination that ought to prevail between Britain and the colonies; the destruction of the Massachusetts constitution coming from the political maneuvers of the whigs;

[and] the positive benefits flowing from the mother country."[102]

In response, John Adams, writing as "Novanglus" asserted that "America is not any part of the British realm," and warned that Britain was preparing to conquer and crush the colonies.[103] Adams grounded his defense in natural law, human reason, and the British revolutionary tradition of resistance to tyranny: "My friends, human nature itself is evermore an advocate for liberty . . . that all men by nature are equal; that Kings have but a delegated authority, which the people may resume, are the revolution principles of 1688; as are the principles of Aristotle, of Livy and Cicero, of Sidney, Harrington, and Locke, of nature and eternal reason."[104]

Adams rejected the notion that Britain is an empire and that the colonies owe obedience to the "imperial crown," and argued instead that Britain was more like a republic than any other form of government, for Adams defines a republic as "a government of laws, and not of men."[105] In answering "Massachusettensis," who pointed out that attachment to only the person of the king threatened liberty because Parliament had circumscribed royal prerogatives, Adams insisted that the ultimate source of liberties was the law of nature, and moreover, that the rights of Englishmen, were "sufficiently known" and secured:

> English liberties are but certain rights of nature reserved to the citizen, by the English constitution, which rights cleaved to our ancestors when they crossed the Atlantic, and would have inbred in them, if instead of coming to New-England they had gone to Outaheite, or Patagonia, even altho' they had taken no patent or charter from the king at all.[106]

Alexander Hamilton's *The Farmer Refuted*

In a pamphlet called *The Farmer Refuted*, published in 1775 in New York, a young Alexander Hamilton laid the ground work for the rights which would later become pillars of the Declaration of Independence. After quoting Blackstone's definition of the law of nature, Hamilton continued:

> Upon this law, depend the natural rights of mankind, the supreme being gave existence to man, together with the means of preserving and beatifying that existence. He endowed him with rational faculties, by the help of which, to discern and pursue such things, as were consistent with his duty and interest, and invested him with an inviolable right to personal liberty, and personal safety.

> Hence, in a state of nature, no man had any *moral* power to deprive another of his life, limbs, property or liberty; nor the least authority to command, or exact obedience from him; except that which arose from the ties of consanguinity.

Hence also, the origin of all civil government, justly established, must be a voluntary compact, between the rulers and the ruled; and must be liable to such limitations, as are necessary for the security of the *absolute rights* of the latter; for what original title can any man or set of men have, to govern others, except their own consent? To usurp dominion over a people, in their own despite, or to grasp at a more extensive power than they are willing to entrust, is to violate that law of nature, which gives every man a right to his personal liberty; and can, therefore, confer no obligation to obedience.[107]

In espousing his belief that our rights do not stem from the king or any government, nor can they be abridged by such, Hamilton passionately declared an argument he would one day reject when he would become the Secretary of the Treasury Department under President George Washington: "[s]acred Rights of mankind are not to be rummaged for among old parchments or musty records. They are written, as with a sunbeam, in the whole volume of human nature, by the hand of Divinity itself, and can never be erased or obscured by mortal power."[108]

Thomas Paine's Common Sense

Thomas Paine's *Common Sense* (1776), which, according to Professor Bailyn, is "the most brilliant pamphlet written during the American Revolution, and one of the most brilliant pamphlets ever written in the English language,"[109] was remarkably written by an Englishman, not an American. In this brief work, Paine outlined the internal political program of the libertarian wing of the American Revolution, which "consisted of rule by democratically elected legislatures established by proportionate representation and responsible to checks upon them by the people."[110] The aim of such government was to protect every man's natural rights of liberty and property: "Securing freedom and property to all men, and above all things, the free exercise of religion…"[111] Paine compared this to "absolute governments…(the disgrace of human nature)" and the British constitution, which he believed was "a tangle of complexities, and hence vague and devoid of a focus of responsibility."[112] In particular, he charged, the so-called checks and balances led to the aggrandizement of monarchical tyranny over the other branches of government:

But where, say some, is the King of America? I'll tell you, friend, he reigns above, and doth not make havoc of mankind like the Royal Brute of Great Britain…. For as in absolute governments the King is law, so in free countries the law ought to be king; and there ought to be no other. But lest any ill use should afterwards arise, let the Crown at the conclusion of the ceremony be demolished, and scattered among the people whose right it is.

A government of our own is our natural right: and when a man seriously reflects on the precariousness of human affairs, he will become convinced, that it is infinitely wiser and safer, to form a constitution of our own in a cool deliberate manner, while we have it in our power, than to trust such an interesting event to time and chance.[113]

Paine concluded the introduction of his magnificent pamphlet with these rousing lines:

The cause of America is, in a great measure, the cause of all mankind. Many circumstances have, and will arise, which are not local, but universal, and through which the principles of all lovers of mankind are affected, and in the event of which, their affections are interested. The laying a country desolate with fire and sword, declaring war against the natural rights of all mankind, and extirpating the defenders thereof from the face of the earth, is the concern of every man to whom nature hath given the power of feeling; of which class, regardless of party censure is the AUTHOR.[114]

Anonymous, The People the Best Governors or, A Plan of Government Founded on the Just Principles of Natural Freedom

The anonymous author of the brief pamphlet published in New Hampshire, *The People the Best Governors or, A Plan of Government Founded on the Just Principles of Natural Freedom* (1776), was, in a sense, the intellectual leader of Massachusetts Left, and declared that the people "best know their wants and necessities and therefore are best able to govern themselves."[115] He grounded his program squarely on natural rights and natural law: "God gave mankind freedom by nature, made every man equal to his neighbor, and has virtually enjoined them to govern themselves by their own laws ....

[Everyone's] right to freedom is the same."[116] In particular, according to Rothbard, the author "attacked upper houses armed with veto power and not directly responsible to the people as engines of oppression."[117] Instead, the author wanted representation proportionate to the population, a judiciary and an executive elected annually by the people.[118] Thus he sensibly opposed not so much a judiciary independent of the legislature as a judiciary independent of the people. He also suggested that in each colony a house of representatives armed with some judicial power be the supreme court of appeals in the province, especially since, as he perceived, judges' decisions are often a camouflaged form of legislation.

These ancient liberties and natural rights referenced by Bailyn, remained central to the revolutionary ideology; the promulgators of revolutionary ideology used evidence of ancient liberties enshrined in natural law from sources in heralded antiquity as well as their contemporary intellectual thought leaders to advance pro-Revolution arguments. "In the realm of political ideas, the colonial agitator used classical sources to prove both the existence and validity of a law *superior to all positive law*, and to laud again and again the high value of individual freedom."[119] In many ways, "[t]he colonists did not seek to change; they set out to defend a constitutional system which had been established, they believed, with the Glorious Revolution of 1688" in which James II was overthrown and replaced with William III.[120] This regime change led to the Declaration of Right (also known as the Declaration of Rights), and, later the English Bill of Rights of 1689. This Bill of Rights remained in the minds of the colonial patriots.[121]

As a result, natural law language, echoing the rights made positive by the English Bill of Rights, as opposed to strictly positive law language, substantially supplied the legal and substantive arguments for the American break from Britain. Grievances against King James listed in the English Bill of Rights would resurface in the language of the Declaration of Independence.[122] Many of these rights, a positive embodiment of the natural rights recognized as an English birthright, would factor into the eventual revolution carried out by colonial patriots.

"Revolution and war spread from a fatal breakdown in politics, and accompanied a broad rejection of the fundamental philosophies which maintained the status quo."[123] The vanguards of the Revolution sought to reshape the nature of rights as those of free persons, members of a community, a nation, rather than those of subjects of the Crown.[124] Bradburn argues that "[l]egally, at least, 'Americans' did not exist as a people independent of the British Empire before 1776, or perhaps 1778 when they were officially recognized by France, or perhaps 1783 when King George acknowledged American independence."[125] Though not using this particular rhetoric, the American pamphleteers often made arguments surrounding rights inherent to the nature of humanity, i.e., natural rights, and thus those to which English subjects were entitled. However, unlike their English counterparts, American pamphleteers were "profoundly reasonable people" who "sought to convince their opponents" rather than "the English pamphleteers of the eighteenth century [who aimed] to annihilate them."[126] Professor Bailyn asserted that this pragmatic approach suited well their purpose, to convince their readers rather than alienate them,

> [f]or the primary goal of the American Revolution, which transformed American life and introduced a new era in human history, was not the overthrow or even the alteration of the existing social order but the preservation of political liberty threatened by the apparent corruption of the institution, and the establishment in principle of the existing conditions of liberty.[127]

These vaunted and valued political liberties were inextricably tied to the notion of natural rights and accompanying the rich common law tradition embracing natural law principles. Consequently, Bailyn further argued,

> [w]hat was essentially involved in the American Revolution was not the disruption of society, with all the fear, despair, and hatred that that entails, but the realization, the comprehension and fulfilment, of the inheritance of liberty and of what was taken to be America's destiny in the context of world history.[128]

THE AMERICAN RESPONSE TO THE COLONISTS' CALL TO ACTION: THE FIRST CONTINENTAL CONGRESS (1774)

Doubtless, the Founders understood the significance of the events in which they found themselves embroiled. The colonists felt that their inheritance of liberty—the "'English Liberties'—the rights and privileges of subjects which were protected and defined by established institutions" such as "jury trials, assemblies, and chartered governments, time-honored traditions, and customary law" were at risk.[129] These liberties "were understood to be much more than a legacy of Englishness; for 'English Liberties' ultimately protected and embodied the natural rights of individuals—rights which could not be taken away or legislated out of existence."[130]

However, Parliament, the colonists felt, had attempted to do just that—a legislative eradication of natural rights. It was essentially over this question, Parliament's jurisdiction in the colonies, that the First Continental Congress assembled and "met [in Philadelphia] for just seven weeks in September and October of 1774 [...] to define and assert the colonies' rights and decide on joint measures to defend them."[131]

The First Continental Congress was not originally set upon the notion of breaking allegiance to the Crown; "[m]any delegates still desired reconciliation with Great Britain," like John Jay, John Rutledge, James Duane, and Joseph Galloway.[132] A committee was formed on colonial "Rights, Grievances and Means of Redress" that pondered whether the colonists should "employ natural rights as found in the 'Law of Nature' as the basis for their grievances against parliament [...] [o]r [...] restrain themselves to their liberties within the British Constitution[.]"[133] In that committee, "the leading Patriots of the 1760s," recognized as "men who could not tolerate ambitious and abstract claims for rights," clashed with demagogues like Richard Henry Lee of Virginia and pragmatists like John Adams of Massachusetts who supported reserving natural law as a later resource for redress, if necessary.[134] They relied on, according to Charles F. Mullet, "[t]his higher law, known variously as the law of God, Natural Law, reason, or merely as *law*" as "short of war, [their] last resort."[135]

Adams fervently argued that natural law should be "retained 'as a Resource [sic] to which we might be driven, by Parliament much sooner than we are aware.'"[136] The reluctance Adams displays in deploying natural law as an opening volley does not represent a rejection of Natural Law theory but instead a recognition of his understanding, as well as his peers, of the universality of natural law. Far from rejecting the relevance of natural law, Adams advocated for additional grounds upon which to initiate a break with England while holding natural law as a reserve, a sort of omnipresent and enduring catch-all to which they could turn when their reasoning based on positive law failed them.[137]

The First Continental Congress preferred natural law reasoning in its condemnation of the behavior of the English government. In particular, the Declaration and Resolves of the First Continental Congress outlined colonial objections to the Intolerable Acts, and provided a detailed list of grievances, which "[u]ltimately [...] was the first of many compromises in which the members agreed 'to found our rights upon the Laws of Nature, the Principles of the English Constitution, & Charters & Compacts.'"[138] The prevailing wisdom sought not to displace the natural law with the positive law of constitutions, charters, and compacts; it sought to run them as parallel or complementary.

Nothing now known in the language of the time suggests that the founding generation eschewed natural law theories but only questioned the proper manner in which to use them in their arguments. The ubiquity of natural law theory at the time, its presence in significant legal treatises, judicial opinions, accepted legal arguments, and widely-read pamphlets, suggests that any rejection of such beliefs would require a much more vocal reprobation than absence by omission. Consequently, the Second Continental Congress would eventually fall back upon natural law arguments in the Declaration of Independence.

THE SECOND CONTINENTAL CONGRESS (1775-1781), THE DECLARATION OF INDEPENDENCE AND THE ARTICLES OF CONFEDERATION

Though "fifty of the sixty-five delegates had attended the previous" Congress,[139] the Second Continental Congress was "a feistier lot than [the First Continental Congress] because the delegates were chosen mostly by *ad hoc* conventions and Committees of Safety rather than broad-based colonial assemblies."[140] This new Congress "[was] forced by events [such as the Siege of Boston] either to leave new England to its fate—in which case their own colonies might be next to face British steel— or else begin to act like a provisional government."[141] Accordingly, "[w]ithout declaring independence, congressmen began to act as the leaders of a sovereign nation."[142]

Eventually, the Congress elected to break allegiance with England and to form both a new nation and a new Rule of Law. In doing so, however, the

Founders fundamentally rejected the philosophy of the previous generation whose members had largely clung only to British constitutional liberties as the articulated sources of their rights.

> The revolutionary separation from the mother country involved a radical break with [the] past, the transformation of English subjects into American citizens and of the rights of Englishmen into the rights of nature.

> The very strongly developed consciousness of English national traditions and rights ... had to be reinterpreted ... by concepts taken from the natural rights philosophy.[143]

In particular, the Lockean/Jeffersonian language of the Declaration approved by this Congress bears this out: When in the Course of human events, it becomes necessary for one people to dissolve the political bands which have connected them with another, and to assume among the powers of the earth, the separate and equal station to which *the Laws of Nature and of Nature's God entitle them*, a decent respect to the opinions of mankind requires that they should declare the causes which impel them to the separation.[144]

Enshrined within the first portion of the Preamble to the Declaration of Independence persists an enduring and explicit embrace of natural rights. The Declaration does not begin by citing rights as Englishmen. Nor does it focus on the "British Constitution, and not on the Law of Nature" as John Rutledge, the future Supreme Court justice and brother of signer Edward Rutledge, had earlier argued.[145] Jefferson could have taken the subsequent language of men being "*endowed by their Creator with certain unalienable Rights*, that among these are Life, Liberty and the pursuit of Happiness,"[146] directly from Locke regarding life, liberty, and estate,[147] and from Aquinas regarding happiness as the ultimate end of the exercise of practical reason.[148] Asserting "that to secure these rights, Governments are instituted among Men, deriving their just powers from the consent of the governed," Jefferson's Declaration draws directly from Locke's natural law theories regarding consent as the *sine qua non* for government's moral legitimacy. Jefferson laments the tendency of mankind to endure an authoritarian government rather than "right themselves by abolishing the forms to which they are accustomed,"[149] but declares a "'long train of abuses and usurpations' tending toward despotism confronts the people with the duty, let alone the right, to revolt and abolish such a government."[150]

The Declaration of Independence was more than just a rebellious missive offered by daring, young, radical, hotheads looking to secede from an empire. It was a declaration of independents, a declaration of ideas, and a declaration of war. It also served as a formal recognition of a growing and irreparable divide between a tired monarchy and a burgeoning republic. Though the Declaration announced the philosophical ideals and aspirations of a new nation, it also served as positive acknowledgement of open hostilities between England and her colonies and marked a point of inflection in their relationship. It was a point of no return. Following the issuance of the Declaration, popular support for the ongoing war would spread.[151]

The colonists who welcomed the Declaration, understood the natural law as universal and enduring. They embraced it in their legal arguments, their polemic pamphlets, and their private writings. It inspired their indignance and nurtured their outrage. It was through the natural law that the colonists viewed the legacy of the common law they inherited from their English forbearers and cultivated through their communities and institutions. It was the natural law, bolstered by positive recognition of natural rights through instruments like the English Bill of Rights, that patriots murmured in the alleyways of Philadelphia and Boston, resonated in the ale houses and parlor rooms, and finally resounded in the Pennsylvania Statehouse in Philadelphia on July 4, 1776.

To the patriots of 1776, the natural law served as much more than a convenient retreat upon which to justify the assertion of their rights but rather a vital component of civil society. The natural law lives within the fabric of the Declaration every bit as much as the iron gall ink absorbed in the very parchment as it bled from Jefferson's quill. All that remained was for the colonists to win a war against the largest imperial power the world had ever seen. Stemming from wartime urgency, the Continental

Congress adopted the Articles of Confederation on November 15, 1777 and submitted them to the states for the required unanimous ratification. However, ratification by all thirteen states did not occur until March 1, 1781, after the Revolutionary War ended.[152] The establishment of a formal confederation was unnecessary to win the war, as "[it] was fought and won by the states informally but effectively united in a Continental Congress; fundamental decisions, such as independence, had to be ratified by every state."[153] Nevertheless, the Articles were "a momentous step from the loose but effective unity of the original Continental Congress to the creation of a powerful new central government;"[154] one whose long-term effects would result in highly conservative policies:

> There was no particular need for the formal trappings and permanent investing of a centralized government, even for victory in war. Ironically, the radicals were reluctantly pulled into an arrangement which they believed would wither away at the end of the war, and thereby helped to forge an instrument which would be riveted upon the people only in time of peace, an instrument that proved to be a halfway house to that archenemy of the radical cause, the Constitution of the United States.[155]

Consequently, "the vast majority of Americans regarded the Confederation

Congress as some distant irrelevancy and their local and state governments as their only meaningful sources of political authority."[156]

Eventually, the War for Independence was fought and won. General Charles Cornwallis, a leading British general, formally surrendered on October 19, 1781 at Yorktown, Virginia, marking the end of major hostilities in North America. On April 11, 1783, Congress called for the cessation of all hostilities.[157] Four days later, Congress ratified a preliminary treaty of peace.[158] Three days after that, General George Washington declared an end to the fighting.[159]

Several months later, George Washington submitted a circular, a letter intended for wide distribution, written from his "Head-quarters" at Newburgh, New York.[160] In the letter, Washington unambiguously articulated profuse and extravagant references to natural law. Concluding the second paragraph of the letter with references to natural, political, and moral thought, Washington brilliantly touched upon the three prevailing and pervasive thought engines of the time; Nature, politics, and morality: Impressed with the liveliest sensibility on this pleasing occasion, I will claim the indulgence of dilating the more copiously on the subjects of our mutual felicitation—When we consider the magnitude of the prize we contended for, the doubtfull [sic] nature of the Contest, and the favorable manner in which it has terminated, we shall find the greatest possible reason for gratitude and rejoycing [sic]—This is a theme that will afford infinite delight to every benevolent & liberal Mind, whether the event in contemplation be considerd [sic] as the source of present enjoyment or the parent of future happiness; and we shall have equal occasion to felicitate ourselves, on the lot which Providence has assigned us, whether we view it in a natural, a political, or a moral point of light.[161]

Such flowery language, uncharacteristic of the taciturn man, underscores the import of the letter itself. Washington wrote for an audience larger than the addressees of his missive. He knew that it would be widely circulated and applied general congratulatory language and ideas reflective of the social and political mores of the time.[162]

Washington made declarations to his audience and, through a rhetorical flourish, welcomed them as possessed of "benevolent and liberal Mind[s]" embracing the promise of the new land through multiple lenses; natural, political, and moral. In other words, no matter the priorities of the individuals, when considered with an eye to the natural world, political institutions, or morals guiding social interaction, all people can agree in the boundless potential of the new nation. Later, Washington applauded that "[t]he foundation of our empire was not laid in the gloomy age of ignorance and superstition, but at an Epocha [sic] when the rights of mankind were better understood and more clearly defined, than at any former period[.]"[163] Here, Washington recognized that the rights of mankind were not inscribed into the organ of human understanding at the moment of conception.

He saw that, as societies progress and changes to the social and political orders reveal new challenges and reframe public and private understandings of the rights of mankind, that our own conception of the scope and privileges of these rights will only increase. With each passing year, human understanding of natural rights reaches a new peak, a new pinnacle. And, at the time of Washington's circular, the great mean recognized that the victory over England marked a milestone in the progress of the understanding of the rights of mankind. Washington demonstrated his belief that the revolutionaries set the foundation of the United States at the zenith of an enlightened age set to elevate the human condition since: "[r]esearchers of the human mind after social happiness have been carried to a great extent: The treasures of knowledge acquired by the labours of philosophers, sages and legislators, though a long succession of years, are laid open for use, and their collected wisdom may be happily applied in the establishment of our forms of government[.]"[164]

Numbering among the factors designed to augment happiness, Washington named "[t]he free cultivation of letters: The unbounded extension of commerce: The progressive refinement of manners: The growing liberality of sentiment, and, above all, pure and benign light of Revelation."[165] Washington believed all these elements "have had a meliorating influence of mankind, and encreased [sic] the blessings of society."[166] At this auspicious period, the United States came into existence as a Nation, and if her citizens should not be completely free and happy, the fault would be entirely their own.[167]

He proposed four necessary actions, including "an indissoluble Union of States under one federal head[;]"[168] "[a] sacred regard to public Justice[;]"[169] "[t]he adoption of a proper Peace Establishment[;]"[170] and:

> "[t]he prevalence of that pacific and friendly disposition among the people of the United States, which will induce them to forget their local prejudices and policies, to make those mutual concessions which are requisite to the general prosperity, and, in some instances, to sacrifice their individual advantages to the interest of the community."[171]

To Washington, these were "the pillars on which the glorious fabrick [sic] of our Independancy [sic] and National Character must be supported — Liberty is the basis[.]"[172] He also warned that "whoever would dare to sap the foundation or overturn the Structure under whatever specious pretexts he may attempt it, will merit the bitterest execration and the severest punishments which can be inflicted by his injured Country."[173] Washington understood the import of the new American experiment and how fragile the nascent republic would be. The Treaty of Paris, signed on September 3, 1783, officially ended the Revolutionary War and finally recognized American independence.[174]

In the meanwhile, lawyers were successfully employing natural law arguments in colonial courts. It is that drama to which we now proceed.

CHAPTER 4

NATURAL LAW ARGUMENTS
IN COLONIAL CASELAW

The Argument

Seminal figures in the early patriot movement like Thomas Jefferson, James Otis, George Mason, and John Adams, relied on arguments that had been propounded by the great philosophers and jurists of Europe like Aquinas, Grotius, Hobbes, Locke, Coke, and Blackstone. Cases argued by the leading lawyers of the American colonial era frequently propounded natural law arguments with now-familiar supporting authorities.

***

[E]ven an Act of Parliament made against natural equity, as to make a man a judge in his own case, is void in itself: for *jura naturae sunt immutabilia*, and they are *leges legum*.[1]

– Chief Justice Henry Hobart (1560-1620)

EARLY COLONIAL CASELAW

Well before blood was drawn at Lexington and Concord, colonial lawyers and jurists relied on Natural Law theories in arguing and deciding cases. In pondering the origin of laws in the colonies, John Adams queried, "How […] do we New Englandmen derive our laws?"[2] Answering his own question, he continued, "I say, not from parliament, not from common law, but from the *law of nature, and the compact made with the king in our charters*[,]" Adams demonstrated the deep-rooted belief in the Natural Law Tradition and the power of the Lockean theory of social compact.[3] And, in terms of actual practice, rather than the tools of practice, the use of Natural Law theories as substantive legal arguments in court was extensive both before and after the Revolution.

Paxton's Case: The Colonists Protest Limitless Searches and Seizures

In 1761, James Otis, the famous attorney and powerful voice in the early patriot movement, gave a full throated argument for natural law in *Paxton's Case*, also known as the *Writs of Assistance Case*. Specifically, he advocated for formal judicial recognition of natural law over positive law and for judicial supremacy in ascertaining natural law. In *Paxton's* case, over 50 Boston merchants challenged the request of a customs official, James Paxton, for a writ of assistance that would allow nearly limitless authority to search private property for contraband. A writ of assistance was a document issued in the name of the king, which lasted for the life of the reigning monarch, and "ordered a wide variety of persons to help the customs man make his search;" ultimately, it was akin to a "permanent search [warrant] placed in the hands of custom officials."[4] In particular, these general warrants were used to combat the common practice of smuggling in the American colonies, implemented to avoid the harsh taxation regime of the King, and operated as follows: "the man who did the seizing, known as the informer, would initiate the proceedings to condemn the goods. The successful informer would receive a portion of the goods condemned, making the informer the beneficiary..."[5] Since "[w]rits were not issued as a result of any information that contraband was stored at a specified place...the customs officials could search wherever they chose[.]"[6]

Many colonists felt the almost absolute and unlimited discretion granted to officials and their informers to search anywhere they desired interfered with their rights to privacy. In *Paxton's case*, the merchants' attorney James Otis provides an example of how the authority granted by general warrants was abused, when a certain "Mr. Ware retained delegated authority under a general warrant held by a Mr. Pew. When Ware was hailed into court to answer an unrelated charge for breach of the Sabbath, he used the warrant as a license to seek revenge against the constable who arrested him and the judge who presided over his case by subjecting both of their homes to lengthy and invasive searches 'from the garret to the cellar.'"[7] Incidentally, these infringements, and the use of such writs to enforce taxation mandated by the British crown, spurred the first gathering of colonial representatives, known as The Stamp Act Congress in New York in October 1765.

When again, "new writs of assistance were requested following the expiration of the previously issued writs due to the death of the king [, a] group of Boston merchants opposed the proposed writs, [and retained] James Otis to represent their cause."[8] The main issue of *Paxton's* case was "whether the Superior Court should continue to grant the writs in general and open-ended form or whether it should limit the writs to a single occasion based on particularized information given under oath."[9] Otis's argument comes to us from his own notes, the notes of Chief Justice Thomas Hutchinson, before whom the arguments were made,[10] and the writings of a young John Adams who observed the trial and took extensive notes.[11] Based on all such sources, we know that Otis punctuated his argument with natural law principles.

After addressing the Court, Otis began, "I will to my dying day oppose, with all the powers and faculties God has given me, all such instruments of slavery on the one hand, and villainy on the other, as this writ of assistance is."[12] Otis maintained:

> In the first place, the writ is universal…every one with this writ may be a tyrant; if this commission be legal, a tyrant in a legal manner, also, may control, imprison, or murder any one within the realm. In the next place, it is perpetual; there is no return….by this writ not only deputies, etc., but even their menial servants, are allowed to lord it over us.[13]

In essence, "[e]very man prompted by revenge, ill humor, or wantonness to inspect the inside of his neighbor's house, may get a Writ of Assistance."[14] Otis forewarned the court that the continued use of the writs, "the worst instrument of arbitrary power, the most destructive of English liberty and the fundamental principles of law" would only result in "tumult and in blood."[15]

Quoting from Coke in *Dr. Bonham's Case*, Otis asserted "that in many cases[,] the common law will control Acts of Parliament and adjudge them to be utterly void; for where an Act of Parliament is against common rights and reason or repugnant or impossible to be performed, the common law will control and adjudge it to be void."[16] And, since the common law is the perfection of reason, it can override Parliament when that body's actions run contrary to reason. Moreover, according to letters from John Adams to William Tudor, Otis insisted that the writs were "inconsistent with the fundamental law, the natural and constitutional rights of the subjects."[17]

In doing so, Otis provides further reinforcement for the sentiment that the natural law in and of itself is superior to the laws of Parliament. Nevertheless, Chief Justice Hutchinson gave Otis' argument little weight, and held that because general writs were used in England, it was "sufficient to warrant the like practice in the province."[18] The people of Massachusetts were outraged by this ruling, and as we will soon see, widespread outcry ensued. From the passive pamphleteering culture and the publishing of Otis' arguments, to aggressively burning down the home of Chief Justice Hutchinson during the Stamp Act riots of 1765, manifested their rage.[19]

Years after the case was decided, John Adams remained in awe of Otis as a scholar, orator, attorney, and patriot. "Otis was a flame of Fire!" Adams explained to William Tudor in a letter in March 1817.[20] Teeming with admiration, "[w]ith the Promptitude of Clasical [sic] Allusions, a depth of Research, a rapid Summary of Historical Events and dates, a profusion of legal Authorities, a prophetic glare

[...] of his eyes into futurity, and a rapid Torrent of impetuous Eloquence, he hurried away all before him," Adams, over half a Century later, appears transported to the Boston courtroom in 1761.[21] "American Independence [sic] was then and there born," Adams argued, because "[t]he seeds of Patriots and Heroes to defend the *non sine Diis animosus infans* [not without the gods is the infant courageous], to defend the vigorous Youth, were then and there sown."[22] Otis cast such a spell over the crowd as to cause "[e]very man of an [immense] crowded Audience to go away, as [did Adams], ready to take up Arms against Writts [*sic*] of Assistants [*sic*]."[23] To Adams, this "was the first scene of the first Act of Opposition to the arbitrary Claims of Great Britain."[24]

In addition, Chief Justice Hutchinson himself wrote that in the aftermath of the case, "Otis's efforts encouraged those in opposition to the government and 'taught' the people that the practices were 'incompatible with English liberties.' The people perceived Otis's actions as springing from a 'sincere concern for the liberties of the people' and elected him as their representative in the next election to the general assembly."[25]

Hancock's Case: The Denial of Jury Trial Causes an Uproar in Boston

We also see natural law arguments utilized to guard the subject's right to jury trial. For example, in 1768, John Adams defended the wealthy merchant and patriot, John Hancock – *the* John Hancock – in an unreported prosecution colloquially deemed *Hancock's case*. Recall that in the fall of 1767, the British had established the American Board of Commissioners to ramp up the collection of customs mandated under the Townshend Acts, and the Board's goal was to show colonists that the government would no longer turn a blind eye to smuggling.[26] Partly on the evidence of a perjured witness, customs officials claimed that Hancock had unloaded from his ship, *Liberty*, quantities of undeclared wine valued at 3,000 pounds and therefore, according to the Sugar Act, was liable for such smuggling, treble the costs the offense.[27] As a result, the admiralty court "accepted the case against Hancock *in personam*, issued a warrant for his arrest, and demanded and got bail of 3,000 pounds, an exorbitant amount for a case of this kind."[28]

Not content merely to defend Hancock against a smuggling charge, Adams, "like James Otis seven years earlier in the famous writs of assistance case, transcended the immediate issue and defined fundamental principles which were to become stock in trade in the Revolutionary movement."[29] In his eloquent defense, Adams "questioned the validity of the legislation under which the case was tried, because it denied his client the right of a jury trial and thus, by repealing 'Magna Charta, as far as America is concerned,' 'degraded [Hancock] below the Rank of an Englishman.'"[30]

Adams, who has transcribed the defense in his Admiralty Notebook, was much more interested in challenging the validity of the Sugar Act itself than in the specific charge of its violation, and "attacked with considerable eloquence the legislative authority of Parliament and in particular, admiralty court jurisdiction in America."[31] Specifically, Adams "harangued at length about subjection to laws which the colonists had not approved. In words which must have maddened and at the same time amused the ministry and Parliament when they read them, he boldly remarked of the statute in question: 'My Clyant Mr Hancock never consented to it.'"[32] Moreover, Adams argued:

> not only was the Sugar Act passed without the colonists' approval... the penalties inflicted by it...out of all proportion to the severity of the crime; but... violations of this act, these penalties and forfeitures are 'to be heard and try'd -how? Not by a Jury, not by the Law of the Land,' but by the civil law before a single judge, contrary to the will of the ancient barons who, in similar circumstances, had answered in one voice: 'We will not that the laws of England be changed, which of old have been used and approved.'[33]

Ultimately, Adams' defense was so successful that the government withdrew its charges,[34] and after the trial concluded "colonial presses, adept at the use of propaganda, were fed a running account of what occurred behind the closed doors of the court," while Adams himself lifted whole sections of his argument against admiralty courts and "incorporated them into Boston's instructions to its representatives in the General Court where they would receive wide currency," as was discussed earlier in the chapter.[35]

The Boston Massacre Trial: Self-Defense as a Natural Right for All

Indeed, "it was not uncommon for colonial lawyers and colonial courts to regard Natural Law and ancient principles of the common law as superior to ordinary legislative acts."[36] For instance, during the Boston Massacre trial of 1770, in which John Adams and Josiah Quincy II *defended* British soldiers accused of killing innocent colonial civilians, Adams asserted a self-defense justification.[37] Adams was advised, Roscoe Pound maintained, by Jeremiah Gridley, "the father of the Boston bar, [...] that [the] study of the natural, i.e. ideal, law, set forth in the Continental treatises on the law of nature and nations, if unnecessary in England, was important for the American lawyer."[38] Quincy argued for one of the soldiers by dispelling the notion forwarded by the Crown, that "the life of a *soldier* was of very little value; of much less value than others of the community."[39] Quincy argued that "we all reluct at death [...] God and Nature hath implanted this love of life.—Expel therefore from your breasts an opinion so unwarrantable by any law, human or divine[.]"[40] He then quoted Blackstone, who, as discussed in Chapter 2 of this work, unmistakably invokes

the natural law: The law by which the prisoners are to be tried, is a law of mercy—
a law applying to us all—a law, judge *Blackstone* will tell us "*founded in
principles that are permanent,* uniform *and* universal, always comfortable *to the
feelings of* humanity *and the indelible rights of mankind.*"[41]

Quincy was quick to remind the jury of the earlier natural law claim he
asserted with Adams, including a citation to John Locke.[42] Adams, in his closing
discussion of justifiable homicide, also invoked Blackstone and "the laws of
nature," signaling the powerful sway of natural law arguments on juries and the
bench at the time.

Of course, as any trial attorney will attest, judges and juries often decide cases
on many factors beyond the persuasiveness of the attorneys and compassionate
presentation of the defendants or victims. A colonial Boston jury, some scant
three-and-a-half years before the signing of the Declaration of Independence, was
not sympathetic to a cadre of British soldiers who had just killed or injured several
of their fellow Bostonians. However, the natural law appeals of Adams and
Quincy were rational rather than sympathetic; and they won the day resulting in
the acquittal of six of the soldiers, and convictions for manslaughter, instead of
murder, for the remaining two.[43]

Robin v. Hardaway: Laws Legitimizing the Enslavement of Indians Violate Natural law

For yet another use of natural law arguments in court rooms during the
colonial era, we explore the 1772 case, *Robin v. Hardaway.*[44] At issue were "the
right of traders to sell the descendants of [Native Americans] as slaves, based
upon an act of the colony of Virginia of 1682[.]"[45] George Mason believed that
another act passed in 1705 negated the prior act. A series of individuals descended
from "Indian women brought into [the colonies] by traders, at several times
between [...] 1682 and 1748, and by [the traders] sold as slaves under" a 1682
Virginia law challenged their status as slaves.[46] They brought a series of claims
such as "actions of trespass, assault and battery [...] against persons who held
them in slavery, to try their titles to freedoms."[47]

Mason, acting as an attorney for the Native Americans, questioned:

If natural right, independence, defect of representation, and disavowal of
protection, are not sufficient to keep [the Indians] from the coercion of
our laws, on what other principles can we justify our opposition to some
late acts of power exercised over us by the British legislature?[48]

He answered that "all acts of the legislature apparently contrary to natural
right and justice are, in our laws, and must be in the nature of things, considered
as void."[49] Mason relied upon the prevailing natural law attitude, namely, that
God designed the laws of nature and they therefore maintain supremacy over any

laws of man.[50] He even echoed the now-familiar refrain of Aquinas, that "[a]ll human constitutions which contradict His laws, we are in conscience bound to disobey."[51] Mason concluded his argument by invoking *Dr. Bonham's Case* to assert that the law in question was "originally void, because [it ran] contrary to natural right and justice."[52] Thomas Jefferson, from whose account the record of the case survives, appeared more interested in the arguments of both counsel. He took over 14 pages to record the arguments made by all the attorneys.[53] He summarized the outcome in 26 words: "The court adjudged that neither of the acts of 1684 or 1691, repealed that of 1682, but that it was repealed by the act of 1705."[54] So, it appears as though George Mason's clients, the plaintiffs suing for their freedom, prevailed, and natural law arguments proved persuasive.[55]

As we have just seen, the heart of many arguments was "for the supremacy of fundamental British common or constitutional law, expressive… of God-given natural rights, whether it was Otis arguing against illegal search warrants, [or] John Adams opposing restrictions on jury trials."[56] Natural Law language, echoing the rights made positive by the English Bill of Rights, as opposed to strictly positive law language, supplied many of the legal and substantive arguments for the colonists' ultimate break from Britain. The promulgators of revolutionary ideology used evidence of ancient liberties enshrined in natural law from sources in heralded antiquity as well as their contemporary intellectual thought leaders to advance pro-Revolution arguments.

In the end, these "legal arguments of the colonial bar led to the discovery of a great truth: that the contractual promises of English liberties in the charters and the residuum of natural rights guaranteed by Magna Carta and the other documents of the British constitution were meaningless in the absence of Britain's recognition, within the Empire, of a separate American sovereignty not subject to the London Parliament."[57] Colonial agitators "used classical sources to prove both the existence and validity of a law *superior to all positive law*, and to laud again and again the high value of individual freedom."[58]

In light of the importance of natural rights arguments in popular public expression like pamphlets, as well as case law during the founding era, Bradburn's conclusory argument that "[i]t is impossible to deny the crucial importance of Natural Law and 'inalienable natural rights' to the ultimate meaning of American citizenship in the Founding Era[,]"[59] is essentially unassailable.

Could all these arguments find their way into a new fundamental law for the colonies? It is to the influence of the Natural Law Tradition at the American Constitutional Convention to which we now proceed, looking for the answer.

CHAPTER 5

THE FOUNDERS, NATURALLY AND CONVENTIONALLY

The Argument

The delegates of the several states met in Philadelphia to amend the Articles of Confederation. Four months of collaboration, debate, and revision would see the production of the Constitution of the United States which would be passed on to the governments of the several states for what the delegates hoped would be their ratifications.

The original meaning of the documents related to this process is critical because, as Professor Randy Barnett astutely noted, "we are interested in the Framers' intentions not because they are a surrogate for the difficult-to-discern will of the majority of 1789, but because we respect their opinions . . ." and "Framers are viewed as designers or architects of the lawmaking 'machine.' We consult them when we want to know how the machine is supposed to work, not because they are a surrogate for the majority . . . but because they might have special insight into the machine that they designed."[1]

***

In no country, is education so general— in no country, have the body of the people such a knowledge of the rights of men and the principles of government. This knowledge, joined with a keen sense of liberty and a watchful jealousy, will guard our constitutions, and awaken the people to an instantaneous resistance of encroachments.[2]

– Noah Webster (1758-1843)

THE CONSTITUTIONAL CONVENTION: A CALL TO RECAST THE FOUNDING DOCUMENT AND THE ENSUING DEBATE BETWEEN FEDERALISTS AND ANTI-FEDERALISTS

The Influence of Shays' Rebellion

Capitalizing on the 1786–1787 tax revolt in Massachusetts known as Shays' Rebellion, largely through the impetus of James Madison, the Federalists were able to secure a convention in Philadelphia in the spring of 1787 for the purpose of revising the Articles of Confederation. Shays' Rebellion was a revolt against excessive burdens on the taxpayer for the benefit of public creditors.[3] Oppressed by taxes and frustrated by the imprisonment of those who could not pay them, mobs throughout western Massachusetts and their supporters seized courthouses, and closed the courts until a redress of the people's grievances were achieved.

This outburst of anarchist freedom had a counterreaction, as Shays' Rebellion conservatized many state leaders who felt that the Confederation and individual state governments were too weak to prevent such uprisings from recurring. Such events served to spur nationalist sentiment by providing fuel for demagogic attacks about the dangers of weak government under the Confederation.

> True, democracy may be turbulent, as presumably in the Shays episode, 'But weigh this against the oppression of monarchy, and it becomes nothing . . . [and] even this evil is productive of good. It prevents the degeneracy of government and nourishes a general attention to the public affairs . . . It is a medicine necessary for the sound health of government.'[4]

Moreover, state jealousies among one another which manifested in tariffs and monopolies, were beginning to become a cause for concern as some states sought to protect the business and industries within their borders by taxing competing goods imported from other states. For example, New Jersey, "relied heavily on New York as a port for its foreign imports. [However, w]hen New York imposed a tariff on foreign goods, much of the burden of the tariff fell on New Jersey residents, while the tariff revenue went to New York."[5] The disdain for New York's ability to raise revenue due to its draconian imposition of tariffs on neighboring states was well acknowledged. "In N. York they pay well because they can do it by plundering N. Jersey & Connecticut..."[6] Oliver Ellsworth of Connecticut, echoed these concerns when he proclaimed, "[t]he state of New York raises 60 or £80,000 a year by impost. Connecticut consumes about one third of the goods upon which this impost is laid, and consequently pays one third of this sum to New York."[7]

Ultimately, these urban merchants and artisans, as well as many slaveholding planters, came together in support of a strong nation-state that would use the coercive power of a distant central government to grant them privileges and subsidies. With such a backing, nationalist forces were able to execute a political *coup d'état* which, according to Professor Murray Rothbard, illegally and surreptitiously liquidated the Articles of Confederation and replaced it with the Constitution.

James Madison, whose notes provide us with the most complete record we have of the Constitutional Convention, proved a towering figure in the formation of the Constitution. Often labeled "the Father of the Constitution,"[8] Madison began planning his *coup* in 1786, when he pushed through the Virginia legislature a "proposal for a convention of commissioners from *all* states to provide for uniform commercial regulations and for 'the requisite augmentation of the power of Congress over trade.'"[9]

The meeting at Philadelphia in 1787 for the sole and express purpose of revising the Articles of Confederation, got the name of a Convention (I believe before long that of a Conspiracy would have been more Significant), [and] paid no more regard to their orders and credentials than Caesar when he passed the Rubicon. Under an Injunction of Secrecy they carried on their works of Darkness until the Constitution passed their usurping hands.[10]

Eager to prepare, James Madison arrived in Philadelphia on May 3, 1787, eleven days before the Constitutional Convention was scheduled to commence.[11] Madison was so cautious about what he was really planning for Philadelphia in the summer of 1787 that he revealed his true objectives only to his close personal friends. What were those plans? Not enhanced commercial arrangements, but instead the beginning of radical political reform.

The Early Influence of Scottish Natural Law Theorists on James Madison

Madison was "a small man, slight of figure [... with] a quiet voice,"[12] who studied at Princeton[13] "just as the ideas of the Scottish Enlightenment[,]" which emphasized the importance of human reason—and called for the rejection of authorities unsupported by reason [14] were sweeping the university.[15] Scottish Enlightenment ideals provided fertile soil for natural law ideas to flourish. "Scots intellectuals[,]" recognizing many of the same issues observed by Grotius, "saw human beings as a volatile mixture of reason and passion."[16] "They learned how to temper dreams of what humanity might become with an appreciation of the immutability of human nature. They looked at themselves and the wild Highlanders alike, admitting even the most erudite scholar could err and even an ignorant herdsman grasp truth."[17] Consequently,

Scottish Enlightenment thinkers, became, in short, consummate realists
who imagined no stylized states of nature or utopias crafted by man
[...but] believed instead in what [eighteenth Century Scottish
philosopher Thomas Reid] called *common sense*: the innate power
common to *all* human beings to apprehend reality through the senses,
mind, intuition, and conscience and then exploit that grip on reality to
advance what [eighteenth Century Irish-born Scottish philosopher
Frances Hutcheson] called *the pursuit of happiness*.[18]

Such ideas had a lasting influence on the young James Madison.

A gifted and hard-working student, Madison "zipped through the college's
undergraduate curriculum in two years rather than the usual three or four, and then
stayed for another year to study ethics and Hebrew."[19] Walter A. McDougall,
Pulitzer Prize-winning historian and Professor of History at the University of
Pennsylvania, notes that "Madison relished Princeton's regimen. He rose at 5
A.M., prayed at 6, attended class all day, and studied well into the night."[20] Given
his motivation, intellect, dedication, and ambition, Madison naturally arrived in
Philadelphia early to prepare for the enormous undertaking of the Convention.

"Of the entire delegation," historian and biographer Catherine Drinker
Bowen notes, "no one came better prepared intellectually [than Madison]."[21]
Historian James MacGregor Burns, after explaining the reluctance that historians
have in characterizing an actor as a "heroic figure, galloping to the rescue [to
snatch] victory from the jaws of defeat and [change] the destiny of a nation"
nonetheless recognized Madison as exactly such a figure "who almost literally did
gallop across the New Jersey flatlands in 1787 to take the lead in confronting and
resolving, for a time at least, the dilemma of 'liberty versus order' through the
Convention."[22]

Difficulties in Reaching a Quorum at the Convention

It remains no mystery, then, why Madison grew frustrated when, by May 14,
the number of delegates who had arrived proved insufficient to satisfy a quorum.[23]
In a letter to Jefferson, who was in Paris as the U.S. Ambassador to France at the
time, Madison bemoaned the lack of timely delegates. "Monday last was the day
for meeting of the Convention. The number as yet assembled is but small."[24]
Madison went on to blame the "late bad weather[,]"[25] referring to heavy
rainstorms that had pounded the East Coast the first two weeks of May.[26] Even
the stoic George Washington, who had arrived in Philadelphia on May 13,
expressed disappointment at the lack of quorum.[27] "Not more than four states were
represented yesterday[,]" wrote Washington in a letter to his friend and neighbor,
Arthur Lee.[28] "These delays greatly impede public measures, and serve to sour the
temper of the punctual members who do not like to idle away their time[.]"[29]

The tardiness of the other delegates proved providential since it allowed

Madison to forge alliances and friendships with several influential members of the Convention before the arrival of the quorum.[30] "The eleven day period between May 14 and May 25 formed a bond not only between the delegations of the country's two most powerful and populous states [Virginia and Pennsylvania] but, equally important, among some of the most active and intellectually-gifted delegates who would participate in the Convention."[31]

The Convention would be marked by alliances, factions, and coalitions. Two main groups emerged: The Federalists and the Anti-Federalists. The Federalists, like James Madison, Alexander Hamilton, John Jay, George Washington, and Benjamin Franklin, who pushed for a stronger central government, "were[,] on average[,] ten to twelve years younger than [the Anti-Federalists][32] who feared a strong central government would threaten liberties and individual rights. Nearly 'half the Federalists' leaders made their careers after 1775," while the Anti-Federalists, "[b]y contrast, [...] including Patrick Henry, George Mason, George Clinton, and Sam Adams [made their careers] before the war and within their own colonies."[33] It was chiefly the Anti-Federalists, whose members—both among those who attended the convention, like Luther Martin, George Mason, and Richard Henry Lee, and those who did not, like George Clinton, Patrick Henry and Samuel Adams—were often remembered as the more colorful and incendiary of the founding generation. However, the records that remain, which inform our understanding of history demonstrate that brash and bombastic rhetoric from the mouths of larger-than-life personalities may make for good drama but, in an age embracing human reason over human reaction, could essentially carry the day.

We should note that among this gathering of America's great men at the Convention there were "conspicuous absences[;] men who were more often than not deeply skeptical or at least ambivalent about the prospects of a convention,"[34] such as, John Adams of Massachusetts and Thomas Jefferson of Virginia, who were away as ambassadors to England and France. Others, like Richard Henry Lee and Patrick Henry of Virginia, were chosen as delegates but declined to attend, "undoubtedly from deep suspicion...[for example,] Patrick Henry declared that he 'smelt a rat.'"[35] Sam Adams, was similarly skeptical and chose, instead, to use his influence in getting the Massachusetts Resolution to restrict the scope of the convention and remain with the Confederation.[36]

Historical Records of the Convention

Because the participants elected to keep the proceedings secret, we only have a handful of records of the convention. Concerned with secrecy, but understanding the need for a record for posterity, the Convention elected William Jackson as secretary. Though Jackson had lobbied vigorously to serve as Secretary, he proved a terrible note taker.[37] Were it not for Madison's fastidious notes, we would today have only a small glimpse into the proceedings of the convention. Though other delegates scribbled personal notes and recollections, in addition to Jackson's account, none of the other records of the convention were as thorough and comprehensive as Madison's legislative diary.[38]

Madison's extraordinary notes on the convention provide contemporary readers with the most complete account of the proceedings of the Convention. Scholars and historians have long praised and relied on Madison's Notes as a thorough and accurate chronicle of events.[39] However, some modern scholars have suggested that Madison may have made more substantive changes to the Notes than the "few alterations and additions" noted by Gaillard Hunt in the introduction to his 1902 edition of Madison's Notes.[40] Despite the possibility that Madison's Notes may have been altered, they remain the single most important contemporaneous resource available to our understanding of the Constitutional Convention of 1787.

One historian has argued that "[t]he revisions do not detract from the manuscript's significance; they enhance it."[41] Regardless of speculation over the provenance of certain passages of Madison's Notes, they still comprise the most important and thorough single account of the issues discussed and arguments made that provide contemporary historians and scholars with insight into the intellectual and philosophical focus and energy of the debates themselves. Today, we know from the brilliant scholarship of Boston College Law School Professor Mary Sarah Bilder that Madison wrote the Notes primarily for his own use and to share with his friend Jefferson. Despite the alterations, the Notes remain the best source for scholars to understand what transpired at the Convention.[42]

Substantive Issues Raised at the Convention and the Federalist's Coup d'etat

From Madison's notes, we know that much of the debate focused on how to structure the government of the burgeoning nation. As Madison waited for a quorum to assemble, he, along with the Virginia delegation, drafted the Virginia Plan. Once the Convention proceedings opened, Virginia Governor Edmund Randolph presented its revolutionary resolutions, which consisted of the following recommendations:

1. Voting in the national legislature to be proportionate to tax revenue or population, rather than by equality of states.
2. Two branches of the national legislature, the lower house to be selected by the people of each state, not by the state legislatures.
3. Election of the smaller upper house for long terms by the lower house out of persons nominated by the state legislatures.
4. Congress to be empowered "to legislate in all cases to which the separate States are incompetent," the ramifications to be presumably decided by Congress, and Congress to have veto power over all state laws which it considered to be inimical to the Confederation, and to force the states to

obey. Thus the rule of the state legislatures were to be enormously reduced to being a pool for nominations for the national upper house.

5. Establishment of a national executive to be chosen by the Congress, its salary to be fixed and chosen by Congress, and the executive to be limited to a single term.

6. A national judiciary of supreme and inferior courts, and with supreme jurisdiction for interstate cases.

7. The creation of a Council of Revision composed of the executive and some of the national judiciary to examine every act of the legislature and to exert a veto power over it, which could be overridden.

8. Finally, this government would be submitted by the old Congress, not to state legislatures as under the Articles, but to special state conventions chosen by the people for this purpose.[43]

It was evident that the Virginians had wanted not a "merely federal" union, but a "national government … consisting of a supreme judicial, legislative, and executive[;]"[44] In essence, Madison meant political revolution rather than reform of the Articles of Confederation. Gouverneur Morris further clarified this nationalist view: the old federal government was "a mere compact resting on the good faith of the parties" while the new national government was to have "a compleat [sic] and compulsive operation."[45] Even Randolph conceded, the proposal was "not intended for a federal government— [but] a strong consolidated union, in which the idea of states should be nearly annihilated."[46]

The next two weeks were spent debating the Virginia Plan, which, as Rothbard notes, "was in itself a benefit for the nationalists because they were able to get from the beginning the frame of reference for the convention's debates."[47] One crucial issue concerned Virginia's demand over proportional representation in Congress (either by population or by contributions of revenue).[48] The Federalists, or nationalists, emphasized a popular election of the large house, for two reasons: first, the populous states (i.e., Virginia, Pennsylvania, and Massachusetts, who shared nearly half of the American population between them[49]) wanted to dominate the new government by ensuring that there would be no equality of states' voting, and second, "to destroy the power of the state legislatures, which were severely hated by the nationalists as being overly democratic and inimical to a powerful central government."[50] Madison shrewdly "provided lip service to the necessity of popular election of one legislative branch as 'essential to every plan of free Government[,]'"[51] yet, he also revealed the purpose of the plan by assuming that popular elections would be refined "by successive filtrations" and that such filtrations of the Senate (the upper house), the judiciary, and the executive would effectively place the all-powerful national government beyond popular control.[52]

[A] popular election of the House would free the national government from state control and thus raise "the federal pyramid to a considerable altitude" by giving it "as broad a basis as possible." Thus, national power could really be removed from more popular control while at the same time, popular election would mislead the people into placing their necessary confidence in the government.[53]

For "no government could long subsist without the confidence of the people. In a republican Government this confidence was peculiarly essential."[54]

On June 15, in an effort to block the acceptance of the Virginia Plan, William Paterson outlined the contrasting New Jersey Plan,[55] which gave the smaller states a voice in that confederation. Instead of the Virginia Plan's bicameral legislature, the New Jersey Plan stuck with the current confederation's unicameral legislature, and each state had only one vote.[56] Paterson also took the opportunity to remind the convention that the express object was to amend the Confederation, and that the articles of confederation were therefore the proper basis of all the proceedings of the Convention. We ought to keep within its limits, or we should be charged by our constituents with usurpation. ... the people of America [are] sharp sighted and not to be deceived. ... The idea of a national Govt. as contradistinguished from a federal one, never entered into the mind of any. ... We have no power to go beyond the federal scheme, and if we had the people are not ripe for any other.[57]

Madison attacked the New Jersey Plan, arguing that "a newly revised Articles would not prevent the states from violating national treaties, would not ensure good state laws, and did not supply sufficient force to suppress state insurrections such as Shays' Rebellion."[58] On June 19, the convention voted 7-3-1 to reject the New Jersey Plan in favor of the Virginia Plan, but the small states were still weary. Gunning Bedford of Delaware asserted the concerns of the small states, "that there was no middle way between a perfect consolidation and a mere confederacy of the States."[59] In addressing those who voted in the affirmative for the Virginia Plan, Bedford continued, "I do not, gentlemen, trust you. If you possess the power, the abuse of it could not be checked; and what then would prevent you from exercising it to our destruction?"[60]

Peppered throughout the discussion are numerous references to natural law in various forms. Madison, for instance, when debating on May 31, 1787, whether the federal government should have "[l]egislative power in all cases to which the State Legislatures were individually incompetent" gave voice to his views through the language of natural law.[61] Though presenting a "strong bias in favor of an enumeration and definition of the powers necessary to be exercised by the national Legislature[,]" Madison believed he "should shrink from nothing which should be found essential to such a form of [government] as would provide for the safety, liberty and happiness of the community."[62] By this point in time, it seems that happiness and liberty served as stand-ins for the natural law.

In addition to Madison, several other participants relied on natural law arguments to underscore their views. James Wilson of Pennsylvania, who would later be appointed to the Supreme Court by George Washington, described personal sovereignty in a State of Nature. Discussing the notion that the federal legislature should have "a negative" over the laws of the states that "might be contrary to the articles of Union, or Treaties with foreign nations,"[63] Wilson argued:

> Abuses of the power over the individual person may happen as well as over the individual States. Federal liberty is to the States, what civil liberty, is to private individuals, and States are not more unwilling to purchase it, by the necessary concession of their political sovereignty, that the savage is to purchase Civil liberty by the surrender of the personal sovereignty, which he enjoys in a State of nature.[64]

Wilson, a Federalist, feared that rivalries between the states would tear apart the Union. Just as an individual concedes some privileges when entering into society, so should the States, felt Wilson, cede some power to the federal government.[65] In a victory for the Anti-Federalists, the vote to allow the new Congress to void potentially contradictory state laws failed.[66]

The failure of an extrapolated-natural-law-consentto-sovereignty-theory does not signal a rejection of natural law principles. Rather, the failure of Wilson's argument demonstrates a larger disagreement between the Federalists, and the Anti-Federalists, many of whom preferred the more autonomous approach of the Articles of Confederation to the stronger central government favored by the Federalists. The Anti-Federalists were not ready to cede the sovereignty of their states to some larger federal organ. However, Wilson, perhaps, made his arguments for his Federalist comrades, or, instead, hoped to win over some of the less-entrenched members of the convention. He would continue to rely on these natural law arguments throughout the convention.

Several days later, Wilson returned to his analogy, comparing the relationship between the individual and the state, and the state and the federal government. On June 9, the gathered delegates debated the election of the national legislature.[67] Wilson observed: We have been told that each State being sovereign, all are equal. So each man is naturally a sovereign over himself,[68] and all men are therefore naturally equal. Can he retain this equality when he becomes a member of Civil Government. [sic] He can not [sic]. As little can a Sovereign State, when it becomes a member of a federal [government]. If [New Jersey] will not part with her sovereignty it is vain to talk of [central government].[69]

Wilson expressed his frustration over the reluctance of the New Jersey delegates, who feared marginalization at the hands of more populous states to agree to proportional representation in a new legislature.[70] Wilson viewed the states as a collection of individuals, each of whom should have a voice in government and viewed the lack of proportional representation as a fault in the

Articles of Confederation which he sought to remedy according to his understanding of the natural law.[71] However, other members of the Convention would rely on natural law rhetoric to illustrate the status of the states to argue against proportional representation.

For instance, Luther Martin "considered the separation from [Great Britain as placing] the 13 States in a state of Nature towards each other[,]" and "that they would have remained in that state [...] but for the confederation[,]"[72] and therefore advocated for equal votes amongst the states.[73] Maintaining "that the States like individuals were in a State of nature equally sovereign [and] free," Martin "read passages from Locke..."[74] and used such "[t]o prove that the case is the same with States till they surrender their equal sovereignty."[75]

Madison's Notes show that the Framers felt the works of Locke to be dispositive and not merely theoretical. Madison did not invoke Locke as a mere example, standing for the proposition of equal sovereignty and the necessity to yield certain rights when entering into a collective society, but as *proof* of the sacrifices necessary to enter into a society. And Martin did not cite to Locke merely as support for his arguments, but rather as proof of their accuracy and veracity.

These arguments informed the tenor of the debate and, though the remainder of Madison's Notes do not reveal many natural law arguments made after July 1787, they show continued debate on the structure of government, how to apportion representation, and the contentious issue of slavery. In the remaining months, a draft version of the Constitution would be assembled, circulated, debated, and revised. Delegates spent hours laboring over particular language, clauses, and the rights of states. Through their discussions, it became clear that the Anti-Federalists would not be satisfied with merely a Constitution, but also would need an instrument of equal power and validity—a Bill of Rights—to restrain the new government.

MADISON AND ROTHBARD

The emphasis of this work, is of course, to highlight the prevalent and vital role of the natural law tradition during the American founding, and the ratification of the Constitution, and beyond. As such, James Madison is often depicted throughout these pages as not only the scrivener of the Constitution, but as a hero of the Bill of Rights, and a true defender of inalienable claims to personal liberty against the government. Some historians, however, paint a different picture of Madison as a shrewd tactician, who cunningly crafted a highly nationalist document with unbridled power in the central government. One such historian is a personal hero to your author, Murray Rothbard. In his recently discovered Volume 5 of *Conceived in Liberty*, Rothbard sheds a different light on Madison, as the mastermind of the Machiavellian nationalist forces and champion of big government.[76] Rothbard describes a political *coup d'etat,* which, headed by

Madison, violated the express instructions of Congress, illegally liquidated the Articles of Confederation, and replaced it with the Constitution.[77]

Madison had four phases to his public life. He was a revolutionary against the king. He was a Federalist who crafted centralized power. He was an anti-Federalist as Secretary of State and for most of his presidency. Yet before he retired, at the end of his second term, he caved to the banking and nationalistic instincts he had resisted since his days in the House of Representatives, and signed the bill creating another national bank in direct defiance of his iconic bank speech. With his signature in 1816, he repudiated his brilliant logic of 1791.

Rothbard was unforgiving. In Volume 5, he spends ample time discussing the "devious and sinister machinations" of Madison throughout the debates at the Constitutional Conventions over issues such as Virginia's demand for proportional representation in Congress and the election of congressmen by popular vote.[78] According to Rothbard, Madison "shrewdly provided lip-service to the necessity of popular election of *one* legislative branch as 'essential to every plan of free Government.' But then he revealed the purpose of the plan by assuming that popular elections would be refined 'by successive filtrations' and that such filtrations of the Senate (the upper house), the judiciary, and the executive would effectively place the all powerful national government beyond popular control."[79]

Rothbard further takes issue with Madison's insistence that a main purpose of government is to defend the rights of various minorities, and that a bigger and farther-reaching government would be best suited to do so.[80] In contrast, Rothbard argues that "the centralizing of power into one large juggernaut provides far more of an opportunity—and more of an incentive—for trampling the rights of minorities. The stakes are larger and restraints weaker, not greater, because power is concentrated and consolidated."[81] Similarly, in recounting the debates over the term of senators, Rothbard asserts that Madison, championing an extension from a seven year term to a nine year term, "saw the main danger to liberty in the people and wished to build up an even stronger oligarchical rule in central government to exert power against the menace of the people."[82] In discussing the pattern of representation in the Senate, Madison made clear that he would rather split the Union and form a separate nation with the large states and simply let the small ones exist as best they could. In doing so, Rothbard states, "Madison displayed not the broad flexible nature of the compromiser that has often been attributed to him, but rather the rule-or-ruin tactician of the hardline ultra-nationalist who settled for nothing less than total victory and was willing to see the Union dissolve rather than give up his program."[83]

Ultimately, Rothbard contends that Madison would become the reluctant author of the Bill of Rights, only because he believed it would head off the call of the anti-Federalists for a second constitutional convention by offering concessions. In fact, Rothbard points out that in Federalist No.45, Madison tried to prevent the need for a bill of rights by spreading "the myth that reserved powers under the Constitution ineluctably belong to the states."[84] Rothbard has been far more critical of Madison than your author, yet his observations are well founded. For further discussion on this alternate view of Madison's role in the drafting and ratification of the Constitution, as well as the Bill of Rights, your author invites the reader to delve deeper in Murray Rothbard's Volume 5 of *Conceived in Liberty*.

BEYOND THE CONVENTION: GEORGE WASHINGTON'S STAMP OF APPROVAL

Once the language of the Constitution was approved by the delegates, it was sent by George Washington to the Congress with a letter in which Washington recognized the significance of the enclosed document and intoned natural law language in his missive of conveyance.

> It is obviously impracticable in the federal government of these states; to secure all rights of independent sovereignty to each, and yet provide for the interest and safety of all:

> Individuals entering into society, must give up a share of liberty to preserve the rest. The magnitude of the sacrifice must depend as well on situation and circumstance, as on the object to be obtained. It is at all times difficult to draw with precision the line between those rights which must be surrendered, and those which may be reserved; and on the present occasion this difficulty was increased [sic] by a difference among the several States as to their situation, extent, habits, and particular interests.[85]

Washington's letter serves as a capstone to a monument to natural law. He encapsulated the embrace of the ideas of the philosophers and jurists whose works provided the ideological and legal guidance to bridge notions of the natural and common law to a burgeoning government founded not on the persistence of feudalistic monarchy but instead upon the deeply-rooted belief in the power of Reason and the Lockean notion of social compact based on individual consent. Washington expressed the understanding of the Convention that the power of government should only extend as far into natural rights as is necessary to "secure [the] freedom and happiness" of those who have consented to be governed.[86] Similarly, for Madison the possibility of reconciling governmental power and personal liberty rested on the existence of "clear boundaries to governmental power publicly agreed-upon by an enduring majority of the people of the United State."[87] In an essay published in the *National Gazette*, Madison wrote:

> In Europe, charters of liberty have been granted by power. America has

set the example and France has followed it, of charters of power granted by liberty. This revolution in the practice of the world, may, with an honest praise, be pronounced the most triumphant epoch of its history, and the most consoling presage of its happiness.[88]

Washington also recognized that some states may express some reluctance to embrace the Constitution. Writing "[t]hat it will meet the full and entire approbation of every state is not perhaps to be expected," Washington nonetheless believed each state would recognize the sacrifices to their own sovereignty that would be necessary for the compromises inherent in a united government.[89]

What would remain was for the states to debate the Constitution and determine whether to ratify it. In examining that process, we can glean an understanding of what the ratifiers believed they were creating. It is to an analysis of that public understanding to which we now proceed.

CHAPTER 6

RATIFICATION: IT PLAYS IN PHILADELPHIA, BUT WILL IT PLAY IN PROVIDENCE?

The Argument

There had been disagreement during the debate at the Convention which led to eventual compromise reflected in the unanimous approval of the draft Constitution that was sent to the states. Public reaction to the Constitution reflected many of the discussions that had been held in secret at the Convention. Since the Constitution itself provided for the ratification process, it was turned over to the states, which had employed numerous tools to designate delegates to their own ratifying conventions.

The Federalists, who advocated for a strong central government, saw a bill of rights as a danger to rights and liberties since it could be understood by some as protection for only those rights expressly enumerated. The anti-Federalists, however, wary of a strong central government, felt the absence of a bill of rights would render their rights vulnerable to abrogation by a federal government untethered by any meaningful negative constraints.

Though the Federalists achieved early victories in several state ratifying conventions, they claimed a pyrrhic victory in Massachusetts where the delegation voted for ratification with an understanding that the absence of a bill of rights in the proposed Constitution would be remedied at the first opportunity. Several states adopted the compromise reached in Massachusetts and ratified while urging revision.

It became clear that, though the several states supported the Constitution, they, together, clamored for some guarantee of protection for personal liberty and state sovereignty. Thus, the Constitution, so exhaustively debated and carefully constructed, would need to be amended in its infancy. And those amendments would all spring from a general understanding and embrace of the natural law.

***

Government requires make-believe. Make believe that the king is divine, make believe that he can do no wrong or make believe that the voice of the people is the voice of God. Make believe that the people have a voice or make believe that the representatives of the people are the people. Make believe that governors are the servants of the people. Make believe that all men are equal or make believe that they are not.[1]

– Edmund S. Morgan (1916-2013)

RATIFICATION DEBATES
WITHIN AND AMONGST THE STATES

Many people eagerly awaited the outcome of the Philadelphia Constitutional Convention. "By the morning of September 18, the day after the convention adjourned, [the publishers] of the *Pennsylvania Packet*, had printed five hundred official six-page broadsides that included the Constitution, the Convention's letter to the president of Congress, and its additional resolutions on ratification procedure."[2] By the following day, six newspapers in Philadelphia had printed the Constitution, and "[w]ithin three weeks, at least fifty-five newspapers had published the document, and another twenty joined the list by late October."[3] Pauline Maier notes that editorials and essays favoring the Constitution had the earliest widespread publication, but they were soon followed by fierce opposition to its adoption.[4]

As with the public discourse recorded in the newspapers and pamphlets over a decade earlier, the reasoning and arguments supporting and opposing the Constitution varied greatly. Those who favored the Constitution argued for its rapid ratification and considered any calls for delay or opposition "akin to treason."[5] However, opponents of speedy ratification raised several objections that supporters could not easily dismiss. Chief among these objects was the absence of a federal Bill of Rights.

The Absence of a Bill of Rights as a Point of Contention

James Wilson, a signer of the Declaration of Independence and a vocal Pennsylvania delegate to the Constitutional Convention, spoke to some of the objections raised in the public discourse to the Constitution. On October 6, 1787, Wilson "became the first member of the Convention to defend the Constitution publicly."[6] At the Pennsylvania Statehouse, "Wilson had to explain," notes Maier, "why the Constitution did not, like several state constitutions, include a Bill of Rights."[7] Recounting that "[t]hrough the state constitutions, the people gave their governments 'every right and authority which they did not in explicit terms reserve,'" Wilson contrasted that to the federal constitution which "carefully defined and limited the powers of Congress," perhaps in a direct response to the actions of Parliament's Intolerable Acts, "so that the body's authority came 'not from tacit implication, but from the positive grant' of specific powers in the Constitution."[8] In other words, "[u]nder the state constitutions, 'every thing which is not reserved is given,' but under the federal Constitution 'every thing which is not given is reserved.'"[9] What would the Federalist Wilson think of the federal government today?

Wilson's argument represents a position thoroughly consistent with prevailing notions of natural law and the role of government: Government may exercise only those powers delegated to it to safeguard the liberty, security and happiness of the people who, or the states which, granted to it their consent. The Constitution aimed to codify the powers delegated to the federal government, and the nine state ratification requirement was meant to serve as positive assent to delegate those powers necessary to allow the functioning of government.

To Wilson, "it would be 'superfluous' to say that Congress could do something [...] that the Constitution gave it no power to do," which also made superfluous a federal Bill of Rights.[10] Further, Wilson recognized that express guarantees, such as freedom of the press, could lead to ambiguities and arguments that the Congress would, absent such a provision, have the power to regulate the press.[11] Such syllogistic logic would soon be extended to demonstrate that Congress *must* have powers extending beyond the boundaries of the document itself since express limitations on legislative authority would only be necessary to curtail some existing authority.[12]

Wilson's arguments had great success in Pennsylvania. However, Maier reminds her readers that "Wilson was preaching to the converted: Philadelphia was a Federalist enclave."[13] Nonetheless, Wilson's arguments, an account of which "first appeared in an 'extra' edition of the *Pennsylvania Herald* on October 9, [...] [were] reprinted in every state except perhaps Delaware," which Maier believes "probably received copies enough from nearby Philadelphia."[14] Accordingly, "Federalists through[out] the country welcomed Wilson's speech— and then silently absorbed his arguments into their own essays and oratory."[15] While history remembers Madison as the most important figure in the debates at the Constitutional Convention, perhaps it should initiate James Wilson into the pantheon of demigods of the American founding since his "October 6 speech became a fundamental text for [Federalists to use in] the ratification debates."[16]

Opposition to Wilson's speech expressed disbelief and concern over the Constitution's lack of a Bill of Rights. Opponents dismissed Wilson's arguments as ephemeral wordplay, called Wilson's "distinctions [...] 'dictum' of his invention, a 'play of words' without substance, [and] 'a distinction without a difference.'"[17] They remained skeptical of the absence of a positive monument enumerating individual rights or a negative restraint on them, and pointed to the vagueness of the "necessary and proper clause" which they believed "gave

Congress a grant of power so open-ended that it was meaningless to say its powers were carefully defined and limited."[18] John Marshall, where are you?

Richard Henry Lee of Virginia, a signer of the Declaration of Independence and the sixth President of the Confederation Congress, remained un-swayed by Wilson's arguments about a bill of rights and derided them in a letter to Samuel Adams. Lee considered them "a distinction without a difference," since he felt, like many others, that the Constitution *had*, in fact, "imposed certain reservations on Congress."[19] Why would the Constitution expressly impose some limitations on government if government could exercise power to which it had been granted? Why, for instance, prohibit interference "with the slave trade for twenty years" as well as prohibiting "grant of titles of nobility" if the government would not otherwise have had that power?[20] Maier argues that Lee believed that "[t]hose explicit limits on congressional power indicated that – whatever Wilson claimed – members of the federal Convention had assumed 'that what was not reserved was given.'"[21] Many others began to raise similar objections.

Virginia's George Mason, who, along with three other Virginia delegates to the convention who had refused to sign the Constitution, circulated his objections privately which provided Elbridge Gerry of Massachusetts with the chance to beat Mason to the newspapers.[22] Gerry's objections, printed on November 3 in the *Massachusetts Centinel*, raised some of the same concerns enumerated by Mason.[23] Included among Gerry's arguments was his objection that "some of the powers given Congress were 'ambiguous, and others indefinite and dangerous'" [...] "and [that] 'the system is without the security of a bill of rights.'"[24] Gerry questioned whether the existing confederation government should be dissolved, whether the state governments should, as he saw it, be subsumed by this new constitution, and, lastly, "[w]hether in lieu of the *federal* and *State* Governments, the *national* Constitution now proposed [should] be substituted without amendment?"[25] Gerry, however, conceded that, "in many respects, [...] it has great merit, and, by proper amendments, may be adapted to the 'exigencies of government,' and preservation of liberty."[26] Like Mason, Gerry's opposition to the Constitution in its presented form did not necessarily call for its wholesale rejection. He recognized that the Constitution contained perhaps the best compromise that could be expected and viewed the failure to ratify as an invitation to anarchy.[27]

However, other prominent figures, like Noah Webster – printer, educator, and lexicographer – turned their attention and efforts to the defense of the Constitution. He wrote and published a lengthy pamphlet on October 10, 1787, in which he delivered a glowing endorsement of the Constitution and a point-by-point refutation of the prominent critiques that had circulated by that point in time.[28] In his pamphlet, addressed to "His Excellency, Benjamin Franklin, Esq. President of the Commonwealth of Pennsylvania and Member of the Late Convention, Held at Philadelphia for the Purpose of Devising a Constitution for the Government of the United States"[29] – titles were more formal, wordy, yet descriptive then – Webster provided both effusive praise and a thorough defense of the Constitution.

Though Webster does not point to critics by name, he evidently intended to deflate the arguments of the Anti-Federalists. Webster, like James Wilson and Luther Martin debating at the Convention, and George Washington, in his letter to the President of the Continental Congress, echoes Locke, and applies Locke's theories on the formation of society to the formation of the Union. "Considering the states as individuals, on equal terms, entering into a social compact, no state has a right to any power which may prejudice its neighbors."[30]

Beginning his critique, "[m]ost of the objections I have yet heard to the constitution, consist in mere insinuations unsupported by reasoning or fact[,]" Webster, whether by deliberate intention or unconscious inclusion, invokes our old friend, Reason, the engine of natural law; and thematic and oblique references to natural law pervade Webster's pamphlet. After restating and refuting major critiques of the Constitution raised by Anti-Federalists, Webster indulges in a discourse on freedom and tyranny.[31] Though "[m]any people[,]" Webster opines, "seem to entrain an idea, that liberty consists in *a power to act without any control*[,] [...] [t]his is more liberty than even the savages [those who have not entered into civil society] enjoy."[32] However, showing his postitivistic/ majoritiarian side, "in civil society, political liberty consists in [...] *acting conformably to a sense of a majority of the society*."[33] Per Locke on consent, "[i]n a free government[,] every man binds himself to obey the *public voice*, or the opinions of a majority; and the *whole society* engages to *protect each individual*," Webster endorsed the familiar notion of choice and the need for individuals to entrust certain rights to the organ selected to act for the safety of those rights.[34] Though, "[i]n such a government a man is *free* and safe[,]" if "every man [were] to act without control or fear of punishment[,] [...] every man would be free, but no man would be sure of his freedom one moment."[35] In other words, "[e]ach would have the power of taking his neighbor's life, liberty, or property; and no man would command more than his own strength to repel the invasion."[36]

Concluding, "[t]he case is the same with the states[,]" Webster, a staunch federalist, emphasized the need for the states to entrust some portions of their sovereignty to a central government.[37] He feared that, "[i]f the states should not unite into once compact society, every state may trespass upon its neighbor, and the injured state has no means of redress but its own military force." Webster called on the states to ratify the proposed Constitution, despite its faults.[38]

"Perfection is not the lot of humanity. Instead of censuring the small faults of the Constitution, I am astonished that so many clashing interests have been reconciled—and so many sacrifices made in the *general interest!* The mutual concessions made by the gentlemen of the convention, reflect the highest honor of their candor and liberality; at the same time, they prove that their minds were deeply impressed with a conviction, that such mutual sacrifices are *essential to our union.* They *must* be made sooner or later by every state; or jealousies, local interest and prejudices will unsheathe the sword, and some Cæsar or Cromwell will avail himself of our divisions and wade to a throne through streams of blood."[39]

As if to remind his readers of the natural law belief in the equality of all persons, and the ability of each to apply his own reason, Webster reminds us, "[i]t is not our duty as freemen, to receive the opinions of any men however great and respectable, without an examination."[40] Though he urged for the adoption of the Constitution, he, like any adherent to natural law principles, invited readers to draw their own conclusions.

And many did draw their own conclusions. Some called for a stronger central government,[41] a weaker central government, while still others raised fundamental opposition to the structure of government proposed by the Constitution.[42] Mainly, however, Anti-Federalists complained about the lack of a Bill of Rights while the Federalists remained largely opposed or indifferent to the need for a Bill of Rights since they possessed greater faith in the ability of the Constitution to rein in a strong central government.

The Federalists argued that a Bill of Rights would likely expand upon enumerated powers and encroach upon non-enumerated rights as they stood as a check against government power.[43] This argument has two distinct veins: first, that "enumeration could be used to justify an unwarranted expansion of federal powers," since, by implication, only those named rights would fall within the aegis of positive protection, and second, that "any right excluded from an enumeration would be jeopardized[,]" since some might argue their absence from a list could indicate deliberate exclusion for purposes of exposure to federal targeting.[44]

Stated differently, the Federalists argued, the simple act of creating a list of rights could lead some in the government to believe that those rights not on the list fell outside the protection of the positive perimeter surrounding those named rights. On the other hand, the Anti-Federalists took the approach that the exclusion of *any* enumeration jeopardized *all* rights and *all* liberties of any character.

The Federalists took early victories in several states. Delaware held its convention on December 3, and the delegates unanimously voted to ratify the Constitution four days later.[45] Pennsylvania ratified on December 12,[46] and New Jersey on December 18.[47] On December 31, after debating the Constitution over one Saturday, Georgia's delegates voted unanimously to ratify.[48] Connecticut ratified on January 8, 1788.[49] However, the Anti-Federalists did not relent and continued to make strong showings in the remaining states.

A. SOLUTION FOR ALL:
THE MASSACHUSETTS COMPROMISE

At the Massachusetts ratifying convention, which met from January 9, 1788 to February 5, 1788, Anti-Federalist leaders Samuel Adams and John Hancock famously negotiated a position that would assure passage of the Constitution in Massachusetts: Ratify now, and amend later. Members of the convention, including an attendee named Gen. William Heath believed that "[e]very exertion should be made" to secure unanimity within the convention and across the land.[50] -After frequent conversations with those who opposed the Constitution, John Hancock arrived at a proposition aimed "to remove the doubts and quiet the apprehensions of gentlemen."[51] To do so, the Massachusetts Compromise stated that the transmission of notice of ratification would include very strong recommendations for amendments at the First Congress—particularly a Bill of Rights. With that a similar "compromise" approach, the Constitution was ratified, with proposed amendments, in South Carolina,[52] New Hampshire,[53] Virginia,[54] and New York.[55] In pleading with the people of New York to ratify the proposed Constitution, Madison invoked "the great principle of self-preservation; to the transcendent law of nature and of nature's God, which declares that the safety and happiness of society are the objects at which all political institutions aim, and to which all such institutions must be sacrificed."[56] After the Massachusetts Compromise was reached, only Maryland did not attach amendments.[57]

The Massachusetts Compromise proves essential to understanding constitutional history. Without the Federalist concession of the promise of a future Bill of Rights, Anti-Federalist interests would have defeated the Constitution.[58] Thus, the general intentions of Massachusetts, South Carolina, New Hampshire, Virginia, and New York ratifiers were not only ascertainable with respect to individual rights, but were also integral to the democratic legitimacy of constitutional clauses in the originalist interpretive exercise.

Because the ratifying conventions of these states thoroughly and unambiguously discussed and acted on these concerns, primarily over natural rights, we have an understanding today of what the ratifiers publicly understood they were ratifying. As we will discover, the Bill of Rights is a negation on the federal government from impairing a non-exhaustive amalgam of pre-political, pre-constitutional, fundamental human liberties, which we can rationally call natural rights. Such a contention over the enumeration of certain rights and liberties necessarily presupposes that such rights and liberties exist! Though both the Federalists and Anti-Federalists possessed fundamentally different positions on the need to codify fundamental rights and liberties, they both appealed to Natural Law theory for support.

The language used by the Massachusetts Compromise reflects the reasoning of two competing schools, Federalist and Anti-Federalist, over the wisdom of enumerating a list of reserved rights. However, what is clear, as evidenced by both sides of the Federalist/Anti-Federalist argument and by the language of the debates in the state ratifying conventions, is that the question at issue was not *whether* liberty is constitutional or pre-political, but *how best to protect* pre-political liberty in America's foundational governmental instrument.

Most commonly in those debates, delegates used natural law arguments when discussing the necessity of a written bill of rights. What is gained from this examination of the ratification and the Massachusetts Compromise, in a general sense, is the understanding that the *sine qua non* to the passage of the Constitution by nine or more states was the express eventual written recognition of pre-political, natural rights in the document: "The necessity of amendments is universally admitted. It is a word which is reechoed from every part of the continent," remarked Virginia's Patrick Henry.[59] Even Madison agreed to this. "[I]t may not be thought necessary to provide [enumerated constitutional] limits for the legislative power in [England], yet a different opinion prevails in the United States."[60] In fact, when amendments were proposed to the first Congress, Madison's friend, fellow Federalist Representative Alexander White of Virginia,[61] noted that:

> I hope we shall not dismiss [consideration of a bill of rights] altogether [in remitting it to committee], because I think *a majority of the people who have ratified the Constitution* did it under the expectation that Congress would, at some convenient time, examine its texture and point out where it was defective, in order that it might be judiciously amended.[62]

More specifically, the Massachusetts Compromise resulted in natural law-specific precursors to the Bill of Rights in the Virginia suggestions for amendment. In moving toward the actual drafting of the first ten amendments, and thus the actual intentions of the drafters, this background of natural law and natural rights in the ratification does not dissipate, but is rather bolstered. This is particularly true because "James Madison, [the] drafter of the Bill of Rights . . . referred to and relied on these proposals [for amendment from the states]."[63] A bill of rights of this nature was widely demanded in Anti-Federalist writings and the Compromise was used to avoid the clamor of Anti-Federalists for a second constitutional convention.[64]

After months of debate, hundreds of pamphlets, letters, circulars, and speeches, the majority of the states had ratified the Constitution. The Federalists managed to win the majority of delegates in each state convention through newspaper propaganda, bribery, malapportionment of delegates, threats of secession, hostile retaliatory trade legislation on resistant states, and the promise of restrictive amendments. Though the Federalists began with a tremendous lead, securing ratification victories in Delaware, Pennsylvania, New Jersey, Georgia, and Connecticut, the Anti-Federalists, with their key victory in Massachusetts, impressed upon enough state conventions their desire for a bill of rights to secure more firmly fundamental liberties and freedoms— natural rights—against what they viewed as a hungry federal leviathan that would surely, they feared, metastasize and soon gorge upon their closely-guarded rights. All the states that chronologically followed Massachusetts, except for Maryland, ratified the proposed Constitution with the strong imperative that a Bill of Rights should immediately follow.

As we shall see in the upcoming debates around the Bill of Rights, the Federalists and Anti-Federalists differed greatly on how to collect and codify the rights that they all understood every free individual to possess. What now remained for the burgeoning Republic was to appease the demands of the several states for a Bill of Rights by amending the new Constitution.

But which rights would they codify? How would they articulate the need to inscribe some particular rights without the risk of degrading others by omission? These questions plagued James Madison who would eventually arrive at a simple and elegant solution. First, however, a government infrastructure needed to be built; then a Bill of Rights could come about. We turn next to those historic tasks and the role of the natural law in each.

CHAPTER 7

THE BILL COMES DUE

The Argument

The colonists had scrambled from conflict to panic for nearly 15 years. What began as resistance turned into rebellion. What became rebellion turned into war. What began as war turned into independence. And what began as independence had turned again into conflict.

Unlike the Revolution, however, this conflict was not against a foreign enemy, but rather a domestic one. The Federalists and Anti-Federalists needed once again to reach a compromise; this time, over how to amend the Constitution.

The elected members of the House and Senate slowly made their way to New York City, then the nation's capital, to meet at the newly-renovated Federal Hall. Without controversy, in early spring 1789, they counted and certified the electoral votes, and found that the Electoral College unanimously elected George Washington as President.

They then set about establishing committees and passing rules, but, within a couple months, moved onto the discussion of amending the Constitution. Madison, as usual, had been preparing for this, and suggested several amendments which provided the basis for the Bill of Rights. Though words were massaged, excised, added, or substituted, the spirit of Madison's suggested amendments survived. Besides addressing the specific complaints enumerated in Anti-Federalist speeches, circulars, essays, and letters, Madison offered a rather laconic and wryly significant suggestion that further enshrined natural law and natural rights into the U.S. Constitution: one of his greatest achievements – the Ninth Amendment.

***

Liberty, the highest of natural endowments, being the portion only of intellectual or rational natures, confers on man this dignity – that he is "in the hand of his counsel" and has power over his actions. But the manner in which such dignity is exercised is of the greatest moment, inasmuch as on the use that is made of liberty the highest good and the greatest evil alike depend. Man, indeed, is free to obey his reason, to seek moral good, and to strive unswervingly after his last end. Yet he is free also to turn aside to all other things; and, in pursuing the empty semblance of good, to disturb rightful order and to fall headlong into the destruction which he has voluntarily chosen.[1]

– Pope Leo XIII (1810-1903)

THE LANDSCAPE OF THE UNITED STATES AT THE TIME OF THE FIRST CONGRESS: DIFFICULTIES IN REACHING A QUORUM

In 1789, "[m]ost Americans lived in what [were] essentially little more than hamlets that had been cut from the wilderness only a generation or two earlier," many of them at the confluence of well-worn paths or along navigable waterways, but most far from any population centers.[2] With a total population of around 3 million,[3] the burgeoning nation boasted only a handful of cities. The largest, Philadelphia, housed around 43,000 people, followed distantly by New York City with 33,000, followed further by Boston with 18,000, Charleston with 16,000 and Baltimore with 13,000.[4] By comparison, London maintained a size of around 1,000,000, and metropolitan Paris, around 500,000.[5] The combined totals of the new nation's five largest urban centers barely amounted to one tenth of the size of the imperial heart of Great Britain and one fifth the romanticized heart of France.[6]

At this time, the United States possessed little industry beyond agriculture and timber. At the time of Washington's inauguration, two states had not yet ratified the Constitution, and, despite the parchment blueprint for what Webster had called an *"empire of reason,"* a new government had yet to be crafted and implemented.[7] Far from concentrating around urban centers, the majority of the nation's 3 million people lived scattered up and down the Atlantic coast and struggled daily against weather, wilderness, and sporadic attacks from varying tribes of the lands' first, and ever-marginalized occupants.

Despite the provincial landscape of the United States, news had spread of the adoption of a new government, and those states that had ratified had elected representatives to convene at New York's Federal Hall for the meeting of the First Congress on March 4, 1789. The Federalists' supporters had turned out in larger numbers at the polls than those who supported the Anti-Federalists. "As election results for the new Congress trickled in from the states – there was no fixed day for elections—the results proved vastly more favorable than Washington, Madison, and their fellow supporters of the new Constitution had hoped."[8] Madison and Washington, and their Federalist allies must have rejoiced since "Federalists had won overwhelming majorities in both houses of Congress."[9]

At the time of the First Congress, "New York City [...] occupied only the southern tip of Manhattan Island and still bore the visible ravages of the seven-year British occupation during the Revolutionary War."[10] The city itself "extended from the Battery northward barely one-third of the way to Greenwich Village and east along the East River only as far as the present site of the Manhattan Bridge."[11] Despite its status as one of the New World's preeminent cities, New York City had "few buildings that rose [taller] than three stories, [yet] for the many members of Congress who hailed from rural areas, it was phantasmagorically cosmopolitan."[12] To modern sensibilities, a city with "streets [...] badly paved, [which were] very dirty [and] narrow as well as crooked [and] filled up with a strange variety of wooden, stone [and] brick houses [and] full of hogs [and] mud [...and] excrement" hardly imbues us with a sense of spectacle and wonder.[13]

However, amidst the undoubtedly arresting combination of sights, smells, and sounds stood an undeniably extravagant love letter to America's classical intellectual heritage and aspirational ideals: Federal Hall. Originally built in the Greek revival style in the late seventeenth century, the hall served as New York's first City Hall. The building had already served as a meeting place of the Stamp Act Congress in 1765, and, later, the Confederation Congress.[14] In 1788, Pierre Charles L'Enfant, who would win George Washington's approval to design the new nation's capital on the Potomac River, began to supervise the revision of the edifice to accommodate the First Congress.[15] The renovation "was the largest construction project in New York City at the time."[16] Journalist and author Richard Labunski notes that "[t]wo hundred artisans, carpenters, and unskilled laborers would labor for almost eight months on the [renovation] project."[17]

Though many marveled "at the Hall's harmonious redesign and elegant, up-to-date interiors," some, like Senator William Maclay, no doubt a victim of the ubiquitous Quaker demand for simplicity within his native Pennsylvania, derided the building with the pejorative nickname, the "Great Baby House[, which was] a play on words [since] L'Enfant's name meant 'child.'"[18]

In America of 1789, transportation was unreliable, and the roads, where they existed, poor; and travel, in general, hazardous. No atlas of America had yet been published,[19] and "shipwrecks were not unusual, and drownings were common even on crossings of the Hudson River from New Jersey to Manhattan."[20] Despite the resonant boom of guns "at noon on March 4 to signal the openings of Congress [...] both houses fell short of the quorum required to do business."[21] Of the eight Senators and thirteen Representatives who showed up, those in attendance were largely from Massachusetts, Connecticut, and Pennsylvania. Those members not in attendance "blamed bad weather, bad health, bad roads and bad luck for their absence."[22] Whatever the cause, the members present grew weary in their idleness.

The Congressional Record reflects the same. On Wednesday, March 4, 1789, it chronicles the anticlimactic nature of the proceedings. "This being the day for the meeting of the new Congress, the following members of the Senate appeared and took their seats."[23] After listing the names of the eight present senators, the record reflects succinct disappointment. "The members present not being a quorum, they adjourned from day to day until WEDNESDAY, MARCH 11. When the same members being present as on the 4th instant, it was agreed that a circular should be written to the absent members, requesting their immediate attendance."[24]

When Representative James Madison finally reached "New York on March 14, he found that only two more Congressmen and no additional Senators had arrived."[25] Once again, Madison grew easily frustrated by inaction wrought by circumstance. "When a quorum will be made up in either House, rests on vague conjecture, rather than on any precise information," grumbled Madison in a March 19 letter to Washington.[26] Continuing, "[i]t is not improbable I think that the present week will supply the deficiency in one, if not both of them," Madison shows his eagerness to get down to the business of government.[27] In the rest of his letter, Madison bemoans New York's still open polls and speculates as to which candidates will ultimately represent New York. Ever the tactician, Madison clearly had begun to figure the strategic calculus of the first congressional session. However, "[w]ithout quoroums[,] the new government didn't really exist. The ballots for president and vice president [from the electors] couldn't be counted. No legislation could take place. Courts couldn't be created. Revenues couldn't be raised."[28] Such a failure would be an unmitigated embarrassment.

Interestingly, it had been a rivalry between Madison, and his fellow Virginian, Patrick Henry, that resulted in Madison's presence in the House of Representatives. This rivalry would serve to drive Madison away from his Federalist roots and closer toward the Anti-Federalist camp which would later culminate in Madison's partnership with Jefferson to form the Democratic Republicans during the Adams Administration in the late 1790s.

Still bitter from the battles over ratification, Patrick Henry, who controlled the Virginia House of Delegates, conspired to keep Madison from being one of Virginia's two U.S. senators.[29] After losing the Senate election, a defeat orchestrated by Henry, Madison was distraught.[30]

However, "[f]or Madison[, ...] personal feelings were beside the point. The more serious problem was the victory for the opponents of the Constitution."[31] At the urging of friends, Madison decided to run for a House seat.[32] Because Henry adjusted the boundaries of Madison's congressional district to make it an Anti-Federalist stronghold in Virginia's first case of partisan gerrymandering,[33] Madison needed to appeal to the Anti-Federalist sentiments of his neighbors.[34] Madison would need to endorse a bill of rights.

However, "[e]ndorsing a bill of rights would show that Madison did not consider the Constitution perfect."[35] To show his approval for modifying the Constitution, Madison published a series of open letters explaining how changes in circumstances could warrant a careful, studied, and moderated approach to amending the Constitution.[36] He explained that it was his "sincere opinion that the Constitution ought to be revised, and that the first Congress meeting under it, ought to prepare and recommend" such modifications—a bill of rights.[37] It was clearly Madison's belief that if his Constitution were to be changed, it would be done under his guidance, supervision, and editorial control. Some of these changes, "would include, he proposed, 'particularly the rights of conscience in the fullest latitude, the freedom of the press, trial by jury, security against general warrants, etc.'"[38] While Patrick Henry's meddling drove Madison to change his position on a bill of rights, it was with his singular purpose and energy that Madison went to New York for the first Congress.

GEORGE WASHINGTON TAKES THE HELM, GUIDED BY JAMES MADISON

When the House of Representatives finally eked out a quorum on a snowy April 1, around four weeks behind schedule,[39] it elected Pennsylvania's Frank Muhlenberg as its first speaker.[40] Three days later, the Senate mustered up its quorum.[41] With a few days' head start, the House had already begun to select members for its ad hoc committees. With the arrival of Virginia's Richard Henry Lee the Senate's quorum, the new government needed to recognize its executive heads: The President and Vice President.

Though boredom and tedium had marked the passage of the month of March as Senators and Representatives awaited quorums, the selection of the nation's first president produced neither real suspense, nor excitement. The Electoral College votes for Virginia's George Washington as President,[42] and Massachusetts' John Adams as vice president were counted and accepted by both houses of Congress.[43] And, though expected by all, Washington's official ascension to the presidency was met with jubilation.

A humble and quiet man, Washington tried to avoid the festivities awaiting him at every stop from Mount Vernon to New York.

> Though he slipped the crowds when he could, he agreed when pressed to deliver addresses in Baltimore, Wilmington, and Philadelphia, where twenty thousand people—half the city's population—thronged the cobbled streets shouting, 'Long live the father of his people!,' and a laurel wreath fit for a Roman emperor was placed on his head.[44]

When he arrived in Elizabeth, New Jersey on April 23, "he was met by a committee of both houses of Congress, John Jay, numerous New York officials, in the uniformed rotundity of his Revolutionary War colleague Henry Knox."[45]

Doubtless, Washington graciously accepted the grandiosity of his reception, though he would later write in his diary

> The display of boats which attended and joined us on this occasion, some with vocal and some with instrumental music on board; the decorations of the ships, the roar of cannon, and the loud acclamations of the people which rent the skies, as I passed along the wharves, filled my mind with sensations as painful (considering the reverse of this scene, which may be the case after all my labors to do good) as they are pleasing.[46]

Washington, as he would note in his inaugural address, only reluctantly accepted the burden of the presidency. On Thursday, April 30, 1789, Washington was welcomed by both houses of Congress, and recited his oath. After thunderous applause, and cheers of *"Long live George Washington, President of the United States*![,] [Washington], having returned to his seat, after a short pause arose, and addressed the Senate and House of Representatives[.]"[47]

Beginning after addressing the body, "[a]mong the vicissitudes incident to life, no event could have filled me with greater anxieties than that of which the notification was transmitted by your order, and received on the 14th day of the present month[,]" Washington humbly admitted his trepidation at accepting responsibility for such an awesome task: shaping the office of the president.[48]

Written mainly by Madison,[49] Washington's speech extolled the natural law roots of individual personal liberty in a free society. Far from urging its occasional nurture with the blood of patriots and tyrants, Washington called for greater unity under the banner of freedom, Providence, and happiness. Madison, still a disciple of the Scottish Enlightenment evangelist and Princeton University President, John Witherspoon, often used the word "happiness" as it was used in the language of the Scottish Enlightenment; as the goal of a life lived under the natural law.

In Washington's speech, Madison tipped his hat to Adam Smith, the famous Scottish Enlightenment thinker who conducted an exhaustive deconstruction of, at the time, the little understood economic forces that shaped markets. Though he wrote on several subjects, Smith secured his canonization amongst the sanctified of the social scientists through his exegesis, commonly referred to as *The Wealth of Nations*, which he published, coincidentally, in 1776.[50] Smith created a simple and elegant metaphor to explain how forces within a free market, chiefly among them supply and demand, led to the efficient distribution of goods and services based on the wants and wills of the consumers and investors within a market. The "invisible hand," according to Smith, would guide the market toward a natural harmony of supply and demand where a market would creep toward inevitable equilibrium maximizing happiness. This theory presumed the absence of government interference with the invisible hand.

Washington, by declaring "[n]o people can be bound to acknowledge and adore the *invisible hand* which conducts the affairs of men more than the people of the United States," simultaneously embraced natural law ideals while surreptitiously endorsing Smith's free market principles.[51] He pledged to remain impartial, not to side with "local prejudices or attachments[,]" and to govern in a manner so as to ensure "that the foundations of [the government's] national policy will be laid in the pure and immutable principles of private morality, and the preeminence of free Government be exemplified by all the attributes which can with the affections of its citizens, and command the respect of the world."[52] By invoking private – i.e., *secular* or, Grotian – notions of morality, Washington declares that he, and his example as President, would embrace a rule of law using morality as a polestar with the recognition that he, and the new government, could be counted upon to labor under the watchful eye of Thomas Aquinas' old friend, Reason.

He continued:

> I dwell on this prospect with every satisfaction which an ardent love for my country can inspire: since there is no truth more thoroughly established, than that there exists, in the economy and course of nature, an indissoluble union between virtue and happiness; between duty and advantage; between the genuine maxims of an honest and magnanimous policy, and the solid rewards of public prosperity and felicity: since we ought to be no less persuaded that the propitious smiles of Heaven can never be expected on a nation that disregards *the eternal rules of order and right, which Heaven itself has ordained*; and since the preservation of the sacred fire of liberty, and the destiny of the republican model of Government, are justly considered as deeply, perhaps as finally, staked, on the experiment entrusted to the hands of the American people.[53]

Economy and course of nature, virtue, happiness, eternal rules of order and right, liberty entrusted to the hands of the American people; Madison and Washington, using incontrovertible watchwords of the natural law, could not have more resoundingly and emphatically enshrined the natural law in the first president's first public address.

Washington's speech also acknowledged that this first Congress planned on revising the Constitution. After the above-quoted section reminding the assembled houses of government of the importance of natural law values, Washington indulged in a rather candid admonition urging temperance and consideration. "Besides the ordinary objects submitted to your care," Washington continued, "it will remain with your judgment to decide how far an exercise of the occasional power delegated by the fifth article of the Constitution," the article that outlines the rules and procedure for amending the Constitution, "is rendered expedient at the present juncture, by the nature of objections which have been urged against the system or by the degree of inquietude which has given birth to them."[54]

Clearly, in the eyes of both Madison and Washington, amendment, at this point in late April 1789, was inevitable. He vowed not to push a personal agenda, but rather encouraged the gathered senators and representatives to decide for themselves, "I shall again give way to my entire confidence in your discernment and pursuit of the public good."[55] Yet he cautioned against overreach:

> I assure myself, that whilst you carefully avoid every alteration which might endanger the benefits of a united and effective Government, or which ought to await future lessons of experience; a reverence for *the characteristic rights of freemen*, and a regard for the public harmony, will sufficiently influence your deliberations on the questions, how far the former can be more impregnably fortified, or the later be safely and advantageously promoted.[56]

The message was clear: Washington sought to preserve harmony and confidence in government and the Constitution by recognizing the prevalent desire to amend the Constitution, thereby addressing Anti-Federalist narratives of the new Federal government as the second coming of George III, while simultaneously bolstering the position of the Federalists by providing them with a verbal imprimatur—the desire that future lessons of experience temper the actions of Congress—to insist on more circumspect approach to amendment. Still, Madison could not resist putting more natural law language on Washington's tongue, by referencing "the characteristic rights" of free persons.[57]

MADISON'S IMPASSIONED PLEA FOR AMENDING THE CONSTITUTION, AND HIS SECRET WEAPON: THE NINTH AMENDMENT

Congress slogged through weeks of business before it was able to take up the topic of amending the Constitution. On Monday, June 8, James Madison addressed the House, announcing that he "considered [himself] bound in honor and in duty to do what [he had] done on this subject" and promised that he would "proceed to bring the amendments before [Congress] as soon as possible[.]"[58] After further discussion in the House, Madison delivered a speech in which he laid out his proposed amendments. Ever organized and careful, Madison systematically laid out all his proposed amendments.[59] Doubtless, many members would have struggled to grasp the subtlety and nuance of all the provisions Madison had crafted. Each of Madison's proposed amendments addressed a concern voiced by an Anti-Federalist in a speech, pamphlet, circular, broadside, or editorial. Each member of the gathered body must have been captivated by a proposed amendment which spoke to his concerns.

When Madison finished listing his proposed amendments, he candidly acknowledge[d], that, […] he [did] conceive that the Constitution may be amended; that is to say, if all power is subject to abuse, that then it is possible the abuse of the powers of the General Government may be guarded against in a more secure manner than is now done [by the current Constitution], while no one advantage arising from the exercise of that power shall be damaged or endangered by it.[60]

Madison's speech to the House echoed Washington's inaugural speech to the Congress. "We have in this way something to gain, and, if we proceed with caution, nothing to lose. And in this case it is necessary to proceed with caution; for while we feel all these inducements to go into a revisal of the Constitution, we must feel for the Constitution itself, and make that revisal a moderate one."[61] Madison probably spoke more to the Anti-Federalists in Congress hoping to reinforce Washington's message of moderation.

Madison's speech occupies over eleven pages in the Annals of Congress, and in it, he touched upon nearly all the issues we now know to be in the Bill of Rights. Several of the Amendments we know debuted nearly verbatim in his speech. Madison restated all the popular arguments for and against the Bill of Rights. Many of those against it, he dismissed handily. One against, however, he believed, had merit.

It has been objected also against a bill of rights, that, by enumerating particular exceptions to the grant of power, it would disparage those rights which were not placed in that enumeration; and it might follow by implication, that those rights which were not singled out, were intended to [be assigned] into the hands of the General Government, and were consequently insecure.[62]

Adding, "[t]his is one of the most plausible arguments I have ever heard urged against the admission of a bill of rights into this system; but, I conceive, that it may be guarded against," Madison laid the groundwork for his plan which would become the Ninth Amendment.[63] Humbly, Madison submitted, "I have attempted it, as gentlemen may see by turning to the last clause of the fourth resolution;" he had earlier stated a perhaps innocuous-sounding bundle of words discussing particular rights retained by the people.[64]

By now, of course, we know this as the forerunner to the Ninth Amendment.

The exceptions here or elsewhere in the Constitution, made in favor of particular rights, shall not be so construed as to diminish the just importance of other rights retained by the people, or as to enlarge the powers delegated by the Constitution; but either as actual limitations of such powers, or as inserted merely for greater caution.[65]

Like Madison's other suggested amendments, this proposal, what amounted to a draft of the Ninth and Tenth Amendments, reflected a careful and considered approach to the issue of amendment. By suggesting that an amendment be included that would make explicit that the Bill of Rights did not contain an exhaustive list of rights, Madison would be able to put upon the Anti-Federalist required enumeration of rights a capstone to assuage any concerns that he, and his Federalist colleagues harbored, that the simple act of giving voice to certain rights could lead future congresses, future executives, future jurists, and future generations to believe themselves only to be possessed of the rights explicitly listed in the federal constitution.

Madison, in crafting the Bill of Rights, needed to manage two competing arguments: the disingenuous argument of Alexander Hamilton, that any enumeration of rights "could be used to justify any unwarranted expansion of federal power" as the government is of enumerated powers, and to enumerate rights implies areas of rights the government can reach into beyond those enumerated, on the one hand; and, the Madisonian argument that "any right excluded from enumeration would be jeopardized," on the other hand.[66] Madison, in this initial proposal to the House "ran together both of these concerns."[67]

His proposals went to a select committee (of which he was a member) for consideration, and "[e]ventually, the two ideas were unpacked" into the Ninth and Tenth Amendments, which deal with "rights" and "powers," respectively.[68] That is the Barnett-libertarian view of the Ninth and Tenth Amendments, which Professor Randy Barnett, whose work is discussed more fully in Chapter 16, termed as power-constraint: The two amendments act to constrain the federal government from either expanding its own powers at the expense of individual persons and of the States, or from infringing on the other unenumerated natural rights of individual persons.

Such a bundle of amendments dispels any argument that the founders disavowed natural law and natural rights. Why else would such a clause exist? What other rights could there be? Of course, there were the state bills of rights, but Madison addressed that concern too! "The powers not delegated by this Constitution, nor prohibited by it to the States, are reserved to the States respectively."[69] So, after setting up the Bill of Rights to contain a provision to protect non-enumerated rights, Madison returned to protect the rights of the states which created the Constitution and to emphasize that the Constitution provided government only with the powers that the states ceded to it, and nothing more.

The amendments would go through Committee, revision, debate, transmission to the Senate, more revision, and, a return to the House, and then, finally, dissemination to the states for their ratification or rejection.[70] When dissected, the principle in what would later become the Tenth Amendment,[71] (limiting the powers and jurisdiction of the federal government to those powers set forth in the Constitution itself and reserving all others to the states or the people) finds support in the involvement of Roger Sherman in crafting the final language of that amendment. Sherman, a strong states' rights advocate, who had opposed the Bill of Rights, offered the language "nor prohibited to it by the states," instead of "nor prohibited to the States."[72] Sherman's motion to alter the last clause of the Tenth Amendment earned unanimous approval in the House of Representatives, and leaves us with a clear record as to the Tenth Amendment's reach to preserve State power and autonomy against implied federal powers.[73] Conversely, the Ninth amendment makes no reference to the states, but to "other rights," an umbrella phrase relating to pre-political natural rights and essential constitutional civil liberties incorporated into the Bill of Rights by the Ninth Amendment. The historical record, when examined, backs this distinction and indeed gives a fairly clear picture of the public understanding embraced by the Ratifiers and the Framers in adopting and drafting the Ninth Amendment.[74]

The level of public attention directed at the legislature likely prompted legislators who represented many different, and sometimes conflicting positions. In campaigning first for their sides in the convention of 1787, and then for ratification, and then for proper amendments, members of Congress often needed to straddle precarious positions that required excruciatingly careful application of precise language. For example, Madison was careful never to state that a majority of the eligible voters in the country did not agree to the Constitution nor imply they would have not done so but for consideration of their specific amendments. In fact, "the Constitution was not 'an expression of the clear and deliberate will of the whole people,' nor of a majority of the adult males, nor at the outside of one fifth of them."[75] Yet, in the same breath he did not avoid admitting it necessary to "satisfy the public," and to "extinguish from the bosom of every member of the community, any apprehensions."[76] Those carefully chosen words, designed to maintain legitimacy while shoring up weaknesses in that same legitimacy, represent a hallmark in Madisonian rhetorical strategy. Moreover, the admitted necessity of compromise, the efforts of ardent Anti-Federalists to stop such compromise and sink the new Constitution through subsequent efforts, and the chicanery of parliamentary procedure provided plenty of opportunity to cause difficulty.

The Ninth Amendment, through the use of "retained," incorporates the "principle that constitutions are not made to create rights in the people, but in recognition of, and in order to preserve them, and if any are specifically numerated and specially guarded, it is only because they are peculiarly important or peculiarly exposed to invasion."[77] Indeed, according to Madison, the Constitution is not intended to "descend to recount every minutiae," for, in the somewhat snarky words of Theodore Sedgewick, if the list was intended to exhaust the enforceable rights of mankind, "they [the select committee] might have gone into a very lengthy enumeration of rights; they might have declared that a man should have a right to wear his hat if he pleased . . . ."[78]

The House of Representatives devolved into "desultory conversation" and adjourned several times while drafting the Bill of Rights.[79] The Bill of Rights is a creature of ruthless congressional compromise that is reasonably consistent, and is emphatically not a complete statement of the higher natural and civil liberties of the people. However, it contains the assurances of the Ninth Amendment, crafted to protect the unenumerated natural rights of all persons, and essential unenumerated civil liberties against government encroachment, and the Tenth Amendment which reserves the powers not delegated to the federal government to the States, and to the people.[80]

Madison said as much in a speech to Congress opposing the creation of a National Bank in February 1791 as Congress awaited the ratification of the proposed amendments by the states, an event that would happen ten months later on December 15.[81] On February 2, Madison rose to speak in response to a bill from the Senate, spearheaded by Secretary of the Treasury, Alexander Hamilton, proposing the creation of the Bank of the United States.[82] He "began with a general review of the advantages and disadvantages of banks,"[83] and mentioned Adam Smith, whom he called "the most enlightened patron of banks," as a source to support his argument about certain disadvantages.[84] Madison went on to restate the Anti-Federalist and Federalist views on the powers of government, and perhaps most importantly, emphasized that the "necessary and proper clause" did not provide Congress with limitless power to issue decrees.[85] He proclaimed:

> The essential characteristic of the Government, as composed of limited and enumerated powers, would be destroyed, if, instead of direct and incidental means, any means could be used, which, in the language of the preamble to the bill, 'might be conceived to be conducive to the successful conducting of the finances or might be conceived to tend to give facility to the obtaining of loans.'

> If[…] Congress, by virtue of the power to borrow, can create the means of lending, and in pursuance of these means, can incorporate a Bank, they may do any thing whatever creative of like means.[86]

He read several of the proposed amendments to clarify his position, "remarking particularly on the [Ninth] and [Tenth]; the former as guarding against a latitude of interpretation; the latter, as excluding every source of power not within the Constitution itself."[87] Madison then traced the history of the Ninth Amendment "in the state conventions,[88] through the drafting process, and into the Virginia Assembly"[89] and argued that the Ninth Amendment ought to be read "as guarding against a latitude of interpretation."[90] In doing so, Madison made it clear that he intended the Ninth Amendment to represent a bulwark against interference with unenumerated natural rights.

Ultimately, he believed the bank was *ultra vires* the powers of Congress, despite Hamilton's assertion that the creation of a federal bank was implied as incident to express powers of taxation and financing debt. Moreover, Madison believed that there existed a natural right to have government remain within the confines of its founding charter. Not only did he offer a philosophical defense of pre political rights, but his speech in response to the Bank Bill was a political argument over the distribution of power under the constitutional framework.

Although Madison may have lost the battle when the Bank Bill passed and was signed into law on February 25th, he won the war.

> In the months following Madison's speech, antifederalist efforts in Virginia waned, and later that same year, on December 15, 1791, Virginia ratified the proposed amendments without further debate and the Bill of Rights became part of our Constitution. There is no historical evidence that Madison's speech actually tilted Virginia toward ratification…[but] [i]t is nevertheless significant that Virginia's ratification vote took place following this public articulation of the meaning of the Ninth Amendment by Virginia's own congressional representative.[91]

The Bill of Rights would pass, and the words of Madison's proposed Ninth amendment were made even more concise, "The enumeration in the Constitution, of certain rights, shall not be construed to deny or disparage others retained by the people."[92]

NATURAL RIGHTS PRINCIPLES IN THE REMAINING AMENDMENTS

Beyond the Ninth Amendment, many of the other rights protected from federal encroachment by the Bill of Rights were in fact fundamental rights in and of themselves, and thus morally mandated; or were manmade mechanisms for enforcing fundamental rights. For example, the First Amendment protection of speech[93] stemmed from the invocation of the fundamental right to expressive freedom in works like Madison's proposal for the amendments, in which he sought to safeguard "natural rights, retained—as Speech, Con[science]."[94] Moreover, in the committee that revised Madison's proposed Bill of Rights, Roger Sherman argued that the people have "'certain natural rights which [we] retained,' including the right 'of [s]peaking, writing and publishing . . . with decency and freedom.'"[95] As for the origins of the First Amendment's defense of freedom of religion, Madison wrote "that in matters of Religion no man's right is abridged by the institution of Civil Society and that Religion is wholly exempt from its cognizance."[96]

Additionally, the Second Amendment,[97] incorporated the natural law understanding that individuals have a pre-political, inalienable right to defend themselves, not only against individual violence but from tyranny of the government itself.[98] Professor Barnett noted, "the right to keep and bear arms is protected – just as all the rights retained by the people are protected by the unamended Constitution – by the fact that the Constitution gives the federal government no power to dispossess the people of their preexisting natural rights."[99] He continues that the Second Amendment should be understood in light of "the axiomatic truths in the allied systems of natural rights and civic republicanism the Founders embraced," including: "[t]he right of personal self-defense is inalienable, being the cardinal natural right,"[100] and "the derivative right... of individuals to join together for collective defense... [against acts] perpetrated by apolitical criminals or for political purposes by a tyrant or his thugs."[101]

The Third Amendment,[102] drafted in response to the detestable British practice of forcing colonists to house British troops in their homes without their consent, aimed to codify the natural right to enjoy the bundle of property rights (use, alienation, and exclusion) of one's real property. Madison suggested a uniquely worded quartering amendment, which not only prohibited forced billeting during times of peace, but "at any time...in a manner warranted by law."[103] Moreover, Madison's draft of the Third Amendment "substituted the mandatory imperative 'shall' for the 'oughts' that had characterized those earlier documents [offered by the states]; thus making the provision a true 'right.'"[104] Such a change by Madison was likely "implying that, above and beyond statutory and constitutional restraints, quartering ought to conform with natural law."[105]

The Fourth Amendment[106] guarantee against unreasonable searches and seizures,[107] a reaction to the almost unlimited use by British customs officials of writs of assistance to break into any house at any time to search for contraband goods,[108] was created to preserve the fundamental right to privacy, or the age old maxim that "a man's home is his castle." Even "in ancient times there were evidences of that same concept in custom and law, partly as a result of the natural desire for privacy, partly an outgrowth, in all probability, of the emphasis placed by the ancients upon the home as a place of hospitality, shelter, and protection."[109]

Similarly, the Eighth Amendment's[110] prohibition of cruel and unusual punishment, as well as excessive fines relates to the natural right to proportionality of punishment, dates as far back as the teachings of the Bible, and was adopted by St. Thomas Aquinas: "the judgment of God is such that a man has to suffer in proportion with his deeds, according to Matthew 7:2: 'With what measure you judge, you shall be judged: and with what measure you mete, it shall be measured to you again.'"[111] Before being included in the Eighth Amendment, the language "first appeared in the English Bill of Rights of 1689, in response to the sentencing practices of royal judges in the reign of King James II. It appeared once again in 1776, across the Atlantic, in the Declaration of Rights that George Mason drafted for the Commonwealth of Virginia. It appeared a third time, in 1788, among the amendments recommended by the Virginia convention when it ratified the United States Constitution."[112] Moreover, it is widely accepted, including by a recent (at this writing) Supreme Court opinion, that "[p]rotection against excessive punitive economic sanctions secured by the Clause is, to repeat, both 'fundamental to our scheme of ordered liberty' and 'deeply rooted in this Nation's history and tradition.'"[113]

On the other hand, some rights listed by the framers in the Bill of Rights were not pre-political, but inserted as man-made mechanisms for enforcing fundamental principles, like the Fifth Amendment's[114] prohibition against double jeopardy, or the Sixth[115] and Seventh Amendment's[116] requirement of trial by jury in criminal and civil cases. During the debate in the House of Representatives over the Bill of Rights, Madison himself acknowledged, that "trial by jury cannot be considered as a natural right, but a right resulting from a social compact which regulates the action of the community, [nevertheless, it] is as essential to secure the liberty of the people as any one of the pre-existent rights of nature."[117]

The fact that the Bill of Rights amalgamates civil liberties and pre-political natural liberties should not reflect a rejection of the latter for the former, or an equation of the latter to the former, but is merely representative of the importance of particular procedural or substantive civil liberties or natural rights in practice, such that enumeration was deemed prudent as an extra precaution in the recent history of particular rights violations.[118]

Madison could not know that the widely-held ideas of natural law and natural rights incorporated in the Bill of Rights would soon give way to a detached, somewhat literalistic approach to law that would sap it of notions of fairness, equity, morality, and restraint. The erosion of natural law and natural rights, however, had already begun. Thinkers and philosophers like Jeremy Bentham began applying a more mechanical, industrial approach to law and jurisprudence that emphasized process, political legitimacy, and promulgation. Little did Madison know that his Ninth Amendment, a simple, elegant approach to remind the people that they had rights beyond simply those that the government recognized, would become so incredibly important, and yet utterly ignored, decades after its adoption.

CHAPTER 8

EXPANSION AND CONTRACTION: POTENCIA ABHORRET VACUUM[1]

The Argument

While the Congress had passed the Bill of Rights and awaited ratification by the several States, the Federalists had begun to construct a new government, and would correct vulnerabilities as they emerged in practice that had eluded construction in theory.

As the Congress debated issues and politics, the Supreme Court began the unenviable task of interpreting the new Constitution, the new amendments, and the new laws.

The highest court of the land slowly began to decide such questions as jurisdiction, separation of powers, the boundaries of the rights of persons, and powers of the states and the federal government. With time, the Supreme Court came to recognize that its opinions reached far beyond the pages of the Supreme Court reporter and judicial chambers to the desks of legislators and arguments of the public. Consequently, justices began to preach from the bench the virtues of republican government, lend support to the efforts of the legislature, and bolster their federalist allies. The approach of this early Supreme Court represents the pinnacle of juridical and jurisprudential thought contemporary to the founding generation.

Though many justices subscribed to natural law principles, others began to decamp to the emerging side of positivism. Such a move marked the commencement of a gradual shift in jurisprudential approaches, with occasional returns to the natural law, that would impact nearly a century-and-a-half of Supreme Court jurisprudence.

***

The truth was, that all men having power ought to be distrusted to a certain degree.[2]

– James Madison (1751-1836)

EARLY SUPREME COURT CASES INTERPRETING THE NEW CONSTITUTION

In the early days of the American Republic, as the branches of the federal government challenged one another, and the governments of the several states pushed back against the federal government, the United States itself faced threats from abroad. Having only just emerged as a nation, the United States confronted potentially existential threats to its founding charter, the Constitution. However, the Supreme Court, through its continued reliance on natural law principles, safeguarded personal liberty against the smothering tide of executive and legislative overreach emanating from both the federal and state governments.

With the Constitution as its astrolabe and natural law as its polestar, the Supreme Court navigated the complex series of issues it confronted as the nascent Congress adjusted the levers and switches of the federal government. At the same time, the Supreme Court took up the role of lantern-keeper and assured that the Constitution, guided by the light of natural liberty, did not find itself dashed upon the rocks of legislative or executive despotism.

While members of Congress debated laws and policies in Federal Hall, the Supreme Court first convened on February 2, 1790 "at the Royal Exchange Building on Broad Street [in Manhattan], a few steps" away.[3] John Jay was confirmed as Chief Justice, and William Cushing, James Wilson, and John Blair as associate justices.[4] Initially, the justices had little to do since budding cases would need time to develop and ripen to the point of reaching the Supreme Court.[5] As a result, the Court heard fewer than a dozen cases during its first several years of operation, and those cases were largely decided on procedural grounds and handled in a few paragraphs. The Constitution limited the Supreme Court's *original jurisdiction* only to cases involving ambassadors (or other public ministers and consuls) and cases in which a state was a party.[6] Accordingly, the Supreme Court, reflecting the Madisonian understanding of the Constitution, could not claim jurisdiction over cases and controversies other than those expressly permitted by Article III. In other words, the Supreme Court enjoyed jurisdiction *only* over those types of cases *explicitly* granted to it by the Constitution.

Thus, those cases which properly reached the Supreme Court during its first few years of its existence were often technical and largely unilluminating for a study of natural law.[7] However, in August 1792, the Court finally heard a case so complex that the opinion it delivered occupied over sixty pages in the Supreme Court Reporter and created the first significant conflict between the Supreme Court and Congress.

Chisholm v. Georgia: Popular Sovereignty, Natural Law, and a Precursor to the Eleventh Amendment

In *Chisholm v. Georgia*, Alexander Chisholm, the executor of the estate of a South Carolina loyalist – a man supportive of Great Britain during the time of the Revolution – brought a claim against the state of Georgia over debts it allegedly owed to the estate for goods supplied by the deceased during the Revolution.[8] The *seriatim* opinion issued by the court – at that time, each Justice issued his individual opinion separately – reads as if it came from a classroom at John Witherspoon's Princeton or, perhaps, a lecture hall at Edinburgh, Aberdeen, or St. Andrews, or even the University of Bologna.

As a procedural matter, the State of Georgia had essentially pretended that the case did not exist. It refused to appear in court. It refused even to acknowledge the existence of the case. Georgia tried to ignore its obligations under the new Constitution by adorning the cloak of sovereign immunity. So, after trying his luck in state and federal courts in Georgia, Chisholm brought his case to the Supreme Court. Though the court eventually found that the State of Georgia could not claim sovereign immunity and continue to refuse to acknowledge the suit, each Justice meandered through an effusive natural law discourse to arrive at his conclusion.

The ubiquitous references to natural law principles in a decision like *Chisholm*, one that pitted concepts of states' rights, state sovereignty, and the relative power of the federal judiciary presents strong evidence that the charter members of the Supreme Court – many of whom had signed the Declaration of Independence, served as delegates to the Constitutional Convention of 1787, and served as delegates to the many state constitutional conventions—relied on Natural Law theories in deciding cases consistent with the Constitution.

For instance, Justice James Iredell, in addressing whether the Supreme Court could exert jurisdiction over a state, engaged in a monologue exploring the rights of Congress. In concert with the wonderfully circular custom of the time, Iredell brought in a bit of tautological syllogistic reasoning[9] before explaining that the only limit upon the authority of Congress was the Constitution.[10]

Justice Iredell acknowledged constitutional supremacy and the inherent, internally-consistent, reasoned approach, that any act contravening such positively delegated authority "would be utterly void, because it would be inconsistent with the Constitution."[11] Such a delimited hierarchical strategy mirrored the earlier approach promulgated by Coke and furthered by Blackstone, that an act of Parliament contravening the laws of nature is, on its face, void. However, where Blackstone venerated the natural law, Justice Iredell appears to honor the Constitution over natural law — a sentiment he would advance five years later in *Calder v. Bull*, which we shall soon see.

Justice Iredell employed a social compact analysis of the issues in *Chisholm* by comparing the relationship between states in a union and individuals within a state. Where individuals joining together to form a state endow, in trust, certain rights and authorities in order for the state to protect freedom and property and to promote the happiness of its individual participants, so, too, did the states, manifested through their acceptance of the Constitution, agree to subjugate certain rights and privileges for the sake of greater harmony.

Ignoring such a pledge by refusing to honor the limits imposed upon it by the Constitution, the State of Georgia tried to exceed its authority. Explaining "[e]very State in the Union, in every instance where its sovereignty has not been delegated to the United States, I consider to be as completely sovereign, as the United States are in respect to the powers surrendered," Justice Iredell invokes the Tenth Amendment to the Constitution in application, though not in name.[12] Since "[t]he United States are sovereign as to all the powers of government actually surrendered [to it by the States]," Iredell continues, "[e]ach State in the Union is sovereign as to all the powers reserved."[13] Despite the clarity of the Tenth Amendment, "[t]he powers not delegated to the United States by the Constitution, nor prohibited by it to the States, are reserved to the States respectively, or to the people,"[14] Justice Iredell appeared compelled to restate and clarify the amendment.[15] He stressed that those powers that were *not* delegated to the federal government by the Constitution therefore remained within the purview of state privilege.[16]

To Justice Wilson, Natural Law theory reigned supreme, and he used it as the basis for his analysis. After opening pleasantries,[17] Justice Wilson turned to foundational natural law reasoning.[18] According to Wilson, the state acquired its importance based on the natural, "native dignity" of those who erected it. "When I speak of a State as an inferior contrivance," Wilson continued, "I mean that it is a contrivance inferior only to that, which is divine: Of all human contrivances, it is certainly most transcendently [sic] excellent."[19] His construction echoed the sentiments of Aquinas who distilled eternal and divine law through man's reason to discover the natural law and create man-made law.

Looking to Locke, "[t]he only reason, I believe, why a free man is bound to human laws, is, that he binds himself," Justice Wilson underscored the importance to early American political and juridical thought of the widely held belief that the consent of the governed remains the *sine qua non*[20] essential to the legitimacy of all government.[21] And the courts existed as an organ of that selfsame government: "Upon the same principles, upon which he becomes bound by the laws, he becomes amenable to the Courts of Justice, which are formed and authorized [sic] by those laws."[22] Reasoning, "[i]f one free man, *an original sovereign*, may do all this; why may not an aggregate of free men, a collection of original sovereigns, do this likewise?" Wilson concludes that "the dignity of each singly is undiminished; the dignity of all jointly must be unimpaired."[23] In other words, a state, an artificial creation coalesced through the collective consent of its constituent voluntary human parts, becomes a pseudo independent entity when, at the direction of its members, it associates with a larger union of similarly-situated collectives.[24] Wilson continued his line of reasoning by explaining that the State of Georgia, though it existed before the establishment of the United States, failed to remain a completely independent sovereign because of its incorporation within the United States.[25] Crucial to Wilson's distinction was that individuals retained their sovereignty as a non-enumerated, non-surrendered right protected by the Ninth Amendment.

Since *Chisholm* involved a claim brought against a state for debts alleged to have occurred before the Revolution, none of the justices needed to indulge in exploratory discourse on political concepts of popular sovereignty. The Supreme Court could have simply stated that a citizen could sue the government of a state since the Constitution did not carve out any special immunities for state governments. Or, the Court could have dismissed the case and provided some stodgy reasoning under the protracted European assumption that "[t]he king can do no wrong; he can break the law; he is below the law, though he is below no man and below no court of law."[26] In the end, the Court opted instead to announce that the States themselves would not exist above the law and therefore would find themselves subject to the jurisdiction of the federal judiciary. Unlike the subjects to the Crown of England,[27] the people of the United States would possess the right to hold accountable their state governments for civil violations and seek damages from them in the federal courts.

Ultimately, the Court held for the plaintiff, reasoning that Article 3, Section 2 of the Constitution abrogated the custom of sovereign immunity enjoyed by states before they became part of the United States; because in effect, they granted federal courts the affirmative power to hear disputes between private citizens and themselves. Georgia would need to make an appearance before the bench or risk a default judgment. Perhaps the justices sensed that the decision, which would allow a citizen of one state to sue the government of another, would create a sense of disquietude in the state legislatures. Perhaps the understanding of the gravity of the decision inspired the grandiose introductions leading into each justice's formal opinion.

The Court effectively announced its intent to interpret the Constitution in favor of the rights of individuals to pursue contract claims against the states over the longstanding principle of sovereign immunity, the accountability of state governments to the people of the United States, and the supreme authority of the federal judiciary over the government of the several states.

The decision in *Chisholm* "provoked immediate outrage."[28] In fact, a day after the Court released the decision, "an amendment was introduced in Congress aimed at overturning it."[29] Eventually, the states ratified the Eleventh Amendment in 1795 to correct what they apparently believed to be a mistake of the Supreme Court.[30] The Eleventh Amendment, though it redefined the nature of claims that citizens could bring against states, did not place such claims completely beyond the reach of the federal judiciary. Georgia had pushed the courts, and the Supreme Court pushed back harder. Congress weighed in with the Eleventh Amendment and regained some ground, but, in the aggregate, the Court concluded the skirmish in a more favorable position than before: It refused to give into the type of popular sentiment that drew support for the Eleventh Amendment and sent a strong message to Congress and the people that the Court would remain an independent, and, if necessary, a counter majoritarian institution. If the Congress or the people disagreed with the manner in which the Court interpreted a statute of constitutional provision, then the Congress would need to change the law or amend the Constitution. If the members of the Supreme Court had not considered that legislators would scrutinize their opinions, they must have certainly realized it after the reaction following *Chisholm*. Perhaps the justices foresaw the consequences of holding a state responsible to standards similar to those of a natural person. Such an understanding could go far to explain why the Court took so much care to document the case so exhaustively and support its arguments over the course of sixty pages.

Penhallow v. Doane's Administrators: Using Reason to Determine Appropriate Jurisdiction

By 1794, the year following the release of its opinion in *Chisholm*, the Court was well aware that it needed to write its opinions for more than just an audience of judges, lawyers, and scholars. Consequently, the Supreme Court took nearly every subsequent opportunity to expound upon and fortify the Constitution. For instance, in the case of *Penhallow v. Doane's Administrators* the Supreme Court explored several topics ranging from the power of Congress and the executive, pre-Revolutionary parliamentary history, to general maritime jurisdiction, though the case related to a rather straightforward jurisdictional question.[31] In particular, *Penhallow* confronted jurisdiction in prize cases[32] and found that the federal courts enjoyed original jurisdiction over prizes rather than the Courts of Appeals in Cases of Capture that had been established by the Confederation Congress in January 1780.[33] Though the questions in *Penhallow* do not initially appear too controversial, since Article III of the Constitution gave federal courts original maritime jurisdiction, the matters at stake related to fundamental questions about the relationship between the states and the new federal government.

At its core, the *Penhallow* case questioned the power of the Continental Congress to overturn a decree from a New Hampshire state court.[34] The dispute that gave rise to the case "originated in 1777 when [a privateering ship], owned by John Penhallow and other New Hampshire merchants, captured the brigantine *Lusana*, belonging to Elisha Doane of Massachusetts, and brought her into Portsmouth harbor as a prize."[35] According to the captain and crew of the privateer, the *Lusana* "was a British vessel in service to the British war effort"[36] and therefore eligible for capture under the practices of wartime maritime tradition.

The facts of the case grow increasingly complex since the *Lusana* had set sail for England from Cape Cod in September 1775, before the outbreak of the Revolution, and her captain and crew had dithered with respect to loyalties throughout her journey and return in attempts to avoid harassment.[37] All of this clouded whether "the *Lusana* and her cargo were British or American-owned and whether she had been carrying supplies intended to aid the enemy."[38] If the courts decided that the *Lusana* was a British-owned ship carrying materiel intended for the enemy, the privateers would get their prize. If the courts decided otherwise, then Doane would get back his ship and cargo, and perhaps some supplemental damages.

The case passed through several levels of the courts of New Hampshire and the courts established by the Continental Congress.[39] On September 17, 1783, the Court of Appeals in Cases of Capture established under the Confederation Congress overturned the most recent decision in the case by the Superior Court of New Hampshire that had favored the privateers and ordered the *Lusana* and her cargo be returned to her original owners.[40]

More shenanigans ensued, and the privateers presented themselves to the New Hampshire legislature as good New Hampshire citizens whose rights were trampled under the boots of the Confederation.[41] The New Hampshire legislature complained to the Confederation Congress which, in turn, brought the issue to a committee,[42] and ultimately, the case ended up before the U.S. Circuit Court of Appeals in New Hampshire. By this time, John Adams,[43] New Hampshire Attorney General John Sullivan,[44] and James Wilson,[45] had all represented one of the parties in the case before some court, and even Thomas Jefferson, sitting as a Virginia delegate, had drafted the committee report for the Confederation Congress on the grievance raised by the New Hampshire legislature.[46]

The issue now before the U.S. Circuit Court of Appeals in New Hampshire in October 1793 related to whether the Court of Appeals in Cases of Capture, the court established under the authority of the Confederation Congress, "had possessed the authority to overturn the decree of the New Hampshire superior court."[47] The Circuit decided that Penhallow now owed Doane damages since Penhallow had earlier refused "to comply with the decision of the Confederation prize court" which had ruled that he was to return the *Lusana* and her cargo to Doane.[48] Justice John Blair, riding the circuit, appointed a commission to determine the amount of damages; the commission eventually arrived at an amount of $38,000 and $154 in costs in October 1794.[49] Penhallow, who had just lost the case, "obtained a writ of error to bring the case before the Supreme Court."[50]

Several procedural issues arose involving sureties (or guarantees for the privateers) which created hurdles to continuing the case, but were eventually addressed by section 22 of the Judiciary Act of 1789, which allowed a judge to sign a writ of error with sureties that covered legal costs but not damages at the higher court.[51] Now, almost 20 years after the events that set the case in motion, the case was finally before the Supreme Court. Ultimately, the Supreme Court concluded "that the Court of Appeals had possessed the jurisdiction to hear and decide the case,"[52] and "had erred in its apportioning of the damages."[53] The Court did not overturn the 1794 decree, but rather adjusted it to reflect its opinion as to the damages.[54] The *seriatim* opinion, including the syllabus, like *Chisholm*, occupies over sixty pages in the Supreme Court Reporter.

After noting the importance of the case[55] and restating the questions presented, Justice Iredell took the time to distinguish republics from monarchies.[56] He appeared compelled to repeat the mantra of equality between citizens of a republic and its grounding within Locke's social compact theory.[57] Such expository discourse hardly seems germane to a case involving jurisdictional questions—as would any that had begun relating to matters authorized and somewhat decided by a prior government. The question remains as to why the Supreme Court so thoroughly and exhaustively explored the issues in the case. Perhaps the length and complexity of the case warranted such discourse. Over nearly twenty years, the case had drawn in some of the most significant figures in the American founding.

Whatever the reason, and unlike the *Chisholm* court, in which Justice Iredell dissented, the *Penhallow* court was unanimous in deciding that the federal courts enjoyed jurisdiction over the case which resolved the crucial question presented.[58] However, it seems likely that the Supreme Court took extra care once again to help enshrine a certain basic natural law principle in the fabric of American common law through its exhaustively thorough opinion; namely, that a court of last resort, even one of limited jurisdiction, can use Reason to assess right and wrong and act accordingly. Ultimately, the Court in *Penhallow* agreed with the holding of the Circuit Court, that Penhallow needed to return the ship and its cargo with damages to Doane's estate, but it disagreed over the apportioning of damages.[59]

Calder v. Bull: A Power Struggle Between the Court and Legislature

A few years later, the Supreme Court confronted a strange case called *Calder v. Bull*, in which a dispute arose between heirs over the disposition of a will. The case called for the Court to test the limits of the natural law concept of fairness in the application of *ex post facto* laws.[60] After a Connecticut Court had a decided the issue, the Connecticut state legislature passed a law changing the formerly expired statute of limitations which had allowed the Calders to file a time-barred claim. The case that reached the Supreme Court arose over this specific action by the state legislature of allowing the reopening of a civil case, and therefore, one of the chief questions presented was whether the Constitution's *ex post facto* clause extended to civil cases in state courts.[61] While the majority of the Court found that the *ex post facto* clause only applied to criminal cases, a few of the justices, as in *Chilsholm* and *Penhallow*, seized the opportunity to write about the nature of republican government, the rights of persons, and the powers granted to government.

With Jefferson in mind, Justice Chase, averred, "[i]t appears to me a self-evident proposition that the several State Legislatures, retain all the powers of legislation, delegated to them by the State Constitutions; which are not EXPRESSLY taken away by the Constitution of the United States."[62] Though by 1798, the Tenth Amendment was nearly seven years old, Justice Samuel Chase of Maryland, a signatory to the Declaration of Independence—which he invoked in his opinion—nonetheless restated the principle of the Tenth Amendment. And where the Tenth Amendment appears, the Ninth accompanies it; or, at least, is a corollary. "All the powers delegated by the people of the United Sates to the Federal Government are defined, and NO CONSTRUCTIVE powers can be exercised by it," wrote Justice Chase, "and all the powers that remain in State Governments are indefinite[.]"[63]

Justice Chase railed against the potential corrupting influence of positive law as the result of "flagrant abuse of legislative power [...] as to authorize manifest injustice by positive law" and concluded that such an act would run contrary to the principles of natural law. "An ACT of the Legislature[,]" wrote Justice Chase, using *act* rather than *law*, "(for I cannot call it a law) contrary to *the great first principles of the social compact*, cannot be considered a rightful exercise of legislative authority."[64] Once again, a state legislature probed the Constitution's defenses seeking weaknesses it could exploit to aggrandize its own power at the expense of personal liberty. Nevertheless, the Supreme Court remained vigilant and repelled the Hamiltonians at the gates.

Though, the Court ultimately found that the Constitution's *ex post facto* provisions applied only to the criminal law, and that the Supreme Court lacked jurisdiction to determine whether a state statute was consistent with a state's constitution, the Supreme Court staked out some guide posts that it would later unearth in a case we shall soon encounter, in which Chief Justice Marshall announced the Supreme Court *did* have the power to invalidate federal laws that ran contrary to the Constitution. Though the Supreme Court had introduced the notion of judicial review in *Calder v. Bull*, a significant victory it would realize in *Marbury v. Madison* in 1803, it began to show some vulnerability to the corrupting force of positive law. And Justice James Iredell, the lone dissenter in *Chisholm*, would give the legislature a roadmap to expanding its powers.

Justice Iredell, though he concurred with the outcome in *Calder*, did so for different reasons.[65] Whereas Justice Chase believed the Supreme Court did not have the power to rule on the constitutionality of acts of the state legislature, he remained ambivalent as to whether the Supreme Court enjoyed that power over Congress. Justice Iredell, however, believed the Court incapable of such declarations. "It is true, that some speculative jurists have held, that a legislative act *against natural justice* must, in itself, be void[,]" noted Justice Iredell. Noting, however, "I cannot think that, under such a government, any Court of Justice would possess a power to declare it so," Justice Iredell expressed a view that more than a violation of natural law would be necessary for a court of limited jurisdiction to declare a law void.[66]

However, Justice Iredell, betrayed some troubling emergent positivist tendencies. He interpreted the constitutions of the states and the federal government as having "define[d] with precision the objects of the legislative power, and restrain its exercise within marked and settled boundaries" not as a framework designed to foster development of natural law , but rather as a positive expression delineating and delegating powers of the legislatures.[67] Though he clearly believed that the natural law alone was insufficient to permit a federal court to declare void a positive law passed by a state legislature, Justice Iredell believed in the supremacy of the Constitution over any act of any legislative body. "If any act of Congress, or of the Legislature of a state, violates those constitutional provisions, it is unquestionably void."[68] However, Justice Iredell admits that such "authority to declare [a law] void is of a delicate and awful nature," so that "the Court will never resort to that authority but in a clear and urgent case."[69]

Therefore, to Justice Iredell, a court may declare void only those laws that directly contravene the express powers articulated in the Constitution. To include within the reasons to void a law the principles of natural law, to the mind of Justice Iredell, could result in chaos. "The Court cannot pronounce [a law] to be void, merely because it is, in [its] judgment, contrary to the *principles of natural justice*."[70]

The problem that Justice Iredell believed inherent to the natural law was that "[t]he ideas of natural justice are regulated by no fixed standard."[71] Accordingly, the ablest and the purest men have differed upon the subject; and all that the Court could properly say, in such an event, would be that the Legislature (possessed of an equal right of opinion) had passed an act which, in the opinion of the judges, was inconsistent with the abstract principles of natural justice.[72]

Justice Iredell gave voice to what would become a common critique of Natural Law theory based on a fundamental misunderstanding of the tenets of natural law. This critical view finds purchase in the belief that natural law emerges not from the purity of reason, but rather from the subjective opinion of the adjudicator.[73] Early legal positivists, like Jeremy Bentham, would seize upon such lines of argument in their rebukes of natural law and its uses. However, to Justice Iredell, and those who shared in his positivist leanings, only the Constitution could serve as grounds to invalidate a law that contravened it principles, even though the Constitution itself – expressly via the Ninth and Tenth Amendments, and implicitly in numerous clauses – unambiguously embraces the natural law.

As we can see, the story of the early American Republic shows the counter-play between the three branches of government, the states, and the people as each body and group flexed its muscles and tested the strength of the boundaries erected by the Constitution. The Supreme Court proved able and capable of reigning in the federal executive and legislative branches, as well as the legislatures of the several states. When the Supreme Court perhaps exceeded its authority, Congress and the states tamped down the Court with the Eleventh Amendment.

Meanwhile, though Madison, the Congress, and the states had erected tremendous natural law fortifications within the armor of the Constitution, and several justices of the Supreme Court attempted to buttress those protections, others began to lose faith in the persuasive power of the core principles of the natural law, turning instead to what they wrongly perceived as the straightforward and more consistent approach offered by positivism. To Justice Iredell, the natural law was not invalid, but rather an artifact much less applicable to his modern times.

Such a diminution of the natural law would help create a void to be filled with the strict Positivism of England's Jeremy Bentham as will be seen in Chapter 11. But first let us examine how unexpected forces – foreign and domestic – would assault the natural law in the American Republic's infancy.

CHAPTER 9

THREATS FOREIGN AND DOMESTIC, AND THE EMERGENCE OF THE DEMOCRATICREPUBLICANS

The Argument

The embroiled federal government of the 1790s struggled to manage international relations while disagreements over the separation of powers split the ruling Federalists into two factions.

Helmed by Thomas Jefferson and James Madison, the Democratic-Republicans pushed back against Alexander Hamilton and the administration of John Adams. They feared the Federalists had begun to adopt monarchical tendencies at the cost of the republican ideals and natural law principles, ubiquitous in the Founding Era and baked into the Constitution.

The Federalists in government took actions that angered many people who, and states which, in turn, engaged in behavior aimed to oppose, embarrass, and disrupt. People rebelled, and states adopted resolutions condemning actions by the Federalists who seemed to abandon protection of natural rights in favor of expanding federal power.

The Democratic-Republicans – basically, the Anti-Federalists plus their newest convert and member, James Madison – embraced the natural law principles of the American founding and presented a powerful alternative to the corrupted Federalists who sought to aggrandize federal power at the expense of the powers of the states and the liberties of the people. They responded to the concerns of the people and states and ousted the Federalists in the election of 1800.

***

Emergency does not create power. Emergency does not increase granted power or remove or diminish the restrictions imposed upon power granted or reserved. The Constitution was adopted in a period of grave emergency. Its grants of power to the federal government and its limitations of the power of the States were determined in the light of emergency, and they are not altered by emergency. What power was thus granted and what limitations were thus imposed are questions which have always been, and always will be, the subject of close examination under our constitutional system.[1]

– **Charles Evans Hughes (1862-1948)**

APPEALS TO THE LAYPERSON: AN EXAMINATION OF EARLY AMERICAN LEGAL ARGUMENTS IN HISTORICAL CONTEXT OF GROWING DISCONTENT WITH THE FEDERALISTS

An examination of the decisions of the early Supreme Court can provide insight into the thought processes and beliefs of the nation's educated elite but does not necessarily reveal the thoughts and opinions of the governed. The Supreme Court wrote largely for an audience of lawyers, judges, and legislators, but it virtually never dealt with juries.[2] Juries, in many ways the standins for the people in the judicial system, remained largely the purview of the lower courts. As a result, the types of arguments offered by lawyers in jury trials can provide insight into the mind of the public in the early American Republic. Stated differently, attorneys then, like today, presented arguments to lay jurors they thought would resonate. The arguments made by trial lawyers to juries stand as some of the most compelling records of the sorts of reasoning persuasive to the minds of the public at large. That would be the same public that participated in ratification debates and votes.

Washington's Neutrality Proclamation, the Citizen Genêt Affair and Henfield's Case

For instance, the line of reasoning presented in *Henfield's Case* (1793), a case that questioned what role the fledgling nation should have in the conflict in Europe between Great Britain and Revolutionary France, is rife with natural law references.[3] Before we turn to the arguments put forth, it is imperative that we discuss the historical context in which the case arose. The French Revolution began the same year that Washington assumed office as President, and lasted until around 1799, the year of Washington's death. The French revolutionaries, under the battle cry of *liberté, égalité, fraternité* (liberty, equality, fraternity), coined by French politician, lawyer, and vanguard of the Revolution, Maximilien Robespierre,[4] sought to overthrow the centuries-old feudal monarchical model— known as the Ancien Régime— characterized by hereditary title, and a ruling class disposed to preserving the old power structure. In the spring of 1792, the French had declared war on Prussia and Austria and would go on to skirmish with most of the remaining European powers like Great Britain, Russia, Spain, and Portugal.

Washington sought to avoid diplomatic entanglements resulting from the pugilistic attitude of revolutionary France. After France declared war on Great Britain, George Washington, sounding like his Secretary of State, Thomas Jefferson, issued a proclamation of Neutrality in April 1793. "Whereas it appears that a state of war exists between Austria, Prussia, Sardinia, Great Britain, and the United Netherlands of the one part[,]" it began, "and France on the other, and the duty and interest of the United States require that they[5] should with sincerity and good faith adopt and pursue a conduct friendly and impartial toward the belligerent powers[.]"[6] The proclamation explained that those who violated this dictat would be subject to trial and sanction by the government of the United States.[7]

The Federalist Party, perhaps caught in the gravity of George Washington's corpulent Vice-President, John Adams, who maintained grandiose and expansive views of executive power, had engaged in more unilateral executive actions, like the Neutrality Proclamation, which many understood as a move closer toward what the Anti-Federalists had feared during the Constitutional Convention of 1787. Hamilton remained a devout Federalist, while Madison had decamped from the Federalists sometime around 1792[8] and formed the Democratic-Republican Party with Thomas Jefferson to combat the trend of accumulation and centralization of power happening under the Washington administration.[9]

The rift between the Anti-Federalists and the Washington/Adams/Hamilton Federalists had festered since Washington had declared neutrality with regard to France.[10] Until the Neutrality Proclamation, "the divisions between Madison and Jefferson's Republicans and Hamilton's Federalists had centered on more domestic issues: the system of finance and the Constitution."[11] However, now the divisions "were transposed into the realm of foreign affairs. Hamilton and the Federalists were on the side of Britain [... and] Madison, Jefferson and the [Democratic-Republicans] were on the side of France."[12]

The executive creation of a criminal statute in Washington's Neutrality Proclamation seemed to confirm the fears of the Democratic-Republicans, fears that the Federalist factions in government aimed to centralize power in the federal government and federal power in the presidency. Hamilton, aware of the criticism of his policies, and the fervor surrounding Washington's unilateral executive proclamation, invited Madison to engage in a public discussion that became known as the *Pacificus Helvidius* Debates.

Using the name *Pacificus*, Hamilton, represented the Federalist position, and argued the executive had the authority to declare neutrality.[13] Hamilton, over his series of seven letters, outlined effusive arguments for broad presidential powers at the expense of the ability of Congress to intervene. He "began with the position that foreign policy was executive by its very nature. Congress was not the 'organ of intercourse' with foreign nations, while the judiciary could only 'decide litigations in particular cases.' Declaring neutrality, therefore, must 'of necessity belong to the Executive.'"[14]

Madison, reluctantly at first, engaged in the debate and chose the pseudonym *Helvidius*. Even Thomas Jefferson begged Madison to pick up his quill. Despairing, "[n]obody answers [Hamilton] & his doctrine will therefore be taken confessed," Jefferson feared Hamilton's view would gain purchase.[15] "For god's sake, my dear Sir," Jefferson continued in a letter to James Madison, "take up your pen, select the most striking heresies, and cut [Hamilton] to pieces for the sake of the public. There is nobody else who can & will enter the lists with him."[16] Perhaps, at his friend's urging, Madison decided to respond to Hamilton. Whatever the reason for Madison's initial delay[17] – Hamilton published all his *Pacificus* essays before Madison published his first – the Father of the Constitution needed only five essays to counter Hamilton's seven and "cut him to pieces" as Jefferson had wished. Unsurprisingly, Madison stuck firmly to his view that the only powers possessed by the three branches of the federal government were those granted to them by the Constitution, and the sacred separation of powers was not to be trifled with. In his first *Helvidius* letter, Madison quoted extensively from Article II of the Constitution, and addressed his immediate concern that the proclamation intruded on Congress's power to declare war.[18] He characterized the Hamiltonian-Federalist positions on executive war-making and executive treaty-making as monarchical in their scope and execution: "The power of making treaties and the power of declaring war, are *royal prerogatives* in the *British government*, and are accordingly treated as Executive prerogatives by *British commentators*."[19] Such a rhetorical approach brilliantly captured the tenor of the disagreement between the Federalists and the Democratic-Republicans who believed that the Federalist policies, particularly those of Alexander Hamilton's Treasury Department, more closely resembled the types of actions undertaken by monarchies and therefore did not conform to the high standards of activities to be undertaken by a republic.

On a deeper level, Madison feared "placing the power to start and wage war in the same hands risked tyranny. 'Those who are to conduct a war cannot in the nature of things be proper or safe judges whether a war ought to be commenced, continued, or concluded.' Since, 'war is in fact the true nurse of executive aggrandizement.'"[20]

Despite the debates between Hamilton's *Pacificus* and Madison's *Helvidius*, Washington's Neutrality Proclamation remained in effect, and, in many ways, exacerbated American relations with Great Britain which, despite the conclusion of the Revolutionary War more than ten years earlier, remained strained. President Washington had dispatched Chief Justice John Jay to negotiate a treaty with Great Britain to address outstanding matters and avoid another war. At this point in time, the United States occupied a somewhat precarious and insecure role on the international stage. It could not survive another armed conflict with Great Britain.

Now, returning to *Henfield's Case*, it was among this backdrop of the Neutrality Proclamation that Gideon Henfield, an American mercenary soldier/ sailor serving aboard the French privateer, *Citizen Genêt*, obtained a letter of marque and reprisal from France and began privateering English ships in American waters, despite Washington's proclamation prohibiting sailors from doing so.[21] In May 1793, Henfield, was arrested after he piloted a captured British vessel, the *William*, into the port of Philadelphia.[22] Shortly thereafter, Henfield was indicted for violating President Washington's Neutrality Proclamation. At the trial, Henfield did not dispute the fact that he had signed on as a crew member on the French privateer *Citizen Genêt*, but instead argued that he had "exercised his 'natural right of expatriation,' one of the inalienable and universal rights of mankind."[23]

The case went before Justice James Wilson who also sat as a judge in the federal circuit court (then a trial court) in Pennsylvania.[24] Wilson instructed the jury that while "much had been said on this occasion, by the defendant's counsel, in support of the natural right of emigration . . . little of it is truly applicable to the present question."[25] Despite this, the jury found Henfield not guilty; newspapers like the *National Gazette* hailed the verdict as a "startling affirmation of 'the rights of man,'" and Democratic-Republican societies offered toasts to Henfield (an important social gesture at the time) which indicated widespread public support of a jury verdict – contrary to the court's instructions – based upon natural law principles.[26]

The United States continued to confront domestic unrest and international conflicts that threatened the stability of the new nation during critical stages of early development when the three branches of the new federal government still needed to test the limits of their authority within the system of checks and balances sculpted by the Constitution. France, which, under Louis XVI, had supported the colonial rebels in America, had been dealing with a rebel problem of its own since the late 1780s. The conclusion of *Henfield's case* and the *Citizen Genêt* Affair did not end the troubles between the United States and France.

The Jay Treaty and the X, Y, Z Affair

Negotiated and signed in 1794, ratified by the U.S. Senate and British government in 1795, and coming into effect on February 29, 1796, the Treaty of Amity, Commerce, and Navigation, Between His Britannnic Majesty – King George III – and the United States of America, commonly known as the "Jay Treaty," resolved several lingering issues unaddressed by the Treaty of Paris in

1783. However, the Jay Treaty, which created a special relationship between Britain and the United States with respect to maritime channels of commerce and rules of trade, drew ire from the French who perceived the treaty as an American betrayal.[27]

Since Washington had declared American neutrality in the conflicts between France and the rest of Europe, revolutionary France felt justified in its anger. The French ignored the fact that the United States, still a young nation and still struggling to manage debts accrued during the American Revolution, possessed neither an imposing army nor formidable navy and could not afford a war with Great Britain. Eventually, however, discord between the United States and France approached a flashpoint, so President John Adams dispatched John Marshall, the man whom Adams would later appoint as Chief Justice, along with Charles Cotesworth Pinckney, and Elbridge Gerry to France to help sort out the issue.

The diplomatic mission, however, ended in disaster when the American delegation took offense to demands from their French counterparts, identified with the pseudonyms X, Y, and Z, who solicited bribes and large loans for France. Disgusted, the American delegation departed without meeting with France's foreign minister. News of the XYZ affair erupted in the United States creating uproar and calls for war, ultimately leading to the passage of the Alien and Sedition Acts under a Federalist Congress and signed by President John Adams.

The Alien and Sedition Acts

Passed in 1798, the Alien and Sedition Acts granted sweeping powers to the federal government[28] including, most contrary to the Constitution's natural law principles, as well as the plain language of the First Amendment, the criminalization of making false statements that criticized the federal government. James Madison, the Father of the Constitution, "condemned the Alien Act as unconstitutional."[29] The Alien Act authorized the president to restrain or deport any alien that he judged "dangerous to the peace and safety of the United States."[30] The Sedition Act, on the other hand, was designed to guard against the subversive efforts of citizens. The first section made it a crime to enter into a conspiracy to "oppose any measure" of the United States government, while the remainder of the act prohibited the "writing, printing, uttering or publishing of any false, scandalous, and malicious writing" tending to bring the government, Congress, or the president into "contempt or disrepute."[31] Many Democratic-Republicans and even some Federalists perceived this program as a conscious assault on organized political opposition.[32] Federalist justifications of the Sedition Act rested on the argument that reputation was an essential privilege owed protection by the Constitution and the rule of law. They warned of an "army of spies and incendiaries scattered through the continent," working in league with France; in essence, the acts were necessary to protect true Americans from foreign undermining.[33]

Democratic-Republicans, on the other hand, perceived the Sedition Act as an attempt to shield the government from all criticism and to drive a wedge between Democratic-Republican legislators and their constituents.[34] They argued that the freedom of speech and the liberty of the press were natural rights that had received explicit constitutional protection under the First Amendment. However, many felt the laws were highly xenophobic and oppressive of the freedom of speech, a natural right; even worse, the laws represented the epitome of oppression perfected by George III. How could the same generation, in some cases the same human beings, that wrote "Congress shall make no law...abridging the freedom of speech..." enact a law that did just that? Only by rejecting the natural law could the Federalists have justified this. And Madison bristled at this rejection of natural law principles. In fact, "[t]he Sedition Act roused Madison to an impressive and even magisterial attack."[35]

Madison denounced the power to punish seditious libel despite what the Act's supporters may have said about the common law powers of the legislature.[36] He invoked the freedom of speech and the press and pointed to the Bill of Rights, which he had, himself, initially found unnecessary, to underscore the importance of free speech to a modern and enlightened society.[37] The First Amendment, Madison argued, placed regulation of speech outside the purview of Congress— otherwise what was the purpose of the First Amendment that had been adopted fewer than ten years earlier.[38] Noah Feldman, the Felix Frankfurter Professor of Law at Harvard Law School, whose biography of Madison offers much insight, explained that Madison's point was powerful. The Federalists claimed that the First Amendment prohibited only prior censorship, not punishment of words already spoken or published. "It would seem a mockery," Madison wrote, "that no law should be passed, preventing publications from being made, but that laws might be passed punishing them in case they should be made."[39]

As they had during the Revolution, people formed and printed newspapers and pamphlets decrying the Alien and Sedition Acts and asserting that "the right of states and individuals to disobey unconstitutional laws"[40] was a natural right. Their writings demonstrate the anger and fury prompted by any government encroachments upon their inalienable rights such as freedom of speech and assembly. They exercised their speech through fiery pamphlets, letters, and circulars. As the people grew angrier, they gathered in larger numbers. In Lexington, Massachusetts, around four thousand persons attended a public gathering and voted to pass a resolution against the Alien and Sedition Acts.[41] At a mass meeting in Fayette County, Kentucky, Colonel George Nicholas was "carried away in triumph" after giving a speech extolling "the preservation of the rights of man."[42]

The Kentucky and Virginia Resolutions

Legislators rallied in Virginia and Kentucky and passed and issued a series of statements—they were not really laws or regulations—that became known as the Virginia and Kentucky Resolutions in a blatant act of defiance of the federal government. Although written anonymously, it is now widely understood that the Kentucky Resolution was authored by Jefferson and the Virginia Resolution was authored by Madison.[43] The Kentucky Resolution provided a clear argument in favor of a natural law interpretation and states' rights view of the Constitution, which it referred to as a compact.[44] Indeed, the Kentucky legislature even expressly invokes the Tenth Amendment to show that the federal government lacks the ability to encroach upon non-delegated powers which shall remain with the states, or the people. They believed that the values expressed in the Ninth and Tenth Amendments "[were] true as a general principle [...] and that no power over the freedom of religion, freedom of speech, or freedom of the press being delegated to the United States by the Constitution, nor prohibited by it to the States"[45] was available to the federal government.

The Virginia House of Delegates put forward and adopted the Virginia Resolution, in which the Virginians gave voice to similar concerns as their Kentucky brethren regarding the powers allowed to the federal government as understood through an analysis of what the people and the states permitted through the Constitution.[46] In no uncertain terms, the Virginia House of Delegates condemned the actions of the federal government in passing the Alien and Sedition Acts as outside the scope of the authorities granted to it by the Constitution.

Virginia, in agreeing to join the United States, did not consent to such a grant of authority as asserted by the Adams administration and the Federalist Congress and therefore felt "duty bound[,]" through its assent and adherence to the Constitution and its principles, to reject and combat such excesses and rein in the federal government. Virginia believed itself obliged to protect its powers as a state, since the Tenth Amendment protected them, and the natural rights of its people against this federal encroachment since the Ninth Amendment protected the natural, pre-political rights not enumerated elsewhere in the Constitution.[47]

THE DOWNFALL OF THE FEDERALISTS: DISCONTENT AND UPRISING IN THE RURAL COUNTRY

As disgruntled legislatures embarrassed the Adams administration and Congress, angry citizens began to rise up in response to the increase in taxes designed to address the debt created by the quasi-war with France.[48] Federalist tax policies created deep discontent in rural areas, such as Western and Central Pennsylvania, sparking conflicts like the Fries Rebellion in 1799.[49] Several enraged regions also began to erect liberty poles, as Americans had done before the Revolution against the British, which "soon spread throughout the Mid-

Atlantic and even into Federalist New England."[50] As Bradburn notes, "[t]he poles were so thick in eastern Pennsylvania by early 1799 that, months before the open conflicts that became known as the Fries Rebellion, the Federalists began organizing associations to 'destroy the sedition poles.'"[51]

Songs, such as "[o]ne untitled song by 'A DEMOCRAT,' published in the (now extremely rare) Nashville Paper *The Rights of Man*," contained lyrics calling for the "bless[ings][of] the *Rights of Man!*"[52] Tens of thousands of signatures were collected on petitions for repeal of the acts—a serious accomplishment when the total population of the country was between 3.7 million and 5 million (including women, minors, other persons except Indians not taxed, and non-free persons).[53] The clear divisions on matters of domestic and foreign policy between the Democratic-Republicans and Federalists approached a breaking point.

The Democratic-Republicans believed something drastic needed to be done. "By 1800," Professor Feldman explained, "Jefferson and Madison had decided that the only solution was to defeat the Federalists in a national election."[54] Their partnership grew stronger since by the late 1790s, they "were now functioning as a political team, poised to lead a serious attempt to gain power for the [Democratic-Republican] Party. Their alliance had never been closer. And the stakes of their joint efforts had never been higher."[55] They seized upon the public outrage over the actions of the Adams administration and the Federalist Congress that had alienated many people in the country and mounted a challenge to Adams in what became one of the most politically vicious campaign seasons in history.

Supporters of Jefferson and his running mate, Aaron Burr—who later gained much notoriety for killing Alexander Hamilton in a pistol duel in Weehawkeh, new Jersey—positioned Adams as a dogmatic Anglophilic monarchist bent on waging war against France,[56] while Federalists derided Jefferson as promoting policies that would undermine the moral values of America resulting in anarchy.[57] A Federalist Connecticut newspaper proclaimed that "[m]urder, robbery, rape, adultery, and incest will all be openly taught and practiced. [...] The air will be rent with the cries of distress, the soil will be soaked with blood, and the nation black with crimes[,]"[58] if the Democratic-Republicans won the election. Confronted with a choice between a second Adams term rife with diplomatic uncertainty and domestic unrest and an emerging party extolling the virtues of the Constitution and a restricted reading of the powers of the federal government, Americans turned out to the polls in huge numbers. Voter participation reached nearly 70% of the eligible voting population in some states in the election of 1800, and the Federalist disparagement of the natural rights, along with its legislative supremacy, was soundly rejected.[59]

In the popular uprising, called the Revolution of 1800, "a watershed transformation [occurred] in participatory democracy in the United States[,]"[60] and widespread opposition to the Federalist rejection of natural and state rights was expressed in various ways. With their fierce opposition to the Alien and

Sedition Acts, the people rose up to protect the Republic rather than relying on the Supreme Court to resolve the matter. The Madisonian view, that the Ninth Amendment protected the non enumerated rights of the people and the Tenth, the nondelegated powers of the States, was embraced in the public consciousness as expressed through their legislative resolutions and their votes for president.

The generation following the one that supported the First Congress and its radical Declaration of Independence, ousted the Federalists in 1800, after the Federalists applied a novel, expansive constitutional philosophy that was profoundly counter to revolutionary principles, and thus counter to the Natural Law Tradition.[61] While the judiciary preserved the separation of powers and protected the natural rights of the people,[62] the people themselves had taken action against government that had used the power of the federal government to disparage their natural rights as the people understood them; all in contravention of the Ninth Amendment.

Legislatures passed resolutions, people rebelled, and eventually ousted a corrupted party that had given them the Constitution and replaced them with a party that embraced the original founding principles. John Adams, however, in the dwindling days of his administration, sought to install as many Federalists as possible into positions of government to combat the rising tide of the Democratic Republicans. Among the many Federalists he appointed to positions of power was John Marshall, an emissary in the XYZ affair, who, a product of a Scottish Enlightenment education, would become perhaps the most important Chief Justice of the Supreme Court, who shaped it into the powerful institution it is today, capable of invalidating congressional and state statutes and defying presidents. Did Marshall & Co. defend the natural law, or did they succumb to the rising tide of Positivism? We turn to addressing that question next.

CHAPTER 10

THE EARLY SUPREME COURT AND THE NATURAL LAW TRADITION

The Argument

The early Supreme Court struggled to maintain its independence and legitimacy until the appointment of Chief Justice John Marshall. Influenced by Scottish Enlightenment ideals, Marshall took the founding Supreme Court and set it on the path to becoming the rarified institution as we know it today.

Under his stewardship for over three decades (from 1801 until 1835) – the longest tenure of any Chief Justice to this day – Supreme Court justices took tremendous strides to solidify the Natural Law Tradition into their decisions. In a series of opinions, Marshall and his brethren considered a range of issues through a natural law lens as if to send a message to future generations of judges and lawyers about the importance of the natural law. In particular, the jurisprudence of the Marshall Court enshrined the then scarcely debated Contracts Clause, into a powerful bastion of property rights.

Moreover, in perhaps his most significant ruling, Marbury v. Madison, Chief Justice Marshall himself left the judiciary a powerful tool, and the natural law, a powerful protection.

***

If, on tracing the right to contract, and the obligations created by contract, to their source, we find them to exist anterior to, and independent of society, we may reasonably conclude that those original and pre-existing principles are, like many other natural rights, brought with man into society; and, although they may be controlled, are not given by human legislation.[1]

– Chief Justice John Marshall (1755 -1835)

NATURAL LAW EMERGES AS A CORNERSTONE OF CHIEF JUSTICE MARSHALL'S JURISPRUDENCE

In part, this work aims to explain the development of Natural Law Tradition as a jurisprudential discipline, the central role it played in the American Revolution and founding, its institutionalization into positive law in the Ninth and Tenth amendments to the Constitution, and its continued – albeit often unstated and unrecognized – role in contemporary jurisprudence and at the heart of our nation's founding documents. A fuller understanding and appreciation of the critical role that the natural law plays and should play in contemporary discussions of the Constitution and Bill of Rights requires a familiarity with the legal doctrines and philosophical approaches that had begun to take its place. By examining the decisions of the Supreme Court in the early nineteenth century, beginning with the appointment of John Marshall as Chief Justice in 1801 until his death in 1835, we can see not only the Court's employment of Natural Law theory, but also the influence of new modes of thought that sought to overcome the Natural Law theory in favor of dogmatic reliance on statutory law.

Appointed by President John Adams in a set of circumstances more providential than planned,[2] John Marshall, a Federalist from Virginia, became the fourth, and, arguably, most significant Chief Justice of the Supreme Court. Though he and Thomas Jefferson were second cousins,[3] Marshall had never really gotten along with the Madisonian and Jeffersonian Virginians.[4] Their animus toward Marshall continued even as Marshall's Chief Justiceship continued through both terms of both of their presidencies. As a Federalist Chief Justice presiding over a largely Federalist Supreme Court, Marshall needed to tread carefully under the administration of a Democratic Republican or Anti-Federalist president like Thomas Jefferson.[5]

Under Marshall, the Court appeared to rely more heavily on precedent and took a more fastidious approach to the inclusion of direct citations. As the available corpus of law from Congress grew as well as the available volumes of case reporters from Cranch and Dallas alike, the Supreme Court had little choice but to utilize these tools available to it. And Marshall sought to find ways to bolster the Court's legitimacy in the eyes of the people.

The Supreme Court had a public perception problem in its early years.[6] It had a hard time holding onto justices. "Of the six original appointees to the Court in 1789, only William Cushing remained on the bench" at the time of Marshall's appointment twelve years later.[7] It also had not issued many opinions. "For the first year and a half of its existence, the Supreme Court did not decide a single case."[8] As noted, it took Congress time to set up the several courts of varying jurisdictions in the United States, and it would take time for the cases and controversies to bubble up through the newly-minted judicial infrastructure. In fact, the Supreme Court only decided sixty-three cases between 1790 and 1800, and "[fewer] than a dozen [of those] were significant."[9]

However, "[d]uring Marshall's tenure from 1801 to 1835, the Court issued more than one thousand decisions— nearly all unanimous—and about half that number were written by Marshall."[10] As evidenced by the cases discussed in Chapter 8, questions remained as to the power of the Court when pitted against the legislative or executive branches. "Washington had placed a distinctive stamp on the office and with his neutrality proclamation had already established the president's authority to interpret the Constitution."[11] And Congress, too, in the popular view, commanded some of the same reverence that the English legal system felt toward Parliament.[12] Under Marshall, the Supreme Court reined in the federal government and disabused the American people of the notion that Congress reigned supreme.

Early Influences on Chief Justice Marshall

Marshall grew up in a relatively remote area in Virginia where his parents took up the task of educating their many children.[13] Marshall's father boasted an exceptional library including "works by Livy, Horace, Pope, Dryden, Milton, and Shakespeare."[14] Marshall later recalled to Justice Joseph Story "how, at the age of twelve, he had [copied] the works of Alexander Pope."[15] His father, Thomas Marshall, "was listed among the charter subscribers" to the first American edition of *Blackstone's Commentaries*.[16] Later, Marshall became "one of eightyodd students who enrolled at William and Mary when the term commenced on May 1, 1780, and one of the forty or so who chose to attend the [law] lectures of Chancellor [George] Wythe."[17]

As a student of Wythe, whose pioneering lectures in law brought significant changes in the way people became lawyers in America, Marshall numbered among the disciples of Scottish Enlightenment like his classmates, many of whom would comprise the judicial elite in the new Republic.[18] Wythe, whose chair was "the first of its kind in America" shaped his curriculum around Blackstone.[19] "Wythe was wedded to Blackstone in his teaching, and his inaugural lecture was cast in Blackstonian terms, stressing the fundamental principles of the law."[20] His students started their mornings with Blackstone before moving onto other treatises and traditional legal texts.[21] The curriculum also included philosophy and featured the writings of Montesquieu and Hume.[22] Marshall did not learn the law merely by apprenticing with established attorneys, which was the traditional method, but rather through the new method of carefully guided study and deliberate examination of the texts. His legal training no doubt prepared Marshall to become the intellect who most shaped the Supreme Court.

Understanding Marshall's background and legal training provides insight into the approach Marshall took in issuing opinions. Appointed by the Federalists serving under the Democratic-Republican, Anti-Federalist Jefferson whom

Marshall distrusted, inheriting a Supreme Court precariously squeezed between a powerful executive and a legislature possessed of a historic reverence endowed by English tradition, Marshall managed to reshape the practice of the Court, reclaim the Court's constitutional birthright, and position it as the first branch among equals *vis-à-vis* the meaning of the law. Perhaps concerned about the future role of the Court, Marshall, in 1803, installed within judicial precedent a sort of judicial reset switch in his opinion in *Marbury v. Madison*, one of the most significant decisions in American history, and one brimming with Natural Law theory.[23]

Marbury v. Madison: Establishing Judicial Review as a Check on Legislative Supremacy

William Marbury, who had been appointed a justice of the peace by John Adams in the waning days of his administration, sought an order from the Supreme Court forcing the new Jefferson administration to deliver him his commission. In the election of 1800, Adams narrowly lost his bid for a second term.[24] Breaking with tradition, Jefferson had run on a joint-ticket with Aaron Burr, so the electoral ballots cast for team Jefferson/Burr did not actually signal which of the two Democratic-Republican candidates should serve as President and which should serve as Vice-President.[25] Accordingly, the votes for President and Vice-President would go to the House.[26] Adams knew he would not maintain office for a second term. Since the President was not inaugurated until March, Adams had a lame duck session that lasted for several months.

The people had spoken through their representatives in the House of Representatives and favored the Democratic-Republicans over the Federalists, so Adams, fearing a takeover by the opposition party, scrambled to position the Federalists to maintain a stronghold in the federal government. In addition to appointing Marshall as Chief Justice of the Supreme Court, Adams sought to appoint dozens of Federalists to various judgeships.

One of these fellows – whose name lives in jurisprudential greatness – was William Marbury. His nomination was confirmed by the Senate while it was still under Federalist control, yet he never received the physical commission granting him the position of justice of the peace before Jefferson assumed office. When Marbury sought the physical piece of paper granting him his position, Jefferson's Secretary of State, James Madison, refused. As a result, Marbury sued Madison, the veritable father of the U.S. Constitution alleging that Madison was acting unconstitutionally. Marbury sought a writ of mandamus from the Supreme Court to compel Madison to deliver him his Commission. Such a writ, if issued, would judicially require the Jefferson administration, acting through Madison, to deliver to the Federalist Marbury his commission.

In reality, although the suit bears Madison's name as the defendant, Marbury's actual claim was against Thomas Jefferson. In many ways, the case served as a stunt by the ousted Federalists to embarrass the newly minted Jeffersonians in the government by accusing them of violating the Constitution. To add to the controversy, John Marshall had been serving as Secretary of State under Adams, and *it was Marshall's office that had been responsible for the failed delivery of Marbury's commission in the first place.*

To send a message to the Supreme Court, Jefferson and the Democratic-Republican Congress refused to budget a term of the Supreme Court in an unambiguous threat to the Court. The Jeffersonians had also begun impeachment proceedings against John Pickering, a Federalist federal judge in New Hampshire, in another signal to the Supreme Court.[27]

Marbury v. Madison features several peculiar issues about jurisdiction and separation of powers since Marbury took his case directly to the Supreme Court. Could the Court could compel the executive branch through a writ of mandamus to act against its will? Marbury claimed the Supreme Court had original jurisdiction over the case not under Article III of the Constitution, but rather under the Judiciary Act of 1789 which asserts, in Section 13, that the Supreme Court has original jurisdiction over cases involving writs of mandamus.[28]

Marshall could have accepted the argument, decided the case upon the merits and held that the law entitled Marbury to his commission and issued a writ of mandamus. Alternatively, Marshall could have decided that the law did *not* entitle Marbury to his commission and decline to issue the writ. Marshall, however, took a third path and found that the Constitution, which severely limited the Court's original jurisdiction,[29] also explained the Court's appellate jurisdiction, and perhaps most importantly, gave Congress the authority to change it.[30] He reflected further, using Madisonian reasoning, that the legislature only possessed the power to alter the Court's *appellate* jurisdiction because such authority was expressly granted to Congress by the Constitution. Accordingly, nowhere in the Constitution was Congress expressly or even impliedly granted the power to expand the Court's *original* jurisdiction.[31] Absent such an explicit provision, Congress could not claim such a power. Therefore, Marshall found that the provision of the Judiciary Act of 1789 that granted the Supreme Court original jurisdiction over writs of mandamus, an act drafted, adopted, and passed by a Federalist legislature and signed by a Federalist president, was unconstitutional. In effect, Marshall slyly gave Jefferson a victory in battle, and the Court a victory in war as it now had the power to invalidate federal statutes.

This move by Marshall, consistent with the Natural Law Tradition, announced strong limitations on the power of Congress, preventing it from exceeding the authority granted to it by the Constitution. The Constitution, the supreme law of the land, conferred upon Congress only certain powers. In other words, while Congress possessed the power to color within the bright lines drawn in ink by the Constitution of the United States, it did not, on its own, have the power to expand those boundaries, at least not in 1803. Congress, then, an artifice created by the Constitution, remained specifically subject to its limitations. In his view, the creature, Congress, could not alter its creator, the Constitution. Thus, Marshall explained that the Constitution remained the supreme law of the highest order, and, by invalidating the relevant portion of the congressional statute, Marshall solidified the role of the Court as the Constitution's chorus, oracle, and protector.

Marshall's ruling in *Marbury v. Madison* dealt a significant blow to the notion of legislative supremacy, the anachronistic holdover from the English parliamentary system. He also provided the Court with a powerful lever to correct the course of errant legislation and provided future courts with a weapon against constitutional excess. These future courts could negate future laws, laws that could be passed through a legitimate process by a legitimate authority, and promulgated, if the Court decided that they ran contrary to the Constitution; including the Ninth Amendment which provides protections for unenumerated rights retained by the people.

Ex Parte Bollman: Marshall Continues to Defend the Role of the Court

Marbury did not stand alone as the only case in which Marshall employed natural law reasoning to safeguard the authority of the Court. For instance, well into Jefferson's second term, when the Court contemplated its authority to issue a writ, in this particular case, a writ of *habeas corpus*,[32] Marshall delivered a fair opinion while markedly protecting the powers of the Court. *Ex Parte Bollman* involved an alleged plot by Aaron Burr, and others, to create an independent country within the United States by "separate[ing] some of this country's newly acquired western territories from their allegiance to the United States."[33] Erick Bollman and Samuel Swartwout, Burr's alleged co-conspirators, became implicated in the cabal and were eventually arrested and committed without trial in the District of Columbia Circuit Court of Appeals on charges of treason.[34]

The issue before the Supreme Court was whether the two "prisoners [could] access [...] the federal writ of *habeas corpus* to test the legality of their confinements"[35] or more specifically, whether the Supreme "court has the power generally of issuing the writ."[36] Despite the scandalous and politically-charged nature of the accusations,[37] Marshall began the opinion by placidly examining the legal elements before the Court, and in doing so signaled his intent to relay a non-controversial opinion. "As preliminary to any investigation of the merits of this motion, this court deems it proper to declare that it disclaims all jurisdiction not given by the constitution [sic], or by the laws of the United States."[38]

Distinguishing between common-law courts and courts established by statute, Marshall created a separation between courts whose authority generally comes from tradition, such as, many English courts or American state courts, and U.S. federal courts established by the Judiciary Act of 1789, pursuant to the

Constitution.[39] Concluding that the Court had statutory authority to issue the writ of *habeas corpus*, Marshall turned to the constitutional issue framed by *Marbury* and, "decided in a few terse sentences that the jurisdiction 'which the court is now asked to exercise is clearly appellate. It is the revision of a decision of an inferior court, by which a citizen has been committed to jail.'"[40] Furthermore, Marshall chose to insulate the federal judiciary against future incursion by other branches. This opinion is not to be considered as abridging the power of the courts over their own officers, or to protect themselves, and their members, from being disturbed in the exercise of their functions. It extends only to the power of taking cognizance of any question between individuals, or between the government and individuals.[41]

The Chief Justice wanted to make clear to others they should not construe the opinion on *Ex Parte Bollman* as limiting the power of the courts. However, Marshall nonetheless believed that "[t]o enable the court to decide on such question, [the question in the present case,] the power to determine it must [b]e[42] given by written law."[43] After determining that the Court did indeed have the power to issue the writ, the Court examined the merits of the petition and ruled that the evidence against the petitioners was insufficient to support an indictment for treason. Ultimately, the Marshall Court decided to order "the Jefferson administration to release the prisoners, but he wrote a decision softened with placatory dictum."[44]

Marshall, concerned with the perceived legitimacy of the Supreme Court, carefully defended the role of the Court in *Marbury* and *Ex Parte Bollman*. In fact, the Marshall Court, staked out several boundaries through a series of landmark decisions defining the limits and refining the scope of the powers of Congress. Since the Constitution was still relatively young, and many of its culverts, peaks, and valleys had yet to be mapped, it needed a stalwart cartographer to begin to compile its atlas. With so many of the Constitution's rules and clauses still in *terra incognita* beyond the reach of judicial reconnaissance, the Supreme Court needed to take the cases as they came and use the opportunities presented to announce how the Constitution would be applied to legislative action. This pioneering court defined the meanings of a range of restrictions placed on government and explored these themes over a series of cases such as those implicating the Contracts Clause and the Commerce Clause as they applied to the actions of state legislatures.

Fletcher v. Peck: Natural Law Reasoning As a Protector for Contract Rights

In 1810, the Supreme Court ruled on the first case involving an impairment of the obligation of contracts. In *Fletcher v. Peck*,[45] the Supreme Court applied natural law principles of fairness and equity and ultimately ruled in favor of the right to contract, strengthening the power of the Contracts Clause of the

Constitution – itself an articulation of the natural right to engage in voluntary commercial transactions and exchanges – against incursions by state legislatures, and setting a roadmap for future cases to follow.[46]

Two land speculators, Robert Fletcher and John Peck, had disputed whether Peck held proper title to land he had acquired that was part of a legislative grant by the State of Georgia. In 1795, "a Georgia Legislature, bribe induced, had deeded thirty-five million acres of land in its western territories, from which were later formed the present day states of Mississippi and Alabama, to [four companies]... of land speculators for a low consideration."[47] Almost immediately, the legislation and ensuing sale "produced great indignation ... throughout the States [... since] [i]t was felt that the legislature had given away a quantity of the public property sufficient, if properly administered, to yield a large sum to the State and furnish land in abundance to all the citizens."[48] Since "the sale had become a political issue[, a] group of enterprising politicians, campaigning for rescission of the deed of sale, had swept into power in the ensuing election."[49] Before the newly elected Georgia lawmakers could reverse the act of their predecessors, which they did in 1796, one of the companies that had been deeded the land began to sell parcels to buyers in New England.[50]

The issue in *Fletcher v. Peck*, then emerged when Fletcher, who was under contract to purchase land from Peck, sought to invalidate their contract based on the Georgia state legislature's reversal of the initial land grant, which called into question Peck's actual ownership of the property.[51] As the Supreme Court contemplated whether it even possessed the authority to invalidate an act of the state legislature,[52] it also wondered if the Contracts Clause conflicted with the actions of the State of Georgia.

In addition to the underlying contract issue, the case presented troubling issues and allegations of corruption at the highest levels of state government,[53] which caused Marshall to question "[h]ow far a court of justice would, in any case, be competent, on proceedings instituted by the state itself, to vacate a contract thus formed, and to annul rights acquired, under that contract, by third persons having no notice of the improper means by which it was obtained?"[54] What could the Supreme Court do when faced with the will of the majority of the people within a state?[55]

Marshall contemplated whether legislative corruption is a condition sufficient to warrant judicial nullification, and pondered the limits of the Supreme Court's own power to nullify state laws.[56] He was uncomfortable with prescribing specific rules for judicial intervention in state legislative action. Marshall even questioned the limits that society naturally places on its legislature and indicated his belief that one which permits arbitrary and compensation-less seizure of private land as, perhaps, tyrannical: "It may well be doubted whether the nature of society and of government does not prescribe some limits to the legislative power; and, if any be prescribed, where are they to be found, if the property of an individual, fairly and honestly acquired, may be seized without compensation."[57] Such a statement undercuts the doctrinal English belief in parliamentary supremacy, and in turn, elevates Natural Law Tradition. Marshall's inclusion of the consideration of *the nature of society* demonstrates his belief in the existence of external forces (rational reliance on natural law) that provide limitations on the power of government.

Marshall did not question that legislatures have power to legislate, but rather whether a legislature could pass an act taking property away from a person without compensation.[58] If not for the Natural Law Tradition of rights, fairness, and justice, why would Marshall question such a limitation on the power of a legislature? He explored the extent that legislatures could act when facing silence or ambiguity within the Constitution.[59] Finally, Marshall concluded that, though it remained dubious as to whether the legislature of the Georgia could pass such an act, the Court could remain silent on the issue since the matter, when examined in the context of the federal Constitution, Georgia was barred from passing any "*ex post facto* law, or law impairing the obligation of contracts."[60] The message was clear: *Even if* the land grant had been made under the cloud of corruption, once it had been done and then the land further sold to a person who was not a party to the corrupt act, the State of Georgia could not interfere with that sale.[61] Once again, the natural right to contract – to engage in enforceable voluntary exchanges – secured by the Constitution, could not be overcome by an act of a state.

Marshall could have invalidated the act of the Georgia legislature on natural law grounds alone. Indeed, some of his reasoning regarding fairness to innocent third parties,[62] smacks of natural law language and reasoning. However, as consistent with the emerging trend of reliance on the Constitution and positive law to justify court decisions, Marshall managed to maintain natural law principles and natural law reasoning while grounding his decision in positive law like the Contracts Clause of the U.S. Constitution. The Constitution, perhaps the most deliberate posited document in Western history, replete with undeniable expressions of natural law principles, and first used to bolster natural law theories, began to have meaning with them.

Terrett v. Taylor: Using Natural Law to Restrain Legislative Authority Over Private Property

The idea of "extra-constitutional limitations on state power pursuant to natural law continued to appear in decisions issued by the Court after *Fletcher*," for example in *Terrett v. Taylor* (1815), where "the Court had before it a Virginia statute which attempted to divest the Episcopal Church of its property in that state."[63] During the colonial era, the Episcopal Church, the official church of Virginia, was granted lands in addition to those that its members owned. However, several years later in 1798, the state legislature adopted a law repealing prior state gifts of property to the Church, "asserted the right to sell all Episcopal Church property and directed the parish overseers of the poor to sell any vacant lands."[64]

Justice Story, writing for a majority of the Court, "stated that a legislature cannot repeal a legislative grant of the right to hold property based 'upon the principles of natural justice, upon the fundamental laws of every free government, [and] upon the spirit and letter of the Constitution.'"[65] Invoking natural law principles, he ruled that "the land still belonged to the church and that the overseers should be enjoined from claiming title;"[66] there was no scenario, he believed, in which a legislative grant of land could be revocable. Allowing such would "uproot the very foundations of almost all the land titles in Virginia, and it utterly inconsistent with a great and fundamental principle of a republican government, the right of citizens to the free enjoyment of their property legally acquired."[67]

Dartmouth College v. Woodward: Marshall Further Strengthens the Obligation to Contract

In 1819, the Marshall Court once again contemplated whether the Contracts Clause could withstand an assault from a state legislature in *Trustees of Dartmouth College v. Woodward*. This time, the conflict arose when in 1816, the state of New Hampshire attempted via statute, to amend Dartmouth College's charter, install several members of the New Hampshire state government as trustees, and make William H. Woodward the college's president.[68] It is hard to imagine a more egregious attempt by a state legislature against a private corporation as these steps effectively aimed to impose public supervision. Unsurprisingly, the majority of Dartmouth's trustees "refused to accept this amended charter, and [...] brought [a] suit for the corporate property, [such as the Corporate Seal] which [was] in possession of a person holding by virtue of the acts" of the state legislature: one William H. Woodward.[69] In effect, the college trustees argued that the charter of a private corporation constituted a contract and was therefore protected against state impairment under the Contracts Clause of the Constitution.[70]

Chief Justice Marshall, writing the opinion for the court, reasoned that the Contracts Clause must be read in a narrow sense.[71] He believed that the Contracts Clause aimed to protect the natural right to contract and prevent "the legislature from violating the right to property."[72] Marshall explained how, before the Constitution, many of the states had taken actions contrary to the natural law by passing legislation that had "weakened the confidence of man in man, and embarrassed all transactions between individuals, by dispensing with faithful performance of engagements."[73]

> To correct this mischief, by restraining the power which produced it, the state legislatures were forbidden 'to pass any law impairing the

obligation of contracts,' that is, of contracts respecting property, under which some individual could claim a right to something beneficial to himself; and that, since the clause in the constitution must in construction receive some limitation, it may be confined, and ought to be confined, to cases of this description; to cases within the mischief it was intended to remedy.[74]

Accordingly, the legislation that interfered with Dartmouth's charter was "repugnant to the constitution of the United States[,]"[75] and therefore invalid. *Trustees of Dartmouth College v. Woodward* represents yet another case in which the Supreme Court under Marshall rejected an act of a state legislature that conflicted with natural rights safeguarded by the Constitution.

Chief Justice Marshall's record on the Contracts Clause shows him to be strongly in favor of the individual natural right to contract. His opinions echo Blackstone's famous defense of property rights: "so great . . . is the regard of the law for private property, that it will not authorize the least violation of it; no not even for the general good of the whole community."[76] Marshall, like Blackstone, understood that many, under the battle cry of "the greater good" often seek to trample on individual liberty and autonomy because of *their* conception of what might be good for themselves.

Ogden v. Saunders: Marshall's Only Dissent Riddled with Locke and Natural Law

Another poignant example of Marshall's devotion to property rights can be seen in *Ogden v. Saunders* (1827), the case that decided the ability of states to create their own bankruptcy laws. It contains the only dissent written by Marshall during his term as Chief Justice and is brimming with natural law language in support of an individual right to contract.[77] Marshall biographer Jean Edward Smith explains the intricacies and context of the *Ogden* case:

[In a prior case decided in 1819], *Sturgis v. Crowninshield*,[78] the Court had rejected the application of New York's insolvency law to contracts entered into before the act [of the legislature] was passed. But the effect of the law on debts contracted *after* its passage remained unclear. This latter issue had first come before the Court in 1824 when George Ogden sought to discharge his debt to John Saunders. Ogden was a citizen of New York; Saunders, a citizen of Kentucky. Their contract had been made after the New York law was adopted. [...] Marshall, Story, and Duvall believed that federal bankruptcy jurisdiction was exclusive and that all such state legislation violated the contract clause of the Constitution. That interpretation would have closed the loophole left open in *Sturgis v. Crowninshield*. Justices Washington, Johnson, and Thompson, on the other hand, thought the New York legislation was valid. Congress had not yet acted in the matter, and the parties to the contract had notice of the state's insolvency law when their agreement was entered into.[79]

In his dissent, Chief Justice Marshall "maintained that [the] act of the legislature [in question] could not be resorted to as a bar to [seeking the judicial enforcement of the obligations arising from the underlying claim by Saunders against Ogden]."[80] As in *Fletcher v. Peck* and *Dartmouth College v. Woodward*, Marshall maintained that the right to contract could supersede the attempts of the state to interfere with it, even to produce a more just result. He argued that:

> So far back as human research carries us, we find the judicial power as a part of the executive, administering justice by the application of remedies to violated rights, or broken contracts. We find that power applying these remedies on *the idea of a pre-existing obligation on every man to do what he has promised* on consideration to do; that the breach of this obligation is an injury for which the injured party has a just claim to compensation, and that society ought to afford him a remedy for that injury.[81]

Marshall invoked the concept of pre-existing universal obligations – that a man's promises must be kept – that apply to *every man*. Such an idea echoes Grotius who spoke of "the obligation to fulfil promises" as one of the principles in harmony with the Natural Law.[82] Moreover, Marshall recognized the role of human law in the enforcement of contracts when he noted:

> We find allusions to the mode of acquiring property, but we find no allusion, from the earliest time, to any supposed act of the governing power giving obligation to contracts. On the contrary, the proceedings [...] evince the idea of a pre-existing intrinsic obligation which human law enforces.[83]

He endorsed the Lockean principle of the acquisition and transfer of property, and the necessity of even application of the law to all members of society.[84] He even commented on the universality of the honoring of contracts.[85] Explaining "[i]n a state of nature, these individuals may contract, their contracts are obligatory, and force may rightfully be employed to coerce the party who has broken his engagement[,]" Marshall declared the sanctity of contracts as he acknowledged and accepted the idea that parties to a contract possess the natural right to pursue remedies to enforce those contracts.[86]

Marshall engaged in a discourse on the nature of the relationship between rights and society so elegant and expository that it is reproduced here in full so as not to diminish or disparage its poetry and persuasiveness. What is the effect of society upon these rights? When men unite together and form a government, do they surrender their right to contract, as well as their right to enforce the observance of contracts? For what purpose should they make this surrender? Government cannot exercise this power for individuals. It is better that they should exercise it for themselves. For what purpose, then, should the surrender be made? It can only be, that government may give it back again. As we have no evidence of the surrender, or of the restoration of the right; as this operation of surrender and restoration would be an idle and useless ceremony, the rational inference seems to be, that neither has ever been made; that individuals do not derive from government their right to contract, but bring that right with them into society; that obligation is not conferred on contracts by positive law, but is intrinsic, and is conferred by the act of the parties. *This results from the right which every man retains to acquire property, to dispose of that property according to his own judgment, and to pledge himself for a future act. These rights are not given by society, but are brought into it.* The right of coercion is necessarily surrendered to government, and this surrender imposes on government the correlative duty of furnishing a remedy. The right to regulate contracts, to prescribe rules by which they shall be evidenced, to prohibit such as may be deemed mischievous, is unquestionable, and has been universally exercised. So far as this power has restrained the original right of individuals to bind themselves by contract, it is restrained; but beyond these actual restraints the original power remains unimpaired.[87]

And, as though such a passage did not present any reader with enough convincing explanation, Marshall added, "This reasoning is, undoubtedly, much strengthened by the authority of those writers on natural and national law, whose opinions have been viewed with profound respect by, the wisest men of the present, and of past ages."[88] Since the wisest men understood the importance of individual liberty, and they recognized the importance of natural law, they also honored the right to contract as perhaps the most important of conventions essential to commerce, enterprise, prosperity, and temporal happiness. The foundations of business would crumble if the government could, with the stroke of a pen, obliterate agreements, void contracts, negate remedies, and thus prevent trade and economic relationships between members of society.

Gibbons v. Ogden: Federal Government Retains Power over Interstate Commerce

In *Gibbons v. Ogden* (1824), the Court needed to determine the scope of the commerce power afforded to Congress by the Constitution in light of a monopoly on steamboats in New York.[89] The state legislature had passed a series of laws granting Robert R. Livingston and Robert Fulton exclusive rights to navigation privileges for a certain number of years on all waters in New York for boats that used fire and steam as a means of propulsion.[90] Eventually, one of the businessmen who had purchased a license to operate some steamboats from

Livingston and Fulton, former New Jersey Governor Aaron Ogden, sought an injunction against Thomas Gibbons, to prevent Gibbons from freely operating his own steamboats.[91] The New York court upheld the injunction against Gibbons, and he appealed.[92]

The Supreme Court questioned whether the state of New York had the authority to issue the monopolistic grant awarded to Livingston and Fulton or whether the Commerce Clause of the Constitution prevented the states from issuing such grants. So, well into the second term of James Monroe, the fifth President of the United States, the Supreme Court still puzzled through the interplay between state power and federal constraints. Even 36 years after the ratification of the Constitution, the United States still struggled to define which powers had been granted to the federal government, and which had been reserved by the states.

After explaining that the states, which had once been sovereign, had ceded some authority to the new federal government,[93] a Lockean analysis, Chief Justice Marshall explained that "[the Constitution] contains an enumeration of powers expressly granted by the people to their government."[94] It is odd, yet typical of Marshall, to argue in the same breath that the federal government's powers came from that which was ceded by the formerly sovereign states and that these powers were granted by the people themselves. In either case, how should the Supreme Court interpret congressional powers under the Commerce Clause?

> It has been said, that these powers ought to be construed strictly. But why ought they to be so construed? Is there one sentence in the constitution which gives countenance to this rule? In the last of the enumerated powers, that which grants, expressly, the means for carrying all others into execution, Congress is authorized 'to make all laws which shall be necessary and proper' for the purpose. But this limitation on the means which may be used, is not extended to the powers which are conferred; nor is there one sentence in the constitution, which has been pointed out by the gentlemen of the bar, or which we have been able to discern, that prescribes this rule.[95]

The Court concluded that it should rely on the plain and simple understanding of the words in the document.[96] So, in interpreting the limitations of the Commerce Clause, since "[t]he subject to be regulated is commerce; and our constitution being, as was aptly said at the bar, one of enumeration, and not of definition, to ascertain the extent of the power, it becomes necessary to settle the meaning of the word."[97]

In interpreting the meaning of commerce and the power to regulate commerce granted to Congress by the Constitution, Marshall opined that the people *must* have contemplated the power over interstate commerce when forming the United States.[98] After establishing that Congress has the exclusive authority to regulate interstate commerce, Marshall contemplated the extent of that power:

> It is the power to regulate; that is, to prescribe the rule by which commerce is to be governed. This power, like all others vested in Congress, is complete in itself, may be exercised to its utmost extent, and acknowledges no limitations, other than are prescribed in the constitution. [...] The wisdom and the discretion of Congress, their identity with the people, and the influence which their constituents possess at elections, are, in this, as in many other instances, as that, for example, of declaring war, the sole restraints on which they have relied, to secure them from its abuse. They are the restraints on which the people must often rely solely, in all representative governments.[99]

So, this power of Congress to regulate commerce, is limited only by the constraints placed upon it by the Constitution, constraints which often serve as the sole force reigning in tyranny. The Court felt bound to consider carefully the limitations of such authority.

However, just because a government authority attempts to exercise a power does not mean that it has that power.[100] As a result, when a question arises as to the authority of a governmental body in the United States, the Court must turn to the Constitution to find the answer.

And the Constitution, according to Marshall, and thus the Court, foresaw conflicts between the actions of the states and those of the federal government:

> But the framers of our constitution foresaw this state of things, and provided for it, by declaring the supremacy not only of itself, but of the laws made in pursuance of it. The nullity of an act, inconsistent with the constitution, is produced by the declaration, that the constitution is the supreme law. The appropriate application of that part of the clause which confers the same supremacy on laws and treaties, is to such acts of the State Legislatures as do not transcend their powers, but, though enacted in the execution of acknowledged State powers, interfere with, or are contrary to the laws of Congress, made in pursuance of the constitution, or some treaty made under the authority of the United States. In every such case, the act of Congress, or the treaty, is supreme; and the law of the State, though enacted in the exercise of powers not controverted, must yield to it.[101]

Here, we must also remember that evidence of the framers' understanding of "to regulate" supports a narrow reading of the Commerce Clause. As Professor Randy Barnett argues, "knowing the scope of these terms is the first essential step towards determining if some other power is really incidental to and *for the purpose* of the regulation of commerce among the states."[102] By looking to evidence from the Constitutional Convention and ratification debates, we see that:

"Congress's power 'to regulate Commerce . . . among the several States' was meant to foster the free flow of interstate commerce, not curtail it. For over one hundred years after the Founding, the country adhered to this view of Congress's interstate commerce power. Few even argued otherwise, and at no point did Congress act as if it possessed the power to ban markets in goods that the states would allow. This history calls into question any easy assumption that the power 'to regulate' commerce necessarily includes the power to eradicate it."[103]

There were scarcely any references to interstate commerce during the Convention and Ratification debates. Instead, "many participants declared, without challenge, that everyone agreed that the Commerce Clause would be especially beneficial" without elaborating further what it meant.[104] Putting ourselves in the shoes of the founders, you will recall that during the post-Revolutionary period, in an attempt to promote business activities in their home states and protect local manufacturers, states employed a practice of discriminatorily taxing and regulating domestic imports, as well as restricting access to local ports by out of state vessels. In addition to retaliating against each other by levying on commerce coming from other states, it was not uncommon for states to negotiate separately with foreign countries on trade. Thus, the primary reason for granting Congress the domestic commerce power was "*to facilitate* interstate trade and protect it against the sort of protectionist state trade policies that occurred all too frequently under the Articles of Confederation." [105] In *Federalist 42*, Madison expressed his concern about the effect of such interstate competitive measures on the national economy and political unity. He stressed that the Commerce Clause provision to regulate trade "among the several States" was to make and keep regular the trade between people of different states and ultimately, further the essential power of regulating trade with foreign nations:

The defect of power in the existing Confederacy to regulate the commerce between its several members is in the number of those which have been clearly pointed out by experience.... [W]ithout this *supplemental provision*, the great and essential power of regulating foreign commerce would have been incomplete and ineffectual.

A very material object of this power [regulating foreign commerce] was the relief of the States which import and export through other States, from the improper contributions levied on them by the latter. Were these at liberty *to regulate the trade between State and State*, it must be foreseen that ways would be found out to load the articles of import and export, during the passage through their jurisdiction, with duties which would fall on the makers of the latter and the consumers of the former. We may be assured by past experience, that such a practice would be introduced by future contrivances; both by that and a common knowledge of human affairs, that it would nourish unceasing animosities, and not improbably terminate in serious interruptions of the public tranquility.[106]

Many years later, Madison once again confirmed that the power to regulate commerce among the several States was granted to the federal government in order to ensure free trade between the people of different states, and

> ... grew out of the abuse of the power by the importing States, in taxing the non-importing; and was intended as a negative & preventive provision agst. injustice among the States themselves; rather than as a power to be used for the positive purposes of the General Govt. in which alone however the remedial power could be lodged. And it will be safer to leave the power with this key to it, than to extend to it all the qualities & incidental means belonging to the power over foreign commerce, as is unavoidable, according to the reasoning I see applied to the case.[107]

Professor Barnett agrees that to Madison and the drafters of the Commerce Clause, the power to regulate does not generally include the power to prohibit. Instead, looking to the definition of "to regulate" at the time of the drafting, we see that it means "1. To adjust by rule or method. . . . 2. To direct,"[108] as distinguished from "to prohibit," which was defined as "1. To forbid; to interdict by authority. . . . 2. To debar; to hinder."[109] In this sense, we can see that the term "to regulate" means "to make regular," as your author has argued elsewhere.[110]

Ultimately, the Court in *Gibbons v. Ogden* held that the state law affecting the navigable waters of New York was an impermissible incursion into the federal power to regulate interstate commerce – even though Congress had theretofore been silent on the matter – and concluded its decision with an encomium to the natural law:

> The conclusion to which we have come, depends on a chain of principles which it was necessary to preserve unbroken; and, although some of them were thought nearly self evident, [sic] the magnitude of the question, the weight of character belonging to those from whose judgment we dissent, and the argument at the bar, demanded that we should assume nothing.

> Powerful and ingenious minds, taking, as postulates, that the powers expressly granted to the government of the Union, are to be contracted by construction, into the narrowest possible compass, and that the original powers of the States are retained, if any possible construction will retain them, may, by a course of well digested, but refined and metaphysical reasoning, founded on these premises, explain away the constitution of our country, and leave it, a magnificent structure, indeed, to look at, but totally unfit for use. They may so entangle and perplex the

understanding, as to obscure principles, which were before thought quite plain, and induce doubts where, if the mind were to pursue its own course, none would be perceived. In such a case, it is peculiarly necessary to recur to safe and fundamental principles to sustain those principles, and when sustained, to make them the tests of the arguments to be examined.[111]

Marshall explained how the Court followed natural law reasoning, reasoning dependent upon "a chain of principles which it was necessary to preserve unbroken." Principles "nearly self evident [sic]"[112] that call for a return to "safe and fundamental principles" of natural law and equity. State governments, it appeared, remained too interested and too invested in engaging in protectionist practices that, if furthered, would foster rivalries, encourage jealousies, and infringe upon the right to contract in matters affecting more than one state. Marshall needed to remind the states that, while they maintained much autonomy under the Tenth Amendment, each could not engage in anticompetitive practices targeting other states and those living within them. Rather, the federal government, a government designed by the Constitution not to allow favorites, reserved the right to maintain and control certain aspects of commerce defined within the Constitution.

Tactfully navigating political issues from the bench, Marshall managed to unify the court and produce fair and well-reasoned opinions that raised the Supreme Court above partisan politics, insulated it against party squabbles, and elevated its independence. And, hardly a parting gift since it was one of the first cases over which Marshall presided, he gave America *Marbury v. Madison*, a decision which empowered the Court to override legislative and executive action by declaring it unconstitutional. Though the Marshall court would almost never wield this power, it would hang, like a Sword of Damocles, over the Legislative and Executive branches, and eventually be rediscovered by the courts of the twentieth century and its most important weapon against legal positivism and legislative and executive overreach.

CHAPTER 11

LEGAL POSITIVISM
BEGINS TO TAKE HOLD

The Argument

Though the Natural Law Tradition retained a prominent place in the Marshall Court, it faced a serious intellectual threat emerging from Great Britain. This threat did not come at the end of a sword but the quill of Jeremy Bentham.

Bentham concocted a "scientific" approach to jurisprudence that sought to eradicate from its roots the moral component of the law and replace it with a slavish adherence to process and words of the statutes themselves. Bentham felt his solution cured the legal profession of what he considered foolish sentimentally which allowed for subjective decisions on abstract principles such as morals and reason, two crucial components to the discovery and application of the natural law.

The increased proliferation of collected cases and laws had provided lawyers and judges with a larger corpus of cases and statutes to cite, and influential thinkers, like Bentham, argued for reliance on these cases and statutes rather than the application of reason.

While the Court under Marshall generally ruled in a manner consistent with the Natural Law theory, it did, from time to time, rely on tenets of legal positivism and rendered its decision in McCulloch v. Maryland where it drastically expanded the power of the federal government to pass expansive statutes eroding natural rights and liberties.

***

Fear, that is the prospect of pain, the latter: fear, the offspring of superstitious fancy: the fear of future punishment at the hands of a splenetic and revengeful Deity. I say in this case fear: for of the invisible future, fear is more powerful than hope.[1]

– **Jeremy Bentham (1748-1832)**

THE RISE OF POSITIVISM: A SCIENTIFIC APPROACH TO JURISPRUDENCE

Social and political changes often inspire new modes of thinking that result in new approaches to understanding the philosophy of law. Whereas science discards old models in favor of the new iterations, in jurisprudence, we accumulate, rather than replace, philosophical methods.[2]

Though approaches derived from the Natural Law Tradition had retained a prominent position since the early modern period, readers familiar with jurisprudence and legal theory will recall several other schools jockeying for supremacy atop the pyramid of judicial philosophy.

Despite the unambiguous recognition of the Natural Law Tradition by Chief Justice Marshall in the nineteenth century, the jurisprudence began to cede ground to philosophies made more popular by wider promulgation of casebooks and newly collected volumes of statutes. With the advent of Supreme Court reporters and volumes of collected statutes, the trend shifted toward greater reliance on positive law, whether in the form the recorded common law or published statutory law. As a result, the Marshall Court began to create a legal environment in which positivism would later thrive. The prescient Chief Justice likely saw the trend towards an approach that would try to rob the Court of its humanity and attempt to replace it with the "science" of legal positivism.

By the late eighteenth and early nineteenth centuries, technology and more established postal routes and shipping channels had developed and allowed for more widespread distribution of enacted statutes and judicial opinions interpreting them.[3] With the lack of a more contemporary definitive treatise on law, American lawyers and judges eagerly awaited the chance to have greater access to legal materials, such as legal treatises, case reporters, and volumes of collected statutes. In 1772, the American publication of Blackstone's *Commentaries* was welcomed in legal communities with open arms, as before Blackstone, lawyers were left to study Coke's *Institutes*, a series of volumes, as we have seen, bereft of organization and rife with dubious and tendentious accounts of history.[4] Blackstone had offered readers more than Coke's collection of cases with poorly-supported, sometimes seemingly arbitrary conclusions. He supplemented decisions with *commentary* explaining the techniques and philosophy behind the decisions of those who happened to occupy the bench.

John Adams, for instance, lamented in his diary the disorganization and frenetic nature of Coke's *Institutes* while extolling the cohesiveness and fluidity of Blackstone:

> I this day got through, my folio of Lord Coke, which has been hanging heavy upon me, these ten weeks. It contains a vast deal of Law learning; *but heaped up in such an incoherent mass that I have derived very little*

benefit from it. Indeed I think it a very improper book to put into the
hands of a student just entering upon the acquisition of the profession. I
am perswaded [sic] I might have spent the Time which has been
employ'd in reading this book, to much better advantage, and that a
twelvemonth hence I could have read it in less time and with more profit:
but if this be the case how much more laborious must the study have
been, when this was the only elementary book of the profession. The
addition of Wood's Institutes and more especially of Blackstone's
commentaries, has been an inestimable advantage of the late students in
the profession.[5]

The common law approach of Blackstone, much like the natural law
methodology proposed by Aquinas, refined by Grotius, and made relevant to
government by Locke had given judges and lawyers a systematic technique for
arguing and deciding cases in a time when volumes of cases were rare and
expensive. A few publishers sought to address this deficiency.

The Advent of Supreme Court Reporters

In 1790, the legal community was further given an opportunity to understand
and anticipate rulings of the Supreme Court when the Court's first chronicler,
Alexander James Dallas (1759-1817),[6] published what would become the first in
several volumes of judicial decisions he organized, at great effort and personal
expense, as a public service to the Court. In his preface to the first volume of
United States Reports,[7] which, incidentally, contained only Pennsylvania
decisions, Dallas explained his motivations for collecting and publishing such
decisions. After humbly taking responsibility for any faults or errors in the
volume, Dallas noted that he:

anticipate[d] with pleasure, that, as a consequence of such
encouragement and indulgence, some one [sic], more able, will be
tempted to follow [his] example, and render an essential service to his
country, by preserving the principles on which the future judgments of
our Courts are founded; —a matter that, in every point of view, whether
we consider the present political situation of the Union, [...] the
advancement of agriculture, or the extension of commerce, must daily
become more interesting and important to the liberty, peace, and
property of every citizen.[8]

In addition, Dallas believed that the volumes would also "serve to facilitate
the labors of the student" by making him aware "of those points of law which
have already been discussed and decided,"[9] as well as "furnishing some hints for
regulating the conduct of Referees [judges], to whom, according to the present
practice, a very great share of administration is entrusted."[10] Judges, too, in
Dallas's mind, needed a published record of decisions in order to keep the

administration of the law in order.

In 1804, William Cranch (1769-1855), the second collector of Supreme Court cases echoed his predecessor. "Much of that *uncertainty of the law*, which is so frequently, and perhaps so justly, the subject of complaint in this country, may be attributed to the want of American reports."[11] He did not blame ambiguous laws or bad decisions for the inconsistency and uncertainty surrounding the law, but rather pointed to the dearth of American published reports. Continuing, "[u]niformity, in such cases, can not [sic] be expected where the judicial authority is shared among such a vast number of independent tribunals, unless the decisions of the various courts are made known to each other," Cranch explained the challenges inherent to the limited recording and transmission of case law.[12] "Even in the same court," Cranch added, "analog of judgement can not [sic] be maintained if its adjudications are suffered to be forgotten."[13] Even in 1804, Cranch, like Dallas before him, recognized the difficulties with consistent adjudication in a complex, and growing society. And that was 215 years ago.

Considering the tasks of collecting, editing, and publishing reports of the Supreme Court in America in the late eighteenth and early nineteenth centuries, one can appreciate the prominence of Coke's *Institutes* despite its well-reported shortcomings, and the enthusiasm with which practitioners welcomed copies of Blackstone's *Commentaries*. Blackstone had provided some relief from the uncertainty wrought by vastly differing approaches to deciding matters of law. Blackstone endorsed an analytic scheme that called on judges to take into account natural law concepts based upon human reason to determine case outcomes. However, some believed this approach left judges with too much discretion to decide cases based on their own moral attitudes. Chief among those critics was a dour Englishman named Jeremy Bentham (1747-1832) who would come up with a scheme that later became known as legal positivism.[14]

Jeremy Bentham: Focus on Text and Process rather than Morals

Bentham, the father of legal positivism, focused not on morals, a hallmark of the Natural Law Tradition, or ethics, a doctrinal requirement necessary to weigh outcomes, or reason, the backbone of NLT; but rather on text and process.[15] He "rejected the notion that law was either divine or natural [… but] [r]ather, […] espoused the theory of legal positivism, which preserved a separation between legal and moral principles."[16] To Bentham, the law lived independent of its moral content (or lack of it). Accordingly, "the defining slogan of legal positivism […] is that '[t]he existence of law is one thing, its merit or demerit is another.'"[17] Whereas the jurisprudence of the Natural Law Tradition focuses on the rightness of a matter as judged through reason, legal positivism seeks to examine law as one might a science by relying only on concrete observation, usually only the observation of the text of a statute and the process by which it became law.[18]

"[A]ccording to [the tradition of legal positivism], law is not derived necessarily from fundamental moral principles but rather is simply 'posited' by human beings and human institutions."[19]

Bentham "heaped criticism on (what he took to be) Blackstone's failure to" distinguish law as what it actually was from what Blackstone felt it ought to have been.[20] "[W]hat Bentham found fundamentally wrong in Blackstone's work was the place he gave to tradition and history, factors that are of no value whatsoever in assessing the merit of the law[.]"[21] Distinguishing between "antiquities" and "jurisprudence," Bentham declared "'[t]he past is of no value but by the influence it preserves over the present and the future. . . .Let us reflect that our first concern is to learn how the things that are in our power ought to be. . . .'"[22]

Bentham eschewed anything he could not empirically measure.[23] Accordingly, "[a] theme running through Bentham's work is the need to eradicate imaginary 'fictions' that bedevil thought, and to restate our knowledge on firm empirical grounds."[24] Bentham "had unbounded contempt for the common law, despised legal fictions, mocked the bar and the judiciary [...] and in many other respects made clear that prescribing change in how the law operated and how the legal system was structured was one of his central goals."[25] Bentham, who attended Blackstone's lectures as a student,[26] wrote to supplant the common law,[27] which he believed was weakened to the point of unsustainability by legal fictions.[28] To Bentham, Blackstone's common law approach neglected to justify the source of the authority of judge-made law and to take into account the superiority of statutory law.[29]

Bentham held nothing but disdain for the natural law. "The various systems that have been formed concerning the standard of right and wrong, may be reduced to the principle of sympathy and antipathy," Bentham asserted.[30] Ruefully, Bentham dismissed these prior approaches to jurisprudence.

> One account may serve for all of them. They consist all of them in so many contrivances for avoiding the obligation of appealing to any external standard, and for prevailing upon the reader to accept the author's sentiment or opinion as a reason and that a sufficient one for itself.[31]

He viewed the common law, and the natural law, as arbitrary tautologies. He believed there existed "no necessary connection between law and morals."[32] Professor Anthony Sebock explained that Bentham felt "[t]he appeal to Natural Law was not only an appeal to an unprovable chimera, but it allowed each law-applier [i.e., judges] to inject his own morality into the law."[33] And, Bentham had some choice words about morality. He "had little patience for moral discourse, which he described with characteristic acerbity: 'While Xenophon was writing History, and Euclid teaching Geometry, Socrates and Plato were talking nonsense, on pretence [sic] of teaching morality and wisdom.'"[34] As far as natural rights,

Bentham declared, "'Natural rights is simple nonsense: natural and imprescriptible rights, rhetorical nonsense, *nonsense upon stilts*.'"[35]

Mirroring the prevailing scientific approaches of the time, Bentham sought to explain the law as an ordered set of restraints and inducements, and human nature as an inconvenient side effect of consciousness. Indeed, beginning his debut exegesis, "[n]ature has placed mankind under the governance of two sovereign masters, *pain* and *pleasure*," Bentham reveals his overly reductionist view of the complexity of the human condition.[36] In an incredibly telling construction for a legal positivist, Bentham reveals his belief as to the more compelling of the two forces he believes control human behavior by listing *pain* before *pleasure*. Bentham, however, erred by ignoring the forces that contribute to human behavior that Aquinas and Grotius had recognized centuries earlier; reasoning to right and wrong and accounting for human emotion.

Bentham tried to create an approach to law he believed more scientific, repeatable, and consistent than natural law or common law. Like a scientist running an experiment, Bentham apparently believed that identical inputs should result in identical outcomes when confronting the same forces. To Bentham, the inputs comprised the facts of the case, the law comprised the forces, and the court produced the outcome. Bentham's scheme did not allow for judges to consider issues outside the words of the law but called instead for judges to examine only *written* law and *settled* law. However, this method of deciding cases relied on ready and unrestricted access to *written* law and *published* decisions. Today, this Benthamite analysis is the essence of positivism: *Only laws that are written and ratified are valid and enforceable.*

So, why discuss the writings of a man so diametrically opposed to the chief subject of this book? Legal positivism, though Bentham never referred to it by such a name, became the chief antagonist to Natural Law theory, and its influence had far-reaching implications for legal thought throughout the nineteenth and twentieth centuries. So strong was its influence that it even caused the great Chief Justice to stray from his reliance on natural law tenets when he wrote his most important opinion after *Marbury*, namely *McCulloch v. Maryland*.

McCulloch v. Maryland: A Grave Aberration on Marshall's Record of Fidelity to Natural Law

In *McCulloch v. Maryland* (1819), the Court wrestled with the power of Congress to engage in legislative behavior outside the boundaries delimited by the Constitution and rendered a decision that would allow the federal government to brandish the Necessary and Proper Clause to pass a wide range of far-reaching, and never-contemplated-by-the-Framers intrusive legislation. In 1818, Maryland's legislature enacted a law that *nominally* taxed all banks not chartered by the state. On its face, the law appeared fair and nondiscriminatory. However, the only non-state-chartered bank in Maryland was the Second Bank of the United

States, a bank incorporated by an 1816 federal act. Any observer could recognize that Maryland targeted this new federal bank. The central issue in this case concerned the power of Congress to incorporate a bank.[37] Congress had already created the First National Bank of the United States, and Marshall acknowledged that its presence influenced the decision at hand; positivism invading the reasoning of the bench.[38] However, Marshall also recognized the intrinsic problem in allowing Congress to engage in activities beyond those expressly permitted under the Constitution.

After a review of the text of the Constitution, the Court concluded that "[a]mong the enumerated powers, *we do not find that of establishing a bank or creating a corporation.*"[39] However, it also noted that "there is no phrase in the [Constitution] which, like the articles of confederation, excludes incidental or implied powers; and which requires that everything granted shall be expressly and minutely described."[40] Indeed:

> Even the 10th amendment, which was framed for the purpose of quieting the excessive jealousies which had been excited, omits the word 'expressly,' and declares only, that the powers 'not delegated to the United States, nor prohibited to the states, are reserved to the states or to the people;' thus leaving the question, whether the particular power which may become the subject of contest, has been delegated to the one government, or prohibited to the other, to depend on a fair construction of the whole instrument.[41]

This logic represents an inverse positivism: relying on words that might have been written, but were not, in order to justify an interpretation of words that were written. Thus, Marshall concluded that it would have been too unwieldy for the Founders to have included *all* the details of government in a single document.[42] "But it may with great reason be contended, that a government, intrusted [sic] with such ample powers, on the due execution of which the happiness and prosperity of the nation so vitally depends, must also be intrusted [sic] with ample means for their execution."[43]

The quandary, then, emerged when the court needed to consider what means were available to the Congress to achieve the ends which the Constitution called for it to reach.[44] Marshall writing for the Court, eventually decided that, since all legislative power relates to sovereignty, an action of the Court preventing Congress from creating a corporation as a sufficiently essential means by which to affect an end prophesied by the Constitution, would interfere with Congress's ability to fulfil its role.[45]

Though *McCulloch* is to blame for the expansive reading of the Necessary and Proper Clause of the Constitution, Marshall could not have foreseen the extent to which future Congresses and courts would turn to that case as grounding for the justification for the expansion of legislative power. True, the opinion permitted the formation of a bank not expressly ordained by the Constitution. True, Marshall again argued, as the Supreme Court had before, that the states had necessarily ceded some sovereignty to the federal government through accession to the Constitution.[46] Therefore, "[t]he Government which has the right to do an act, and has imposed on it, the duty of performing that act, must, according to the dictates of reason, be allowed to select the means[,]" and those opposed to the proposed means have the burden of demonstrating those means are out of bounds.[47] However, the Court reasoned that "The power of creating a corporation is never used for its own sake, but for the purpose of effecting something else."[48] Accordingly, "[n]o sufficient reason is, therefore, perceived, why it may not pass as incidental to those powers which are expressly given, if it be a direct mode of executing them."[49]

Yet, "the constitution of the United States has not left the right of congress to employ the necessary means, for the execution of the powers conferred on the government, to general reasoning[,]"[50] but rather relied on the Necessary and Proper clause as the standard against which to judge the actions of Congress.[51]

It is both necessary and proper that a legislature pass laws. "That a legislature, endowed with legislative powers, can legislate, is a proposition too self-evident to have been questioned."[52] However, what it can legislate remains subject to limitations.

Congress is not empowered by it to make all laws, which may have relation to the powers confered [sic] on the government, but such only as may be 'necessary and proper' for carrying them into execution. The word 'necessary' is considered as controlling the whole sentence, and as limiting the right to pass laws for the execution of the granted powers, to such as are indispensable, and without which the power would be nugatory. That it excludes the choice of means, and leaves to congress, in each case, that only which is most direct and simple.[53]

The Court questioned how *necessary* things must be to fall within the purview of congressional scrutiny and action.[54] Marshall "uses twenty-four different terms for his interpretation of 'necessary and proper,' creating potential ambiguities about the scope of the implied powers."[55] On one hand, words and phrases like 'convenient,' 'useful,' 'conducive,' 'adapted,' and 'free use of means' suggest more latitude for Congress.[56] However, Marshall's inclusion of other words in the discussion such as "direct," "needful," "requisite," "required" and "essential" seem more restrictive on Congress' ability to legislate.[57]

While reasonable people could disagree as to what specific means were *necessary* to achieve a specific end, such a decision was not always subject to the jurisdictional review of the judiciary as Marshall understood it: "[t]o employ the means necessary to an end, is generally understood as employing any means calculated to produce the end, and not as being confined to those single means, without which the end would be entirely unattainable."[58]

In other words, Marshall concluded, *necessary* did not mean *absolutely necessary* but rather some other, vaguer abstraction of necessity since "[i]t would have been an unwise attempt to provide, by immutable [positive] rules, for exigencies which, if foreseen at all, must have been seen dimly, and which can be best provided for as they occur."[59] In a perverse use of inverse positivism that not even Jeremy Bentham would have ascribed to, because James Madison[60] did not use the words "absolutely necessary," Marshall argued:

> A thing may be necessary, very necessary, absolutely or indispensably necessary. To no mind would the same idea be conveyed by these several phrases. The comment on the word is well illustrated by the passage cited at the bar, from the 10th section of the 1st article of the constitution. It is, we think, impossible to compare the sentence which prohibits a state from laying 'imposts, or duties on imports or exports, except what may be absolutely necessary for executing its inspection laws,' with that which authorizes congress 'to make all laws which shall be necessary and proper for carrying into execution' the powers of the general government, without feeling a conviction, that the convention understood itself to change materially the meaning of the word 'necessary,' by prefixing the word 'absolutely.' This word, then, like others, is used in various senses; and, in its construction, the subject, the context, the intention of the person using them, are all to be taken into view.[61]

There you have it. Through an adroit use of inverse postivism, the incorporation of a bank by Congress was constitutional,[62] and Maryland's attempt to tax that bank was unconstitutional.[63]

Recall Madison's observations on the Bank Speech regarding overbroad readings of enabling language in key legal documents such as the Constitution:

> No argument could be drawn from the terms "common defence and general welfare." The power as to these general purposes was limited to acts laying taxes for them; and the general purposes themselves were limited and explained by the particular enumeration subjoined. To understand these terms in any sense that would justify the power in question would give to Congress an unlimited power; would render nugatory the enumeration of particular powers; would supercede [sic] all the powers reserved to the state governments.[64]

> It appeared on the whole, [Madison] concluded, that the power exercised by the [bank] bill was condemned by the silence of the Constitution; was condemned by the rule of interpretation arising out of the Constitution; was condemned by its tendency to destroy the main characteristic of the

Constitution; was condemned by the expositions of the friends of the Constitution whilst depending before the public; was condemned by the apparent intention of the parties which ratified the Constitution; was condemned by the explanatory amendments proposed by Congress themselves to the Constitution; and he hoped it would receive its final condemnation, by the vote of this house.[65]

Madison, speaking in February of 1791, even referred to what would become the Ninth and Tenth Amendments in December of that year as if they had been ratified already by describing them as "guarding against a latitude of interpretation [and] as excluding every source of power not within the constitution itself."[66] Madison's views on the issue being well known, it appears strange that Marshall would so broadly interpret the powers of Congress as to permit the incorporation of a bank when Madison, the seminal figure in the drafting and adoption of the Constitution and its first ten amendments, opposed the bank so forcefully in the first place.

However, Marshall seemed to be of two minds on the warmth the states had for the Constitution at the outset of the nation. As discussed by the historian Charles A. Beard, Marshall chronicled two different attitudes toward the origins and power limits of the federal government.[67] In his biography of George Washington, written between 1804 and 1807, Marshall noted:

So balanced were the parties in some of [the states], that, even after the subject had been discussed for a considerable time, the fate of the constitution could scarcely be conjectured; and is small, in many instances, was the majority in its favour, as to afford strong ground for the opinion that, had the influence of character been removed, the intrinsic merits of the instrument would not have secured its adoption. Indeed, *it is scarcely to be doubted that in some of the adopting states, a majority of the people were in opposition.* In all of them, the numerous amendments which were proposed, demonstrate the reluctance with which the new government was accepted; and that a dread of dismemberment not an approbation of the particular system under consideration, has induced an acquiescence to it.[68]

Such a record contradicts Marshall's words written fifteen years later in *McCulloch* where he wrote that:

No political dreamer was ever wild enough to think of breaking down the lines which separate the states, and of compounding the American people into one common mass. Of consequence, when they act, they act in their states. But the measures they adopt do not, on that account, cease to be the measures of the people themselves, or become the measures of the state governments.

From these conventions, the constitution derives its whole authority. The government proceeds directly from the people; is "ordained and established," in the name of the people; and is declared to be ordained, "in order to form a more perfect union, establish justice, insure domestic tranquility, [sic] and secure the blessings of liberty to themselves and to their posterity." The assent of the states, in their sovereign capacity, is implied, in calling a convention, and thus submitting that instrument to the people. But the people were at perfect liberty to accept, or reject it; and their act was final. It required not the affirmance, and could not be negatived, [sic] by the state governments. The constitution, when thus adopted, was of complete obligation, and bound the state sovereignties.[69] While we may never know why in March 1819 Chief Justice Marshall more fondly remembered the extent to which the public had embraced the Constitution at the time of its ratification, than he did in the years of 1804 to 1807, we can certainly observe the sharp contrast between conflicting viewpoints. In Marshall's first version of events, the Constitution barely survived its gestation and managed to pass through cajoling and threats yet with only "one fourth or one fifth" of eligible voters' approval.[70] In the other version, "the people were at perfect liberty to accept, or reject it; and their act [of full acceptance] was final."[71]

Marshall's opinion in *McCulloch* became notorious for more than dubious records of history. Future Supreme Courts would cite to *McCulloch* and invoke Marshall as the Supreme Court's Oracle, to justify some of the most governmental-expansive opinions in history.[72] This diminished use of natural law supplanted with increased reliance on positive law, even inverse positive law, in the Marshall Court continued as legal positivism slowly replaced the natural law at the Supreme Court. Increased reliance on and deference to legal positivism permitted the Court repeatedly to abdicate its role to vouchsafe natural rights and liberties. In many ways, the Court used legal positivism as a sort of "Get of Jail Free card" when it faced difficult decisions and perhaps feared the social and political fallout that could result if the Court invalidated outdated practices and policies that should have never been tolerated in an enlightened society.[73]

Though *McCulloch* appeared only as an aberration in Marshall's record of fidelity to Natural Law theory, the opinion became more sinister, and perhaps more protracted, and even perverse, because of the preeminence and general unimpeachability of its author. Since Marshall holds a special place of reverence in the field of American constitutional jurisprudence, it remains doubtful whether *McCulloch* would have withstood the test of time and grown to serve as one of the most dangerous precedents used by the government to justify incursions into personal liberty if it had been written by another justice.

Despite the damage done by the Court in *McCulloch*, it continued to apply natural law principles to cases it decided under Marshall's leadership to defend and preserve those matters and principles beyond the perfidious reach of *McCulloch*. After Marshall's tenure as Chief Justice, some courts continued to use positivism as a tool to avoid uncomfortable outcomes, and some relied on natural law to correct profound errors. It is to this continued friction throughout the twentieth century, that we now turn.

CHAPTER 12

INTEREST RETURNS AFTER
A CENTURY OF LEGAL POSITIVISM

The Argument

Following the end of the Marshall Court, as court reporters and collected volumes of statutes became more prevalent, legal positivism provided to courts an excuse to avoid opining on difficult cases or fulfilling their role as the counter-majoritarian institution it became under Marshall.

The tradition of legal positivism persisted and eventually allowed for the emergence of governments that were possessed of legitimate authority that, through a legitimate process, adopted and promulgated laws so egregious and offensive as to shock the conscience.

Following the conclusion of World War II, legal scholars struggled to find philosophical grounding for prosecution of the Nazis when legal positivism failed to supply sufficient legal justification.

Renewed interest in Natural Law theory inspired a natural law renaissance which gave birth to a new generation of legal philosophers and critics who modernized our understanding of Natural Law theory and its role in contemporary jurisprudence.

***

At every stage, there has been a wealth of theoretical argument to support the economically convenient opinion.[1]

– Bertrand Russell (1872-1970)

THE SUPREME COURT'S DETRIMENTAL RELIANCE ON POSITIVISM

Thus far, we have focused on the development of Natural Law theory from the days of Aristotle and later Augustine and Aquinas and then Grotius and Bracton through the first five decades of the American federal republic, with the goal of explaining how the founding generation understood and applied natural law principles in the design and interpretation of the Constitution and Bill of Rights. We must not approach law as a loose interpretive exercise which permits wild and creative personal speculation about the meanings of words and phrases or the intent – or lack of intent – of its authors. Unlike poetry or most other written works, laws manifest through a collaborative, albeit sometimes adversarial process, including debate, amendment, review, and revision. To suggest the suspected intent of just *one* law giver – even giants like Madison, Jefferson, and Marshall, should control future understanding of a statute and consequently guide from the grave its interpretation and execution would reveal a fundamental misunderstanding of the appropriate methods of constitutional and statutory interpretation. Contrary to this view are the originalists, who are addressed in Chapter 17.

A wholistic approach, however, requires understanding of ideas and principles widely held by those involved in the crafting and passage of a statute. Legal positivism rejected the belief that understanding a statute required more than understanding only the words contained within the four corners of the page on which the statute is written. This Benthamite attitude removed conscience from law and permitted judges to render opinions bereft of considerations of morality; even of obvious right and wrong. Separating conscience – individual judicial conscience or collective societal conscience – from analysis of law allowed for courts to operate in a moral vacuum and deliver some of the most detestable and reprehensible decisions rendered in history. An imperfect human institution, the Supreme Court of the United States has made and continues to make many errors. Sometimes the errors are minor, such as scrivener's error misattributing the publication year of a book,[2] and, rarely, the errors, on the wrong side of history, prove to be so egregious and perfidious as to undermine the public faith and harm the credibility of the institution and the government. Sometimes these poor decisions, rejected by jurists, scholars, and the public, fail to ossify in the record of *stare decisis* but rather come up again under the scrutiny of a future Supreme Court unbounded by attitudes and approaches that may have plagued earlier judicial line-ups. When the Court confronts an issue it decided prior and poorly, will it correct the matter?

While reasonable people may disagree over which historical decisions should draw the ire of fair-minded students of the law, we shall focus our discussion on several cases that the Supreme Court itself has, in time, repudiated for want of reason, want of principle, or want of legal or philosophical grounding. Most of these cases disproportionately relied on legal positivism that approximated a philosophical basis behind reckless decision-making condemned by dissenting justices and civil-minded members of society. We shall explore cases, often not only repudiated by dissenting opinions but also later overturned by the Supreme Court itself.

Plessy v. Ferguson: The Majority Errs in Upholding Forced Segregation but Harlan's Dissent Sheds Light on the Civil and Natural Rights Violations

Originalism again emerges in the Supreme Court's decision in *Plessy v. Ferguson* (1896).[3] The notorious case that gave us the standard of "separate, but equal" turned to positivism to avoid deciding a case based on principles well-known to the Framers – right and wrong – because such an analysis would produce an outcome that would profoundly disturb the *status quo*. In 1892, Homer Plessy, a man whose lineage claimed one-eighth African descent, bought a first-class ticket to ride the Louisiana intra-state railroad, and took a seat in the whites only car. Several years earlier, Louisiana had passed a law called the Separate Car Act which required that railroads create completely separate accommodations for blacks and whites such as separate train cars. Since he was of one-eighth African descent, Plessy fell into the classification that state law required he ride in the "colored" car.

A civil rights group called *The Citizens' Committee* convinced Plessy to purchase the ticket to use his example as a test case.[4] The East Louisiana Railroad had been informed of Plessy's lineage and intent to ride the car designated for whites. Plessy was arrested for violating the state ordinance and challenged the law, first in Louisiana by seeking a writ of prohibition against Judge John H. Ferguson, the judge for the criminal district court for the parish of New Orleans, first in the Supreme Court of Louisiana, and then, following its ruling, via petition to the Supreme Court of the United States.[5] The Supreme Court refused to invalidate the state law professing to be bound by the Constitution.[6]

The Court, after quoting the Louisiana statute, explained Plessy's plight as follows: The petition for the writ of prohibition averred that petitioner was seven eighths Caucasian and one eighth African blood; that the mixture of colored blood was not discernible in him, and that he was entitled to every right, privilege and immunity secured to citizens of the United States of the white race; and that, upon such theory, he took possession of a vacant seat in a coach where passengers of the white race were accommodated, and was ordered by the conductor to vacate said coach and take a seat in another assigned to persons of the colored race, and having refused to comply with such demand he was forcibly ejected with the aid of a police officer, and imprisoned in the parish jail to answer a charge of having violated the above act.[7]

In so doing, the Court revealed its own biases and predispositions to render a decision steeped wholly with the barrel dregs of racism. To the majority, odious *cultural distinctions* based upon race could be enforced by a state government so long as those distinctions did not threaten or result in disparate *legal treatment* based upon race. A statute which implies merely a legal distinction between the white and colored races — a distinction which is founded in the color of the two races, and which must always exist so long as white men are distinguished from the other race by color — has no tendency to destroy the legal equality of the two races, or reestablish a state of involuntary servitude.[8]

In other words, the Court maintained that separation based on race was not intrinsically wrong because mere *de jure* segregation did not necessarily imply, in the minds of the judges, that one racial or ethnic group was superior or inferior to the other. The Court explained that it:

> consider[ed] the underlying fallacy of the plaintiff's argument to consist in the assumption that the enforced separation of the two races stamps the colored race with a badge of inferiority. If this be so, it is not by reason of anything found in the act, but solely because the colored race chooses to put that construction upon it.[9]

The Court actually reasoned that forced segregation did not imply judicial or governmental favoritism between racial groups. Nor should it have made African Americans, who, the Court pointed out, simply *happened* to be the numerical minority in this case: [Plessy's argument] necessarily assumes that if, as has been more than once the case, and is not unlikely to be so again, the colored race should become the dominant power in the state legislature, and should enact a law in precisely similar terms, it would thereby relegate the white race to an inferior position. We imagine that the white race, at least, would not acquiesce in this assumption. The argument also assumes that social prejudices may be overcome by legislation, and that equal rights cannot be secured to the negro except by an enforced commingling of the two races. We cannot accept this proposition.[10]

The majority believed that "[i]f the two races are to meet upon terms of social equality, it must be the result of natural affinities, a mutual appreciation of each other's merits, and a voluntary consent of individuals."[11] It clearly felt that opposition to segregation presented some form of social engineering aimed at improving race relations. After all, the Court believed that the whole issue must take root in some underlying social insecurity felt by members of an entire designated race that had been nearly completely enslaved a mere 32 years earlier.[12] The majority felt: Legislation is powerless to eradicate racial instincts or to abolish distinctions based upon physical differences, and the attempt to do so can only result in accentuating the difficulties of the present situation. If the civil and political rights of both races be equal one cannot be inferior to the other civilly or politically. If one race be inferior to the other socially, the Constitution of the United States cannot put them upon the same plane.[13]

In affirming the statute,[14] the Court validated segregation its lone dissenter lampooned as "separate but equal."[15] Only Justice John Marshall Harlan dissented in *Plessy* and pointed to violations of civil and natural rights endemic to the majority's ruling. Denying that "that any legislative body or judicial tribunal may have regard to the race of citizens when the civil rights of those citizens are involved," Justice Harlan demonstrated the Natural Law belief in equality in shared humanity.[16] Continuing, "[i]ndeed, such legislation, as that here in question, is inconsistent not only with that equality of rights which pertains to citizenship, National and State, but with the personal liberty enjoyed by every one [sic] within the United States," Justice Harlan reveals a preference for Natural Law theories by invoking personal liberty.[17] Justice Harlan cites to Blackstone in explaining the meaning of personal liberty. "'Personal liberty,' it has been well said, 'consists in the power of locomotion, of changing situation, or removing one's person to whatsoever places one's own inclination may direct, without imprisonment or restraint, unless by due course of law.' 1 Bl. Com. *134."[18] Justice Harlan recognized the pejorative popular view of activist courts.[19]

The prescient Justice Harlan lamented, "[i]n my opinion, the judgment this day rendered will, in time, prove to be quite as pernicious as the decision made by this tribunal in the *Dred Scott* case."[20] "I am of opinion that the statute of Louisiana is inconsistent with the personal liberty of citizens, white and black, in that State, and hostile to both the spirit and letter of the Constitution of the United States."[21] That spirit would be the protection of the natural right to travel.

Lochner v. New York: A Glimmer of Hope for Natural Rights, Once Again Used to Uphold Contract Obligations

From time to time, however, the Court would opine on a matter in such a way as to give natural law adherents some glimmer of hope. In 1905, the Supreme Court ruled on a case called *Lochner v. New York* in which it found in favor of economic liberty over the power of a state legislature.[22]

Joseph Lochner, a bakery owner, challenged a New York law limiting the number of hours that bakers could work. He had been indicted for violating the statute, convicted, and fined $50.[23] He proceeded through the appellate courts in the state of New York which all found against him.[24] He eventually brought a Fourteenth Amendment Due Process Clause argument before the Supreme Court to challenge his conviction for "... permit[ing] an employee working for him to work [voluntarily] more than sixty hours in one week," in violation of a state law requiring New York bakery employees to work not more than fifty hours a week.[25] The Supreme Court found that:

> [t]he statute necessarily interferes with the right of contract between the employer and employees, concerning the number of hours in which the latter may labor in the bakery of the employer. The general right to make a contract in relation to his business is part of the liberty of the individual protected by the Fourteenth Amendment [Due Process Clause] of the Federal Constitution. . . . The right to purchase or to sell labor is part of the liberty protected by this amendment, unless there are circumstances which exclude the right.[26]

Despite the existence, at the time, of "somewhat vaguely termed police powers" which states possessed and which the "exact description and limitation of which have not been attempted by the courts[,]" the Supreme Court did not believe states had the power to encroach upon the right to contract for labor.[27] In the court's view, the absolute right to contract, however, is not completely sacrosanct. Limitations do exist. For instance, those "[c]ontracts in violation of a statute, either of the Federal or state government, or a contract to let one's property for immoral purposes, or to do any other unlawful act, could obtain no protection from the Federal Constitution, as coming under the liberty of person or of free contract."[28]

And, while certain circumstances may arise under which a state may rightfully set limitations on certain kinds of labor, or certain kinds of laborers, none of the acceptable reasons for doing so were present in the case of the New York statute in *Lochner* regulating the number of hours bakers could voluntarily work. In fact, the Court aggressively refuted the reasoning of the State of New York.

> There is no reasonable ground for interfering with the liberty of person or the right of free contract, by determining the hours of labor, in the occupation of a baker. There is no contention that bakers as a class are not equal in intelligence and capacity to men in other trades or manual occupations, or that they are not able to assert their rights and care for themselves without the protecting arm of the State, interfering with their independence of judgment and of action. They are in no sense wards of the State. Viewed in the light of a purely labor law, with no reference whatever to the question of health, we think that a law like the one before us involves neither the safety, the morals nor the welfare of the public, and that the interest of the public is not in the slightest degree affected by such an act.[29]

Certain classes of workers, such as sailors, were often treated to greater protections from the Court, because of the power disparity between sailors and officers, and the nearly limitless power of the captains of vessels when at sea. The courts also smiled kindly upon certain wards of the state. Miners whose arduous labor presented specific health risks as a result of exposure to the byproducts of mining also received special consideration. However, as the Court explained, bakers did not need such special attention and special consideration. "We think the limit of the police power has been reached and passed in this case," the Court expounded.[30] "There is, in our judgment, no reasonable foundation for holding this to be necessary or appropriate as a health law to safeguard the public health or the health of the individuals who are following the trade of a baker."[31]

Though the majority of the Court, speaking though Justice Rufus Peckham, embraced Natural Law theory regarding the natural right to contract, several justices dissented, including the scion of American Legal Realism, Justice Oliver Wendell Holmes. Holmes believed the Court's decision ran contrary to the popular belief in economic theory.[32] He argued that:

> It [was] settled by various decisions of this court that state constitutions and state laws may regulate life in many ways which we as legislators might think as injudicious or if you like as tyrannical as this, and which equally with this interfere with the liberty to contract.[33]

To Holmes, the fact that the courts had contemplated and ruled on the matter should prove sufficient to put it to rest. Holmes's version of legal positivism focused more on the common law than statutes, and argued, with a peculiar sense of propriety, on the power of judges to render decisions based on precedent and the Constitution so long as Holmes agreed with them.

"The liberty of the citizen to do as he likes so long as he does not interfere with the liberty of others to do the same," Holmes explained, "is interfered with by school laws, by the Post Office, by every state or municipal institution which takes his money for purposes thought desirable, whether he likes it or not."[34] To Holmes, such a history demonstrated a sufficient rational basis for the New York law. With so many interferences with personal liberty, why quibble at one more? Holmes, a Legal Realist, felt that "[e]very opinion tends to become law," and that "the word liberty in the Fourteenth Amendment is perverted when it is held to prevent the natural outcome of a dominant opinion."[35] Though he admits that such a use would be fine when "a rational and a fair man necessarily would admit that the statute proposed would infringe fundamental principles as they have been understood by the traditions of our people and our law."[36] Though Holmes had earlier condemned dogmatic adherence to law encrusted with the patina of age,[37] he seems to have forgotten himself while scrambling for philosophical grounding in his dissent. Such is the way of the Legal Realist and legal positivism and such would persist as the United States sought to justify egregious violations of natural rights nearly 40 years later.

Wickard v. Filburn: Paternalism During the New Deal Leads to an Invasion of Natural Rights

In 1942, as war consumed Europe and the United States engaged Japanese forces in the Pacific Theatre, the Supreme Court still sat, still heard cases, and rendered a decision on a subject as innocuous sounding as acres of wheat, but it created ripples so resonant as to permit Congress to regulate the otherwise lawful activity of growing crops on one's own property for one's own personal use. In *Wickard v. Filburn*, the Supreme Court upheld a ruling that Roscoe Filburn, an Ohio farmer, who had planted around 12 acres of wheat, .09 acres more than the 11.1 acres set by the Agricultural Adjustment Act of 1938, was therefore subject to fines. This Act, the court held, did not violate the Commerce Clause of the

Constitution.[38] Filburn "operated a small farm in Montgomery County, Ohio," and "maintain[ed] a herd of dairy cattle, selling milk, raising poultry, and selling poultry and eggs."[39] He would plant and grow a small amount of winter wheat, sell a bit of it, use the rest in feed for his livestock, grind into flour for home use, and then hold the remainder for seeding his crops the following year.[40] Filburn argued that his growth and consumption of the additional wheat remained a local matter and thus did not fall within the reach of the Commerce Clause which grants Congress the power to regulate interstate commerce.[41]

In the view of the Court, Congress already had the power to regulate the prices of commodities since those commodities travel in interstate commerce and the conditions of that commerce impacts prices.[42] "One of the primary purposes of the Act in question," the Court held, "was to increase the market price of wheat, and to that end to limit the volume thereof that could affect the market."[43] So, according to the Court, if Congress intended to regulate the price of wheat, it could do so through expansive means such as setting limits on the volume that could be produced.

Despite acknowledging that one family's production alone would likely have an *immeasurable impact* on the overall price of wheat,[44] the Supreme Court adopted its aggregation theory and held that when combined with other personal producers of immeasurable impact, the effect could, in the aggregate, be substantial enough to make the activity measurable and thus subject to congressional regulation:

> The maintenance by government regulation of a price for wheat undoubtedly can be accomplished as effectively by sustaining or increasing the demand as by limiting the supply. The effect of the statute before us is to restrict the amount which may be produced for market and the extent as well to which one may forestall resort to the market by producing to meet his own needs. That appellee's own contribution to the demand for wheat may be trivial by itself is not enough to remove him from the scope of federal regulation where, as here, *his contribution, taken together with that of many others similarly situated*, is far from trivial.[45]

Such inanity, bordering on insanity, characterized much of the paternalistic New Deal-Era sentiment of government and arguably represents the most far reaching example of Congress's authority to regulate under the Commerce Clause.[46] *Wickard* is not merely an evasion of the natural right to grow food supplies for one's family, it is an invasion of that right.

Korematsu v. United States: Positivism and Racism in the Majority, and Many Dissenters Who Look to Natural Rights

The Supreme Court again turned to positivism in the twentieth century to justify an opinion that today ranks with the *Dred Scott* opinion as an embarrassing positivistic reach in order to please political forces at play. In 1942, Fred Korematsu, an American of Japanese ancestry born in Oakland, California, was convicted of violating a federal order[47] issued by an Army general acting under powers granted via presidential authority and, authorized by congressional statute.[48] The "law" Korematsu was convicted of violating was an order from the general; it was not a federal statute.

Following the attack on Pearl Harbor on December 7, 1941, the United States, swept up in a frenzied fear of invasion, resorted to the lesser angels of human nature and branded all persons in the country with Japanese heritage as potential saboteurs, loyal not to the United States – despite the fact that most were natural-born U.S. citizens – but rather to the Emperor of Japan. A series of military rules never voted upon by Congress, governing civilians were put into place giving the military powers to take sweeping steps in the name of "protection against espionage and sabotage."[49]

The U.S. District Court for the Northern District of California originally found Korematsu guilty of violating the order and determined that Korematsu should be placed under probation for five years and that the judgement be suspended.[50] He appealed to the Circuit Court of Appeals for the Ninth Circuit, which questioned whether it enjoyed jurisdiction over the case since the determination had been probation rather than a formal sentencing.[51] The Supreme Court found that the order was final and appealable, and remanded the case back to the lower courts.[52] Having settled the jurisdictional question, the Ninth Circuit affirmed Korematsu's conviction,[53] and he appealed to the Supreme Court once again which agreed to hear his case.[54]

While Justice Hugo Black, writing for the Supreme Court acknowledged "that all legal restrictions which curtail the civil rights of a single racial group are immediately suspect[,]" he nonetheless added, "[t]hat is not to say that all such restrictions are unconstitutional [...but rather that ...] courts must subject them to the most rigid scrutiny."[55] Foreshadowing the Court's conclusion, he explained that while "[p]ressing public necessity may sometimes justify the existence of such restrictions; racial antagonism never can."[56] Accordingly, he reasoned that:

Compulsory exclusion of large groups of citizens from their homes, except under circumstances of direct emergency and peril, is inconsistent with our basic governmental institutions. But when under conditions of modern warfare our shores are threatened by hostile forces, the power to protect must be commensurate with the threatened danger.[57]

> Contrary to natural reason, the Court found that: Korematsu was not excluded from the Military Area because of hostility to him or his race. He was excluded because we are at war with the Japanese Empire, because the properly constituted military authorities feared an invasion

of our West Coast and felt constrained to take proper security measures, because they decided that the military urgency of the situation demanded that all citizens of Japanese ancestry be segregated from the West Coast temporarily, and finally, because Congress, reposing its confidence in this time of war in our military leaders — as inevitably it must — determined that they should have the power to do just this.[58]

Relying on positivistic lines of argument, the majority of the Court ignored *Marbury v. Madison* and its progeny, and failed to conclude that the rules targeting those of Japanese descent solely for their ancestry run contrary to the principles of the Natural Law theory and, indeed, the Constitution itself. Despite the majority's coy use of language, it was clear to nearly everyone, but the military and the Roosevelt administration, it seems, that the rules targeted certain people not because of the character of their actions but rather for the character of their genes.

The Court was not unanimous, however. Justice Owen Roberts opened his dissent with a bang: "I dissent, because I think the indisputable facts exhibit a clear violation of Constitutional rights."[59] Contrary to the opinion of the majority, Roberts found: On the contrary, it is the case of convicting a citizen as a punishment for not submitting to imprisonment in a concentration camp, based on his ancestry, and solely because of his ancestry, without evidence or inquiry concerning his loyalty and good disposition towards the United States. If this be a correct statement of the facts disclosed by this record, and facts of which we take judicial notice, I need hardly labor the conclusion that Constitutional rights have been violated.[60]

He also criticized the Court for what he believed was a decision that changed the rules, and he did so hinting at the Augustinian/Thomistic rubric that an unjust law is no law:

> Again it is a new doctrine of constitutional law that one indicted for disobedience to an unconstitutional statute may not defend on the ground of the invalidity of the statute but must obey it though he knows *it is no law* and, after he has suffered the disgrace of conviction and lost his liberty by sentence, then, and not before, seek, from within prison walls, to test the validity of the law.[61]

Clearly, Justice Roberts was furious with the Court's decision.[62] And Owen Roberts was not the only dissenter. Justice Frank Murphy, a former U.S. Attorney General, began his dissent with an even weightier declarative than Justice Roberts:

> This exclusion of "all persons of Japanese ancestry, both alien and nonalien," from the Pacific Coast area on a plea of military necessity in the absence of martial law ought not to be approved. Such exclusion goes

over "the very brink of constitutional power" and falls into the ugly abyss of racism.[63]

Responding to the claims aimed at justifying the military's rules, Murphy argued:

> In support of this blanket condemnation of all persons of Japanese descent, however, no reliable evidence is cited to show that such individuals were generally disloyal, or had generally so conducted themselves in this area as to constitute a special menace to defense installations or war industries, or had otherwise by their behavior furnished reasonable ground for their exclusion as a group.[64]

After explaining the faulty grounds upon which the military orders had been issued,[65] he accepted that while *some* people of Japanese descent may have given aid to Japan, that there were also those of Italian and German descent in the United States, too—and, yet none of them faced that same treatment as those of Japanese heritage.[66] Justice Murphy lamented the uniform treatment of Japanese Americans as though they presented some monolithic threat rather than the recognition that every person is an individual possessing natural rights.[67] He concluded:

> I dissent, therefore, from this legalization of racism. Racial discrimination in any form and in any degree has no justifiable part whatever in our democratic way of life. It is unattractive in any setting but it is utterly revolting among a free people who have embraced the principles set forth in the Constitution of the United States. All residents of this nation are kin in some way by blood or culture to a foreign land. Yet they are primarily and necessarily a part of the new and distinct civilization of the United States. They must accordingly be treated at all times as the heirs of the American experiment and as entitled to all the rights and freedoms guaranteed by the Constitution.[68]

Justice Robert Jackson, another former U.S. Attorney General, who would later serve as Chief United States Prosecutor at Nuremberg, also dissented from the majority's opinion. He underscored Justice Murphy's reasoning as to the disparate treatment of Japanese Americans compared to descendants from the other warring nations.[69] He feared the impact of the Court's opinion as to the military exclusion order: But once a judicial opinion rationalizes such an order to show that it conforms to the Constitution, or rather rationalizes the Constitution to show that the Constitution sanctions such an order, the Court for all time has validated the principle of racial discrimination in criminal procedure and of transplanting American citizens.[70]

He feared that "*[t]he principle then lies about like a loaded weapon ready for the hand of any authority that can bring forward a plausible claim of an urgent need.*"[71] Justice Jackson felt that the decision enshrined within the common law "discrimination on the basis of ancestry" and that, as a result, "[n]ow the principle of racial discrimination is pushed from support of mild measures to very harsh ones, and from temporary deprivations to indeterminate ones."[72]

Rather, he argued:

> I should hold that a civil court cannot be made to enforce an order which violates constitutional limitations even if it is a reasonable exercise of military authority. The courts can exercise only the judicial power, can apply only law, and must abide by the Constitution, or they cease to be civil courts and become instruments of military policy.[73]

POST-WORLD WAR II: THE REEMERGENCE OF MORALITY AS A LODESTAR AND A RETURN TO NATURAL LAW PHILOSOPHICAL DEBATES

Though legal positivism had clearly displaced Natural Law Tradition as the preferred mode of approaching constitutional and statutory interpretation through most of the nineteenth and early twentieth centuries, it failed to correct for egregious abuses executed by foreign governments. Following World War II, "jurisprudential thinking generally moved towards a theoretical interest in Natural Law justifications."[74]

The failure of legal positivism to allow for the charges levied in the Nuremberg Trials, such as "Crimes against Humanity" left scholars struggling to find some theoretical foundation upon which to justify the prosecutions. Professor Anthony Lisska of Denison University, a specialist in Thomism explained, "[i]f the Nuremberg Trials with their accompanying charges of 'Crimes against Humanity' were to have a theoretical foundation, then one needed a radically different account of the nature of law from that proposed by the then reigning theory, legal positivism."[75] Stated differently, "the positivist view of law steeped in the voluntarist tradition could not make the theoretical case for 'Crimes against Humanity' so central to the war crimes trial."[76] As a result, legal scholars scrambled to find rational justifications to bring such charges against the accused Nazi war criminals.

Since legal positivism required a legitimate authority to adopt a law through a legitimate process and promulgate it, how could the war's victors prosecute bad actors unless the prosecuting authority enjoyed some preexisting jurisdiction? "The fundamental postulate of positivism – that law must be strictly severed from morality – seems to deny the possibility of any bridge between the obligation to obey law and other moral obligations."[77]

Moreover, many questioned whether "legal positivism, as practiced and preached in Germany, had... any causal connection with Hitler's ascent to power" to begin with.[78] Lon Fuller (1902-1979), the noted Harvard Law professor and American legal theorist, argued the "German legal positivism not only banned from legal science any consideration of the moral ends of law, but it was also indifferent to ... the inner morality of law itself."[79] In a resilient rebuke of positivism, and a subtle embrace of Thomism and the strict adherence to the written law it commands, Professor Fuller proclaimed:

> When a system calling itself law is predicated upon a general disregard by judges of the terms of the laws they purport to enforce, when this system habitually cures its legal irregularities, even the grossest, by retroactive statutes, when it has only to resort to forays of terror in the streets, which no one dares challenge, in order to escape even those scant restraints imposed by the pretence of legality - when all these things have become true of a dictatorship, *it is not hard for me, at least, to deny to it the name of law.*[80]

With positivism as the intellectual basis for the Nuremberg laws and all the legal atrocities they brought about in the Nazi regime, it is no wonder the world shunned such modern-day Benthamism in favor of a Thomistic approach that emphasized moral reasoning.

Scholars soon welcomed Natural Law theory back into the jurisprudential canon[81] as legal positivism lacked the grounding and flexibility to bring about renewed global order following the industrial and mechanized atrocities carried out in Fascist Europe on a scale nearly inconceivable to human imagination. "From mid-century onwards, several philosophers of law from different philosophical perspectives produced monographs dealing with different aspects of natural law jurisprudence," Lisska observed.[82] "While some were developed in more detail and general agreement with Aquinas than others, most referred to Aquinas's account of natural law as the classical foundation for such discussion in Western philosophy."[83] This renewed interest in Natural Law theory spawned critical examinations of its concepts from legal theories and scholars seeking to recast the ideas of thinkers and philosophers like Aquinas into contemporary terms and considering the changes in law, moral philosophy, and society since the times of Aquinas.[84]

Between 1950 and 1965, Leo Strauss published *Natural Right and History* (1953), H.L.A. Hart published *The Concept of Law* (1961), and Lon Fuller published *The Morality of Law* (1964), the latter of which will be visited in the following chapters. Each of these thinkers sought to develop and expand further the theories traceable to Aquinas on the necessary moral character of law to aid in the establishment of a harmonious and just society, while maximizing government defense of personal liberty.

Leo Strauss

Straus (1899-1973) began his work, *Natural Right and History*, by revisiting Jefferson's oft-quoted natural law axiom, regarding equality in creation, and the inalienability of life, liberty, and the pursuit of happiness.[85] Though published in 1953, Strauss's book actually began as a series of lectures that he delivered at the University of Chicago in 1949, three years after the conclusion of the trials at Nuremberg. He focused on the lamentable departure from Natural Law theory and the consummate impact of such a departure from the moral landscape of Germany.[86] Strauss agreed with prominent German scholars that the German departure from natural law principles, in part, yielded ground to "unqualified relativism"[87] which, if not contributed to, permitted the barbaric practices of Nazi Germany. In light of such atrocities, Strauss both lamented and sought to dispel the "[p]resent-day American social science, as far as it is not Roman Catholic social science, [which had been] dedicated to the proposition that all men are endowed by the evolutionary process or by a mysterious fate with many kinds of urges and aspirations, but certainly no natural right."[88]

The general academy, much to his chagrin, had sought to reduce humanity and human behavior to measurable biological impulses rather than exquisite beings endowed with the spark of Reason, rejecting the concept that the exercise of Reason upon natural aspirations is meaningless without robust recognition of natural rights.

Strauss would have none of this. He urged a return to the acknowledgement and consideration of theories of natural rights. Writing just four years after the conclusion of World War II, he argued "the need for natural right is as evident today as it has been for centuries and even millennia."[89] He continued, "[t]o reject natural right is tantamount to saying that all right is positive right," and, as a result, "what is right is determined exclusively by the legislators and the courts of the various countries."[90] Misplaced reliance on permission from organs of government to create rights plows fertile ground for governmental despotism, rejecting that the exercise of reason upon natural aspirations is meaningless without natural rights, and is the plaything of the positivist, Mr. Bentham!

Strauss even spoke of the consideration of when a law or decision is "unjust"[91] as requiring some independent standard of right and wrong that exists outside of the positive framework created by legislators.[92] He explained the need to manage the competing values within a society and concludes that the "problem posed by the conflicting needs of society cannot be solved if we do not possess knowledge of natural right."[93] Accordingly, "[t]he contemporary rejection of natural right leads to nihilism— nay, it is identical with nihilism."[94] Finally, Strauss brought himself to acknowledge that Natural Law theory is more than just "urges" and "aspirations;" and does not require an acceptance of Roman Catholic "social science [sic.]" (by which he must have meant the social justice teachings of Pope Leo XIII, promulgated in his encyclical *Rerum Novarum* in 1891).

To Strauss, the contemporary problem with natural rights was "a matter of recollection rather than [a matter] of actual knowledge."[95] It appears Strauss believed the ground well-trodden, if forgotten. Therefore, he called for exhaustive study and analysis.[96] The two camps, as Strauss saw them, "liberals of various descriptions" and "Catholic and non-Catholic [often scholarly Jewish] disciples of Thomas Aquinas"[97] needed to come to a common, contemporary understanding of natural right which, "in its classic form is connected with a theological view of the universe,"[98] for, "in the case of man, reason is required for discerning [the operations of life and order]."[99] Strauss believed that "reason determines what is by nature right with ultimate regard to man's natural end."[100] Aquinas could not have said it better.

Strauss's work took an extensive and expansive historical approach to framing natural right through analysis of thinkers from Plato and Aristotle to Strauss's own contemporaries. He explored the notions of natural right in classical antiquity and modern history, with special attention to Hobbes and Locke, and Rousseau and Burke. Strauss's foundational work marked the beginning of a rebirth of academic interest in natural law and natural rights. In many ways, Strauss's *Natural Rights and History*, in the tradition of Coke's *Institutes*, became the harbinger of natural rights theory in the twentieth century.

Edwin S. Corwin

A contemporary of Strauss, who also contributed greatly to the field of natural law jurisprudence was longtime Princeton Professor Edwin S. Corwin (1878-1963). Corwin published extensively on the Constitution and its power over American law and was widely read, including by your author as a Princeton undergraduate, where I studied politics in Corwin Hall. In a series of articles, later collected as a book called *The Higher Law Background of American Constitutional Law*, Corwin viewed the dual-sources of the constitutions *legality* and *supremacy* as originating from two competing beliefs.[101] First, the "the so-called 'positive' conception of law as a general expression merely for the particular commands of a human lawgiver, as a series of acts of human will[,]" and the other, "that the highest possible source of such commands, because the highest possible embodiment of human will, is 'the people.'"[102] Corwin believed, however, that "[t]he attribution of supremacy to the Constitution on the ground solely of its root[s] in popular will represents... a comparatively late outgrowth of American constitutional theory" since "supremacy accorded to constitutions was ascribed less to their putative source than to their supposed content, to their embodiment of essential and unchanging justice."[103] He felt, rather that:

> There are, it is predicated, certain principles of right and justice which are entitled to prevail of their own intrinsic excellence, altogether regardless of the attitude of those who wield the physical resources of the community. Such principles were made by no human hands; indeed,

if they did not antedate deity itself, they still so express its nature as to bind and control it. They are external to all Will as such and interpenetrate all Reason as such. They are eternal and immutable. In relation to such principles, human laws are, when entitled to obedience save as to matters indifferent, merely a record or transcript, and their enactment act not of will or power but one of discovery and declaration.[104]

Moreover, Corwin believed that:

The Ninth Amendment of the Constitution of the United States, in its stipulation that 'the enumeration of certain rights in this Constitution shall not prejudice other rights not so enumerated,' illustrates this theory perfectly, except that the principles of transcendental justice have been here translated into terms of personal and private rights. The relation of such rights, nevertheless, to governmental power is the same as that of the principles from which they spring and which they reflect. They owe nothing to their recognition in the Constitution - such recognition was necessary if the Constitution was to be regarded as complete.[105]

In so concluding, Corwin explained that the inclusion of the Ninth Amendment to the Constitution manifests in the *supremacy* of the Constitution a concept that commands the government to protect rights beyond those solely on the words on the page: "*Thus the legality of the Constitution, its supremacy, and its claim to be worshipped, alike find common standing ground on the belief in a law superior to the will of human governors.*"[106]

Following Strauss and Corwin, scholars and theorists, such as H.L.A. Hart and Lon Fuller, began to explore the role of competing schools of jurisprudence in the modern age and how we could apply such principles and ideas in a world that had survived the horrors of the world wars, and was facing the rise of Communism, the Korean War, the baby boomers, and the changes to society along gender and racial lines following the end of World War II.

This new generation of mid-twentieth century scholars, beginning with Corwin and Strauss, examined Aquinas and labored to update Natural Law theories to fit a contemporary understanding of legal and moral philosophy responding to the vicissitudes wrought by the first half of the twentieth century. Each added to and refined the theories of those who came before and established a modern foundation for the later twentieth century scholars who would follow. This includes H.L.A. Hart who took on Lord Patrick Devlin and Professor Lon Fuller; brilliant scholars locked in lifelong, jolly academic combat. They debated morality and law in the late 1950s and elevated the tenor of discussion from mere rhetorical, armchair philosophy to the main battleground of judicial philosophy that may represent the most significant modern conflict over the soul of American jurisprudence. To this illuminating debate we now turn.

CHAPTER 13

EARLY MODERN NATURAL LAW THEORY AND NEW POSITIVISM

The Argument

While legal positivism dominated the field of jurisprudence, two of Bentham's disciples distinguished themselves and made their own significant contributions to the field. John Austin built upon Bentham's approach to laws and morals, while John Stuart Mill explored Bentham's ideas of Utilitarianism.

In the twentieth century, H.L.A. Hart carried Austin's torch and elevated modern notions of legal positivism, while Lon Fuller became the standard bearer in modern Natural Law theory in which he incorporated some of the Millian Harm Principle.

Hart debated all comers, such as Professor Lon Fuller, the renowned English judge Lord Patrick Devlin, and, as we shall visit later, the American legal theorist Ronald Dworkin.

To many, Hart represented the spiritual successor to Bentham and the largest positivist lighting rod worthy of the most serious and thorough criticism.

Through debate with the boogeyman of Hart and his new positivism did the early modern Natural Law theorists strengthen and clarify their arguments and develop modern approaches to natural law more consistent with contemporary sensibilities.

***

No one will deny that wrong statutes can be and are enforced, and we should not all agree as to which were the wrong ones.[1]

– Oliver Wendell Holmes, Jr. (1841-1935)

THE DEBATE BETWEEN
JOHN AUSTIN AND JOHN STUART MILL

Though the field of American jurisprudence was dominated by legal positivism in the nineteenth and early twentieth centuries, some scholars and thinkers strived to develop or discover alternative philosophies by which to evaluate and interpret the manner in which societies organized and self-regulated. In many ways, it can be said that the two most prominent thinkers with the largest influence on western jurisprudence were both descended from a common philosophical ancestor who has been in these pages before, Jeremy Bentham. The story of nineteenth century jurisprudential thought is a tale of two Johns; John Austin and John Stuart Mill.

Mill and Austin were friends. Each knew and admired Bentham. Each, influenced by Bentham's ideas, explored different reasoned outcomes of Bentham's precepts. Austin (1790-1859) very much advanced the Benthamite desire to purge from manmade law any consideration of natural or moral content or influence.[2] To Austin, law came from a sovereign[3] who ensured compliance in a population through the threat of sanction or punishment. The existence of such laws, said Austin, accompanied by threat of sanction, had the effect of creating legal obligations to comply.

The Austinian model considers a sort of top-down approach in which a cloistered body of superiors establishes the rules that supposedly govern themselves and actually govern their inferiors. A reflection of the times, Austin, no doubt sought ways to legitimize the English parliamentary model in which unlike counterparts in the United States, English men and women remained not *citizens* of England but rather *subjects* to their royal sovereign. H. L. A. Hart, whom we will visit in this chapter, faulted Austin for many oversights, such as the failure to consider and discuss laws that create no threat of sanction but rather grant powers to officials or create rights for citizens, such as the right to vote.

John Stuart Mill (1806-1873), sixteen years younger than Austin, explored government power and political relationships, with an eye to how society at large exerted power over individuals. Whereas Austin focused on the ways, in his mind, to exert power properly over individuals and to justify that use of power, Mill appeared more interested in understanding it. To that end, he engaged in a series of explorations into the origins of liberty, or, essentially, the relationship between rights and privileges of the citizenry and how those rights and privileges wax and wane in the shadows cast by government.

During his lifetime, Mill published a number of books, treatises, essays, and monographs on a range of subjects as diverse as liberty,[4] positivism,[5] utilitarianism,[6] the subjection of women,[7] political economy,[8] logic,[9] religion,[10] and representative government.[11] Mill developed Bentham's notion of *felicity calculus*, or the idea that we can measure the beneficial utility of any action by evaluating the level of aggregate pleasure or pain a particular action would cause. Through a thorough and studied application of considerations which Bentham referred to as *circumstances*, one could approach every decision through a scientific algorithm to seek to create the greatest benefit.[12] Extrapolated and applied to the whole of society, the doctrine could become an axiomatic approach which called for steps to ensure the greatest good, or happiness for the greatest number of people. This is a theory of government, based on positivism, for the societal or collective good; decidedly not for the protection of the individual.

Mill recognized the absurdity of Bentham's wholly detached approach and argued for a modified version. "It is quite compatible with the principle of utility to recognize the fact, that some *kinds* of pleasure are more desirable and valuable than others," Mill observed.[13] Continuing, "[i]t would be absurd that while, in estimating all other things, quality is considered as well as quantity, the estimation of pleasures should be supposed to depend on quality alone," Mill rejected Bentham's calculus of scale and argued instead for an approach that, structurally, bears similarities to Thomistic Natural Law theory.

While Aquinas advocated for reliance on human reason to derive a rational set of rules aimed at doing good and avoiding evil, Mill adopted a more secular approach arguing that humanity functioned at its best when it sought to achieve the maximum amount of happiness for the largest number of people. Mill believed that each of us seeks to maximize our own pleasure so, in turn each of us should desire to maximize the pleasure of society at large. Whereas Bentham's legal positivism focused on inputs and rules to guide outcomes, Mill's utilitarianism focused on creating desired outcomes, such as the maximization of collective happiness, through rules.

Mill also introduced a principle of the use of power in relation to harm that now bears his name. The *Millian Harm Principle* states that "the only purpose for which power can be rightfully exercised over any member of a civilized community, against his will, is to prevent harm to others."[14] This idea, explored later by lower case "L" liberal and eventually libertarian philosophers, speaks to the principles of limited powers of government reflective of a doctrinal approach which prohibits interference in the liberty of a man or woman unless he or she acts in a manner to interfere with the liberty of others. As we shall soon see, economists and philosophers like Ludwig von Mises and Murray Rothbard, advanced and updated Mill's Harm Principle so as to expand its prescience and applicability to twentieth century sensibilities, and pronounced it as the Non-Aggression Principle, which is examined at length in Chapter 16.

One can see Mill turning from the influence of Bentham in *On Liberty*, where Mill explains:

[t]he object of [On Liberty was] to assert one very simple principle, as entitled to govern absolutely the dealings of society with the individual

in the way of compulsion and control, whether the means used be physical force in the form of legal penalties, or the moral coercion of public opinion.[15]

Mill opposed tyranny[16] and believed that individuals could best judge their own needs.[17]

Mill explained three conditions necessary for a society consistent with human liberty. First the society must not restrict thought or opinion.[18] Second, people must have the ability to pursue their own interests and ends so long as they do not aim to harm others.[19] Finally, individuals shall remain free to unite with others or around others, so long as they do not join others in order to harm them, and that they have reached adulthood and not joined under threat or coercion.[20] "No society in which these liberties are not on the whole, respected, is free, whatever may be its form of government; and none is completely free in which they do not exist absolute and unqualified."[21] This is far more Grotius and Rothbard than it is Bentham.

Mill advocated for an approach to the organization of a society that aimed for specific outcomes, such as the maximization of happiness, through a minimalistic government that encroached on personal liberty *only* when necessary to prevent harm to others. This philosophy had little need for process, and little need for a Benthamite-like complex series of rules and procedures, but rather questioned only whether the rules involved sought to maximize the happiness of those in the society while inflicting the fewest and least encroachments on individual liberty. Such a system of beliefs could lead to outcomes seemingly contrary to the process-obsessed positivists like Bentham, and his twentieth century disciple H. L. A. Hart.

H.L.A. HART CARRIES THE TORCH OF AUSTIN

Hart (1907-1992), a longtime Oxford professor of jurisprudence, carried on the work of Bentham and Austin and addressed many of the oversights that critics had recognized over the decades since Austin's death.[22] For instance, Hart announced a distinction between primary legal rules, such as laws that govern behavior like criminal conduct, and secondary rules, such as those that dictate procedures and the manner of enforcement of primary rules.[23] In Hart's view, "law may most illuminatingly be characterized as a union of primary rules of obligation with such secondary rules."[24] Those secondary rules focused mostly on how the process of primary rules came into existence.[25]

Hart laid out a series of three principal secondary rules. The "Rule of Recognition," based on the notion of the *grundnorm* or basic norm first promulgated by the Austrian legal philosopher, Hans Kelsen, which called for some publicly available means by which members of a society could learn of the existence of a primary rule.[26] This rule of promulgation need not exist in an explicit fashion, but could rather take the form of a normative or customary approach to the manner in which a society promulgated its rules.[27]

Societies, however, never remain static, so Hart suggested the addition of a second rule, called the "Rule of Change," which provided for the ability and process by which to alter, adjust, amend, or abandon old rules.[28] Finally, in the event that a member of a society was suspected of violating a primary rule, a secondary set of "Rules of Adjudication" must exist to designate a process as well as persons to oversee that process to evaluate suspected violation of the rule and mete out the appropriate consequences.[29]

While Hart made several contributions to the field of jurisprudence, he also became a rather popular antagonist to other legal philosophers, and served as the other half of a series of significant debates with Lord Patrick Devlin, Lon Fuller,[30] and, later, Ronald Dworkin.

The Debate Between H.L.A Hart and Lon Fuller

Lon Fuller argued for a structured secular form of Natural Law theory that responded to twentieth century critiques of Natural Law theory. Born in 1902 in Texas, Fuller lived through both World Wars, the roaring twenties, the Great Depression, and the rise and fall of totalitarianism and fascism in Europe. Witnessing the dangerous consequences of moral relativism in Europe and dogmatic adherence to legal positivism in the United States, Fuller grew dissatisfied with the existing explorations and explanations of law and morality. Indeed, he began his 1964 book, *On Law and Morals* by declaring, "[t]he content of these chapters has been chiefly shaped by a dissatisfaction with the existing literature concerning the relationship between law and morality."[31]

In *On Law and Morals*, Fuller explored themes and levelled charges famously laid against Hart in the Harvard Law Review in 1958.[32] Fuller, using a rhetorical flourish, levied cutting arguments against Hart, but walked them back by excusing them as merely his initial impressions. At first, Fuller accused Hart of making confusing, inconsistent arguments.[33] Like a good legal positivist, Hart echoed Bentham's distinctions between what "is" and "what ought to be." Fuller, in turn, mocked Hart: "It is not clear, in other words, whether in Professor Hart's own thinking the distinction between law and morality simply 'is,' or is something that 'ought to be' and that we should join with him in helping to create and maintain."[34] Though Fuller dismissed these as simple initial impressions,[35] he published them nonetheless.

Fuller's response to Hart comes down to a fundamental difference, in many ways, of perception. Fuller explained this difference as one in which different camps disagreed on causes and meanings. "On the one side, we encounter a series of definitional fiats," Fuller wrote.[36] "A rule of law is – that is to say, it really and simply and always is – the command of a sovereign, a rule laid down by a judge, a prediction of the future incidence of state force, a pattern of official behavior, etc."[37] However, "[w]hen we ask what purpose these definitions serve, we receive the answer, 'Why, no purpose, except to describe accurately the social reality that corresponds to the word 'law.'"[38] Fuller showed that, to the legal positivist, a dogmatic servant of process and procedure, a law represents what simply *is*.

Just as with the laws of physics, such as gravity, laws exist to a positivist as a tautological series of facts. A Hartian positivist does not care *why* a society has deemed theft a crime but only that a society *has* deemed theft a crime and taken the proper and appropriate steps to *announce* its criminality and prepare for adjudication in the instance of a suspected theft. To Fuller, and all Natural Law theorists, theft is a crime because it materially interferes with property rights, which are natural. Fuller also points out that a procedural Natural Law theorist would object to the Hartian formulation and response to the query about the reason for a rule of law. Whereas the positivist accepts without question that the law simply is, the Natural Law theorist disagrees: "'But it doesn't look like that to me[.]'" to which the positivist replies, "'Well, it does to me.' There the matter has to rest."[39]

Fuller's chief objection arises out of what he perceived as the persistent obstinance of legal positivists to recognize and acknowledge that the reasons for rules of law emanate from a source tied to our shared humanity. "Our dissatisfaction [with the positivistic approach] arose not merely from the impasse we confronted, but because this impasse seemed to us so unnecessary."[40] Fuller saw the possibility of détente were the positivists simply to acknowledge that their "definitions of 'what law really is' are not mere images of some datum of experience, but direction posts for the application of human energies."[41] Positivists had fought to remove the humanity from manmade law and replace it with some peculiar simplistic formulation of fact and process without an understanding or acknowledgement of the human factor. Fuller was astounded that any person, positivist or not, could make this argument with memories of twentieth century Europe still fresh.

Fuller recognized in Hart's arguments "a new and promising turn."[42] Hart had defended Bentham and Austin by explaining that none ever "denied that, as a matter of historical fact, the development of legal systems had been profoundly influenced by law, so that the content of many legal rules mirrored moral rules or principles."[43] Further, Hart explained that none rejected or denied the existence of morals, or that "by explicit legal provisions moral principles might at different points be brought into a legal system and form a part of its rules, or that courts might be legally bound to decide in accordance with what they thought just or best."[44]

Instead, Hart argued, that Bentham and Austin "were anxious to assert" that a rule of law that violated moral standards could still be a law, and that a rule consistent with standards or morality did not mean that such a rule achieved the status of a law.[45] In other words, to Hart, moral rules and norms could influence and inspire the creation of some laws, but such an incursion better represented the normative attitudes of those members of society charged with creating primary rules rather than comprising a component necessary to their legitimacy. Stated differently, to Bentham, Austin, and Hart, the sovereign could make theft of property legal. Both Hart and Fuller, however, seem to have agreed upon the necessity of respect for and fidelity to the law.[46]

Fuller proposed that law in a society eventually achieves its own implicit morality if it is to achieve its own ends and goals.[47] Eventually, unjust or inconsistent regimes that fail to command the respect of the governed can correct course or fail to supply that society with what can be justly called "law." Fuller called this process "the internal morality of law" and explained how Hart neglected to account for it in his writings.[48] Fuller believed that shared morality can always catch up with and modify positive law, lest revolution do so. Failing to understand how law achieves a moral equilibrium, Hart provided a seemingly thorough, but hollow, explanation for the structure of law without exploring its purpose which echoed the sentiments of Bentham and Austin that ossified jurisprudence for over a century.

However, the ossification of jurisprudential thought wrought by positivism did not always result in the retardation of social progress. In 1957, a committee advising the British Parliament released a report, popularly referred to as the Wolfenden Report finding that the United Kingdom should no longer consider consensual homosexual behavior between adults to be criminal.[49] The Departmental Committee on Homosexual Offences and Prostitution in Great Britain was set up by the Home Office under Sir John Wolfenden as Chairman.[50] John Frederick Wolfenden, Baron Wolfenden, CBE, (1906-1985) was an "educationalist and public servant."[51] H. L. A. Hart wrote in favor of the report in *The Morality of Criminal Law*.[52] While Hart acknowledged that the Millian Harm Principle could well explain many proscriptions achieved by criminal law, such as in the cases of murder and rape, such a principle could "not explain the criminalization of consensual conduct which by its nature does not cause harm to others[.]"[53] Lord Patrick Devlin, an English baron and judge who criticized the findings of the Wolfenden Report, argued for the ability of a sort of popular, majoritarian morality to override, in some instances, the notion of the Millian Harm Principle, and reject the natural right to privacy.

Lord Patrick Devlin Inserts Himself into the Debate

Devlin argued that societies should have an interest in and a right to protect themselves.[54] Modern societies must also acknowledge that they grapple with multiple, and occasionally competing, moral principles shared across that society.[55] Societies also possess a right to use their institutions to deem certain conduct as criminal and to create certain sanctions for such criminal conduct.[56]

Following that, since societies have the right to establish their own rules based on tradition and collective morality, they can do so in such a manner as to punish a variety of offenses, including those generally regarded as immoral, though they should not do so to those offenses only arguably immoral and harmless.[57] Devlin believed that societies could punish immoralities when they cause *discomfort* in the majority that rises to "intolerance, indignation, and disgust."[58] While we have acceded that individuals within a society can forfeit their rights to protection and safety by violating the rules of the society, but do they *also* lose the privileges and protections of society for engaging in behavior that offends provincial social custom, arbitrary moral schema, local taboos, or religious doctrine?

Devlin argued that "the criminal law is not (just) for the protection of individuals but also for the protection of society — 'the institutions and the community of ideas, political and moral, without which people cannot live together.'"[59] Hart responded to Devlin in a radio broadcast and then a series of lectures he delivered at Stanford in 1962 and later published.[60] Peter Cane (b. 1950), Distinguished Professor of Law, Emeritus at the Australian National University and a Senior Research Fellow at Christ College, Cambridge, explained: Hart interpreted Devlin's case for what has come to be called "legal moralism" (or "legal enforcement of morality") as resting on two arguments, which he dubbed "the moderate thesis" and "the extreme thesis" respectively. According to the former, a society is entitled to enforce its morality in order to prevent the society falling apart at the seams, as it were. According to the latter, a society is entitled to enforce its morality in order to preserve its distinctive communal values and way of life.[61]

Therefore, "Hart attacked the moderate thesis on the ground that it implied factual claims for which Devlin did not provide, and (in Hart's view) could not have provided, substantial empirical support."[62] In other words, Hart felt that Devlin's claims about the fragile détente arrived at by centuries of English society could crumble in the face of permitting consensual homosexual behavior rang false. "For this reason," Cane continued, "Hart read the moderate thesis as resting on a tautologous equation of a society with its morality and, therefore, true by definition: to attack a society's morality is to attack society itself."[63]

When it came to the extreme thesis, "Hart rejected [it since] it potentially justified legal enforcement of moral values, regardless of their content, simply because they were widely held." Such an approach that endorsed *legal enforcement of normative social values* helped fuel autocratic majoritarian regimes like the national socialists in Germany, the fascists in Italy, and a countless number of oppressive and authoritarian regimes that acted under the aegis of preservation of "traditional" values or culture. One simply needs to look at the number of tyrannical governments today that control nearly all aspects of human interaction and autonomy to preserve some unattainable moral ideal to see any of the many flaws in Devlin's argument. "Other important elements of Hart's case against legal moralism were distinctions between harm and offence, paternalism and moralism, positive and critical morality; and, within the criminal law, between principles of liability and principles of sentencing."[64] A major element of Hart's critique of Devlin, which related to the conflation of offense and harm, was exhaustively examined by Princeton Professor, Joel Feinberg.

Joel Feinberg's Magnum Opus, *The Moral Limits of the Criminal Law*

Joel Feinberg (1926-2004) explored these very questions over four volumes in *The Moral Limits of the Criminal Law*, the definitive twentieth century American work on the interplay between morality and criminal law.[65] Professor Feinberg's work is a superb and exhaustive delineation of the different species of harm principles and the seeming variety of normative bases for their employment. It lays out an influential hierarchy within which liberty-restricting principles fit, according to harm prevention, legal moralism, and legal paternalism. Moreover, it is one of the deepest and most profound discussions of a classical liberal scheme of harm prevention *qua* primary and supplemental liberty restraint principles in existence.

In a similar vein, Feinberg also examined the relationship between offense and harm to begin to probe the threshold at which matters, ranging from a malodorous cloud emerging from public transit rider or strident conversationalist to graphic public sex acts, cross the Rubicon from distasteful and offensive to harmful.[66] He distinguishes between harm and non-harmful offenses, or that category of acts "cover[ing] the whole miscellany of universally disliked mental states."[67] However, Feinberg's arguments produce a dissonance between classifying the species of act subject to this principle as harmless, when arguing that "it is a misconception to think of offenses as occupying the lower part of the same scale of harms."[68]

Is there a right not to be offended? Of course not, yet this issue exposes a false dichotomy. Feinberg presumes that harmful offenses must have an immediate physical cause in order to have a "harmful" immediate physical effect. Thus, per his argument, as not all of the species of offensive acts results in harm, the harm must be some related-but-non-causal effect of subsequent physical harm.[69]

However, this is to confuse the effect and cause of harm: Harm is an effect to human rights felt by the acted upon party. A physical act can cause harm, but that is not the sole species of harmful acts. Non-physical harmful acts, such as the passage of laws that restrict natural liberty, can be harmful in their chilling effects, even if no one ever touches a person to enforce the law. Offenses fall in the category of non-physical harmful acts. The false dichotomy that seems to be underlying Feinberg between physical harm and non-physically harmful acts that have harmful effects is based on a failure to distinguish properly between harmful effects and harmful acts. This is why I think Feinberg appears to be uneasy with admitting that some offenses "may become so offensive as to be actually harmful, in a minor sort of way."[70] He attempts to account for this in terms of wrongfulness of offense, in that a serious wrongful offense, while not harmful, can be as wrongful as a harm. This distinction, however, collapses upon examination.[71] All in all, Feinberg has both feet in the Millian Harm Principle/ Rothbard Non-Aggression Principal camps.

H.L.A. Hart, however, in his disagreement with Lord Devlin, considered offense and harm in terms of the dangers they might cause to society. He contended that not every act that evinces in a majority "intolerance, indignation, and disgust" rises to the level of an existential threat to society.[72] Though Hart and Devlin argued extensively with one another through footnotes, neither induced a satisfactory response from the other. Surprisingly, the fundamental disagreement between Hart and Devlin grew from divergent beliefs over the "should" of law. The positivist in Hart cared about the enforcement of established rules passed through legitimate process, but the utilitarian in Hart objected to a law that placed significant restrictions on individual liberty absent the legitimizing and necessary predicate of a substantial harm. The Natural Law theorist in Devlin wanted the government to leave personal liberty to individual judgment. But the moralist in him wanted government to punish even private harmless behavior that the majority condemned when it learned of it.

Since the positivists and Natural Law theorists diverge on the role of morality in creation of law, they seem likely to talk around one another. A Natural Law theorist argues that laws should at minimum acknowledge secular moral standards, and, ideally, contemplate them. Some laws, such as procedural ones dealing with the administration of government, may not implicate significant moral dilemmas. For instance, a rule that gives a person 30 days to contest or accede to an administrative fine for exceeding time allotted by a parking meter is rational and thus fair; but purely positivistic. Dismissing the reasons for the placement of the meter in the first place, the cost of parking, and the time allotted relative to parking cost, we can examine the limit of 30-day period for response. Is 30 days intrinsically more moral than 25 days or less moral than 35?

The debates over law and morality, like the ones between Hart and Devlin, and between Hart and Fuller often come down to the differences in the way that positivists and Natural Law theorists view government. While each remains concerned with the acceptance and adherence to law, each uses a different metric to evaluate government and to predict often parallel outcomes. The Natural Law theorist believes that government laws achieve their legitimacy through contemplation of notions of fairness and justice rooted in their protection of individual freedom and property. The positivists, in general, care little about the reasons for a rule of law to exist but rather on the processes and procedures that they believe grant that rule its legitimacy.

In both instances, free societies through the corrective force of normative behavior will influence the laws and procedures adopted by that society, and how that society changes and enforces those laws. The legal positivists, however, failed to explain the behavior of judges who render decisions that contravene the rules of law established by the legitimate authority through a legitimate process. The U.S. Supreme Court certainly rendered decisions rooted in legal positivism, such as the ones we have discussed like *Dred Scott*, *Plessy*, *Korematsu*, *Wickard*, and others.

However, following the conclusion of World War II, the Supreme Court mandated the desegregation of U.S. schools based on fairness and reason,[73] ruled on a trio of cases in favor of reproductive rights based on privacy and reason,[74] and rendered decisions that broadly expanded privacy.[75] While Hart might have criticized such decisions by the Court as improper or inappropriate for the judiciary, he could not explain why the Court consistently rendered decisions in opposition to established rules of law. Devlin's arguments about the ability of a society to regulate private behavior that offended majoritarian views on morality also failed to explain how and why government bodies routinely passed rules or rendered decisions unpopular to the normative beliefs and behaviors.

Despite the attempts of these intellectual titans to erect a monument to legal positivism so large that not even Bentham could climb it, they failed to address the perpetual fault of legal positivism, that its complete blindness to universal concepts of right and wrong, rendered it so powerful an instrument of tyranny that only bloodshed could negate it. Even following the atrocities committed in the twentieth century with the approval of legal positivism, many great minds, as we have seen, sought to resurrect it with the addition of meager impediments against tyranny and despotism so low as to allow even an unmounted Napoleon to hurdle them with ease. It would be the American legal philosopher Ronald Dworkin who would not only provide one of the most salient and pointed critiques of Hart but also put forth a comprehensive theory of Natural Law that considered judicial decision-making as essential to the preservation of personal liberty.

CHAPTER 14

NATURAL LAW AND CIVIL RIGHTS

The Argument

The social and political changes in the latter half of the twentieth century saw shifts in the makeup of important national institutions and attitudes. Some of these began as small shifts in policies by state legislatures while others coalesced almost together on a national scale.

A series of court cases and public incidents pushed forward this new era, and the Supreme Court began to render decisions that radically expanded notions of created civil rights that often overlapped with natural law principles of fairness, due process, and inalienable, pre-governmental rights.

While this ethos of court-driven rights-creation dominated the second half of the twentieth century through the present, the Court occasionally returned to legal positivism when it was unable, or, more likely, unwilling to render a decision too radical, or, as was often the case, on the wrong side of history.

***

A man's natural rights are his own, against the whole world; and any infringement of them is equally a crime, whether committed by one man, or by millions; whether committed by one man, calling himself a robber, (or by any other name indicating his true character,) or by millions, calling themselves a government.[1]

– Lysander Spooner (1808-1887)

THE SUPREME COURT FOLLOWS: A RETURN TO NATURAL LAW JURISPRUDENCE

Whereas legal positivism dominated the judicial landscape of the nineteenth and early twentieth centuries, natural law theory jurisprudence began to reemerge and win small victories starting in the middle of 1946 and persisting through today. That is not to say that the Supreme Court adopted a doctrinal approach that examined matters before it with strong deference to natural law and natural rights, but rather that activist and conservative Courts alike ruled on matters in such a fashion as to incorporate into lofty *stare decisis* certain natural law principles. All of this occurred much to the chagrin of simple fairweather positivists, who grumbled about statutory law, and so-called legal realists, who believe in the importance and primacy of judicial precedent, though, it seems, only when such reliance suited their ends.

We see now that around the end of the second World War a return to Natural Law theories emerged with renewed vigor. During this time, the Third Reich had revealed to humanity the devastation and atrocities of which contemporary society became capable when deploying modern methods of engineering, science, and manufacturing to sinister, horrific and protracted ends *and grounding them in positivism*. We have also observed the means by which societies sought to safeguard against future abuses through the passage of laws and rules holding government more accountable, such as the Federal Tort Claims Act in 1946[2] in the United States, which allowed injured persons to sue the federal government in certain limited circumstances, and the Crown Proceedings Act in 1947 in England, which granted English "subjects" (how I loathe the word when referring to persons) the right to sue the Crown without first obtaining a royal fiat.[3]

Shelley v. Kramer: Restrictive Covenants – Natural but not Enforceable

While legislators passed reforms and legal thinkers and scholars theorized, the courts wrestled with matters more immediate and direct to those affected than finer points of philosophy. Take, for instance, the case of *Shelley v. Kraemer*, a 1948 case in which the Supreme Court confronted restrictive land covenants that prevented landowners in an area of St. Louis from selling their property to "any person not of the Caucasian race."[4]

The matter that set the case in motion began years earlier in 1911 when thirty property owners in a St. Louis, Missouri neighborhood signed and enacted a racially restrictive covenant designed to keep the neighborhood singularly monochromatic for fifty years.[5] In 1945, the Shelley's, an African-American family, having no knowledge of the restrictive agreement, purchased a parcel and moved into the neighborhood.[6] Louis Kraemer, owner of another parcel in the neighborhood covered by the restrictive covenant, brought suit to enforce the covenant, and prevent the Shelley's from acquiring title and moving into their house.[7] The Supreme Court of Missouri held the agreement effective and concluded that enforcement of its provisions violated no rights guaranteed to the Shelley's by the federal Constitution.[8] The Shelley's then appealed to the United States Supreme Court.

The Supreme Court, under Chief Justice Fred Vinson, an appointee of President Harry Truman, needed to reconcile the time-honored notion of nearly limitless ability to contract – a right reinforced by the Supreme Court in *Lochner* in 1905, a mere six years before the specific restrictive covenant at issue was erected (and later overturned by *West Coast Hotel Co. v. Parrish* in 1937)[9] – and the availability of federal courts to enforce such racist covenants entered into between private parties.

Lawyers for the white homeowners seeking to uphold covenants argued that private individuals had the right to sign whatever contracts they wished. Such an argument, though condemnable in this instance, does, however, align with principles of a natural right to enter into private contract. This covenant, though despicable in its aim, could be argued to be no business of the government. The justices agreed, and the opinion, by Chief Justice Fred Vinson, specifically declared that such restrictive covenants fell outside the scope of protections extended by the 14th Amendment and consequently remained legal. "We conclude, therefore, that the restrictive agreements *standing alone* cannot be regarded as violative of any rights guaranteed to petitioners by the Fourteenth Amendment," Chief Justice Vinson opined.[10] "So long as the purposes of those agreements are effectuated by voluntary adherence to their terms, it would appear clear that there has been no action by the State and the provisions of the [Fourteenth] Amendment have not been violated."[11]

It appeared as though the Supreme Court sat poised to reverse its reversal of *Lochner*! Could it be possible that the Supreme Court would uphold a state minimum wage law in Washington yet refuse to act when a party sought to use a restrictive land covenant aimed solely at excluding non-whites? Perhaps in the Taney or Fuller Court, but not the Vinson Court.

While the Supreme Court elected to preserve the rights of contract in the private action of private individuals, it did recognize that certain actions, such as private contracts between private individuals covering private matters cease to remain private when one or more of the parties involved invokes the courts for their enforcement. The Supreme Court in *Shelley v. Kraemer* ultimately found that state enforcement of this particular restrictive covenant was a violation of the Fourteenth Amendment.

In ruling this way, the Supreme Court had handed down a decision that navigated the straits between the sanctity of voluntary commitments and the government keeping its hands clean of racism by leaving undisturbed certain private rights of contract but closing the courts as a means of enforcement to purveyors of such contracts. While preserving natural rights of contract, the Supreme Court simultaneously struck a tremendous blow against the use of government institutions to advance racist ends, a movement the Supreme Court boldly catapulted to the forefront of the American psyche in a series of cases captioned *Brown v. Board of Education*. After all, the natural law is – thankfully – color-blind.

Brown v. Board of Education: The Court Asserts its Moral Natural Authority to Right Wrongs

Colloquially referred to as *Brown I* and *Brown II*, this pair of Supreme Court rulings obliterated the "separate but equal" holding of *Plessy v. Ferguson* and commenced the beginning of the end of the terrible chapter of institutional educational segregation in our nation's history.[12]

The Supreme Court combined five cases under the heading of *Brown v. Board of Education* (1954), from Delaware, Kansas, South Carolina, Virginia, and Washington, DC.[13] In each of the cases, schools had denied African-American students admittance based on local or state laws allowing, and in some cases requiring, racial segregation in public education.[14] The lower courts had relied on *Plessy*, believing racially segregating public facilities remained endorsed by the Supreme Court so long as such separate accommodations maintained an "equal" character. The Supreme Court, however, found such arguments unconvincing. Announcing, in a unanimous opinion, "[w]e conclude that in the field of public education the doctrine of 'separate but equal' [established in *Plessy v. Ferguson* in 1896] has no place."[15] Stating as *dicta* that "separate educational facilities are inherently unequal," the Supreme Court ended segregation in government schools.[16] And that should have concluded the matter. However, because the court did not order an immediate remedy of integrating schools of the various jurisdictions, the changes it called for in *Brown I* did not materialize. As a result, the parties re-appeared before the Supreme Court in *Brown II*, and the district courts, in all but one of the cases were ordered "to take such proceedings and enter such … decrees consistent with this opinion as are necessary and proper to admit to public schools on a racially nondiscriminatory basis with all deliberate speed the parties to these cases."[17]

In deciding the case, the Supreme Court rejected any approach that relied on the idea that laws become fixed in time when adopted, like a painting or photograph. Rather than accepting the ossification of laws, Chief Justice Warren explicitly condemned such fixation theses. "In approaching this problem," he wrote for the Court, "we cannot turn the clock back to 1868 when the [Fourteenth] Amendment was adopted, or even to 1896 when Plessy v. Ferguson was written."[18] Rather, the Chief Justice opined, the Supreme Court "must consider public education in the light of its full development and present place in American life throughout the Nation."[19]

Such a ruling in the *Brown* cases by the Warren Court, certainly consistent with the Fourteenth Amendment, also happened to coincide with natural law principles of fairness and equality. In its discussion of the matter, the Warren Court seems to have *avoided* discussion of natural law and natural rights favoring instead the language of civil rights.[20] Chief Justice Warren reasoned that, when the state endeavors to create some sort of positive right – really a privilege, not a right – such as the right to a free and public education, that it "must be made available to all on equal terms," because government like nature and reason, must be color-blind.[21]

Some resisted. For instance, "[i]n August 1957, someone hurled a stone through the window of the home of an Arkansas N.A.A.C.P. leader, Daisy Bates. An attached note said: 'Stone this time, dynamite next.'"[22] Though the District School Board of Little Rock, Arkansas, erected a plan to desegregate its schools, some other Arkansas agencies and figures opposed the move.[23] "On September 2, 1957, one day before nine black students were scheduled to be admitted to Central High School in Little Rock, [Governor Orval Faubus] of Arkansas dispatched units of the Arkansas National Guard to the school grounds and placed the school 'off limits' to black students."[24] Apparently, "Governor Faubus proclaimed that he was going to deploy National Guard troops around Central High School because of 'evidence of disorder and threats of disorder.'"[25] As the crisis mounted, President Dwight D. Eisenhower got involved. On September 5, 1957, the President sent Governor Faubus a telegram in which he warned Faubus that "[w]hen I became President, I took an oath to support and defend the Constitution of the United States. The only assurance that I can give you is that the Federal Constitution will be upheld by me by every legal means at my command."[26]

Only a few brave figures in Arkansas, such as Harry Ashmore, of the Little Rock Gazette whose editorials on the crisis garnered him a Pulitzer Prize, took public stands against the popular Arkansas Governor.

> Recalling those days, Henry Woods, a Federal district judge in Little Rock who was a leading Little Rock lawyer in 1957, said: "Harry was the central figure in the crisis. He was the leader of the opposition to mob rule, and all of us who opposed [Governor] Faubus rallied around him. The thing I admire most was the great courage Harry displayed. He received daily threats against his life and his family, but he stood in the breech and held the walls against the barbarians."[27]

Apparently, Ashmore's actions endangered more than himself. "During the crisis, Mr. Ashmore's editorials caused declines in advertising revenue and circulation," an action that at this writing would draw ire from publishers in an age of advertising-driven media coverage.[28] Some argued that segregation remained an essential role in the "southern way of life."[29] Such declarations should dispense with any idea that segregation in many areas in the 1950s continued merely as some anachronistic holdover from a bygone era persisting in blind imitation of the past. Rather, segregation remained a seemingly popular institution in large pockets of the American south, and in many inner cities in the Northeast and Midwest.

As such, the decision of the Supreme Court did not find warm receptions in every corner of every county of every state in the U.S. Had such ideas already gained wider acceptance throughout the country, the Supreme Court would not have needed to render a ruling invalidating the practice of segregation as a violation of the Fourteenth Amendment to the U.S. Constitution. In the *Brown* cases, as with many others in this era of American history, the Supreme Court of the United States embraced its role as a *counter-majoritarian* institution entrusted with interpreting and safeguarding the Constitution no matter the external pressure, no matter the risks, no matter the popular will. Natural Law theory, as well, does not take into consideration the popular will.

Here is a subtle yet important distinction between Natural Law theory reasoning and the capital "p" Progressive activism of the Warren Court. In rendering its decision in *Brown I*, the Warren Court spent a great deal of time discussing the disparate impact of a separation of Caucasian children and children of color. "To separate them from others of similar age and qualifications solely because of their race[,]" the Chief Justice opined, again in *dicta*, "generates a feeling of inferiority as to their status in the community that may affect their hearts and minds in a way unlikely ever to be undone."[30]

While undebatable in theory and practice, such reasoning appears unnecessary to the natural law scholar. The natural law does not need to resort to suppositions of feelings—no matter how well-considered or universally accepted—to determine that some practice or policy contravenes simple principles of fairness and reason. True, public education cannot be considered a *natural right*, since natural rights exist independent of government, but a privilege once created by statute, policy, or fiat, must necessarily be shared equally amongst those within its ambit. Here we see an example not of the creation of a *civil* right, or a right that may not exist in a state of nature, but rather a privilege erected by the people through government.

The pair of *Brown* cases have grown to become marked by many as the beginning of the modern Civil Rights era. It was in 1955 that Montgomery, Alabama, authorities arrested Claudette Colvin, an African American woman for refusing to give up her seat on a bus. In the same year, in neighboring Mississippi, a pair of white men murdered 14-year-old Emmett Till, an African American teenager, who supposedly flirted with a white woman, Carolyn Bryant. Bryant's father and husband kidnapped Till, beat him, shot him, and dumped his corpse in a nearby river. An all-white jury acquitted them the following month. In December, Montgomery authorities arrested Rosa Parks for the same violation for which they had arrested Claudette Colvin. Colvin, who was 15 at the time of her arrest in 1955, became one of four plaintiffs in a 1956 case, *Browder v. Gayle*, in which the United States District Court for the Middle District of Alabama found that racial segregation on a government owned bus violated the Fourteenth Amendment.[31] Parks' case became entangled in the Alabama state courts, but, nonetheless, she became a pivotal figure in the civil rights movement.

THE ROLE OF NATURAL LAW IN THE CIVIL RIGHTS MOVEMENT BEYOND THE COURTS

Over the next decade, countless individuals through countless acts of bravery, perseverance, and great personal risk and sacrifice organized and participated in boycotts, sit-ins, marches, and other non-violent forms of protest to call attention to and fight against the despicable "Jim Crow" legacy of the post-Reconstruction South. We can fill libraries with the tremendous works of history and journalism that capture this pivotal era in modern world history. Suffice it to say that this was a period of great turmoil in the United States where the federal government frequently clashed with the governments of the states, and authorities on both sides resorted to drastic measures in attempts to stand firm on their positions.

Martin Luther King's Letter from a Birmingham City Jail

One such example is Reverend Martin Luther King's *Letter from a Birmingham City Jail* (April 16, 1963), in which King "anchor[ed] the defense of civil rights, and of his own actions in their behalf, in the idea of natural law and natural rights."[32] In order to protest racial injustice in Birmingham, Alabama, which at the time, was known as "the most segregated city in America,"[33] Martin Luther King Jr. (1929-1968) and his followers organized a campaign of civil disobedience called "Project Confrontation," in which they planned to "picket the downtown stores, sit-in at lunch counters… march on segregated city facilities, [and] call for 'kneel-ins' at white churches."[34] One week after such demonstrations began, King was served with an injunction prohibiting further action on the basis that such demonstrations had "violated the parade permit laws and trespassing laws, and thus endangered the city's peace and safety."[35] Despite such an order from a court, King decided to press on with the protest, and was promptly arrested: At about 2:15 p.m., 52 persons emerged from the church. They formed up in pairs on the sidewalk and began to walk in a peaceful, orderly, and nonobstructive way toward City Hall. They walked about forty inches apart, carried no signs or placards and observed all traffic lights. At times they sang. . .. The walk proceeded about four blocks-to the 1700 block of Fifth Avenue where all the participants were arrested.[36]

After his arrest, the *Birmingham News* published "A Call for Unity," a statement from eight local white clergy, urging for the demonstrations to end; although they agreed with Martin Luther King that social injustices existed in their city, they argued that the battle against racial segregation should be fought in the courts, not the streets. In response, to the suggestion that he should wait for the courts to act, King endeavored to justify civil disobedience in the face of unjust laws as not only permissible, but as required in certain circumstances.[37]

[T]here are two types of laws: just and unjust. I would be the first to advocate obeying just laws. One has not only a legal but a moral responsibility to obey just laws. Conversely, one has a moral responsibility to disobey unjust laws. I would agree with St. Augustine that *"an unjust law is no law at all."*[38]

He continued:

To put it in the terms of St. Thomas Aquinas: *An unjust law is a human law that is not rooted in eternal law and natural law.* Any law that uplifts human personality is just. Any law that degrades human personality is unjust. All segregation statutes are unjust because segregation distorts the soul and damages the personality. It gives the segregator a false sense of superiority and the segregated a false sense of inferiority .... Hence segregation is not only politically, economically and sociologically unsound, it is morally wrong and sinful.... I can urge [disobedience to] segregation ordinances, for they are morally wrong.[39]

King's letter and invocation of natural law giants like Thomas Aquinas had a widespread impact, including on "the Catholic bishop who signed the letter to which King responded. That bishop, Joseph Aloysius Durick of Nashville, Tennessee, ultimately became known as a strong voice for civil rights. Over local opposition, he put in place the decrees of Vatican II that were intended to eliminate racial divisions and show compassion for the poor and socially marginalized."[40]

The Civil Rights Act of 1964

The Civil Rights Era, beginning in the mid-1950s, and deeply influenced by the actions and writings of people like Martin Luther King, culminated with the passage of the Civil Rights Act of 1964 in July of that same year. The Civil Rights Act of 1964 outlawed discrimination based on race, color, religion, sex, or national origin. It prohibited tactics often used to preclude African-Americans from voting in elections, and ended racial segregation in schools, employment, and public accommodations. This landmark piece of legislation aimed to usher in a new era of equality in the United States bringing certain natural law principles of fairness and equity to public civil rights.[41]

Though many critics and opponents of the Civil Rights Act doubtlessly object to its goals and aims for racist and bigoted reasons, a few took exception not to its ends, but rather its means. One of these critics was Arizona Senator and 1964 Republican Presidential Candidate, Barry Goldwater. Goldwater, (1909-1998) a five-term Arizona senator, voiced his concerns on June 18, 1964 during the debate on the Civil Rights Act.[42]

Goldwater saw no constitutional impediment to a federal statute barring the states from using race as a basis for government behavior, but he saw no constitutional basis for a federal statute abolishing race or any other means of discrimination on private property, lest the property owner be divested of his natural law right to exclude. Goldwater feared that Title II (which related to injunctive relief against discrimination in places of public accommodation) and Title VII (which related to equal employment opportunity) of the Civil Rights Act, represented government overreach.[43] He explained: I find no constitutional basis for the exercise of Federal regulatory authority in either of these areas; and I believe the attempted usurpation of such power to be a grave threat to the very essence of our basic system of government; namely, that of a constitutional republic in which 50 sovereign States have reserved to themselves and to the people those powers not specifically granted to the Central or Federal Government.[44]

Goldwater was no racist[45] – in fact, he had supported the Civil Rights Act of 1957 and the Civil Rights Act of 1960[46] – but he was a man deeply concerned with process. He expressed concern that the 1964 Civil Rights Act contained within it prescriptions that exceeded the authority granted to the federal government by the U.S. Constitution. If the American people wanted to grant the federal government such authority, Goldwater reasoned, then they should amend the Constitution.[47] He argued further that for this [the Senate] to ignore the Constitution and the fundamental concepts of our governmental system is to act in a manner which could ultimately destroy the freedom of all American citizens, including the freedoms of the very persons whose feelings and whose liberties are the major subject of this legislation.[48]

He feared that the Act would require "the creation of a Federal police force of mammoth proportions" in order "[t]o give genuine effect to the prohibitions" contained in the Act.[49] He did not oppose the idea of a legislative attempt to address the systematic problem of racism and bigotry in America, but rather felt that the Civil Rights Act of 1964 contained within it provisions that would lead to the erosion of natural rights – particularly property rights – and a rejection of the ability of the free market to correct for social factors into addition to economic ones.[50] Goldwater explained:

> I repeat again: I am unalterably opposed to discrimination of any sort and I believe that though the problem is fundamentally one of the heart, some law can help   but not law that embodies features like these, provisions which fly in the face of the Constitution and which require for their effective execution the creation of a police state. And so, *because I am unalterably opposed to any threats to our great system of government and the loss of our God-given liberties*, I shall vote "no" on this bill.[51]

THE WARREN AND BURGER COURTS: NATURAL LAW PRINCIPLES ALIGN WITH CONTEMPORARY PROGRESSIVE IDEALS

Griswold v. Connecticut:
Goldberg Embraces the Ninth Amendment

A year later, in 1965, the Supreme Court would again seek to address a matter consistent with natural law principles in *Griswold v. Connecticut*. Although natural law principles would make only a cameo appearance in the Court's majority opinion, they would rise from understudy to starring role in both the concurrence and dissent. In *Griswold v. Connecticut* (1965), the Supreme Court struck down Connecticut's anti-contraceptive law on the basis of the "right to privacy" not expressly stated in the Constitution. The Court addressed a Connecticut law that punished the use of contraceptives and those who facilitated the use of contraceptives.[52] Estelle Griswold, the Executive Director of the Planned Parenthood League of Connecticut, conspired with a physician to violate the law so as to have standing to challenge it.[53]

Justice William O. Douglas delivered the opinion of the Court and appeared to avoid mentioning Natural Law theories and principles, opting instead to perform positivistic acrobatics with the peculiar language of penumbras and emanations of rights. He reasoned that the courts had found a freedom of association under the First Amendment that was not *expressly* mentioned in the Bill of Rights.[54] Likewise,

> [t]he right to educate a child in a school of the parents' choice—whether public or private or parochial—is also not mentioned. Nor is the right to study any particular subject or any foreign language. Yet the Frist Amendment has been construed to include certain of those rights.[55]

Justice Douglas saw within these cases the prevalent theme of "protect[ing] the 'freedom to associate and privacy in one's actions[.]'"[56] These, he found, created within the First Amendment some peculiar "penumbra where privacy is protected from governmental intrusion."[57] He went on to list several cases that he believed "suggest that specific guarantees in the Bill of Rights have penumbras, formed by emanations from those guarantees that help give them life."[58]

Justice Douglas did, however, acknowledge the Ninth Amendment[59] before announcing that the court, in the present case, "deal[t] with a right of privacy older than the Bill of Rights—older than our political parties, older than our school system."[60] Though, here, Justice Douglas spoke, of course, of the institution of marriage, he was invoking, without mentioning, notions of natural, prepolitical rights such as those protected by the Ninth Amendment.

Justice Arthur Goldberg, joined with Chief Justice Warren, and Justice William J. Brennan, placed more reliance on the Ninth Amendment than did Douglas for the majority opinion. Though Justice Goldberg and his colleagues agreed "that the concept of liberty protects those personal rights that are fundamental, and is not confined to the specific terms of the Bill of Rights," he concluded "that the concept of liberty is not so restricted that it embraces the right of marital privacy though that right is not mentioned explicitly in the Constitution" and such a view finds support both in numerous decisions by the Court "and by the language and history of the Ninth Amendment."[61]

Justice Goldberg's extended discussion of the Ninth Amendment went further. "The language and history of the Ninth Amendment reveal that the Framers of the Constitution believed that there are additional *fundamental* rights, protected from governmental infringement, which exist alongside those fundamental rights specifically mentioned in the first eight constitutional amendments."[62] Justice Goldberg, here channeling James Madison, spoke directly to the principles of natural law shared by the Founders but opted instead to use the more contemporary, secular term *fundamental* rather than the more traditional and familiar term *natural* which remains vulnerable to criticism because of its historical association with religious moralism. Unlike Justice Goldberg, this book uses the term that the language and history demand, which the legal academy has taken to viewing as unfashionable for purely semantic reasons: natural law.

After quoting the text of the Ninth Amendment, Justice Goldberg spoke to its origin. Recalling "[t]he Amendment is almost entirely the work of James Madison[,]" he explained that "[i]t was introduced in Congress by him and passed the House and Senate with little or no debate and virtually no change in language."[63]

He continued to recount the debate between the Federalists and the Anti-Federalists, that the proposed amendment "was proffered to quiet expressed fears that a bill of specifically enumerated rights could not be sufficiently broad to cover all essential rights and that specific mention of certain rights would be interpreted as a denial that others were protected."[64]

After further discussion of the Ninth Amendment, a discussion that ranges as far back as the writings of Justice Joseph Story, Justice Goldberg wrote that the statements of Madison and Story "[made] clear that the Framers did not intend that the first eight amendments be construed to exhaust the basic and fundamental rights which the Constitution guaranteed to the people."[65] Justice Goldberg wanted posterity to understand the importance of an amendment that "the court has had little occasion to interpret."[66] He lamented that "[t]he Ninth Amendment to the Constitution may be regarded by some as a recent discovery and may be forgotten by others," but argued that "since 1791 it has been a basic part of the Constitution which we are sworn to uphold."[67] He continued, "[t]o hold that a right so basic and fundamental and so deep-rooted in our society as the right of privacy in marriage may be infringed because that right is not guaranteed in so many words by the first eight amendments to the Constitution is to ignore the Ninth Amendment and to give it no effect whatsoever."[68] Consequently, "a judicial construction that this fundamental right is not protected by the Constitution because it is not mentioned in explicit terms by one of the first eight amendments or elsewhere in the Constitution would violate the Ninth Amendment[.]"[69]

However, Justice Goldberg also sought to counter Justice Black's dissent and explain that he did not suppose to identify the Ninth Amendment as a source of limitless independent power to the judiciary. "I do not mean to imply that the Ninth Amendment is applied against the States by the Fourteenth[,]"[70] Justice Goldberg observed.[71]

> Nor do I mean to state that the Ninth Amendment constitutes an independent source of rights protected from infringement by either the States or the Federal Government. Rather, the Ninth Amendment shows a belief of the Constitution's authors that *fundamental rights exist that are not expressly enumerated in the first eight amendments and an intent that the list of rights included there not be deemed exhaustive.* [...] The Ninth Amendment simply shows the intent of the Constitution's authors that other fundamental personal rights should not be denied such protection or disparaged in any other way simply because they are not specifically listed in the first eight constitutional amendments. I do not see how this broadens the authority of the Court; rather it serves to support what this Court has been doing in protecting fundamental rights.[72]

Justice Goldberg embraced a view of the Ninth Amendment that is certainly consistent with the view shared by Madison and the majority of the Founders. He believed, "the Ninth Amendment simply lends strong support to the view that the 'liberty' protected by the Fifth and Fourteenth Amendments from infringement by the Federal Government or the States is not restricted to rights specifically mentioned in the first eight amendments."[73] How could a handful of justices maintain such a position absent a belief in some specie of the natural, pre-political rights?

Loving v. Virginia: The Freedom to Marry, a Natural Right Without Calling it So

The Warren Court would go on to make several rulings consistent with natural law principles and notions of natural rights while merely alluding to them. In *Loving v. Virginia* (1967), the Supreme Court invalidated a Virginia law punishing interracial couples.[74] Mildred Jeter, an African-American woman, and Richard Loving, a white man, were lawfully married in Washington, D.C. in 1958, since they could not marry in Virginia where they lived.[75] One night in July in 1958, as the two were in their bedroom in their Virginia home, the county sheriff, flanked by two deputies, showed up at their home and confronted the couple.[76] Acting on an anonymous tip, the three law enforcement officials "burst into [the Lovings'] bedroom and shined flashlights in their eyes. A threatening voice demanded, 'Who is this woman you're sleeping with?'"[77] Mrs. Loving responded that she was Loving's wife and indicated the D.C. marriage certificate.[78] "The sheriff responded, 'That's no good here[,]'" and hauled the couple to jail beginning their legal journey that would end in the Supreme Court of the United States.[79]

About six months later, they pleaded guilty to violating the Virginia law banning interracial marriages.[80] Though they were sentenced to one year in jail, the trial judge offered to suspend the sentence for 25 years so long as the Lovings left the state and agreed not to return together for 25 years.[81] So, they traded Virginia for the District of Columbia and, a few years later, filed a complaint in the D.C. Superior Court to vacate the judgment of the Virginia court, and set aside their sentence.[82]

The Supreme Court recounted and rejected the argument of the State of Virginia and found "[t]he clear and central purpose of the Fourteenth Amendment was to eliminate all official state sources of invidious racial discrimination in the States."[83] The Court could have settled the matter as soon as it found that "[t]here [could] be no question but that Virginia's miscegenation statutes rest solely upon distinctions drawn according to race."[84] However, in the home stretch of its opinion, the Court gave a nod to natural law principles. "The freedom to marry has long been recognized as one of the vital personal rights essential to the orderly pursuit of happiness by free men."[85] Isn't it strange that the Warren Court would seem to embrace natural law principles without articulating and declaring them so and instead resort to vague allusions to natural law watchwords such as "personal rights essential to the orderly pursuit of happiness," in its opinions? Who pursues happiness "orderly?"

While the Warren Court, sometimes seemingly by accident, incorporated principles of natural law and natural rights into its decisions, it did not mark the beginning of a glorious return to natural law ideals to the opinions of the Supreme Court. Just as the nineteenth and early twentieth century jurisprudence reflected a predominantly oppressive adherence to legal positivism with the occasional nod to natural law in cases like *Lochner* and dissents like those in *Plessy* and *Korematsu*, the late twentieth and early twenty-first centuries, though frequently marked by sympathetic overtures toward natural law, occasionally fell back to the simple, clean, suffocating embrace of legal positivism.

Bowers v. Hardwick: The Court Stops
Short of Recognizing Extra-textual Rights

Twenty years after *Griswold*, the Supreme Court upheld Georgia's anti-sodomy law. In *Bowers v. Hardwick* (1986), the State of Georgia had charged Michael Hardwick with violating the Georgia statute that criminalized sodomy.[86] He challenged the matter in federal court and landed before nine justices who, by this point were hardly those who concurred in *Griswold*.

It appears that the Burger Court sought to focus more on procedure than policy and made careful distinctions about process and order in response to what it likely considered the free-wheeling wild-west-style openness of the Warren Court. Justice Byron White, writing for the majority, took pains to narrow the decision to one of scope and procedure.[87] He condemned prior cases[88] and wanted to explain that the Court must carefully determine the nature of the extratextual rights protected in the Bill of Rights.[89]

However, after the court criticized decisions made by a prior roster, accepting, but not mentioning Holmes's Legal Realism, it veered off into Benthamite/Austinian positivism by looking to statutory precedent. "Sodomy was a criminal offense at common law and was forbidden by the laws of the original thirteen States when they ratified the Bill of Rights[,]" the Court explained.[90] Continuing, "[i]n 1868, when the Fourteenth Amendment was ratified, all but 5 of the 37 States in the Union had criminal sodomy laws[,]"[91] the Supreme Court forecasted its decision to turn to legal positivism to excuse itself from rendering an antimajoritarian outcome it found distasteful. As if reassuring itself, it continued, "[i]n fact, until 1961, all 50 States outlawed sodomy, and today, 24 States and the District of Columbia continue to provide criminal penalties for sodomy performed in private and between consenting adults."[92] Adding, "Nor are we inclined to take a more expansive view of our authority to discover new fundamental rights imbedded in the Due Process Clause[,]" the Supreme Court clearly sought to reject what it believed was the judicial alchemical prestidigitation of the Warren Court which it believed had conjured penumbra from precedent and transmuted that into rights.[93]

The Burger Court did not stop at oblique attacks on the Warren Court. Justice White proclaimed, "[t]he Court is most vulnerable and comes nearest to illegitimacy when it deals with judge-made constitutional law having little or no cognizable roots in the language or design of the Constitution."[94] There was no mention of Justice Goldberg's use of the Ninth Amendment to underscore privacy or Justice Brandeis' famous leave-me-alone jurisprudence.[95]

Eventually, the Court rejected arguments of due process at issue and distinguished the case from others involving public regulation of private behavior.[96] "And if respondent's submission is limited to the voluntary sexual conduct between consenting adults, it would be difficult, except by fiat, to limit the claimed right to homosexual conduct while leaving exposed to prosecution adultery, incest, and other sexual crimes even though they are committed in the home[,]" the Supreme Court reasoned.[97] Presenting such a parade of horribles falls below our expectations for the standard of jurisprudence of our nation's highest court. It is unbecoming of courts of last resort to avoid rendering a proper decision, and many critical things can be said of the Court for rendering its decision in such a manner. However, as the court said in *Bowers v. Hardwick*, "[w]e are unwilling to start down that road."[98]

Lawrence v. Texas: Righting the Wrong of Bowers and Acknowledging the Natural Right to Choose a Sexual Partner

Bowers smacks of the debates between Lord Patrick Devlin and Professor H. L. A. Hart over England's repeal of its anti-sodomy laws. The Supreme Court adopted a view similar to Devlin's belief in the popular majority when it came to matters of private morality; even if tyrannical.[99] Though the Court was unable to find any Devlin-like public harm due to private acts, and it came nowhere near Feinberg's distinctions between harm and offense, the Supreme Court would recognize its error and overturn *Bowers v. Hardwick* in the 2003 case, *Lawrence v. Texas*. The Supreme Court rejected its prior holding in *Bowers*, and recognized the substantive due process right – another secular phrase for natural right – to choose a sexual partner, including for the purpose of engaging in consensual homosexual sodomy:

> The laws involved in *Bowers* and here are, to be sure, statutes that purport to do no more than prohibit a particular sexual act. Their penalties and purposes, though, have more far-reaching consequences, touching upon the most private human conduct, sexual behavior, and in the most private of places, the home. The statutes do seek to control a personal relationship that, whether or not entitled to formal recognition in the law, is within the liberty of persons to choose without being punished as criminals.[100]

Professor Laurence Tribe aptly explains the Court's change of heart:

> When the Bowers majority nonetheless transmuted that claim as advanced by Michael Hardwick into a "fundamental right to engage in homosexual sodomy," it became easier to deride Hardwick's position as "at best, facetious." But that transparent transmutation also made it easier for the *Lawrence* Court to conclude that the *Bowers* majority had inadvertently "disclose[d] the Court's own failure to appreciate the extent of the liberty at stake."[101]

In questioning "whether the majority may use the power of the State to enforce these views on the whole society through operation of the criminal law," the court in *Lawrence v. Texas* held "[o]ur obligation is to define the liberty of all, not to mandate our own moral code."[102] Justice Anthony Kennedy in his concurring opinion went even further:

> ...we think that our laws and traditions in the past half century are of most relevance here. These references show an emerging awareness that liberty gives substantial protection to adult persons in deciding how to conduct their private lives in matters pertaining to sex. "[H]istory and tradition are the starting point but not in all cases the ending point of the substantive due process inquiry."[103]

RECENT SUPREME COURT RULINGS: POSITIVISM TAKES BACK THE HELM

Were *Bowers v. Hardwick* the only temporary misstep in recent Supreme Court history, we would have cause to rejoice. However, such is not the case. In 2005, two years after the court overturned its holding in *Bowers v. Hardwick*, the Supreme Court rendered two decisions rife with legal positivism in a pair of cases that each, in their own way, radically expanded and reinforced government overreach at the cost of natural rights.

Gonzales v. Raich: Expansive Reading of the Necessary and Proper Clause Threatens Non Enumerated Rights

In the first of these cases, *Gonzales v. Raich* (2005), the Supreme Court seized authority from the dustbowl of *Wickard v. Filburn* to find that private growers of private supplies of marijuana for medicinal purposes fully sanctioned by the laws of the State of California could be found to violate the Federal Controlled Substances Act on the grounds that the Commerce Clause power granted to the Congress by the Constitution and expanded beyond recognition by the Court in *Wickard* somehow *also* "applied to the intrastate, noncommercial cultivation and possession of cannabis for personal medical purposes as recommended by a patient's physician pursuant to valid California state law."[104]

Like a bad penny, *Wickard v. Filburn* refuses to disappear. The Supreme Court itself appeared unable to abandon its holding and unwilling to overturn it. Justice John Paul Stevens, writing for the majority in *Gonzales* opined, "[t]he similarities between this case and *Wickard* are striking. Like the farmer in *Wickard*, respondents are cultivating, for home consumption, a fungible commodity for which there is an established, albeit illegal, interstate market."[105] The Court in *Gonzalez* drew further parallels between the law there and in *Wickard*, the Agricultural Adjustment Act[,] was designed 'to control the volume [of wheat] moving in interstate and foreign commerce in order to avoid surpluses...' and consequently control the market price, [...], a primary purpose of the [Controlled Substances Act] is to control the supply and demand of controlled substances in both lawful and unlawful drug markets.[106]

According to the Court, so long as Congress waved the flag of interstate commerce, it could control, seemingly without limitation, any product of any kind that at any point could potentially, in the aggregate, have the minutest effect on a matter that could touch or concern interstate commerce.[107] Again, Justice Stevens wrote, "[i]n both [*Wickard* and *Gonzalez v. Raich*], the regulation is squarely within Congress' commerce power because production of the commodity meant for home consumption, be it wheat or marijuana, has a substantial effect on supply and demand in the national market for that commodity."[108] This is not only lacking in reason, it is anti-reason.

The Court held that "[i]n assessing the scope of Congress' authority under the Commerce Clause, we stress that the task before us is a modest one. We need not determine whether respondents' activities, taken in the aggregate, substantially affect interstate commerce in fact, but only whether a 'rational basis' exists for Congress so concluding[.]"[109] In so doing, the Court renewed with invidious foreboding the power of the legislature to take far-reaching and intrusive action to regulate the personal freedoms of those residing in the United States.

Justice Clarence Thomas recognized this great danger. He observed:

> Respondents Diane Monson and Angel Raich use marijuana that has never been bought or sold, that has never crossed state lines, and that has had no demonstrable effect on the national market for marijuana. If Congress can regulate this under the Commerce Clause, then it can regulate virtually anything — and the Federal Government is no longer one of limited and enumerated powers.[110]

In lambasting the ease with which the "substantial effects test" can be manipulated, Justice Thomas chastised the majority's attempt to define economic activity "in the broadest possible terms as 'the production, distribution, and consumption of commodities,'" so as to avoid the restriction on federal power from regulating *noneconomic* activity:

> This carves out a vast swath of activities that are subject to federal regulation. If the majority is to be taken seriously, the Federal Government may now regulate quilting bees, clothes drives, and potluck suppers throughout the 50 States. This makes a mockery of Madison's assurance to the people of New York that the "powers delegated" to the Federal Government are "few and defined," while those of the States are "numerous and indefinite."[111]

Justice Thomas added, "[b]y holding that Congress may regulate activity that is neither interstate nor commerce under the Interstate Commerce Clause, the

Court abandons any attempt to enforce the Constitution's limits on federal power."[112] He recognized that "[t]he Necessary and Proper Clause is not a warrant to Congress to enact any law that bears some conceivable connection to the exercise of an enumerated power."[113]

An expansive reading of the Necessary and Proper Clause as well as the Commerce Clause, as exhibited by the majority in *Raich* jeopardizes the non-enumerated rights protected under the Ninth Amendment and the entire natural law order. By claiming necessity or invoking that some component of some item in some fashion contemplates some action or requires some piece that even faintly touches or concerns interstate commerce, Congress could, using *Raich*, impose regulations and restrictions on daisies, lawn clippings, twigs, and snowballs. We know they can already regulate a farmer's private growth of wheat for personal use or a couples' private, state compliant growth of cannabis for personal, medicinal use.

Kelo v. New London:
Eminent Domain Overtakes Natural Rights

In yet another blow to personal liberty – here property rights— the same Court issued a ruling in a case that permitted the seizure of land from a private person under the banner of the Takings Clause of the Fifth Amendment to transfer such a parcel to another private person. In *Kelo v. New London* (2005), a city in Connecticut, as part of a revitalization effort, granted authority to a private nonprofit development corporation to acquire several contiguous parcels of land to serve as the anchor of this new initiative.[114] When one homeowner, Susette Kelo, refused to sell her property, the City claimed eminent domain and sought to seize it.[115]

The government often invokes eminent domain, a compulsory government action in which private property owners are forced by government to sell their property to the government "for public use" so long as such a party receives "just compensation," when it wants to seize a person's property to build a park, road, bridge, or other physical construct that the public can use.[116] The question, as it came before the Supreme Court, related to whether the "public use" requirements of eminent domain could be satisfied if the seizure from one private entity was designed to transfer the seized property to another private entity.[117] However, "[f]or more than a Century, [the Court's] public use jurisprudence has wisely eschewed rigid formulas and intrusive scrutiny in favor of affording legislatures broad latitude in determining what public needs justify the use of the takings power."[118] As a result, the Court deferred to the City.[119] And, "[j]ust as [it] decline[d] to second-guess the City's considered judgments about the efficacy of its development plan, [it] also decline[d] to second-guess the City's determinations as to what lands it need[ed] to acquire in order to effectuate the project."[120]

In *Kelo*, it seems, the Court felt its "authority... extend[ed] only to determining whether the City's proposed condemnations [were] for a "public use" within the meaning of the Fifth Amendment to the Federal Constitution[.]"[121] Blaming positivism, "over a Century of our case law interpreting [the takings clause] dictates an affirmative answer to that question, we may not grant petitioners the relief that they seek[,]" the Supreme Court, relying on precedent, granted local authorities license, under the claims of an expansive view of "public use" that included raising tax revenue of all things, to seize private property from private individuals and transfer that property to other private individuals.[122] Such a decision contravenes nearly all notions of fairness and notions of the sanctity of one's property so cherished by the founding generation. In her dissent, Justice Sandra Day O'Connor cautioned:

> The Court rightfully admits, however, that the judiciary cannot get bogged down in predictive judgments about whether the public will actually be better off after a property transfer. In any event, this constraint has no realistic import. For who among us can say she already makes the most productive or attractive possible use of her property? The specter of condemnation hangs over all property. Nothing is to prevent the State from replacing any Motel 6 with a Ritz– Carlton, any home with a shopping mall, or any farm with a factory.[123]

Absent *Raich*, which recognized nearly limitless commerce power to the legislature, it becomes difficult to imagine a modern case more dangerous and threatening to the natural right to own, use, and enjoy private property.

The unprecedented and egregious use of eminent domain in *Kelo* shocks the conscience to such a degree that it calls into question the legitimacy of the entire principle of eminent domain. Here, once again, we see the peculiarity that emerges in some forms of government in which the newly formed entity of government claims dominion over some authority greater than that which any of its voluntary members possesses. In a Lockean state of nature, no man or woman may assert a claim over the property of another solely because he or she feels such property would fare better under new ownership.[124] Yet, when people band together to form a society for the mutual protection of themselves, their rights, and their property, such societies often magically imbue their governing bodies with rights and powers beyond those at the command of any individual member. Such is the case with Eminent Domain, a flagrant violation of the Jeffersonian notion of voluntarism when it comes to private property transfer.[125] How can those joining society consent to give government a power which they themselves lack?

Despite the trend in the past several decades in which judges have ruled to align precedent more closely with a natural law understanding of rights and liberties, the Supreme Court has occasionally erred in destructive ways in opinions stained with the corrupting influence of legal positivism. This is not to say that the Vinson and Warren courts aimed to embrace the natural law. Nor does it suggest that they did so unconsciously. Instead, it so happened that principles of natural law and natural justice so allied with progressive ideals contemporary to those time periods. The enduring appeal of Natural Law theory rests in its ability to transcend social mores and popular majoritarian attitudes to guide those willing to explore it to decisions and opinions that almost always err on the side of recognizing the pre-existence in all individuals of the deposit of personal liberty, choice, and the ability to act according to how each wants to pursue his or her own happiness in a manner so as to minimize his or her impact on the ability of others to do the same; and to do this free of government interference.

The most significant contemporary legal scholars all explore the matters central to all of the cases discussed in this chapter. John Rawls examined the relationship between equality and freedom, Robert Nozick the boundaries of the state's ability to encroach upon individuals' rights, even in a complex, modern society, Ronald Dworkin on the integrity of legal systems, and Randy Barnett, whose work on the Ninth Amendment has contributed immensely to its rebirth and modern recognition.

We will soon visit the poignant works of each of these scholars in turn and explore how they have sought to explain how we should best understand the working of the legislature, executive branch, courts, and our relationship with these organs of government and with one another so as to maximize the recognition of natural rights and minimize the positivistic assault on those rights.

CHAPTER 15

THE TREATMENT OF THE INSTITUTION OF SLAVERY UNDER NATURAL LAW

The Argument

We take a brief detour to discuss how the natural law dealt with the institution of slavery throughout the years. The story is not always a happy one. Greats like Aristotle, Aquinas, and Augustine championed individual liberty, but left a gaping hole in their philosophies when, like so many of their time, they voiced no objections to slavery.

In the colonies, founders like Jefferson publicly denounced slavery, but privately owned many slaves. No one seemed to want to challenge the status quo, and so three clauses maintaining the substandard condition of African Americans were written into the Constitution without much debate. When antislavery champion Lysander Spooner began rallying against the slave trade, we saw an emergence of natural law ideals being used to justify abolition.

For many, however, including Chief Justice Marshall, while the African slave trade was contrary to the law of nature, it was not prohibited by the positive law of nations, and so we see in America, for far too long, the perpetuation of an unequal system of justice based on race.

***

If there be such a principle as justice, or natural law, it is the principle, or law, that tells us what rights were given to every human being at his birth; what rights are, therefore, inherent in him as a human being, necessarily remain with him during life; and, however capable of being trampled on, are incapable of being blotted out, extinguished, annihilated, or separated or eliminated from his nature as a human being...[1]

– Lysander Spooner (1808-1887)

Regrettably, not every part of the original Constitution was consistent with the natural law principles enshrined in the Declaration and the Ninth amendment. Although slavery had been a fiercely debated political issue during the Constitutional Convention, the morality of the institution seems to have been largely undisputed on this large stage. Notwithstanding that, the words "slave" or "slavery" do not appear in the Constitution, the institution was first discussed among the delegates in the context of representation in the House of Representatives, which was to be based on population. States in the South stood to gain an advantage if slaves were to be included when calculating their population, while northern states adamantly opposed doing so since slaves were denied virtually every liberty recognized by the Constitution; after all, they were not citizens and could not vote.

Hypocritically, the Southern states wanted slaves to "count" where it helped them, but not to count when it really mattered – i.e., in terms of humanity and liberty.[2] In the end, a compromise was reached, such that each slave would be counted as three-fifths of a free person when determining population.[3] The slaves themselves, of course, had no say whatsoever in their constitutional standing. Widely considered to be the chief pro-slavery clause in the Constitution, the Three-Fifths Compromise epitomized the racism inherent in the document, and became a reflection of the inferiority Blacks would come to endure in the coming decades.

Yet another point of contention at the Constitutional Convention was the status of fugitive slaves who had escaped to free states.[4] Generally, the power structures in Southern states were concerned that fugitive slaves would not be returned to their owners, while their northern counterparts generally wanted to see the slaves freed. In another compromise viewed as necessary to assure ratification of the Constitution among the states, the Constitution provided that fugitive slaves were to be returned regardless of their physical location in a free state.[5]

In discussing the powers denied to Congress, there arose a third bargain between the North and South: the slave trade clause[6] prohibited the federal government from limiting the importation of "persons" where existing state governments allowed such actions, but only until twenty years after the Constitution was adopted. Moreover, this clause is one of only two in Constitution that is rendered exempt from being amended.[7]

Deliberately shrouded in ambiguity so that both sides could proclaim victory when returning home to their ratifying conventions, these clauses allowed those in the South, whose livelihood and riches were predicated on the use of inexpensive slave labor, to assuage their constituents, while those in the North could tout the end of the slave trade was imminent, and the Union remained an achievable goal; these clauses were seen by many as a necessary evil.

For example, Roger Sherman, the delegate from Connecticut, voiced no objection. According to Madison's *Notes on the Constitutional Convention,*

Sherman "disapproved of the Slave-trade: yet as the States were now possessed of the right to import slaves, as the public good did not require it to be taken from them, and as it was expedient to have as few objections as possible to the proposed scheme of government, he thought it best to leave the matter as we find it."[8] Delegates from the South justified slavery and invoked fairness as a value. South Carolina's John Rutledge denied that religion or humanity had anything to do with the matter, but proclaimed it would not be fair to states like South Carolina if slavery were curtailed.

> If slavery be wrong, it is justified by the example of all the world. He cited the case of Greece, Rome, and other ancient states; the sanction given by France, England, Holland, and other modern states. In all ages one half of mankind have been slaves. If the Southern States were let alone, they will probably of themselves stop importations. He would himself, as a citizen of South Carolina, vote for it. An attempt to take away the right, as proposed, will produce serious objections to the Constitution, which he wished to see adopted.[9]

And so, with these three clauses ingrained in the Constitution, the Founders created an abhorrent exception for their otherwise pervasive use of natural law. It is the Founders' greatest failure that they presumed to pick and choose whose rights to respect and whose to reject, and that they did so based on race. Nevertheless, it is important to delve further into the history of natural law philosophy and the discussion of natural law theorists regarding the morality of slavery. Two hundred years before the American Revolution, and nearly three hundred before the American Civil War, issues of political self-determination and slavery were debated – and much to my dismay, we may not like the arguments that some, albeit not all, natural law theorists have put forth.

THE NATURAL LAW GIANTS' INCOMPREHENSIBLE DEFENSE OF SLAVERY: ARISTOTLE, AUGUSTINE, AND AQUINAS

It is important to address Aristotle, Saint Augustine, and Saint Thomas Aquinas on slavery in order to familiarize ourselves with the justifications historically voiced in defense of slavery, and to understand now, how natural law stands in sharp contrast to the institution of slavery.

Slavery was the very basis of the Greek social and economic system, so it is no surprise that Aristotle did not outwardly condemn it. Instead, in book I of the *Politics*, Aristotle defines natural slavery in two parts: first, the natural slaves' characteristics, and second, how they interact with their master. To Aristotle, a natural slave was "anyone who, while being human, is by nature not his own but of someone else..." ... "a piece of property; and a piece of property is a tool for action separate from its owner."[10] Aristotle addresses the question of whether slavery is contrary to nature, by stating: Those who are as different [from other men] as the soul from the body or man from beast— and they are in this state if their work is the use of the body, and if this is the best that can come from them— are slaves by nature. For them it is better to be ruled in accordance with this sort of rule, if such is the case for the other things mentioned.[11]

Aristotle aims to justify the belief that certain men, incapable of being educated to virtue were, by nature, unfit for citizenship.[12] Since such men could not truly reason and, thus, were ruled by their passions, they ought to be ruled in the form of ownership as slaves by those who had higher faculties.[13] "Slaves by nature, were, therefore, men who could obey reason, although they were unable to exercise it."[14] Aristotle distinguishes this slavery "by nature" from slavery based on "conquest" or "force of law," in which he did see an injustice.[15] Some have argued, on the other hand, that Aristotle was "evidently uncomfortable with his argument for slavery, since in his will he freed his slaves… and ultimately was true to his words that 'it is wise to offer all slaves the eventual reward of emancipation.'"[16] It would be insincere to focus on this last act by Aristotle, when he spent his life writing about the ways it was justified.

Saint Augustine believed that slavery was inevitable; not because of the natural laws of the universe – for he preached that in a pure world slavery would be quite unnatural – but as the consequence of sin and the Fall of Man.

> The prime cause, then, of slavery is sin, which brings man under the dominion of his fellow – that which does not happen save by the judgment of God, with whom is no unrighteousness, and who knows how to award fit punishments to every variety of offence.[17]

Saint Augustine continues, "this is why we do not find the word 'slave' in any part of Scripture until righteous Noah branded the sin of his son with this name. It is a name, therefore, introduced by sin and not by nature."[18] *Furthermore*, "servitude is… penal, and is appointed by that law which enjoins the preservation of the natural order and forbids its disturbance; for if nothing had been done in violation of that law, there would have been nothing to restrain by penal servitude. And therefore the apostle admonishes slaves to be subject to their masters, and to serve them heartily and with good-will."[19]

Saint Thomas Aquinas built upon the reasoning of Aristotle and Augustine, but did not go as far as to condemn slavery. He believed the subjection of one person to another could not be derived from the natural law, but in certain circumstances, it could be appropriate based on the subjugated individual's actions. According to Aquinas, the natural structure of the universe, which gave some men authority over others, mirrored the hierarchical nature of heaven, where some angels were superior to others.[20] He also uses a similar argument to Aristotle, that "men of outstanding intelligence naturally take command, while those who are less intelligent but of more robust physique, seem intended by nature to act as servants."[21] However, he did consider that slaves had some restricted rights. A son, as such, belongs to his father, and a slave, as such, belongs to his master; yet each, considered as a man, is something having separate existence and distinct from others. Hence in so far as each of them is a man, there is justice towards them in a way: and for this reason too there are certain laws regulating the relations of father to his son, and of a master to his slave; but in so far as each is something belonging to another, the perfect idea of 'right' or 'just' is wanting to them.[22]

Saints are heroic, not perfect. In one of philosophy's bitterest ironies, the three human beings most responsible for the promulgation of NLT in the West had a blind spot for slavery – arguably the most profound rejection of NLT imaginable. And, as is discussed below, their American successors were no better.

BARTOLOMÉ DE LAS CASAS, GROTIUS, BLACKSTONE, AND LOCKE

Meanwhile, in Spain, two centuries before the American Revolution, natural rights in the new world were being addressed as issues of political self-determination and slavery was debated in terms of Natural Law theory by Bartolomé de Las Casas (1484-1566), who "worked and wrote tirelessly for the natural rights of [Native Americans] to political liberty and property."[23] Las Casas had first left Spain in 1502 for the Indies at age 18, and "lived and worked among the natives for twenty years before he entered the Domincan Order and turned to a systematic study of theology and law."[24] In 1509, he served as a chaplain on the Spanish conquest of Cuba and took up residence on Hispaniola, where "he lived off the toil of the Indians of his encomienda—the system by which Spanish colonists were given tracts of land and the rights to the forced labor of the native people in return for a promise to instruct them in the faith."[25] This firsthand experience opened his eyes to atrocities that he would later denounce, and "after a profound conversion of conscience in 1514, Las Casas arranged to free his slaves and began a lifelong, passionate devotion to the cause of just and humane treatment of the indigenous peoples."[26] He then "crisscrossed Spanish America from Peru to Guatemala, campaigning against conquest," against the encomienda system, and provided sensational accounts of the cruelty of the conquistadores on many occasions where he pled his case before Spanish court.[27]

Las Casas' most well-known defense occurred in 1550, in response to an order of the King of Spain, Charles V, that all conquests in the New World be suspended until a council of theologians and jurists could decide a just method of conducting them.[28] Referred to as "The Battle at Valladolid," the council heard both Las Casas and his principal intellectual adversary, the theologian Juan Ginés de Sepúlveda, debate the lawfulness of the Spanish occupation of the Americas as they set out to discern whether it was lawful for the "the King of Spain to wage war on the Indians, before preaching the faith to them, in order to subject them to his rule, so that afterward they may be more easily instructed in the faith."[29]

Once before the council, Sepúlveda read the conclusions of his work *Democrates Alter, Sive de Justis Belli Causis apud Indos* [A Second Democritus: On the Just Causes of War with Indians] and argued that the subjugation of certain indigenous people was warranted because of "their sins against Natural Law; that their low level of civilization required civilized masters to maintain social order; that they should be made Christian and that this in turn required them to be pacified; and that only the Spanish could defend weak Indians against the abuses of the stronger ones."[30] For instance, Sepúlveda wrote:

> The Spaniards rule with perfect right over the barbarians who, in prudence, talent, virtue and humanity are as inferior to the Spaniards as children to adults, women to men, the savage and cruel to the mild and gentle, the grossly intemperate to the continent, I might almost say as monkeys to men.[31]

In response to such racist and foul arguments Las Casas argued that "the Indians were not uncivilized nor lacking social order; that peaceful mission was the only true way of converting the natives; and that some weak Indians suffering at the hands of stronger ones was preferable to all Indians suffering at the hands of Spaniards."[32] In arguing so, Las Casas often presented the Indians as morally and intellectually superior people; he described them as "gentle, patient, and humble," endowed with "excelled, subtle, and very capable minds."[33] Las Casas continued:

> Not only have [the Indians] shown themselves to be very wise peoples and possessed of lively and marked understanding, prudently governing and providing for their nations…and making them prosper in justice; but they have equaled many diverse nations of the world, past and present, that have been praised for their governance, politics and customs, and exceed by no small measure the wisest of all these, such as the Greeks and Romans, in adherence to the rules of natural reason.[34]

In effect, while his rival argued that the Native Americans were beastlike "natural slaves," Las Casas appealed to the ancient Stoic concept of a universal brotherhood of man when he proclaimed:

> All the races of the World are men, and of all men and of each individual there is but one definition, and this is that they are rational. All have understanding and will and free choice, as all are made in the image and likeness of God. . . . Thus the entire human race is one.[35]

Las Casas' rested his case "on the first principle of the unity of the human family [which] puts his notion of natural rights on a decidedly universal plane."[36] This is reiterated in the closing of his argument, when he ends with the lines: "The Indians are our brothers, and Christ has given his life for them. Why then, do we persecute them with such inhuman savagery when they do not deserve such treatment?"[37] According to Paolo G. Carozza, "the rights that Las Casas sought for the native peoples were theirs simply by virtue of their humanity—a humanity common to all of God's children."[38] For this reason, we can infer that Las Casas' stress on the fundamental humanity of Native Americans "meant that they were created with freedom" – in other words, endowed with natural rights.[39]

Ultimately, no winner was declared between Sepúlveda and Las Casas – each claiming the victory for himself. The debate, however, did cement Las Casas' position as the defender of natural rights for all persons and a staunch opponent of slavery. In one of his last works before his death, *De Thesauris in Peru*, he reiterated his belief in the free nature of the Indians:

> Whenever a free person, and still more, a free people or community is to be obliged to accept some burden or pay some due and generally when it is a question of something prejudicial, especially to many, it is fitting that all whom the matter touches be called and their free consent obtained; otherwise what is done has no validity.

According to Brian Tierney, Las Casas, who had been ordained a bishop in 1545 by Pope Paul III, laid the groundwork for a doctrine of natural rights that was independent of religious revelation "by drawing on a juridical tradition that derived natural rights and natural law from human rationality and free will, and by appealing to Aristotelian philosophy."[40] Ultimately, the transition from classical medieval doctrines of natural law to modern conceptions of natural rights was achieved in no small part by Spanish scholastics like Las Casas.

Yet another philosopher discussed in Chapter 1, Hugo Grotius explicitly refutes the argument that slavery can be imposed on those who might be naturally suited to it.[41] In his masterpiece *De Jure Belli (The Rights of War and Peace)*, Grotius criticizes those who claim rights of 'discovery' over lands already occupied by less enlightened individuals.[42] He discusses the utility of slavery, from the slaves' standpoint, suggesting that the fundamental right to preserve oneself is what led to the legitimacy of voluntary slavery. In other words, if an individual's circumstances were such that the only course of action that would keep one alive would be to subject oneself to a master, Grotius supported it.

> [P]erfect and utter Slavery, is that which obliges a Man to serve his Master all his Life long, for Diet and other common Necessaries; which indeed, if it be thus understood, and confined within the Bounds of Nature, has nothing too hard and severe in it; for that perpetual Obligation to Service, is recompensed by the Certainty of being always

provided for; which those who let themselves out to daily Labour, are often far from being assured of....[43]

Grotius believed that systems of rights could be alterable through the manner in which people choose to dispose of those rights. Individuals can choose to alienate whatever rights they wish, even up to the extreme of enslaving themselves to another. In effect, Grotius repurposes Aristotle's doctrine that some individuals are naturally suited to be slaves, not as grounds for imposing slavery but rather as an explanation for why a people might choose of their own accord to hand over their full rights to the government of another.

In a similar vein, the rhetoric of 17th-century England was rife with the teachings of those who opposed the increasing power of the kings and claimed that the country was headed for a condition of slavery. In his *Second Treatise of Government*, John Locke facetiously asks under what conditions such slavery might be justified. For the first time amongst the theorists we have studied, we read that slavery cannot come about as a matter of contract. This is the perfect condition of *slavery*, which is nothing else, but *the state of war continued, between a lawful conqueror and a captive*: for, if once compact enter between them, and make an agreement for a limited power on the one side, and obedience on the other, the *state of war and slavery* ceases, as long as the compact endures: for, as has been said, no man can, by agreement, pass over to another that which he hath not in himself, a power over his own life. I confess, we find ... that men did sell themselves; but, it is plain, this was only to drudgery, not to slavery: for, it is evident, the person sold was not under an absolute, arbitrary, despotical power: for the master could not have power to kill him, at any time, whom, at a certain time, he was obliged to let go free out of his service; and the master of such a servant was so far from having an arbitrary power over his life, that he could not, at pleasure, so much as maim him, but the loss of an eye, or tooth, set him free....[44]

Locke adamantly argued that to be a slave is to be subject to the absolute, unbridled, arbitrary power of another. As men do not have this power, even over themselves, they cannot sell or otherwise grant it to another.

> The natural liberty of man is to be free from any superior power on earth, and not to be under the will or legislative authority of man, but to have only the law of nature for his rule. The liberty of man, in society, is to be under no other legislative power, but that established, by consent, in the commonwealth; nor under the dominion of any will, or restraint of any law, but what that legislative shall enact, according to the trust put in it. … freedom of men under government is, to have a standing rule to live by, common to every one of that society, and made by the legislative power erected in it; a liberty to follow my own will in all things, where the rule prescribes not; and not to be subject to the inconstant, uncertain,

unknown, arbitrary will of another man: as freedom of nature is, to be under no other restraint but the law of nature.[45]

As one may not submit to slavery, there is a moral injunction to attempt to throw off and escape it whenever it looms: submission to absolute monarchy is a violation of the law of nature, for one does not have the right to enslave oneself.

We also see a discussion of slavery in the first chapter of Blackstone's *Commentaries of the Laws of England* (1753), where he dealt with rights of individuals and discussed two major arguments against slavery: "firstly, that traditional arguments in its favor are wrong (the right of capture in war, selling oneself into slavery); and secondly, that it historically has had no place in English law."[46] Blackstone believed "the law of England acts upon general and extensive principles: it gives liberty, rightly understood, that is, protection, to a Jew, a Turk, or a heathen, as well as to those who profess the true religion of Christ."[47] Blackstone argued that the spirit of liberty was so implanted in the English constitution, its meaning and character, that "a slave or negro, the moment he lands in England, falls under the protection of the laws, and with regard to all natural rights becomes *eo instanti* a freeman."[48]

> I have formerly observed that pure and proper slavery does not, nay, cannot, subsist in England: such, I mean, whereby an absolute and unlimited power is given to the master over the life and fortune of the slave. And indeed it is repugnant to reason, and the principles of natural law, that such a state should subsist anywhere.[49]

Blackstone found slavery repugnant, but he was not willing to go far enough to exclude slaves from the right of contract; on the contrary, he argued that even in England, the slave could still be tied up in the perpetual contractual relationship that he/she had entered with his/her master.

DISCOURSE ON SLAVERY IN THE COLONIES: THOMAS JEFFERSON, LYSANDER SPOONER

In the fledgling United States, Thomas Jefferson regularly opposed slavery in public and private, calling it a "moral depravity"[50] and a "hideous blot."[51] Jefferson's immortal words in the Declaration attached the new nation's soul to the natural law, but when he personally owned 600 slaves to work at his plantation in Monticello, Jefferson rejected the natural law for himself. It becomes hard to square the circle when giants like Jefferson spoke of natural law and inalienable rights but at the same time engaged in such a deplorable practice that remains a stain on the history of the United States.

Jefferson himself voiced his concern that slavery was contrary to the laws of nature and knew that such an institution was a crime against humanity.

If a slave can have a country in this world, it must be any other in preference to that in which he is born to live and labour for another; in which he must lock up the faculties of his nature, contribute as far as depends on his individual endeavours to the evanishment of the human race, or entail his own miserable condition on the endless generations proceeding from him. With the morals of the people, their industry also is destroyed. For in a warm climate, no man will labour for himself who can make another labour for him. This is so true, that of the proprietors of slaves a very small proportion indeed are ever seen to labour. *And can the liberties of a nation be thought secure when we have removed their only firm basis, a conviction in the minds of the people that these liberties are of the gift of God?* That they are not to be violated but with his wrath?[52]

Jefferson could feel the tensions rising, and "a change already perceptible" when he wrote, "[i]ndeed I tremble for my country when I reflect that God is just: that his justice cannot sleep for ever: that considering numbers, nature and natural means only, a revolution of the wheel of fortune, an exchange of situation is among possible events: that it may become probable by supernatural interference!"[53] He believed that "the spirit of the master is abating, that of the slave rising from the dust... preparing, under the auspices of heaven, for a total emancipation, and that this is disposed, in the order of events, to be with the consent of the masters, rather than by their extirpation."[54]

In 1778, he drafted a Virginia law that prohibited the importation of enslaved Africans,[55] but decided not to put it to a vote in the Virginia House of Delegates for, as he later wrote, "[t]he public mind would not yet bear the proposition, nor will it bear it even at this day," forty years later.[56] "[T]he day is not distant when it must bear and adapt it, or worse will follow. Nothing is more certainly written in the book of fate than that these people are to be free. "[57] Despite such rhetoric, Jefferson always maintained that the decision to emancipate slaves would have to be part of a democratic process; abolition would be thwarted until slaveowners *consented* to free their human property together in a large-scale act of emancipation. To Jefferson, it was anti-democratic and contrary to the principles of the American Revolution for the government to enact abolition or for only a few planters to free their slaves. Instead, he believed, that the laws governing were not the purview of Congress, but rather, a matter to be handled within each individual state government, the most direct expression of the will of the citizens. When called upon to discuss the Missouri Compromise (1820), a deal brokered between the North and the South, and passed by Congress that allowed for admission of Missouri as a slave state, Maine as a free state, and effectively excluded slavery from all remaining territories in the Louisiana Purchase north of Missouri, Jefferson wrote that "this momentous question, like a fire bell in the night, awakened and filled me with terror."[58]

[T]o regulate the condition of the different descriptions of men composing a state…certainly is the exclusive right of every state, which nothing in the constitution has taken from them and given to the general government. Could congress, for example say that the Non-freemen of Connecticut, shall be freemen, or that they shall not emigrate into any other state?[59]

One man who adamantly invoked natural law principles in his support of emancipation was the American philosopher, entrepreneur, and pamphleteer, Lysander Spooner (1808-1887). By relying on the interpretive canon that 'all language must be construed strictly in favor of natural right' Spooner rejected any interpretation of constitutional language that would have reconciled slavery with the Constitution and developed an argument of constitutional theory that would have rendered slaveholding unconstitutional even before the adoption of the thirteenth amendment. In his manifesto, *The Unconstitutionality of Slavery* (1845), Spooner argued that not one state government of the slave states specifically authorized slavery, and that the *intentions* of the delegates to the Constitutional Convention have no legal bearing on the document they created.

Spooner set out to show "that the constitution of the United States, not only does not recognize or sanction slavery, as a legal institution, but that, on the contrary, it presumes all men to be free; that it positively denies the right of property in man; and that it, *of itself*, makes it impossible for slavery to have a legal existence in *any* of the United States."[60] In response to the argument that the Framers *intended* to sanction slavery, Spooner replied, in a foretaste of modern Originalism, that their objectives are irrelevant, and we should only be concerned with the legal meaning of the words they used.

[N]o intention, in violation of natural justice and natural right (like that to sanction slavery,), can be ascribed to the constitution, unless that intention be expressed in terms that are *legally competent* to express such an intention; and, 2d, that no terms, except those that are plenary, express, explicit, distinct, unequivocal, *and to which no other meaning can be given*, are legally competent to authorize or sanction anything contrary to natural right.[61]

He refused to look at what the Framers said about the Constitution, specifically the notes of James Madison, as a source to understand the constitutional meaning, but instead referred to these as "meagre [sic] snatches of argument, intent or opinion, uttered by a few only of the members; jotted down by one of them, (Mr. Madison,) merely for his own convenience, or from the suggestions of his own mind; and only reported to us fifty years afterwards by a posthumous publication of his papers."[62] Spooner believed where words are susceptible to two meanings, one consistent, and the other inconsistent with justice and natural right, *only the* meaning which is consistent with natural right, shall be attributed to them— unless other parts of the instrument overrule that interpretation. In support of these rules, Spooner quoted Chief Justice John Marshall's dissenting opinion in *Ogden v. Saunders*:

> The intention of the instrument must prevail; that this intention must be collected from its words; that its words are to be understood in that sense in which they are *generally used* by those for whom the Instrument was intended; that its provisions are neither to be restricted into insignificance, nor extended to objects not comprehended in them, nor contemplated by its framers.[63]

As for the Fugitive Slave Clause (Art. IV, sect. 2, cl. 3), during the Constitutional Convention it was widely accepted that this clause was *meant* to apply to runaway slaves, but Spooner denied the relevance of what the delegates meant to say. Their intentions were not germane to the *legal* meaning of the text. To Spooner, because the clause does not mention slaves at all, it should not be construed as pertaining to slaves, rather, "[i]t must be construed, if possible, as sanctioning nothing contrary to natural right."[64]

In addressing the three-fifths rule (Art. I, sect. 2, cl. 3), it is commonly understood that "free Persons" stood in contrast to unfree persons, so "all other Persons" clearly meant slaves. Spooner argued, however, that prior to the Convention, "free Persons" was never used (either in common law or in American legal documents) in contrast to slaves. Instead, he argued "free persons" referred to Americans with the full rights of citizenship, in contrast to immigrants and others who did not enjoy all the privileges of citizenship.

As for the Slave Trade Clause (Art. I, sect. 9, cl. 1), Spooner focused on the popular understanding and construction of the word importation. When applied to "persons," Spooner argued it does not convey the idea of property, but "only when it is applied distinctly to 'slaves,' that any such idea is conveyed; and then it is the word 'slaves,' and not the word 'import,' that suggests the idea of property." Since importation can apply to anybody on a ship, any classification of imported people as slaves would be based entirely on the recognition of foreign laws.

Ultimately, Spooner regarded the Constitution as a type of contract, and since the Preamble to the Constitution specifies "we the people" as the contracting parties, we must assume that Blacks and well as Whites are among those people. And it would be unreasonable and absurd to assume that Blacks contracted for their own enslavement. After all, Spooner stated:

> A man's natural rights are his own, against the whole world; and any infringement of them is equally a crime, whether committed by one man, or by millions; whether committed by one man, calling himself a robber, (or by any other name indicating his true character,) or by millions, calling themselves a government.[65]

In a later work, *Natural Law*, Spooner argued that natural law and its concrete expression in terms of natural rights, are the only legitimate basis for political obligation. He believed legislators are incapable of changing the natural law, so in instances when they pass laws that are in *violation of* natural rights, those laws have no moral authority whatsoever.

> What, then, is legislation? It is an assumption by one man, or body of men, of absolute, irresponsible dominion over all other men whom they can subject to their power. It is the assumption by one man, or body of men, of a right to subject all other men to their will and their service. It is the assumption by one man, or body of men, of a right to abolish outright all the natural rights, all the natural liberty of all other men; to make all other men their slaves; to arbitrarily dictate to all other men what they may, and may not, do; what they may, and may not, have; what they may, and may not, be. It is, in short, the assumption of a right to banish the principle of human rights, the principle of justice itself, from off the earth, and set up their own personal will, pleasure, and interest in its place. All this, and nothing less, is involved in the very idea that there can be any such thing as human legislation that is obligatory upon those upon whom it is imposed.[66]

As an aside, Lysander Spooner was no stranger to challenging the constitutionality of the government's actions. In 1844, Lysander Spooner created the American Letter Mail Company[67] in order to challenge the constitutionality of the United States Post Office's government enforced monopoly on the delivery of mail, noting that, in the absence of competition, "government functionaries" had no incentive to innovate or provide good service. While the Constitution granted the United States Government the ability to create postal roads and post offices, there was no intention for it to have a monopoly on mail delivery

> Universal experience attests that government establishments cannot keep pace with private enterprise in matters of business — (and the transmission of letters is a mere matter of business.) Private enterprise has always the most active physical powers, and the most ingenious mental ones. It is constantly increasing its speed, and simplifying and cheapening its operations. But government functionaries, secure in the enjoyment of warm nests, large salaries, official honors and power, and presidential smiles — all of which they are sure of so long as they are the partisans of the President — feel few quickening impulses to labor, and are altogether too independent and dignified personages to move at the speed that commercial interests require. They take office to enjoy its honors and emoluments, not to get their living by the sweat of their brows.[68]

In just a few short months after being established, Spooner's American Letter

Mail Company had "engrossed the bulk of the service between Boston, New York, Philadelphia, and Baltimore."[69] "Hoping to drive Spooner out of business… the Postmaster General resorted to some extra-legal measures,"[70] for example, "transport companies were told that they would lose their government contracts unless they stopped carrying American Letter Mail Company mail," while "the government began to arrest and prosecute Spooner's agents in district court."[71] In response to the "depressing loss of customers to Spooner's American Letter Mail Company," the Postal Reduction Act of 1845 "nearly [was enacted and] halved the postal rates,"[72] effectively driving Spooner out of business, but not before achieving his goal of "unmask[ing] the hypocrisy"[73] of the government.

ADDRESSING SLAVERY IN THE COURTS

Many justices in the Supreme Court, as we shall soon see, used natural law principles to address the myriad of issues before them. Chief Justice Marshall's opinion in *The Antelope* (1815) addressed the question of whether the slave trade violated international law. The facts of the case are lengthy with multiple parties and claims, but can be best summarized as follows:

> The Antelope, a Spanish-licensed ship, left Cuba on Aug. 24, 1819, on a voyage to Africa, where it took on slaves before being captured by the Arraganta, a privateer under the Uruguayan flag. After seizing the Antelope and its slaves, the Arraganta stole additional slaves from Portuguese ships that it then destroyed. The Arraganta and the hijacked Antelope, carrying more than 300 chained Africans, recrossed the Atlantic to Brazil, where the Arraganta was wrecked in a storm. The privateer crew then took the Antelope north and sailed near St. Augustine, in what is now Florida [but at that, was Spanish territory]. On June 29, 1820, the ship, with 281 remaining captives, was captured by the Dallas, a U.S. Navy cutter. The Africans were transported to Savannah, Ga., where they waited for their fates to be decided. The wait lasted seven years (for those who lived), as the case went through local courts and was appealed to the Supreme Court three times.[74]

The issue before Chief Justice Marshall was the legal standing of the captives, and the rights of the parties (Spain, Portugal, the privateer captain of the Arraganta, and the captain of the Dallas) who each claimed the African captives as their property, as well as "the United States, represented by the Georgia attorney Richard Wylly Habersham, who maintained that the Africans were free under the 1819 Slave Trade Act,"[75] which prohibited the importation of slaves and outlawed the slave trade. Marshall had to decide, had the captives been illegally transported to the United States and thus free, requiring them to be sent back to Africa, or were they in fact still slaves? And if so, to whom did they belong?

Marshall begins by addressing the right to liberty, and writes that there is no question of the immorality of the slave trade.

> That it [the slave trade] is contrary to the law of nature will scarcely be denied. That every man has a natural right to the fruits of his own labour, is generally admitted; and that no other person can rightfully deprive him of those fruits, and appropriate them against his will, seems to be the necessary result of this admission...[76]

Unfortunately, Marshall did not stop there, but as he did many times at Chief Justice, subordinated natural rights to positive law.

> Slavery, then, has its origin in force; but as the world has agreed that it is a legitimate result of force, the state of things which is thus produced by general consent, cannot be pronounced unlawful.[77]

Marshall writes that throughout the continent of Africa, the consensus is undeniably that captive prisoners are to be considered slaves, and the slave trade considered legitimate commerce "sanctioned by universal assent." While "each [country] may renounce it for its own people," Marshall questions whether such renunciation can affect others. He answers in the negative. In particular, Marshall writes,

> Each legislates for itself, but its legislation can operate on itself alone. A right, then, which is vested in all by the consent of all, can be devested only by consent; and this trade, in which all have participated, must remain lawful to those who cannot be induced to relinquish it. As no nation can prescribe a rule for others, none can make a law of nations; and this traffic remains lawful to those whose governments have not forbidden it.

> The supposed inconsistency of the slave trade with the law of nature, will not alone condemn it in the view of a Court of justice, so as to authorize all nations to treat it as a crime, or to enforce its prohibition by the confiscation of the property of those engaged in it. It becomes all reflecting men to think seriously, and speak cautiously, on the subject of the illegality of a trade, which was once universally participated in by the civilized nations of Europe and America.[78]

> Whatever might be the answer of a moralist to this question, a jurist must search for its legal solution, in those principles of action which are sanctioned by the usages, the national acts, and the general assent, of that portion of the world of which he considers himself as a part, and to whose law the appeal is made. If we resort to this standard as the test of international law, the question, as has already been observed, is decided

in favour of the legality of the trade. Both Europe and America embarked in it; and for nearly two centuries, it was carried on without opposition, and without censure. A jurist could not say, that a practice thus supported was illegal, and that those engaged in it might be punished, either personally, or by deprivation of property.[79]

Ultimately, Marshall held that the international slave trade was legal, and in devising a legal solution, established a mathematical formula by which the claimants received the "property" on board, and ordering the return of the captives to their respective foreign owners.

In the context of slavery, Justice Joseph Story (17791845),[80] who served alongside Chief Justice Marshall, believed, like Aquinas and Grotius, that "natural law identifies both those human purposes which positive institutions should further and those human tendencies which positive institutions must, if they are to achieve their ends, recognize."[81] In *United States v. La Jeune Eugenie* (1822), Justice Story, while riding circuit in Massachusetts, offered an opinion in an admiralty case in which a commissioned American vessel had seized a French ship, *La Jeune Eugenie*, suspected of engaging in the trafficking of slaves off the coast of Africa.[82] The American captain argued such trafficking violated the law of nations as well as the American Slave Trade Acts. Story's opinion begins by asserting that the law of nations rests on "the eternal law of nature," which can be "deduced by correct reasoning from the rights and duties of nations[] and the nature of moral obligation."[83] Story was careful to note, however, that as a judge, he only had the authority to enforce the law of nations if it has not been "relaxed or waived by the consent of nations" as seen in their "general practice[s] and customs."[84] As to the slave trade itself, Story condemned it as "breach[ing] . . . all the maxims of justice, mercy and humanity," involving "corruption, and plunder, and kidnapping" and as "incurably unjust and inhuman."[85] He continued that slavery was: a violation of some of the first principles which ought to govern nations. It is repugnant to the great principles of Christian duty, the dictates of natural religion, the obligations of good faith and morality, and the eternal maxims of social justice.... When any trade can be truly said to have these ingredients [it is impossible] that it can be consistent with any system of law that purports to rest on the authority of reason or revelation.[86]

Ultimately, Justice Story ruled that the French slave trade vessel seized on high seas in peacetime would have been tortuously seized only if it were not involved in piracy. Here, he ruled, slave trading was piracy since it was unlawful under laws of the country of the boat seized, thus, Story declined to order the return of the French vessel to its owners.

Justice Story had occasion once again to invoke natural law principles in the face of a case that sought to determine the status and fate of slaves discovered onboard a ship in the waters of the United States, in *United States v. Schooner*

Amistad (1841). On June 27, 1839, the Spanish ship *The Amistad* left the port of Havana, Cuba, with Captain Ransom Ferrer, two passengers (Jose Ruiz and Pedro Montez) and 53 African slaves on board. During the voyage, the slaves mounted an uprising in which they killed the captain, took possession of the ship, and "spared the lives of Ruiz and Montez, on condition that they would aid in steering the Amistad for the coast of Africa, or to some place where negro slavery was not permitted by the laws of the country."[87] Under a ruse, Ruiz and Montez tricked the slaves and steered the Amistad for the United States, where they landed off the coast of Long Island.

The Spanish government asked that the ship, cargo and slaves be restored to Spain under the Pinckney Treaty of 1795[88] between Spain and the United States, and as a result, the United States filed a claim on behalf of Spain. On the other hand, the alleged slaves argued that they were native-born, free Africans who had been unlawfully and forcibly kidnapped to be sold as slaves. The district court agreed with the federal government and held that the alleged slaves should be delivered to the President of the United States to be transported back to Africa. The Circuit Court affirmed.

When the case was heard by the Supreme Court, the great statesman, attorney, and former president, John Quincy Adams (1767-1848) represented the alleged slaves.

In advocating for the rights of the Africans, Adams cited to many of the tried and true abolitionist arguments, including appealing to the natural law.

> The Africans were in possession, and had the presumptive right of ownership; they were in peace with the United States; the Courts have decided, and truly, that they were not pirates; they were on a voyage to their native homes--their dulces Argos; they had acquired the right and so far as their knowledge extended they had the power of prosecuting the voyage; the ship was theirs, and being in immediate communication with the shore, was in the territory of the State of New York; or, if not, at least half the number were actually on the soil of New York, and entitled to all the provisions of the law of nations, and the protection and comfort which the laws of that State secure to every human being within its limits.[89]

Pointing to a copy of the Declaration of Independence hanging in the courtroom, Adams continues:

> I know of no law, but one which I am not at liberty to argue before this Court, no law, statute or constitution, no code, no treaty, applicable to the proceedings of the Executive or the Judiciary, except that law... I know of no other law that reaches the case of my clients, but the law of nature and of Nature's God on which our fathers placed our own national

existence. The circumstances are so peculiar, that no code or treaty has provided for such a case. That law, in its application to my clients, I trust will be the law on which the case will be decided by this Court.[90]

After dismissing the application of any international treaties to this case, Adams then invokes the individual nature of personal liberty.

Is it possible that a President of the United States should be ignorant that the right of personal liberty is individual. That the right to it of every one, is his own – JUS SUUM ["legal right"]; and that no greater violation of his official oath to protect and defend the Constitution of the United States, could be committed, than by an order to seize and deliver up at a foreign minister's demand, thirty six persons, in a mass, under the general denomination of all, the Negroes, late of the *Amistad*.[91]

And finally, in his summation, Adams again returns to the importance of adhering to the Declaration of Independence and it's call to uphold natural law.

In the Declaration of Independence the Laws of Nature are announced and appealed to as identical with the laws of nature's God, and as the foundation of all obligatory human laws. But here Sir William Scott proclaims a legal standard of morality, differing from, opposed to, and transcending the standard of nature and of nature's God. This legal standard of morality must, he says, in the administration of law, be held, by a Court, to supersede the laws of God, and justify, before the tribunals of man, the most atrocious of crimes in the eyes of God. With such a principle it is not surprising that Sir William Scott should have found a difficulty in maintaining that the African slave trade was legally criminal, nor that one half the Supreme Court of the United States should have adopted his conclusions. It is consolatory to the friends of human virtue and of human freedom to know, that this error of the first concoction, in the moral principle of a British judge, has been, so far as relates to the African slave trade, laid prostrate by the moral sense of his own country, which has overcome the difficulty of finding the slave trade criminal, by the legal and national abolition of slavery itself.[92]

This argument obviously resonated with Justice Story, who, writing for the majority of the court, echoes Adams sentiment:

Did the people of the United States, whose government is based on the great principles of the revolution, proclaimed in the Declaration of Independence, confer upon the federal executive or judicial tribunals the power of making our nation accessories to such atrocious violations of human rights?

Is there any principle of international law or law of comity which requires it? Are our Courts bound, and if not, are they at liberty, to give effect here to the slave trade laws of a foreign nation, to laws affecting strangers never domiciled there, when to give them such effect would be to violate the natural rights of men?[93]

Ultimately, Story appealed in his decision both to positive international law and to the "eternal principles of justice." He believed that the treaty with Spain could not have intended "to take away the equal rights of all foreigners, who should contest their claims before any of our Courts, to equal justice; or to deprive such foreigners of the protection given them by other treaties, or by the general law of nations."[94] Upon the merits of the case, then, Story held there was no doubt "that these negroes ought to be deemed free..."[95]

Not all cases addressing slavery had as happy an ending. For instance, the Supreme Court, following positivist principles, held in *Dred Scott v. Sandford* (1857) that a former slave now free, who descended from African slaves who had been kidnapped and brought in chains to the United States, could not become a U.S. citizen, was not among those referenced as "men" in the Declaration of Independence, or a "person" as the Constitution used that word, and therefore, was not entitled to protection under the U.S. Constitution.[96]

In April 1846, Dred Scott filed a suit in the Circuit Court for the District of Missouri, a state trial court, on behalf of himself, his wife, and their two daughters against their owner's wife, for their freedom.[97] After being taken from Missouri to military posts in Illinois and the Louisiana Territory by his owner, a surgeon in the Army, Scott argued that his residency in Illinois (then, a free state in the Union) as well as his and his family's residency in Fort Snell in the Louisiana Territory (where slavery was forbidden by the Missouri Compromise of 1820), made them free.[98] Nevertheless, "[a]fter six years of complicated litigation which included victory for the Scotts in the Missouri trial court, the Missouri Supreme Court, on March 22, 1852, held, by a 2-1 vote, that since the Scotts resided in Missouri, a slave state, Missouri law prevailed; the Scotts were not free."[99]

Scott appealed to the U.S. Supreme Court, and ignoring the principles and usages of Natural Law theory, the Supreme Court returned arguably its most regrettable decision in its history.[100] In *Dred Scott v. Sandford*, Chief Justice Roger Brooke Taney engaged in a discourse embracing a sort of proto-Originalism whereby he ignored foundational natural law principles and, instead, concluded that when Jefferson wrote "all men are created equal" he *really* only meant adult white males. Taney even dared to profess his civil inclinations while claiming to be handcuffed by the "original" meaning of the Constitution.[101] Holding that Dred Scott was not, therefore, a "citizen" of Missouri, and thus could not sue in the courts of the United States, the suit was dismissed for want of jurisdiction. The *Dred Scott* case is one of the earliest instances of the use of

Originalism – Originalism, which produced the result that living post-natal human beings were not "persons" – in American jurisprudence.[102]

The *Dred Scott* case offers a premonition of the debate as to whether judges should avail themselves of moral theories in adjudicating constitutional cases, but in the end, the problem was settled by the deaths of 750,000 Americans in the war between the states and then by the Thirteenth Amendment after the Civil War. Abolitionist enthusiasm for natural justice found expression in the legislative rather than the judicial arena, and thankfully, the *Dred Scott* holding was overruled by the Thirteenth Amendment, enacted and ratified in 1865, which abolished slavery; and by the *Slaughter-House* cases, decided in 1873, in which the Court held that the amendment superseded the *Dred Scott* ruling. But the essence of Chief Justice Taney's opinion was not overruled. Blacks were still treated like second-class citizens, a fact that was fueled by the positivist idea that government can write any law, enact any policy, and enforce any cultural norm, so long as the measure has popular support. Relying on positivism, the government permitted, condoned, and protected the most horrific abuse imaginable to Blacks, and to some of the whites who protested.

Without a fundamental, obvious public rejection of positivism and embrace of the natural law by the government, the courts should presume that what the government seeks to do is unconstitutional; the government should be compelled to justify constitutionally, under the natural law and morally, whatever it wants to do, whenever and wherever it wants to do it. When the government protects freedom and respects natural rights, it is doing its job. When it ceases to protect freedom and when it violates natural rights, it is the duty of the people to alter or abolish it.

CHAPTER 16

CONTEMPORARY NATURAL LAW THEORISTS

The Argument

In the present age, theorists and philosophers have sought to update the ideas of their predecessors to accommodate Natural Law theory to changes in contemporary society.

Even modern scholars who challenged Natural Law theory relied heavily on the ideas of Hobbes and Locke. John Rawls argued for government to prioritize justice to help the less advantaged, while Robert Nozick argued that the government lacks the moral authority to transfer wealth, even for justice's sake. Joseph Raz buttressed Hartian Legal Positivism, and Randy Barnett argued for a return to first principles in a modified minimalist version of Originalism.

These formulations inspired new debates and deeper exploration into the roles and goals of government and challenged long-held conceptions of the limitations of the state vis-à-vis individual liberty.

***

Individuals have rights, and there are things no person or group may do to them (without violating their rights).[1]

– **Robert Nozick (1938-2002)**

MODERN NATURAL LAW DEBATES

As the scholars and theorists informed judicial minds in England and America, so did the social, political, and legal environments inform the work of the scholars. We have already seen how the Nuremberg trials prompted a return to natural law principles; and, in the later part of the twentieth century, philosophers and scholars challenged and buttressed once again the role of government in the planning and administration of societies.

Though thinkers like Hobbes, Locke, and Blackstone wrote at times of great political upheaval, revolution, and a sea change of political thought against the notion of hereditary monarchy, many American minds turned to concepts of justice and government in a nuclear age of mutual assured destruction.

John Rawls

In 1971, John Rawls published *A Theory of Justice* in which he advocated for a pseudo-socialistic model of distributive justice which called for some mechanism to distribute societal rights and burdens in, what he considered, a socially fair fashion. Robert Nozick responded with *Anarchy, State, and Utopia* in 1974 in which he disputed Rawls's argument for a maximal government and instead favored a minimal state whose functions were constrained to the protection of its members and their property, and enforcement of private contracts.

Years later, Ronald Dworkin explored how to regulate the conditions under which governments could and should use force to coerce compliance and conformity, and Randy Barnett – courageously questioning whether any person now living in America has ever consented to the Constitution or the government – advocated for a return to a sort of originalist appeal to jurisprudence emphasizing natural liberty as a bulwark against popular sovereignty.

Many contemporary American philosophers turned to some of the earliest political theorists to search for an answer. They reexamined the ideas critical to early American political thought such as those of John Locke. Recall from Chapter 1, that the Lockean account of rights, an account very familiar to Jefferson and Madison, supposes the pre-existence of certain pre-governmental rights emanating from the very nature of our humanity. Since no contemporary uniform account of the scope of those rights existed, beyond that posited by Locke himself, such notions of rights remained subject to differences of opinion, especially when we consider that rights outside of abstract conceptions of what legal or moral space they occupy, are essentially claims. Thus, what one man wishes to leave alone in Locke's state of nature may contrast with what another man wishes to address by force.

When two individuals with equal rights disagree over which of them owns a parcel of land, how can they adjudicate the matter? Imagine by some circumstance, each has equal claim to the same parcel. Since each would presumably benefit from owning the parcel in question and each wants to claim ownership over it, neither will be able impartially to decide to whom the parcel should legally belong. To solve such matters, we would need to separate the power of ownership and the power of adjudication of that ownership. As Barnett has argued, we have now arrived at a morally legitimate role for a minimalist government – even in the absence of consent – a government that only enforces natural rights. Accordingly, the Lockean State of Nature seems to argue government from necessity alone to enforce natural liberty according to reason.[2] And, of course, the Lockean model requires some form of consent or social compact between individuals in order for such a government to work.

John Rawls (1921-2002) sought to offer a counterpoint to John Stuart Mill's utilitarianism and reimagined the notion of social contract comprising the beliefs and attitudes of Locke and others.[3] Born in 1921 in Baltimore, Maryland, Rawls served as a combat infantryman in the South Pacific in World War II, and later returned to Princeton, where he had studied as an undergraduate, to earn a doctorate in philosophy.[4] In 1971, he published his book *A Theory of Justice* at a time of concerted national debate over the Vietnam War and the fight for racial equality.[5]

Rawls argued that social institutions should prioritize justice,[6] and if such institutions become unjust, they lose their legitimacy and must either be fixed or eliminated.[7] He was concerned that laws and institutions under the utilitarian model focused too much on maximizing public benefit at the cost of liberty or freedom of others. Rawls rejected what he believed to be the philosophical corruption of utilitarian theories, namely that greater public welfare could justify the overriding of one's rights and liberties.[8] He argued that the enduring persistence of such belief structures came not from their value—of which he perceived very little—but rather from the lack of meaningful alternatives.[9] Rawls provided an alternative theory of society designed to maximize the distribution of justice to all its participants instead of focusing on ideology that called for actions that considered the greatest good for the greatest number of people in society. He supposed that the role of society gathered around a common conception of justice aimed to distribute "the benefits and burdens of social cooperation."[10]

To Rawls, justice relates to how social institutions administer the distribution of rights and responsibilities in the name of social cooperation. "For [Rawls,] the primary subject of justice is the basic structure of society, or more exactly, the way in which the major social institutions distribute fundamental rights and duties and determine the division of advantages from social cooperation."[11] He understands that, at a basic level, "political constitution and the principal economic and social arrangements [in a society] [...] define men's rights and duties and influence their prospects, what they can expect to be and how well they can hope to do."[12] Accordingly, "the institutions of society favor certain starting places over others" and cause "especially deep inequalities."[13]

He called the idea that all individuals were equal in a state of nature "the original position" of the Lockean Compact and argued for a model where each person remained ignorant of his or her abilities, knowledge, skills, and future allocation of assets.[14] Only then, Rawls believed, could such circumstances give rise to a society to benefit all persons maximally, since each member would act in his or her own self-interest in creating the rules under this veil of ignorance as to their own attributes and assets.[15]

Rawls eventually announced key principles and priorities that lay out a scheme he believed would maximize individual liberty while minimizing inequality. First, he argued that "[e]ach person is to have equal right to the most extensive total system of equal basic liberties compatible with a similar system of liberty for all."[16] Second, he called for the prioritization of "social and economic inequalities [...] such that they are both: (a) to the greatest benefit of the least advantaged [...] and (b) attached to offices and positions open to all under conditions of fair equality of opportunity."[17]

Whereas Locke argued for interested parties to band together to form societies designed to protect the natural rights in the group, falling short of infringement of natural rights, Rawls called for the imposition onto society of some deterministic sense of social justice aimed to benefit the least advantaged. He borrowed from natural law language to describe his counter-thesis and called justice "happiness according to virtue" while acknowledging "that this ideal can never be fully carried out," but that "it [was] the appropriate conception of distributive justice, at least as a prima facie principle, and society should try to realize it as circumstances permit."[18] Rawls, however, believed that "justice as fairness reject[ed] this conception" of justice.[19] He engaged in a circular discussion where he invoked socialistic notions of distributive shares based on work, as well as notions of conceptually deserved outcomes that warrant actual outcomes, and implied that, in a Rawlsian society, cloaked in language of morals, virtue and a sense of entitlement, a "well-ordered society," one "in which institutions are just and this fact is publicly recognized[,]""each [person] is to receive what the principles of justice say he [or she] is entitled to[.]"[20]

Stated differently, Rawls believed that rights, justice, and material wealth should be allocated by government from each according to his ability; to each according to his needs. This emerges because:

> In a well-ordered society individuals acquire claims to a share of the social product by doing certain things encouraged by the existing arrangements. The legitimate expectations that arise are the other side, so to speak, of the principle of fairness and the natural duty of justice. For in the way that one has a duty to uphold just arrangements, and an obligation to do one's part when one has accepted a position in them, so a person who has complied with the scheme and done his share has a right to be treated accordingly by others. They are bound to meet his legitimate expectations. Thus when just economic arrangements exist, the claims of individuals are properly settled by reference to the rules and precepts (with their respective weights) which these practices take as relevant.[21]

Rawls all but states that the society itself can decide, through majoritarian approaches to fairness and justice, how to distribute shares of social product. In other words, so long as these arrangements fall in line with the ideas that societies should organize to shift burdens from the less-advantaged to the more advantaged, the government may *create* and *distribute* rights in a manner in which it treats differently different classes of citizens based on notions of *fairness* and *social justice*. This is arguably more offensive to Natural Law theory than pure positivism which is occasionally a ratification of natural law.

While Rawls did not dismiss notions of natural rights and natural law in pre-governmental societies, he appeared to believe that, as soon as people came together to form a society, their collective force somehow created a system less bounded than the sum of its parts. So, when people, from a Rawlsian baseline "original position" come together to form a society, they should organize around a common goal of ensuring that those endowed with greater gifts (whether in property, talent, or personality) become forced through some societal mechanism to ensure that those less fortunate shoulder a lesser burden than those more capable, or less affected by doing so. To Rawls, a society can impose restrictions on natural liberty and create, from the ether, new rights for some that could, in many cases, contravene the natural rights of others so long as doing so benefitted the less advantaged. Stated differently, somehow, what individuals cannot do personally and alone – like take property and redistribute it – they may and *must* do collectively. Rawls is the anti-Locke.

Robert Nozick

Through such a formulation, Rawls believed he had improved upon and furthered the social compact model, and he received many accolades for his work. However, in the wonderfully competitive spirit of academia, when Robert Nozick (1938-2002) disagreed with Rawls, he decided to write a book which he named *Anarchy, State, and Utopia.*

Born to Jewish parents in Brooklyn in 1938, Nozick excelled in school, as an undergraduate at Columbia University, and as a Ph.D. student at Princeton, and landed a full professorship at Harvard University by age 30.[22] Though respected and well-known in academic circles in the northeastern United States, Nozick did not rise to fame and notoriety until he published *Anarchy, State, and Utopia* in 1974 in response to Rawls's *A Theory of Justice.*

Unlike Rawls, who took the necessity of the state as given, Nozick questioned the assumption that we need states.[23] He asked readers to imagine the worst Hobbesian state of nature and to compare it to the worst iteration of the state.[24] He then set up the same thought experiment with the best version of each and used such an experiment to explore the boundaries of the morally-justified state.[25] Nozick concludes that:

> A theory of a state of nature that begins with fundamental general descriptions of morally permissible and impermissible actions, and of deeply based reasons why some persons in any society would violate

these moral constraints, and goes on to describe how a state would arise from that state of nature will serve our explanatory purposes, even if no actual state ever arose that way.[26]

Eventually, he concluded that "[t]he just state is the minimalist state [... which] provides protection for its citizens' [natural] rights without violating the rights of anyone."[27] Asserting that "[t]he minimal state is the most extensive state that can be justified[,]"[28] Nozick suggested "[a]ny state more extensive violates people's rights."[29] He criticized the Rawlsian model as overly simplistic[30] before cautioning the reader to recognize that "[t]here is no *central* distribution, no person or group [morally] entitled to control all the resources, jointly deciding how they are to be doled out."[31] He proposed the "Entitlement Theory" to counter Rawls's "distributive justice." Nozick's Entitlement Theory presented a simple and elegant explanation of the Natural Law theory of property. He stated:

1. A person who acquires a holding in accordance with the principle of justice in acquisition is entitled to that holding.
2. A person who acquires a holding in accordance with the principle of justice in transfer, from someone else entitled to the holding, is entitled to the holding.
3. No one is entitled to a holding except by (repeated) applications of 1 and 2.[32]

Such a formulation echoes the sentiments of Thomas Jefferson who observed in 1823 that "[t]he laws of civil society, indeed, for the encouragement of industry, give the property of the parent to his family on his death, and in most civilized countries permit him even to give it, by testament, to whom he pleases."[33] In other words, a core notion of the right of property ownership relates to its limitless voluntary alienation by those who hold its title in fee simple absolute, for, as Jefferson wrote, "[t]he true foundation of republican government is the equal right of every citizen in his person and property and in their management."[34] Jefferson also believed – like Murray Rothbard, whom we shall soon discuss – that private property rights remained essential to personal liberty since the only moral transfers of property are those which are fully voluntary.[35]

Similarly, Madison began his brief essay on "Property" by paraphrasing Blackstone, without attribution: "This term in its particular application means 'that dominion which one man claims and exercises over the external things of the world, in exclusion of every other individual.'"[36] In the next line, however, Madison seems to channel Jefferson – who argued that the sole limit on the exercise of natural rights is the natural rights of others – when he says: "In its larger and juster meaning, it embraces every thing to which a man may attach a value and have a right, and which leaves to every one else the like advantage."[37]

This Nozickian explanation, consistent with Jeffersonian thought, justified a historical chain of property from its original acquisition to its current owner. He later used an example of ten Robinson Crusoes on separate islands who, after two years of isolated independence, simultaneously discover radios on their separate islands that allow them to communicate with one another.[38] Once they established communication, would those more capable Crusoes or those Crusoes lucky enough to land on more bountiful islands then become obliged to "rectify these arbitrary facts and inequities[?]"[39] Rawls might argue that such a situation would require some redistribution to achieve his concept of justice, but Nozick found "[i]t [...] pellucidly clear in this situation who is entitled to what so [that] no theory of justice is needed."[40] To Nozick, social cooperation did not require some new and just distribution of goods as Rawls had assumed. To Nozick, forming a social compact did not grant society the license to redistribute goods in attempts to smooth the edges of inequality. To Nozick, society could only create a minimalist state constrained to keeping order, establishing rule of law, and protecting its members from crimes and harm.

However, the modern academy sees the argument from consent or contract, and says it has deep flaws in many of its veins.[41] Much of the antipathy toward the consent or contract theory relates to the difficulty in justifying continuous consent based on the actions of people who lived over 230 years ago. "Those who think that consent is the foundation of authority cannot tolerate the supposition that the current generation is subject to the law [i.e., the Constitution] because it enjoyed the consent of the population living two hundred years ago."[42] *The notion of a social compact having normative validity by virtue of the consent of the governed is a myth.* The most notable recent discussion of this topic was from Professor Barnett, who attacked the notion of contractual social consent on any meaningful level in his recent work, *Restoring the Lost Constitution.*[43]

Randy Barnett

Randy Barnett (b. 1952) argues that from a contractual perspective consent must be personal, direct, absolute, and unanimous.[44] He identifies the problem with consent theories as characterized by a pointed lack for choice since in order "[f]or consent to bind a person, there must be a way to say 'yes' as well as 'no.'"[45] Some argue that those who do not consent can move outside the boundaries of that society. Accordingly, their continued presence within such a jurisdiction subject to certain rules implies a tacit consent to the authority that governs that jurisdiction. To combat such tacit consent theories,[46] Barnett advances several arguments. First, in discussing tacit consent to the outcome of a referendum merely by voting, he argues that to give rise to a duty of obedience within a legal order, a referendum may be sufficient to represent consent, but "it does not follow that individual voters, by voting, have consented to be bound [by the outcome] themselves."[47] With respect to abstentions, a theory must then claim that the mere option of participating in universal suffrage is what encapsulates consent. However, any such theory falls apart "when one realizes that, if consent is an expressing of willingness to go along with something, then this presupposes it is possible to express an unwillingness to go along"—voting for, against, or abstaining represents consent under that scheme.[48] "It is a queer sort of consent where there is no way to refuse consent."[49] That is stating a truism mildly.

In discussing tacit consent by residency, wherein a person implicitly consents to a legal order by remaining within its geographical jurisdiction, Barnett contends that one's failure to emigrate does not equate to consent to an entire legal regime, as the reasoning would be circular.[50] He considers a similar demand:

Suppose one refused to take the oath [to obey the law]. Would one then not be bound to obey the laws of the United States? Or would one then be expelled from the country? The latter prospect presupposes that the person who is demanding we take an oath is an authority who has the right to expel us if we refuse, but it is his authority that is at issue in the first place and that supposedly demands [or requires] our consent.[51]

He supports this notion with the historical fact that "[b]efore the Holocaust—and even after it began—many Jews remained in Germany when they had a chance to escape, but chose to stay for a variety of reasons."[52] Further, "[w]hatever else we can say about their decisions, we cannot conclude that, merely by their presence, they tacitly assented to the Nuremberg laws."[53]

When it comes to tacit consent by a failure to revolt, as constituting tacit consent, Barnett notes that "the failure of enough people to band together to overthrow a government tells us nothing about the consent of the individual to be bound by the commands of the government and therefore it tells us nothing about why the laws are binding on the individual."[54] While that argument could be rehabilitated by arguing a failure to attempt to amend the scheme implies consent, such an argument is defeasible on the same grounds as the argument about emigration.[55]

Barnett rejects Edmund Morgan's theory of tacit consent—that there is a fictional consent that derives from general acquiescence—effectively arguing that this is a flawed theory.[56] By and large, it confuses a Hartian rule of recognition "with the conditions of constitutional legitimacy"—something also decried by Joseph Raz.[57] This confounds the issue of consent to a legal regime, and thus its normative force, with the fact of the existence of that legal scheme in the first place.[58]

Barnett argues that theories of hypothetical consent, or rational choice theories, "may well provide an argument in favor of certain moral or political principles, [however] such an argument is not based on the real-world consent of anyone [now living] to anything [now being enforced]."[59] He relies on the work of Lysander Spooner to show that "everyone cannot be presumed—in the absence of express or actual [personal] consent—to have given up their rights."[60]

Spooner's is the classic Lockean formulation of the natural law argument about consent and surrender of some limited rights to a government charged with protecting all natural rights. For if natural rights are personal and thus integral to individuals, they are not subject to majoritarianism. I can surrender certain of my rights, but I can neither surrender any of yours nor justify or authorize a government seizure of them, absent due process.

With respect to the consent of the founders, or the argument that the consent of the founding generation alone is relevant to this issue, Barnett notes that the argument is susceptible to "the exact same problems here as we saw with voting, only once removed. Now we are talking about deficiencies in other people's consent, not ours."[61]

Joseph Raz (b. 1939), an Israeli disciple of Hart, and co-editor of the second edition of Hart's *The Concept of Law*, takes a broader form of attack in his book, *Between Authority and Interpretation: On the Theory of Law and Practical Reason.*[62] He begins by embracing Barnett's argument that the dead simply cannot consent for the living, so any form of dead hand control is illicit as a moral principle.[63] He argues that whatever merit is left in hypothetical consent lacks the normative force of real consent, "which hypothetical consent does not have."[64] However, Raz asks a puzzling question: "If consent to authority is effective only when based on adequate reasons to recognize the authority, why are these reasons not enough in themselves to establish that authority?"[65] Raz argues that "many areas of government action are matters of setting up schemes to facilitate conformity with precepts of justice and morality, and these are typical of matters where obligations that are not voluntary abound."[66]

Barnett, on the other hand, has a different account of the Lockean limitations implied by the "state of license" and that of liberty, and accordingly the extent of human freedom. Largely, Barnett and your author are in agreement about many fundamentals about the natural law. First, we both proceed in large part from a Lockean, rather than a Hobbesian State of Nature, in that we both recognize that natural rights and the duty to respect them preexist a constitution or government in a state of equality. We both recognize that natural law can have a religious origin, per Saint Thomas Aquinas and Hugo Grotius – God the Father, God the Creator – or a secular one, per Murray Rothbard: Man the Reasoner.[67] We both find that necessity is an important aspect to a normative account of government. We also both have a cognitivist account of human action underlying our theory of government. Barnett in *Structure of Liberty* poses the following for the origin of normative force:

> The normative force of Natural Law can therefore be seen as the imperative of "if—then." If you want to achieve Y, then you ought to do Z. If you want to live and be happy, then you ought not jump off tall buildings or drink poison. If you want to facilitate the pursuit of

happiness by those living in a society with others, then you ought to adhere to certain basic principles. . . . [E]ven if natural rights generated only a "prudential" or "hypothetical obligation, this would be plenty significant. For the hypothetical at issue is: if we want a society in which persons can survive and pursue happiness, peace, and prosperity, then we should respect the liberal conception of justice—as defined by natural rights—and the rule of law.[68]

The link between if-and-then, given the examples provided, presupposes the ability to reason—and that relatedly, per Aquinas and Locke, reason governs all human action.[69]

Barnett argues that: "... a law is *just*, and therefore binding in conscience, if its restrictions are (1) *necessary* to protect the rights of others and (2) *proper* insofar as they do not violate the preexisting rights of the persons on whom they are imposed."[70] Here, Barnett takes three normative sources for laws in order to justify a *prima facie* duty of obedience: justice, necessity, and propriety. Justice, the overarching concept and source of normative force, is achieved by adherence to the other two. Necessity in the literal sense (as opposed to its bastardization by Chief Justice Marshall in *McCulloch v. Maryland*, discussed in Chapter 11), is relatively self-explanatory. Propriety does away with the "need to obtain the consent of the person on whom a law is imposed," so normative reasons outside of consent have the force to bind, absent interference with that which they aim to preserve.[71]

That is the large point of distinction between Barnett and your author. While Barnett's theory implies that there remains an area of natural liberty to which human license does not extend before the limits of another's rights or one's duties, your author does not. There is no space for such propriety when referencing preexisting rights and then stating, what is the equivalent of a rule of recognition. The state of liberty articulated by John Locke includes the right to choices, behaviors, or experience not proscribed by natural obligations; that is, the presence or exercise of others' natural rights.

Rather, necessity to preserve the core of natural liberty requires the recognition of the right to do anything within the bounds of natural law, and that core of natural rights or liberties (as opposed to purely positive or political ones) may not be imposed on anyone without express consent. Moreover, the sphere of rights that is natural and inalienable may not be abrogated even *with* consent; I cannot morally be a slave to a person or the government. This argument gives weight to a broader range of actions than, say, consent, but roughly the same force as a Barnett like concept of justice. The argument in favor can be stated inductively and deductively.

Recall Nozick's argument for a moral state arising out of the need to separate adjudication and ownership. Without it, such a government, as Nozick states, the scheme of purely private enforcement between two parties would lead to "feuds, to an endless series of acts of retaliation and [] compensation;" moreover, "there is no firm way to *settle* such a dispute, to *end* it and to have both parties know it is ended[,]"[72] other than the positivistic notion of might making right. The overarching theme of this inductive account is that individuals have rights, but only have self-help in the state of nature to vindicate claims; for a scheme of rights to preserve its meaning and benefit—and not be an empty set or a vacuous bundle— rights must have meaning. Therefore, out of necessity, a central monopolization for authorizing and distributing force may be created for equal vindication of rights. That immediately controlling government will not have to defend its legitimacy to authorize force against the legitimacy of other organizations (except states and revolts). The resultant normative force of a scheme is exactly to the extent that such a scheme is *necessary* to preserve the individual's liberty (natural rights) in an overall scheme of ordered – as opposed to state of nature – liberty.

Importantly, this is only a *prima facie* duty in the law of nature. There is a right to self-help (that can be limited by government) which permits an enforcement of a duty or rights structure (noting that rights assertion is a claiming activity); however, collectivization of wills for common defense will normally be necessary to preserve the greatest amount of freedom. That is, we can more capably parse minimal suppressions of liberty to our own social rules by virtue of collective decision-making than we can stand up to an army, or even a stronger neighbor.[73]

But how may we measure the extent to which we may exercise our own conceptions of the boundaries of our rights and liberties? Professor Barnett has argued that, [w]hile the Necessary and Proper Clause has long been used to greatly expand congressional power, [...] that, to the contrary, it provides a two--part standard against which all national legislation should be judged: Such laws shall be "necessary and proper." According to this standard, laws that are either unnecessary or improper are beyond the powers of Congress to enact.[74]

Barnett prefers to revisit a Madisonian interpretation of the word "necessary" through exploration of Madison's Bank Speech (as discussed in Chapter 7).[75] In short, in opposition to Marshall's expansive reading of the Necessary and Proper Clause in *McCulloch*, discussed in Chapter 11, Barnett believes that what is *necessary* should be determined by the courts, since *per Marbury*, determining the meaning of words and phrases in the Constitution is not a proper legislative function. "In sum, a Madisonian or strict conception of necessity is a matter of constitutional principle and within the purview of judicial review, whereas a Marshallian or loose conception of necessity is a matter of legislative policy and outside the purview of courts."[76] For Barnett, and your author, only an independent judiciary sworn to uphold natural rights can decide what is necessary and proper; as the legislature will *always* find its legislation to be necessary and proper. As well, the legislature is constitutionally incompetent to determine what the law means. Barnett invoked Madison arguing that:

> Thus, for Madison, whether or not a proposed action of government that restricted the liberty of the people was necessary, and therefore within the powers of Congress to enact, required some assessment of whether the means chosen were essential to the pursuit of an enumerated end. Without this assessment, the scheme of limited enumerated powers would unravel. In his words, allowing the exercise of a power that was neither specifically enumerated nor fairly inferred from one that it "involves the guilt of usurpation, and establishes a precedent of interpretation levelling all the barriers which limit the powers of the General Government…"[77]

But how may we measure the extent to which we may morally exercise our liberties and reach their boundaries? Recall the two important formulations: The Millian Harm Principle and Rothbardian Non-Aggression Principle. If the NAP sounds familiar, it is because it parallels the Millian Harm Principle. Both the Harm Principle and the Non-Aggression Principle are species of a similar principle. However, between the two of them there is a formulation of the Non-Aggression Principle and the Harm Principle that I believe to be a defensible central ethic of the natural law, and thus protected from government disparagement by the Ninth Amendment—the principal constitutional instrument that protects non-enumerated rights.

Murray Rothbard and The Non-Aggression Principle

Professor Murray Rothbard (1926-1995) believed in the sanctity of private property rights and understood all rights as emerging from or relating to property. Born in New York City in 1926, Rothbard was an economist and social philosopher who "fiercely defended individual freedom against government intervention…"[78] Rothbard contended, "every person, at any time or place, can be covered by the basic rules: ownership of one's own self, ownership of the previously unused resources which one has occupied and transformed; and ownership of all titles derived from that basic ownership—either through voluntary exchanges or voluntary gifts."[79] Whereas Jeremy Bentham sought to separate morality from law and reformulate law as a rules-based approach to human interaction, Rothbard sought instead to ignore existing rules and recast all oppositional human interaction into acts of aggressor and victim. While "peaceful cooperation and voluntary interpersonal relation" remained the optimal form of human interaction, Rothbard acknowledged that conflict could arise. He explained, "[t]here is, however, another and contrasting type of interpersonal relation: the use of aggressive violence by one man against another. What such aggressive violence means is that one man invades the property of another without the victim's consent."[80]

Accordingly, if all of a person's rights flow from his or her bodily ownership, or his or her ownership of physical property, then any violation of those bounded property rights, in the Rothbardian terms, becomes some form aggression or violence against them, and violates the Non-Aggression Principle (NAP).[81] Rothbard explained: The invasion may be against a man's property in his person (as in the case of bodily assault), or against his property in tangible goods (as in robbery or trespass). In either case, the aggressor imposes his will over the natural property of another—he deprives the other man of his freedom of action and of the full exercise of his natural self ownership.

Rothbard's ideas required new definitions for property rights and criminality. There is a "right of every individual to own his person and the property that he has found and transformed, and therefore 'created,' and the property which he has acquired either as gifts from or in voluntary exchange with other such transformers or 'producers.'"[82] *We thus have a theory of the rights of property:* that every man has an absolute right to the control and ownership of his own body, and to unused land resources that he finds and transforms. He also has the right to give away such tangible property (though he cannot alienate control over his own person and will) and to exchange it for the similarly derived properties of others. Hence, all legitimate property-right derives from every man's property in his own person, as well as the "homesteading" principle of unowned property rightly belonging to the first possessor.[83]

Rothbard continued, "[w]e may define anyone who aggresses against the person or other produced property of another as a *criminal*. A criminal is anyone who initiates violence against another man and his property [, as well as] anyone who uses the coercive 'political means' for the acquisition of goods and services."[84]

> We also have a theory of *criminality*: a criminal is someone who aggresses against such property. Any criminal titles to property should be invalidated and turned over to the victim or his heirs; if no such victims can be found, and if the current possessor is not himself the criminal, then the property justly reverts to the current possessor on our basic "homesteading" principle.[85]

So, in Rothbardian terms, external acts directed at a person without his or her consent that in any way negatively impact or impair his or her rights become an act of violence or aggression against them, even if done by the government. In Rothbard's world, every nonconsensual, unwelcome, non-trivial act committed by one person against the person or property of another becomes an act of aggression, and thus violates the NAP. To keep order between people, then, Rothbard proclaimed that "no one may threaten or commit violence ('aggress') against another man's person or property."[86] Accordingly, "[v]iolence may be employed only against the man who commits such violence; that is, only defensively against the aggressive violence of another."[87] So, in Rothbardian terms, "no violence may be employed against a nonaggressor."[88] Through such an expression as his NAP, Rothbard believed he had distilled "the fundamental rule from which [could] be deduced the entire corpus of libertarian theory."[89] Rothbard stands as the intellectual hero to contemporary libertarians, including your author, because of this distillation and all that flows from it.

To explore the NAP further, suppose Professor Rothbard decided to host a small party on his private property in his backyard. Let us imagine that Rothbard's backyard exists in some alternate reality where time would not prevent him from including figures that had long passed, such as Madison and Jefferson, Bentham, Mill, Locke, and other great minds and figures that we have already examined. Suppose, as well, that Rothbard posted, on his property, a clear set of rules or guidelines regarding the behavior he expects from his guests. Imagine, as well, that this version of Rothbard, for some inexplicable reason, wildly diverges from his libertarian ethos and decides to impose some arbitrary, tyrannical rules upon his guests:

1. No guns.
2. No smoking tobacco.

Such an arrangement could lead to tremendous conflicts between Rothbard and his guests.

Hobbes, for instance, who famously considered life "solitary, poore, [sic] nasty, brutish, and short[,]"[90] also believed in the supreme power of the sovereign so long as those over whom the sovereign ruled have agreed to some compact under which to band together. Because "Hobbes's analysis pertains to life in a state of anarchy," we must recognize that he begins from a completely stateless society.[91] As we saw in Chapter 1, he argued that people should cede certain rights to the sovereign in exchange for the sovereign's protection against others. However, Hobbes believed the default position of stateless men and women was that of a harsh, uncaring, nasty, poor, solitary, brutish, and short existence. To Hobbes, a world of limitless violence abounded absent some *Leviathan* form of government to keep order based on rules established by the people.[92] Therefore, to Hobbes, so long as the rules of the society in which Rothbard's property sits observe certain prohibitions on violent crimes against one's person or property, Hobbes might attend Rothbard's party and leave his guns and tobacco at home.

John Locke, too, would probably attend Rothbard's party. Locke, as we saw in Chapter 1, focused on the importance of social contract as a legitimizing force behind the power of government over the people who agreed to subject themselves to it. Locke, like Hobbes, believed that government should therefore claim some form of legitimacy through the consent of those to be bound. While Locke might have bristled at the Rothbard's rules, he would likely have weighed the benefits from the temporary constraints on his liberties with the chance of getting to have some of Rothbard's canapes and a chat with Jefferson.

While Rothbard's rules may have presented little more than a temporary quandary for the likes of Hobbes and Locke, they would likely present a greater challenge to some Rothbardian purists who would consider any unwelcome restriction on their rights as an act of aggression. So Rothbard invites Bardroth, a NAP absolutist to his party. Before Bardroth enters Murray's property, Murray points out the rules, and Bardroth nods, and then sets foot onto Murray's private property. Bardroth then decides to flout Murray's rules by lighting up a cigar. What, then can Murray do against Bardroth? Were Bardroth on his own property, for instance, he could smoke a cigar if he so chose. However, Bardroth is not on his property: he is on Murray Rothbard's property, and Murray does not permit smoking. So, Bardroth's act would be considered an act of aggression in the NAP scheme. What, then is Rothbard's recourse? He believed "it is not the business of *law*—properly the rules and instrumentalities by which person and property are violently defended—to make people moral by use of legal violence."[93] It is, however, "the business of legal violence to defend persons and their property from violent attack, from molestation or appropriation of their property without their consent."[94] Rothbard endorsed the need for proportionality.[95] So, a "criminal, or invader, loses his own right *to the extent* that he has deprived another man of his."[96] As a result, "[i]f a man deprives another man of some of his self-ownership or its extension in physical property, to that extent does he lose his own rights."[97] Accordingly, Murray Rothbard would be able to respond to

Bardroth's act with some proportionate response. Clearly, Murray cannot shoot Bardroth for smoking a cigar on Murray's property. He needs to find some proportionate response, and, absent the arrival at such a proportionate response, consider the continuous refusal to conform to the rules of the property as a ramping up of hostilities. In the event that hostilities elevate to the point of the need for government intervention, however, "police can never be allowed to commit an invasion that is worse than, or that is more than proportionate to, the crime under investigation."[98]

Now, what if, rather than lighting up a cigar, Bardroth had decided to bring a gun onto Rothbard's property?[99] The gun, a mechanical extension of the right to self-defense, could easily be mistaken for a sign of hostility. What if Rothbard himself had guns on his property but he prohibited others from bringing guns onto his property? Presumably, offensive use of force by Rothbard against those who merely bring guns onto his property would fail the element of proportionality. However, it appears to remain the task of human reason to determine appropriate proportionate responses. And, once again, the appeal to human reason brings us back into the realm of Natural Law theory.

However, difficulties arise when trying to reconcile Rothbard's NAP with Natural Law theory. Natural Law theory, as we discussed in Chapter 1, addresses and reconciles the relationship between the law and human nature.[100] Rothbard, on the other hand, proposed a principle that focused on the boundaries that he believed should govern proper human interaction and government restraints. Rothbard's NAP provides a good framework for how people may behave toward one another in a society mostly free from the hindrance of government. He believed that "[a]bsolute freedom […] need *not* be lost as the price we must pay for the advent of civilization [since] men *are* born free, and need *never* be in chains."[101] Accordingly, "[m]an may achieve liberty *and* abundance, freedom *and* civilization,"[102] but only with a government that recognizes and respects NLT and NAP. His formulation of the NAP argues that a society, comprising individuals, remains bounded by the rules governing each person as an individual actor. So, any form of coercion compelling some sort of activity, whether based on labor, such as compelled work, or some form of mandatory tribute to a sovereign authority, such as taxes, become acts of aggressive coercion under NAP and therefore registers as immoral and unconscionable.

This approach to interpersonal relationships provides the strongest moral support for the primacy of the individual over the state – any state, authoritarian or majoritarian. In this, Rothbard is the polar opposite of Rawls: To Rothbard, a collective – the government – may only do what its constituents may morally do individually.[103] In other words, Rothbard's NAP formulation considers most heavily the rules and practices that should govern how people act towards one another, and Rothbard maintains that such an approach translates directly to the limitations of government. This is not necessarily inconsistent with NLT. He reasons that just as John Doe many not claim ownership over part of his neighbor Jane Roe's property because he feels that he may put it to better use than Jane Roe, so too, the government may not do the same to individuals. But Rothbard extends this argument to *all* interaction between people and government. He – like your author – criticizes and condemns certain long-accepted government practices and customs, like taxation, as violative of NAP.

When it comes to the moral component of criminal laws, laws designed to prohibit certain behavior under threat of punishment, how may we properly construct laws to be *objectively* moral rather than just reflections of popular majoritarian beliefs?

This question remains, and, unfortunately, no modern legislator has made any significant contribution to the field of jurisprudence. Instead, philosophers have endeavored to explore notions of society and the limits of the powers of government over individuals. John Rawls suggested government should focus on ensuring the burden of justice falls disproportionately less on the disadvantaged, while Robert Nozick argued for a purer form of government that essentially leaves individuals alone and that treats each individual the same with respect to his or her rights regardless of the unique traits or advantages that came from birth. Joseph Raz argued along Benthamite-Austinian-Hartian lines, that laws should consider social facts rather than abstract moral principles. Randy Barnett appealed to the libertarian notions of a Lockean formulation of society bound by NLT that considered, as their main constituent, limitations imposed on governments by the existing natural rights of others. And Murray Rothbard arguably saved NLT from rejection by many non-religionists, when he re-formulated it to NAP, conjoined by the truism of self-ownership. However, none of these great philosophers ever sat on the bench, so they could only hope to influence government through the osmotic effect of papers, articles, and arguments. Save for the occasional amicus brief, these giants rarely laid out cases and arguments before judges.[104]

In our nation's history, only 115 individuals have served as justices of the Supreme Court. These individuals, together, have had a tremendous impact on the law, as we have seen and as we will continue to see.

Few, in recent history, have been as vocal, as pithy, as sincere, and as intellectually rigorous as your author's dear friend and intellectual sparring partner, the late Justice Antonin Scalia who became the most significant and prominent champion of a theory of jurisprudence known as Originalism; which became the chief contemporary antagonist to NLT jurisprudence. To this antagonism, we turn next.

CHAPTER 17

A TALE OF TWO ORIGINALISTS

The Argument

Though legal positivism had served as the chief antagonist to NLT jurisprudence for centuries, the two forms of jurisprudence may find common ground in a modified form of legal positivism that reflects and respects the commands of the Ninth Amendment.

Justice Antonin Scalia, one of the foremost proponents of a version of positivism known as "Originalism," brought to the Supreme Court a conservative doctrinal approach that called for the narrow interpretation of statutes and constitutional provisions consistent with the original public understanding of the words in question at the time they were ratified or enacted.

Far from using Originalism as a straitjacket, Justice Scalia advocated for a considered approach to interpretation that looked to the original public understanding of the words of the text but allowed for the occasional divergence from anachronistic sensibilities in favor of a reasonable, contemporary outlook.

His approach, along with Professor Randy Barnett's emphasis on the power of the Ninth Amendment allows for an originalist approach to jurisprudence that also firmly incorporates Natural Law theories through the Ninth Amendment.

Borrowing from Rothbard and working within the framework of a natural law and positivist methodology, one can formulate a new series of principles designed to minimize government overreach and maximize individual freedom.

***

I try to be an honest originalist! I will take the bitter with the sweet![1]

– Antonin Scalia (1936-2016)

AN OVERVIEW OF ORIGINALISM

Though typically at loggerheads, Natural Law theory and legal positivism can find common purchase through soft-hearted approaches to Originalism that factor in the principles behind the Ninth Amendment to the U.S. Constitution. Justice Antonin Scalia, one of the most significant figures in the spread and modern development of Originalism, brought what he believed to be a greater sense of order and consistency to the bench by calling for judges to restrict their decisions in a narrow fashion by adhering to Originalism, a philosophy he believed would lead toward more authentic and honest interpretation of laws and the Constitution itself.

As time passes, language can undergo semantic shift in which the popular meanings of words change.[2] So, in order truly to understand a statute, some argued, one needed to seize the mantel of the historian and endeavor to determine what was meant by a statute at the time of its passage rather than interpreting the statute according to the contemporary meaning of its words. In 1982, Paul Brest, then a professor at Stanford Law School, coined the term "Originalism" which he defined as "the familiar approach to constitutional adjudication that accords binding authority to the text of the Constitution or the intention of its adopters."[3] According to Brest, "[a]dherence to the text and original understanding arguably constrains the discretion of decision makers [i.e., judges] and assures that the Constitution will be interpreted consistently over time."[4]

Different flavors of Originalism focus on different original elements involved in the drafting, creation, adoption, and passage of various elements of the Constitution, its amendments, and legislation written under its authority. The textualists look to the language of the text in question.[5] "The plain meaning of a text is the meaning that it would have for a 'normal speaker of English' under the circumstances in which it is used."[6] Though textualists focus mainly on the words of the text in question, they will occasionally consult outside sources to determine exactly what a word or a term of art meant to the general public at the time the particular provision was adopted or passed. In other words, they may look to newspapers, other legislation, books, speeches, circulars, broadsides, treatises, or treaties contemporaneous to the particular language they seek to understand. However, such an approach looks to extratextual material only in so far as it clarifies the meaning of the words involved in the piece in question and is not used to try to understand what may have been the intent of those who adopted the law. The textualists care only about the plain public meaning *of the words* at the time they were written, not the intent of the authors.

Intentionalists, on the other hand, seek to divine the intentions of those who adopted or passed a piece of legislation or provision.[7] They endeavor to do so by considering the text of the law or provision as a persuasive—though not controlling—authority.

Intentionalists will look to a nearly endless variety of sources related, directly, or even imaginarily, to the piece in question. The camps of intentionalists diverge or sometimes disagree over *whose* intent they should consider. Some believe that the intent of the drafters of a piece should carry more weight when it comes to its interpretation, while others argue for heavier consideration of the intent of those who adopted it. Further wrinkles arise when others advocate for the inclusion of ideas of legal structuralism, calling for evaluation of the relationships between the various branches of government at the time of the passage of language in question to determine how different organs of government relate to and interact with one another.

Justice Scalia and Faint Hearted Originalism

With all the different approaches to Originalism vying for supremacy, Scalia favored and promulgated a modified version of Originalism which became known as "Faint-Hearted Originalism" which argued for a strict, limited, interpretive, textual approach that bound judges to narrow interpretations based on dogmatic adherence to the concept of original public understanding. Justice Scalia believed such a dogmatically conservative approach would diminish judicial activism in favor of a studied approach relying on exhaustive analysis of the words of a law in question, irrespective of the judicial outcome.

Conservative interpretation of constitutional provisions and laws with strict consideration to their content may sound a lot like legal positivism. In many ways, Originalism is like legal positivism in that it explores only the content of the law or provision without factoring in the moral component (or absence thereof) in a given statute. In this manner, Originalism presents an amoral doctrinal approach to jurisprudence. Laws adopted by and passed by tyrants would lead to interpretations just as tyrannical and oppressive in the hands of an originalist as they would in the hands of a Benthamite, Austinian, or Hartian. Likewise, laws passed by a Rawlsian or Nozickian would likely take the character of their framers when interpreted by an originalist. In many ways, an originalist becomes a bit of a cipher, an uncritical diachronic detective exploring subjective and selective accounts of history – as opposed to reason – and striving to interpret a statute and apply its tenets in a way consistent to the manner in which they believe those who adopted it and passed it would have understood it.

Justice Scalia argued that originalist methodology leads to more predictable, authentic, and consistent interpretation of statutes. Laws can often be very clear. Interpreting ambiguities in favor of the usages and practices consistent with the time of a law's adoption can lead to greater judicial consistency which, in turn, he argued leads to more predictable outcomes, and greater confidence for those attempting to behave in a manner consistent with the rules of society in an effort to avoid sanction. However, as Justice Scalia observed, an originalist approach can lead to somewhat awkward results when analyzing texts of passages from bygone eras.

Take, for instance, the Eighth Amendment to the Constitution which prohibits cruel and unusual punishment.[8] Attempts to interpret the original public understanding of the Eighth Amendment could lead to arguments for permitting the use of stocks, flogging, branding, or any number of formerly typical punitive measures from the 1790s, happily eschewed today. Notions of cruelty, too, certainly differed in the late eighteenth century. Are we then to permit, in perpetuity, punishments that shock the modern conscience – such as branding – but remained pedestrian in 1791?

When your author confronted Justice Scalia with such a question in 2014 in front of an audience of several thousand at the Brooklyn Academy of Music, he admitted that he was more of a "faint-hearted" originalist who did not insist we export popular eighteenth century cultural concepts, such as notions of cruelty and punishment to modern times.[9] He may have argued that inclusion of the word *unusual* in the Eighth Amendment indicated the presence of a sliding scale that allows for consideration of the how societal attitudes about punitive measures change over time.

Though a version of legal positivism, Originalism does not necessarily exist exclusive of consideration to Natural Law Theory. Indeed, Justice Scalia, with his "softhearted" approach creates some room for an understanding of Natural Law theories to enter into the originalist's interpretive canon.

Randy Barnett's Originalism

Professor Barnett, for instance, argues for adherence to both natural law and originalist principles. In *Restoring the Lost Constitution*, Barnett argues for an originalist approach, not too different from that called for by Justice Scalia, in which one could reconcile the belief in NLT jurisprudence with the desire to combat the occasional practice of judges to engage in judicial activism where they seek to further some social or political end better left and constitutionally delegated to other branches of government or to social institutions. Barnett explained that "[T]he Ninth Amendment does more than merely refer to these unenumerated natural rights and affirm their existence, however. It also mandates how they are to be treated: they are not to be 'denied or disparaged.'"[10] But how should one determine the scope of those rights? If you ask an originalist, he will tell you "look to the era and the words of those involved in its crafting and passage!"

Madison, as we saw in Chapter 7, drafted the language of the Bill of Rights. Barnett reminds us that "all of Madison's proposals were referred to a Select Committee of the House, which decided to list the amendments after the body of the original Constitution rather than insert them in the text."[11] Madison had originally suggested the government shall not "diminish the importance of" certain rights in the Constitution, but it was the House committee that changed the words to "the stronger phrase 'deny or disparage.'"[12] Barnett invoked Madison's opposition to the national bank, discussed in Chapter 7.[13] "Madison viewed the Ninth Amendment as providing authority for a rule against the loose construction of [government powers]— especially the Necessary and Proper Clause—when legislation affected the rights retained by the people."[14]

Barnett argued that "Madison's use of the Ninth Amendment shows that, like the natural rights that were enumerated, the unenumerated rights retained by the people provide[d] a twofold check on government power."[15] Consistent with an originalist approach, "both the plain and original meanings of the Ninth Amendment require the strict construction of any power that restricts the exercise of individual liberty, whether that liberty is enumerated or unenumerated."[16] Thus, according to Barnett – and your author totally agrees – *any judge, despite his or her personal philosophy, should always err on the side of liberty when adjudicating any matter that concerns the exercise of individual liberty, particularly if the liberty in question may be recognized as natural.*

In other words, any philosophical approach which calls for examination of the original public understanding of the Constitution and the Bill of Rights must look not only to those documents for guidance but also consider them, NLT, and NAP in their entirety. The Ninth Amendment explicitly commands that the government honor, respect, and protect non-enumerated rights. And, as we have demonstrated, those who drafted, crafted, and adopted the Bill of Rights strongly believed in inalienable rights retained by individuals that they could limitlessly exercise without the fear of government infringement and without fear of sanction. Yet, this is Professor Barnett's version of Originalism, not Justice Scalia's.

Any approach to American jurisprudence that ignores, dismisses, or otherwise passes over considerations of NLT and NAP necessarily fails to maintain its internal consistency by selectively rejecting the Ninth and (according to Madison) the Tenth Amendments. All forms of American jurisprudence must acknowledge the supremacy of the Constitution and its amendments, including the Ninth and the Tenth. Consequently, no decision may diminish or disparage the non-enumerated rights retained by the people. Originalists who do not factor into their calculus how a decision may run afoul of the Natural Law Tradition and the Non-Aggression Principle disingenuously follow their elected doctrine. Even Justice Scalia overlooked the importance of the incorporation of NLT and NAP into constitutional interpretation and application. Barnett, on the other hand, allowed for the comingling of NLT, NAP, and Originalism through studied consideration of the Ninth Amendment.

However, Ninth Amendment jurisprudence, an oft neglected field, remains underdeveloped when compared to the record of cases examining most of the other amendments and clauses of the Constitution. Rather, the Supreme Court has explored the role of the Natural Law Tradition in the context of cases and controversies that explored the natural rights of those implicated in civil and criminal processes. Though many of these cases did not expressly involve the Ninth Amendment, each did subject to the scrutiny of the Court some natural right, whether contained expressly within the Constitution or otherwise protected by the aegis of the Ninth Amendment. The rulings and dissents in these cases demonstrate an obstacle-strewn journey of the Natural Law Tradition in the Supreme Court and underscore the challenges it faces in light of competing forms of jurisprudence. We examine that journey next.

CHAPTER 18

THE SISYPHEAN JOURNEY OF NATURAL LAW IN AMERICAN COURTS IN THE NINETEENTH CENTURY

The Argument

Despite its universal beginnings, Natural Law theory has ebbed and flowed, caught in the orbital gravity of social and political thought. While it yielded ground to legal positivism during the waning days of the Marshall Court, it was never truly abandoned in American jurisprudence.

Throughout its existence, the Supreme Court has, from time to time, turned to Natural Law theory when contemplating fundamental rights and the limits of state action.

***

There is no doubt that if there were a super Supreme Court, a substantial proportion of our reversals of state courts would also be reversed. We are not final because we are infallible, but we are infallible only because we are final.[1]

– Robert H. Jackson (1892-1954)

COMPREHENSIVE REVIEW OF SUPREME COURT CASES THAT ADDRESS NATURAL LAW[2]

Philosophy does not develop in a vacuum. Through thorough study, we can trace the lineage of philosophical thought to the beginning of recorded history. Some ideas never die, no matter how naïve, erroneous, or perfidious. Luckily good ideas persist as well. Though occasionally neglected and at times intentionally forgotten, Natural Law Tradition jurisprudence never went away. Legal positivism and all its variations failed to snuff out the light of reason from the pages of the Supreme Court Reporter. Since the early days of John Jay, the justices of the Supreme Court have used every means of interpretation and jurisprudence available to them in aid of interpreting laws, treaties, and the U.S. Constitution.

The natural law, once the prevailing theory in western jurisprudence, has fallen in and out of favor for centuries. But, since it addresses and reconciles the relationship between law and human nature, it should always have a place in jurisprudence. Chapters 8, 9, 10, 11, and 14 of this work explored some of the major cases implicating the juxtaposition between natural law and legal positivism. Now, we will explore how courts have woven Natural Law theories into positive jurisprudence, and also how they have attacked it.

Like Theseus, one can follow the thread through labyrinthine court reporters spanning over two-and-a quarter centuries. Winding our way through opinions, pouring through lines of cases spanning social and political epochs, we can trace the rise and fall of natural law trends in decision-making. While the Natural Law Tradition has never quite returned to the same prominence it reached in its American apex during the days of the early federal republic, it has enjoyed a resurgence and rediscovery following the conclusion of the Second World War. However, a keen eye can find signposts pointing to NLT principles peppered throughout the Supreme Court Reporter following the first major blow to it in *McCulloch v. Maryland.*

Wilkinson v. Leland

Even more occasionally, the Supreme Court tossed about small references to natural law principles and theories of natural rights to remind us that it was never too far from the justices' minds. In 1829, the Supreme Court considered whether a state legislature could interfere with ownership rights to private property in *Wilkinson v. Leland.*[3] In the case, "the state of Rhode Island had attempted by statute to confirm title to Rhode Island real estate."[4] Specifically, "[t]he property had been sold by an executrix of an insolvent New Hampshire testator pursuant to authority granted by a New Hampshire probate court."[5] However, "[b]ecause the United States Supreme Court held that the title was valid without regard to the legislation, it did not need to decide the question of the constitutionality of the statute."[6] Nonetheless, Justice Story examined the issues and declared: The fundamental maxims of a free government seem to require, that

> *the rights of personal liberty and private property should be held sacred.* At least no court of justice in this country would be warranted in assuming, that the power to violate and disregard them; a power so repugnant to the common principles of justice and civil liberty lurked under any general grant of legislative authority, or ought to be implied from any general expressions of the will of the people. The people ought not to be presumed to part with rights so vital to their security and well being, without very strong and direct expressions of such an intention.[7]

The Supreme Court invoked "common principles of justice[,]" a secular phrase for the principles of natural law. And, it would again turn to ideas of reason, common principles of justice, and common sense.

Harris v. Hardeman

In 1852 in *Harris v. Hardeman*, the Supreme Court set aside a judgement against a defendant, affirming the holding of the U.S. Circuit Court for the Southern District of Mississippi which found service of process had been deficient.[8] The Court felt that precedent "as well as of reason and common sense" could "amply sustain [the] conclusions of law."[9] Justice Peter Daniel quoted Chief Justice Smith Thompson of the Supreme Court of New York in explaining the necessity of notice "is not considered as growing out of any thing peculiar to proceedings by attachment, but is founded on more enlarged and general principles."[10] These "more enlarged and general principles" echoed by the Supreme Court can only be the enlarged and general principles of natural law. How under NLT can someone be sued without notice?

Cummings v. Missouri

In 1867 in *Cummings v. Missouri*, the Supreme Court rejected a Missouri state law on the grounds that it punished actions taken prior to its enactment – that it constituted an *ex post facto* law.[11] After commenting on the concepts of state sovereignty and the surrenders made to the federal government by each state upon its entrance to the United States,[12] Justice Steven Field explained that the Court viewed the deprivation of rights a form of punishment.[13] He declared that:

> The theory upon which our political institutions rest is, that all men have certain inalienable rights—that among these are life, liberty, and the pursuit of happiness; and that in the pursuit of happiness all avocations, all honors, all positions, are alike open to every one, and that in the protection of these rights all are equal before the law. Any deprivation or suspension of any of these rights for past conduct is punishment, and can be in no otherwise defined.[14]

The Court recognized that people had a right – a right some could still call *inalienable* – to know the law before assessing how to comply with it.

The Slaughter-House Cases

In a series of cases that became known as the *Slaughter-House Cases* (1872), the Supreme Court first interpreted the range and scope of the Fourteenth Amendment.[15] The seminal case involved an act of the Louisiana legislature to charter a private corporation to which it granted a 25-year monopoly on the slaughtering of livestock in efforts to combat the issue of offal flowing from the numerous New Orleans slaughterhouses contaminating the Mississippi River and municipal water supply, and spawning outbreaks of disease such as cholera. The city's butchers challenged the law using the rather new Fourteenth Amendment.

As it puzzled through the meaning of the "privileges and immunities" contained in Article IV, Section 2, Clause 1 of the Constitution, the Court looked to the work of the Circuit Court for the District of Pennsylvania and the work of Justice Washington in the 1812 case of *Corfield v. Coryell*.[16]

> 'The inquiry,' he says, 'is, what are the privileges and immunities of citizens of the several States? We feel no hesitation in confining these expressions to those privileges and immunities which are fundamental; which belong of right to the citizens of all free governments, and which have at all times been enjoyed by citizens of the several States which compose this Union, from the time of their becoming free, independent, and sovereign. What these fundamental principles are, it would be more tedious than difficult to enumerate. They may all, however, be comprehended under the following general heads: protection by the government, with the right to acquire and possess property of every kind, and to pursue and obtain happiness and safety, subject, nevertheless, to such restraints as the government may prescribe for the general good of the whole.'[17]

The Supreme Court accepted the "definition of privileges and immunities of citizens of the States [...] in [the] recent case of *Ward v. The State of Maryland*."[18] Almost echoing the Ninth Amendment, the Court explained: The description [of fundamental rights], when taken to include others not named, but which are of the same general character, embraces nearly every civil right for the establishment and protection of which organized government is instituted. They are, in the language of Judge Washington, those rights which are fundamental. Throughout his opinion, they are spoken of as rights belonging to the individual as a citizen of a State. They are so spoken of in the constitutional provision which he was construing. And they have always been held to be the class of rights which the State governments were created to establish and secure.[19]

Ultimately, the majority held that the butchers were not deprived of their property without due process for they were still able to earn a living; the Fourteenth Amendment bans the states from depriving Blacks of equal rights, it does not, however, require that all citizens should receive equal economic privileges by the states. The rights of the butchers to work as *butchers* is, therefore, not fundamental and unprotected by the privileges and immunities clause of the 14th Amendment.

There were, however, several substantial and significant dissents to the opinion of the majority. Justice Field explained that the Fourteenth Amendment aimed to secure "the like protection to all citizens in [a state] against any abridgment of their common rights, as in other States."[20] The Fourteenth

Amendment, he noted, "was intended to give practical effect to the declaration of 1776 of inalienable rights, rights which are the gift of the Creator, which the law does not confer, but only recognizes."[21] He continued:

> So fundamental has this privilege of every citizen *to be free from disparaging and unequal enactments, in the pursuit of the ordinary avocations of life*, been regarded, that few instances have arisen where the principle has been so far violated as to call for the interposition of the courts. But whenever this has occurred, with the exception of the present cases from

> Louisiana, which are the most barefaced and flagrant of all, the enactment interfering with the privilege of the citizen has been pronounced illegal and void.[22]

Justice Bradley also dissented from the opinion of the Court, but he concurred with Justice Field. He argued: "A violation of one of the fundamental principles of that constitution in the Colonies, namely, the principle that recognizes *the property of the people as their own*, and which, therefore, regards all taxes for the support of government as gifts of the people through their representatives, and regards taxation without representation as subversive of free government, was the origin of our own revolution.

> This, it is true, was the violation of a political right; but personal rights were deemed equally sacred, and were claimed by the very first Congress of the Colonies, assembled in 1774, as the undoubted inheritance of the people of this country; and the Declaration of Independence, which was the first political act of the American people in their independent sovereign capacity, lays the foundation of our National existence upon this broad proposition: 'That all men are created equal; that they are endowed by their Creator with certain inalienable rights; that among these are life, liberty, and the pursuit of happiness.' Here again we have the great threefold division of the rights of freemen, asserted as the rights of man. Rights to life, liberty, and the pursuit of happiness are equivalent to the rights of life, liberty, and property. These are the *fundamental rights* which can only be taken away by due process of law, and which can only be interfered with, or the enjoyment of which can only be modified, by lawful regulations necessary or proper for the mutual good of all; and these rights, I contend, belong to the citizens of every free government."[23]

Butchers' Union Slaughter-House & Live-Stock Landing Co. v. Crescent City Live-Stock Landing & Slaughter-House Co.

In 1884, the Supreme Court once again confronted the issue of a state-guaranteed monopoly as it had in the *Slaughter-House cases*.[24] Crescent City Live-stock Landing and Slaughter-House Company sought an injunction in the Circuit Court for the Eastern District of Louisiana to prevent the Butchers' Union Slaughter-House and Live-stock Landing Company from operating within certain limits of the parishes of New Orleans, Jefferson, and St. Bernard, Louisiana.[25] The Court upheld the monopoly-granting law. Justice Field concurred. As in our intercourse with our fellow men certain principles of morality are assumed to exist, without which society would be impossible, so certain inherent rights lie at the foundation of all action, and upon a recognition of them alone can free institutions be maintained. These inherent rights have never been more happily expressed than in the declaration of independence, that new evangel of liberty to the people: 'We hold these truths to be self-evident'-that is, so plain that their truth is recognized upon their mere statement-'that all men are endowed'-not by edicts of emperors, or decrees of parliament, or acts of congress, but 'by their Creator with certain inalienable rights.' that is, rights which cannot be bartered away, or given away, or taken away, except in punishment of crime-'and that among these are life, liberty, and the pursuit of happiness; and to secure these' not

> grant them, but secure them 'governments are instituted among men, deriving their just powers from the consent of the governed.' Among these inalienable rights, as proclaimed in that great document, is the right of men to pursue their happiness, by which is meant the right to pursue any lawful business or vocation, in any manner not inconsistent with the equal rights of others, which may increase their prosperity or develop their faculties, so as to give to them their highest enjoyment.[26]

Monongahela Nav. Co. v. U.S.

In 1893, in *Monongahela Nav. Co. v. U.S.*, the Supreme Court confronted limitations of eminent domain.[27] "The question presented [was] not whether the United States [had] the power to condemn and appropriate [...] property of the Monongahela Company, for that is conceded, but how much it must pay as compensation therefor."[28] Writing for the Court, Justice Brewer spoke of the principle of just compensation for the taking of land that existed *prior* to the Fifth Amendment.[29] However, he found that the court "need not have recourse to this natural equity,"[30] and that it was not "necessary to look through the constitution to the affirmations lying behind it in the Declaration of Independence, for in this fifth amendment there is stated the exact limitation on the power of the government to take private property for public uses."[31]

Chicago, B. & Q.R. Co. v. City of Chicago

In 1897, Justice Harlan, who dissented in *Plessy*, delivered an opinion for the Court in a case brought by a railroad company against the City of Chicago.[32] In *Chicago, B. & Q.R. Co. v. City of Chicago*, the Court tackled a similar issue to that in *Monongahela Nav. Co.* The City wanted to widen a street and sought to take land as well as a right of way owned by the Chicago, Burlington & Quincy Railroad Company in order to do so.[33] For the right of way, the railroad company was awarded just one dollar, and it challenged the award.[34]

> Writing for the Court, Justice Harlan noted: The requirement that the property shall not be taken for public use without just compensation is but 'an affirmance of a great doctrine established by the common law for the protection of private property. *It is founded in natural equity, and is laid down as a principle of universal law.* Indeed, in a free government, almost all other rights would become worthless if the government possessed an uncontrollable power over the private fortune of every citzen [sic].'[35]

Oblique references to concepts of "natural equity" and "universal law" are secular references to Natural Law theory. Justice Harlan just as easily could have cited to caselaw without quoting Justice Story and his *Commentaries*. Justice Harlan could have relied solely on the language of the Fifth Amendment, which makes clear, in no uncertain terms that "private property [shall not] be taken for public use, without just compensation."[36] However, in an action once again showing Justice John Marshall Harlan to be worthy of his namesake, he harkened back to natural law principles, showing that natural rights maintained a place in Supreme Court jurisprudence.

This series of cases demonstrates the ember of the Natural Law Tradition which varying justices on the Supreme Court protected from the stifling air of legal positivism. These cases, spanning nearly a century characterized by wars, westward expansion, and developments in technology so profound as to prompt an industrial revolution, show that, despite the rapidly changing character of American society, the Supreme Court refused to abandon the principles upon which the nation was founded. Though the Court could have walked away from the Natural Law Tradition and turned instead to new, emerging doctrines such as legal positivism or utilitarianism. However, it consciously elected to embrace NLT when it confronted cases where adherence to other philosophies would permit conclusions consistent with concepts of natural law and equity.

Changes to society will bring new challenges. Waiving the banners of national security, immigration, climate change, gun violence, terrorism, public safety, and any number of specters, politicians will always seek aggrandizement of their roles, their powers, their influence at the cost of some right, some liberty. Such was the case, as we saw with *Lochner* in Chapter 12, a small victory and recent highpoint in Natural Law Theory principles. And so, we turn next to the pages of the Supreme Court Reporter written in the twentieth century in search of more modern invocations of the natural law.

CHAPTER 19

THE NATURAL
REASONING BEHIND DUE PROCESS

The Argument

Following the Supreme Court's decision in Lochner v. New York, several justices used the Due Process clauses of the Fifth and Fourteenth Amendments as well as the Privileges and Immunities Clause of the Fourteenth as avenues through which they could enshrine natural law principles into constitutional jurisprudence.

Various cases provided opportunities for the Court to recognize more expansive views of property rights and further develop principles of due process as understood through reason, common sense, and fairness.

The Court recognized that, as society changes, new circumstances emerge that require due consideration of how our understanding of natural law and natural rights extend to these evolving facets within society. Changes, the Court found, provide new opportunities to discover new areas of natural law theory.

***

[M]orality, compassion generosity are innate elements of the human construction; that there exists a right independent of force; that a right to property is founded in our natural wants, in the means with which we are endowed to satisfy these wants, and the right to what we acquire by those means without violating the similar rights of other sensible beings; that no one has a right to obstruct another, exercising his faculties innocently for the relief of sensibilities made a part of his nature; that justice is the fundamental law of society; that the majority, oppressing an individual is guilty of a crime, abuses it's [sic] strength, and by acting on the law of the strongest breaks up the foundations of society[.][1]

– **Thomas Jefferson (1743-1826)**

THE USE OF NATURAL LAW REASONING TO UNCOVER AND ENFORCE NEW LIBERTIES

For many, the twentieth century high water mark of Natural Law theory jurisprudence in the U.S. Supreme Court came toward the beginning of the century in the 1905 case, *Lochner v. New York*.[2] As discussed in Chapter 12, the case involved an attempt of the New York legislature to regulate the number of hours worked by bakers in that state. The Supreme Court, heavily relying on Natural Law theory, rejected the reasoning of the state of New York and ruled in favor of economic liberty and the right to contract. Over the course of the twentieth century, however, many legal scholars, judges, and justices began to deride and decry the Supreme Court's reasoning in *Lochner* and turned the name of the petitioner into a derisive intransitive verb so prevalent in common legal usage as to garner an entry in a popular legal dictionary.[3]

Although certain legal circles rejected the Court's reasoning in *Lochner*, they could not eliminate the pockets of natural law resistance that persisted in the first half of the twentieth century. Though marginalized, *Lochner* further incorporated natural law principles into the judicial understanding of due process under the Fifth and Fourteenth Amendments, as well as the Privileges and Immunities clause of the Fourteenth. Recall that in *Lochner*, by invalidating a New York law restricting the number of hours that bakers could work, the Supreme Court found that "[t]he statute [regulating the number of hours that a baker could work] necessarily interferes with the right of contract between employer and employes, [sic] concerning the number of hours in which the latter may labor in the bakery of the employer[,]" and, as such, violated the Fourteenth Amendment's provision that required that "no State can deprive any person of life, liberty, or property without due process of law."[4] The court could have said "… the natural right of contract…" Following this line of reasoning articulated in *Lochner*, many subsequent petitioners during the twentieth century argued that their property or liberty rights related to the right to contract, often in the context of employment contracts, or, more broadly, a natural right in economic liberty made positive through the incorporation of the protection of the Bill of Rights as applied to the states through the Fourteenth Amendment.[5]

David Bernstein's Rehabilitating Lochner

Professor David E. Bernstein (b. 1967) in *Rehabilitating Lochner: Defending Individual Rights Against Progressive Reform*, challenges much of the mythology that has been built up around the *Lochner* line of cases; namely, the "conventional wisdom that liberty of contract jurisprudence was in conflict with judicial protection for individual rights," and moreover, that "[progressive] critics of that jurisprudence farsightedly sought to replace liberty of contract with protection for civil liberties against the states."[6] In fact, they planned to fill that gap with the benefits of exercising the state's police power in the sphere formally allocated to personal autonomy.[7] The modern blending of New Deal liberals, who twisted the banner of individual liberty into something which ignored the economic sphere, with early 1900s Progressives, who believed that many individual liberties such as life, liberty, property, and privacy, were subordinate to the state, is disingenuous. Bernstein's account of economic liberties as a species of personal civil liberty lines up with the *Lochner* doctrine of liberty to contract, and Bernstein's description of *Lochner*-izing as declining to distinguish between civil and economic liberties is difficult to refute.

Adair v. United States: Enshrining the Natural Right to Contract for Labor and Employment

In October 1907, the Supreme Court heard *Adair v. United States*, a case in which the petitioner challenged part of an 1898 federal statute targeting unrest in the railroad industry.[8] Specifically, the section of the statute in question prevented companies from discriminating against employees or potential employees who joined or were already members of a labor union.[9] William Adair, an "agent and employee" of the Louisville & Nashville Railroad Company had fired O. B. Coppage for Coppage's "membership in [the Order of Locomotive Firemen]."[10] After his indictment, Adair "pleaded not guilty, and after the trial[,] a verdict was returned of guilty on the [on the charge of violating Section 10 of the Erdman Act] and a judgement rendered that he pay to the United States a fine of $100[,]"[11] the lowest fine permissible by statute.[12] However, once before the Supreme Court, Justice John Marshall Harlan found the relevant part of the Erdman Act of 1898 unconstitutional.

Since the case involved a law that interfered with liberty and property, the court needed to consider if it involved:

> a fair, reasonable, and appropriate exercise of the policepower [sic] of the state, or is it an unreasonable, unnecessary, and arbitrary interference with the right of the individual to his personal liberty or to enter into those contracts in relation to labor which may seem to him appropriate or necessary for the support of himself and his family[.][13]

Justice Harlan, writing for the court, contemplated the extent to which the state and federal governments could interfere with personal liberty and economic liberty— secular twentieth century watchwords for natural rights. He explained that Section 10 of the Erdman Act of 1898:[14] [I]s an invasion of the personal liberty, as well as of the right of property, guaranteed by [the Fifth] Amendment. Such liberty and right embrace the right to make contracts for the purchase of the labor of others, and equally the right to make contracts for the sale of one's own labor; each right, however, being subject to the fundamental condition that no contract, whatever its subject-matter, can be sustained which the law, upon reasonable grounds, forbids as inconsistent with the public interests, or as hurtful to the public order, or as detrimental to the common good.[15] Central to the Court's reasoning was the nearly boundless right to economic liberty—namely, the natural right to contract for labor and employment.[16]

The Court went on to note that certain elements surrounding the right to contract extend *beyond* the reach of government:

> While, as already suggested, the right of liberty and property guaranteed by the Constitution against deprivation without due process of law is subject to such reasonable restraints as the common good or the general welfare may require, *it is not within the functions of government*—at least, in the absence of contract between the parties—*to compel any person, in the course of his business and against his will, to accept or retain the personal services of another, or to compel any person, against his will, to perform personal services for another.*[17]

And, while the Court continued to enshrine some natural law principles in the corpus of American constitutional law, it inexplicably managed to stumble when confronted with whether certain codified natural rights, such as the right against self-incrimination and compelled speech, could stand up to the tyranny of overreaching state government.

Twining v. State of New Jersey: The Natural Right to Silence

In *Twining v. State of New Jersey* (1908),[18] the Court tackled a case in which two men charged with fraud invoked their Fifth Amendment rights and refused to testify at trial.[19] The lower court judge instructed the jury that "they might draw an unfavorable inference against [the charged] from [their] failure to testify," and the pair were subsequently convicted,[20] and the men appealed their case to the Supreme Court on the grounds that the trial jury instructions violated their Fifth Amendment rights. In exploring the issues before the court, Justice William Moody, writing for the Court, questioned whether the right against self-incrimination should be included in the notion of due process:

> Is it a *fundamental* principle of liberty and justice which inheres in the very idea of free government and is the *inalienable right* of a citizen of such a government? If it is, and if it is of a nature that pertains to process of law, this court has declared it to be essential to due process of law. In approaching such a question it must not be forgotten that in a free representative government *nothing is more fundamental than the right of the people, through their appointed servants, to govern themselves in accordance with their own will*, except so far as they have restrained themselves by constitutional limits specifically established, and that, in

our peculiar dual form of government, nothing is more fundamental than the full power of the state to order its own affairs and govern its own people, except so far as the Federal Constitution, expressly or by fair implication, has withdrawn that power.[21]

Despite a promising recognition of the right against self incrimination as a natural right consistent with fundamental principles of liberty and justice, the Court erred and found that the Fifth Amendment only constrained the federal government; a blunder it would repeat once more before correcting itself in 1964.[22] Justice John Marshall Harlan dissented and applied the now-familiar rhetoric of due process that parallels NLT reasoning and argumentation.[23] Harkening back to the English heritage of the United States, Justice Harlan mused:

> What, let me inquire, must then have been regarded as principles that were fundamental in the liberty of the citizen? Every student of English history will agree that, long before the adoption of the Constitution of the United States, certain principles affecting the life and liberty of the subject had become firmly established in the jurisprudence of England, and were deemed vital to the safety of freemen, and that among those principles was the one that no person accused of crime could be compelled to be a witness against himself. [...] The liberties of the English people had then been placed on a firmer foundation. *Personal liberty was thenceforward jealously guarded. Certain it is, that when the present government of the United States was established it was the belief of all liberty-loving men in America that real, genuine freedom could not exist in any country that recognized the power of government to compel persons accused of crime to be witnesses against themselves.*[24]

He cited to our old friend Justice Story, noting the rights universally recognized as those belonging to Englishmen— rights that the early colonial patriots argued had been abridged by the King and Parliament, as discussed in Chapter 3; and how emigration across the Atlantic did not diminish those rights.[25] Justice Harlan reviewed prior decisions of the Supreme Court that invoked Sir Edward Coke's writings[26] before raising the crucial question overlooked by the majority: "[W]hen, [...], there is placed in the Constitution [...] a declaration that 'no State shall deprive any person of life, liberty, or property without due process of law,' can a State make any thing due process of law which, by its own legislation, it chooses to declare such?"[27] "To affirm this [decision]" he recognized, "is to hold that the prohibition to the States is of no avail, or has no application where the invasion of private rights is affected under the forms of state legislation."[28] Accordingly, he concluded:

> I cannot support any judgment declaring that immunity from self incrimination is not one of the privileges or immunities of national citizenship, nor a part of the liberty guaranteed by the 14th Amendment

against hostile state action. The declaration of the court, in the opinion just delivered that immunity from self incrimination is of great value, a protection to the innocent, and a safeguard against unfounded and tyrannical prosecutions, meets my cordial approval. And the court having heretofore, upon the fullest consideration, declared that the compelling of a citizen of the United States, charged with crime, to be a witness against himself, was a rule abhorrent to the instincts of Americans, was in violation of *universal American law*, was contrary to the principles of free government, and a weapon of despotic power which could not abide the pure atmosphere of *political liberty and personal freedom*[.] I cannot agree that a state may make that rule a part of its law and binding on citizens, despite the Constitution of the United States. No former decision of this court requires that we should now so interpret the Constitution.[29]

Ultimately, Justice John Marshall Harlan recognized that certain political liberties and personal freedoms were enshrined in universal American law as descended from the natural rights and liberties understood and recognized by the traditions and usages of history.

Coppage v. State of Kansas: The Natural Right to Contract

In 1915, the Supreme Court heard *Coppage v. State of Kansas*, a case so similar to *Adair* that the Court itself recognized that "[i]n [*Adair*], this court had to deal with a question not distinguishable in principle from the one now presented."[30] T. B. Coppage, the Superintendent of the Frisco Lines, in Fort Scott, Kansas, for the St. Louis & San Francisco Railway Company, asked a switchman named Hedges to sign an agreement saying he would withdraw from the Switchmen's Union of North America.[31] Coppage told Hedges that he needed to sign the paper to keep his job.[32] When Hedges refused to sign, Coppage fired him.[33] After recalling the facts and holding of *Adair*, Justice Mahlon Pitney, writing the opinion of the Court, found that the Supreme Court of Kansas, whose decision fell under the Supreme Court's scrutiny, attempted to distinguish *Coppage* from *Adair* on the grounds that in *Adair*, the railroad company had as a condition of employment a requirement that its employees not be involved in unions whereas in *Coppage*, the superintendent decided to terminate the switchman *because of* his membership in a union.[34] Pages later, the Court opined that the case was indistinguishable from *Adair*.[35]

So, why would the Court bother to rehash the issues it decided less than a decade before? Clearly, "[t]he decision in [*Adair*] was reached as the result of elaborate argument and full consideration."[36] Yet, in *Coppage*, the Court was "asked, in effect, to overrule [*Adair*]; and in view of the importance of the issue, [the Court ...] reexamined the question from the standpoint of both reason and authority [... and felt] constrained to reaffirm the doctrine [...] applied [in *Adair*]."[37] In sum:

The principle is fundamental and vital. Included in the right of personal liberty and the right of private property— partaking of the nature of each —is the right to make contracts for the acquisition of property. Chief among such contracts is that of personal employment, by which labor and other services are exchanged for money or other forms of property. If this right be struck down or arbitrarily interfered with, there is a substantial impairment of liberty in the long-established constitutional sense. The right is as essential to the laborer as to the capitalist, to the poor as to the rich; for the vast majority of persons have no other honest way to begin to acquire property, save by working for money.

An interference with this liberty so serious as that now under consideration, and so disturbing of equality of right, must be deemed to be arbitrary, unless it be supportable as a reasonable exercise of the police power of the state.[38]

The Supreme Court invalidated the Kansas law.[39]

Rochin v. California: Reason as a Guide to Uncover Natural Rights

In 1952, the Supreme Court heard the landmark case *Rochin v. California*, in which Antonio Richard Rochin, who had been arrested and convicted for morphine possession, challenged his conviction[40] on the basis that the Los Angeles police had engaged in behavior so outrageous that it "shock[ed] the conscience."[41] The police, who had information that Rochin was selling drugs, went to his home, entered through the open outer door and forced their way into Rochin's room.[42] As Rochin sat on the side of his bed, partially dressed, the police, who had just entered, saw on the nightstand two capsules.[43] When the deputies asked about who owned the capsules, Rochin grabbed them and swallowed them.[44] "A struggle ensued, in the course of which the three officers 'jumped upon [Rochin] and attempted to extract the capsules" from his mouth.[45] When they realized they would not be able to retrieve the capsules, the police handcuffed Rochin and took him to a hospital where they had a doctor "[force] an emetic solution through a tube into Rochin's stomach against his will."[46] This, of course, caused Rochin to vomit, and he expelled two capsules which were tested and found to contain morphine.[47] Over Rochin's objections, the California court allowed the entrance into evidence of the two capsules— despite the barbaric means through which they were retrieved—which proved to be the "chief evidence" against Rochin.[48] The California Second District Court of Appeals affirmed the conviction,[49] and the U.S. Supreme Court granted certiorari "because a serious question [was] raised as to the limitations which the Due Process Clause of the Fourteenth Amendment imposes on the conduct of criminal proceedings by the States."[50]

The Supreme Court, careful to respect the sovereignty of the states when adjudicating their criminal laws,[51] nonetheless acknowledged that just as Congress and the state legislatures have a responsibility to the Constitution, so, too does the Court.[52] Accordingly:

> Regard for the requirements of the Due Process Clause 'inescapably imposes upon [the Supreme] Court an exercise of judgment upon the whole course of the proceedings (resulting in a conviction) in order to ascertain whether they offend those canons of decency and fairness which express the notions of justice of English-speaking peoples even toward those charged with the most heinous offenses.'[53]

However, "[t]hese standards of justice are not authoritatively formulated anywhere as though they were specifics."[54] So, "[d]ue process of law is a summarized constitutional guarantee of respect for those personal immunities [which ...] are 'so rooted in the traditions and conscience of our people as to be ranked as fundamental,' [..] or are 'implicit in the concept of ordered liberty.'"[55]

Curiously, the Court engaged in an atypical digression exploring the shifting meaning of language and the evolution of human understanding as it pertains to the dictates of reason.

> The Court's function in the observance of this settled conception of the Due Process Clause does not leave us without adequate guides in subjecting State criminal procedures to constitutional judgment. In dealing not with the machinery of government but with *human rights*, the absence of formal exactitude, or want of fixity of meaning, is not an unusual or even regrettable attribute of constitutional provisions. Words being symbols do not speak without a gloss. On the one hand the gloss may be the deposit of history, whereby a term gains technical content. Thus the requirements of the Sixth and Seventh Amendments for trial by jury in the federal courts have a rigid meaning. No changes or chances can alter the content of the verbal symbol of 'jury'—a body of twelve men who must reach a unanimous conclusion if the verdict is to go against the defendant. On the other hand, the gloss of some of the verbal symbols of the Constitution does not give them a fixed technical content. *It exacts a continuing process of application.*[56]

The peculiarity of this digression rests in the Court's attack on the hallmarks of legal positivism such as the concept of fixed technical meaning. In the same breath, the Court endorsed natural law principles such as human rights and the need for continued application of reason in the discovery of the tenets of due process. As a result, writing for the majority, Justice Felix Frankfurter explained: When the gloss has thus not been fixed but is a function of the process of judgment, *the judgment is bound to fall differently at different times and differently at the same time through different judges.* Even more specific provisions, such as the guaranty [sic] of freedom of speech and the detailed protection against unreasonable searches and seizures, have inevitably evoked as sharp divisions in this Court as the least specific and most comprehensive protection of liberties, the Due Process Clause.[57]

Justice Frankfurter continued:

> The vague contours of the Due Process Clause do not leave judges at large. We may not draw on our merely personal and private notions and disregard the limits that bind judges in their judicial function. Even though the concept of due process of law is not final and fixed, these limits are derived from considerations that are fused in the whole nature of or judicial process. See Cardozo, The Nature of the Judicial Process; The Growth of the Law; The Paradoxes of Legal Science. *These are considerations deeply rooted in reason* and in the compelling traditions of the legal profession. The Due Process Clause places upon this Court the duty of exercising a judgment, within the narrow confines of judicial power in reviewing State convictions, upon interests of society pushing in opposite directions.[58]

Frankfurter, clearly familiar with the popular critiques of NLT, preemptively silenced critics no doubt voicing Benthamite arguments that NLT could allow for judges to inject their own personal sensibilities into their opinions. Judges simply cannot make sweeping declarations claiming natural law as a defense and justification. No, true appeals to NLT require a more studied approach considering the practices and usages of the law *deeply rooted in reason.*

Accordingly, "[d]ue process of law thus conceived is not to be derided as resort to a revival of 'natural law.'"[59] Neither, too, should people turn to legal positivism to combat NLT:

> To believe that this judicial exercise of judgment could be avoided by freezing 'due process of law' at some fixed stage of time or thought is to suggest that the most important aspect of constitutional adjudication is a function for inanimate machines and not for judges, for whom the independence safeguarded by Article III of the Constitution was designed and who are presumably guided by established standards of judicial behavior.[60]

These standards "[demand] of judges the habit of selfdiscipline and self-criticism, incertitude that one's own views are incontestable and alert tolerance toward views not shared."[61] However, "these are precisely the presuppositions of our judicial process. They are precisely the qualities society has a right to expect from those entrusted with ultimate judicial power."[62] In reversing Rochin's conviction, Frankfurter wrote for the Court: Restraints on our jurisdiction are selfimposed only in the sense that there is from our decisions no immediate appeal short of impeachment or constitutional amendment. But that does not make due process of law a matter of judicial caprice. The faculties of the Due Process Clause may be indefinite and vague, but the mode of their ascertainment is not self-willed. "In each case 'due process of law'

> requires an evaluation based on a disinterested inquiry pursued in the spirit of science, on a balanced order of facts exactly and fairly stated, on the detached consideration of conflicting claims, see Hudson County Water Co. v. McCarter, 209 U.S. 349, 355, 28 S.Ct. 529, 531, 52 L.Ed. 828, on a judgment not ad hoc and episodic but duly mindful of reconciling the needs both of continuity and of change in a progressive society.

> *Applying these general considerations to the circumstances of the present case, we are compelled to conclude that the proceedings by which this conviction was obtained do more than offend some fastidious squeamishness or private sentimentalism about combatting crime too energetically. This is conduct that shocks the conscience.* Illegally breaking into the privacy of the petitioner, the struggle to open his mouth and remove what was there, the forcible extraction of his stomach's contents—this course of proceeding by agents of government to obtain evidence is bound to offend even hardened sensibilities. They are methods too close to the rack and the screw to permit of constitutional differentiation."[63]

In parsing the meaning and significance of Due Process, the Court underscored the importance of reliance on reason and explained how an evolving understanding of the concept could result in further development and discovery.

Palmer v. Thompson: A Roadmap to Uncover New Rights

In 1971, the Supreme Court decided *Palmer v. Thompson*, a case where the City of Jackson, Mississippi, closed several city pools after being forced to desegregate them by a federal court case ruling in accordance with the *Brown* cases.[64] Though the Supreme Court's majority found that the decision to construct and maintain or close and tear down pools remained solely within the purview of the city,[65] Justice William O. Douglas, a vocal defender of the jurisprudence of Natural Law theory – yet unwilling to call it by its name – dissented in the case and turned to the Ninth Amendment to explain his disapproval with the majority's opinion.[66]

Justice Douglas argued that "[r]ights, not explicitly mentioned in the Constitution, have at times been deemed so elementary to our way of life that they have been labeled as basic rights."[67] With respect to the Ninth Amendment, "[t]he 'rights' retained by the people within the meaning of the Ninth Amendment may be related to those 'rights' which are enumerated in the Constitution."[68] However, "[the Supreme Court has] held that that enumerated 'right' also has other facets commonly summarized in the concept of privacy."[69] And, the shifting landscape of discovery and advancements in human understanding can lead to the recognition of new rights. While "[t]here is, of course, not a word in the Constitution [...] concerning the right of the people to education or to work or to recreation by swimming or otherwise."[70]

Could such a right fall within the unenumerated rights retained by the people? Justice Douglass mused that, perhaps "[t]hose rights, like the right to pure air and pure water, may well be rights 'retained by the people' under the Ninth Amendment. May the people vote them down as well as up?"[71] He concluded that such rights could not be subject to the wishes of the majority. "A constitutional right [including those protected by the Ninth Amendment] cannot be so burdened."[72] The Supreme Court "stated in *West Virginia State Board of Education v. Barnette*, [...] that: 'One's right to life, liberty, and property ... and other fundamental rights may not be submitted to vote; they depend on the outcome of no elections.'"[73] Justice Douglas continued, "[a]nd, we added in *Lucas v. Forty Fourth Colorado General Assembly*, [...] 'A citizen's constitutional rights can hardly be infringed simply because a majority of the people choose that (they) be.'"[74]

He added:

Much has been written concerning the Ninth Amendment including the suggestion that the rights there secured include 'rights of natural endowment.'2 B. Patterson, The Forgotten Ninth Amendment 53 (1955).

Mr. Justice Goldberg, concurring in *Griswold v. Connecticut*, supra, 381 U.S., at 492, 85 S.Ct., at 1686, said:

'(T)he Ninth Amendment shows a belief of the Constitution's authors that fundamental rights exist that are not expressly enumerated in the first eight amendments and an intent that the list of rights included there not be deemed exhaustive.'

We need not reach that premise in this case. We deal here with analogies to rights secured by the Bill of Rights or by the Constitution itself. Franklin, The Ninth Amendment as Civil Law Method and its Implications for Republican Form of Government[.].[75]

He believed:

[I]t is in the penumbra of the policies of the Thirteenth, Fourteenth, and Fifteenth Amendments and as a matter of constitutional policy should be in the category of those enumerated rights protected by the Ninth

Amendment. *If not included [in the protections of the Ninth Amendment], those rights become narrow legalistic concepts which turn on the formalism of laws, not on their spirit.*[76]

Such decisions are not surprising coming from the same Court that gave us tremendous privacy decisions throughout the 1970s.

Obergefell v. Hodges: The Natural Right to Choose One's Own Mate

More recently, the Supreme Court recognized the Due Process Clause and Equal Protection Clause of the Fourteenth Amendment also protects the *fundamental* right to choose a marital partner. In 2015, the Court decided *Obergefell v. Hodges*.[77] Justice Anthony Kennedy began the opinion with a positive, definitive declaration setting the tone for the rest of the 5-4 decision.

The Constitution promises liberty to all within its reach, a liberty that includes certain specific rights that allow persons, within a lawful realm, to define and express their identity. The petitioners in these cases seek to find that liberty by marrying someone of the same sex and having their marriages deemed lawful on the same terms and conditions as marriages between persons of the opposite sex.[78]

He then discussed the histories of several of the plaintiffs and historical approaches and attitudes towards marriage as a societal institution. Then, Justice Kennedy pivoted.

"Under the Due Process Clause of the Fourteenth Amendment," Kennedy wrote, "no State shall 'deprive any person of life, liberty, or property, without due process of law.' The fundamental liberties protected by this Clause include most of the rights enumerated in the Bill of Rights."[79] However, "these liberties extend to certain personal choices central to individual dignity and autonomy, including intimate choices that define personal identity and beliefs."[80] It is up to the Court to *identify* and protect fundamental liberties.[81] "That responsibility, however, 'has not been reduced to any formula.'"[82] Accordingly, such a responsibility:

requires courts to exercise reasoned judgment in identifying interests of the person so fundamental that the State must accord them its respect. [...] That process is guided by many of the same considerations relevant to analysis of other constitutional provisions that set forth broad principles rather than specific requirements. History and tradition guide and discipline this inquiry but do not set its outer boundaries. [...] That method respects our history and learns from it without allowing the past alone to rule the present.[83]

And, "[o]ver time and in other contexts, the Court has reiterated that the right to marry is fundamental under the Due Process clause."[84]

The Court found its "analysis compels the conclusion that same-sex couples may exercise the right to marry."[85] Justice Kennedy explained that "[a] first premise of the Court's relevant precedents is that the right to personal choice regarding marriage is inherent in the concept of individual autonomy."[86] The "abiding connection between marriage and liberty is why *Loving* invalidated interracial marriage bans under the Due Process Clause."[87] He added "[l]ike choices concerning contraception, family relationships, procreation, and childrearing, all of which are protected by the Constitution, decisions concerning marriage are among the most intimate that an individual can make."[88] Marriage has been an important societal institution, such that "[t]he nature of marriage is that, through its enduring bond, two persons together can find other freedoms, such as expression, intimacy, and spirituality. This is true for all persons, whatever their sexual orientation."[89] By finding the universality of the right of same sex couples to marry, the Court rendered a decision wholly consistent with the principles of Natural Law Theory.

Your author recognizes, as perhaps Justice Kennedy did, that arguing that NLT undergirds the *Obergefell* decision is like poking a hornets' nest with a stick to traditionalist Roman Catholics in the academy, the courts, the media, and in the pews. Suffice it to say, this book is not about Catholic moral teaching, which unambiguously teaches that homosexual acts are intrinsically disordered and thus inconsistent with NLT. Yet, this book, written by a traditionalist Catholic, is about secular courts recognizing constitutionally unarticulated rights, unconnected to Catholic moral teachings and about how those rights ought to be exercised. This book is about the relationship of human beings to government, not to Holy Mother Church. The essence of the Natural Law Tradition insulates the human heart from the government's touch when the heart's acted-upon yearnings are harmless to others. As Rothbard argued[90] mirroring Aquinas, the instrument by which we ascertain the universality of human rights, is reason, not passion or grace or revelation – but reason. Reason led the *Obergefell* court to ask, effectively: Can governments in America – state or federal – constitutionally reach and regulate the stirrings of human hearts as individuals make decisions that violate neither the Non-Aggression Principle nor the Millian Harm Principle? They cannot.

Despite how far we have come as an enlightened, modern society, we continue to make strides in the discovery and understanding of natural law and natural rights. Through the use of the Due Process Clause of the Fifth and Fourteenth Amendments as well as the Privileges and Immunities Clause of the Fourteenth, and the unenumerated rights in the Ninth Amendment, the Court has taken significant strides to utilize natural law jurisprudence to protect natural rights. And it will continue to recognize and protect rights in favor of personal autonomy and individual liberty so long as it harkens back to the natural law principles woven throughout the Constitution, the Bill of Rights, dictates of reason, and principles of fairness and equity.

These cases demonstrate that natural rights exist that were inconceivable to the sharpest minds of the founding generation, like Madison and Jefferson, and most staunch defenders of NLT, like Chief Justice John Marshall and Justice James Wilson. Whether economic liberty was explicitly contemplated by the Founders, the Supreme Court in *Lochner* recognized that right as fundamental. Likewise, prior generations did not contemplate same-sex marriage, yet, through the lens of NLT, the right is clear. As society moves forward, doubtless the Court will continue to discover natural rights we do not have the means to discover. In time, we shall see what universal natural rights become clear in light of advances in society. Of course, there is another side to the wonderful use of NLT to liberate individuals from the heavy hand of government. To that side of this seemingly endless debate we now turn.

CHAPTER 20

JUDICIAL CONFRONTATIONS OF NATURAL LAW THEORY

The Argument

Many prominent jurists and thinkers in the nineteenth and twentieth centuries have opposed the Natural Law Tradition in favor of doctrinal offshoots and successors to legal positivism and utilitarianism.

Justice Holmes, an outspoken critic of NLT and significant figure in the legal realism movement, and Justice Scalia upheld unfavorable opinions with deferential reliance to federal or state legislatures, and opposed rulings they believed veered too far from the well-trodden path of tradition—whether in the common law or stare decisis.

Contemporary Natural Law theorist Robert P. George has artfully refuted most of Holmes's critiques of NLT. However, his arguments could not sway contemporary positivists, such as Justice Antonin Scalia, who, like Holmes, often voted to uphold lower court rulings unless he felt they overtly violated the letter of the Constitution.

Both Holmes and Scalia endorsed an approach that remained internally consistent but which occasionally aligned with the Natural Law theory so long as they considered its principles to be articulated directly within parts of the Constitution.

***

Yet though liberty is beyond doubt an end-in itself, it is also of the highest value, to repeat, as a means to most of our other ends. We can pursue not only our economic but our intellectual and spiritual goals only if we are free to do so. Only when we are free do we have the power to choose. And only when we have the power to choose can our choice be called right or moral. Morality cannot be predicated of the act of a slave, or of any act done because one has been coerced into doing it. (The same does not apply, of course, to immorality. If a man flogs someone else because he fears that he will otherwise be flogged himself, or murders someone else, under orders, to save his own life, his act is still immoral.)

Liberty is the essential basis, the sine qua non, of morality. Morality can exist only in a free society; it can exist to the extent that freedom exists. Only to the extent that men have the power of choice can they be said to choose the good.[1]

– Henry Hazlitt (1894-1993)

ANTAGONISTS OF NATURAL LAW: BEYOND THE POSITIVISTS

In every century since the founding of the United States, a prominent philosopher or jurist has debuted a form of jurisprudence that ushered in a new era of scholarship, philosophy, and legal reasoning designed to promote this new form as legal science in its ultimate, purest form. Each new jurisprudential era proclaims this new approach to cure the ills of the law and recast all prior doctrines as foolish anachronisms and reduce those who faithfully adhere to them as cultists who continue to worship at the altars of long-forgotten pagan deities. The nineteenth century had Bentham, the early twentieth century had Oliver Wendell Holmes, Jr., and the early twenty-first century had Antonin Scalia.

While we have focused on the rivalries and jealousies between adherents to NLT and acolytes of older forms of legal positivism, we must also examine the competition between newer interpretive schema and NLT.

Justice Oliver Wendell Holmes

Oliver Wendell Holmes, Jr. (1841-1935) was nominated to the Supreme Court by President Theodore Roosevelt in 1902,[2] and served under four Chief Justices before resigning on January 11, 1932, due to faltering strength and his advanced age.[3] A veteran of the American Civil War,[4] Holmes sat as a Supreme Court Justice through the Great War, most of Prohibition, and the beginnings of the Dust Bowl, and the Great Depression.

Despite the reverence and esteem with which Justice Holmes was held by the legal community,[5] Oliver Wendell Holmes, Jr., did not appear to return that respect, especially when it came to legal traditions and the natural law. While sitting as an Associate Justice on the Massachusetts Supreme Judicial Court, Holmes published an article called *The Path of the Law* in the Harvard Law Review.[6] In this famous piece, he disparaged Natural Law theory and explained his own version of jurisprudence, known as *legal realism*, which recast the pseudo-scientific underpinnings of legal positivism in the motifs and rhetoric of the late nineteenth and early twentieth centuries with an almost obsessive focus on inputs and outcomes attempting to reduce law from an art to a science. All

Holmes cared about was the effect of the law and not the content of its character.

To Holmes, as to Bentham and Austin, there was no need to factor considerations of morality into the law. Despite his intellect and achievements, Holmes had a blind spot — a deep-rooted bias or aversion — when it came to Natural Law theory. In his famous law review article, Holmes focused on the outcomes of the laws rather than the reasons behind them when he wrote, "I think it desirable at once to point out and dispel a confusion between morality and law, which sometimes rises to the height of conscious theory, and [...] constantly is making trouble in detail without reaching the point of consciousness."[7] Continuing, "...a bad man has as much reason as a good one for wishing to avoid an encounter with the public force," Holmes concluded "therefore you can see the practical importance of the distinction between morality and law."[8]

Declaring, "[a] man who cares nothing for an ethical rule which is believed and practised [sic] by his neighbors is likely nevertheless to care a good deal to avoid being made to pay money, and will want to keep out of jail if he can," Holmes betrayed his simplistic outcome-based approach.[9] In other words, Holmes measured the efficacy of the law by how it deterred bad actors, and held people in both ambivalence and disdain. Those good people who believed in "morals" would behave in a manner according to their creed and avoid engaging in behavior that offended the law, so far as their morals aligned with it or such behavior might offend the sensibilities of their neighbors. Those individuals who behaved badly would not care about the reasons behind a law but care only of its outcomes. Thus, to him, a law consistent with a Constitution allowing the state to sterilize those suffering from mental illness could stand, while another that prevented the government from seizing private property to sell to other private individuals would not.

Holmes attempted to appear reasonable, to make mild concessions to his somewhat absolutist attitude,[10] but he rejected that which he could not easily quantify, such as morals, or a traditional acceptance of and adherence to natural law principles deeply rooted in history. To Holmes, the study and practice of law could include its history, and "the history of the moral development of the [human] race," but should focus on results and outcomes.[11] However, he argued for the use of history *only* as far as it could shed light on the present.[12] Rather, those who wish to know the law, though they can learn about the history and utility of carrots, should concern themselves mostly with the judicious application of the stick. "If you want to know the law and nothing else," then Holmes argued, "you must look at it as a bad man, who cares only for the material consequences which such knowledge enables him to predict, not as a good one, who finds his reasons for conduct, whether inside the law or outside of it, in the vaguer sanctions of conscience."[13] Once again, Holmes, ever concerned with outcomes over motives, cared not about the reasons behind a law, but only what it seeks to accomplish and whether it accomplishes that end. To Holmes, it seems, law must be studied in light of how it affects the behavior of the worst members of society.

Trying to understand the moral component to a law, in his eyes, served only to waste time and confuse. "The law talks about rights, and duties, and malice, and intent, and negligence, and so forth, and nothing is easier, or, [...] more common in legal reasoning, than to take these words in their moral sense, at some stage of the argument, and so to drop into fallacy."[14] To Holmes, moral considerations led only to fanciful arguments and impotent analysis. To Holmes, morals were vagaries and had no place in his jurisprudence, which he took to mean "simply law in its most generalized part."[15] He believed that "every word of moral significance could be banished from the law altogether, and other words adopted which should convey legal ideas uncolored by anything outside the law."[16] Instead, Holmes espoused a "practical" view of the law as a way for people to make informed decisions about their behavior through the predictive model afforded by understanding judicial outcomes.

Holmes derided Natural Law theory as a mere succumbing to the human desire to seek superlatives. "It is not enough for the knight of romance that you agree his lady is a very nice girl—if you do not admit that she is the best that God ever made or will make, you must fight."[17] Thus it is, Holmes argued, with the desire to seek the natural law. "It seems to me that this demand is at the bottom of the philosopher's effort to prove that truth is absolute and of the jurist's search for criteria of universal validity which he collects under the head of natural law."[18] Holmes believed that truth and universal validity were not absolutes but were subject to interpretation. "Certitude is not the test of certainty. We have been cock-sure of many things that were not so."[19]

Therefore, Holmes believed, those who sought to discover natural law aimlessly tilted at subjective windmills:

> The jurists who believe in natural law seem to me to be in that naïve state of mind that accepts what has been familiar and accepted by them and their neighbors as something that must be accepted by all men everywhere. No doubt it is true that, so far as we can see ahead, some arrangements and the rudiments of familiar institutions seem to be necessary elements in any society that may spring from our own and that would seem to us to be civilized — some form of permanent association between the sexes — some residue of property individually owned — some mode of binding oneself to specified future conduct — at the bottom of all, some protection for the person. But without speculating whether a group is imaginable in which all but the last of these might disappear and the last be subject to qualifications that most of us would abhor, the question remains as to the *Ought* of natural law.[20]

Rather than attempting to understand NLT, Holmes preferred to dismiss its adherents as naïve, brainwashed masses too afraid to take positions outside the realm of the familiar or to question the foundational principles that have governed their lives. To Holmes, subscribers to the principles of natural law had not reached these positions after careful consideration and study, but rather continued to adhere to NLT in an act worthy of Holmes's sharpest disdain: "blind imitation of the past."[21]

Robert P. George

Robert P. George (b. 1955), McCormick Professor of Jurisprudence and Director of the James Madison Program in American Ideals and Institutions at Princeton University, has dissected Holmes's views on the Natural Law theory. "While I have my own reasons for admiring some of Holmes's work, [...] I think that everything Holmes thought and taught about natural law is wrong."[22] Because "Holmes disbelieve[d] in the possibility of *normative* science or rationality—the use of intellectual faculties to ascertain objective truths about what one *ought* to want, what is *worth* wanting and what is not," George argued that Holmes based his attacks upon and disdain for NLT on faulty premises.[23] George reminded his readers that "Hitler's hatred of Jews, or ancient Rome's quest for glory in the conquest and domination of other peoples, are, or were, expressions of subjective values."[24] Accordingly:

> Under Holmes's view, they are intrinsically neither more nor less rational than the opposing values of others-say Mother Teresa and the Quakers. Of course, reason—positive science—can inquire whether Hitler really *hated* Jews, and, if he did, *what caused* his hatred; it can inquire whether the Romans *really* sought glory in conquest and domination, and, if so, *why*. But reason is, according to the account Holmes provides, powerless to judge the rightness or wrongness of Hitler's values or Rome's, whatever they were; nor can it identify the values of Mother Teresa as rationally superior to Hitler's, or the values of the Quakers as more reasonable than those of the Romans.[25]

George objected to Holmes' oversimplified syllogistic logical chain that resulted in Holmes's conclusion that "people's values are just fact."[26] A number of factors contribute to the value structures held by different people at different times, and many of these values express themselves in social conventions, such as wearing a tuxedo to a formal event rather than a bathing suit or a toga. While each of these outfits carries with it a cultural cachet, man in the state of nature would not intrinsically consider one more proper than another. In other words, our perception of these social conventions is largely arbitrary and based solely on custom and tradition.[27] Holmes had "very little respect for the conventions 'in themselves[.]'"[28] However, the relationship between social conventions and law, Holmes seemed to ignore, had been addressed centuries earlier by the Angelic Doctor. George noted that:

> It would, perhaps, not particularly please Holmes to know that an important dimension of these basic ideas about the role and importance of social conventions was elaborated skillfully by Thomas Aquinas in his discussion of the relationship of positive to natural law. Famously, Aquinas held that all just positive law is derived, in some sense, from natural law. Of course, natural law, for Aquinas, was nothing like Holmes's caricature of a "brooding omnipresence in the sky" ... as Aquinas understands the matter, the task of the legislator is to give effect to relevant principles of right order and natural justice in the shape of positive laws for the common good of society.[29]

In other words, one does not write natural law, we *discover* it; or rather we *uncover* it, much like peeling back the many layers of an onion over a period of thousands of years.[30]

While some laws derive from practical moral considerations related to the need to regulate the behavior of people within a society, such as prohibitions on theft and murder, other rules, like those limiting campaign contributions or requiring the payment of parking fines within 30 days, do not have direct moral roots. Steven Pinker, the cognitive psychologist and linguist, examined a study that attempted to gauge the role of human intuition in judgments of morality, and wrote:

> The psychologist Jonathan Haidt has underscored the ineffability of moral norms in a phenomenon he calls moral dumbfounding. Often people have an instant intuition that an action is immoral, and then struggle, often unsuccessfully, to come up with reasons *why* it is immoral. When Haidt asked participants, for example, whether it would be all right for a brother and sister to have voluntary protected sex, for a person to clean a toilet with a discarded American flag, for a family to eat a pet dog that had been killed by a car, for a man to buy a dead chicken and have sex with it, or for a person to break a deathbed vow to visit the grave of his mother, they said no in each case. But when asked for justifications, they floundered ineffectually before giving up and saying, "I don't know, I can't explain it, I just know it's wrong."[31]

George would argue that Aquinas, unlike Holmes, recognized that Haidt tried to test that humans have some hard-wired inarticulable sense of right and wrong. While some may argue that such views come down to social convention, George explained that: Values may be objective even if nobody considers them to be so, and even if lots of people, or indeed, everyone, does not

> accept or hold them. Differences of wants, or of beliefs about what people should want, do not negate the possibility that people can have reasons to want things even if they happen not to want them, or the

possibility that people can have reasons not to want things that they happen to want.[32]

To Holmes' argument on the subjectivity of natural law, that people accept that which is familiar to them and their neighbors as universal, George asserts that "this is plainly a false charge [since ...] [i]t certainly does not apply to Aquinas or his most influential forbears and successors in the tradition of natural law theorizing."[33] "Indeed," George added, "as Leo Strauss observed in *Natural Right and History*, it is the diversity of human practices and moral opinions that *motivates* the philosophical quest to discover principles of natural law or natural right that provide criteria for their moral-critical evaluation."[34] While science searches to classify variations across the human genome, moral philosophy seeks to find what unites our species through common elements contained within universal human inclinations.

As George recounted, "theories of natural law are reflective critical accounts of the constitutive aspects of the well-being and fulfillment of human persons and the communities they form."[35] So, "[n]atural law theories, then, propose to identify principles of right action – moral principles – specifying the first and most general principle of morality, namely, that one should choose and act in ways that are compatible with a will towards integral human fulfillment."[36] Contained within "these principles is a respect for rights people possess simply by virtue of their humanity – rights which, as a matter of justice, others are bound to respect and governments are bound not only to respect but, to the extent possible, also to protect."[37] He explained:

Theorists of natural law understand human fulfillment – the human good – as variegated. There are many irreducible dimensions of human wellbeing. This is not to deny that human nature is determinate. It is to affirm that our nature, though determinate, is complex. We are animals, but rational. Our integral good includes our bodily well-being, but also our intellectual, moral, and spiritual well-being. We are individuals, but friendship and sociability are constitutive aspects of our flourishing. We form bonds with others not only for instrumental purposes, but because of our grasp of the inherent fulfillments available in joining together in a wide variety of formal and informal types of association and community. In ways that are highly relevant to moral reflection and judgment, man truly is a social animal.[38]

George believes that "[t]here are human rights if there are principles of practical reason directing us to act or abstain from acting in certain ways out of respect for the well-being and the dignity of persons whose legitimate interests may be affected by what we do."[39] To George,

This natural law understanding of human rights is connected with a particular account of human dignity. Under this account, the natural human capacities for reason and freedom are fundamental to the dignity of human beings – the dignity that is protected by human rights. The basic goods of human nature are the goods of a rational creature – a creature who, unless impaired or prevented from doing so, naturally develops and exercises capacities for deliberation, judgment, and choice. These capacities are God-like (albeit, of course, in a limited way). In fact, from the theological vantage point they constitute a certain sharing – limited, to be sure, but real – in divine power. This is what is meant, I believe, by the otherwise extraordinarily puzzling Biblical teaching that man is made in the very image and likeness of God.[40]

George's formulation of NLT relies on human reason to determine rights with respect to intrinsic notions of human dignity and the intrinsic value associated with that dignity.[41] And, if these notions of value are intrinsic to all mankind, how come so many societies do not recognize them?[42] "As human beings," George explained, "we are rational animals, but we are imperfectly rational."[43] As a result, "We are prone to making intellectual and moral mistakes and capable of behaving grossly unreasonably, especially when deflected by powerful emotions that run contrary to the demands of reasonableness. Even when following our consciences, as we are morally bound to do, we can go wrong."[44] Sometimes we even do wrong when trying to do right:[45]

The will can err, as we discussed in Chapter 1. While George believes that a purpose-focused approach to law consistent with NLT allows for the passage of laws that respect human dignity and morality, Holmes cared *only* about results.

With his focus on product rather than process, Holmes endorsed darker outcome-based ideas associated with eugenics and social engineering aimed at producing a better society.[46] And, Holmes, as a powerful member of the Supreme Court, had a platform upon which to endorse or validate egregious government overreach.

Holmes would again defer to the positivism of a state legislature in a contemptible decision in *Buck v. Bell* (1927). The Supreme Court, speaking through Holmes, affirmed a Virginia state law that permitted the forced sterilization of individuals with "hereditary forms of insanity, imbecility, [etc.]"[47] Since "Carrie Buck is a feeble minded white woman who was committed to [a state care facility and ....] is the daughter of a feeble minded mother in the same institution, and the mother of an illegitimate feeble minded child,"[48] she could be sterilized since "[t]hree generations of imbeciles are enough."[49] Justice Butler was the lone dissenter but did not appear to issue a separate opinion.

In the wake of the decision in *Buck v. Bell*, "[t]hirty states ultimately approved legislation [allowing forced sterilization], and more than eighteen thousand people in the United States were sterilized involuntarily following the Court's decision."[50]

As modern society struggled to reconcile complicated feelings regarding achievements of historical figures when taken out of the context of the time periods in which they operated, we all too often focus on the bad at the cost of diminishing, or, in some cases, overlooking the good. Baked into the notion of due process rests the profound admission of the limitlessness of human fallibility—that the government can get it wrong. The procedural and substantive elements of due process aim to minimize the extent to which the judiciary can err, but such attitudes and approaches do not guarantee perfection.

As we have already seen, the court can and does err because its members, despite their achievements and qualifications, are only human. To hold Holmes to a different standard than we do more contemporary justices is to do Holmes an injustice. We must hold all justices to the highest standards. After all, champions natural law theory, such as the early Chief Justice John Marshall erred (see, *McColluch v. Maryland*) as did others such as Justice Louis D. Brandeis, for failing to dissent in *Buck v. Bell*, and other justices whose failure to dissent when called upon by NLT to do so at best turned a deaf ear to principle, and at worse gave tacit assent to legislative and executive despotism. We now turn to those infamous dissents.

Justice Hugo Black

In *Adamson v. California* (1947),[51] a case similar to *Twining v. State of New Jersey*, discussed in Chapter 19, Justice Hugo Black dissented from the majority and harshly criticized the natural law. Admiral Dewey Adamson was charged with first-degree murder and chose not to testify.[52] A California law allowed for prosecutors to comment on the failure of a defendant to testify and imply that such a failure could be seen by the jury as an admission of guilt.[53] Again, the similarities to *Twining* are striking. And, as in *Twining*, the Court failed to render a proper decision and found that the Fifth Amendment right against self-incrimination would have been violated had Adamson been tried in federal court, but that Fifth Amendment did not require that defendants be afforded the same rights in state trials.[54]

Justice Black, joined by Justice Douglas, dissented in spectacular fashion, and, while he argued for the application of the first eight amendments in the Bill of Rights to the states, throughout his entire line of reasoning, he needlessly disparaged the natural law. This decision reasserts a constitutional theory spelled out in *Twining v. New Jersey*, […] that this Court is endowed by the Constitution with boundless power under "natural law" periodically to expand and contract constitutional standards to conform to the Court's conception of what, at a particular time, constitutes "civilized decency" and "fundamental liberty and justice." Invoking this *Twining* rule, the Court concludes that, although comment upon testimony in a federal court would violate the Fifth Amendment, identical comment in a state court does not violate today's fashion in civilized decency and fundamentals, and is therefore not prohibited by the Federal Constitution, as amended.[55]

So, Justice Black, following a Holmesian line of reasoning, would argue for a different outcome—one that in fact would have been more consistent with a natural law approach— but only invoked the incorporation of the first eight amendments to the Constitution and stopped just short of the one that promises the retention by the people of NLT rights. However, Black noted that:

> Conceding the possibility that this Court is now wise enough to improve on the Bill of Rights by substituting natural law concepts for the Bill of Rights, I think the possibility is entirely too speculative to agree to take that course. I would therefore hold in this case that the full protection of the Fifth Amendment's proscription against compelled testimony must be afforded by California. This I would do because of reliance upon the original purpose of the Fourteenth Amendment.[56]

Black believed that, rather than protecting the rights afforded to the people, the Bill of Rights served in fact to restrict those rights!

> It is an illusory apprehension that literal application of some or all of the provisions of the Bill of Rights to the States would unwisely increase the sum total of the powers of this Court to invalidate state legislation. The Federal Government has not been harmfully burdened by the requirement that enforcement of federal laws affecting civil liberty conform literally to the Bill of Rights. Who would advocate its repeal? It must be conceded, of course, that the natural-law-due-process formula, which the Court today reaffirms, has been interpreted to limit substantially this Court's power to prevent state violations of the individual civil liberties guaranteed by the Bill of Rights.[57]

This dissent makes clear that Justice Black held some peculiar views on the role of the natural law in the Court's decision calculus. It seems that he felt that the natural law had become a tool in the hands of those seeking to constrain the rights of the people rather than defend them. The Court's alleged use of the natural law to allow for the state selectively to incorporate the Bill of Rights remains misplaced. However, if the Court had tried to use NLT to justify such intrusions, one could argue that Justice Black's irregular disdain for it could stem from witnessing its bastardization. Whatever the root cause, Justice Black would continue to rail against the use of NLT in the Court.

In *Griswold v. Connecticut*, the 1965 case in which the Supreme Court invalidated a Connecticut anticontraception statute, Justice Hugo Black yet again delivered a blistering dissent in which he decried the reasoning harmonious with NLT held by the majority.

Justice William O. Douglas, who wrote for the majority, extolled the Ninth Amendment and found within the Constitution certain penumbral rights emanating from the guarantees contained within the Bill of Rights.[58] Justices Harlan and White, in separate opinions in which they concurred in the judgment, felt more comfortable relying on due process to invalidate the state law. To Justice Black, however, such formulations were inadequate.

> The due process argument which my Brothers HARLAN and WHITE adopt here is based, as their opinions indicate, on the premise that this Court is vested with power to invalidate all state laws that it consider to be arbitrary, capricious, unreasonable, or oppressive, or this Court's belief that a particular state law under scrutiny has no 'rational or justifying' purpose, or is offensive to a 'sense of fairness and justice.' If these formulas based on 'natural justice,' or others which mean the same thing, are to prevail, they require judges to determine what is or is not constitutional on the basis of their own appraisal of what laws are unwise or unnecessary.[59]

And, like Justice Holmes, yet sounding like Justice Scalia, Justice Black believed that:

> The power to make such decisions is of course that of a legislative body. Surely it has to be admitted that no provision of the Constitution specifically gives such blanket power to courts to exercise such a supervisory veto over the wisdom and value of legislative policies and to hold unconstitutional those laws which they believe unwise or dangerous.[60]

Justice Black echoed the common ill-conceived contra-NLT refrain that the natural law could become a dangerous weapon in the hands of unscrupulous judges. He also attacked Justice Goldberg's concurrence: My Brother GOLDBERG has adopted the recent discovery that the Ninth Amendment as well as the Due Process Clause can be used by this Court as authority to strike down all state legislation which this Court thinks violates 'fundamental principles of liberty and justice,' or is contrary to the 'traditions and (collective) conscience of our people.' He also states, without proof satisfactory to me, that in making decisions on this basis judges will not consider 'their personal and private notions.' One may ask how they can avoid considering them. Our Court certainly has no machinery with which to take a Gallup Poll. And the scientific miracles of this age have not yet produced a gadget which the Court can use to determine what traditions are rooted in the '(collective) conscience of our people.' Moreover, one would certainly have to look far beyond the language of the Ninth

Amendment to find that the Framers vested in this Court any such awesome veto powers over lawmaking, either by the States or by the Congress.[61]

Furthermore, Justice Black argued that the built-in process to amend the Constitution in order to reflect changing attitudes and demands of society negated the need to resort to the application of Due Process or natural law to invalidate any law. Because the framework of amendment exists, Justice Black argued he "[could not] rely on the Due Process Clause or the Ninth Amendment or any *mysterious and uncertain natural law concept* as a reason for striking down this state law."[62] He attacked the Court's economic due process formulation in *Lochner*:

> That formula, based on subjective considerations of 'natural justice,' is no less dangerous when used to enforce this Court's views about personal rights than those about economic rights.[63]

And, while Justice Black did not mind that the Court could invalidate legislative action running contrary to the limits imposed by the Constitution, he felt that judges should only do so in select circumstances.[64] Consequently: But to pass upon the constitutionality of statutes by looking to the particular standards enumerated in the Bill of Rights and other parts of the

> Constitution is one thing; to invalidate statutes because of application of 'natural law' deemed to be above and undefined by the Constitution is another. 'In the one instance, courts proceeding within clearly marked constitutional boundaries seek to execute policies written into the Constitution; *in the other they roam at will in the limitless area of their own beliefs as to reasonableness and actually select policies, a responsibility which the Constitution entrusts to the legislative representatives of the people.*' Federal Power Commission v. Natural Gas Pipeline Co., 315 U.S. 575, 599, 601, n. 4, (Footnotes omitted.)[65]

In his blistering dissent, Justice Black lashed out a sarcastic and derisive style less in accord with the custom and practice of his time and more aligned with the rhetorical flourishes and command of history that would feature more prominently in the Rehnquist Court and the Roberts Court from Justice Antonin Scalia.

Justice Antonin Scalia

Justice Scalia became the most important and influential figure in parallel, related movements in jurisprudence known as Originalism and textualism, consanguineous progeny of legal positivism focusing alternatively on notions of *the original public understanding* of the texts in question and an insistence on the dispositive and controlling nature of only the words within the body of the text (absent, of course, specific references to delimited portions of extratextual material, such as when a statute says something such as "For the purposes of this statute, the definition of *fraud* shall take the same meaning as it does in 18 U.S.C §, etc.,"). As a result of his views, "Justice Scalia [...] disdained the use of legislative history – statements from members of Congress about the meaning and purpose of laws – in the judicial interpretation of statutes."[66] "He likened judges' use of secondary sources such as committee reports or statements made by members of Congress during floor debates to 'looking over the faces of the crowd at a large cocktail party and picking out your friends.'"[67] In other words, he feared that judges used only selective snippets as soon through rose-colored glasses to validate and reinforce only those views which coincided with their own. He also told your author many times that no one should give credence to statements made by legislators concerning their public "votes." "They only have one reason to vote as they do and it is always the same – to get re-elected."

Scalia's jurisprudence, though perhaps internally consistent, oscillates between concordance with NLT and disdain for it. Though considered by many a jurist who allowed his personal beliefs to cloud his opinions, Justice Scalia rendered decisions consistent with his own interpretive schema largely agnostic with respect to political beliefs. Indeed, "[i]n Justice Scalia's hands, [O]riginalism generally led to outcomes that pleased political conservatives, *but not always*."[68]

He relished "debating his critics at law schools[69] and in public appearances," Supreme Court journalist Robert Barnes noted; and never disappointed his audiences delivering often animated and clever retorts when faced with difficult questions.[70] Despite his affable and jovial nature, Justice Scalia could be a fierce academic opponent and an imposing presence from beneath the robe. In his nearly 30 years on the Supreme Court, Justice Scalia elevated the dissent to an artform and never allowed a careless turn of phrase or a missing step in a logical chain to remain unaddressed. He studied the law and history with the patient and methodical approach of a Catholic school teacher in the 1950s, and the meticulous and interdisciplinary scrutiny of a professor of romance languages.

Justice Scalia was, of course, intimately familiar with the writings of St. Thomas Aquinas. With respect to Aquinas's assertion that laws running contrary to the natural law had no binding force, Scalia felt that such authority should not rest in the hands of a judge.[71] He noted that:

Now in my view natural law does make its demands upon judges – but not the demand that they render judgments that contradict positive law. Where positive law places judges in the position of being the instrument of evil, the judge must recuse from the case or (if there are many such cases) resign from the bench. Thus, if I were a judge in Nazi Germany, charged with sending Jews and Poles to their death, I would be obliged to resign my office (and perhaps lead a revolution).[72]

Scalia remained faithful to his brand of Originalism which he believed more narrowly bounded judges than abstract appeals to morals. However, Scalia's brand of Originalism drove him to repeat the same sorts of errors that plagued disciples of the schools of Bentham, Austin, and Hart; namely, that the only way to negate a law duly passed through a legitimate process by a legitimate authority would be if some superior positive law, such as a Constitution, precluded in whole or in part the inferior law. Justice Scalia viewed his role as more of an umpire, merely calling balls and strikes, rather than one of nine arbiters in the last line of defense against executive and legislative tyranny.

Justice Scalia fiercely dissented in *Lawrence v. Texas*, the 2003 case that invalidated state laws criminalizing homosexual activity between consenting adults. "Most of the rest of today's opinion has no relevance to its actual holding – that the Texas statute 'furthers no legitimate state interest which can justify' its application to petitioners under rational-basis review[,]" Scalia grumbled.[73] His concern – the majority's analysis fails to "declare that homosexual sodomy is a 'fundamental right' under the Due Process Clause[,]" and, it also, accordingly does not "subject the Texas law to the standard of review that would be appropriate (strict scrutiny) if homosexual sodomy *were* a 'fundamental right.'"[74] Instead, the Court "simply describes [Lawrence and Garner's] conduct as 'an exercise of their liberty'—which it undoubtedly is—and proceeds to apply an unheard-of form of rational-basis review that will have far-reaching implications beyond this case."[75] In a multi-page argument, Scalia systematically attacked the reasoning behind the majority's inconsistencies and carelessness with language arguing against the reasoning behind the Court's decisions. He explained that "[w]e have held repeatedly, in cases the Court today does not overrule, that *only* fundamental rights qualify for this so-called 'heightened scrutiny' protection — that is, rights which are deeply rooted in this Nation's history and tradition[.]"[76] He pointed out that in *Bowers v. Hardwick*, the Supreme Court cited legislative and common-law prohibitions on homosexual sodomy in the 13 original colonies, which indicated "that a right to engage in homosexual sodomy was not deeply rooted in this Nation's history and tradition."[77] Why go through such a fuss? Because the Supreme Court, in Scalia's mind, was changing the rules. He pointed this out: Realizing that [homosexual sodomy is not a fundamental right 'deeply rooted in this Nation's history and tradition'], the Court instead says: [W]e think that our laws and traditions in the past half century are of most relevance here. These references show *an emerging awareness* that liberty gives substantial protection to adult persons in deciding how to conduct their private lives *in matters pertaining to sex.*[78]

He added:

Apart from the fact that such an "emerging awareness" does not establish a "fundamental right," the statement is factually false. States continue to prosecute all sorts of crimes by adults "in matters pertaining to sex": prostitution, adult incest, adultery, obscenity, and child pornography.[79]

Scalia did not mention natural law, natural rights, or universal standards. In fact, he deliberately lampooned the majority's consideration of the approach of the international community. He even acknowledged that the exercise of intimate relations between Garner and Lawrence were *undoubtedly* an exercise of their liberty. Why, then, did Scalia oppose the majority's ruling?

Certainly, if we were to scratch the veneer of the language of *stare decisis*, the principle of general adherence to precedent, and of the limitations of the federal courts to encroach upon the rights of the state to police the health, safety, welfare, and general morality of people in the states, some would argue that we would find, peaking through, not Justice Scalia, the staunch originalist, but rather Nino Scalia, the devout Catholic who, like the rest of us, had his blind spots. However, I would disagree with such an assessment. Justice Scalia was imminently concerned with the limitations of the powers of the federal government. He was wary of any decision that subjectively expanded or created rights from the bench. To Scalia, the power to create rights did not emanate from the gavel of the judge, but rather the gavel of the Speaker of the House, or whichever state legislative body is charged with the creation of its laws, subject, of course, the bright lines—and Nino loved bright lines—indicated by the Constitution.

This is pure positivism and a rejection of even the Thomistic mantra of using reason to discern and recognize – not create – rights.

In *Kerry v. Din* (2015), Fauzia Din, a U.S. citizen, sued the Department of State because it denied her husband, Kanishka Berashk, an "Afghan citizen and former civil servant in the Taliban regime" a visa.[80] Din brought the claim since her husband did not have standing to challenge the decision. Writing for a plurality, Scalia spoke of the historical background of due process,[81] before turning to the powers of the court.

> Despite this historical evidence, this Court has seen fit on several occasions to expand the meaning of "liberty" under the Due Process Clause to include certain implied "fundamental rights." (The reasoning presumably goes like this: If you have a right to do something, you are free to do it, and deprivation of freedom is a deprivation of "liberty"— never mind the original meaning of that word in the Due Process Clause.) These implied rights have been given more protection than "life, liberty, or property" properly understood. While one may be dispossessed of property, thrown in jail, or even executed so long as proper procedures are followed, the enjoyment of implied constitutional rights cannot be limited at all, except by provisions that are "narrowly tailored to serve a compelling state interest."[82]

To Scalia, the Court, from time to time, detoured from its ultimate responsibility and has *created* rights outside its constitutional purview.

I think it worth explaining why, *even if one accepts the textually unsupportable doctrine of implied fundamental rights*, Din's arguments would fail. Because "extending constitutional protection to an asserted right or liberty interest ... place[s] the matter outside the arena of public debate and legislative action," *Washington v. Glucksberg*, 521 U.S. 702, 720, 117 S.Ct. 2258, 138 L.Ed.2d 772 (1997), and because the "guideposts for responsible decision making [sic] in this unchartered area are scarce and openended," *Collins v. Harker Heights*, 503 U.S. 115, 125, S.Ct. 1061, 117 L.Ed.2d 261 (1992), "[t]he doctrine of judicial self-restraint requires us to exercise the utmost care whenever we are asked to break new ground in this field," *ibid.*

Accordingly, before conferring constitutional status upon a previously unrecognized "liberty," we have required "a careful description of the asserted fundamental liberty interest," as well as a demonstration that the interest is "objectively, deeply rooted in this Nation's history and tradition, and implicit in the concept of ordered liberty, such that neither liberty nor justice would exist if [it was] sacrificed." *Glucksberg, supra*, at 720721, 117 S.Ct. 2258 (citations and internal quotation marks omitted).[83]

Scalia refused to acknowledge the idea of fundamental rights not supported by the text of the Constitution and Bill of Rights and believed that the court needs to exercise the utmost care in recognizing, or, as Scalia might quip, *creating* new rights.

In 1987, Scalia voted and wrote to uphold the right of a criminal defendant to suppress evidence obtained from his apartment in an unlawful search in *Arizona v. Hicks*.[84] When a bullet had been fired through Hicks's floor and hit a man on the floor below, police entered Hicks's apartment in search of the shooter.[85] Once inside, the police found several weapons, a stocking-cap mask, and two sets of expensive stereo equipment.[86] Though the police had responded because of the gunshot and not to investigate a robbery, the police moved some of the equipment in Hick's apartment to read, and subsequently record the serial numbers and later check them against records of stolen property.[87] Once the police determined that the stereo equipment had in fact been stolen, Hicks was indicted for the robbery, and "the state trial court granted his motion to suppress the evidence that had been seized, and the Arizona Court of Appeals affirmed."[88]

While the investigation of the stereo equipment might have fallen into the plain view doctrine,[89] a judicial acceptance of evidence obtained when outside the scope of a warrant if the evidence is likely to be discovered by an officer nevertheless, such as bloody knife on a kitchen table, a firearm on a sofa, or drug paraphernalia on a coffee table,[90] Justice Scalia noted that the Court needed "to decide whether this 'plain view' doctrine may be invoked when the police have less than probable cause to believe that the item in question is evidence of a crime or is contraband."[91] Incidentally, the Court examined its prior decisions to see whether it had yet decided the standard for inclusion of evidence on the plain view doctrine—whether an officer needed only a *reasonable suspicion* or the higher standard of *probable cause*.[92] It resolved the issue in determining that "probable clause is required[,] [since] [t]o say otherwise would be to cut the 'plain view' doctrine loose from its theoretical and practical moorings."[93] Scalia observed, "there is nothing new in the realization that *the Constitution sometimes insulates the criminality of a few in order to protect the privacy of us all*."[94] The Supreme Court upheld the suppression of the evidence against Hicks.[95] While Scalia hid behind the language of the Fourth Amendment, preventing unreasonable search and seizure, his decision aligns with the Natural Law Tradition regarding notions of privacy. The amendment itself even contains the word *unreasonable*, inextricably related to *reason*, a building block of the Natural Law Tradition, as the standard by which to judge government action. And, of course, the Pope of Originalism and King of Textualism would be the first to remind his critics that the word "privacy" appears nowhere in the constitutional text!

Fundamentally, however, Scalia's beliefs regarding rights and government were at odds with the view of Ludwig von Mises, that "Government is essentially the negation of liberty[,]"[96] since, at its core, it seeks to regulate human behavior in such a fashion as to ignore natural rights when it is convenient for government to do so and dispense civil rights only when it is required. Scalia rejected the Misean inalienable individualism for the Thomistic "common good." Only there did he come close to NLT.

In a state of nature, human beings exist at the apex of their personal liberty, and, when burdened by government, they can fall to liberty's lowest ebb. Scalia's Originalism seemed to arise out of a desire to adhere strictly to the bright lines drawn by the Founders in the Constitution. To an originalist, like Scalia, the only way to constrain the government was to follow the rules laid out in the instruction manual for the federal government: The Constitution.

With the failure of legal Realism and Originalism to cure properly the ills they purport to treat, lawyers and jurists must explore new means by which to fulfil the prophesying goal of law suggested by Holmes, and the narrowly-bounded path the law should take according to Scalia's process-and-history-based approach to jurisprudence. Rather than concocting new interpretive schemes or glancing backwards to a fixed point in history, we should open our minds and turn to a secure, flexible, and bounded method that judges used for centuries to lend the law consistency, to satisfy Holmes, while rooted in longstanding tradition and the practices and usages of the law to satisfy Scalia. Through the marriage of traditional natural law theory and contemporary libertarian principles, we can satisfy both difficult men while preserving natural rights and natural liberties.

CHAPTER 21

LIMITING THE ROLE OF POSITIVE LAW: CRIMINALIZING ONLY ACTS WHICH PRODUCE PALPABLE HARM

The Argument

In order to assess the moral legitimacy of our positive law, particularly criminal law, the Declaration of Independence instructs us to use natural law as a guiding principle. The fundamental natural law principle that individuals have a right to engage voluntarily in acts that harm no one but themselves informs our belief that the state should punish an individual only if one has caused harm to another. We trace this principle, known to us by many different names, the Millian Harm Principle, Rothbard's Non-Aggression Principle to name a few, from its origin to its continued invocation today.

***

Of liberty I would say that, in the whole plenitude of its extent, it is unobstructed action according to our will. But rightful liberty is unobstructed action according to our will within limits drawn around us by the equal rights of others. I do not add 'within the limits of the law,' because law is often but the tyrant's will, and always so when it violates the right of an individual.[1]

– Thomas Jefferson (1743-1826)

The nature of mankind and the proper role of government were two philosophical questions with which the Founders grappled in 1776. In particular, they contemplated fundamental questions such as, "Which is the higher authority, the State or the People? [And c]an a state properly create a moral system through law and then use the authority of law to enforce it?"[2] The collective answer to these quandaries was clearly articulated in the Declaration of Independence, and later in clauses of the Constitution, such as the Ninth and Tenth amendments. As discussed earlier, the Declaration of Independence set forth the Founders' collective belief that as a direct function of the "Laws of Nature and of Nature's God" and as a self-evident truth, "all men are created equal, that they are endowed by their Creator with certain unalienable Rights."[3] The Declaration clarified that "proper government" is "instituted by the people, who in essence delegate limited powers to their chosen governing bodies in order to help *secure* these rights, not to create them, and certainly not to interfere with them."[4] After all, as Thomas Jefferson stated, "[a] free people [claim] their rights as derived from the laws of nature, and *not* as the gift of their chief magistrate."[5]

We see then, that through this reference to the "Laws of Nature and of Nature's God," the Founders envisioned a government structure that was (and still claims to be) dependent on natural law for both its context as well as its content. Specifically, the government created by the Framers would operate as "an entity of limited authority and must therefore work within the *context* of the superior rights of its creators, the people," in order to protect the people's inalienable rights "from the tendency of all government to overstep its bounds while not exceeding the restrictions imposed upon it within the natural law framework."[6] In other words, under Natural Law Theory, the only true purpose of government is "to guard the fundamental rights of persons without infringing upon them."[7]

Stated differently, under NLT, government must avoid impairing rights while allowing individuals to conduct their daily affairs with the greatest amount of freedom. One obligation that flows from this role is the state's duty to acknowledge that under natural law all persons must refrain from harming one another; this in turn "requires the creation of legal *content* in the form of positive law rules and regulations"[8] which comport with the natural law.

In order to determine the content of such positive law, the Declaration points us towards natural law as the lodestar. The central tenet of the natural law teaches that harm to another is wrong unless warranted by extraordinary and exceptional circumstances, such as self defense. The idea that the state should punish an individual only if one has caused harm to another is an essential feature not only of a liberal state, but one founded on natural law principles. It is important, therefore to trace the origins of the idea that natural law "incorporates a morality that places limits on personal (as well as governmental) behavior, claiming ... that freedom does not extend to allowing people to harm one another, as individuals or as a society."[9]

Beginning with Saint Thomas Aquinas, we see that the natural law is "binding and valid at the level of morality, laying out comprehensive and obligatory moral standards applicable to all."[10] For example, individuals have inclinations to "[(1)]the preservation of their own being, according to their natures... [(2)] the preservation of the species, towards actions such as sexual intercourse, education of offspring and so forth...[and (3)] know the truth about God and to live in society."[11] Ultimately, the purpose of positive law "is to specify more concretely the demands of the natural law in actual circumstances and to bring to bear the authority and the coercive sanctions of the state in service to the natural law."[12] In fact, the "natural law need not stand diametrically opposed to the positive law…[but instead,] directed immediately to each other. The natural law calls imperatively for specification by positive enactments, even though it is at the same time the measure and guideline of the positive law."[13]

Aquinas himself understood that natural law required enactment by earthly authority, and that such positive law, or,

> [h]uman law is framed for the mass of men, the majority of whom are not perfectly virtuous. Therefore human law does not prohibit every vice from which virtuous men abstain, but only the more serious ones from which the majority can abstain, especially those that *harm others* and which must be prohibited for human society to survive, such as homicide, theft, and the like.[14]

This no-harm rule became the linchpin for the Millian Harm Principle and the Rothbardian Non-Aggression Principle. It was further articulated by John Locke in the seventeenth century, widely shared by the framing generation in the eighteenth century, entrenched in modern philosophy and law by John Stuart Mill in the nineteenth century, and further elaborated on in the twentieth century by Joel Feinberg.

For centuries, the United States has held individual autonomy in high regard and viewed paternalistic legislation with great mistrust. After Aquinas, the American Founders greatly valued the work of John Locke, seeing a fundamental Thomistic truth in his observation that natural law provides the standard by which one may know of the justice of any government.[15] In fact, Thomas Jefferson placed Locke alongside Isaac Newton and Francis Bacon as "the three greatest men the world had ever produced,"[16] so it is likely that this drafter of the Declaration of Independence read Locke's 1689 masterpiece, *Two Treatises of Government*, which proclaimed:"[t]he state of nature has a law of nature to govern it, which obliges every one . . . that being all equal and independent, no one ought to harm another in his life, health, liberty, or possessions."[17]

Jefferson himself echoed Locke by writing in 1787 that "the legitimate powers of government extend to such acts only as are injurious to others."[18] Locke's *Second Treatise* continues by discussing his "workmanship argument," which highlights an individual's calling not to harm one another, and can be summarized as follows:

> The beginning point is God the Creator. Human beings are the creation or "workmanship" of God; they therefore belong to God and are His property. From this fact derives a set of prescriptions under the natural law. These prescriptions mainly take the form of limitations on what human beings may do: they may not use force (may not directly harm

each other), for they belong to God, not to each other; they may not harm themselves (they may not commit suicide, for example) for the same reason; and they may not indirectly harm each other through taking more than their fair share of the goods of the external world.[19]

Furthermore, Locke contends that while man is endowed with free will and the law of nature is known by reason, it is not necessarily universally obeyed. Instead, "the very freedom requisite to a Lockean state of nature implies that there will be individuals who choose to act outside of the boundaries of the law."[20] By disobeying the tenets of the law of nature, such an "offender" declares himself to live by another rule than that of reason and common equity, which is that measure God has set to the actions of men for their mutual security; and so he becomes dangerous to mankind, the tie, which is to secure them from injury and violence, being slighted and broken by him.[21]

As a result, the rational man has the right to punish such offenders – criminals – "[f]or if no one had such a right the law of nature would be in vain."[22]

In Locke's opinion, for punishment to be justified, two things are required: "[f]irst, that he who does it has commission and power so to do . . . [s]econdly, that it be directly useful for the procuring some greater good."[23] In order to meet the first prong, the government's right to punish in civil society, "like all governmental rights, must be composed of the redistributed natural rights of citizens, rights that the citizens must therefore have been capable of possessing in a nonpolitical state of nature."[24] Locke further points out that the bounds of government are natural law:

> A Man, as has been proved, cannot subject himself to the Arbitrary Power of another; and having in the State of Nature no Arbitrary Power over the Life, Liberty, or Possession of another, but only so much as the Law of Nature gave him for the preservation of himself, and the rest of Mankind; this is all he doth, or can give up to the Common-wealth, and by it to the Legislative Power, so that the Legislative can have no more than this. Their Power in the utmost Bounds of it, is limited to the publick good of the Society .... Thus the Law of Nature stands as an Eternal Rule to all Men, Legislators as well as other. The Rules that they make for other Mens [sic] Actions, must, as well as their own and other Mens [sic] Actions, be conformable to the Law of Nature, i.e. to the Will of God, of which that is a Declaration, and the fundamental Law of Nature being the preservation of Mankind, no Humane Sanction can be good, or valid against it.[25]

Beyond the liberal philosophies of Enlightenment thinkers like Locke, arguments about the proper role of government also found support in nineteenth-century philosophers such as John Stuart Mill. In 1869, Mill published his treatise, *On Liberty*, which set forth a bold standard for defining the sphere of individual liberty and a utilitarian view of government. In what has now become known colloquially as the "Harm Principle," Mill began by stating:

> The object of this Essay is to assert one very simple principle, as entitled to govern absolutely the dealings of society with the individual in the way of compulsion and control, whether the means used be physical force in the form of legal penalties, or the moral coercion of public opinion. That principle is, that *the sole end for which mankind are warranted, individually or collectively, in interfering with the liberty of action of any of their number, is self-protection.* That the only purpose for which power can be rightfully exercised over any member of a civilized community, against his will, is *to prevent harm to others.* His own good, either physical or moral, is not a sufficient warrant. He cannot rightfully be compelled to do or forbear because it will be better for him to do so, because it will make him happier, because, in the opinion of others, to do so would be wise, or even right... The only part of the conduct of anyone for which he is amenable to society is that which concerns others. In the part which merely concerns himself, his independence is, of right, absolute. Over himself, over his own body and mind, the individual is sovereign.[26]

According to Mill, the liberty of the individual may only be restricted "by the active interference of mankind," "when one, without justifiable cause, do[es] harm to others."[27] Such harm or injury, according to Mill, must be direct and specific to particular individuals:

> [W]ith regard to the merely contingent or, as it may be called, constructive injury which a person causes to society by conduct which neither violates any specific duty to the public, nor occasions perceptible hurt to any assignable individual except himself, the inconvenience is one that society can afford to bear, for the sake of the greater good of human freedom.[28]

To "harm" another, in Mill's sense, is to violate an individual's moral or legal interests or rights, "which, either by express legal provision or by tacit understanding, ought to be considered as rights..."[29] There must be "a definite damage, or a definite risk of damage, either to an individual or to the public."[30] In sum, to be the basis of legal or moral concern, Mill argued, the harm must be tangible, secular, palpable material – physical or financial, or, if emotional, focused and direct – rather than moral or spiritual. He contrasts this with "acts of an individual [that] may be hurtful to others, or wanting in due consideration for their welfare, without going to the length of violating any of their constituted rights."[31] Here, an offender may be "justly punished by opinion, though not by law." [32]

In citing to Mill to assess a state constitution's ban on same-sex marriage, Judge Richard Posner recently wrote,

> "[T]here is a difference… between the distress that is caused by an assault, or a theft of property, or an invasion of privacy, or for that matter discrimination, and the distress that is caused by behavior that disgusts some people but does no (other) harm to them.

Mill argued that

> neither law (government regulation) nor morality (condemnation by public opinion) has any proper concern with acts that, unlike a punch in the nose, inflict no temporal harm on another person without consent or justification."[33]

Mill went on to categorize two spheres of individual activity: the "self-regarding" and the "other-regarding;" he cautioned that society may rightfully interfere only in the latter.

> The only part of the conduct of any one, for which he is amenable to society, is that which concerns others. In the part which merely concerns himself, his independence is, of right, absolute.[34]

Once any part of a person's conduct "affects prejudicially the interests of others, society has jurisdiction over it," however, "there is no room for entertaining any such question when a person's conduct affects the interests of no persons besides himself."[35] Specifically, Mill believed there were three regions of human liberty in the "self regarding sphere" that should remain exempt from any political or social restrictions: (1) "liberty of conscience, in the most comprehensive sense," including "absolute freedom of opinion and sentiment on all subjects, practical or speculative, scientific, moral, or theological" (2) "liberty of tastes and pursuits; of framing the plan of our life to suit our own character," and (3) "freedom to unite for any purpose not involving harm to other persons."[36] Any society that did not respect these liberties could not be "free, whatever may be its form of government…

> The only freedom which deserves the name, is that of pursuing our own good in our own way, so long as we do not attempt to deprive others of theirs, or impede their efforts to obtain it. Each is the proper guardian of his own health, whether bodily, or mental and spiritual. Mankind are greater gainers by suffering each other to live as seems good to themselves, than by compelling each to live as seems good to the rest."[37]

Thus, the Millian Harm Principle holds that the only legitimate justification for the state to limit the liberty of the individual, *vis a vis* the creation of positive criminal law, is the prevention of harm to third parties.[38] The state has no right to enact laws which limit any individual's action, whether committed alone or in union with others, that does not bring about direct, material, palpable harm to another.

Mill derived these principles "from a rights-based conception of the essential spheres of self-governing moral independence," and was concerned that "society should be skeptical about enforcing moral perfectionism on the community at large."[39] Mill espoused the traditional liberal view that criminal law should restrict freedom only to prohibit conduct, not to demand it; he strongly cautioned against the "increasing inclination to stretch unduly the powers of society over the individual, both by the force of opinion and even by that of legislation," out of fear that "the tendency ... is to strengthen society, and diminish the power of the individual."[40] He continued,

> This disposition of mankind, whether as rulers or as fellow-citizens, to impose their own opinions and inclinations as a rule of conduct on others, is so energetically supported by some of the best and by some of the worst feelings incident to human nature, that it is hardly ever kept under restraint by anything but want of power; and as power is not declining, but growing, unless a strong barrier... can be raised against the mischief, we must expect, in the present circumstances of the world, to see it increase.[41]

Mill's Harm Principle has become the primary philosophical, political, and legal rationale for interfering with individual autonomy. Others, such as the philosopher Joel Feinberg, have gone on to consider "whether it is the *only* valid liberty-limiting principle, as John Stuart Mill declared."[42] In his four-volume *magnum opus, The Moral Limits of the Criminal Law* (1984), also discussed in Chapter 13, Feinberg, by his own account aims both to "vindicate the traditional liberalism derived from Mill's *On Liberty*" and "to try to go as far as possible with the harm principle alone...."[43] Eventually, he ends up "applying it to the difficult and controversial areas case by case, [to] try to determine to what extent, if any, it must be modified or supplemented,"[44] and in doing so, attempts "to identify a set of constraints that a state (as represented by its legislature) can use to ensure that criminal legislation does not illegitimately contravene individual liberty."[45]

In defending and fleshing out Mill's Harm Principle, Feinberg examines four traditionally accepted "categories of justification for criminal sanction": (1) harm to others, (2) offense to others, (3) harm to the actor herself, and (4) harmless wrongdoing. Neither of the two final principles are morally acceptable as a basis for criminal prosecution to Feinberg, who says that the overall goal of his four volume work is to defend "the view that the harm and offense principles, duly clarified and qualified, between them exhaust the class of morally relevant reasons for criminal prohibitions."[46]

Throughout the first volume, Feinberg argues that in order to legitimize a decision to criminalize conduct, the notion of harm must be based on two elements, present at the same time: (1) The conduct must produce a *setback to interests* in which one has a stake, and (2) The conduct must entail the violation of a person's right.[47] "'Interests'" are defined as longer-term desires and goals, as opposed to passing wants or fancies.[48] In other words, harm is not merely an interference with another person's *preference*, but only a significant, wrongful interference with those rights in which the other person has a stake. In essence, "harm" that may be criminalized is: "harm to one's body, psyche, or purse."[49] In narrowing the idea of harm, Feinberg echoes many of Mill's arguments, for example, by stating that neither actions that an individual does to *himself*,[50] nor injurious actions to which the individual consents[51] fall within the harm principle. In an attempt to make the harm principle a *limiting* principle, he devotes his first volume "largely to the most problematic applications of this principle, posing questions such as whether a failure to prevent harm qualifies as harm, whether the voluntary consent of the person harmed absolves the actor, [and] whether one can be harmed posthumously..."[52]

In his second volume, Feinberg goes beyond Mill and argues that some laws criminalizing *offenses* to others will be justified under the harm principle. Here, "offense" refers to unreflective or emotional reactions like irritation, disgust, or humiliation.[53] Stated differently, in certain circumstances, mental discomfort can rise to the level of harm. Drawing largely from the law of nuisance, Feinberg concludes that an offensive action may be punished as a harm "where the time, place, or manner of the act is beyond the bounds of reason, and the unwilling observer's reaction of disgust, shock, or outrage is itself reasonable."[54] This principle is used to justify actions like banning open lewdness in public places or prohibiting loud amplifiers in quiet neighborhoods, and of course, is demonstrated by reference to Feinberg's famous Ride on the Bus.[55] However, Feinberg limits such by stating "it will be insufficient to invoke this justification by merely alleging that someone (or the community at large) is offended by the *knowledge* that otherwise harmless, though perhaps repulsive, activity is going on somewhere in private."[56]

In his third volume, Feinberg addresses Mill's discussion of "legal paternalism," or the use of the criminal law to "prevent harm (physical, psychological, or economic) to the actor himself."[57] Feinberg, like Mill, rejects this position as a valid justification for criminal statutes because it interferes with personal autonomy. Feinberg does, however, distinguish "hard paternalism" from "soft paternalism," which he believes is reasonable and warrants state interference with dangerous self-regarding behavior "only when that conduct is substantially nonvoluntary, or when temporary intervention is necessary to establish whether it is voluntary or not."[58] Feinberg concludes that soft paternalism is not clearly paternalistic "because this type of government act does not seek to veto decisions that are genuinely autonomous, but merely to assure that they truly are autonomous..."[59] Feinberg's fourth volume considers harmless wrongdoing. While harm consists of physical, psychological or economic injury, it "excludes simple moral harms and in Feinberg's view, renders unacceptable any attempt to justify a criminal prohibition simply on the ground that its existence will lead to the elevation of the character of an individual or of society."[60]

In summation, Feinberg sets out to offer moral, natural law based guidelines to "'an ideal legislature in a democratic country' regarding coherent and plausible principles that should represent the basis for the drafting of penal laws."[61] "It is not my purpose," Feinberg observes, "to try to specify what such a body would choose to include in its ideally wise and useful penal code, but rather what it may include, if it chooses within the limits that morality places on legislative decisions."[62]

The works of Murray Rothbard are addressed in Chapter 16 where this book delves into his discussion on property and liberty, and the boundaries he sets to protect both. We first see an iteration of his Non-Aggression Principle in *War, Peace, and the State* (1963) which appeared in *Egalitarianism as a Revolt Against Nature and Other Essays*, and becomes a theme throughout his subsequent works:

No one may threaten or commit violence ('aggress') against another man's person or property. Violence may be employed only against the man who commits such violence; that is, only defensively against the aggressive violence of another. In short, no violence may be employed against a non-aggressor. Here is the fundamental rule from which can be deduced the entire corpus of libertarian theory.[63]

In 1982, Rothbard published *The Ethics of Liberty*, in which he sought to establish the validity of natural law, as an approach to moral inquiry based on the distinctive nature, faculties, and tendencies of the human being. In the preface Rothbard writes: "Since questions of property and crime are essentially *legal* questions, our theory of liberty necessarily sets forth an ethical theory of what law concretely *should* be. In short, as a natural-law theory should properly do, it sets forth a normative theory of law in our case, a theory of 'libertarian law.'"[64] He begins Chapter 9 (Property and Criminality) by applying the Non-Aggression principle to positive law, "We may define anyone who aggresses against the person or other produced property of another as a *criminal*. A criminal is anyone who initiates violence against another man and his property: anyone who uses the coercive 'political means' for the acquisition of goods and services."[65] In another work published that same year, Rothbard goes on to address a concern that legal and political theory have "fail[ed] to pinpoint physical invasion as the only human action that should be illegal and that justifies the use of physical violence to combat it."[66]

The normative principle I am suggesting for the law is simply this: No action should be considered illicit or illegal unless it invades, or aggresses against, the person or just property of another. Only invasive actions should be declared illegal, and combated with the full power of the law. The invasion must be concrete and physical.[67]

Rothbard explains that there are degrees of such invasion (i.e., burglary versus robbery), and hence, different degrees of restitution or punishment, but the most important axiom is that "man is a self owner, having absolute jurisdiction over his own body."[68] In fact, physical invasion or molestation need not be actually "harmful" or inflict damage in order to be proscribed. For example, spitting in someone's face or ripping off someone's hat are batteries, for although "the actual damage may not be substantial, in a profound sense we may conclude that the victim's person was molested, was *interfered with*, by the physical aggression against him, and that hence these seemingly minor actions have become legal wrongs."[69]

Today, since the introduction of Feinberg's Offense Principle, the Harm Principle would apply to victimless crimes, "a large number of *offenses against morals* in which there are no victims, such as gambling, consumption of liquor or homosexuality, whose characteristic feature is that . . . the persons affected are those who take part in the act of their own free will and are responsible for the suffering which is self-inflicted."[70] Instead of an injured individual seeking reparation from a public authority, "it is the public authority which is offended against and which must *seek out* the transgressor."[71] The extent that the right to privacy is understood in Millian terms, "it would immunize from constitutional attack all such laws [which prohibit private activity done to, and with, other consenting adults], at least to the extent that they do not directly harm third parties."[72]

Yet, NLT has taught that where fundamental rights are involved, private morality alone cannot justify their abridgment, and as Justice John Marshall Harlan II wrote: "the mere assertion that the action of the State finds justification in the controversial realm of morals cannot justify alone any and every restriction it imposes."[73] The Supreme Court put it more bluntly; "under our form of government, the state does not attempt to control the citizen except as to his conduct to others."[74] For this reason, the Feinberg extension of the Millian Harm Principle contradicts the Lockean understanding of NLT.

The reality is that our current lawmakers have a considerably broad idea of harm, which in turn, in their minds, justifies greater government intervention into the personal sphere than Mill would have defended or Rothbard would have condoned. This approach, however, interferes directly with the 'right to do as one pleases,' a core natural law principle and surely one of the "individual rights [that] exist independently of government,"[75] and are protected by the Ninth Amendment.[76]

Natural Law Theory is a constant reminder, nevertheless, that the Declaration and its explicit reference to natural law provide a lens through which to interpret the Constitution and subsequently limit the litany of criminal laws to those that prosecute palpable harm. "The right to do as one pleases' does not continue with the phrase, 'as long as you are a middle or upper class member of society;' instead this right is blind to race, blind to religion and blind to socioeconomic status. The 'right to do as one pleases' continues with 'so long as you do not interfere with the fundamental rights of others.'"[77] Afterall, even Thomas Jefferson wrote, "No man has a natural right to commit aggression on the equal rights of another: and this is all from which the laws ought to restrain him."[78] This longstanding vision held by the Founders was reinforced by the Supreme Court, which in the past has held,

> There are, of necessity, limits beyond which legislation cannot rightfully go. ... [T]he courts must ... upon their own responsibility, determine whether in any particular case, these limits have been passed. ... If, therefore, a statute purporting to have been enacted to protect the public health, the public morals, or the public safety, has no real or substantial relation to those objects, ... it is the duty of the courts to so adjudge, and thereby give effect to the Constitution.[79]

Thus, under Natural Law Theory, all definitions of crime must contain a reference to harm; for under Natural Law Theory, without palpable harm to others, there can be no crime. Afterall, "in the United States of America, the great barrier to the inevitable mischief of governmental intrusion upon personal liberty is the Constitution,"[80] including of course, the Ninth Amendment's protection of unenumerated liberties.

CHAPTER 22

CONCLUSION

The Argument

We have examined the path of the natural law from the time Thomas Aquinas refined it to a series of tenets. We saw how it became secularized by Hugo Grotius, acknowledged by Hobbes, refined by Locke, and applied by Edward Coke and William Blackstone.

We then explored how the American Revolutionaries embraced the Natural Law Tradition, revered it in the Declaration of Independence, and enshrined it in the U.S. Constitution.

The Supreme Court, receptive to natural law arguments in its earliest days, took major steps to weave it into the fabric of American jurisprudence despite the occasional divergence like McCulloch.

After the death of John Marshall, the majority of the Supreme Court fell to the false luster of legal positivism which permitted it to endorse simply awful decisions under the banner of legal positivism.

The atrocities committed by governments during the Second World War turned the Court back to the Natural Law Tradition and begat several generations of thinkers, scholars, and jurists who reexamined the relationship between government and the governed through the lens of NLT.

One of the most significant contemporary formulations running adjacent to the Natural Law Tradition came from Murray Rothbard in his Non-Aggression Principle. However, his NAP neglected certain principles and usages of NLT.

Can the Natural Law Tradition and the Non-Aggression Principle be combined to assure greater individual autonomy?

***

There can be no truly moral choice unless that choice is made in freedom; similarly, there can be no really firmly grounded and consistent defense of freedom unless that defense is rooted in moral principle.[1]

– **Murray Rothbard (1926-1995)**

In reality, we possess the highest degree of natural liberty in that vaunted state of nature so grimly portrayed by Hobbes and so warmly embraced by Locke. In that state of nature, we command ourselves and answer to one another only so far as our rights and liberties confront the rights of others. However, savage and more atavistic tendencies, whether spurred on by avarice or some primordial desire to conquer, can, in turn, drive one to exercise dominion or control over some form or property rightfully belonging to another. Or, perhaps, a genuine dispute emerges in light of ambiguous boundaries or borders, or a good faith error or mistake of one or both of the parties. In any case, as observed by the great minds of the centuries, those in a state of nature often come together to form a society for the mutual protection of their rights and property. In so doing, those who have banded together agree to grant, in trust, certain rights and privileges to whatever artifice they have ordained to administer that society.

The simple act of forming a society for mutual protection *requires* the partial diminution of certain rights for the sake of order and legitimacy. Many flourish when such societies confer upon their members benefits that allow for activities as basic as collective child rearing, to the fulfilment of societal needs that allow for the exercise of competitive advantage, wherein members of a society can rely on others to perform the tasks and duties to which they are best suited – fostering barter, free trade, and the wealth and happiness that the invisible hand shepherds forward in such a minimally-fettered society. Such providence, such blessings of liberty, however, can lead to larger and more complex societies that can bring with them increased human density and, often, a perceived need for additional rules, regulations, and restrictions – negations of liberty – which further erode those liberties that had formerly been accepted as unspoken and simply natural. Slowly, villages can become towns, towns become cities, cities become nations, and nations become empires. When an empire grows to the point of unsustainability, it begins to buckle and strain. Pressure often mounts in its imperial heart; and government, in an attempt to placate those within a stone's distance of the seat of power, treats others within the empire as a lower class of citizen or subject somehow, by dint of proximity, entitled to lesser protections and fewer civil (or, often natural) rights than those at home.

Such was the case with the British Empire, and such was the lot of the colonists, whose rights of equal representation somehow lost the ability to traverse the Atlantic Ocean. And, as those ill-treated by the powers that run society are wont to do, they demanded the restoration of the rights to which they felt they were guaranteed. They marched, skirmished, rebelled, and eventually won. Weary of the loss of their rights under the English Crown and aware of the trajectory of imperial civilizations,[2] the founding generations labored to ensure the protection of our natural rights and liberties though the Constitution, its restraints on government, and the positive language of the Ninth and Tenth Amendments. Despite their best efforts, however, as we have seen, the United States grew more complicated, and issues began to emerge uncontemplated by the even the most brilliant minds of the eighteenth and early nineteenth centuries. The graph of natural rights and liberties is reminiscent of a far-off mountain range. Following such a path, societies often slowly creep away from the light of reason, the knowledge and control of their natural rights and liberties toward some form of despotism against which they rebel, as did the Founders, to form a new society whose rules and protections exist in a fashion more harmonious than they did under the prior government.

Such has been the path of natural law in the United States. From its apogee following the American Revolution, it has, over time, engaged in trajectory on a fall from grace caught perhaps in the omnipresent gravity of executive and legislative rapaciousness, or, and perhaps more appalling, administrative indolence and judicial indifference. However, from time to time, some fight the forces seeking to hamper natural rights and liberties to further some government end and elevate the field of jurisprudence above the cacophony of voices calling for Positivism, Originalism, Legal realism, Formalism, Structuralism, Constructionism, or Living constitutionalism.

The purpose of this book is to explore the path of the Natural Law Tradition going back to the thirteenth century through the first two decades of the twenty-second century. This has addressed American caselaw, over the course of our country's history, in which the Supreme Court has recognized and protected many of our core, fundamental rights identified by theorists, and exalted by the Framers.

Perhaps the most easily recognizable embodiment of such rights is Jefferson's oft-quoted natural law maxim – the divine origin and inalienability of individual rights to *life*, *liberty*, *and the pursuit of happiness*. The first and foremost inalienable right being that of life, the right to protect oneself from harm from both individual violence as well as the tyranny of the government. This natural right is protected in the Second Amendment's right to keep and bear arms. From this natural right to self-defense stems the right to proportionality of punishment, also incorporated in the Bill of Rights via the Eighth Amendment.

At its core, the rights embraced by Jefferson's concept of "liberty" include the natural right to privacy – to keep the government out of your personal affairs and bedroom, including but not limited to the right to the control and ownership of one's own body, the fundamental right to marital privacy, and of course, the right to choose a sexual partner. Perhaps most emblematic of this fundamental right to privacy is the Fourth Amendment guarantee against unreasonable searches and seizures, an effort to uphold the age old maxim that "a man's home is his castle," and not even the government may trample on our rights in this domain. Moreover, liberty encompasses our fundamental expressive freedom – freedom of speech and conscience embodied in the First Amendment.

Lastly, Jefferson's call to protect "the pursuit of happiness" includes our desire to seek a better life – chiefly the natural right to own, use, enjoy, and exclude others from one's real property, as well as the right to travel free from government-imposed, often nativistic-inspired impediments. Similarly, we have seen the Court protect our natural right to economic liberty – the right to enter into contract for employment, or the right to engage in voluntary commercial transactions and exchanges, as well as the right to pursue remedies to enforce such contracts/transactions. Perhaps most importantly, this list of natural rights is not exhaustive – in fact, the courts may uncover additional natural rights as time progresses and circumstances warrant. The Founders were acutely aware of this fact, and through the Ninth Amendment, sought to protect these innate, but perhaps undiscovered rights when they proclaimed: "the enumeration in the Constitution, of certain rights, shall not be construed to deny or disparage others retained by the people." By stressing the *rights* of the people, there can be no mistake – there is no grant to the government of power to dispossess the people of their preexisting natural rights.

We have also explored different theories of jurisprudence, which sometimes took hold in decades, or years. As we saw with Bentham, Mill, and Austin, ideas of legal positivism and utilitarianism captured the imagination of jurisprudential and political thought and helped usher in changes in modes of thought that allowed society to abandon morals and reason and instead cede ground to philosophies extolling the virtues of vague and subjective claims of judicial "science" and the greater good. However, people quickly forgot that the founding generation sought to prepare a new nation, a constitutional republic unlike any that had ever been erected, for the greatest good: the preservation of individual liberty and natural rights.

While the founding generation may have felt more strongly about the contents of those rights, and may have been more familiar with their expression and their limitations, they left us a gift to ensure that we did not lose sight of them. That gift is the Ninth Amendment, which serves as a safeguard to future generations that when government tries to diminish, discard, or disparage those unenumerated rights, it must stop and proceed in reverse.

The passage of time, the damage of wars, and the difficulty of economic hardship have drawn our attention away from our natural rights. Unlike muscles that atrophy from lack of use, rights do not weaken or diminish when neglected. It is only our neglect and reluctance to assert these rights that have led us toward complacency and the perpetual victims of government overreach. As we have seen, we do not need to decamp into tribalism over interpretive approaches. Originalists in the United States can remain true to their slavish adherence to the words on the page. Intentionalists need to waiver when reading centuries-old tea leaves or performing interpretive séances to divine what existed in the mind of the legislators or adopters of a law or provision. All can set their sextant to the polestar of the NLT and breathe easily that, in so doing, they have not violated their sacred vows to the gospel of the text of the thing. The Constitution – the supreme law of the land – bestows its benediction to the inclusion of the NLT and NAP because "[t]he enumeration in the Constitution, of certain rights, shall not be construed to deny or disparage others retained by the people."[3]

Originalists, who proclaim that their one true method of jurisprudence demands the consideration of the original public understanding of the text, *must*, when it comes to the Constitution and the Bill of Rights, explore the widely held public understanding of political and social theory held by the Framers and the American people in the early days of our Republic from 1776 through 1791.

The research for this book began with examinations of the speeches, arguments, broadsides, pamphlets, essays, circulars, and letters of the colonial revolutionaries, legislators, and thinkers who became the Founding Fathers, and the Framers of the Constitution of the United States. By exhaustive review of what they read, how they argued, and how these men thought of government, your author and his researchers worked backwards to read, analyze, and understand those thinkers who influenced these great men. Your author did not begin with St. Thomas Aquinas by accident. Our discussion of Hugo Grotius, Thomas Hobbes, John Locke, John Milton, William Blackstone and Edward Coke in the first two chapters of this endeavor was not happenstance.

This review began at a particular point in time and traced a thread of Natural Law theory from a crucial point in its development through the first few decades of the federal Republic in an effort to demonstrate a rhythm of thought, a motif in the tapestry of philosophy and jurisprudence to show the development and evolution in Natural Law theory as it informed, shaped, and then became enshrined in the Declaration of Independence, Constitution, and Bill of Rights; and, perhaps most importantly for these pages, *how Natural Law Tradition became positive law through the guarantee of natural rights demanded under the Ninth Amendment.*

Rather than halting at the adoption of the Bill of Rights in 1791, we saw how the Supreme Court, the ultimate arbiter of law in the United States, the preeminent court of last resort, confronted issues that implicated Natural Law theory and notions of natural rights at a time when the nation was fresh and, as a society, Americans needed to decide which rights to preserve as integral to humanity, and which had been ceded to or *stolen* by government overreach.

As we saw in Chapters 6 and 7, state legislatures and bands of people drew battle lines and tested the power of both the state and federal governments. As the Supreme Court decided cases, constitutional amendments and federal laws were passed to reverse some of those outcomes. As states and Congress passed new laws, the Supreme Court, on occasion invalidated them. When government overreached, the people pushed back. And occasionally, the government pushed back harder.

And, as we have seen, attitudes, approaches, and ideas did not become ossified in 1776, 1783, 1787, 1789, 1791, or any other year. As new ideas were developed, these ideas informed the agencies and instrumentalities of government, and the social institutions in our society. The legislative, executive, and judicial branches of government are not the only agents of change. The rise and fall of societies and advances in social thought and science *should* inform enlightened societies and result in vicissitudes designed to uphold first principles, such as the pursuit of happiness and our security in our property and ourselves. Natural Law theory, the Non-Aggression Principle, Professor Barnett's views on the importance of unanimous actual consent, and Justice Scalia's calls for focus on the original public understanding of the text of the Constitution and its amendments need not present us with mutually exclusive propositions. Nor should we need to enlist our greatest minds to concoct insular scenarios in which some overlapping ideas would grant us the luminary brilliance of a single polestar to guide us to a single instance of mutuality between these ideas. Building upon NLT and NAP, we can construct a modified, simple coda comprising six tenets that succinctly and properly addresses the limitations of the power the state can exercise over individuals.[4]

Accordingly, here is your author's six part coda:

1. All human beings have natural rights which are utterly inalienable unless expressly surrendered by unambiguous conduct.

2. The state is an artificial construct based on a monopoly of force in a defined geographical location. It is at its essence the negation of liberty.

3. The state may only justly use force against any person without his or her consent, to repel unwelcome aggression, including fraud or its equivalents, against another individual, a group, their autonomy, or their property.

4. Other principles of offense, legal moralism, legal paternalism or their analogs become permissible subjects for legal prescription and proscription only in so far as they are absolutely necessary and utterly proper to preserve the liberty and autonomy of the individual from substantial or future derogation by harm.

5. Since human liberty is the default position, and government is essentially the negation of liberty, all that government does beyond the direct protection of individual liberty shall, at every turn, be presumed to be beyond its lawful authority.

6. Reason, necessity, and propriety together dictate the exact contours and definitions— and indeed the very recognition of acceptable principles and rules.

The Jeffersonian reformulation of Aquinas is embedded in American theory and culture, though widely rejected in practice. Nevertheless, without it in America, NLT and NAP would devolve into battles over property rights.

Diverging from Feinberg (see Chapter 12), your author believes that offense is not a species of harm, or at least is not an area of sensibility and sentiment which government has a moral basis for the exercise of force, absent actual consent. There is no natural right not to be offended.

Barnett's definition of propriety ultimately permitted imposition on the natural liberty of the individual without establishing the necessity of doing so (absent that individual's consent). In other words, Barnett would allow *some* impositions on the individual absent his or her consent so long as those impositions related to natural law and natural rights. This formulation of a necessary condition leaves unmolested the space for personal autonomy and choice where such action does not harm another individual. For, as Gerald Dworkin ably argued, "Paternalism is justified only to preserve a wider range of freedom for the individual in question... [The question that remains is discerning principles of] acceptable use of paternalistic power."[5] However, more akin to Barnett than Gerald Dworkin, consent is not the only acceptable way of delineating a justifiable area of paternalism; rather, necessity – absolute necessity – can provide a sufficient and narrow alternative account.[6] Thus, contra to the lesson of *Les Miserables*, the right to life trumps the right to property. Rothbard would probably disagree, but under NLT, if you are starving and unable to acquire nourishment to stave off death, you may morally steal my loaf of bread and consume it; Police Inspector Javert notwithstanding.[7]

The requirement of "substantial or future" in the fourth prong specifically addresses a point made by Gerald Dworkin in criticizing John Stuart Mill's justifications of paternalism. The only two ways in which an unharmed person may become harmed is immediately or in the future. Mill argued that the type of harm paternalism should protect is limited to the future variety, which Dworkin disproves by using Mill's own example of prohibiting the sale of oneself into slavery:

> While it is true that *future* choices of the slave are not reasons for thinking that what he chooses is desirable for him, what is at issue is limiting his *immediate* choice; and since that choice is made freely, the individual may be correct in thinking that his interests are best provided for by entering [into] such a contract. The main consideration for not enforcing such a contract, however, is the obligation of government to preserve the liberty of the person to make future choices.[8]

Gerald Dworkin is, of course, correct. There is an entire set of substantial concerns present in Mill's example, such as the derogation of the autonomy of the individual and the alienability of certain rights from humanity, to name a few.

The presence of property in the third prong does not mean that the overall principle, including the remaining tenets, could not *derive* from a scheme of property instead of presupposing one. For instance, in a state where government exists by necessity (i.e., without consent and only to protect natural rights), it could easily be necessary to prevent imminent harm (by mistaken or excessive self help) by delineating rules of ownership and transfer of property. Perhaps, even if a state does not *begin* from a moral position, it can evolve to fill a role consistent with a moral position. The only possible presupposition contained with respect to property is that it is possible to own, use, alienate, and exclude others – including the government– from one's property. However, that becomes only as effective as arguing that harm prevention as a fundamental principle presupposes that one can be harmed—the scheme respecting how to deal with species of harm follows, not precedes. Thus, the species of principle and rules regulating how to bound proper ownership follows from necessity, it does not precede it.

An alternative way of considering that objection considers harm prevention as assuming self-ownership. If it is improper to harm a person then there must be a more fundamental reason why, which takes the form of self-ownership and/or individual autonomy. Then, it becomes wrong to harm an *autonomous* being. Thus, even a precept based on pure harm prevention would require a scheme of proper self-ownership. Accordingly, a scheme of property may flow from the notion of individual political autonomy that requires, at the very least, the ownership of the self. Moreover, this goes to show the necessity of adding to the NAP formulation, a scheme of dealing with paternalism necessary to preserve greater autonomy and self ownership in a politically meaningful way.[9]

We may distinguish between authority and justice in hopes of clarifying a concept of propriety (different from Barnett's approach) to accompany the definition of necessity.[10] Underlying this discussion is the Feinberg notion that attaching values of right or wrong to an act is necessarily an act of claiming.

An action that may be authorized by law could remain unjustified by superior positive law or the pre-political moral or natural order. A necessarily *proper* action must be both *justified* by the positive and non-positive orders and *authorized* by the existing legal scheme. Ultimately, the meaningfulness of a legal scheme's claim becomes tied to how effectively the legal scheme operates with respect to its institutional core mission to protect and reinforce individual autonomy *qua* justice, and *contra* its arbitrariness. Essentially, the legal scheme must relate to its outcomes through a lens of preservation of individual autonomy and personal choice.

As such, in order for government action to be proper, it must either conform to NLT, NAP, or the variant set forth above. However, just because an action does not offend the rules under an existing legal scheme – which could make them sufficient – does not necessarily also mean that such an action is necessary. Certain rules or actions may not run afoul of the existing legal order in as much as positive law may not *prohibit them*. But just because a government action does not offend the existing legal order does not mean that it is *absolutely* necessary when undertaken by the government. The government should *only* undertake actions that are both *absolutely necessary* to fulfill its mandate of preserving individual liberty, but also *sufficiently proper* under the existing legal rules.

An individual can claim that an action is just, but proclaiming it as such does not make it so.[11] Sometimes, however, an action may seem necessary, but may not be proper in the existing legal order. And, other times, government action may be neither necessary *nor* proper *nor* authorized by the legal regime. To answer H.L.A. Hart's oft-raised Nazi paradigm: Their actions were sufficiently proper under their positivist order, but upon even cursory examination, unquestionably unjust as violative of the Natural Law Tradition and the Non-Aggression Principle. We have already seen in Chapter 12 how the absence of moral considerations when crafting first-order laws often leads to disaster.

Accordingly, we must continue to guide ourselves using principles designed to consider the default position as liberty and individual autonomy. We must rely on Reason when evaluating new positive rules, and when confronting ideas and positions, no matter how their bearers cloak them. Rules and actions that contravene Reason should not escape scrutiny because those in favor of them call for appeals to vague notions of "justice" or "fairness" when simultaneously requiring the diminution of our liberties, rights, and freedoms.

Tyrannical governments rarely retain power over an informed populace that defends its rights against government incursion and sublimation. Through vigilance, study, and application of these principles, we may continue to flourish in a society that embraces natural law principles, defers to the Non-Aggression Principle, and, through understanding and application, creates environs amenable to the growth of individual liberty.

Was Jefferson partly right about the tree of Liberty occasionally, and only when absolutely necessary, soaking up the blood of patriots and tyrants in order to survive? Or was he right when he observed that in the long march of history, governments grow and liberty shrinks? Or, were intellectual giants from Aquinas to Rothbard right when they argued that so long as we can reason, we will have liberty?

But to exercise reason, we must have free will. Both free will and natural law principles have been imprinted in us. Positive law not faithful to the natural law principles is an artificial fabrication of humans, usually for their own good or tenure in power. Yet all rational adults have natural inclinations to know good from evil.

The issues this work addresses are not those of individual fidelity to natural law principles, but government infidelity to them. Government fidelity to natural law principles assures individual choices, personal autonomy, and authorship of one's own life. Isn't that the definition of personal liberty – freedom bounded, as Jefferson said, only by the natural rights of others? Isn't that the pursuit of happiness?

Short of a government committed to the preservation of natural rights, there is darkness and chaos.

As Voltaire argued, people often believe the loudest voice, not the most rational. And anyone who can persuade you to believe absurdities can persuade you to commit atrocities. Only a government faithful to natural law principles – Kołakowski's "uncompromising demon" – no matter the winds of fortune or change, can prevent that.

ABBREVIATIONS

AML — Fred. D. Miller, Jr., *Aristotle's Theory of Political Rights, published in* ARISTOTLE AND MODERN Law (Richard O. Brooks & James Bernard Murphy eds., 2003)

ATOJ — JOHN RAWLS, A THEORY OF JUSTICE REVISED EDITION (1999) (1971)

BENTHAM'S MORALS — JEREMY BENTHAM, AN INTRODUCTION TO THE PRINCIPLES OF MORALS AND LEGISLATION (J.H. Burns, H. L. A. Hart eds., 1996) (1776)

COKE'S FIRST INSTITUTE — J. H. THOMAS, ESQ., LORD COKE'S FIRST INSTITUTE OF THE LAWS OF ENGLAND 1 (R.H. Helmholz, Bernard D. Reams, Jr. eds., 1986) (1818)

DE LEGIBUS — FRANCISCO SUÁREZ, TRACTATUS DE LEGIBUS ET LEGISLATORE DEO, Bk. I, Ch. 2, P 5, in 5 Opera Omnia 5 (Carolo Berton ed., Paris, Ludovicum Vivès 1856)

DHRC — DOCUMENTARY HISTORY OF THE RATIFICATION OF THE CONSTITUTION, (MERRILL JENSEN, JOHN P. KAMINKSI, ET AL., EDS.,) (1976-)

DJBP — HUGO GROTIUS, DE JURE BELLI AC PACIS (Francis W. Kelsey, ed. 1925) (1625)

ELLIOT'S DEBATES — THE DEBATES IN THE SEVERAL STATE CONVENTIONS ON THE ADOPTION OF THE FEDERAL CONSTITUTION AS RECOMMENDED BY THE GENERAL CONVENTION AT PHILADELPHIA IN 1781 (Jonathan Elliot ed., 1996)

GPMNL — GROTIUS, PUFENDORF AND MODERN NATURAL LAW (Knud Haakonssen, ed.) (1999)

GPT — GREAT POLITICAL THINKERS 1 GROTIUS (John Dunn and Ian Harris, eds., 1997)

HENLE'S AQUINAS	Summa Theologiae, I-II, *q*. 90, *a*. 4, *ad* 1. in ST. THOMAS AQUINAS THE TREATISE ON LAW [BEING *SUMMA THEOLOGIAE*] (R.J. Henle, S.J. ed. 1993)
HUNT'S MADISON	Gaillard Hunt in 3 WRITINGS OF JAMES MADISON ix (Gaillard Hunt ed., 1902)
MAIER'S RATIFICATION	PAULINE MAIER, RATIFICATION THE PEOPLE DEBATE THE CONSTITUTION, 1787-1788 (2010)
NLIC	R. H. HELMHOLZ, NATURAL LAW IN COURT: A HISTORY OF LEGAL THEORY IN PRACTICE (2015)
NAP	NON-AGGRESSION PRINCIPLE
NLIC	R. H. HELMHOLZ, NATURAL LAW IN COURT: A HISTORY OF LEGAL THEORY IN PRACTICE 2 (2015)
NLT	NATURAL LAW TRADITION
PHD	ALEXANDER HAMILTON & JAMES MADISON, THE PACIFICUS-HELVIDIUS DEBATES OF 1793-1794 (Morton J. Frisch, ed. 2007)
POTC	PAMPHLETS ON THE CONSTITUTION OF THE UNITED STATES PUBLISHED DURING ITS DISCUSSION BY THE PEOPLE 1787-1788 (Paul Leicester Ford, ed., De Capo Press 1968) (1888)
ROTHBARD'S EGALITARIANISM	MURRAY N. ROTHBARD, EGALITARIANISM AS A REVOLT AGAINST NATURE AND OTHER ESSAYS (Ludwig von Mises Institute 2000) (1974)
ROTHBARD'S ETHICS	MURRAY N. ROTHBARD, THE ETHICS OF LIBERTY (New York University Press 1998) (1982).
TUCKER'S BLACKSTONE	BLACKSTONE'S COMMENTARIES: WITH NOTES OF REFERENCE TO THE CONSTITUTION AND LAWS OF THE FEDERAL GOVERNMENT OF THE UNITED STATES; AND THE COMMONWEALTH OF VIRGINIA (St. George Tucker, ed., William Young Birch & Abraham Small, Philadelphia 1803)

NOTES[1]

[*] Murray N. Rothbard, Conceived in Liberty xv-xvi (Ludwig Von Mises Institute 2011).

INTRODUCTION

[1] Leszek Kołakowski, Is God Happy? On Natural Law 250 (2013).

[2] Patrick Devlin, The Enforcement of Morals 7 (Oxford University Press 1970).

[3] See, e.g., 1 William Blackstone, Commentaries *53-54, *38-45, *121-40.

[4] Id. at *160.

[5] 1 William Blackstone, Commentaries *41.

[6] Letter from Thomas Jefferson to Noah Webster, Jr. (Dec. 4, 1790) reprinted in 18 Papers of Thomas Jefferson 132 (Julian P. Boyd ed., 2d printing, Princeton Univ. Press 1985) (1971).

[7] James Otis, Rights of British Colonies Asserted and Proved (Pamphlet) 1763.

[8] Murray N. Rothbard, Conceived In Liberty 1052 (Ludwig Von Mises Institute 2011).

[9] The Trial of The British Soldiers of The 29th Regiment of Foot 46 (William Emmons, Boston, 1863) (quoting 4 William Blackstone *3) (emphasis in original)).

[10] 3 The Debates in The Several State Conventions on The Adoption of The Federal Constitution as Recommended by The General Convention at Philadelphia in 1781, 315 (Jonathan Elliot ed., 1996) (statement of Patrick Henry) [hereinafter Elliot's Debates].

[11] 1 Annals of Cong. 436 (1789) (J. Gales & W. Seaton eds., 1834) (statement of Rep. Madison) (introducing his proposed amendments).

[12] Randy E. Barnett, James Madison's Ninth Amendment, in 1 Rights Retained by The People: The History and Meaning of The Ninth Amendment 12 (Randy Barnett ed., 1989).

[13] U.S. Const. amend. IX (emphasis added).

---

[1] Some endnotes refer the reader to sources referenced in other endnotes throughout this work and to pages in those sources.

[14] Thomas Cooley, The General Principles of Constitutional Law In The United States of America 36 (1880).

[15] Douglas Bradburn, The Citizenship Revolution: Politics and The Creation of The American Union, 1774-1804, 102 (2009).

[16] *Id.* at 172, 178.

[17] *McCulloch v. Maryland*, 17 U.S. 316, 415 (1819) (Marshall, C. J.).

[18] *Scott v. Sandford*, 60 U.S. 393, 405 (1857).

[19] John Stuart Mill, On Liberty 23 (2 ed. 1863) (1859).

[20] *Shelley v. Kraemer*, 34 U.S. 1, 5 (1948).

[21] *Griswold v. Connecticut*, 381 U.S. 479, 480 (1965). (Douglas, J.).

[22] *Id.* at 486-487 (Goldberg, J., *concurring*) (footnote omitted).

[23] *Bowers v. Hardwick*, 478 U.S. 186, 194 (1986).

[24] MILL, Introduction, note 19, at 33.

CHAPTER 1

[1] Federalist No. 51 (James Madison).

[2] "Natural law, apparently killed and buried more times than any of us can count, keeps returning from the dead, both in the scholarly world and in popular thinking about morality." Michael Zuckert, *The Fullness of Being: Thomas Aquinas and the Modern Critique of Natural Law*, 69 Rev. of Pol. 28, 28 (2007). Zuckert also noted in 1997 that:

> Less than thirty years ago, a very competent student of political theory gave this assessment of the subject of this Symposium: "Natural law, which was for many centuries the basis of the predominant Western political thought, is rejected in our time by almost all students of society who are not Roman Catholics ....[N]atural law is today primarily not more than a historical subject." Michael P. Zuckert, *Do Natural Rights Derive From Natural Law?*, 20 Harv. J. L. & Pub. Pol'y 695, 695 (1997) (quoting Leo Strauss, Studies in Platonic Political Philosophy 137 (1983)).

[3] "Natural law theory thus began, and still begins, with an assumption of congruence between law and basic features of man's nature as they are thought to have existed from the beginning of time." R. H. Helmholz, Natural Law in Court: A History of Legal Theory in Practice 2 (2015) [hereinafter NLIC].

[4] Regarding the philosophy underlying the Declaration of Independence, Thomas Jefferson once wrote: "All its authority rests ... on the harmonizing sentiments of the day, whether expressed in conversation, in letters, printed essays, or in the elementary books of public right, as Aristotle..." Letter from

Thomas Jefferson to Henry Lee, Monticello (May 8, 1825) *reprinted in* 7 Works of Thomas Jefferson 407 (H. A. Washington ed., 1884).

5   Tomislav Han, The Transformation of Aristotelian Political Epistemology in Eighteenth-Century American Constitutional Discourse 35 (2003). "Perhaps no other single idea had such a hold on republican ideology as the notion that man is a political animal whose participation in politics is determined by a naturally defined station in a well-ordered republic." *Id.*

6   *Id.*

7   Fred. D. Miller, Jr., *Aristotle's Theory of Political Rights, published in* Aristotle and Modern Law 309 (Richard O. Brooks & James Bernard Murphy eds., 2003) [hereinafter AML]. Miller, however, has his critics with respect to his theories about Aristotle's notions of rights. *See* Malcolm Schofield, *Sharing in the Constitution,* 49 Rev. of Metaphysics 831-858 (1996) *reprinted in* AML at 353-380; Roderick T. Long, *Aristotle's Concept of Freedom,* 49 Rev. of Metaphysics 775-802 (1996) *reprinted in* AML at 383-410; and, Martha C. Nussbaum, *Capabilities and Human Rights,* 66 Fordham L. Rev. 273-300 (1997) *reprinted in* AML at 413-440.

8   *Id.* at 311.

9   John Kroger, *The Philosophical Foundations of Roman Law: Aristotle, The Stoics, and Roman Theories of Natural Law,* 2004 Wis. L. Rev. 905, 916 (2014) (citing Aristotle on Rhetoric: A Theory of Civic Discourse, 1373b, 1375a, at 102, 107-10 (George A. Kennedy trans., 1991).

10   Miller, Chapter 1, note 7, at 309.

11   Donald R. McConnell, *Nature in Natural Law,* 2 Liberty U. L. Rev. 797, 807 (2008).

12   Howard P. Kainz, Natural Law: An Introduction and Reexamination 7 (2004).

13   Kroger, Chapter 1, note 9, at 917 (citing Aristotle On Rhetoric: A Theory of Civic Discourse, 1373b,1368b, 1375a).

14   The Rhetoric of Aristotle 92-93 (J. E. C. Weldon, M.A. ed., trans, 1886).

15   *Id.* at 101-102 (emphasis in original).

16   Howard P. Kainz, Natural Law: An Introduction and Reexamination 7 (2004); *see also* John Kroger, *The Philosophical Foundations of Roman Law: Aristotle, The Stoics, and Roman Theories of Natural Law,* 2004 WIS. L. REV. 905, 918 (2014) ("This appears, however, to be a claim about what to say, and not what is. [Here,] Aristotle does not assert that positive or specific laws can, as an empirical matter, actually violate the laws of nature.")

17   Edwin S. Corwin, *The Natural Law and Constitutional Law,* 1949 Institute Proceedings, 47. We will discuss Professor Corwin further in Chapter 12, but for now we should note that his presentation on the "Natural Law and the

Constitution" remains an extraordinary contribution to the scholarship in this field. He famously begins: "the documentary Constitution is still, in important measure, Natural Law under the skin." *Id.*

18   The *Politics* is broken into three sections: books 1-3 consist of an introduction to political science, books 4-6 discuss practical politics, and books 7-8 consider the ideal state.

19   Kroger, Chapter 1, note 9, at 918.

20   Aristotle, Politics Book 1, chapter 5, 1254a at 21.

21   Kroger, Chapter 1, note 9, at 919.

22   For Aristotle, a free man is not merely any man who lives in a free society, but one "who possesses certain traits of character that allow him to govern himself responsibly and attain happiness." Tibor R. Machan, Liberty and Democracy 36-37 (1 ed. 2002).

23   "St. Augustine's decisive influence on the major trends of jurisprudential thought can be discerned for almost a millennium." Anton-Hermann Chroust, *The Fundamental Ideals in St. Augustine's Philosophy of Law*, 18 Am. J. Juris. 57, 58 (1973) (citing Anton Hermann Chroust, *The Philosophy of Law from St. Augustine to St. Thomas Aquinas*, 20 The New Scholasticism, 26, 26-71 (1956)).

24   *Id.* at 57.

25   *Id.*

26   *Id.* at 59.

27   *Id.* at 60 (footnote omitted).

28   Augustine, On The Free Choice of The Will, on Grace and Free Choice, and Other Writings 8-10 (Peter King ed., trans., 2010) (emphasis added).

29   2 Henry De Bracton, On The Laws and Customs of England 26 (George E. Woodbine ed., Samuel S. Thorne trans. 1968) (c. 1235).

30   *Id.*

31   *Id.*

32   *Id.*

33   "The Philosophic and jurisprudential achievements of St. Thomas Aquinas [...] constitute the high point of scholastic or mediaeval [sic] philosophy." Anton-Hermann Chroust, *The Philosophy of Law of St. Thomas Aquinas: His Fundamental Ideas and Some of His Historical Precursors*, 19 AM. J. Juris. 1, 1 (1974).

34   Charles P. Nemeth, questions whether Aquinas had access to Plato (4), but feels confident enough to Aristotle (6), St. Augustine of Hippo (7-8), Isodore of Seville (10), and nearly every other significant scholar or philosopher preceding and contemporary to Aquinas. Charles P. Nemeth, Aquinas in The

Courtroom: Lawyers, Judges, and Judicial Conduct (2001). *Accord*, Anton-Hermann Chroust, *The Philosophy of Law of St. Thomas Aquinas: His Fundamental Ideas and Some of His Historical Precursors*, Chapter 1, note 33, at 1.

35   NLIC, Chapter 1, note 3, at 2. Or, as Nemeth states it:

St. Thomas plants his feed in the soil of meaning, articulating a legal ideology that is consistent with his teleological approach, where law is a far more esoteric principle than simple enactment, where law draws in the comprehensive whole, the perfection of God and his creation, the natural, rational orders of the human species, and the ends and purposes of human existence. Nemeth, Chapter 1, note 34, at 3.

36   Summa Theologiae, I-II, *q.* 90, *a.* 4, *ad* 1. in St. Thomas Aquinas The Treatise on Law [Being *Summa Theologiae*] 124 (R.J. Henle, S.J. ed. 1993) [hereinafter Henle's Aquinas].

37   Zuckert, *Do Natural Rights Derive From Natural Law?*, Chapter 1, note 2, at 704.

38   *Id.*

39   "Law is an ordinance of reason, since every human agent is endowed with rational faculties." Nemeth, Chapter 1, note 34, at 17. "St. Thomas confidently asserts that 'law is something pertaining to reason' and a measure of human activity (*Ergo lex est aliquid rationis*)." *Id.* at 26 (footnote omitted).

40   "Human law is the derivative of practical reason which directs humans to known or knowable principles applicable to matters of human conduct." R.J. Araujo, S.J., *Thomas Aquinas: Prudence, Justice, and the Law*, 40 Loy. L. Rev. 897, 902 (1995) (footnote omitted) (citing to Thomas Aquinas, Summa Theologiae Ia-IIae, Q. 91, art. 3 (Anton Pegis trans., 1945)).

41   Ralph McInery and John O'Callaghan, *Saint Thomas Aquinas*, Stanford Encyclopedia of Philosophy, Summer 2018 Edition, Edward N. Zalta (ed.), *available at* https://plato.stanford.edu/archives/sum2018/entries/ aquinas/ ("When Thomas referred to Aristotle as the Philosopher, he was not merely adopting a *façon de parler* of the time. He adopted Aristotle's analysis of physical objects, his view of place, time and motion, his proof of the prime mover, his cosmology. He made his own Aristotle's account of sense perception and intellectual knowledge. His moral philosophy is closely based on what he learned from Aristotle and in his commentary on the *Metaphysics* he provides a cogent and coherent account of what is going on in those difficult pages.").

42   "The Aristotelian-Thomist[ic] theory of natural law [...] holds that the natural law is *universal* in its validity, in that it sets justified prescriptive requirements or precepts for the conduct of all human beings." Alan Gewirth, *The Ontological Basis of Natural Law: A Critique and An Alternative*, 29 Am. J. Juris. 95, 95 (1984).

43 *Id.*

44 *Id.*

45 Araujo, Chapter 1, note 40, at 902 (footnote omitted) (citing to Thomas
Aquinas, Summa Theologiae at Ia-IIae, Q. 90, art. 1 (Anton Pegis trans.,
1945)). "Law is a rule and measure of acts whereby man is induced to act or
is restrained from acting […] for *lex* (law) is derived from *ligare* (to bind),
because it binds one to act." Henle's Aquinas Chapter 1, note 36, at 141.
"Reason is law, for it ordains the actor towards those ends the intellect
unequivocally prescribes." Nemeth, Chapter 1, note 34, at 18.

46 Araujo, Chapter 1, note 40, at 902 (footnote omitted) (citing to Thomas
Aquinas, Summa Theologiae at Ia-IIae, Q. 90, art. 2, obj 1. "Law, properly
speaking, regards first and principally the order to the Common Good.").
Henle's Aquinas, Chapter 1, note 36, at 139.

47 "[T]he Common Good belongs either to the whole people or to one who is
represents the whole people. And therefore, to establish law belongs either to
the whole people or to a public official who has care of the whole community,
because, as in all other matters, to order an end belongs to him who that end
most properly belongs." *Id.* "Thomistic jurisprudence is planted in the mind
of man, forged and burned into the intellect and delivering predictable and
reliable messages about what ends are." Nemeth, Chapter 1, note 34, at 1.

48 Nemeth, Chapter 1, note 34, at 37.

49 *Id.* at 35 (quoting St. Thomas Aquinas, Summa Theologica, I-II Q. 94 a. 2, c.
) "[Aquinas] insists that [the Natural Law] contains but one supreme precept
or principle, namely, to do good and avoid evil." *Anton-Hermann Chroust,
The Philosophy of Law of St. Thomas Aquinas: His Fundamental Ideas and
Some of His Historical Precursors*, Chapter1, note 33, at 28.

50 John Finnis, *Natural Law and Legal Reasoning*, 38 Clev. St. L. Rev. 1, 1
(1990). "The doctrine of Natural Law is part of an older conception of nature
in which the observable world is not merely a scene of such regularities, and
knowledge of nature is not merely a knowledge of them. Instead, on this older
outlook every nameable kind of existing thing, human, animate, and
inanimate, is conceived not only as tending to maintain itself in existence but
as proceeding towards a definite optimum state which is the specific good—
or the end […] appropriate for it." H. L. A. Hart, The Concept of Law 188-
189, (3d ed. 2012).

51 "Law is seen not simply as the act of the legislator, but a product intended
toward a specific end of happiness and the virtuous life." Nemeth, Chapter 1,
note 34, at 18. "Being a virtuous person is synonymous with the moral
practice of law." *Id.* at 57 "Virtuous conduct, to be sure, is geared to the
human person's proper ends, but these ends extend to a higher, supernatural
order." *Id.* at 57-58.

52 Nemeth, Chapter 1, note 34, at 37.

53 St. Thomas Aquinas, Summa Theologica Ia-2ae. xc. 4, *in* St. Thomas Aquinas Philosophical Texts 354 (Thomas Gilby, trans.) (1952).

54 *Id.* at Ia-2ae. xc. I, c. & ad 3.

55 *Id.*

56 *Id.*

57 *Id.*

58 "Reason is the supreme measure for St. Thomas, and he is opposed to any conception of law that is fundamentally tied to the will of man or God." Nemeth, Chapter 1, note 34, at 8 (2001). "The model St. Thomas provides is not one of will, but of intellect, of reason in the human person. [...] [Aquinas] indicates that law is a dictate, an ordination of reason, standing in a superior position to human will." *Id.* at 28.

59 *Id.*

60 *Id.*

61 *Id.*

62 *Id.* at 355. [63] *Id.*

64 "So too the power to enact laws belongs either to the whole people or to the public authority who is the guardian of the community." *Id.*

65 "To lay an obligation a law must be applied to the men who have to be regulated, and this means that it must be brought to their knowledge by promulgation." *Id.*

66 "No one is obliged to obey a precept unless he be reasonably informed about it." St. Thomas Aquinas, Quaestiones Disputatae De Veritate XVII 3, *in* St. Thomas Aquinas Philosophical Texts 355 (Thomas Gilby, trans., 1952).

67 Gewirth, Chapter 1, note 42, at 96.

68 Nemeth, Chapter 1, note 34, at 37.

69 St. Thomas Aquinas, Summa Theologica Ia-2ae. xc. 4, *in* St. Thomas Aquinas Philosophical Texts 354 (Thomas Gilby, trans.) (1952).

70 *Id.*

71 Steven J. Brust, *Retrieving a Catholic Tradition of Subjective Natural Rights from the Law Scholastic Francisco Suarez, S.J.* 10 Ave Maria L. Rev. 343 (2002). 72 *Id.* at 346.

73 Francisco Suárez, Tractatus De Legibus Et Legislatore Deo, Bk. I, Ch. 2, P 5, in 5 Opera Omnia 5 (Carolo Berton ed., Paris, Ludovicum Vivès 1856) [hereinafter De Legibus] ("[*S*]*olet proprie jus vocari facultas quaedam moralis, quam unusquisque habet, vel circa rem suam, vel ad rem sibi debitam; sic enim dominus rei dicitur habere jus in re, et operarius dicitur habere jus ad stipendium, ratione cuius dicitur dignus mercede sua.*").

74   *Id.* at Bk. III, Ch. 3, P 6, at 183 (*"Quocirca sicut homo, eo ipso quod creatur et habet usum rationis, habet potestatem in seipsum et in suas facultates et membra ad eorum usum ....").

75   *Id.* at Bk. II, Ch. 14, P 16, at 141 (*"Nam hac ratione libertas est de jure naturae, potius quam servitus, quia natura fecit homines positive (ut sic dicam) liberos cum intrinseco jure libertatis, non tamen ita fecit positive servos, proprie loquendo."*).

76   Brust, Chapter 1, note 71, at 348.

77   *Id.* at 351 (citing Francisco Suárez, Tractatus Secundus: De Voluntario Et Involuntario in Genere, Deque Actibus Voluntariis in Speciali, Bk. I, Ch. 3, P 13, in 4 Opera Omnia 171 (D. M. André ed., Paris, Ludovicum Vivès 1856) (*"[N]otandum est liberum ex primaeva impositione significare id quod est sui juris, et alteri non est subjectum: unde videtur directe excludere relationem servitutis: unde in l. Libertas, ff. de Statu hominum, dicitur, libertas est facultas ejus quod cuique facere libet, nisi quod ei, et lege prohibitum est."*)).

78   *Id.* at 350.

79   *Id.* at 362-363.

80   *Id.* at 357-358.

81   *Id.* at 359.

82   Brian Tierney, The Idea of Natural Rights, Studies on Natural Rights, Natural Law, and Church Law, 1150-1625, 304 (1997).

83   *Id.* at 314.

84   *Id.*

85   *Id.* at 316.

86   Benjamin Straumann, *Is Modern Liberty Ancient? Roman Remedies and Natural Rights in Hugo Grotius's Early Works on Natural Law,* 27 L. & Hist. Rev., 55, 55 (2009).

87   Roscoe Pound, *Grotius and the Science of Law,* 19 Am. J. Of Int'l L. 685, 685 (1925).

88   "At the end of the first quarter of the seventeenth century, the revival of learning, humanism, the Reformation, and the rise of modern nations and breakdown of the academic idea of a universal empire of all Christendom, had put their mark upon the law and the time was ripe for a juristic new start." *Id.* at 685.

89   10 A Treatise of Legal Philosophy and General Jurisprudence:

The Philosophers' Philosophy of Law From The Seventeenth Century to Our Day 16 (Enrico Pattaro, Damiano Canale, Paolo Grossi, Hasso Hoffman, & Patrick Riley eds., 2009).

90   "Only by showing to what extent Grotius relied upon Thomistic sources we may be able to understand more completely his own attitude towards the ultimate grounds and problems of Natural Law." Anton-Hermann Chroust, *Hugo Grotius and the Scholastic Natural Law Tradition*, 17 New Scholasticism 101, 115 (1943) [hereinafter Chroust on Grotius] *in* 7 Great Political Thinkers 1 Grotius 354 (John Dunn & Ian Harris eds., 1997) [hereinafter GPT].

91   Hans Rapp, *Grotius and Hume on Natural Religion and Natural Law*, 68 (3) Archiv Für Rechts-Und Sozialphilosophie 372-386, *in* 7 Great Political Thinkers 2 Grotius 142 (John Dunn & Ian Harris eds., 1997). Some scholars also argue that Grotius did not intend to divorce the natural law from its theological roots. *E.g*, M.B. Crowe, *The "Impious Hypothesis": A Paradox in Hugo Grotius?* 38 Tijdschrift Voor Filosofie, 379 (1976) *in* Grotius, Pufendorf and Modern Natural Law 3 (Knud Haakonssen ed.) (1999) [hereinafter GPMNL].

92   "Grotius divorced Natural Law from Theology by grounding it in the 'social nature' and natural reason of man." Chroust on Grotius, Chapter 1, note 90, at 125 *in* GPT at 364.

93   Crowe, Chapter 1, note 91, at 380 in GPMNL at 4. Crowe attributes the translation to Francis W. Kelsey in Hugo Grotius Prolegomena to The Law of War and Peace (1957). However, it appears that Crowe has taken some liberties with Kelsey's capitalization, and that Crowe's writing convention called for parenthesis for personal additions to quotations rather than brackets. Kelsey's translation, properly quoted, reads:

What we have been saying [about the Natural Law] would have a degree of validity even if we should concede that which cannot be conceded without the utmost wickedness, that there is no God, or that the affairs of men are of no concern to Him.

Hugo Grotius, De Jure Belli Ac Pacis (Francis W. Kelsey ed. 1925) (1625) [hereinafter DJBP], published in Grotius Reader 233 (L.E. Van Holk & C.G. Roelofsen eds., 1983). (The original Latin reads: *"Et haec quide quae iam diximus, locum aliquem haberent etiamsi daremus, quod sine summo scelere dari nequit, non esse Deum, aut non curari ab eo negotia humana."*).

94   John Finnis, professor and legal philosopher, observed that "Grotius is standardly said to have inaugurated a new, modern, and secular era in natural law theorizing by his *etiamsi daremus* [passage] […] [b]ut this standard reading of Grotius is a mere misunderstanding" since it was used merely as a way to fortify to the legitimacy of natural law. John Finnis, Natural Law and Natural Rights 43 (2nd ed. 2011). See also, Peter Judson Richards, *Hugo Grotius, Hosti Humani Generis, and the Natural Law in Time of War*, 2 Liberty U. L. Rev. 881 fn. 52 (2008).

95   M.B. Crowe, Chapter 1, note 91, at 379 *in* GPMNL at 3. B. P. Vermeulen, G. A. Van Der Wal, *Grotius, Aquinas and Hobbes Grotian Natural Law between Lex Aeterna and Natural Rights*, 16 Grotiana 55, 71 (1995).

96   The writings of Grotius would later figure prominently in the philosophical framework of the Founding era in the colonies. Lawyers like James Otis, who was also a well-known pamphleteer during the Revolutionary Era, "quoted at length, Locke, Rousseau, Grotius, and Pufendorf." Bernard Bailyn, The Ideological Origins of The American Revolution 27 (1967). Colonial revolutionaries looked to other prominent writers and jurists. "Sir Edward Coke is everywhere in the literature," Bailyn remarked. *Id.* at 31. Continuing, "the citations are almost as frequent as, and occasionally even less precise than those to Locke, Montesquieu, and Voltaire," Bailyn demonstrated that the minds of the founding era considered the work of these writers and philosophers as incredibly significant. *Id.*

97   *See* Nemeth, Nemeth, Chapter 1, note 34, at 30.

98   "What distinguishes Grotius, however, was an overriding concern to reconcile the ideal of popular liberty, on the one hand, with the necessity of civil government, on the other." Daniel Lee, *Popular Liberty, Princely Government, and the Roman Law in Hugo Grotius's "De Jure Belli Ac Pacis*," 72 J. Hist. Ideas, 371, 373 (2011).

99   *Id.* at 376.

100 Annabel Brett, *Natural Right and Civil Community: The Civil Philosophy of Hugo Grotius*, 45 Hist. J. 31, 32 (2002).

101 "Grotius produced a treatise outlining an international regime of law, systematized upon natural law foundations, that continues to shape the world." Richards, Chapter 1, note 94 at 884 (footnote omitted).

102 "Natural Law is the supreme determinant in the Grotian framework, and customary International Law subordinate to it." C.G. Roelofsen, *Grotius and International Law an Introduction to Some Themes in the Field of the Grotian Studies*, in Grotius Reader, Chapter 1, note 93, at 16.

103 *Id.* at 18.

104 Many, including your author, would take issue with giving the force of "law" to religious interpretations; after all, "the law can no longer rely on doctrines in which citizens are entitled to disbelieve." Patrick Devlin, The Enforcement of Morals 7 (Oxford University Press 1970) (1965).

105 DJBP, Chapter 1, note 93, in Grotius Reader, Chapter 1, note 93, at 233.

106 *Id.* In many ways, Hugo Grotius served as an influence to the preeminent economist and philosopher, Professor Murray Rothbard, who developed a form of Libertarian Natural Law Theory emanating from his famous "Non-Aggression Principle," in which participants in a free society are precluded from violating the property rights of others, in physical property and in their

persons, without committing an act of aggression or violence violative of the tenet of non-aggression toward others. We explore Rothbard and his Non-Aggression Principle at greater length in Chapter 16.

107 Grotius noted:

> For those who have associated themselves with some group, or had subjected themselves to a man or to men [x] [sic] had either expressly promised, or from the nature of the transaction must be understood impliedly to have promised, that they would conform to that which should have been determined, in one case by the majority, in the other by those upon whom authority had been conferred.

Id. at 233-234. Grotius's penetrating observations of human nature led him to conclusions on the intrinsic social nature of man. "For the very nature of man, which even if we had no lack of anything would lead us into the mutual relations of society." *Id.* at 234.

108 *Id.* at 234.

109 As we shall see later in Chapter 16, contemporary legal theorist, Professor Randy Barnett, rejected the notion of majoritarian and implied consent arguing that consent must be unanimous and willful.

110 Hobbes noted:

> The Right of Nature, which writers commonly call *Jus Naturale*, is the liberty each mean has, to use his own power, as he himself, for the preservation of his own nature; that is to say, of his own life; and consequently, of doing anything, which is his own judgment, and reason, he shall conceive to be the [most apt] means thereunto.

Thomas Hobbes, Leviathan, 86 (A. R. Waller ed., Cambridge Univ. Press, 1904) (1651) (spelling and capitalization modernized). "A Law of Nature, (*Lex Naturalis*) is a precept, or a general rule, found out by reason, by which a man is forbidden to do, that, which is destructive of his life, or takes away the means of preserving the same; and to omit, that, by which he thinks it may be preserved." *Id.* (spelling and capitalization modernized).

111 *Id.* at 86 (spelling and capitalization modernized).

112 *Id.* (spelling and punctuation modernized).

113 *Id.* (spelling modernized).

114 Dan Priel, *Jurisprudence Between Science and the Humanities*, 4 Wash. U. Juris. Rev. 269, 285 (2012).

115 Hobbes, Chapter 1, note 110, at 84.

116 Steven Pinker, The Better Angels of Our Nature Why Violence Has Declined 35 (Penguin Books 2012) (2011).

117 Hobbes, Chapter 1, note 110, at 86 (spelling and capitalization modernized).

118 *Id.*

119 The great Austrian-American economist Ludwig von Mises further shed light on the detrimental effect government may have on an individual's natural rights, when he eloquently stated:

> As regards the social apparatus of repression and coercion, the government, there cannot be any question of freedom. *Government is essentially the negation of liberty.* It is the recourse to violence or threat of violence in order to make all people obey the orders of the government, whether they like it or not. As far as the government's jurisdiction extends, there is coercion, not freedom. Government is a necessary institution, the means to make the social system of cooperation work smoothly without being disturbed by violent acts on the part of gangsters whether of domestic or of foreign origin. Government is not, as some people like to say, a necessary evil; it is not an evil, but a means, the only means available to make peaceful human coexistence possible. But *it is the opposite of liberty.*

> Ludwig Von Mises, Liberty & Property, 35 (Ludwig von Mises Institute 2009) (1958) (emphasis added).

120 Hobbes, Chapter 1, note 110, at 189 (capitalization and spelling modernized) (emphasis added).

121 Alice Ristroph, *Sovereignty and Subversion*, 101 VA. L. REV. 1029, 1032 (2015) (emphasis added).

122 *Id.* at 1034 (citing Thomas Hobbes, Leviathan 150 (Richard Tuck ed., Cambridge Univ. Press 1996) (1651)) ("[T]here being no obligation on any man, which arises not from some act of his own; for all men equally, are by nature free."). *Id.*

123 As President, Thomas Jefferson once wrote:

> The world has so long and so generally sounded the praises of [Sidney's] *Discourses on government*, that it seems superfluous, and even pre-sumptuous, for an individual to add his feeble breath to the gale. They are in truth a rich treasure of republican principles, supported by copious & cogent arguments, and adorned with the finest flowers of science. It is probably the best elementary book of the principles of government, as founded in natural right which has ever been published in any language: and it is much to be desired in such a government as ours that it should be put into the hands of our youth as soon as their minds are sufficiently matured for that branch of study.

> Letter from Thomas Jefferson to Mason Locke Weems (December 13, 1804), *available at* https://founders.archives.gov/documents/Jefferson/99-01-02-0824

124 Algernon Sidney, Discourses Concerning Government, 511, ed. Thomas G. West (Indianapolis: Liberty Fund 1996).

125 *Id.* at 510.

126 *Id.* at 30.

127 *Id.* at xx.

128 *Id.* at 402.

129 *Id.* at 548.

130 Sidney's belief in the right to revolution was controversial in England during that time, and because it was a main tenet of his writing, led to his demise when in 1683, he was ultimately executed for treason. His work *Discourses Concerning Government* was denounced at his trial and directly led to his conviction, when Chief Justice Jeffries ruled "*scribere est agree*" [to write is to act]: The only witness, who deposed against Sidney, was lord Howard; but as the law required two witnesses, a strange expedient was fallen on to supply this deficiency. In ransacking the prisoner's closet, some discourses on government were found; in which he had maintained principles, favourable indeed to liberty, but such as the best and most dutiful subjects in all ages have been known to embrace; the original contract, the source of power from a consent of the people, the lawfulness of resisting tyrants, the preference of liberty to the government of a single person. These papers were asserted to be equivalent to a second witness, and even to many witnesses.

David Hume, The History of England From The Invasion of Julius Caesar to The Revolution In 1688, Vol. 6. 436 (Indianapolis: Liberty Fund 1983).

Ultimately, the forced abdication of King James II thwarted the last attempt to impose absolute monarchy on England. In the wake of the Glorious Revolution of 1688, five years after Sidney's death, Parliament reversed his conviction, but a great theorist was already lost.

131 Sidney, Chapter 1, note 124, at 380.

132 *Id.* at 401-402.

133 "Men, being, as has been said, by nature, all free and equal, and independent, no one can be put out of this estate, and subjected to the political power of another, without his own consent." John Locke, Two Treatises On Government 240 (George Routledge and Sons 1884) (1689). *See also*, Brian Tierney, *Historical Roots of Modern Rights: Before and Locke and After*, 3 Ave Maria L. Rev. 23, 29 (2005). Indeed, as Professor Murray Rothbard, who we shall visit again at great length in Chapter 16, stressed, "[i]t was the Lockean individualist tradition that profoundly influenced the later American revolutionaries and the dominant tradition of libertarian political thought in the revolutionary new nation." Murray N. Rothbard, The Ethics of Liberty 21 (New York University Press 1998) (1982) [hereinafter Rothbard's Ethics]. 134 Tierney, Chapter 1, note 133, at 29 (citing John Locke, Two Treatises of

Government 349 (Peter Laslett ed., Cambridge Univ. Press 2d ed. 1970) (1690)) (emphasis original). "Locke emphasized that civil government arises only when people can remove themselves from the state of nature by combining to form a government." Donald L. Doernberg, *"We the people": John Locke, Collective Constitutional Rights, and Standing to Challenge Government Action*, 73 Cal. L. Rev. 52, 59 (1985) (footnote omitted).

135   Tierney, Chapter 1, note 133, at 29, (citing John Locke, Two Treatises of Government 348-51, 355 (Peter Laslett ed., Cambridge Univ. Press 2d ed. 1970) (1690)).

136   *Id.* (citing to Michael P. Zuckert, Natural Rights And The New Republicanism 229 (1994)).

137   *Id.* at 30.

138   *Id.*

139   "Locke himself thought that life in a political community was best for humans, but it was not taken to mean that such societies just came to exist naturally without human artifice." *Id.* "Men came to be under civil government, not because it was thrust on them by some external power (divine or human), but because they themselves deliberately instituted it for their convenience." James C. Corson, *John Locke*, 44 Jurid. Rev. 315, 315-316 (1932).

140   Locke, Chapter 1, note 133, at 192.

141   *Id.* at 193-194.

142   Incidentally, Locke believes that man, in a State of Nature, "has a power to kill a murderer, both to deter others from doing the like injury (which no reparation can compensate) by the example of the punishment that attends it from everybody, and also to secure men from attempts of a criminal who, having renounced reason, the common rule and measure God hath given mankind, hath, by the unjust violence and slaughter he hath committed upon one, declared war against all mankind, and therefore may be destroyed as a lion or a tiger, one of those wild savage beasts with whom men can have no society or security." *Id.* at 196. To Locke, this "power" appears to remain consistent with the Natural Law since "every man has a power to punish a crime to prevent its being committed again, by the right he has in preserving all mankind, and doing all reasonable things he can in order to that end." *Id.*
143   *Id.* at 234.

144   Locke reasoned that:

because no political society can be, nor subsist, without having in itself the power to preserve the property, and, in order thereunto punish the offences of all those of that society, there, and there only, is political society where ever one of the members hath quitted this natural power, resigned it up into the hands of the community in all cases that exclude him not from appealing for protection to the law established by it.

Id. at 234-5. These Lockean principles of voluntary entrance into society will emerge as crucial distinctions in the early days of the American Republic when states would challenge the authority of the federal government as we shall see in Chapters 7, 8, and 9.

145 *Id.* at 235.

146 *Id.*

147 *Id.*

148 *Id.* at 240.

149 Locke later explains that he calls "lives, liberties and estates [...] by a general name—property." *Id.* at 256.

150 *Id.* at 241.

151 The Declaration of Independence para. 2 (U.S. 1776).

CHAPTER 2

1   Yochai Benkler, *The U.S. Supreme Court needs to keep up with our cellphones- and the NSA*, The Guardian (April 29, 2014).

2   J. H. Thomas, Esq., Lord Coke's First Institute of The Laws of England 1 (R.H. Helmholz, Bernard D. Reams, Jr. eds., 1986) (1818) [hereinafter Coke's First Institute].

3   *Id.*

4   *Id.*

5   *Id.* (emphasis added).

6   The 1628 title was "The First Part of the Institutes of the Laws of England or a Commentary Upon Littleton, not the name of the Lawyer only, but of the Law itself." (Spelling modernized).

7   Thomas de Littleton was the Lord of Frankley in Worcester. Sir Edward Coke In Thomas De Littleton, Treatise on Tenures (T.E. Tomlins, Esq., ed. 1841) (1970 reissue) (XXVII). Littleton had served as a judge during the time of Edward IV who reigned from 1461-1470.

8   Coke's First Institute, Chapter 2, note 2, at v. "It has been long regretted, that a book of such acknowledged merit as Lord Coke's First Institute, is, from its defective arrangement and want of order, in a manner lost to the profession." *Id.*

9   James R. Stoner, Jr., Common Law And Liberal Theory Coke, Hobbes, And The Origins of American Constitutionalism 13 (1992) (quoting 15 The Writings of Thomas Jefferson 57 (Andrew Lipscomb ed. 1903)).

10   Despite its erudition, Coke's "writing itself so offends modern standards of scholarship and method as to challenge the patience of even the most painstaking historian." *Id.* at 14. Jefferson was not the only one to carp about the dearth of organization in Coke's writings. Coke's Institutes, Blackstone observed in his *Commentaries*, "have little of the institutional method to warrant such a title." 1 William Blackstone, Commentaries *73. However, despite their want of organization, *Coke's Institutes* marked the development of jurisprudence and legal history. Biographer, Catherine Drinker Bowen, remarked on the impact of the Commentary on Littleton:

> Part One [of Coke's Institutes], *A Commentary upon Littleton*, is the best known of the four [Institutes]. *Coke on Littleton*, as the *Commentary* soon was called, carried Sir Edward's name across the ocean. Throughout three centuries the book was issued and reissued, corrected, amended, abridged, edited with commentaries upon Coke's commentary.

> Catherine Drinker Bowen, The Lion And The Throne: The Life And Times of Sir Edward Coke (1522-1634) 509 (Little Brown & Co., Reissue ed. 1990) (1957) (emphasis original).

11   Letter from Thomas Jefferson to John Minor, (Aug 30, 1814), fn. 1, including undated letter from Thomas to Bernard Moore (emphasis added) in 11 Works of Thomas Jefferson 420-421 (Paul Leicester Ford ed., 1905).

12   "The reason of the law is the life of the law; for though man can tell the law, yet, if he know[s] not the reason thereof, he shall soon forget his superficial knowledge. But when he [finds] the right reason of the law, and so [brings] it to his natural reason, that he [comprehends] it as his own, this will not only serve him for the understanding of that particular case, but of many others; for *cognitio legis est copulata et complicate*; and this knowledge will long remain with him." Coke's First, Chapter 2, note 2, at (183 b).

13   *Compare, e.g.*, Richard H. Helmholz, *Natural Law and Human rights in English Law: From Bracton to Blackstone*, 3 Ave Maria L. Rev. 1.

> 11 n.80 (2005) (quoting Tract on Law And Especially The Law of England, British Library, London, Stowe MS. 159, fols. 303v-04 (describing the "Lawe of Reason" as "written in the hartes of all men") (original spelling) (accessed by the author at the British Library)), *with* Coke's First, Chapter 2, note 2 at bk. 1, ch. 10, § 80 ("Of Tenant per la verge"), *and* bk. 2, ch. 6 § 139 ("of Frankalmoigne"); *see also* 1 William Blackstone, Commentaries *40 ("[God] gave him also the faculty of reason to discover the purport of those [natural] laws.").

14   Calvin's Case is the earliest, most influential theoretical articulation by an English court of what came to be the common-law rule that a person's status was vested at birth and based upon place of birth. *See* Polly J. Price, *Natural Law and Birthright Citizenship in Calvin's Case (1603)*, 3 Yale J. of L. &

Human. 73 (1997). The facts of the case are as follows: In 1607, two civil suits were initiated in the King's Bench and Chancery over two estates in England conveyed to a Scottish child, Robert "Calvin." Calvin was born in Scotland after 1603, the year in which the English throne descended to James. Robert's guardians initiated the suits, claiming that he had been forcibly dispossessed of both estates by the defendants, Nicholas and Robert Smith, who "unjustly, and without judgment, dismissed him of his freehold in Haggard." The defendants responded with a plea "in disability of Robert Calvin's person" that the writs were inadmissible because Calvin was an alien since he had been born "within [James's] kingdom of Scotland, and out of the allegiance of the said lord the King of his kingdom of England." If Calvin were an alien, he would, according to English law, be unable to be seized of a freehold in England. Therefore, the legal issue in the case centered on the status of persons born in Scotland after the accession of James I to the throne of England. *Id.* at 81-82.

15 *Calvin's* Case, 7 Co. Rep. 1a, 4(b), 77 Eng. Rep. 377 (K.B. 1607).

16 *Id.*

17 *Id.*

18 *Id.* at 394.

19 *Id.* at 392 (citations and quotations omitted).

20 Summa Theologiae, I-II, *q.* 90, *a.* 4, *ad* 1. in St. Thomas Aquinas The Treatise On Law [Being *Summa Theologiaee* 124 (R.J. Henle, S.J. ed., 1993).

21 In his list, Coke quips "*Lex et constuetudo parliament. Ista lex est ab omnibus quærenda, à multis ignorata, à paucis cognita.*" Coke's First Institute, Chapter 2, note 2, at 6. Translated, this reads, "The law and custom of parliament[.] This law is sought by all, unknown to many, known to few." Thomas Branch, Principia Legis Et Æquitatis Being An Alphabetical Collection of Maxims, Principles Or Rules, Definitions, And Memorable Sayings In Law And Equity Interspersed With Such Law Terms, And Latin Words And Phrases As Most Frequently Occur, In The Study And Practice Of Law 73(William Waller Hening, ed., 4th ed. 1824).

22 Coke's First Institute, Chapter 2, note 2, at 6.

23 Adams Student Notes (Ca. 1758), 1 Legal Papers of John Adams *microfilmed on* Reel No. 185 (Massachusetts Historical Society, 19541959).

24 Case of Proclamations [1610] EWHC KB J22.

25 *Dr. Bonham's Case*, 77 Eng. Rep. 646 (C.P. 1610), 18 Co. Rep. 114 (1861).

26 *Id.* at 275.

27 *Id* (emphasis added).

28 John Milton, Areopagitica: A Speech to The Parliament of England For The Liberty of Unlicensed Printing, 60 (T. Holt White, Esq. ed., 1819) (1644) (spelling and punctuation modernized).

29 *See* Helmholz, *Natural Law and Human rights in English Law: From Bracton to Blackstone*, Chapter 2, note 13, at 5-11 (emphasis added) (listing the following jurists:

Sir Francis Ashely (d. 1636), Sir Francis Bacon (d. 1626), Matthew Bacon (d. 1759), Henry Ballow (d. 1782), Daines Barrington (d. 1800), William Bohun (fl. 1732), Britton (fl. 1300), John Byrdall (d.c. 1705), Robert Callis (d. 1642), Sir Charles Calthrope (d. 1616), William Cawley (fl. 1680), Sir Edward Coke (d. 1634), Michael Dalton (d. 1644), Sir John Davies (d. 1626), Sir John Doderidge (d.1628), Sir William Dugdale (d. 1686), Thomas Egerton, Lord Ellesmere (d. 1617), Sir Robert Filmer (d. 1653), Heneage Finch, Lord Nottingham (d. 1682), Sir Henry Finch (d. 1625), Fleta (d. 1290), Sir John Fortescue (d.1479), Sir Michael Foster (d. 1763), Abraham Fraunce (d. 1592/93), Sir Geoffrey Gilbert (d. 1726), Edward Hake (d. 1604), Sir Matthew Hale (d. 1676), Sir Christopher Hatton (d. 1591), William Hawkins (d. 1750), Sir John Holt (d. 1710), Giles Jacob (d. 1744), David Jenkins (d. 1663), William Lambarde (d. 1601), Sir Thomas Littleton (d. 1481), Walter Mantell (17th Century), St. Thomas More (d. 1535), William Murray, Lord Mansfield (d. 1793), Roger North (d. 1734), William Noy (d. 1634), Sir Roger Owen (d. 1617), Edmund Plowden (d. 1585), Robert Powell (fl. 1609-42), Charles Pratt, Lord Camden (d. 1794), William Prynne (d. 1669), Ferdinando Pulton (d. 1618), Francis Rodes (d. 1589), Christopher St. German (d. 1540), John Selden (d. 1654), William Sheppard (d. 1674), John Somers (d. 1716), Sir Henry Spelman (d. 1641), Sir William Staunford (d. 1558), William Styles (d. 1679), Sir John Vaughan (d. 1674), William West (d. 1598), Bulstrode Whitelock (d. 1675), Thomas Williams (d. 1566), Edmund Wingate (d. 1656), Edward Wynne (d. 1784), and lastly (although out of order) Anonymous. The list is long, and no doubt could be made longer. *Id.* at 5-11 (footnotes omitted).

30 Writing more than a century after Coke's death Blackstone referred to the Institutes as "a bit pedantic and quant," at least according to Stoner. Stoner, Chapter 2, note 9, at 15 (citing to 1 William Blackstone Commentaries *72). Blackstone wrote: Some of the most valuable of the ancient reports are those published by Lord Chief-Justice Coke; a man of infinite learning in his profession, though not a little infected with the pedantry and quaintness of the times he lived in, which appear strongly in all his works. However, his writings are so highly esteemed, that they are generally cited without the author's name. 1 William Blackstone Commentaries *72 (footnote omitted).

31 "The first American edition of Blackstone's Commentaries on the Laws of England was published in 1772, and Thomas Marshall [John Marshall's father] was listed among the charter subscribers." Jean Edward Smith, John Marshall: Definer of A Nation, 75 (Holt Paperbacks 1998) (1996).

32 *Id.* at 77.

33 *Id.* at 76.

34 *Id.*

35 *Id.* (quoting 3 The Works of John Adams 50 note, (Charles Francis Adams, ed., Boston: Little, Brown 1854) and encouraging consultation of Charles Warren, History of The American Bar 35–38 (1911)).

36 Jean Edward Smith, Chapter 2, note 31, at 76.

37 *Id.*

38 "The few treatises and abridgements available—such as the *Institutes* of Sir Edward Coke; Sir Matthew Hale's *Historia Placitorum Coronae*; and the works of Matthew Bacon—focused on individual precedents and provided little guidance in the way of organizing principles or general concepts." *Id.*

39 *Id.*

40 *Id.*

41 *See, e.g.,* 1 William Blackstone, Commentaries *53-54, *38-45, *121-40.

42 *Id.* at *123-24 (emphasis in original).

43 *Id.* at *124.

44 *Id.* at *129.

45 *Id.* at *160.

46 *Id.* at *54-55 (emphasis added).

47 Blackstone, referring to the will of man's "Maker" writes:

This will of his Maker is called the law of nature. For as God, when he created matter, and endued it with a principle of mobility, established certain rules for the perpetual direction of that motion, so, when he created man, and endued him with free-will to conduct himself in all parts of life, he laid down certain immutable laws of human nature, whereby that freewill is in some degree regulated and restrained, and gave him also the faculty of reason to discover the purport of those laws. *Id.* at *39-40.

48 *Id.* at *40.

49 *Id.*

50 *Id.* "William Blackstone, in conjunction with his claim that commonlaw decisionmaking [sic] was a process of law-discovery and not lawcreation, insisted that immoral law was for that reason deficient law, awaiting to be

perfect *as law* for the very reason of its moral deficiency." Frederick Schauer and Virginia J. Wise, *Legal Positivism as Legal Information*, 82 Cornell L. Rev. 1080, 1084-1085 (1997).

1084-1085 signaling 1 William Blackstone, Commentaries *41 [T]his law of nature being coe[qu]al with mankind and dictated by God Himself, is of course superior in obligation to any other. It is Binding over all the globe in all countries and at all times: no human laws are of any validity, if contrary to this; and such as of them as are valid derive all their force, and all their authority, mediately or immediately, from this original.

Schauer and Wise, at n. 21 (quoting 1 William Blackstone, Commentaries *41).

51 1 William Blackstone, Commentaries *41.

52 *Id.*

53 *Id.*

54 *Id.*

55 *Id.* (footnote omitted). Blackstone hedges such an assertion in the notion that humans, as fallible beings, can manifest a corrupted, or imperfect reason. *Id.* at *41-42. Divine Law, law set down by God, in Blackstone's view, is perfect an incorruptible. *Id.* Since we lack the faculties to comprehend the explicit terms of Divine Law, we can only, "by the assistance of human reason" divine what "we imagine to be the that law." *Id.* at *42.

56 *Id.* at *42.

57 *Id.*

58 *Id.* at *42-43. 59 Blackstone builds on the Lockean notion, that certain powers and rights may be restrained by some power vested with lawmaking and punishment authority by consensual participation by members of society.

60 1 William Blackstone, Commentaries *43. 61 Locke, Chapter 1, note 133, at 235.

62 1 William Blackstone, Commentaries *44 (footnote omitted).

63 *Id.* at *45. Blackstone notes that a "compact is a promise proceeding *from* us, [whereas a] law is a command directed *to* us. *Id.* (emphasis original).

64 *Id.* Municipal law is also "a rule of civil conduct." This distinguishes municipal law from the natural, or revealed; the former of which is the rule of moral conduct, and the latter not only the rule of moral conduct, but also the rule of faith. These regard man as a creature, and point out his duty to God, to himself, and to his neighbour, considered in the light of an individual. But municipal or civil law regards him also as a citizen, and bound to other duties towards his neighbour than those of mere nature and religion: duties, which he has engaged in by enjoying the benefits of the common union; and

which amount to no more than that he do contribute, on his part, to the subsistence and peace of the society. *Id.*

65 *Id.* "It is requisite that this resolution be notified to the people who are to obey it." *Id.*

66 *Id.* at *44, *46.

67 *Id.* at *46. Curiously, Blackstone does not appear to include a definition of legislature in his commentaries. Perhaps this exclusion signals Blackstone's belief in the lack of ambiguity of the term. Blackstone may have considered "legislature" an analog to "parliament," or, even more generally, any body [sic] that exercises "the function or power of legislation" *Legislature, The Oxford English Dictionary,* www.oed.com/view/Entry/107105 (last visited Apr. 2, 2018). Incidentally, the entry in the Oxford English Dictionary cites to the above-referenced quotation from Blackstone!

68 1 William Blackstone, Commentaries *48.

69 *Id.*

70 *Id.*

71 1 William Blackstone, Commentaries *41.; *Compare* Bradburn, Introduction, note 15, 22, 28-29, 187-92, 204 (2009) (discussing the widespread inclination of the "public mind" toward the republican philosophies of the "natural rights of mankind" which was reflected in the outcome of the Revolution of 1800), *with id.* at 304-05 (discussing the aim of Federalist law professionals and the inclination of the generation of law professionals "weaned on Blackstone" to leave a citizen "little appeal against the sovereign command . . . ." (citations and quotations omitted)).

72 Letter from Thomas Jefferson to Noah Webster, Jr. (Dec. 4, 1790) reprinted in 18 Papers of Thomas Jefferson 132 (Julian P. Boyd ed., 2d printing, Princeton Univ. Press 1985) (1971); *see also* 29 The Writings of George Washington 478 (John C. Fitzpatrick ed., 1939) ("[T]he people evidently retained everything which they did not in express terms give up."). [A] young Alexander Hamilton—citing Blackstone, not yet trained in the law—writing enthusiastically in 1775 in terms that presaged language Thomas Paine would later use to shut down Edmund Burke. As Hamilton wrote, "The sacred rights of mankind are not to be rummaged for among old parchment or musty records." The rights of man "are written, as with a sunbeam, in the whole volume of human nature, by the hand of divinity itself, and can never be erased or obscured by moral power." Bradburn, Introduction, note 15, at 28 (citing 1 Papers of Alexander Hamilton 122).

73 1 William Blackstone, Commentaries *53-54.

74 *See* 1 Blackstone's Commentaries: With Notes of Reference To The Constitution And Laws of The Federal Government of The United States; And The Commonwealth of Virginia, Vol. 2 (St. George Tucker, ed., William

Young Birch & Abraham Small, Philadelphia 1803), Note A, at app. 3-6, Note D, at app. 155 [hereinafter Tucker's Blackstone]. Tucker praises the American Revolution as producing "an original written compact formed by free and deliberate voices of individuals disposed to unite in the same social bonds [and] thus exhibiting a political phenomenon unknown to former ages." *Id.* at 4.

75   James Wilson And Thomas Mckean, Commentaries on The Constitution of The United States of America: With that constitution prefixed, in which are unfolded, The principles of free government and the superior advantages of republicanism demonstrated 44 (1792) (emphasis in original).

76   *See* 1 Tucker's Blackstone, *supra* note 74, Note D, at 155:

The boasted constitution of England, has nothing of this visible form about it; being purely constructive, and established upon precedents or compulsory concessions betwixt parties at variance. The several powers of government, as has been elsewhere observed, are limited, though in an uncertain way, with respect to each other; but the three together are without any check in the constitution, although neither can be properly called the representative of the people. And from hence, the union of these powers in the parliament hath given occasion to some writers of that nation to stile it omnipotent: by which figure it is probable they mean no more, than to inform us that the sovereignty of the nation resides in that body; haying by gradual and immemorial usurpations been completely wrested from the people.

Id. The term "Parliamentary sovereignty" refers technically to the right of Parliament to make and unmake laws without the restraint of an entrenched "higher law" as set out in a written constitution. British constitutional authority Michael Pinto-Duschinsky explains, "If all law emanates from Parliament and all power ultimately resides in it, then the line of accountability can easily be traced by the electorate back to those who take the decisions that govern their lives." Michael Pintoduschinsky, Bringing Rights Back Home Making Human Rights Compatible With Parliamentary Democracy In The UK, 21 (2011). This stands in stark contrast to the limited constitutional authority given to the American Congress. When the Framers emerged from the secret convention that drafted the Constitution, they announced, almost uniformly, that the proposed document gave the federal government a limited list of defined powers. In what is probably the most important speech of the ratification process, James Wilson addressed a crowd in front of Independence Hall, where the Constitution had been drafted, in October 1787. Wilson argued that the states had plenary powers, but the federal government did not. "The congressional authority is to be collected, not from tacit implication," he said, "but from the positive grant expressed in the proposed Constitution." The states, he argued, could have powers not mentioned in any document. For the federal government, however, "everything which is not given, is reserved." James Wilson, *Speech to Public Meeting in Philadelphia* (Oct. 6, 1787), *reprinted in* 13 The Documentary History of the Ratification of the Constitution of the United States, Constitutional Documents and Records, 1776-1787 339 (Merrill Jensen John P. Kaminski, et al. eds., 1976-) [hereinafter DHRC].'

CHAPTER 3

1 John Adams to Thomas Jefferson (Aug. 24, 1815) *reprinted in* 8 Papers of Thomas Jefferson, Retirement Series, 1 October 1814 to August to 31 August 1815 682-683 (J. Jefferson Looney ed., 2011).

2 Thomas C. Grey, *Origins of the Unwritten Constitution: Revolutionary Thought*, 30 Stan. L. Rev. 843, 849-850 (1978).

3 *Id.* at 850.

4 *Id.* at 860.

5 *Id.* at 860-861 (emphasis in original).

6 *Id.* at 861.

7 Gordon S. Wood, The American Revolution: A History 4 (Modern Library Paperback Ed., 2002).

8 "The arrival of peace found the [British government's] national debt rising at a perilous rate; it had grown from 72,289,673 pounds in 1755 to 122,693,336 in 1763 and to 129,586,789 in 1764." Edmund S. Morgan & Helen S. Morgan, The Stamp Act Crisis 36 (online version) (1995).

9 Wood, Chapter 3, note 7, at 5.

10 Morgan, Chapter 3, note 8.

11 *Id.*

12 Boden, Chapter 3, note 12, at 7 (1976).

13 *Id.*

14 Richard J. Trethewey, The Economic Burden of the Sugar Act, The American Economist, Vol. 13, No. 1 (Spring, 1969), pp. 141. ://www.jstor.org/stable/25602737.

15 *Id.* at 63.

16 *Id.*

17 *Id.* at 64 (citing Oliver M. Dickerson, *The Navigation Acts and the American Revolution*, Phila., 1951, p. 179).

18 Murray N. Rothbard, Conceived In Liberty 805-806 (Ludwig Von Mises Institute 2011).

19 *Id.* at 819.

20 *Id.*

21 *Id.*

22 Morgan, Chapter 3, note 8, at 71-72.

23 *Id.* at 78-79 (citing Letter from Ingersoll to Whately, July 6, 1764, New Haven Colony Historical Society, *Papers*, 9 (1918), 299300) (emphasis added).

24 Boden, Chapter 3, note 12, at 7.

25 Circular from the Massachusetts Assembly to the Province of Massachusetts Bay (Jun. 8, 1765) *reprinted in* 114 Annals of The American Revolution (Jedidiah Morse, D.D. ed., 1824).

26 The Declaration of Rights And Grievances of The Stamp Act Congress (October 19, 1765).

27 Murray N. Rothbard, Conceived In Liberty 892 (Ludwig Von Mises Institute 2011).

28 *Id.*

29 *Letter from Christopher Gadsden to Charles Garth, December 2, 1765.*

30 *Id.*

31 Massachusetts, Colonial Assembly, 29 October 1765.

32 *Id.*

33 Herbert Aptheker, The American Revolution 1763-1783: A History of the American People, An Interpretation, p. 66, New York: International Publishers (1960).

34 Murray N. Rothbard, Conceived In Liberty 904 (Ludwig Von Mises Institute 2011).

35 *Id.* (emphasis added).

36 *Id.*

37 *Id.* at 930.

38 Thomas K. Clancy, *The Framers' Intent: John Adams, His Era, and the Fourth Amendment*, 86 Ind. L. J. 979, 1003 (2011).

39 Alden Bradford, Speeches of the Governors of Massachusetts from 1765 to 1775: and the answers of the House of Representatives to the same; with their resolutions and addresses for that period and other public papers relating to the dispute between this country and Great Britain which led to the independence of the United States, 424 (Boston: Russell and Gardner 1818) (quoting Massachusetts Circular Letter to the Colonial Legislatures, February 11, 1768)

40 *Id.*

41 Wood, Chapter 3, note 7, at 33.

42 *Id.* at 34.

43 *Id.*

44 John K. Alexander, Samuel Adams: America's Revolutionary Politician 62 (Rowman & Littlefield 2004).

45 Murray N. Rothbard, Conceived In Liberty 946 (Ludwig Von Mises Institute 2011) (emphasis added).

46 Wood, Chapter 3, note 7, at 34.

47 *Id.*

48 Morgan, Chapter 3, note 8, at 40.

49 Alan Taylor, American Revolutions: A Continental History 1750-1804, 112 (W.W. Norton & Company 2016).

50 Morgan, Chapter 3, note 8, at 40.

51 Taylor, Chapter 3, note 49, at 112.

52 Morgan, Chapter 3, note 8, at 40.

53 Murray N. Rothbard, Conceived In Liberty 1013 (Ludwig Von Mises Institute 2011).

54 *Id.*

55 Samuel Adams, The Rights of the Colonists: The Report of the Committee of Correspondence to the Boston Town Meeting (November 20, 1772) (emphases added).

56 Morgan, Chapter 3, note 8, at 40.

57 Taylor, Chapter 3, note 49, at 113.

58 Morgan, Chapter 3, note 8, at 42.

59 *Id.*

60 Walter A. McDougall, Freedom Just Around The Corner A New American History 1585-1812, 226 (2004).

61 Taylor, Chapter 3, note 49, at 113 (citations omitted).

62 McDougall, Chapter 3, note 60, at 227.

63 Morgan, Chapter 3, note 8, at 42.

64 "In the spring [of 1774], Parliament adopted four 'Coercive Acts' by overwhelming margins: the Boston Port Act, Massachusetts Government Act, Impartial Administration of Justice Act, and Quartering Act." Taylor, Chapter 3, note 49, at 114.

65 *Id.* at 114.

66 Boden, Chapter 3, note 12, at 15-16.

67   *Id.*

68   In fact, scholars even argue about whom to label as a Founding Father. "Despite these conventional boundaries, 'founding fathers,' is a protean phrase with varying meanings depending on who has used it and when." *Id.* at 6. Though it "[m]ost often […] includes participants on both sides of the 1787-1788 controversy over ratifying the Constitution[,]" it has been expanded by some to include other figures preceding the founding generation, and even as far as "the late Samuel J. Ervin, Jr. (D-NC), who won fame as the chairman of the Senate's Watergate Committee in 1973-1974, to Brian Lamb, founder of CSpan." R. B. Bernstein, The Founding Fathers Reconsidered 6-7 (2009) (citations omitted). It appears that Warren G. Harding coined the phrase "Founding Fathers" in a 1916 speech as a senator delivering the keynote at the Republican National Convention in Chicago. *Id.* at 1-3.

69   "I give to my son, when he shall arrive at the age of fifteen years, Algernon Sidney's works, — John Locke's works, — Lord Bacon's works, — Gordon's *Tacitus*, — and *Cato's Letters.* May the spirit of liberty rest upon him!" Bailyn, Chapter 1, note 96, at 22 (quoting Last Will and Testament of Josiah Quincy, Jr., 1774). The pamphleteers of the era were steeped in great works of the ancient world. 'Homer, Sophocles, Plato, […] Aristotle, […and] Plutarch, […], among the Greeks; and Cicero, […] Ovid, […] Cato, Pliny, Juvenal, […] Marcus Aurelius, […] Caesar, […] and Justinian among the Romans' – all are cited in the Revolutionary literature; many are directly quoted. *Id.* at 24 (quoting Charles F. Mullet, *Classical Influences on the American Revolution*, 35 Classical J. 92, 93-94 (1939)).

70   Bradburn, Introduction, note 15, at 26 (emphasis added)

71   *Id.* at 27.

72   *Id.*

73   Wood, Chapter 3, note 7, at 58.

74   "The full bibliography of pamphlets relating to the Anglo-American struggle published in the colonies through the year 1776 contains not a dozen or so items, but over four hundred." Bailyn, Chapter 1, note 96, at v.

75   *Id.* at 2.

76   *Id.* at 2-3.

77   *Id.* at 2.

78   *Id.* at 4.

79   *Id.* at 8.

80   *Id.* at 8 (citation omitted).

81   *Id.* at vii.

82 Bradburn, Introduction, note 15, at 27, 29-30 (emphasis added). ("In America, natural rights rhetoric in the midst of war and state formation became the ultimate political weapons—something it had long possessed the potential to be: a Revolutionary language, a complaint and justification of people asserting on original authority based in nature and reason to restructure the assumptions of their world. When we understand as well that the common law was widely thought to be the product and equivalent of *natural law*, it is impossible to deny the crucial importance of natural law and 'inalienable natural rights' to the ultimate meaning of American citizenship in the Founding Era."). *Id.*

83 James Otis, *Rights of British Colonies Asserted and Proved* (Pamphlet) 1763.

84 *Id* (emphasis in original).

85 *Id.*

86 *Id.* The six rights were as follows:

1st. That the supreme and subordinate powers of the legislation should be free and sacred in the hands where the community have once rightfully placed them.

2dly. The supreme national legislative cannot be altered justly 'till the commonwealth is dissolved, nor a subordinate legislative taken away without forfeiture or other good cause. 3dly. No legislative, supreme or subordinate, has a right to make itself arbitrary.

4thly. The supreme legislative cannot justly assume a power of ruling by extempore arbitrary decrees, but is bound to dispense justice by known settled rules, and by duly authorized independant judges.

5thly. The supreme power cannot take from any man any part of his property, without his consent in person, or by representation.

6thly. The legislature cannot transfer the power of making laws to any other hands.

87 *Id.*

88 *Id.*

89 *Id.*

90 *Id.*

91 *Id.*

92 *Id.*

93 *Id.*

94 Murray N. Rothbard, Conceived In Liberty 1052 (Ludwig Von Mises Institute 2011). Murray Rothbard notes, "Since the British king could not impose legislation or taxation without Parliament, such allegiance would

necessarily be more ceremonial and *pro forma* than anything else, and signified an advance to virtual independence from Great Britain." *Id.*

95   Thomas Jefferson, *A Summary View of the Rights of British America* (1774).

96   *Id.*

97   *Id.*

98   *Id.*

99   James Wilson, *Considerations on Nature and Extent of the Legislative Authority of the British Parliament* (1774) (emphasis added).

100 *Id.*

101 Murray N. Rothbard, Conceived In Liberty 1080 (Ludwig Von Mises Institute 2011).

102 Papers of John Adams, vol. 2, December 1773–April 1775, ed. Robert J. Taylor, 216–226 (Cambridge, MA: Harvard University Press, 1977) .

103 Murray N. Rothbard, Conceived In Liberty 1080 (Ludwig Von Mises Institute 2011).

104 John Adams, *To the Inhabitants of the Colony of Massachusetts-Bay, 23 January 1775*," Papers of John Adams, vol. 2, December 1773– April 1775, ed. Robert J. Taylor, 226–233 (Cambridge, MA: Harvard University Press, 1977).

105 *Id.* at 327–337.

106 *Id.*

107 Alexander Hamilton, *The Farmer Refuted*, reprinted in 2 Works of Alexander Hamilton 43-44 (John C. Hamilton ed., John F. Trow 1850) (1775) (emphasis in original).

108 *Id.* at 80.

109 Bernard Bailyn, Faces of The Revolution: Personalities & Themes In The Struggle For American Independence 67 (1990). Bailyn continued, "How it could have been produced by the bankrupt Quaker corset-maker, the sometime teacher, preacher, and grocer, and twice-dismissed excise officer who happened to catch Benjamin Franklin's attention in England and who arrived in America only fourteen months before *Common Sense* was published is nothing one can explain without explaining genius itself." *Id.*

110 Murray N. Rothbard, Conceived In Liberty 1252 (Ludwig Von Mises Institute 2011).

111 Thomas Paine, *The Writings of Thomas Paine*, Collected and Edited by Moncure Daniel Conway (New York: G.P. Putnam's Sons, 1894). Vol. 1. (Originally published as Common Sense: Addressed to the Inhabitants of America, on the following Interesting Subjects, viz.: I. Of the Origin and Design of Government in General; with Concise Remarks on the English

Constitution. II. Of Monarchy and Hereditary Succession. III. Thoughts on the Present State of American Affairs. IV. Of the Present Ability of America; with some Miscellaneous Reflections (January 10, 1776)).

112 Murray N. Rothbard, Conceived In Liberty 1252 (Ludwig Von Mises Institute 2011).

113 Thomas Paine, *The Writings of Thomas Paine, Vol. I (17741779)* [1774] 99.

114 *Id*. at 68.

115 Anonymous, *The People the Best Governors or, A Plan of Government Founded on the Just Principles of Natural Freedom* (1776).

116 Thomas S. Kidd, God of Liberty: A Religious History of The American Revolution 141 (Basic Books, 2010).

117 Murray N. Rothbard, Conceived In Liberty 1263 (Ludwig Von Mises Institute 2011).

118 *Id*.

119 Charles F. Mullet, *Classical Influences on the American Revolution*, 35 Classical J. 92, 94 (1939) (emphasis added).

120 Pauline Maier, From Resistance To Revolution: Colonial Radicals And The Development of American Opposition To Britain, 1765-1776, 271 (Norton Paperback, 1991).

121 Some of the colonists even hoped for some sort of positive guarantee of rights from England. "Significantly, colonial leaders discussed a hypothetical 'American Bill of Rights,' looking back to the English Bill of Rights established in 1689." *Id*. at 299.

122 For instance, the nobleman under King James, expressed concern over the presence of standing armies without consent of Parliament, the suspension of laws of Parliament without its consent, levying taxes without consent of Parliament. *Id*.

123 Bradburn, Introduction, note 15, at 14.

124 *Id*. at 2. The abjuration of allegiance to George III, the rejection of the authority of British-made law, and the Declaration of Independence broke the old colonial system and created a new and untested status—"American citizens"—complicated by the indistinct meaning and revolutionary potential of both "American" and "citizen." *Id*.

125 Bradburn, Introduction, note 15, at 3.

126 Bailyn, Chapter 1, note 96, at 18-19.

127 *Id*. at 19.

128 *Id*.

129 Bradburn, Introduction, note 15, at 5.

130 *Id.* at 5 (citing Pauline Maier, From Resistance To Revolution: Colonial Radicals And The Development of American opposition To Britain, 1765-1776, (1992)).

131 McDougall, Chapter 3, note 60, at 229.

132 Bradburn, Introduction, note 15, at 19-22; *see also* John Adams, *[Notes of Debates in the Continental Congress] Septr. 8 Thursday, in* 2 Diary of John Adams (L. H. Butterfield ed., 1962).

133 Bradburn leaves the words 'states' outside the name of the committee, although he does state that it was the first established. In his notes, John Adams refers to it as the Committee for States Rights, Grievances and Means of Redress, though it seems that it may have originally been called the Committee for Stating Rights, Grievances, and Means of Redress. John Adams, *Septr. 8 Thursday in* 2 Diary of John Adams, Chapter 3, note 132. The Committee on States Rights, Grievances, and Means of Redress was one of the first congressional committees established, and its purpose was to deal with the problem of states and individual rights, as well as to create a plan for redress and resistance to the colonial leadership of Great Britain. In particular, the members met to decide upon the language and justifications that the colonists should use to challenge Parliament. Bradburn, Introduction, note 15, at 22.

134 *Id.* at 21-24.

135 Mullet, Chapter 3, note 119, at 94(citations omitted) (emphasis in original).

136 5 Works of John Adams 373 *reprinted in* 1 Letters of Members of The Continental Congress 46 (Edmund C. Burnett ed., 1921) at fn. 2.

137 At this time, reference to *positive law* did not refer to the philosophy of legal positivism which would emerge nearly a quarter century later introduced by English philosopher and critic, Jeremy Bentham. "The term 'positive law' is of much older provenance than that of [philosophical] positivism or that of 'legal positivism.' The term originated around the twelfth century as the opposite of natural law (although the idea of law laid down by humans is obviously much older than that." Priel, Chapter 1, note 114, at 285.

138 Bradburn, Introduction, note 15, at 24.

139 Taylor, Chapter 3, note 49, at 139.

140 McDougall, Chapter 3, note 60, at 214.

141 *Id.*

142 Taylor, Chapter 3, note 49, at 141.

143 Yehoshua Areli, Individualism And Nationalism In American Ideology 25-26 (Cambridge, Mass; Harvard University Press, 1964).

144 The Declaration of independence para. 1 (U.S. 1776) (emphasis added).

145 Bradburn, Introduction, note 15, at 23 (citations omitted).

146 The Declaration of Independence para. 2 (U.S. 1776) (emphasis added).

147 Locke, Chapter 1, note 133, at 256.

148 St. Thomas Aquinas, Summa Theologica Ia-2ae. xc. 2, *in* St. Thomas Aquinas Philosophical Texts 354 (Thomas Gilby, trans., 1952).

149 The Declaration of Independence para. 2 (U.S. 1776).

150 Murray N. Rothbard, Conceived In Liberty 1292 (Ludwig Von Mises Institute 2011) (citing The Declaration of Independence).

151 Today, the Declaration of Independence is in the United States Code in Front Matter under the heading of Organic Laws. This section includes the Declaration of Independence, Articles of Confederation, Ordinance of 1787, and Constitution of the United States as well as an "Analytical Index to the Constitution of the United States."

152 The Confederation Congress, the legislative branch of government established by the Articles of Confederation, did not have a permanent home and met at several locations, including Princeton's Nassau Hall from June to November of 1783. *See* Brett Tomlinson, *The Continental Congress at Nassau Hall*, Princeton Alumni Weekly, (Oct. 1983) "For a brief time in 1783... the Continental Congress left Philadelphia and convened in Nassau Hall." *Id.*

153 Murray N. Rothbard, Conceived In Liberty 1357 (Ludwig Von Mises Institute 2011).

154 *Id.*

155 *Id.*

156 Joseph J. Ellis, American Creation Triumphs And Tragedies At The Founding of The American Republic 91-92 (2007).

157 Robert W. Coakley & Stetson Conn, The War of The American Revolution Narrative, Chronology, And Bibliography 135 (1975).

158 *Id.* at 136.

159 *Id.*

160 There exist some conflicted attributions regarding to whom this particular letter was addressed and its exact date. "Washington's retained copy is dated 8 June and the latest known copy sent to a state executive is dated 21 June." 13 DHRC, Chapter 2, note 76, at 60. Circular from George Washington, Head-Quarters, Newburgh, Jun. 18, 1783 *reprinted in* 13 DHRC, Chapter 2, note 76, at 62.

161 *Id.* at 63.

162 "In 1783 pamphlet editions of the letter were published in Exeter [New Hampshire], Boston [Massachusetts], Newport [Rhode Island], Hartford

[Connecticut], Philadelphia [Pennsylvania], and Annapolis [Maryland]. The next year it was printed in New York City, and in 1786 it appeared again in New York City and Philadelphia." *Id.* at 61.

163 *Id.*

164 *Id.*

165 *Id.*

166 *Id.*

167 *Id.*

168 *Id.* at 64.

169 *Id.*

170 *Id.*

171 *Id.*

172 *Id.* at 65.

173 *Id.*

174 COAKLEY & CONN, Chapter 3, note 157, at 136.

CHAPTER 4

1 *Day v. Savadge*, Hob. 85, 87a, 80 Eng. Rep 235, 237 (C.P. 1615) (Chief Justice Hobart of the English Court of Common Pleas quoting Lord Coke, translated as "the laws of nature are immutable," and "the law of laws.")

2 IV The Works Of John Adams, Novanglus, Thoughts On Government, Defence of The Constitution 122 (Charles Francis Adams ed., Charles C. Little and James Brown 1851) (1774-1778).

3 *Id.* (*emphasis added*).

4 Clancy, Chapter 3, note 38, at 991 (internal citations omitted); *see also* Michael Dalton, The Country Justice 418 (1746) (citing an example of a general warrant for stolen goods that permitted "diligent Search in all and every such suspected Houses . . . as you and this Complainant shall think convenient").

5 Clancy, Chapter 3, note 38, at 991-992 (internal citations omitted).

6 *Id.* at 991.

7 David Gray and Danielle Citron, *The Right to Quantitative Privacy*, 98 Minn. L. Rev. 62, 144 (2013).

8 Clancy, Chapter 3, note 38, at 992. Prior to the case, "Otis had been advocate of the Admiralty Court, a position which would have obliged him to argue in favor of the writs, but he resigned in order to argue against them. As a result

Otis gained in popularity what [Chief Justice] Hutchinson lost." MORGAN, Chapter 3, note 8, at 219.

9   Clancy, Chapter 3, note 38, at 992.

10   *Id.*

11   "[I]mmediately after his [John Adam's] account of the Writs of Assistance, are the following unfinished notes of the argument." Appendix II to Josiah Quincy, Jr., Reports of Cases Argued and Adjudged in the Superior Court of Judicature of the Province of Massachusetts Bay Between 1761 and 1772 545-546 (Little, Brown & Co. 1865).

12   2 The Works of John Adams, 523 (Charles Francis Adams ed., Charles C. Little and James Brown 1850).

13   *Id.* at 524.

14   *Id.* at 525.

15   *Id.*

16   Josiah Quincy, Jr., Report of Cases Argued And Adjudged In The Superior Court of Judicature of The Province of Massachusetts Bay Between 1761 And 1772 With An Appendix Upon The Writs of Assistance, at app. 521 (Samuel M. Quincy ed., 1865) (citations omitted) (spelling modernized).

17   Clancy, Chapter 3, note 38, at 992 (citing Letter from John Adams to William Tudor, (Jun. 24, 1818), in 10 The Works of John Adams at 323).

18   *Id.* at 993 (quoting Thomas Hutchinson, The History of The Province of Massachusetts Bay, From 1749 to 1774, at 94-95 (1828)).

19   *Id.* at 1003.

20   Letter from John Adams to William Tudor, (Mar. 29, 1817) *reprinted in* 10 Works of John Adams 247 (Charles Francis Adams ed., 1856). John Adams, in a contemporaneous report of the proceedings in Congress on the Declaration of Independence, referred to "the Argument concerning Writs of Assistance, in the Superiour Court, which I have hitherto considered as the Commencement of the Controversy, between Great Britain and America." Letter from John Adams to Abigail Adams (Jul. 3, 1776), *reprinted in* 2 Adams Family Correspondence 28 (L. H. Butterfield & Marc Friedlaender eds.).

21   *Id.* at 187.

22   *Id.* at 187.

23   *Id.* at 187.

24   *Id.* at 187. For a contemporary reiteration of colonists' resentment over general warrants as an impetus to the American Revolution, *see United States v. Rabinowitz*, 339 U.S. 56, 69 (1950) (Frankfurter, J., *dissenting*) (discussing the disdain was so "deeply felt by the Colonies as to be one of the potent

causes of the Revolution"); *Harris v. United States*, 331 U.S. 145, 159 (1947) (Frankfurter, J., *dissenting*) (arguing that the abuses surrounding searches and seizures "more than any one single factor gave rise to American independence").

25 Clancy, Chapter 3, note 38, at 1002 (quoting Thomas Hutchinson, The History of The Province of Massachusetts Bay, From 1749 to 1774, at 94-95 (1828)).

26 *The Liberty Affair- John Hancock Loses a Ship and Starts a Riot*, New England Historical Society *available at* http://www.newenglandhistorical society.com/the-liberty-affair-johnhancock-loses-a-ship-and-starts-a-riot/

27 *See* David S. Lovejoy, "Rights Imply Equality: The Case against Admiralty Jurisdiction in America, 1764–1776," *WMQ*, 3d ser., 16: 459– 484 (Oct. 1959), p. 478–482.

28 *Id.*

29 *Id.*

30 *The Adams Papers*, Diary and Autobiography of John Adams, vol. 3, *Diary, 1782–1804; Autobiography, Part One to October 1776*, ed. L. H. Butterfield. Cambridge, MA: Harvard University Press, 1961, pp. 305–306.

31 Lovejoy, Chapter 4, note 27, at 478–482.

32 *Id.*

33 *Id.*

34 At the end of the record appears this notation, dated 25 March 1769: "The Advocate General prays leave to Retract this Information and says our Sovereign Lord the King will prosecute no further hereon. Allow'd" (Suffolk co. Court House, Records, Court of Vice Admiralty, Province of Massachusetts Bay, 1765–1772).

35 Lovejoy, Chapter 4, note 27, at 478–482.

36 *See* Charles Grove Haines, The American Doctrine of Judicial Supremacy 73 (1914); *see also* Scott Douglas Gerber, to Secure These Rights: The Declaration of Independence And Constitutional Interpretation 106-07 (1995) ("This trend continued after the colonist declared independence.").

37 The Trial of The British Soldiers of The 29th Regiment of Foot 53 (William Emmons, Boston, 1863).

38 Roscoe Pound, The Development of Constitutional Guarantees of Liberty 73 (1957). Editorial Standards in 1957 at the Yale University Press, it seems, failed to notice Pound's error in claiming. The full quotation reads, "In 1725, Gridley, the father of the Boston bar, advised John Adams that study of natural, i.e. ideal, law, set forth in the Continental treatises on the law of nature and nations, if unnecessary in England, was important for the American lawyer." *Id.* Though Jeremiah (sometimes recorded as "Jeremy")

Gridley *was* in fact one of the founders of the Boston bar, he certainly did not give John Adams *any* advice in 1725 since Adams would not be born until 1735. Perhaps this is just a scrivener's error.

39 Trial of The British Soldiers, Introduction, note 9, at 45-46.

40 *Id.* at 45-46.

41 *Id.* at 46 (quoting 4 William Blackstone *3) (emphasis in original).

42 *Id.* at 89-90, 93-95.

43 Ultimately, the jury acquitted six of the soldiers: William Wemms, William M'Cauley, Hugh White, William Warren, John Carrol and James Hartegan. The other two soldiers, Hugh Montgomery and Matthew Killroy, were found not guilty of murder but guilty of manslaughter, therefore escaping the death penalty. *Id.* at 143.

44 *Robin v. Hardaway*, Jeff. 109, 1772 WL 11, (Va. Gen. Ct. Apr. 1772).

45 Charles Grove Haines, Ph.D., The American Doctrine of Judicial Supremacy 72 (1914).

46 *Robin v. Hardaway* at 1.

47 *Id.*

48 *Id.* at 114; *see also* Clarence E. Minton, *The Natural Law Philosophy of the Founding Fathers, in* 1 U. Of Notre Dame Natural L. Inst. Proc. 25 (1949).

49 *Robin v. Hardaway* at 114.

50 "The laws of nature are the laws of God; whose authority can be superseded by no power on earth." *Id.*

51 *Id.*

52 *Id.* "Citing Coke's opinion in Bonham's case, and Hobart's in Calvin's case, Mason argued that the act of 1682, permitting enslavement, was void because it was contrary to natural right and justice." Charles Grove Haines, The American Doctrine of Judicial Supremacy 73 (1914).

53 *Robin v. Hardaway* at 109-123.

54 *Id.* at 123.

55 *Id.*

56 Boden, Chapter 3, note 12, at 10 (1976).

57 *Id.* at 11-12.

58 Mullet, Chapter 3, note 119, at 94 (emphasis added).

59 Bradburn, Introduction, note 15, at 27, 29-30 (emphasis added). ("In America, natural rights rhetoric in the midst of war and state formation became the ultimate political weapons—something it had long possessed the potential to be: a Revolutionary language, a complaint and justification of

people asserting on original authority based in nature and reason to restructure the assumptions of their world. When we understand as well that the common law was widely thought to be the product and equivalent of *natural law*, it is impossible to deny the crucial importance of natural law and 'inalienable natural rights' to the ultimate meaning of American citizenship in the Founding Era."). *Id.*

CHAPTER 5

1   Randy E. Barnett, *The Relevance of the Framer's Intent*, 19 Harv. J. L. & Pub. Pol'y 403, 406, 408 (1996).

2   Noah Webster, An Examination Into The Leading Principles of The Federal Constitution Proposed By The Late Convention Held At Philadelphia With Answers To Principal Objections That Have Been Raised Against The System By A Citizen of America (1787) [hereinafter Webster On The Constitution] *reprinted in* Pamphlets On The Constitution of The United States Published During Its Discussion By The People 1787-1788 61 (Paul Leicester Ford ed., De Capo Press 1968) (1888) [hereinafter POTC].

3   For an in-depth discussion of Shays' rebellion, *see* Murray N. Rothbard, Conceived In Liberty, Volume 5, 111-126 (Ludwig Von Mises Institute 2020).

4   *Id.* at 125-126 (citing Letter from Thomas Jefferson to James Madison, January 30, 1787).

5   Christopher R. Drahozal, *On Tariffs v. Subsidies in Interstate Trade: A Legal and Economic Analysis*, 74 Wash. Univ. L. Rev. 1127, 1182 (1996).

6   *Id.* (citing Letter from William Grayson to James Monroe, (May 29, 1787), in 2 The Records of The Federal Convention of 1787, at 30 (Max Farrand ed., 1966)).

7   Drahozal, Chapter 5, note 5, at 1182 (1996) (citing 2 The Debates In The Several State Conventions On The Adoption of The Federal Constitution 189 (Jonathan Elliot ed., 2d ed. 1836) (remarks of Oliver Ellsworth of Connecticut)).

8   *See, e.g.*, Brent P. Kelly & Arthur M. Schlesinger, James Madison: Father of The Constitution (2000).

9   Rothbard, Chapter 5, note 3, at 130-131.

10 Staughton Lynd, *"Abraham Yates' History of the Movement for the U.S. Constitution,"* The William and Mary Quarterly, 223–45 (April 1963) (citing to a manuscript of Abraham Yates, author of the first (but unpublished) history of the drive for the Constitution in 1789).

11 Richard Beeman, Plain, Honest Men: The Making of The American Constitution 22 (2009).

12   Catherine Drinker Bowen, The Miracle At Philadelphia 13 (Back Bay Books 1986) (1966).

13   The College of New Jersey was founded in Elizabeth, New Jersey, in 1746. Trustees of Princeton University, *History | Princeton University*, Princeton University, *available at* https://www.princeton.edu/meetprinceton/history. A year later, it moved to Newark, New Jersey. In 1748, the university's present charter was granted in New Brunswick, New Jersey. Five years later, 10 acres were deeded in Princeton to the college. In 1756, Nassau Hall was completed, and the College of New Jersey moved from Newark to Princeton. *Id.* Madison left Virginia for Princeton in 1769. McDougall, Chapter 3, note 60, at 280.

14   "It has long been commonplace that the thinkers of the Scottish Enlightenment understood that moral life and moral institutions of humanity in social and historical terms; in fact, they have been seen as pioneers of holistic methods of explanation and historical sociology." Knud Haakonssen, Natural Law And Moral Philosophy, From Grotius to The Scottish Enlightenment 1 (2000).

15   Beeman, Chapter 5, note 11, at 25. It turns out that the Princeton's trustees hired the Scotsman John Witherspoon believing him an "evangelical in the tradition of Jonathan Edwards," the prominent Congregationalist Protestant theologian who had died in 1758. McDougall, Chapter 3, note 60, at 280. However, in Witherspoon was not, as they learned, "a (by now) old-fashioned product of the 'Great Awakening,' but [rather] a novel exponent of the Scottish Enlightenment." *Id.* at 280-281. "For young minds such as Madison's that made all the difference." *Id.* at 281. If Witherspoon's name sounds familiar, it might be because he signed the Declaration of Independence and "served in the Continental Congress." *Id* at 282. He was also "only clergyman to sign the Declaration of Independence." *Id.*

16   McDougall, Chapter 3, note 60, at 281.

17   *Id.*

18   *Id.* at 280-281 (emphasis in original).

19   Beeman, Chapter 5, note 11, at 25.

20   McDougall, Chapter 3, note 60, at 282.

21   Bowen, The Miracle At Philadelphia, Chapter 5, note 12, at 14.

22   Beeman, Chapter 5, note 11, at 27.

23   *Id.* at 22.

24   Letter from James Madison to Thomas Jefferson (May 15, 1787) reprinted in 3 The Records of The Federal Convention OF 1787 20 (Max Farrand ed., 1911).

25   *Id.*

26   Beeman, Chapter 5, note 11, at 23.

27   *Id.* at 34. 28 Letter from George Washington to Arthur Lee (May 20, 1787) *reprinted in* 3 The Records of The Federal Convention of 1787, 22 (Max Farrand ed., 1911).

29   *Id.*

30   Beeman, Chapter 5, note 11, at 41. The Convention would finally reach a quorum "on May 25, a day on the which twenty-seven delegates from seven states attended." *Id.* at 57.

31   *Id.* at 57. These delegates included, among James Madison and George Washington, Edmund Randolph, George Mason, all of Virginia, and the Pennsylvania delegates Gouverneur Morris, James Wilson, Robert Morris, and Benjamin Franklin.

32   McDougall, Chapter 3, note 60, at 292.

33   *Id.*

34   Rothbard, Chapter 5, note 5, at 139.

35   *Id.* at 139-140.

36   *Id.* at 140.

37   Beeman, Chapter 5, note 11, at 69-70.

38   In addition to Jackson's record of the convention, "notes survive from over ten other delegates." Mary Sarah Bilder, Madison's Hand Revising The Constitutional Convention 1, (2015). However, "Madison's notes […] are the only ones that cover every day of the Convention, beginning May 14 and ending on September 17, 1787." *Id.* John Quincy Adams, when he was Secretary of State, began to organize Jackson's notes for publication of the Convention Journal of 1819. BEEMAN, Chapter 5, note 11, at 70. He found them a mess. *Id.* "They essentially consisted of random daily notes, from which, Adams complained, 'the regular journal ought to have been, but was never made out.'" *Id.*

39   Gaillard Hunt, an editor of Madison's works, proclaimed that the Notes "[outrank] in importance all the other writings of the founders of the American Republic." Gaillard Hunt in 3 Writings of James Madison ix (Gaillard Hunt ed., 1902) [hereinafter Hunt's Madison].

40   *Id.* at x. Bilder believes that Madison's Notes may not be a wholly reliable source due to subsequent revisions by or at the direction of Madison though the 1820s. Bilder, Chapter 5, note 38, at 2.

41   *Id.* at 2.

42   *Id.*

43   Rothbard, Chapter 5, note 5, at 146-147.

44   *Id.* at 147.

45   *Id.*

46 *Id.* at 146.

47 *Id.* at 147.

48 *Id.*

49 *Id.*

50 *Id.*

51 *Id.* at 149.

52 *Id.*

53 *Id.*

54 *Id.*

55 *Id.* at 162.

56 *Id.* at 163.

57 Hunt's Madison, Chapter 5, note 39, at 53.

58 Rothbard, Chapter 5, note 5, at 165.

59 *Id.* at 170.

60 *Id.* at 170.

61 Hunt's Madison, Chapter 5, note 39, at 53.

62 *Id.* at 55.

63 *Id.* at 121.

64 *Id.* at 124.

65 *Id.*

66 *Id.* at 127.

67 *Id.* at 129.

68 We will explore this sovereignty-over-self argument in Chapter X.

69 Hunt's Madison, Chapter 5, note 39, at 135.

70 *Id.* at 133-135.

71 Madison's notes read:

Mr. Wilson, hoped if the Confederacy should be dissolved, that a majority—nay, that a minority of the States would unite for their safety. He entered elaborately into the defence of a proportional representation, stating for his first position that as all authority was derived from the people, equal numbers of people ought to have an equal no. of representatives, and different numbers of people different numbers of representatives. This principle had been improperly violated in the Confederation, owing to the urgent circumstances of the time. *Id.* at 134-5.

72 *Id.* at 224. Wilson and Hamilton disagreed with Martin and argued instead that the colonies did not become independent of one another when they separated from Great Britain. *Id.* These arguments did not reject the natural law metaphor but rather argued that the Declaration of Independence transitioned the colonies from English subjection not into a separate and independent states, but that they declared independence "not *individually* but *Unitedly* and that they were confederated as they were independent, States." *Id.* (emphasis in original).

73 *Id.* at 298 (June 27, 1787.

74 *Id.*

75 *Id.* at 298.

76 *See* Rothbard, Chapter 5, note 5.

77 *Id.* at 147.

78 *Id.* at 148.

79 *Id.* at 149.

80 *Id.* at 150.

81 *Id.* at 150-151.

82 *Id.* at 167.

83 *Id.* at 171

84 *Id.* at 270.

85 Letter from George Washington, as President of the Constitutional Convention, to His Excellency, the President of Congress (Sep. 17, 1787) in 1 DHRC 305.

86 *Id.* at 306.

87 James H. Read, *Our Complicated System: James Madison on Power and Liberty*, 23 Pol. Theory, 453 (1995).

88 James Madison, *National Gazette*, (Jan. 19 1792) *reprinted in* 6 Writings of James Madison 1790-1802 83 (Gaillard Hunt ed.) (1906). 89 *Id.* at 306.

CHAPTER 6

1 Edmund S. Morgan, Inventing The People: The Rise of Popular Sovereignty In England And America 13 (W W Norton & Co. 1988).

2 Pauline Maier, Ratification The People Debate The Constitution, 1787-1788, 27 (2010). It was on September 28, 1787, that the congress under our first constitution, the Articles of Confederation, agreed to submit a new Constitution to the states, an act that would render that legislative body obsolete. The new Constitution had been submitted as a report for

consideration, and the twelve state representatives at the Confederation Congress voted unanimously to submit it to the states for ratification.

3   *Id.* at 70. "Before the end of 1787 there were as many as two hundred separate printings for the benefit of "We the People," who would decide, directly or indirectly, the Constitution's fate." *Id.* (citations omitted).

4   *Id.* at 70-71.

5   *Id.* at 71.

6   *Id.* at 78.

7   *Id.*

8   *Id.*; *Contra McCulloch v. Maryland*, 17 U.S. 316 (1819).

9   Maier, Chapter 6, note 2, at 78.

10   *Id.*

11   *Id* at 79.

12   *Id.*

13   *Id* at 80.

14   *Id* at 80-81.

15   *Id* at 81.

16   *Id.*

17   *Id.*

18   *Id.* (citations omitted).

19   *Id.*

20   *Id.* (citations omitted).

21   *Id.*

22   *Id.* at 86-87.

23   *Id.* at 87.

24   *Id.* at 87 (citing Elbridge Gerry, Letter published in the Massachusetts Centinel, (Nov 3, 1787), *reprinted in* 13 DHRC 548550).

25   Elbridge Gerry, Letter to the State Legislature of Massachusetts, Oct 18, 1787, *reprinted in* 2 The Complete Anti-Federalist 7 (Herbert J. Strong ed., 1981) (emphasis in original).

26   *Id.*

27   Gerry saw the citizens of the United States as choosing between "the [Constitution] as it now stands, their liberties lost" or electing to "reject it altogether" in which case "Anarchy may ensue." *Id.*

28   Webster On The Constitution, Chapter 5, note 2, *reprinted in* POTC, at 28-65 (emphasis in original).

29 *Id.* at 29.

30 *Id.* at 46.

31 "But I cannot quit this subject [of the principal objections to the proposed
Constitution] without attempting to correct some of the erroneous opinions
respecting freedom and tyranny, and the principles by which they are
supported." *Id.* at 54 (emphasis in original).

32 *Id.* (internal pagination omitted) (emphasis in original).

33 *Id.*

34 *Id.* at 54-55 (emphasis in original).

35 *Id.* at 55 (emphasis in original).

36 *Id.* (emphasis in original).

37 *Id.* (emphasis in original).

38 *Id.* at 54-55 (internal pagination omitted) (emphasis in original).

39 *Id.* at 63 (internal pagination omitted) (emphasis in original).

40 *Id.* at 63-64.

41 Edmund Randolph, Governor of Virginia, who did not sign the Constitution,
"was a firm supporter of a stronger central government." Maier, Chapter 6,
note 2, at 89. "Randolph said he did not sign the Constitution, in short,
because he advocated amendments and also because he thought the
Convention majority's 'all-or-nothing' strategy would fail and do great harm
to the country." *Id.* at 90. Maier notes that, "[l]ike Mason and Gerry,
Randolph wanted amendments adopted prior to ratification." *Id.*

42 Luther Martin, Robert Yates and John Lansing, Jr. *Id.* at 90-92.

43 A vocal opponent of the Bill of Rights, Alexander Hamilton warned of the
danger of attempting to codify the inherent rights of the people:

I go further, and affirm that bills of rights, in the sense and to the extent
in which they are contended for, are not only unnecessary in the
proposed Constitution, but would even be dangerous. They would
contain various exceptions to powers not granted; and, on this very
account, would afford a colorable pretext to claim more than were
granted. For why declare that things shall not be done which there is no
power to do? Why, for instance, should it be said that the liberty of the
press shall not be restrained, when no power is given by which
restrictions may be imposed?

The Federalist No. 84 (Alexander Hamilton); Randy E. Barnett, *James
Madison's Ninth Amendment*, in 1 Rights Retained By The People: The
History And Meaning of The Ninth Amendment 11-12 (Randy Barnett ed.,
1989); *see also* 1 Annals of Cong. 448, 448-50 (1789) (J. Gales & W. Seaton

eds., 1834) (statement of Rep. Madison) calling enumeration "mistaken in its object").

44 Barnett, *James Madison's Ninth Amendment*, Chapter 6, note 43, in 1 Rights Retained By The People, at 11-12.

45 Maier, Chapter 6, note 2, at 122.

46 *Id.* at 120.

47 *Id.* at 122.

48 *Id.* at 123.

49 *Id.* at 137.

50 *See, e.g.*, 2 Elliot's Debates, Introduction, note 10, at 121 (statements of Gen. Heath, Mr. Hancock).

51 *See, e.g., id.* at 123 (statements of Mr. Hancock).

52 South Carolina ratified on May 23, 1788 and offered four amendments. Maier, Chapter 6, note 2, at 251-252.

53 New Hampshire ratified on June 21, 1788 and offered the same sorts of amendments that were presented by Massachusetts, and they even offered a few additional amendments. *Id.* at 315-316.

54 Virginia ratified on June 25, 1788. *Id.* at 300-307. Virginia also recommended a bill of rights "and an additional twenty amendments to the Constitution that the convention, in the name of the people of the commonwealth, would 'enjoin' their representatives in Congress to 'exert all their influence and use all reasonable and legal methods' to have enacted." *Id.* This recommended bill of rights, "which the convention approved without dissent, was a revised version of the 1776 Virginia declaration of rights" which was penned mainly by George Mason. *Id.*

55 New York ratified on July 26, 1787. *Id.* 396. North Carolina eventually ratified on November 21, 1789, and Rhode Island on May 29, 1790. *Id.* at 457, 459.

56 The Federalist NO. 43 (James Madison).

57 Maryland ratified on April 28, 1788. Maier, Chapter 6, note 2, at 204-207.

58 As we have discussed, concern over the absence of a bill of rights was seized on by Anti-Federalists, particularly in New York and Virginia, as a reason to oppose ratification. Anti-Federalist efforts to defeat the Constitution were ultimately unsuccessful but, in 1789, to appease their concerns and to circumvent any attempt they might make to call for a second convention, Representative James Madison introduced twelve amendments to the First Federal Congress – the last ten of which ultimately became the "Bill of Rights."

59 3 Elliot's Debates, Introduction, note 10, at 315 (statement of Patrick Henry).

60 1 Annals of Cong. 436 (1789) (J. Gales & W. Seaton eds., 1834) (statement of Rep. Madison) (introducing his proposed amendments).

61 Alexander White attended the University of Edinburgh in Scotland and received his legal education in London's Inns of Court, after which he served as King's Attorney for Frederick County and then for the colony of Virginia. In 1788, he served as a delegate to the Virginia's ratifying convention and its second constitutional convention, and spoke of the limits on the federal government:

> There are other things so clearly out of the power of Congress, that the bare recital of them is sufficient, I mean the "rights of conscience, or religious liberty—the rights of bearing arms for defence, or for killing game—the liberty of fowling, hunting and fishing—the right of altering the laws of descents and distribution of the effects of deceased persons and titles of lands and goods, and the regulation of contracts in the individual States." . . . The freedom of speech and of the press, are likewise out of the jurisdiction of Congress.

> Robert G. Natelson, *The Founders Interpret the Constitution: The Division of Federal and State Powers*, 9 Federalist Soc'y Rev. 60, 63 (2018) (citing Alexander White, Winchester Va. Gazette, Feb. 22, 1788, *reprinted in* 8 DHRC, at 401, 404 (internal quotation marks in original)).

62 1 Annals of Cong. 428 (1789) (J. Gales & W. Seaton eds., 1834) (statement of Rep. Alexander White) (emphasis added).

63 Kurt T. Lash, *The Lost Original Meaning of the Ninth Amendment*, 83 Tex. L. Rev. 331, 360 (2004).

64 *See, e.g.*, 2 Herbert J. Storing, The Complete Anti-Federalist, 214-452 (1981) (works of Federal Farmer and Brutus); Kurt T. Lash, *Rejecting Conventional Wisdom: Federalist Ambivalence in the Framing and Implementation of Article V*, 38 AM. J. Legal Hist. 197, 215–21 (1994).

CHAPTER 7

1 Pope Leo XIII, Libertas Prasetantissimum: On The Nature of Human Liberty (June 20, 1888) (footnote omitted).

2 Fergus Bordewich, The First Congress How James Madison, George Washington, And A Group of Extraordinary Men Invented Government 4 (Simon & Schuster Paperbacks 2017) (2016).

3 *Id.*

4 *Id.* at 5.

5 *Id.*

6 *Id.*

7 Webster On The Constitution, Chapter 5, note 2, *reprinted in* POTC, at 29.

8   Bordewich, Chapter 7, note 2, at 20.

9   *Id.*

10   *Id.* at 22.

11   Richard Labunksi, James Madison And The Struggle For The Bill of Rights 180 (2006).

12   Bordewich, Chapter 7, note 2, at 23.

13   *Id.* at 23-24 (citations omitted).

14   Labunski, Chapter 7, note 11, at 182.

15   *Id.* at 183.

16   *Id.* at 182.

17   *Id.* (citing, opaquely, a trail of *ibid* references eventually leading to *Documentary History of the First Federal Congress* 27 (Charlene Bangs Bickford et al. eds., 1992). Labunski, Chapter 7, note 11, at 307, notes 24, 23, and 22.

18   Bordewich, Chapter 7, note 2, at 25.

19   *Id.* at 28.

20   *Id.* at 29.

21   *Id.* at 27.

22   *Id.* at 28.

23   1 Annals of Cong. 15 (1789) (Joseph Gale ed., 1834).

24   *Id.* The record continues in that vein and occasionally marks the arrival of additional senators until a quorum was reached on Monday, April 6, just more than a month after its disappointing debut. *Id.* at 16.

25   Bordewich, Chapter 7, note 2, at 27.

26   Letter from James Madison to George Washington (Mar. 19, 1789) *reprinted in* 5 Writings of James Madison 1787-1790 329 (Gaillard Hunt ed., 1904).

27   *Id.*

28   Bordewich, Chapter 7, note 2, at 27.

29   Noah Feldman, The Three Lives of James Madison Genius, Partisan, President 245-247 (2017).

30   *Id.* at 247.

31   *Id.*

32   *Id.*

33   *Id.* at 247-248.

34   *Id.* at 251-252.

35 *Id.* at 252.

36 *Id.* at 252-253.

37 *Id.* at 253.

38 *Id.* at 252 (citation omitted).

39 *Id.* at 30.

40 *Id.* at 31.

41 "Richard Henry Lee, from Virginia, then appearing, took his seat and formed a quorum of the whole Senators of the United States." 1 Annals of Cong. 16 (Joseph Gale ed., 1834) (1789).

42 Bordewich, Chapter 7, note 2, at 32.

43 Until the Twelfth Amendment was passed in 1804, each state's presidential electors cast two votes for president, and the runner-up became Vice President. *Id.* at 34. "The votes for vice president were, […] in Madison's words, 'sufficient to give John Adams the second dignity,' but only by a plurality. To Washington's sixty-nine, Adams received just thirty-four, a splintered result that greatly embarrassed a man whose *amour propre* was easily wounded…" *Id.* at 32. The remaining 35 electoral votes were split among 10 different candidates.

44 *Id.* at 44.

45 *Id.* at 44.

46 George Washington, Diary Entry (Apr. 23, 1789) *reprinted in* 5 Diaries of George Washington, 1 July 1786–31 December 1789 447 (Donald Jackson & Dorothy Twohig eds., 1979).

47 1 Annals of Cong. 27 (1789) (Joseph Gale ed., 1834) (emphasis in original).

48 1 Annals of Cong. 27 (Joseph Gale ed., 1834) (1789) (statement of Pres. Washington).

49 Bordewich, Chapter 7, note 2, at 52. Washington's inevitable election as President was a forgone conclusion much earlier than his official election in April. "[I]n late February of 1789, a diminutive figure bundled against the cold, had crossed Virginia from his home near the Blue Ridge mountains to see a friend who was also the most famous man in America." Id. at 15. Washington had asked Madison for help writing his inaugural speech. Id. at 16. Though Washington "had first entrusted the job to his aide David Humphreys, who had delivered a seventy-three-page behemoth of an oration full of policy proposals that expressed Washington's support for a powerful federal government and an assertive executive[,]" the retired General opted instead to consult the erudite Madison. Id. Madison feared Humphrey's speech was too long and too broad. Id. "Instead, he urged Washington to speak more simply to a fragile nation that was about to embark on a political experiment whose outcome few could see and many feared." Id.

50 The original title, like so many treatises of that time, was of course much longer. 1 Adam Smith, An Inquiry Into The Nature And Causes of The Wealth of Nations (David Buchanan ed., 1814) (1776).

51 1 Annals of Cong. 27 (Joseph Gale ed., 1834) (1789) (statement of Pres. Washington) (emphasis added).

52 *Id.* at 28 (statement of Pres. Washington).

53 *Id.* (emphasis added).

54 *Id.*

55 *Id. See also* Labunski, Chapter 7, note 11, at 188. "The low-key approach to amendments in the inaugural address reflected Washington's view that he should not tell Congress what to do." *Id.*

56 1 Annals of Cong. 28-29 (Joseph Gale ed., 1834) (1789) (Statement of Pres. Washington) (emphasis added).

57 *Id.*

58 *Id.* at 424 (1789) (statement of Rep. Madison).

59 *Id.* at 434-436 (statement of Rep. Madison).

60 *Id.* at 432 (statement of Rep. Madison).

61 *Id.* at 433-434 (statement of Rep. Madison).

62 *Id.* at 439 (statement of Rep. Madison).

63 *Id.*

64 *Id.*

65 *Id.* at 435 (statement of Rep. Madison).

66 *See* Barnett, Chapter 6, note 43, at 12.

67 *Id.* at 12; *see* 1 Annals of Cong. 435 (Joseph Gale ed., 1834) (1789) (statement of Rep. Madison).

68 1 Annals of Cong. 665; Barnett, Chapter 6, note 43, in 1 Barnett Chapter 6, note 43, at 13. *Contra* Kurt T. Lash, *The Lost Original Meaning of the Ninth Amendment*, Chapter 6, note 63, at 339. Barnett argues quite strongly that Roger Sherman's view of the Ninth amendment also accords with a natural law reading. Randy E. Barnett, *The Ninth Amendment: It Means What It Says*, 85 Tex. L. Rev. 1, 3840 (2006) (quoting Roger Sherman, Draft of the Bill of Rights, in 1 The Rights Retained By The People: The History And Meaning of The Ninth Amendment 351 (Randy Barnett, ed., George Mason University Press 1989)).

69 1 Annals of Cong. 436 (Joseph Gale ed., 1834) (1789) (statement of James Madison).

70 The order of the amendments would finally solidify when adopted by three-quarters of the states in December 1791. For the sake of discussion, we will

refer to the amendments in the order that they were finally adopted rather than the numbers assigned to them during their journey to join with the Constitution.

71 "The powers not delegated to the United States by the Constitution, nor prohibited by it to the States, are reserved to the States respectively, or to the people." U.S. Const. amend. X.

72 1 Annals of Cong. 768 (Joseph Gale ed., 1834) (1789) (statement of Rep. Sherman).

73 1 Annals of Cong. 767-68. (Joseph Gale ed., 1834) (1789).

74 According to Professor Barnett,

The fact that there have been five distinct models of the Ninth Amendment in no way supports a claim that originalism generally, or the original meaning of the Ninth Amendment in particular, is indeterminate. To the contrary, as this body of scholarship developed—often through sharp debate—it produced an increasingly closer, careful, and comprehensive examination of the relevant sources. The more we investigated, the more we learned. We now know much more about the Amendment's original meaning than we used to, and what we know is both internally consistent and generally persuasive.

Barnett, The Ninth Amendment: It Means What It Says, Chapter 7, note 68, at 3.

75 *See, e.g.* Charles Beard, An Economic Interpretation of The Constitution of The United States 244-251, 299 (Dover Publications 2004) (1913) (discussing the number of voters participating in the election of delegates to the state conventions).

76 1 Annals of Cong. 431-32 (statement of Rep. Madison). "The ratification of the constitution in several States would never have taken place, had they not been assured that the objections would have duly been attended to by Congress." *Id.* at 447 (statement of Rep. Elbridge Gerry). Thomas Jefferson gave a bit of a bleaker picture in correspondence and a clearer picture of the Bill of Rights as a creature of ratification compromise:

Our new constitution was acceded to in the course of the last summer by all of the states except N. Carolina and Rhode Island. Massachusetts, Virginia and New York, tho [sic] they accepted unconditionally, yet gave it as a perpetual instruction to their future delegates never to cease arguing certain amendments. N. Carolina insisted that the amendments should be made before she would accede. The most important of these amendments will be effected by adding a bill of rights; and even the friends of the Constitution are become more sensible of the expediency of such an addition were it only to conciliate the opposition. *In fact, this security for liberty seems to be demanded by the general voice of America*, and we may conclude it will be unquestionably added. . . . .

There has been just opposition enough to produce probably further guards to liberty without touching the energy of the government, and this will bring over the bulk of the opposition to the side of the new government [dooming ardent antifederalists to permanent minority].

77 Thomas Cooley, The General Principles of Constitutional Law In The United States of America 36 (1880).

78 1 Annals of Cong. 732, 761 (Joseph Gale ed., 1834) (1789) (statements of Rep. Sedgewick, Rep. Madison); *see also id.* (statement of Rep. Page).

79 *See, e.g.*, 1 Annals of Cong. 661, 717, 749.

80 The text of the Ninth Amendment reads as follows: "[t]he enumeration in the Constitution, of certain rights, shall not be construed to deny or disparage others retained by the people." U.S. Const. amend. IX; *compare* U.S. Const. amend. X ("The powers not delegated to the United States by the Constitution, nor prohibited by it to the States, are reserved to the States respectively, or to the people."). Supreme Court Justice Joseph Story interpreted the phrase "or to the people" to mean that "what is not conferred [to the national government], is withheld, and belongs to the state authorities, if *invested* by *their constitutions of government respectively in them;* and if not so invested, it is retained by the people, as a part of their residuary sovereignty." 3 Joseph Story, Commentaries On The Constitution of The United States 752 (1970) (emphasis added).

81 In his article, *The Ninth Amendment: It Means What It Says*, Professor Randy Barnett contends that "If Madison's explanation of the purpose of the Ninth Amendment in his Bill of Rights speech is the most important evidence of its original meaning, then how he actually used the Ninth Amendment in a constitutional argument in his speech to the House opposing a national bank is a close second." Barnett, *The Ninth Amendment: It Means What It Says*, Chapter 7, note 68, at 55.

82 2 Annals of Cong. 1894 (1790).

83 *Id.*

84 *Id.* at 1895.

85 Madison adverted to a distinction, which he said had not been sufficiently kept in view, between a power necessary and proper for the Government or Union, and a power necessary and proper for executing the enumerated powers. In the latter case, the powers included in the enumerated powers were not expressed, but to be drawn from the nature of each. In the former, the powers composing the Government were expressly enumerated. This constituted the peculiar nature of the Government; no power, therefore, not enumerated could be inferred from the general nature of Government. Moreover, Madison argued "the proposed bank could not even be called necessary to the government; at most it could be but convenient." *Id.* at 1901.

86   *Id.* at 1898.

87   *Id.* at 1901.

88   One of the strongest pieces of evidence for original public understanding is the adoption of Ninth Amendment analogs by the several states. Alaska, Arkansas, California, Iowa, Kansas, Maine, Maryland, Minnesota, New Jersey, Ohio, Oregon, and Rhode Island all adopted language substantially similar to that contained in the Ninth Amendment. *See* Barnett, *The Ninth Amendment: It Means What It Says*, Chapter 7, note 68, at 75-76 & n.321. As Professor Barnett aptly explains,

The implications of this development for . . . [Ninth/Tenth Amendment] models is reasonably obvious. It flatly contradicts the claim that the Ninth Amendment is a reference to state constitutional and common law rights, at least in the sense that such rights may freely be altered by state legislation. Nor is it compatible with the residual rights analysis, as most state constitutions did not contain specific enumeration of state legislative powers. It seems strongly to suggest an individual natural rights reading. After all, such rights were thought to constrain all persons, including persons who serve as state officials. *Id.* at 76.

89   Kurt T. Lash, *The Lost Original Meaning of the Ninth Amendment*, Chapter 6, note 63, at 393.

90   2 Annals of Cong. 1901.

91   Kurt T. Lash, *The Lost Original Meaning of the Ninth Amendment*, Chapter 6, note 63, at 393.

92   U.S. Const. amend. IX.

93   "Congress shall make no law respecting an establishment of religion, or prohibiting the free exercise thereof; or abridging the freedom of speech, or of the press; or the right of the people peaceably to assemble, and to petition the Government for a redress of grievances." U.S. Const. amend. I.

94   Jud Campbell, *Natural Rights and the First Amendment*, 127 Yale L.J. 246, 264 (2017) (citing James Madison, Notes for Speech in Congress (June 8, 1789), in 12 Papers of James Madison 193, 194 (Charles F. Hobson & Robert A. Rutland eds., 1979)).

95   *Id.* at 269 (citing Proposal by Roger Sherman to House Committee of Eleven, July 21-28, 1789 in The Complete Bill of Rights: The Drafts, Debates, Sources, And Origins 83 (Neil H. Cogan ed., 1997)). Campbell goes on to list the frequent discussion of natural rights envisioned in the First Amendment by Madison's contemporaries, such as the "right to speak," "[t]he right of publication," "the natural right of free utterance," the "liberty of discussion," "the liberty of the tongue," and the "exercise of . . . communication." *Id.* at 269 (internal citations omitted).

96 James Madison, A Memorial and Remonstrance (ca. June 20, 1785), *in* 8 Papers of James Madison 298-299 (Robert A. Rutland et al. eds., 1973)

97 "A well regulated Militia, being necessary to the security of a free State, the right of the people to keep and bear Arms, shall not be infringed." U.S. Const. amend. II.

98 *See United States v. Cruikshank*, 92 U.S. 542, 551, 553 (1875) (dealing with the right to assemble and the right to arms and declaring them preexisting rights guaranteed by the Constitution, not rights created thereby); *see also Logan v. United States*, 12 S. Ct. 617, 624 (1892) (distinguishing rights created by federal law from preexisting constitutional rights, expressly including Second Amendment).

99 Randy E. Barnett & Don B. Kates, *Under Fire: The New Consensus on the Second Amendment*, 45 Emory L.J. 1139, 1171 (1996).

100 *Id.* at 1177. For specific examples, Barnett cites to the following:

Sam Adams listed among the 'Natural Rights of the Colonists as Men, the rights to life, liberty and property,' 'together with the right to support and defend these in the best manner they can.' (quoted in Malcolm, Origins, supra note 13, at 149). See also, 3 William Blackstone, Commentaries *4

('Self-defense therefore, as it is justly called the primary law of nature, so it is not, neither can it be in fact, taken away by the law of society.'); Thomas Hobbes, Leviathan 105, 110 (Collier ed., 1962) (1651) (describing the right to self-defense as inalienable: 'a covenant not to defend myself from force, by force, is always void'); 2 James Kent, Commentaries On American Law I (1827) (same); St. George Tucker, Blackstone's Commentaries With Notes of Reference To The Constitution And Law of The Federal Government 300 (1803) ('The right of selfdefense is the first law of nature.'). *Id.* at 1177-1178 & n.184.

101 Barnett & Kates, Chapter 7, note 99, at 1171.

102 "No Soldier shall, in time of peace be quartered in any house, without the consent of the Owner, nor in time of war, but in a manner to be prescribed by law." U.S. Const. amend. III.

103 Tom W. Bell, *The Third Amendment: Forgotten but Not Gone*, 2 WM. & Mary Bill RTS. J. 117, 134 (1993).

104 *Id.* at 135 (internal footnotes omitted).

105 *Id.* (internal footnotes omitted).

106 "The right of the people to be secure in their persons, houses, papers, and effects, against unreasonable searches and seizures, shall not be violated, and no Warrants shall issue, but upon probable cause, supported by Oath or affirmation, and particularly describing the place to be searched, and the persons or things to be seized." U.S. Const. amend. IV.

107 "The precept that was initially proposed by James Madison to govern the issuance of warrants underwent significant changes due to the enterprising efforts of a single congressman. Madison's proposal, 'a one-barrelled affair, directed apparently only to the essentials of a valid warrant,' was altered by Congressman Benson to a 'double barrelled form' that seems to provide for 'two constitutional mandates where only one had existed before.' The changes to Madison's draft escaped the notice of members of the House and Senate, and the altered provision was approved by Congress and ratified by the state constitutional conventions without extensive discussion regarding the precise language of what later became the Fourth Amendment to the Constitution." Tracey Maclin, *The Central Meaning of the Fourth Amendment*, 35 WM. & Mary L. Rev. 197, 208-209 (1993).

108 Thomas E. Towe, *Natural Law and the Ninth Amendment*, 2 PEPP.

L. REV. 2, 302-303 (1975); *Compare* Chester James Antieau, *Natural Rights And The Founding Fathers- The Virginians*, 17 Wash. & Lee L. Rev. 43, 76 (1960) (According to Richard Henry Lee, "[t]here are other essential rights, which we have justly understood to be the rights of freemen; as freedom from hasty and unreasonable search warrants, warrants not founded on oath, and not issued with due caution, for searching and seizing men's papers, property and persons.").

109 Nelson B. Lasson, The History And Development of The Fourth Amendment To The United States 13 (1970).

110 "Excessive bail shall not be required, nor excessive fines imposed, nor cruel and unusual punishments inflicted." U.S. Const. amend. VIII.

111 Thomas Aquinas, Summa Theologiae Ia-IIae, Q. 61, art. 4 (Anton Pegis trans., 1945). Interestingly, Aquinas believed that private individuals lack the authority to punish crimes; only the state may do so: "The care of the common good is entrusted *to persons of rank having public authority: wherefore* they alone, and not private individuals, can lawfully put evildoers to death" *Id.* at Q. 64, art. 3.

112 John F. Stinneford, *The Original Meaning of Unusual: The Eighth Amendment as a Bar to Cruel Innovation*, 102 Nw. U. L. Rev. 1739, 1748 (2008).

113 *Timbs v. Indiana*, 586 U. S. ____, 7 (2019) (citing *McDonald v. Chicago*, 561 U. S., at 767 (2010)).

114 "No person shall be held to answer for a capital, or otherwise infamous crime, unless on a presentment or indictment of a Grand Jury, except in cases arising in the land or naval forces, or in the Militia, when in actual service in time of War or public danger; nor shall any person be subject for the same offence to be twice put in jeopardy of life or limb; nor shall be compelled in any criminal case to be a witness against himself, nor be deprived of life, liberty, or

property, without due process of law; nor shall private property be taken for public use, without just compensation." U.S. Const. Amend. V.

115 "In all criminal prosecutions, the accused shall enjoy the right to a speedy and public trial, by an impartial jury of the State and district wherein the crime shall have been committed, which district shall have been previously ascertained by law, and to be informed of the nature and cause of the accusation; to be confronted with the witnesses against him; to have compulsory process for obtaining witnesses in his favor, and to have the Assistance of Counsel for his defence." U.S. Const. amend. VI.

116 "In Suits at common law, where the value in controversy shall exceed twenty dollars, the right of trial by jury shall be preserved, and no fact tried by a jury, shall be otherwise re-examined in any Court of the United States, than according to the rules of the common law." U.S. Const. amend. VII.

117 1 Annals of Cong. 437 (Joseph Gale ed., 1834) (1789) (statement of Rep. Madison); *See also* Antieau, Chapter 7, note 108, at 43, 46 (1960), ("Some Virginians included in their natural rights such concepts as trial by jury, freedom from ex post facto laws, the right to an impartial judge, and a right to defend their liberties by force, although to Jefferson and others these were more properly deemed 'fences' to assure the enjoyment of the more basic rights indicated earlier.").

118 One can see parallels between the enumerations in the Bill of Rights and the "Catalogue of Charges" contained in the Declaration of Independence. Examining the Article III protections in the original constitution in light of the declaration bolsters this claim as well.

Compare The Declaration of Independence (1776), with U.S. Const. amends. I-X, *and id.* at article III (granting a right to a jury trial in criminal cases and handling treason).

CHAPTER 8

1 Power abhors a vacuum.

2 James Madison, 2 The Debates In The Federal Convention of 1787 Which Framed The Constitution of The United States of America, 237 (Gaillard Hunt & James Brown Scott eds., Prometheus Books 1987) (1902).

3 Bordewich, Chapter 7, note 2, at 195.

4 The record only lists their names, and the date of their appointments. For instance, "WM. Cushing, appointed one of the Justices, 27th *Sept.* 1789." 2 Dallas 399 (1790).

5 The Supreme Court adjourned until August 1790 when the justices recognized James Iredell as another associate justice and then adjourned once again until February 1791. 2 Dall. 400 (1790).

6 U.S. Const. art. III § 2, cl. 2.

7 These cases often involved highly specialized issues relating to jurisdictional and procedural questions, and maritime cases under the Court's Admiralty jurisdiction.

8 Mark David Hall, The Political And Legal Philosophy of James Wilson 1742-1798 169 (1997); *Chisholm v. Georgia*, 2 Dall. 419 (1793).

9 "[The legislature,] [h]aving a right thus to establish the Court, and it being capable of being established in no other manner, I conceive it necessary [sic] follows, that they are also to direct the manner of its proceedings." *Chisholm v. Georgia*, 2 Dall. 419, 433 (1793) (Iredell, J.).

10 "Upon this authority, there is, that I know, but one limit; that is, 'that they shall not exceed their authority.' If they do, I have no hesitation to say, that any act to that effect would be utterly void, because it would be inconsistent with the Constitution, which is a fundamental law paramount to all others, which we are not only bound to consult, but sworn to observe; and, therefore, where there is an interference, being superior in obligation to the other, we must unquestionably obey that in preference." *Id.*

11 *Id.*

12 *Id.*

13 *Id.*

14 U.S. Const. amend. X.

15 "It must necessarily be so, because the United States have no claim to any authority but such as the States have surrendered to them [the United States]: Of course the part not surrenderred [sic] must remain as it did before." *Chisholm v. Georgia*, 2 Dall. 419, 435 (1793) (Iredell, J.).

16 Additionally, Justice Blair also raised the importance of the Constitution. "The Constitution of the United States is the only fountain from which I shall draw; the only authority to which I shall appeal," he begins. *Chisholm v. Georgia*, 2 Dall. 419, 450 (1793) (Blair, J.). "Whatever be the true language of [the Constitution], it is obligatory upon every member of the Union; for, no State could have become a member, but by an adoption of it by the people of that State." *Id.* In other words, reasoned Justice Blair, the states are subordinate to the Constitution because the people of each state, the true guardians of their own sovereignty, elected for their states to join the Union.

17 Justice Wilson begins by acknowledging that "[t]his is a case of uncommon magnitude" since "[o]ne of the parties to it is a State." *Chisholm v. Georgia*, 2 Dall. 419, 453 (1793) (Wilson, J.).

18 "Man, fearfully and wonderfully made, is the workmanship of his all perfect Creator: A State; useful and valuable as the contrivance is, is the inferior contrivance of man; and from his native dignity derives all its acquired importance." *Id.* at 455.

19 *Id.*

20 "Without which, there is nothing."

21 *Chisholm v. Georgia*, 2 Dall. 419, 456 (1793) (Wilson, J.).

22 *Id.*

23 *Id* (emphasis added).

24 As if to drive the point home further, Justice Wilson invoked his own status "[a]s a citizen" to illustrate that "the Government of [Georgia] to be republican; and my short definition of such a Government is, one constructed on this principle, that the Supreme Power resides in the body of the people." *Id.* at 457.

25 "As a Judge of this Court, I know, and can decide upon the knowledge, that the citizens of Georgia, when they acted upon the large scale of the Union, as a part of the 'People of the United States,['] did not surrender the Supreme or Sovereign Power to that State; but, as to the purposes of the Union, retained it to themselves. As to the purposes of the Union, therefore, Georgia is NOT a sovereign State. If the Judicial decision of this case forms one of those purposes; the allegation, that Georgia is a sovereign State, is unsupported by the fact." *Id.*

26 1 Pollock & Maitland, The History of English Law 500 (1st ed. 1895). *See also*, Herbert Barry, *The King Can Do No Wrong*, 11 VA. L. Rev. 349, 353 (1925). Besides the attribute of sovereignty, the law also ascribes to the King in his political capacity absolute *perfection*. The King can do no wrong. The King, moreover, is not only incapable of doing wrong, but even of thinking wrong; he can never mean to do an improper thing. In him is no folly or weakness. 1 William Blackstone Commentaries *245-6 (emphasis in original).

27 English subjects would not earn the independent right to pursue claims against the Crown without royal fiat until the Crown Proceedings Act in 1947 which provided that, "[s]ubject to the provisions of [the] Act, the Crown Shall be subject to all those liabilities in tort to which, if it were a private person of full age and capacity, it would be subject:[...]" The Crown Proceedings Act 10 & 11 Geo. VI, c. 44., 1947, (Eng) (Part I).

28 Hall, Chapter 8, note 8, at 27.

29 *Id.*

30 "The Judicial power of the United States shall not be construed to extend to any suit in law or equity, commenced or prosecuted against one of the United States by Citizens of another State, or by Citizens or Subjects of any Foreign State." U.S. Const. amend. XI.

31 *Penhallow v. Doane's Adm'rs*, 3 Dall. 54, 80-81, 90-91, 97 (1795).

32 Prize cases involved determining the fees, rewards, and costs assigned the various parties when a ship, captain, or crew recaptured another ship that had been taken by pirates or seized by a foreign government.

33   16 Journals of The Continental Congress 61-64 (1780) (Gaillard Hunt &
     Herbert Putnam eds., 1910).

34   6 Documentary History of The Supreme Court of The United States, 1789-
     1800 ("DHSC") 385 (Maeva Marcus, William B. R. Daines, Robert P.
     Frankel, Jr., Anthony M. Joseph, Stephen L. Tull, eds; 1998) (1985-2007).

35   *Id.* 387.

36   *Id.*

37   *Id.* at 388.

38   *Id.* 388.

39   *Id.* at 389.

40   *Id.* Elisha Doane, incidentally, by this time, had been dead for nearly 9
     months.

41   *Id.* at 390.

42   *Id.*

43   *Id.* at 387.

44   *Id.* at 390.

45   *Id.* at 392.

46   *Id.* at 390.

47   *Id.* at 392 (footnote omitted).

48   *Id.* 392.

49   *Id.* at 392-3.

50   *Id.* at 393 (footnote omitted).

51   *Id.*

52   *Id.* at 394.

53   *Id.* at 395.

54   *Id.*

55   "This case, which is of so much novelty and importance, has been argued at
     the bar with very great ability on both sides." *Penhallow*, at 89 (Iredell, J.).

56   *Id.* at 93.

57   He then departs to a masterful digression in which he attacks the inefficiency
     of a complete democracy in a revealing indulgence aimed perhaps at
     lingering critics of representative—rather than direct— democracy:

     Suppose, a state to consist exactly of the number of 100,000 citizens, and
     it were practicable for all of them to assemble at one time and in one
     place, and that 99,999 did actually assemble: the state would not be, in
     fact, assembled. Why? Because the state, in fact, is composed of all the

citizens, not of a part only, however large that part may be, and one is wanting; in the same manner, as 99 [pounds] is not a hundred, because one pound is wanting to complete the full sum. But as such exactness in human affairs cannot take place, as the world would be at an end, or involved in universal massacre and confusion, if entire unanimity from every society was required; as the assembling in large numbers, if practicable, as to the actual meeting of all the citizens, or even a considerable part of them, could be productive of no rational result, because there could be no general debate, no consultation of the whole, nor, of consequence, a determination grounded on reason and reflection, and a deliberate view of all the circumstances necessary to be taken into consideration, mankind have long practised (except where special exceptions have been solemnly adopted) upon the principle, that the majority shall bind the whole.

Id. at 93-4 (Iredell, J.). Though, up to this point, there existed nearly no catalogue of Supreme Court decisions, such expansive exploration of a tangential theme comes across as odd in a time of the quill and pen, and he laborious task of manual typesetting. Some underlying ulterior motive, such as a chance to appeal to the reason of those finding themselves in the minority in some cases.

58 Their unanimity likely arose since the issues at bar were less controversial than those in *Chisholm*. No constitutional amendment was later passed to abrogate the Court's decision in *Penhallow*.

59 For more on the outcome of the case, see 6 DHSC, Chapter 8, note 34, at 394-396.

60 *Calder v. Bull*, 3 U.S. 386, 386 (1798) (Chase, J.).

61 We do not mean to marginalize the other issues decided by the Court in *Calder v. Bull*, such as the Court's inability to nullify state law ("I am fully satisfied that this court has no jurisdiction to determine that any law of any state Legislature, contrary to the Constitution of such state, is vo*id." Id.* at 392 (Chase, J.). Curiously, Justice Chase preceded the aforementioned by carefully declaring, "[w]ithout giving an opinion, at this time, whether this Court has jurisdiction to decide that any law made by Congress, contrary to the Constitution of the United States, is void: I am fully satisfied..." *Id.* Such a phrase indicates the Supreme Court had already begun to contemplate the limits of its own powers which Chief Justice John Marshall would famously declare in *Marbury v. Madison*, 5 U.S. 137 (1803), granting the Supreme Court the power of judicial review.

62 *Calder v. Bull*, at 387 (capitalization in original).

63 *Id.* (capitalization in original). Strangely, Justice Chase added, "except only in the Constitution of Massachusetts." *Id.* Though here Chase sounds incredibly Anti-federalist, he apparently camped firmly within the Federalist

party. Thomas Jefferson, attempting to purge the Court of Federalist influences, would later try to impeach Chase. *Contra McCulloch v. Maryland*, 17 U.S. 316 (1819) (Marshall, C. J.). Chase even digresses in grandiose tangents, recounting the ethos of the revolution and invoking the preamble to the Constitution. "The people of the United States erected their Constitutions, or forms of government, to establish justice, to promote the general welfare, to secure the blessings of liberty; and to protect their persons and property from violence." *Calder v. Bull*, at 388. He mentioned Lockean social compacts:

The purposes for which men enter into society will determine the nature and terms of the social compact; and as they are the foundation of the legislative power, they will decide what are the proper objects of it: The nature, and ends of legislative power will limit the exercise of it.

Calder v. Bull, at 388. He extolled the virtues of republican government: "This fundamental principle flows from the very nature of our free Republican governments, that no man should be compelled to do what the laws do not require; nor to refrain from acts which the laws permit." *Id.* He even explained the limits of federal authority:

There are acts which the Federal, or State, Legislature cannot do, without exceeding their authority. There are certain vital principles in our free Republican governments, which will determine and over-rule an apparent and flagrant abuse of legislative power; as to authorize manifest injustice by positive law; or to take away that security for personal liberty, or private property, for the protection whereof of the government was established. *Id.*

64 *Id.* (capitalization original) (emphasis added).

65 "Though I concur in the general result of the opinions, which have been delivered, I cannot entirely adopt the reasons that are assigned upon the occasion." *Id. at* 398 (Iredell, J.).

66 *Id.* (emphasis added). Justice Iredell appears to ground his reasoning in his interpretation of Blackstone.

Sir William Blackstone, having put the strong case of an act of Parliament, which should authorise a man to try his own cause, explicitly adds, that even in that case, 'there is no court that has power to defeat the intent of the Legislature, when couched in such evident and express words, as leave no doubt whether it was the intent of the Legislature, or no.' 1 Bl. Com. 91. *Id.* at 398-399.

67 *Id.* at 399.

68 *Id.*

69 *Id.*

70 *Id.* (emphasis added).

71 *Id.*

72 *Id.*

73 Natural law "erects barriers that limit positive legislation and do not allow it to legalize attempts to infringe the indestructible dignity that is proper to every human being." Lesek Kołakowski, Is God Happy? On Natural Law 250 (2013). Kołakowski continues to argue, and your author wholeheartedly agrees, that *"[n]atural law should be like an uncompromising demon breathing down the neck of all the legislators of the world." Id.* (emphasis added).

CHAPTER 9

1 *Home Building and Loan Ass'n v. Blaisdell*, 290 U.S. 398, 425-426 (1934) (Hughes, C.J.).

2 Incidentally, although the Supreme Court presided over only three jury trials in its history, only one, *Georgia v. Brailsford*, was ever reported. Lochlan F. Shelfer, *Special Juries in the Supreme Court*, 123 Yale L.J. 208, 211 (2013). The question at issue before the Court was whether an "act of the Legislature of Georgia sequestering debts due to British subjects prevented the recovery of the debt by suit during the continuance of the war, [and] the mere restoration of peace, as well as the terms of the treaty, revived the right of action." *Georgia v. Brailsford*, 3 Dall. 1 (1794). In the only published jury charge that the Supreme Court has ever delivered, Chief Justice Jay instructed the jury that, while judges typically find the law and juries the fact, "you have nevertheless a right to take upon yourselves to judge of both, and to determine the law as well as the fact in controversy." Lochlan F. Shelfer, *Special Juries in the Supreme Court*, 123 Yale L.J. 208, 211212 (2013) (citing *Georgia v. Brailsford*, 3 Dall. 1, 4 (1794)).

3 *See* Henfield's Case, II F. Cas. 1099, 1107 (No. 6360) (C.C.D. Pa. 1793).

4 Robespierre, the rhetorical wizard behind the catchy axiom became the chief architect of a dark period known as the *Reign of Terror* during which, by some estimates, around 17,000 people were executed. Reign of Terror, Encyclopedia Britannica Online, *Reign of Terror* (Apr. 5, 2019) *available at* https://www.britannica.com/event/Reign-of-Terror.

5 Not until after the War between the States did federal officials drop the use of "they" or "them" when referring to the United States of America. The Constitution itself uses "them" and "their" in the Treason Clause. "Treason against the United States, shall consist only in levying war against *them*, or in adhering to *their* enemies, giving *them* aid and comfort…" U.S. Const. art. III, § 3, cl. 1 (emphasis added).

6 George Washington, Proclamation of Neutrality (Apr. 22, 1793) *in* 12 Papers of George Washington 281-282 (Worthington Chauncy Ford ed., 1891).

7 "And I do hereby also make known that whosoever of the citizens of the United States shall render himself liable to punishment or forfeiture under the

law of nations by committing, aiding, or abetting hostilities against any of the said powers, or by carrying to any of them those articles which are deemed contraband by the modern usage of nations, will not receive the protection of the United States against such punishment or forfeiture; and further, that I have given instructions to those officers to whom it belongs to cause prosecutions to be instituted against all persons who shall, within the cognizance of the courts of the United States, violate the law of nations with respect to the powers at war, or any of them." *Id.*

8   *See* James Madison, *A Candid State of Parties*, Nat'l Gazette (Sep. 22, 1792) (discussing the divide between what Madison called the "republican" and the "antirepublican" parties) *reprinted in* 6 Writings of James Madison 1790-1802 106-119 (Gaillard Hunt ed. 1906). It is important to note that at the time, the Democratic-Republicans thought of and referred to themselves as "Republicans" after the notional structure of the United States as a Republic. The name "Democratic-Republicans" is a construction of modern historians and did not emerge until much later.

9   Before the First Party System, Hamilton and Madison were already at odds in terms of ideology for the federal government: "Hamilton wished to re-create a British-inspired fiscal-military state, and to extinguish the importance and influence of the state governments gradually . . . . Madison rejected such a vision, believing the new Constitution provided a good blueprint for an extended republican system—a 'compound republic' . . ." BRADBURN, Introduction, note 15, at 68. Moreover, Madison and Jefferson feared that the fiscal policies of Alexander Hamilton, the first Secretary of the Treasury, including the proposal of a national credit system and a national bank, would create significant problems for the new government and threaten individual liberty. In fact, "the beginnings of political organization can be traced to Washington's cabinet where Alexander Hamilton and Thomas Jefferson faced off as representatives of federalist and republican viewpoints," and "lines of cleavage were already forming in the Congress that paralleled those in the cabinet." Robert M. Chesney, *Democratic-Republican Societies, Subversion, and the Limits of Legitimate Political Dissent in the Early Republic*, 82 N.C. L. Rev. 1525, 1533 (2004).

10   "To Jefferson, the Neutrality Proclamation could have only one meaning: Hamilton was now making foreign policy. Hamilton not only wanted the government of the United States to resemble that of Great Britain; he also favored alliance with that country." Feldman, Chapter 7, note 29, at 373.

11   *Id.*

12   *Id.*

13   *See generally*, Alexander Hamilton & James Madison, The Pacificus-Helvidius Debates of 1793-1794 (Morton J. Frisch, ed. 2007) [hereinafter PHD]. "The enumeration ought rather therefore to be considered as intended by way of greater caution, to specify and regulate the principal articles

implied in the definition of Executive Power; leaving the rest to flow from the general grant of that power, interpreted in conformity to other parts of the constitution and to the principles of free government." Pacificus No. 1 (Alexander Hamilton) *reprinted in* PHD at 13.

14 John Yoo, *George Washington and the Executive Power*, 5 U. St. Thomas J.L. & Pub. Pol'y 1, 28 (2010).

15 Letter from Thomas Jefferson to James Madison, (Jul. 7, 1793) *reprinted in* PHD, Chapter 9, note 13, at 54.

16 *Id.*

17 According to Chernow, Madison, "[f]rom his Virginia plantation, [...] complained to Jefferson that he [Madison] lacked the necessary books and papers to refute 'Pacificus,' and he griped about the summer heat." Ron Chernow, Alexander Hamilton 443 (Head of Zeus Ltd. 2016) (2004).

18 Helvidius I (James Madison) reprinted in PHD, Chapter 9, note 13, at 55-65.

19 *Id.* at 59.

20 Yoo, Chapter 9, note 14, at 29-30.

21 Bradburn, Introduction, note 15, at 101-03. Generally, letters of marque were an authority given to private persons to outfit an armed ship and use it to attack, capture, and plunder of enemy merchant ships in time of war. The U.S. Constitution provides: "The Congress shall have Power ... To declare War, grant Letters of Marque and Reprisal, and make Rules concerning Captures on Land and Water." U.S. Const. art. I, § 8, cl. 11.

22 Bradburn, Introduction, note 15, at 110.

23 *Id.* at 102. The prosecution maintained that an American citizen did not have the right to engage in a hostile action against a friendly power. It is of note that William Rawle, the U.S. attorney prosecuting the case, argued that individuals gave up the right to wage war on their own the moment they entered into a civil society. Otherwise, "a few individuals, for avaricious purposes, might involve the nation in a war." Francis Wharton, State Trials of The United States During The Administrations of Washington And Adams With References Historical And Professional, And Preliminary Notes On The Politics of The Times 79 (1849).

24 Bradburn, Introduction, note 15, at 112-13. The position of Supreme Court Justice was not a full-time position until several decades after John Jay first banged the gavel to open the Court's first session. Justices often sat as judges in other courts in a practice known as "circuit riding." In fact. "the earliest Justices spent most of their time outside of Washington, D.C., serving as judges of the circuit courts and interacting with lawyers and citizens." David R. Strass, *Why the Supreme Court Justices Should Ride Circuit Again*, 91 Minn. L. Rev. 1710, 1710 (2007) (footnote omitted). In many ways, this phenomena was a result of the fact that "the Judiciary Act of 1789 created

circuit courts but no circuit judges." Joshua Glick, *On the Road: The Supreme Court and the History of Circuit Riding*, 24 Cardozo L. Rev. 1753 (2003).

25   Bradburn, Introduction, note 15, at 114.

26   *Id.* at 114-116.

27   "The Jay Treaty produced a strain in Franco-American relations because the French regarded the treaty as markedly favoring Britain, a leader in the coalition with France was at war." Marshall Smelser, *George Washington and the Alien and Sedition Acts*, 59 AM. Hist. Rev. 322, 324 (1954).

28   "The Alien laws made naturalization more difficult than before, and authorized executive action to restrict the freedom of alien friends and enemies." *Id.* at 322.

29   Feldman, Chapter 7, note 29, at 428.

30   Alien Act, 1 Stat. 570-72 (1798).

31   *Id.*

32   Robert Churchill, To Shake Their Guns In The Tyrant's Face: Libertarian Political Violence And The Origins of The Militia Movement, 61-2 (Univ. of Michigan Press, 2012) (2009).

33   *See generally* Charles Slack, Liberty's First Crisis: Adams, Jefferson And The Misfits Who Saved Free Speech, 53-54 (Atlantic Monthly Press 2015)*; see also* 1 Annals of Cong. 567-68, 570-72, 57778, 596-97; Bradburn, Introduction, note 15, at 140, 158.

34   Slack, Chapter 9, note 33, at 53-54.

35   Feldman, Chapter 7, note 29, at 428.

36   *Id.*

37   *Id.* at 429.

38   *Id.*

39   *Id.* seemingly erroneously citing Letter from James Madison to Thomas Jefferson (Jan. 18, 1800) *reprinted in* 17 Papers of James Madison 336. Madison, in fact, made this argument in a report to the Virginia House of Delegates on the Virginia Resolutions (Madison's Report on the Virginia Resolutions to the House of Delegates, Session of 1799-1800, *reprinted in* 4 Elliot's Debates, Introduction, note 10, at 569.

40   Bradburn, Introduction, note 15, at 172, 178.

41   *Id.* These arguments would have found favor with the medieval progenitor of the Natural Law Tradition, St. Thomas Aquinas, who wrote and profoundly believed that because an unjust law is no law, one has a duty to disobey it. Thomas's just-law theory is a compelling and prophetic analysis of the human person's rights and obligations before the law, and further evidence of the law's derivative quality. Considered from various fronts, it is an

account that deals with the justice and the equity of a law itself, the enforceability or obligatoriness of an un- just or just law, and the right to disobey its content. Nemeth, Chapter 1, note 34, at 48.

42 Bradburn, Introduction, note 15, at 168-69.

43 *See* Slack, Chapter 9, note 33, at 164 ("Though he would not acknowledge authorship until decades later, putting pen to paper in such a way represented a real risk, especially by Jefferson's careful, cautious standards. Should he be discovered as the author [of the Kentucky Resolution], essentially suggesting that states could repudiate federal law, he might be opening himself to charges of sedition."). *See also*, *id.* at 165 (discussing "Madison's Virginia Resolutions).

44 Kentucky Resolutions of 1798 and 1799, *reprinted in* 4 Elliot's Debates, Introduction, note 10, at 540. In particular, Kentucky espoused a natural law argument, that which has not been delegated away has been retained, and this use of the notion of natural rights by a state legislature defending its own sovereignty reinforces, as the First Continental Congress realized, the fact that such language was a powerful legal and philosophical argument:

Resolved, That a committee of conference and correspondence be appointed, who shall have in charge to communicate the preceding resolutions to the Legislatures of the several States: to assure them . . . that every State has a natural right in cases not within the compact, (*casus non fœderis*) to nullify of their own authority all assumptions of power by others within their limits: that without this right, they would be under the dominion, absolute and unlimited, of whosoever might exercise this right of judgment for them . . . .That this commonwealth does therefore call on its co-States for an expression . . . . that the co-States, recurring to their natural right in cases not made federal, will concur in declaring these acts void, and of no force, and will each take measures of its own for providing that neither these acts, nor any others of the General Government not plainly and intentionally authorized by the Constitution, shalt be exercised within their respective territories. *Id.* at § 8.

45 *Id.* at § 3; *see also id.* at § 7 (complaining of the "construction" applied to infer constitutional implied powers pursuant to express tax powers).

46 It read:

That this Assembly doth explicitly and peremptorily declare, that it views the powers of the federal government, as resulting from the compact, to which the states are parties; as limited by the plain sense and intention of the instrument constituting the compact; as no further valid that they are authorized by the grants enumerated in that compact; and that in case of a deliberate, palpable, and dangerous exercise of other powers, not granted by the said compact the states who are parties thereto, have the right, and are in duty bound, to interpose for arresting the progress of the evil, and for maintaining within their respective limits, the authorities, rights and liberties appertaining to them. Virginia Resolution of 1798, 4 Elliot's Debates 528, 528 (2 ed.1888).

47 *Id.* at 529. *See also* 3 Elliot's Debates, Introduction, note 10, at 656-59. The reference to other rights refers, likely due to Madison's authorship of the Virginia Resolution, to the essential natural and civil liberties contained in the Ninth Amendment. Madison's Virginia Resolutions, adopted by the Virginia General Assembly in late December, strove to declare the Alien and Sedition Acts unconstitutional – but it did so in a way that was "at once more expansive, optimistic, and hopeful about the future of a united republic than the Kentucky Resolutions." Slack, Chapter 9, note 33, at 165. In particular, Madison "argued forcefully for a strong union and helped recalcitrant Virginians to overcome their doubts." *Id.*

48 The United States, which had owed a tremendous financial debt (some estimate over two million dollars) to the French crown, had argued that the financial debt accrued during the American Revolution and owed to the French crown did not pass unto the government of revolutionary France. Office of the Historian, U.S. Dep't of State, *U.S. Debt and Foreign Loans, 1775–1795, available at* https://history.state.gov/milestones/1784-1800/loans. Consequently, the French, between 1798 and 1800, enfranchised privateers to disrupt U.S. shipping routes and attack and harass U.S. merchant vessels.

49 In 1799, political agitation in Pennsylvania grew directly out of a tradition "of local resistance to taxes, pro-speculation land laws, and pro-creditor monetary policies." Petitioners worried that "new taxes would fall unfairly on Pennsylvania households…[who would] pay much more in the proportion to the value of their property, than the holders of uncultivated land." Bradburn, Introduction, note 15, at 175-76. German settlers, generally known for their Quietist tendencies, were stirred to anger for the first time. The militia was sent to Pennsylvania to suppress a revolt, but when it arrived there was no revolt in sight. It nevertheless seized John Fries, a former officer of the Continental Army, and brought him to Philadelphia to be tried. Fries's anti-tax rhetoric was viewed as an incitement to insurrection under the Alien and Sedition Acts, and he was sentenced to be executed for treason. *Id.* However, President Adams later pardoned Fries since Adams believed that Fries had not tried to overthrow the government of the United States.

50 *See* Bradburn, Introduction, note 15, at 176-77.

51 *Id.* at 177.

52 *Id.* at 179-80 (quotations in original).

53 U.S. Dep't of State, *Return of the Whole Number of Persons Within the Several District of the United States* 2 (1800); U.S. Dep't of State, *Return of*

the Whole Number of Persons Within the Several District of the United States 4 (1790); Bradburn, Introduction, note 15, at 178.

54 Feldman, Chapter 7, note 29, at 430.

55 *Id.*

56 Susan Dunn, Jefferson's Second Revolution: The Election Crisis of 1800 And The Triumph of Republicanism 103 (2004).

57 *Id.* at 2, 64, 118.

58 *Id.* at 1.

59 Susan Dunn, Jefferson's Second Revolution: The Election Crisis of 1800 And The Triumph of Republicanism 275 (2004). "Voter participation, which was high in 1800—almost 70% in some states— continued its upward trend, especially when there was stiff competition between Federalist and Republican candidates." *Id.*

60 Bradburn, Introduction, note 15, at 172.

61 *Id.* at 151. "As we shall see, [Federalists] explicitly rejected the Revolutionary [Era] formulations of citizenship that the Republicans espoused." *Id.*

62 In a number of decisions discussed in Chapter 10, the Supreme Court curtailed the power of the federal government and the governments of the states so as to protect the rights of people from government overreach.

CHAPTER 10

1 *Ogden v. Saunders*, 25 U.S. (12 Wheat) 213, 345 (Marshall, C.J. *dissenting*) (emphasis added).

2 Biographer Jean Edward Smith notes that "[t]here is no evidence that Adams had planned to name Marshall, or that he had even calculated the move beforehand. Instead, the available information suggests that the pace of events forced the choice." Jean Edward Smith, Chapter 2, note 31, at 15 (footnote omitted). As Smith explains:

Adams simply could not afford to delay naming a new chief justice if the Federalists were to retain control of the Court. Marshall was at hand, he was prepared to accept the post, and his personal loyalty to the president had been demonstrated time and again over the past year. By choosing Marshall, the petulant Adams was also demonstrating the power he still retained as president. Most Federalists had assumed the nod would go to William Cushing, who had served on the Court since its inception in 1789, or to the next senior justice, William Paterson of New Jersey. Paterson especially had strong support among the Hamiltonian wing of the party. Yet Adams knew that Marshall's standing was unassailable and that the Senate ultimately would have to go along. *Id.* (footnotes omitted).

3   *Id.* at 4.

4   Smith explains:

Marshall's long-standing aversion to Jefferson was deeply held and cordially reciprocated. It was a character flaw that Marshall and Jefferson shared equally; a flaw that was captured by the historian Henry Adams who, when speaking of Marshall, wrote that "this great man nourished one weakness. Pure in life; broad in mind, and the despair of bench and bar for the unswerving certainty of his legal method; almost idolized by those who stood nearest him ... this excellent and amiable man clung to one rooted prejudice: he detested Thomas Jefferson.... No argument or entreaty affected his conviction that Jefferson was not an honest man."

Id. at 11 (quoting Henry Adams, 1 History of The United States During The Administration of Thomas Jefferson 132 (Earl N. Harbert ed., 1986) (1882)).

5   Adams, a staunch Federalist, scrambled to ensure that the Federalist Party, one that had fought for a stronger central government during the Constitutional Convention of 1787, maintained a strong presence and powerful influence in the impending Democratic-Republican administration of Thomas Jefferson – the parties were different back then. There emerged a handful of peculiarities with the election of 1800. Originally, electors casted ballots for candidates, and the one who received the most votes served as President, and the one who received the second-most served as vice-President.

6   At the time of Marshall's appointment, "[t]he Supreme Court was regarded as nothing more than a constitutional afterthought. The Court had few cases, little dignity, and no genuine authority. In designing the new capital, no one had even planned a building to house the Supreme Court: it ended up in the basement of the U.S. Capitol."

Joel Richard Paul, Without Precedent John Marshall And His Times 3 (2018).

7   Jean Edward Smith, John Marshall: Definer of A Nation, Chapter 2, note 31, at 283. *See* Smith, *id.* at 283-4 explaining the series of resignations, rejected offers to serve on the bench or as Chief Justice, and even the unconfirmed nomination of John Rutledge. "The chief justiceship began to resemble a revolving door." *Id.* (footnote omitted). Adams asked Jay once again adorn the mantel of Chief Justice, but Jay "declined, citing the failure of the Supreme Court to 'acquire the public confidence and respect which, as the last resort of justice of the nation, it should possess.'" *Id.* (quoting Letter from John Jay to John Adams, (Jan. 2, 1801) reprinted in 4 The Correspondence And Public Papers of John Jay, First Chief-Justice of The United States, Member And President of The Continental Congress, Minister To Spain,

Member of The Commission To Negotiate Treaty of Independence, Envoy to Great Britain, Governor of New York, etc. 1794-1826 285 (Henry P. Johnston, A.M. ed., 1890-1893)). Jay explained to President Adams:

I [Jay] left the bench perfectly convinced that under a system so defective it would not obtain the energy, weight, and dignity which are essential to its affording due support to the national government, nor acquire the public confidence and respect which, as the last resort of the justice of the nation, it should possess. Hence I am induced to doubt both the propriety and the expediency of my returning to the bench under the present system; especially as it would give some countenance to the neglect and indifference with which the opinions and remonstrances of the judges on this important subject have been treated. *Id.*

8   Jean Edward Smith, Chapter 2, note 31, at 282 (footnote omitted).

9   *Id.* (footnote omitted).

10 Paul, Chapter 10, note 6, at 3.

11 Jean Edward Smith, Chapter 2, note 31, at 283 (footnote omitted).

12 "The authority of the legislature derived from the concept of legislative supremacy, which the Continental Congress had inherited from the British Parliament." *Id.* (footnote omitted).

13 *Id.* at 33. Marshall grew up in a two-room log cabin shared with fourteen siblings on the hardscrabble frontier of Virginia. His only formal education consisted of one year of grammar school and six weeks of law school. Yet in the space of two decades he went from being a poor, unschooled frontiersman to become a military officer, an influential lawmaker, a successful attorney, a foreign diplomat, a national hero, Washington's biographer, a congressman, secretary of state, and chief justice." Paul, Chapter 10, note 6, at 2.

14 Jean Edward Smith, Chapter 2, note 31, at 33 (footnote omitted).

15 *Id.*

16 *Id.* at 75.

17 *Id.*

18 Among these were Bushrod Washington, future Supreme Court Justice and nephew of the great George Washington, as well as Spencer Roane, who would become "a leading judge on the Virginia court of appeals." *Id.*

19 Charles T. Cullen, *New Light on John Marshall's Legal Education and Admission to the Bar*, 16 Am. J. Legal. Hist. 345, 345 (1972).

20 Jean Edward Smith, Chapter 2, note 31, at 78.

21 *Id.*

22 *Id.*

23 *Marbury v. Madison*, 1 Cranch 137 (1812).

24   "Jefferson received seventy-three electoral votes to the sixty-five of the
     Federalist candidate, John Adams." Gordon S. Wood, Empire On Liberty: A
     History of The Early Republic, 1789-1815 278 (2009).

25   *Id.*

26   In 1800, the Constitution read:

     The Person having the greatest Number of Votes shall be the President,
     if such Number be a Majority of the whole Number of Electors
     appointed; and if there be more than one who have such Majority, and
     have an equal Number of Votes, then the House of Representatives shall
     immediately chuse [sic] by Ballot one of them for President. U.S. Const.,
     art. II, § 1, cl. 3.

27   For an interesting account of the impeachment, see Lynn W. Turner, *The
     Impeachment of John Pickering*, 54 The AM. Hist. Rev. 485 (1949). John
     Pickering's "was the first impeachment to run its full course under the federal
     Constitution, and the first of a judicial officer." *Id.* At 486. Though Pickering
     had served New Hampshire with distinction for decades, he had, in his early
     sixties, begun to fall victim to worsening dementia and drunkenness. *Id.* at
     487-488. While some urged Pickering to resign, others, mainly New
     Hampshire Federalists, feared Pickering's post would go to John Samuel
     Sherburne, a Democratic Republican attorney general. *Id.* at 491.
     Consequently, the deteriorating, drunken Pickering became a political pawn
     in the struggle between the Democratic-Republicans and entrenched
     federalists. Ultimately, he was convicted by the Senate and removed from
     office on March 12, 1804. *Id.* at 505.

28   *Marbury v. Madison*, 1 Cranch 137, 148 (1812).

29   "In all Cases affecting Ambassadors, other public Ministers and Consuls, and
     those in which a State shall be Party, the supreme Court shall have original
     Jurisdiction." U.S. Const. art. III, § 2.

30   "In all the other Cases before mentioned, the Supreme Court shall have
     appellate Jurisdiction, both as to Law and Fact, *with such Exceptions, and
     under such Regulations as the Congress shall make.*" U.S. Const. art. III, § 2
     (emphasis added).

31   *Marbury v. Madison*, 1 Cranch 137, 173-5 (1803) (Marshall, C.J.).

32   Translated as "you have the body," a writ of *habeas corpus* refers to a
     proceeding in which a court reviews the legal sufficiency of an individual's
     imprisonment by ordering the responsible official to bring the prisoner before
     the court and justify the confinement.

33   *Ex Parte Bollman*, 4 Cranch 75, 93-94 (1807) (Marshall, C.J.); Eric M.
     Freedman, *Milestones in Habeas Corpus: Part I Just Because John Marshall
     Said It, Doesn't Make It So: Ex Parte Bollman and the Illusory Prohibition*

on the Federal Writ of Habeas Corpus for State Prisoners in the Judiciary Act of 1789, 51 Ala. L. Rev. 531, 536 (2000) (footnotes omitted).

34 The D.C. Circuit Court was not one of the United States circuit courts established by the Judiciary Act of 1789. Instead, the Circuit Court of the District of Columbia was established on February 27, 1801 by the District of Columbia Organic Act of 1801, 2 Stat. 103, which granted the court the same powers as the U.S. circuit courts *as well as* local civil and criminal jurisdiction within the District of Columbia. The circuit court, district court, and criminal court of the District of Columbia were abolished altogether on March 3, 1863, by 12 Stat. 762, and a new court, the Supreme Court of the District of Columbia (later renamed the "United States District Court for the District of Columbia"), was created in its place.

35 Freedman, Chapter 10, note 33, at 536.

36 *Id.* at 561.

37 "Interest in the argument that followed was at fever pitch, almost the whole of Congress being in attendance." *Id.* (footnote omitted).

38 *Ex Parte Bollman*, 4 Cranch 75, 93 (1807) (Marshall, C. J.).

39 "Courts which originate in the common law possess a jurisdiction which must be regulated by their common law, until some statute shall change their established principles; but courts which are created by written law, and whose jurisdiction is defined by written law, cannot transcend that jurisdiction." *Id.*

40 Freedman, Chapter 10, note 33, at 536 (citing *Ex Parte Bollman*, 4 Cranch 75, 101 (1807) (Marshall, C. J.)).

41 *Ex Parte Bollman*, 4 Cranch 75, 94 (1807) (Marshall, C. J.).

42 The text, as recorded, reads "…it must *he* given by…" though this must be a scrivener's error. *Id.*

43 *Id.*

44 Freedman, Chapter 10, note 33, at 570. For an example of the dicta, see Freedman, Chapter 10, note 33, at 566-570, including "Marshall's claim that the Court had 'repeatedly' explained the reasoning behind the proposition that courts created by written law could only exercise the powers explicitly granted by such laws was false." *Id.* at 566-567 (footnote omitted). Marshall's suggestion-sheer dictum in the case at hand and unsupported by any authority-that Congress could suspend the writ by doing nothing at all certainly would have come as a shock to all of the debaters over the Suspension Clause, whose positions were described in Part II above, particularly since suspension of the writ in England or its colonies had required an affirmative Act of Parliament. *Id.* at 568-569 (footnote omitted).

45 *Fletcher v. Peck*, 6 Cranch 87 (1810); David C. Bayne, *The Supreme Court and the Natural Law*, 1 Depaul L. Rev. 216, 219 (1952).

46   *Id.* (citing the clearly traceable cases as *Satterlee v. Matthewson*, 2 Pet. (U.S.)
     378 (1829); *Poindexter v. Greenhow*, 114 U.S. 270 (1884); *Legal Tender
     Cases*, 12 Wall. (U.S.) 457 (1870); *Chicago, Burlington and Quincy R.R. Co.
     v. Chicago*, 66 U.S. 226 (1896)).

47   Joseph M. Lynch, *Fletcher v. Peck: The Nature of the Contacts Clause*, 13
     Seton Hall L. Rev. 1, 6 (1982) (footnote omitted).

48   C. H. Haskins, *The Yazoo Land Companies*, 5 Papers of The AM. Hist. Ass'n
     395, 418 (1891).

49   Lynch, Chapter 10, note 47, at 6 (footnote omitted). It is of note, that many
     prominent politicians were involved in some of this land speculation, such as
     George Washington, Benjamin Franklin, Albert Gallatin, Patrick Henry,
     Robert Morris, and James Wilson. Haskins, Chapter 10, note 48, at 396.

50   Lynch, Chapter 10, note 47, at 6-7.

51   "Fletcher, under contract to purchase certain Yazoo lands, sought rescission
     of the contract on the ground that Peck could not convey good title because
     the lands were part of the original grant subsequently voided by the Georgia
     legislation of 1796." *Id.* at 8.

52   Marshall wrote:

     The question, whether a law be void for its repugnancy to the constitution
     [of the State of Georgia], is, at all times, a question of much delicacy,
     which ought seldom, if ever, to be decided in the affirmative, in a
     doubtful case. The court, when impelled by duty to render such a
     judgment, would be unworthy of its station, could it be unmindful of the
     solemn obligations which that station imposes. But it is not on slight
     implication and vague conjecture that the legislature is to be pronounced
     to have transcended its powers, and its acts to be considered as vo*id.* The
     opposition between the constitution [of the State of Georgia] and the law
     should be such that the judge feels a clear and strong conviction of their
     incompatibility with each other.

     Fletcher v. Peck, 6 Cranch 87, 128 (1810) (Marshall, C. J.). In his analysis,
     Marshall did not invoke Blackstone on laws that offend our sensibilities
     through injustice against nature or fairness, but rather, he questioned whether
     the law in question would offend the Constitution of the State of Georgia.

53   "That corruption should find its way into the governments of our infant
     republics, and contaminate the very source of legislation, or that impure
     motives should contribute to the passage of a law, or the formation of a
     legislative contract, are circumstances most deeply to be deplored." *Id.* at
     130.

54   *Id.* He also worried that:

     It may well be doubted how far the validity of a law depends upon the
     motives of its framers, and how far the particular inducements, operating

on members of the supreme sovereign power of a state, to the formation of a contract by that power, are examinable in a court of justice.

Id. However, he reasoned that "[i]f the principle be conceded, that an act of the supreme sovereign power might be declared null by a court, in consequence of the means which procured it, still would there be much difficulty in saying to what extent those means must be applied to produce this effect." *Id.*

55 Marshall asked:

Must it be direct corruption, or would interest or undue influence of any kind be sufficient? Must the vitiating cause operate on a majority, or on what number of the members? Would the act be null, whatever might be the wish of the nation, or would its obligation or nullity depend upon the public sentiment? *Id.*

56 He wrote:

If the majority of the legislature be corrupted, it may well be doubted, whether it be within the province of the judiciary to control their conduct, and, if less than a majority act from impure motives, the principle by which judicial interference would be regulated, is not clearly discerned. *Id.*

57 *Id.* at 135.

58 "To the legislature all legislative power is granted; but the question, whether the act of transferring the property of an individual to the public, be in the nature of the legislative power, is well worthy of serious reflection." *Id.* at 136.

59 "It is the peculiar province of the legislature to prescribe general rules for the government of society; the application of those rules to individuals in society would seem to be the duty of other departments. How far the power of giving the law may involve every other power, in cases where the constitution is silent, never has been, and perhaps never can be, definitely stated." *Id.* Here, Marshall likely referred to the Constitution of the State of Georgia.

60 *Id.* (emphasis in original, underline added). He reasoned:

The validity of this rescinding act, then, might well be doubted, were Georgia a single sovereign power. But Georgia cannot be viewed as a single, unconnected, sovereign power, on whose legislature no other restrictions are imposed than may be found in its own constitution. She is a part of a large empire; she is a member of the American union; and that union has a constitution the supremacy of which all acknowledge, and which imposes limits to the legislatures of the several states, which none claim a right to pass. The constitution of the United States declares that no state shall pass any bill of attainder, *ex post facto* law, or law impairing the obligation of contracts. *Id.*

61 Marshall wrote:

It is, then, the unanimous opinion of the court, that, in this case, the estate having passed into the hands of a purchaser for a valuable consideration, without notice, the state of Georgia was restrained, either by general principles which are common to our free institutions, or by the particular provisions of the constitution of the United States, from passing a law whereby the estate of the plaintiff in the premises so purchased could be constitutionally and legally impaired and rendered null and void. *Id.* at 139.

62 "If the original transaction was infected with fraud, these purchasers did not participate in it, and had no notice of it. They were innocent." *Id.* at 132. "If a suit be brought to set aside a conveyance obtained by fraud, and the fraud be clearly proved, the conveyance will be set aside, as between the parties; but the rights of third persons, who are purchasers without notice, for a valuable consideration, cannot be disregarded." *Id.* at 133. Titles, which, according to every legal test, are perfect, are acquired with that confidence which is inspired by the opinion that the purchaser is safe. If there be any concealed defect, arising from the conduct of those who had held the property long before he acquired it, of which he had no notice, that concealed defect cannot be set up against him. He has paid his money for a title good at law, he is innocent, whatever may be the guilt of others, and equity will not subject him to the penalties attached to that guilt. All titles would be insecure, and the intercourse 134*134 between man and man would be very seriously obstructed, if this principle be overturned. *Id.* at 133-134.

63 *Terrett v. Taylor*, 13 U.S. (9 Cranch) 43 (1815); Wilbur D. Preston, Jr., *The Due Process Clause as a Limitation on the Reach of State Legislation: An Historical and Analytical Examination of Substantive Due Process*, 8 U Balt. L. Rev. 1, 10 (1978).

64 James Ely, The Guardian of Every Other Right: A Constitutional History of Property Rights, Oxford University Press 68 (2008).

65 *Terrett v. Taylor*, 13 U.S. (9 Cranch) 43 (1815).

66 Ely, Chapter 10, note 64, at 68.

67 *Terrett v. Taylor*, 13 U.S. (9 Cranch) 50-51(1815).

68 *Trustees of Dartmouth College v. Woodward*, 17 U.S. 518, 626 (1819).

69 *Id.* at 626-627.

70 "No State shall...pass any Bill of Attainder, ex post facto Law, or Law impairing the Obligation of Contracts..." U.S. Const. art. I, § 10, cl. 1.

71 Marshall observed:

Taken in its broad, unlimited sense, the clause would be an unprofitable and vexatious interference with the internal concerns of a state, would unnecessarily and unwisely embarrass its legislation, and render immutable those civil institutions, which are established for purposes of internal government, and which, to subserve those purposes, ought to vary with varying circumstances. That as the framers of the constitution could never have intended to insert in that instrument, a provision so unnecessary, so mischievous, and so repugnant to its general spirit, the term 'contract' must be understood in a more limited sense. *Dartmouth College v. Woodward*, 17 U.S. 518, 628 (1819).

72　*Id.*

73　*Id.*

74　*Id.* at 628-629.

75　*Id.* at 654 (1819).

76　1 William Blackstone Commentaries *139. See *also* Wallace Mendelson, *New Light on Fletcher v. Peck and Gibbons v. Ogden* 58 Yale L. J. 567 (1949).

77　*See Ogden v. Saunders*, 25 U.S. (12 Wheat) 213 (1827) (holding that a state bankruptcy law applying to contracts made *after* the law's passage does not violate the Obligation of Contracts Clause of the Constitution). "On February 18, 1827, the Court announced its decision, and for the first and only time during his tenure as chief justice, Marshall found himself in dissent on a constitutional issue." Jean Edward Smith, Chapter 2, note 31, at 498 (footnote omitted). Incidentally, in the footnote, Smith explains his theory on the dissent:

Marshall's lengthy dissent in *Ogden* was most likely written shortly after the case was argued in 1824 and, anticipating [Justice] Todd's return, was intended to be the opinion of the Court. In it, Marshall made clear that the federal issue was controlling. 'When we consider the nature of our Union; that it is intended to make us, in a great measure, one people, as to commercial objects; that, so far as respects the intercommunication of individuals, the lines of separation between the States are, in many respects, obliterated; it would not be a matter of surprise, if on the delicate subjects of contracts once formed, the interference of State legislation should be greatly abridged, or entirely forbidden.' He also spoke at length about the sanctity of contract, which, he said, 'results from the right which every man retains to acquire property, to dispose of that property according to his own judgment, and to pledge himself for a future act. *These rights are not given by society, but are brought into it.*' 12 Wheaton 346 (emphasis added). *Id.*

78　*Sturgis v. Crowninshield*, 17 U.S. (4 Wheat) 122 (1819).

79　Jean Edward Smith, Chapter 2, note 31, at 498 (footnotes omitted).

80　David C. Bayne, Chapter 10, note 45, at 224.

81   *Ogden v. Saunders*, 25 U.S. (12 Wheat) 213, 344-345 (Marshall, C.J. *dissenting*) (emphasis added).

82   Hugo Grotius, De Jure Belli AC Pacis (Francis W. Kelsey, ed., 1925) (1625), *in* Grotius Reader at 233.

83   *Ogden v. Saunders*, 25 U.S. (12 Wheat) 213, 345 (Marshall, C.J. *dissenting*) (emphasis added).

84   "In the rudest state of nature a man governs himself, and labours for his own purposes. That which he acquires is his own, at least while in his possession, and he may transfer it to another. This transfer passes his right to that other." *Id.* "Superior strength may give the power, but cannot give the right. The rightfulness of coercion must depend on the pre-existing obligation to do that for which compulsion is used. It is no objection to the principle, that the injured party may be the weakest." *Id.*

85   Marshall noted:

Independent nations are individuals in a state of nature. Whence is derived the obligation of their contracts? They admit the existence of no superior legislative power which is to give them validity, yet their validity is acknowledged by all. If one of these contracts be broken, all admit the right of the injured party to demand reparation for the injury, and to enforce that reparation if it be withheld. He may not have the power to enforce it, but the whole civilized world concurs in saying, that the power, if possessed, is rightfully used. *Id.* at 346.

86   *Id.*

87   *Id.* at 346-347 (emphasis added).

88   *Id.* at 347.

89   *Gibbons v. Ogden*, 22 U.S. 1 (1824).

90   *Id.* at 1.

91   *Id.*

92   *Id.*

93   Chief Justice Marshall explained:

As preliminary to the very able discussions of the constitution, which we have heard from the bar, and as having some influence on its construction, reference has been made to the political situation of these States, anterior to its formation. It has been said, that they were sovereign, were completely independent, and were connected with each other only by a league. This is true. But, when these allied sovereigns converted their league into a government, when they converted their Congress of Ambassadors, deputed to deliberate on their common concerns, and to recommend measures of general utility, into a Legislature, empowered to enact laws on the most interesting subjects, the whole character in which the States appear, underwent a change, the extent of which must be determined by a fair consideration of the instrument by which that change was effected. *Id.* at 71.

94   *Id.* Here, it would seem that Chief Justice Marshall means to imply that power was granted from the sovereign people to the federal government, as he later echoes so famously in *McCulloch v. Maryland* and elsewhere from the bench. Yet we will see in Chapter 11, he has written before his appointment to the Supreme Court, that far from proceeding from "the whole people," the Constitution barely escaped defeat altogether. *See, e.g.*, Beard, Chapter 6, note 75, at 296, 299 (Dover Publications 2004) (1913) ("[A]s a historian of great acumen, in which capacity he was not hampered by the traditional language of the bench and bar, Marshall sketched with unerring hand the economic conflict which led to the adoption of the Constitution, and impressed upon the nature of that instrument.")

95   *Gibbons v. Ogden*, 22 U.S. 1, 71 (1824).

96   Marshall wrote:

As men, whose intentions require no concealment, generally employ the words which most directly and aptly express the ideas they intend to convey, the enlightened patriots who framed our constitution, and the people who adopted it, must be understood to have employed words in their natural sense, and to have intended what they have sa*id. Id.*

97   *Id.* at 72.

98   Marshall noted:

The power over commerce, including navigation, was one of the primary objects for which the people of America adopted their government, and must have been contemplated in forming it. The convention must have used the word in that sense, because all have understood it in that sense; and the attempt to restrict it comes too late. *Id.*

99   *Id.* at 75.

100   *See id.* at 79:

In our complex system, presenting the rare and difficult scheme of one general government, whose action extends over the whole, but which possesses only certain enumerated powers; and of numerous State governments, which retain and exercise all powers not delegated to the Union, contests respecting power must arise. Were it even otherwise, the measures taken by the respective governments to execute their acknowledged powers, would often be of the same description, and might, sometimes, interfere. This, however, does not prove that the one is exercising, or has a right to exercise, the powers of the other. *Id.*

101   *Id.* at 82.

102 Randy E. Barnett, *The Original Meaning of the Commerce Clause*, 68 U. Chi. L. Rev. 101, 139 (2001).

103 Barry Friedman & Genevieve Lakier, *"To Regulate," Not "To Prohibit": Limiting the Commerce Power*, 2012 Sup. CT. Rev. 255, 260 (2012).

104 Grant S. Nelson and Robert J. Pushaw Jr., *Rethinking the Commerce Clause: Applying First Principles to Uphold Federal Commercial Regulations but Preserve State Control over Social Issues*, 85 Iowa L Rev 1, 35 n 138 (1999).

105 Barry Friedman & Genevieve Lakier, *"To Regulate," Not "To Prohibit": Limiting the Commerce Power*, 2012 Sup. CT. Rev. 255, 264 (2012) (emphasis in original).

106 James Madison, Federalist 54: The Powers Conferred By The Constitution Further Considered, New York (January 22, 1788) (emphasis added).

107 Letter from James Madison to Joseph C. Cabell, (February 13, 1829)," *Founders Online*, National Archives, *available at* https://founders.archives. gov/documents/Madison/99-02-02-1698.

108 Barnett, *The Original Meaning of the Commerce Clause*, Chapter 10, note 102, at 139 (citing Samuel Johnson, 2 A Dictionary of the English Language (J.F. Rivington, et al 6th ed 1785)).

109 *Id.*

110 *See* Andrew P. Napolitano, *Health-Care Reform and the Constitution: Why hasn't the Commerce Clause been read to allow interstate insurance sales?* The Wall Street Journal (Sept. 15, 2009).

111 *Id.* at 87.

112 *Id.*

CHAPTER 11

1 Jeremy Bentham, An Introduction To The Principles of Morals And Legislation 10 (J.H. Burns, H. L. A. Hart eds., 1996) (1776).

2 Jurisprudence does not offer us the types of interactions and events that lend themselves to empiricization like that of the natural sciences. In a concrete disciplines, such as physics, scientists set out to prove a hypothesis through replicable experimentation. As a result, they enjoy the luxury of objective measurements and collection of data that allow them to draw conclusions based on the quantification of nature. Unlike the hard sciences, in which practitioners push existing models beyond their usefulness only to replace them with a newer one that adjusts for the deficiencies of the former, jurisprudence never completely supplants prior doctrines.

3 For instance, Justice William Paterson, when he had served as Governor of New Jersey, from 1790 to 1793 "had initiated a compilation of the statutes in force in New Jersey" in an attempt to bring greater consistence and coherence

to the administration of government and justice in that state." Jean Edward Smith, Chapter 2, note 31, at 288.

4 Perhaps, Coke's *Institutes* remained so influential in the development of English Law because it, quite literally, remained in a class on its own for over a century. Despite its erudition, Coke's "writing itself so offends modern standards of scholarship and method as to challenge the patience of even the most painstaking historian." Stoner, Chapter 2, note 9, at 14. Coke's *Institutes*, Blackstone observed in his *Commentaries*, "have little of the institutional method to warrant such a title." 1 Blackstone Commentaries *73.

5 Diary of John Quincy Adams (Mar 1788), *reprinted in* Charles Francis Adams, T. Jefferson Coolidfge, Samuel A. Green, and William P. Upham, *Diary of John Quincy Adams: Some Extracts from an Autobiography*, 16 Proc. of Mass. Hist. Soc'y 392 (1902).

6 Alexander J. Dallas would later go on to serve as Secretary of the Treasury under James Madison.

7 On the title page of the reports, Dallas included an epigram from Hugo Grotius, from the Prolegomena to On the Law of War and Peace:

Atque eo magis nece[ss]aria e[s]t hæc opera quod et no[s]tro [s]æculo non de[s]unt et olim non de[s]uerunt. qui hanc juris qui hanc juris partem ita contemnerent. qua[s]i nihil ejus præter inane nomen exi[s]teret.

1 Dallas i (1790). And such a work is the more necessary on this account; that there are not wanting persons in our own time, and there have been also in former times, persons, who have despised what has been done in this province of jurisprudence, so far as to hold that no such thing existed, except as a mere name. Hugo Grotius, De Jure Belli Et Pacis Libri Tres xxviii (William Whewell ed., 1853) (1625).

8 1 Dallas v-vi (1790) (spelling modernized).

9 *Id.* at vi (spelling modernized).

10 *Id.* (spelling modernized).

11 William Cranch, *Preface*, 1 Cranch iii (1804) (spelling modernized) (emphasis in original).

12 *Id.* (emphasis in original).

13 *Id.* (emphasis in original).

14 According to Professor Frederick Schauer of the University of Virginia Law School:

Although Bentham and Austin, among others, talked about "positive law," and although the nineteenth century scientific positivism of Auguste Comte was explicitly described as such, the use of the word "positivism" to describe a legal theory, regime, or attitude first surfaced in the early twentieth century and was made substantially more visible by the anti-positivist Lon Fuller in 1940 in *Law in Quest of Itself*.

Frederick Schauer, *Positivism before Hart*, 24 Can. J. L. & Jurisprudence 455, 457 (2011) (emphasis in original) (footnotes omitted).

15   "Classical [legal] positivism developed in reaction to classical common law theory." Anthony J. Sebok, *Misunderstanding Positivism*, 93 Mich. L. Rev. 2054, 2063 (1995). "To the [legal] positivist, [...] laws and legal systems satisfying certain sociological criteria count as laws and legal systems, regardless of their moral content." Frederick Schauer, *Constitutional Positivism*, 25 Conn. L. Rev. 797, 800 (1993) (footnote omitted).

16   Alan B. Handler, *Judicial Jurisprudence*, 205-OCT N.J. Law. 22, 23 (2000). I have a soft spot in my heart for Justice Handler. He was a justice of the Supreme Court of New Jersey during the years that I was a judge of the Superior Court of New Jersey; and from time to time was a mentor to me. *See also*, Frederick Schauer, Chapter 11, note 15, at 800-801.

[T]he central [legal] positivist claim about the separation of law and morality is not a claim on the existence (or nonexistence) of moral values, nor a denial of the preferability of moral laws and legal systems over immoral ones, but rather simply a claim that the existence of law is conceptually distinct from its moral worth.

Id.

17   Priel, Chapter 1, note 114, at 282 (quoting John Austin, The Province of Jurisprudence Determined 157 (Wilfrid E. Rumble ed., 1995)).

18   "The identification of law and legal systems, therefore, [according to legal positivism], is a matter of identification of some social fact, a process not *necessarily* entailing moral evaluation." Frederick Schauer, *Constitutional Positivism*, Chapter 11, note 15, at 799-800 (footnote omitted).

19   *Id.* at 799 (footnote omitted).

20   Priel, Chapter 1, note 114, at 284. The *what is* versus *what ought to be* comes from David Hume in his Treatise on Human Nature:

In every system of morality, which I have hitherto met with, I have always remark[e]d, that the author proceeds from some time in the ordinary way of reasoning, and establishes the being of a God, or makes observations concerning human affairs; when of a sudden I am surpri[se]d to find, that instead of the usual copulations of propositions, *is*, and *is not*, I meet with no proposition that is not connected with an *ought*, or an *ought not*. This change is imperceptible; but is, however, of the last consequence. For as this *ought*, or *ought not*, expresses some new revelation or affirmation, 'tis necessary that it shou[e]d be observ[e]d and explain[e]d; and at the same time that a reason should be given, for what seems altogether inconceivable, how this new relation can be a deduction from others, which are entirely different from it. But as authors do not commonly use this precaution, I shall presume to recommend it to the readers; and am persuaded, that this small attention wou[l]d subvert all the vulgar systems of morality, and let us see, that the distinction of vice and virtue is not founded merely on the relation of objects nor is perceiv[e]d by reason.

David Hume, A Treatise On Human Nature 469-470 (L.A. Selby-Bigge, M.A. ed., 1888) (1738).

21   Priel, Chapter 1, note 114, at 290.

22   *Id.* (quoting Jeremy Bentham, A Comment on the Commentaries and a Fragment on Government 314 (J.H. Burns & H.L.A. Hart eds., Univ. of London Athlone Press 1977) (1776)).

23   "Positivist philosophy restricts the object of scientific knowledge to matters that can be verified by observation, and thus excludes from its domain all matters of an *a priori*, metaphysical nature." Hans J. Morgenthau, *Positivism, Functionalism, and International Law*, 34 AM. J. Int'l L. 260, 261 (1940) (footnote omitted).

24   Priel, Chapter 1, note 114, at 299.

25   Frederick Schauer, *The Path-Dependence of Legal Positivism*, 101 VA. L. Rev. 957, 964 (2015).

26   "When Bentham was at Oxford, he attended lectures on William Blackstone (1723-80), the first Vinerian Professor of English Law, which were eventually published as the *Commentaries on the Laws of England*." F. Rosen, introduction, Jeremy Bentham, An Introduction To The Principles of Morals And Legislation xxxii (J.H. Burns, H. L. A. Hart eds., 1996) (1776) [hereinafter Bentham's Morals] (footnote omitted). Blackstone must have made an impression on a young Bentham.

27   "Bentham and [later, John] Austin wrote in reaction to Blackstone's theory of common law, which had become the dominant theory of English law before the Nineteenth century." Sebok, Chapter 11, note 15, at 2062.

28   "Bentham was indeed a scathing critic of the use of fiction in the discourse of the law." Nomi Maya Stolzenberg, *Bentham's Theory of Fictions--A "Curious Double Language,"* 11 Cardozo Stud. L. & Literature 223, 223 (1999). "Bentham's views about legal fictions are well known. His contempt for these peculiarities of legal discourse bordered on an obsession." *Id* at 226 (footnote omitted).

29   "Blackstone's theory of law, which set for itself the task of explaining the source and authority of judge-made law, was held to be inadequate by Bentham and Austin not only because it failed to explain statutory law, but because it failed, in their eyes, even to explain the authority of common law." Sebok, Chapter 11, note 15, at 2062.

30   Bentham's Morals, Chapter 11, note 26, at 25.

31   *Id.* at 25-26.

32   Sebok, Chapter 11, note 15, at 2063.

33   *Id.* at 2062 (footnote omitted).

34   Dan Priel, *Toward Classic Legal Positivism*, 101 VA. L. Rev. 987, 997 (2015) (quoting Jeremy Bentham, Deontology 135 (Amnon Goldworth ed., 1983) (1834)).

35   *Id.* at 34, 996 (quoting Jeremy Bentham, *Nonsense upon Stilts* (1816), reprinted in Rights, Representation, And Reform: Nonsense Upon Stilts And Other Writings On The French Revolution 317, 330 (Philip Schofield, et al. eds., 2002) (emphasis added)).

36   Bentham's Morals, Chapter 11, note 26, at 11. Bentham clearly chose to list *pain* before *pleasure*. Readers can draw their own conclusions.

37   "The first question made in the case is — has Congress power to incorporate a bank?" *McCulloch v. Maryland*, 17 U.S. 316, 401 (1819) (Marshall, C. J.).

38   *Id.* at 401.

39   *Id.* at 406 (emphasis added).

40   *Id.*

41   *Id.*

42   "A constitution, to contain an accurate detail of all the subdivisions of which its great powers will admit, and of all the means by which they may be carried into execution, would partake of the prolixity of a legal code, and could scarcely be embraced by the human mind." *Id.* at 407. "It would, probably, never be understood by the public. Its nature, therefore, requires, that only its great outlines should be marked, its important objects designated, and the minor ingredients which compose those objects, be deduced from the nature of the objects themselves." *Id.* He continued, "That this idea was entertained by the framers of the American constitution, is not only to be inferred from the nature of the instrument, but from the language." *Id.*

43   *Id.* at 408.

44   The Court mused:

> It is not denied, that the powers given to the government imply the ordinary means of execution. That, for example, of raising revenue, and applying it to national purposes, is admitted to imply the power of conveying money from place to place, as the exigencies of the nation may require, and of employing the usual means of conveyance. But it is denied, that the government has its choice of means; or, that it may employ the most convenient means, if, to employ them, it be necessary to erect a corporation.

Id. at 409.

45 The Court reasoned:

[A]ll legislative powers appertain to sovereignty. The original power of giving the law on any subject whatever, is a sovereign power; and if the government of the Union is restrained from creating a corporation, as a means for performing its functions, on the single reason that the creation of a corporation is an act of sovereignty; if the sufficiency of this reason be acknowledged, there would be some difficulty in sustaining the authority of congress to pass other laws for the accomplishment of the same objects.

Id.

46 Marshall wrote:

The powers of the general government, it has been said, are delegated by the states, who alone are truly sovereign; and must be exercised in subordination to the states, who alone possess supreme dominion. It would be difficult to sustain this proposition. The convention which framed the constitution was indeed elected by the state legislatures. But the instrument, when it came from their hands, was a mere proposal, without obligation, or pretensions to it.

Id. at 402-403.

47 *Id.* at 409-410.

48 *Id.* at 411.

49 *Id.*

50 *Id.*

51 *Id.* at 412.

52 *Id.* at 413.

53 *Id.*

54 "Is it true, that this is the sense in which the word 'necessary' is always used? Does it always import an absolute physical necessity, so strong, that one thing to which another may be termed necessary, cannot exist without that other?" *Id.*

55 David S. Schwartz, *Misreading McCulloch v. Maryland*, 18 U. Pa. J. Const. L. 1, 73 (2015).

56 *McCulloch v. Maryland*, Introduction, note 17, at 409, 413, 415, 419, 420.

57 *Id.* at 418.

58 *Id.* at 413-414.

59 *Id.* at 415.

60   In speaking to John Quincy Adams, Madison politely deflated the English philosopher, Jeremy Bentham's scheme to rationalize and codify American law: "[Either], I greatly overrate or [Bentham] greatly underrates the task...not only [of digesting] our Statutes into a concise and clear system, but [of reducing] our unwritten to a text law." Ralph Ketcham, James Madison: A Biography, 632 (1990).

61   *McCulloch v. Maryland*, Introduction, note 17, at 414-415. He continued:

We admit, as all must admit, that the powers of the government are limited, and that its limits are not to be transcended. But we think the sound construction of the constitution must allow to the national legislature that discretion, with respect to the means by which the powers it confers are to be carried into execution, which will enable that body to perform the high duties assigned to it, in the manner most beneficial to the people. Let the end be legitimate, let it be within the scope of the constitution, and all means which are appropriate, which are plainly adapted to that end, which are not prohibited, but consist with the letter and spirit of the constitution, are constitutional.

Id. at 421.

62   *Id.* at 425.

63   *Id.* at 435-437.

64   2 Annals of Cong. 1896-1897 (statement of Rep. Madison).

65   *Id.* at 1902 (statement of Rep. Madison).

66   *Id.* at 1902 (statement of Rep. Madison).

67   Beard, Chapter 6, note 75, at 299 (Dover Publications 2004) (1913).

68   John Marshall, 2 The Life Of Washington 127 (2 ed. 1843) (emphasis added).

69   *McCulloch*, Introduction, note 17, at 198-199.

70   Beard, Chapter 6, note 75, at 250-251, 299.

71   *McCulloch*, Introduction, note 17, at 198.

72   "Many of Congress' most consequential actions, including regulations, safety-net programs, and civil rights protections, are not explicitly enumerated in Article 1, Section 8, and have been justified using the reasonableness standard established in McCulloch. And while the powers of states in relation to the federal government have waxed and waned over time, McCulloch established baseline constraints on how states can and cannot react to federal legislation and programs." Johnathan Stahl, *McCulloch v. Maryland: Expanding the power of Congress, available at* https://constitutioncenter.org / blog / mcculloch-v-maryland-expandingthe-power-of-congress.

73 For instance, in the nineteenth century, the Court would adopt a slavish adherence to positivism in its decision-making that would justify opinions as egregious and offensive as *Dred Scott v. Sandford* in which the Supreme Court found it could not properly exercise jurisdiction over the case since Scott, as a former slave descended from kidnapped African slaves, was not a "citizen" of the United States, nor a person who could invoke the jurisdiction of the federal courts. *Dred Scott v. Sandford*, 60 U.S. 393 (1857).

CHAPTER 12

1 Bertrand Russell, The History of Western Philosophy 188 (Simon & Schuster Touchstone 1967) (1945).

2 In *Chisholm v. Georgia*, Justice James Iredell, referring to a text quoted in Blackstone, supposes "the first edition of [*Finch's Nomotexnia*], it seems, was published in 1579" when it was, in fact first published in 1612 in French and in English in 1627. *Chisholm v. Georgia*, 2 U.S. 419, 437 (1793), (Iredell, J.).

3 *Plessy v. Ferguson*, 163 U.S. 537 (1896).

4 Keith Weldon Medley, We As Freemen: Plessy V. Ferguson (2003).

5 The famous case was eventually recorded as *Plessy v. Ferguson*, 163 U.S. 537 (1896).

6 "In the present case no question of interference with interstate commerce can possibly arise, since the East Louisiana Railway appears to have been purely a local line, with both its termini within the State of Louisiana." *Id.* at 548 (Brown, J.).

7 *Id.* at 541-542.

8 *Id.* at 543.

9 *Id.* at 551.

10 *Id.*

11 *Id.*

12 *Id.* at 551-552.

13 *Id.*

14 *Id.* at 552.

15 *Id.* at 553 (Harlan, J. *dissenting*).

16 *Id.* at 554-5.

17 *Id.* at 556.

18 *Id.* at 557 (1896).

19 Justice Harlan noted:

There is a dangerous tendency in these latter days to enlarge the functions of the courts, by means of judicial interference with the will of the people as expressed by the legislature. Our institutions have the distinguishing characteristic that the three departments of government are coordinate and separate. Each must keep within the limits defined by the Constitution. And the courts best discharge their duty by executing the will of the law-making power, constitutionally expressed, leaving the results of legislation to be dealt with by the people through their representatives. Statutes must always have a reasonable construction. Sometimes they are to be construed strictly; sometimes, liberally, in order to carry out the legislative will. But however construed, the intent of the legislature is to be respected, if the particular statute in question is valid, although the courts, looking at the public interests, may conceive the statute to be both unreasonable and impolitic. If the power exists to enact a statute, that ends the matter so far as the courts are concerned. The adjudged cases in which statutes have been held to be void, because unreasonable, are those in which the means employed by the legislature were not at all germane to the end to which the legislature was competent.

Id. at 558-559.

19 *Id.*

20 *Id.* at 559.

21 *Id.* at 563.

22 *Lochner v. New York*, 198 U.S. 45 (1905).

23 *Id.* at 47.

24 *Id.*

25 Andrew P. Napolitano, Suicide Pact: The Radical Expansion of Presidential Powers And The Lethal Threat To American Liberty 110 (2014) (footnotes omitted) (citing *Lochner v. New York*, 198 U.S. 45, 52 (Peckham, J.).

26 *Lochner v. New York*, 198 U.S. 45, 53 (1905) (Peckham, J).

27 *Id.*

28 *Id.* at 53-54.

29 *Id.* at 57.

30 *Id.* at 58.

31 *Id.*

32 "This case is decided upon an economic theory which a large part of the country does not entertain." *Id.* at 75 (Holmes, J. *dissenting*).

33 *Id.*

34 *Id.*

35 *Id.* at 76.

36 *Id.* at 75.

37 In 1897, Holmes wrote:

It is revolting to have no better reason for a rule of law than that so it was laid down in the time of Henry IV. It is still more revolting if the grounds upon which it was laid down have vanished long since, and the rule simply persists from blind imitation of the past.

Oliver Wendell Holmes, *The Path of the Law*, 10 Harv. L. Rev. 457, 469 (1897).

38 *Wickard v. Filburn*, 317 U.S. 111, 114-115 (1942) (Jackson, J.).

39 *Id.* at 114.

40 *Id.*

41 Congress shall have the power "[t]o regulate Commerce with foreign Nations, and among the several States, and with the Indian Tribes." U.S. Const. art. 1, § 3, cl. 8.

42 "It is well established by decisions of this Court that the power to regulate commerce includes the power to regulate the prices at which commodities in that commerce are dealt in and practices affecting such prices." *Wickard v. Filburn*, Chapter 12, note 38, at 128 (footnote omitted).

43 *Id.*

44 "It can hardly be denied that a factor of such volume and variability as home-consumed wheat would have a substantial influence on price and market conditions." *Id.*

45 *Id.* at 127 (emphasis added).

46 *See United States v. Lopez*, 514 U.S. 549, 560 (1995).

47 Civilian Exclusion Order No. 34 of the Commanding General of the Western Command, U.S. Army (May 3, 1942).

48 *Korematsu v. United States*, 324 U.S. 214, 215-216 (1944) (*Korematsu II*).

49 *Id.* at 217.

50 *Korematsu v. United States*, 319 U.S. 432, 432 (1943) (*Korematsu I*).

51 *Id.* at 433.

52 *Id.* at 436.

53 *Toyosaburo Korematsu v. United States*, 140 F.2d 289, 290 (9th Cir. 1943), aff'd, 323 U.S. 214, 65 S. Ct. 193, 89 L. Ed. 194 (1944).

54 *Korematsu v. United States*, 321 U.S. 760, 64 S. Ct. 786 (1944).

55 *Korematsu II* at 216.

56 *Id.*

57   *Id.* at 219-220.

58   *Id.* at 223.

59   *Id.* at 225 (Owens, J., *dissenting*).

60   *Id.* at 226.

61   *Id.* at 233 (emphasis added).

62   *Id.*

63   *Id.*

64   *Id.* at 236 (footnote omitted).

65   Justice Murphy explained:

> Justification for the exclusion is sought, instead, mainly upon questionable racial and sociological grounds not ordinarily within the realm of expert military judgment, supplemented by certain semi-military conclusions drawn from an unwarranted use of circumstantial evidence. Individuals of Japanese ancestry are condemned because they are said to be "a large, unassimilated, tightly knit racial group, bound to an enemy nation by strong ties of race, culture, custom and religion." They are claimed to be given to "emperor worshipping ceremonies" and to "dual citizenship." Japanese language schools and allegedly pro-Japanese organizations are cited as evidence of possible group disloyalty, together with facts as to certain persons being educated and residing at length in Japan. It is intimated that many of these individuals deliberately resided "adjacent to strategic points," thus enabling them "to carry into execution a tremendous program of sabotage on a mass scale should any considerable number of them have been inclined to do so." The need for protective custody is also asserted. The report refers without identity to "numerous incidents of violence" as well as to other admittedly unverified or cumulative incidents. From this, plus certain other events not shown to have been connected with the Japanese Americans, it is concluded that the "situation was fraught with danger to the Japanese population itself" and that the general public "was ready to take matters into its own hands." Finally, it is intimated, though not directly charged or proved, that persons of Japanese ancestry were responsible for three minor isolated shellings and bombings of the Pacific Coast area, as well as for unidentified radio transmissions and night signaling.
>
> The main reasons relied upon by those responsible for the forced evacuation, therefore, do not prove a reasonable relation between the group characteristics of Japanese Americans and the dangers of invasion, sabotage and espionage. The reasons appear, instead, to be largely an accumulation of much of the misinformation, half-truths and insinuations that for years have been directed against Japanese Americans by people with racial and

economic prejudices — the same people who have been among the foremost advocates of the evacuation. A military judgment based upon such racial and sociological considerations is not entitled to the great weight ordinarily given the judgments based upon strictly military considerations. Especially is this so when every charge relative to race, religion, culture, geographical location, and legal and economic status has been substantially discredited by independent studies made by experts in these matters. *Id.* at 236-240 (Murphy, J., *dissenting*) (footnotes omitted).

66 Justice Murphy explained:

No one denies, of course, that there were some disloyal persons of Japanese descent on the Pacific Coast who did all in their power to aid their ancestral land. Similar disloyal activities have been engaged in by many persons of German, Italian and even more pioneer stock in our country. But to infer that examples of individual disloyalty prove group disloyalty and justify discriminatory action against the entire group is to deny that under our system of law individual guilt is the sole basis for deprivation of rights.

Id. at 240.

67 *Id.* at 241.

68 *Id.* at 242.

69 Justice Jackson pointed out:

A citizen's presence in the locality, however, was made a crime only if his parents were of Japanese birth. Had Korematsu been one of four — the others being, say, a German alien enemy, an Italian alien enemy, and a citizen of American-born ancestors, convicted of treason but out on parole — only Korematsu's presence would have violated the order. The difference between their innocence and his crime would result, not from anything he did, said, or thought, different than they, but only in that he was born of different racial stock.

Id. at 243 (Jackson, J., *dissenting*).

70 *Id.* at 246.

71 *Id.*

72 *Id.* at 247.

73 *Id.*

74 Anthony J. Lisska, Aquinas's Theory of Natural Law An Analytic Reconstruction 8 (1996).

75 *Id.* at 8. "Legal positivism did not offer theoretical grounds to warrant claims like 'Crime Against Humanity' which were needed to provide justification for the war crimes trials." *Id.* at 8-9.

76 *Id.* at 9.

77 Lon L. Fuller, *Positivism and Fidelity to Law—A Reply to Professor Hart*, 71 Harv. L. Rev. 630, 656 (1958).

78 Lon Fuller proclaimed, "[d]uring the last half century in this country no issue of legal philosophy has caused more spilling of ink and adrenalin than the assertion that there are 'totalitarian' implications in the views of Oliver Wendell Holmes, Jr." *Id.* at 657. He ultimately concluded, "I cannot see either absurdity or perversity in the suggestion that the attitudes prevailing in the German legal profession were helpful to the Nazis. Hitler did not come to power by a violent revolution. He was Chancellor before he became the Leader. The exploitation of legal forms started cautiously and became bolder as power was consolidated. The first attacks on the established order were on ramparts which, if they were manned by anyone, were manned by lawyers and judges." *Id.* at 659.

79 *Id.* at 659.

80 *Id.* at 660 (1958) (emphasis added).

81 *See, e.g.* Leo Strauss, Natural Right And History 1 (1953); H. L. A. Hart, The Concept of Law, Chapter 1, note 50; Lon. L. Fuller, The Morality of Law (1964).

82 Lisska, Chapter 11, note 74, at 9.

83 *Id.*

84 "While some [aspect of natural law jurisprudence] were developed in more detail and general agreement with Aquinas than others, most referred to Aquinas's account of natural law as the classical foundation for such discussions in Western philosophy." *Id.*

85 Leo Strauss, Chapter 11, note 81, at 1.

86 Strauss wrote:

"About a generation ago, an American diplomat could still say that 'the natural and divine foundation of the rights of man ... is self-evident to all Americans.' At about the same time a German scholar could still describe the difference between German thought and that of Western Europe and the United States by saying that the West still attached decisive importance to natural rights, while in Germany the very terms 'natural right' and 'humanity' 'have now become almost incomprehensible ... and have lost altogether their original life and color.'" *Id.*

87 *Id.* at 2. Strauss looks to Otto Gierke's Natural Law and the Theory of Society, originally published in German in 1882, as his source of the views of German attitudes towards natural law and moral relativism, though Strauss cites to the English translation published in 1934. *Id.*

88 *Id.*

89 *Id.*

90 *Id.*

91 "Now it is obviously meaningful, and sometimes even necessary, to speak of 'unjust' laws or 'unjust' decisions." *Id.*

92 "In passing such judgments[,] we imply that there is a standard of right and wrong independent of positive right and higher than positive right: a standard with reference to which we are able to judge of positive right." *Id.*

93 *Id.* at 3.

94 *Id.* at 5.

95 *Id.* at 7.

96 "We are therefore in need of historical studies in order to familiarize ourselves with the whole complexity of the issue [of natural right]. We have for some time to become students of what is called the 'history of ideas.'" *Id.*

97 *Id.*

98 *Id.*

99 *Id.*

100 *Id.*

101 Edwin S. Corwin, *The "Higher Law" Background of American Constitutional Law*, 42 Harv. L. Rev. 149, 151 (1928).

102 *Id.*

103 *Id.* at 152.

104 *Id.* (emphasis in original) (footnote omitted).

105 *Id.* at 152-3.

106 *Id.* at 153 (emphasis added).

CHAPTER 13

1 Holmes, *The Path of the Law*, Chapter 12, note 37, at 460.

2 Austin, like Bentham, began his exegesis, *The Province of Jurisprudence Determined* without pleasantries or fanfare. Declaring, "[t]he matter of jurisprudence is positive law: law simply and strictly so called: or law set by political superiors to political inferiors[,]" Austin signals to the reader that the following text will present a dense, and rather humorless approach to legal philosophy. John Austin, The Province of Jurisprudence Determined Being The First Part of A Series of Lectures On Jurisprudence, or, The Philosophy of Positive Law 1 (2d ed. 1876) (1831) ("Austin's Lectures"). Before the first "Lecture," Austin indulges in an Author's Preface, detailed table of contents,

outline, and then abstract of the outline which occupy over 80 pages in the work itself. The positivists were always so serious.

3 "Of the laws or rules set by men to men, some are established by *political* superiors, sovereign and subject: by persons exercising supreme and subordinate *government*, in independent nations, or independent political societies." *Id.* at 2.

4 John Stuart Mill, On Liberty (1859).

5 John Stuart Mill, August Comte And Positivism (1865).

6 John Stuart Mill, Utilitarianism (1863).

7 John Stuart Mill, The Subjection of Women (1869).

8 John Stuart Mill, Essays on Some Unsettled Questions of Political Economy (1844), John Stuart Mill, The Principles of Political Economy: With Some of Their Applications to Social Philosophy (1848).

9 John Stuart Mill, A System of Logic (1843).

10 John Stuart Mill, Three Essays on Religion (1874).

11 John Stuart Mill, Considerations on Representative Government (1861).

12 Bentham lays out the principles of felicific calculus in Chapter 4 of An Introduction to the Principles and Morals of Legislation. Bentham's Morals, Chapter 11, note 26, at 25.

13 John Stuart Mill, Utilitarianism 11 (7th ed. 1879) (1863) (emphasis in original).

14 Mill, On Liberty, Introduction, note 19, at 23.

15 *Id.* 22-23. Bentham famously began *On the Principles and Moral of Legislation* discussing pain and pleasure. Mill substituted pleasure for happiness, and pain for the coercive force of legal penalties or public opinion.

16 Mill, however, argued that his principles best applied to mature members of societies advanced beyond existence of "backward states of society in which the race itself may be considered as in its nonage." Mill, On Liberty, Introduction, note 19, at 24. For those backwards societies Mill did not rule out harsh government so long as so long as it served its purpose. "Despotism," Mill observed, "is a legitimate mode of government in dealing with barbarians, provided the end be their improvement, and the means justified by actually effecting that end." *Id.*

17 "In the part [of one's conduct] which merely concerns himself, his independence is, of right, absolute. Over himself, over his own body and mind, the individual is sovereign." *Id.* at 23.

18 "It comprises, first, the inward domain of consciousness; demanding liberty of consciousness, demanding liberty of conscience, in the most comprehensive sense, liberty of though and feeling; absolute freedom of

opinion and sentiment on all subjects, practical or speculative, scientific, moral, or theological." *Id.* at 27-28.

19   "Secondly, the principle requires liberty of tastes and pursuits; of framing the plan of our life to suit our own character; of doing as we like, subject to such consequences as may follow; without impediment from our fellow-creatures, so long as what we do does not harm them, even though they should think our conduct foolish, perverse, or wrong." *Id.* at 28.

20   "Thirdly, from this liberty of each individual flows the liberty, within the same limits, of a combination among individuals; freedom to unite, for any purpose not involving harm to others: the persons combining being supposed to be full age, and not forced or deceived." *Id.* To the NAP, deception and fraud are aggression.

21   *Id.*

22   Anthony Lisska noted,

For many years, Hart was the Professor of jurisprudence at Oxford. He published profusely on matters of jurisprudence. A student of ordinary language philosophy, Hart was attracted by the everydayness of much of John Austin' writings in jurisprudence. Bentham also served as the focal point of much of Hart's writings.

Lisska, Chapter 11, note 74, at 18.

23   "Surely not all laws order people to do or not to do things." H.L.A.

Hart, The Concept of Law, Chapter 1, note 50, at 26 "Is it not misleading so to classify laws which *confer powers on private individuals to make wills, contracts, or marriages*, and laws which give powers to officials, e.g. to a judge to try cases, to a minister to make rules, or a county council to make by-laws?" *Id.* (emphasis added). The language above in italics is profound rejection of NLT, which teaches that humans have natural rights to make wills, contracts, or marriages; the state does not create these rights.

24   *Id.* at 94.

25   "Thus they may all be said to be on a different level from the primary rules, for they are all about such rules; in the sense that while primary rules are concerned with the actions that individuals must or must not do, these secondary rules are all concerned with the primary rules themselves." *Id.*

26   Hart explained that this could take many forms and did not require any complex framework or architecture. In fact, "[i]t [could], as in the early law of many societies, be no more than that an authoritative list or text of the rules is to be found in a written document or carved on some public monument." *Id.*

27   "For the most part the rule of recognition is not stated, but its existence is shown in the way in which particular rules are identified, either by courts or other officials or private persons or their advisers." *Id.* at 101.

28   "The simplest form of such a rule is that which empowers an individual or body of persons to introduce new primary rules for the conduct of the life of the group, or of some class within it, and to eliminate old rules." *Id.* at 95.

29   "The minimal form of adjudication consists in such determinations, and we shall call the secondary rules which confer the power to make them 'rules of adjudication.' Besides identifying the individuals who are to adjudicate, such rules will also define the procedure to be followed." *Id.* at 97.

30   I must confess that my fascination with Fuller began in my high school years when I first read his famed fable "The Case of the Speluncean Explorers," a great tool for fomenting debate among law and graduate students on the moral basis, if any, of generally accepted laws, such as those prohibiting murder. *See* Lon L. Fuller, *The Case of the Speluncean Explorers*, 62 Harv. L. Rev. 66 (1949).

31   Lon. L. Fuller, The Morality of Law 3 (Revised ed. 1969) (1964).

32   Fuller, Chapter 12, note 77, at 630.

33   "At times [Hart] seemed to be saying that the distinction between law and morality is something that exists, and will continue to exist, however we may talk about it. It expresses a reality which, whether we like it or not, we must accept if we are to avoid talking nonsense. At other times, he seemed to be warning us that the reality of the distinction is itself in danger and that if we do not mend our ways of thinking and talking we may lose a 'precious moral ideal,' that of fidelity to law." *Id.* at 630-631.

34   *Id.* at 631.

35   "These were the perplexities I had about Professor Hart's argument when I first encountered it. But on reflection I am sure any criticism of his essay as being self-contradictory would be both unfair and unprofitable." *Id.*

36   *Id.*

37   *Id.*

38   *Id.*

39   *Id.*

40   *Id.* at 631-632.

41   *Id.* at 632.

42   *Id.*

43   H.L.A. Hart, *Positivism and the Separation of Law and Morals*, 71 Harv. L. Rev. 593, 598 (1958).

44   *Id.* at 599.

45   *Id.*

46 "It is now explicitly acknowledged on both sides that one of the chief issues
    is how we can best define and serve the ideal of fidelity to law. Law, as
    something deserving loyalty, must represent a human achievement; it cannot
    be a simple fiat of power or a repetitive pattern discernible in the behavior of
    state officials. The respect we owe to human laws must surely be something
    different from the respect we accord to the law of gravitation. If laws, even
    bad laws, have a claim to our respect, then law must represent some general
    direction of human effort that we can understand and describe, and that we
    can approve in principle even at the moment when it seems to us to miss its
    mark." Lon. L. Fuller, *Positivism and Fidelity to Law – A Reply to Professor
    Hart*, Chapter 12, note 77, at 632.

47 *Id.* at 644-645.

48 "What I have called 'the internal morality of law' seems to be almost
    completely neglected by Professor Hart. He does make *646 brief mention
    of 'justice in the administration of the law,' which consists in the like
    treatment of like cases, by whatever elevated or perverted standards the word
    'like' may be defined." *Id.* at 645-646 (footnote omitted).

49 Report of the Committee on Homosexual Offences and Prostitution (HMSQ,
    1957). Parliament enacted the substance of those recommendations 10 years
    later in the Sexual Offences Act 1967, § 1.

50 H.A. Hammelmann, *Committee on Homosexual Offences and Prostitution*,
    21 The Modern L. Rev. 68, 68 (1958).

51 J. Weeks, *Wolfenden, John Frederick*, Oxford Dictionary of National
    Biography *available at* https://doi.org/10.1093/ref:odnb/31852.

52 H. L. A. Hart, The Morality of Criminal Law (1965).

53 J. Paul McCutcheon, *Morality and the Criminal Law: Reflections on Hart-
    Devlin*, 47 Crim. L. Q., 15, 18-19 (2002).

54 Ronald M. Dworkin, *Lord Devlin and the Enforcement of Morals*, 75 Yale L.
    J. 986, 989 (1965-1966).

55 *Id.*

56 *Id.*

57 *Id.* In Chapter 14, we shall see such a series of arguments come before the
    U.S. Supreme Court twenty years later in a case called *Bowers v. Hardwick*,
    in which a Georgia man challenged the state's anti-sodomy laws after being
    arrested on suspicion of violating such laws with another consenting adult in
    his own home. *Bowers v. Hardwick*, 478 U.S. 186 (1986).

58 Dworkin, Chapter 13, note 54 at 989 (quoting Devlin, The Enforcement of
    Morals (Oxford University Press 1959). Reprinted in Devlin, The
    Enforcement of Morals 17 (Oxford University Press 1965)). *See also*
    Feinberg, Offense To Others *in* 2 The Moral Limits of The Criminal Law 1
    (Oxford University Press 1984) (discussing whether there are any human

experiences that are harmless in themselves yet so unpleasant that we can rightly demand legal protection from them even at the cost of other persons' liberties).

59   Peter Cane, *Taking Law Seriously: Starting Points of the Hart/Devlin Debate*, 10 The J. of Ethics, 21, 22 (2006) (footnotes omitted).

60   "Herbert Hart responded to Devlin, first in a radio broadcast subsequently published in The Listener magazine, and later in three lectures delivered at Stanford University in 1962 and subsequently published under the title *Law Liberty and Morality*." *Id.* (footnotes omitted) (emphasis in original).

61   *Id.* at 23 (footnotes omitted).

62   *Id.*

63   *Id.* "He also thought that the thesis placed an unjustified brake on changes in social mores." *Id.*

64   *Id.*

65   I still enjoy great affection for the late Professor Feinberg since he instilled in me a love of the study of philosophy while I was a freshman at Princeton University.

66   In "A Ride on the Bus," in order to determine, "whether there are any human experiences that are harmless in themselves yet so unpleasant that we can rightly demand legal protection from them even at the cost of other persons' liberties," Professor Feinberg posits 31 vividly sketched tales of a passenger on a crowded public bus and urges readers to "consider hypothetically the most offensive experiences we can imagine," including scenarios from the following six categories: (1) affronts to senses, (2)disgust and revulsion, (3)shock to moral, religious or patriotic sensibilities, (4) shame, embarrassment, and anxiety, (5) annoyance, boredom, frustration, and (6) fear, resentment, humiliation and anger. Joel Feinberg, Offense to Others, *in* 2 The Moral Limits of The Criminal Law 1, 10-13 (Oxford University Press 1984).

67   *Id.* at 1 (citing Feinberg, Harm To Others at ch 1, § 4).

68   *Id.* at 3.

69   *Id.*

70   *Id.*

71   Harms are wrongful because they restrict liberty as the autonomy of the person or the ability of the person to enjoy the range of available human phenomenal experiences. Offenses are wrongful for the same reason, in that they are of the same species of wrong as harm. The problem with either is in its liberty-restrictive harm, whether or not there is a normative difference in quality between the category of acts known as offense and the category of acts known as harm, is of no concern to the essential character of either. Thus,

his distinction is without difference. My affirmative case then is that I find that Feinberg here has committed an error in his categorization, for clearly offense is a lesser species of harm than pure physical harms, and that moral or paternalistic rules may have a limited role under the doctrine of necessity as other species of substantive harms to autonomy. The reasoning for this is because there is no meaningful or "real" distinction between the non-physical act of changing legal status, and the physical act of enforcing that status, with respect to an individual's daily life and expectation of the law's operation. Jerome Frank, Law And The Modern Mind 5-12, 42-47 (Brentano's Publishers, New York 1930) (discussing realism and the law per the 1920s movement); *see also* Karl N. Llewellyn, The Bramble Bush: On Our Law And Its Study 70-81 (Oceana Publications, New York 1951) (discussing "Ships and Shoes and Sealing Wax"). Harmful effects, are by and large the resultant interferences with a person's natural liberty to make choices. Harmful actions are the species of acts which interfere with a person's liberty to cause the resultant effects. The category of harmful actions certainly includes physical liberty-restricting harms, and non-physical harms roughly divided into categories of offense, legal paternalism, and so-called legal moralism.

72 "Professor H. L. A. Hart, responding to its appearance at the heart of the [Devlin's arguments], thought that it rested upon a confused conception of what a society is. If one holds anything like a conventional notion of a society, he said, it is absurd to suggest that every practice the society views as profoundly immoral and disgusting threatens its survival." Dworkin, Chapter 13, note 54, at 990 (footnote omitted).

73 *Brown v. Board of Education*, 347 U.S. 483 (1954).

74 *Poe v. Ullman*, 367 U.S. 497 (1961); *Griswold v. Connecticut*, 381 U.S. 479 (1965); *Roe v. Wade*, 410 U.S. 113 (1973).

75 *Katz v. United States*, 389 U.S. 347 (1967).

CHAPTER 14

1 Lysander Spooner, *No Treason: No. 1*, 7 (1867).

2 28 USC § 1346(b).

3 The Crown Proceedings Act of 1947 provided that, "[s]ubject to the provisions of [the] Act, the Crown Shall be subject to all those liabilities in tort to which, if it were a private person of full age and capacity, it would be subject:..." The Crown Proceedings Act 10 & 11 Geo. VI, c. 44., 1947, (ENG) (Part I).

4 *Shelley v. Kraemer*, 34 U.S. 1, 5 (1948).

5 *Id.* at 4.

6 *Id.* at 5.

7   *Id.* at 6.

8   *Id.* at 6.

9   In *West Coast Hotel Co. v. Parrish*, 300 U.S. 379 (1937), the Supreme Court upheld the constitutionality of a Washington State law establishing minimum wage law since it aimed to protect historically vulnerable groups. *Id.* at 399-400.

10 *Shelley v. Kraemer*, Chapter 14, note 4, at 13 (emphasis added).

11 *Id.*

12 For a discussion of *Plessy v. Ferguson, see* Chapter 12.

13 *Brown v. Board of Education*, 347 U.S. 483, 486 (1954) ("*Brown I*").

    "These cases come to us from the States of Kansas, South Carolina, Virginia, and Delaware. They are premised on different facts and different local conditions, but a common legal question justifies their consideration together in this consolidated opinion." *Id.* (footnote omitted).

14 *Id.* at 487.

15 *Id.* at 495.

16 *Id.*

17 *Brown v. Board of Education*, 349 U.S. 294, 757 (1955) (Warren, C.J.).

18 *Brown I*, Chapter 14, note 13, at 492. The Fourteenth Amendment, adopted in 1868 after the American Civil War, contained several provisions ranging from citizenship, representation, voting, and public debt, to due process, privileges and immunities, and equal protection. U.S. CONST. amend. XIV, §§ 1-5.

19 *Brown I*, Chapter 14, note 13, at 492-3.

20 Chief Justice Warren, speaking for the Court observed:

    Today, education is perhaps the most important function of state and local governments. Compulsory school attendance laws and the great expenditures for education both demonstrate our recognition of the importance of education to our democratic society. It is required in the performance of our most basic public responsibilities, even service in the armed forces. It is the very foundation of good citizenship. Today it is a principal instrument in awakening the child to cultural values, in preparing him for later professional training, and in helping him to adjust normally to his environment. In these days, it is doubtful that any child may reasonably be expected to succeed in life if he is denied the opportunity of an education. Such an opportunity, where the state has undertaken to provide it, is a right which must be made available to all on equal terms.

    Id. at 493.

21 *Id.*

22 Eric Pace, *Harry S. Ashmore, 81, Whose Editorials Supported Integration in Arkansas, Dies*, N. Y. Times, Jan. 22, 1998.

23 Edwin Meese III, *Law of the Constitution*, 61 Tul. L. Rev. 979, 986 fn 24 (1986-1987).

24 *Id.* at fn 24.

25 Pace, Chapter 14, note 22.

26 Telegram, President Dwight D. Eisenhower to Arkansas Governor Orval E. Faubus, Sep. 5, 1957 *available at*

https://www.eisenhower.archives.gov/research/online_documents/civil
_rights_little_rock/Press_release_DDE_telegram_to_Faubus.pdf

27 Pace, Chapter 14, note 22.

28 *Id.*

29 "An unsigned letter was sent to some business people in Little Rock saying that The [Arkansas] Gazette, in taking its anti segregation [sic] stand, was 'playing a leading role in destroying time-honored traditions that have made up our Southern way of life.'" *Id.*

30 *Brown I*, Chapter 14, note 13, at 494.

31 *Browder v. Gayle*, 142 F. Supp 707 (MD Ala 1956), aff'd *Gayle v. Browder*, 352 U.S. 903 (1956).

32 Robert P. George, *The 1993 St. Ives Lecture - Natural Law and Civil Rights: From Jefferson's "Letter to Henry Lee" to Martin Luther King's "Letter From Birmingham Jail,"* 43 Cath. U. L. Rev. 143, 154 (1994).

33 For examples of such injustices and the deep rooted practice of segregation, *see* David Benjamin Oppenheimer, *Martin Luther King, Walker v. City of Birmingham, and the Letter from a Birmingham Jail*, 26 U.C. Davis L. Rev. 791, 794- 797 (1993).

By local ordinance, restaurants in Birmingham were not permitted to serve both African Americans and whites... The ordinance similarly prohibited integrated drinking fountains, bathrooms, or dressing rooms... African Americans were not permitted to ride in taxies used by whites... Local law required completely separate rest room facilities for African Americans and whites, segregation of theaters and ball parks, racially divided jail cells, white or African American only hospitals and cemeteries, segregated hotels, and an absolute ban, subject to criminal penalties, on African Americans and whites together playing cards, checkers, or dice.

Id. (internal citations omitted).

34 *Id.* at 802-803.

35 *Id.* at 805.

36   *Id.* at 812 (citations omitted).

37   Robert P. George, *The 1993 St. Ives Lecture - Natural Law and Civil Rights: From Jefferson's "Letter to Henry Lee" to Martin Luther King's "Letter From Birmingham Jail,"* 43 Cath. U. L. Rev. 143, 155 (1994).

38   Letter from Martin Luther King, *Letter from Birmingham Jail* (Apr. 16 1963), *reprinted in* Christian Century 80 (June 12, 1963): 767, 769.

39   *Id.* (emphasis added).

40   Ronald J. Rychlak, *Natural Law from a Birmingham Jail,* Inside Catholic, Jan 17, 2011.

41   For instance, the Civil Rights Act of 1964 prohibited discriminatory use of literacy tests in voting (§ 101(a)(2)(C)), the desegregation of public facilities (Title III), and the desegregation of public education (Title IV). Some, however, point to the expansive definition of public accommodations in Title II of the Act as a potential incursion on private property and the rights of that property's owner(s). For instance, § 201(b) includes "any inn, hotel, motel, or other establishment that provides lodging to transient guests" with some size restrictions (§201(b)(1)), "any restaurant, cafeteria, lunchroom, lunch counter, soda fountain, or other facility principally engaged in selling food or consumption of the premises, included, but not limited to, any such facility located on the premises of any retail establishment or gasoline station" (§201(b)(2)), "any motion picture hose, theater, concert hall, sports arena, stadium or other place of exhibition entertainment" (§ 201(b)(3)). The Civil Rights Act of 1964, Pub. L. No. 88-352, 78 Stat. 241 (1964). While the legislature clearly felt such an exhaustive list of businesses and organizations necessary to protect the civil rights of African Americans in places where bigotry and hatred still guided the actions and attitudes of the people, the legislature also failed to consider some of the long-term ramifications of such broad government action. The Natural Law approach would likely apply such mandates to government-run institutions and allow racist and bigots to exclude and discriminate on their own property and to allow market forces to address those whose odious practices militate against the modes and practices of an enlightened society.

42   110 Cong. Rec. 14318 (1964) (statement of Sen. Barry Goldwater).

43   *Id.* at 14319.

44   *Id.*

45   He explained:

   I am unalterably opposed to discrimination or segregation on the basis of race, color, or creed, or on any other basis; not only my words, but more importantly my actions through the years have repeatedly demonstrated the sincerity of my feeling in this regard.

This is fundamentally a matter of the heart. The problems of discrimination can never be cured by laws alone; but I would be the first to agree that laws can help-laws carefully considered and weighed in an atmosphere of dispassion, in the absence of political demagogery, [sic] and in the light of fundamental constitutional principles.

Id. at 14318-14319.

46   *Id.* at 14319.

47   He argued:

If it is the wish of the American people that the Federal Government should be granted the power to regulate in these two areas and in the manner contemplated by this bill, then I say that the Constitution should be so amended by the people as to authorize such action in accordance with the procedures for amending the Constitution which that great document itself prescribes.

Id.

48   *Id.*

49   *Id.*

50   *Id.*

51   *Id* (emphasis added).

52   *Griswold v. Connecticut*, 381 U.S. 479, 480 (1965). (Douglas, J.).

53   *Id.* Incidentally, a few years earlier, the case *Poe v. Ullman*, 367 U.S. 497 (1961) saw a challenge to the same Connecticut contraception law. *Id.* at 507. However, in that case, those seeking invalidation of the state law had yet to suffer punishments for violating it. The Court discussed notions of "ripeness" and explained various court doctrines such as "standing." *Id.* 504.

54   *Id.* at 482.

55   *Id.*

56   *Id.* at 483 (quoting *NAACP v. Alabama*, 357 U.S. 499, 462 (1958)).

57   *Id.*

58   *Id.* at 484, signaling, broadly, and self-referentially, *Poe v. Ullman* at 516-522 (Douglas, J. *dissenting*).

59   *Id.* at 484 (Douglas, J.).

60   *Id.* at 486.

61   *Id.* at 486-487 (Goldberg, J., *concurring*) (footnote omitted).

62   *Id.* at 486-487.

63   *Id.* at 488 (emphasis added).

64   *Id.* at 488-489 (footnotes omitted).

65 *Id.* at 490 (footnote omitted).

66 *Id.* (footnote omitted). Specifically, Justice Goldberg noted that the Supreme Court only had occasion to opine on the Ninth Amendment in three prior cases, none of which offered much help. Without any precedent to guide the Court, Goldberg turned to the original understanding of the Founders.

67 *Id.* at 491 (Goldberg, J., *concurring*).

68 *Id.*

69 *Id.* Natural Law recognizes the mutable nature of the human condition— social life in 400 A.D. bears little resemblance to 2018 A.D. Accordingly, precedent such as *Griswold* could be saved because a married couple's decision to use birth control, which has just been invented, relates to a mutable characteristic that touches on privacy. Mistakes as to mutable or immutable nature of characteristics are, if anything obviously endemic to the human condition. These mistakes tend to get weeded out over time, and thus the common law via *jurisprudence constante* is the best, if an imperfect, answer.

70 Such an application would be superfluous.

71 *Id.* at 492 (Goldberg, J., concurring).

72 *Id.* at 492-493 (emphasis added).

73 *Id.* at 493. Incidentally, Justice Black, a longtime opponent of natural-law jurisprudence, vehemently dissented in this case. He wrote, "I cannot rely on the due process clause or the Ninth Amendment or any mysterious and uncertain natural law concept." *Id.* at 522 (Black, J. *dissenting*). He rejected such doctrines, "based on subjective considerations of 'natural justice,'" even if he approved of the policy ends which they served.

74 *Loving v. Virginia*, 388 U.S. 1 (1967).

75 *Id.* at 2.

76 Douglas Martin, *Mildred Loving, Who Battled Ban on Mix-Race Marriage, Dies at 68*, N. Y. Times, May 6, 2008.

77 *Id.*

78 *Id.*

79 *Id.*

80 *Loving* at 3.

81 *Id.*

82 *Id.*

83 *Id.* at 10 (citations omitted).

84 *Id.* at 11.

85 *Id.* at 12.

86   *Bowers v. Hardwick*, 478 U.S. 186, 187-188 (1986).

87   He wrote:

This case does not require a judgment on whether laws against sodomy between consenting adults in general, or between homosexuals in particular, are wise or desirable. It raises no question about the right or propriety of state legislative decisions to repeal their laws that criminalize homosexual sodomy, or of state court decisions invalidating those laws on state constitutional grounds. The issue presented is whether the Federal Constitution confers a fundamental right upon homosexuals to engage in sodomy and hence invalidates the laws of the many States that still make such conduct illegal and have done so for a very long time. The case also calls for some judgment about the limits of the Court's role in carrying out its constitutional mandate.

Id. at 190.

88   Take, for instance, this passage:

Precedent aside, however, respondent would have us announce, as the Court of Appeals did, a fundamental right to engage in homosexual sodomy. This we are quite unwilling to do. It is true that despite the language of the Due Process Clauses of the Fifth and Fourteenth Amendments, which appears to focus only on the processes by which life, liberty, or property is taken, the cases are legion in which those Clauses have been interpreted to have substantive content, subsuming rights that to a great extent are immune from federal or state regulation or proscription. Among such cases are those recognizing rights that have little or no textual support in the constitutional language. *Meyer*, *Prince*, and *Pierce* fall in this category, as do the privacy cases from *Griswold* to *Carey*.

Id. at 191.

89   The Court observed:

Striving to assure itself and the public that announcing rights not readily identifiable in the Constitution's text involves much more than the imposition of the Justices' own choice of values on the States and the Federal Government, the Court has sought to identify the nature of the rights qualifying for heightened judicial protection.

Id.

90   *Id.* at 192 (footnote omitted).

91   *Id.* at 192-193 (footnote omitted).

92   *Id.* at 193-194 (footnote omitted).

93   *Id.* at 194.

94   *Id.* at 194.

95   In the context of the Fourth Amendment, Justice Brandeis argued that the
     Constitution conferred as against the government a right to privacy:

> The makers of our Constitution undertook to secure conditions favorable
> to the pursuit of happiness. They recognized the significance of man's
> spiritual nature, of his feelings, and of his intellect. They knew that only
> a part of the pain, pleasure and satisfactions of life are to be found in
> material things. They sought to protect Americans in their beliefs, their
> thoughts, their emotions and their sensations. *They conferred, as against
> the Government, the right to be let alone—the most comprehensive of
> rights, and the right most valued by civilized men.* To protect that right,
> every unjustifiable intrusion by the Government upon the privacy of the
> individual, whatever the means employed, must be deemed a violation
> of the Fourth Amendment.

> *Olmstead v. United States*, 277 U.S. 438, 478 (1928) (Brandeis, J., *dissenting*)
> (emphasis added).

96   *Bowers* at 195. Specifically, the Court address the matter of *Stanley v.
     Georgia* in which a man who had been arrested for suspicion of gambling
     was later tried for possession of obscene materials when police discovered
     and then reviewed a few reels of pornographic material they had found in a
     drawer. *Stanley v. Georgia*, 394 U.S. 557 (1969). Eventually, the Court found
     that the First Amendment and Fourteenth Amendments rendered such state
     laws inval*id. Id.*

97   *Bowers* at 195-196 (footnote omitted).

98   *Id.* at 196 (footnote omitted). Interestingly enough, the court drops an
     illuminating footnote:

> John and Mary Doe were also plaintiffs in the action. They alleged that
> they wished to engage in sexual activity proscribed by § 16–6–2 in the
> privacy of their home, App. 3, and that they had been "chilled and
> deterred" from engaging in such activity by both the existence of the
> statute and Hardwick's arrest. *Id.* at 5. The District Court held, however,
> that because they had neither sustained, nor were in immediate danger
> of sustaining, any direct injury from the enforcement of the statute, they
> did not have proper standing to maintain the action. *Id.* at 18. The Court
> of Appeals affirmed the District Court's judgment dismissing the Does'
> claim for lack of standing, 760 F.2d 1202, 1206–1207 (CA11 1985), and
> the Does do not challenge that holding in this Court.

> The only claim properly before the Court, therefore, is Hardwick's challenge
> to the Georgia statute as applied to consensual homosexual sodomy. We
> express no opinion on the constitutionality of the Georgia statute as applied
> to other acts of sodomy.

> *Id.* at fn. 2. The dissent, penned by Justice Blackmun in which he was joined
> by Justices Brennan, Marshall, and Stevens, criticizes the Court's opinion:

First, the Court's almost obsessive focus on homosexual activity is particularly hard to justify in light of the broad language Georgia has used. Unlike the Court, the Georgia Legislature has not proceeded on the assumption that homosexuals are so different from other citizens that their lives may be controlled in a way that would not be tolerated if it limited the choices of those other citizens. ... The sex or status of the persons who engage in the act is irrelevant as a matter of state law. In fact, to the extent I can discern a legislative purpose for Georgia's 1968 enactment of § 16-6-2, that purpose seems to have been to broaden the coverage of the law to reach heterosexual as well as homosexual activity. I therefore see no basis for the Court's decision to treat this case as an "as applied" challenge to § 16-6-2, [...] or for Georgia's attempt, both in its brief and at oral argument, to defend § 16-6-2 solely on the grounds that it prohibits homosexual activity. Michael Hardwick's standing may rest in significant part on Georgia's apparent willingness to enforce against homosexuals a law it seems not to have any desire to enforce against heterosexuals. [...] But his claim that § 16-6-2 involves an unconstitutional intrusion into his privacy and his right of intimate association does not depend in any way on his sexual orientation.

Id. at 200-201 (Blackmun, J. *dissenting*) (footnote omitted).

99 The Supreme Court wrote:

Even if the conduct at issue here is not a fundamental right, respondent asserts that there must be a rational basis for the law and that there is none in this case other than the presumed belief of a majority of the electorate in Georgia that homosexual sodomy is immoral and unacceptable. This is said to be an inadequate rationale to support the law. The law, however, is constantly based on notions of morality, and if all laws representing essentially moral choices are to be invalidated under the Due Process Clause, the courts will be very busy indeed. Even respondent makes no such claim, but insists that majority sentiments about the morality of homosexuality should be declared inadequate. We do not agree, and are unpersuaded that the sodomy laws of some 25 States should be invalidated on this basis.

Bowers v. Hardwick, at 196 (footnote omitted).

100 *Lawrence v. Texas*, 539 U.S. 558, 567 (2003).

101 Laurence H. Tribe, *Lawrence v. Texas: The "Fundamental Right" That Dare Not Speak Its Name*, 117 Harv. L. Rev. 1893, 1922–23 (2004) (internal citations omitted).

102 *Lawrence v. Texas*, 539 U.S. 558, 571 (2003).

103 *Id.* at 571-72 (2003) (Kennedy, J., *concurring*) (internal citations omitted). Justice Kennedy could have placed "natural" in front of "liberty."

104 *Gonzales v. Raich*, 545 U.S. 1, 1 (2005) (syllabus).

105 *Id.* at 18.

106 *Id.* at 18-19.

107 The Court observed:

In *Wickard*, we had no difficulty concluding that Congress had a rational basis for believing that, when viewed in the aggregate, leaving home-consumed wheat outside the regulatory scheme would have a substantial influence on price and market conditions. Here too, Congress had a rational basis for concluding that leaving home-consumed marijuana outside federal control would similarly affect price and market conditions.

Id. at 19.

108 *Id.*

109 *Id.* at 22 (citations omitted).

110 *Id.* at 57-58 (Thomas, J. *dissenting*).

111 *Gonzales v. Raich*, 545 U.S. 1, 69 (Thomas, J. *dissenting*) (citing, The Federalist No. 45 (James Madison).

112 *Raich* at 58 (Thomas, J. *dissenting*).

113 *Id.* at 60 (Thomas, J. *dissenting*) (citing *McCulloch v. Maryland*, at 419-421; James Madison Madison, The Bank Bill, House of Representatives (Feb. 2, 1791), in 3 The Founders' Constitution 244 (P. Kurland & R. Lerner eds., 1987) (requiring "direct" rather than "remote" means-end fit); Alexander Hamilton, *Opinion on the Constitutionality of the Bank* (Feb. 23, 1791), in *id.* at 248, 250 (requiring "obvious" means-end fit, where the end was "clearly comprehended within any of the specified powers" of Congress).

114 *Kelo v. New London*, 545 U.S. 469, 469-475 (2005).

115 *Id.* at 475.

116 U.S. CONST. amend. V.

117 *Kelo* at 472.

118 *Id.* at 483.

119 *Id.* at 486-7.

120 *Id.* at 488-489.

121 *Id.* at 489-490.

122 *Id.* at 490.

123 *Id.* at 503 (O'Connor, J., *dissenting*).

124 This, of course, almost always failed to be the case when members of a more technologically, immunologically, or militaristically advanced society

encountered lands previously unknown to them that were already, inconveniently, occupied by others.

125 For a more thorough discussion on Jefferson's views of property, see Chapter 17. Incidentally, Eminent Domain also runs contrary to Professor Murray Rothbard's Non-Aggression Principle, discussed in Chapter 16.

CHAPTER 15

1 Lysander Spooner, Natural Law; or the Science of Justice: A Treatise on Natural Law, Natural Justice, Natural Rights, Natural Liberty, and Natural Society; showing that all Legislation whatsoever is an Absurdity, a Usurpation, and a Crime. Part First, 11 (1882) *available at* https://oll.libertyfund.org/titles/spooner-natural-law-or-the-scienceof-justice-1882.

2 *See* Andrew P. Napolitano, The Constitution In Exile 7 (2006).

3 U.S. CONST. article I, section 2, clause 3 ("Representatives and direct Taxes shall be apportioned among the several States which may be included within this Union, according to their respective Numbers, which shall be determined by adding to the whole Number of free Persons, including those bound to Service for a Term of Years, and excluding Indians not taxed, three fifths of all other Persons.").

4 Regarding this debate, Madison wrote in *Federalist 54*, "We must deny the fact, that slaves are considered merely as property, and in no respect whatever as persons. The true state of the case is, that they partake of both these qualities: being considered by our laws, in some respects, as persons, and in other respects as property." James Madison, Federalist 54, New York (February 12, 1788).

5 U.S. Const. article IV, section 2, clause 3 ("No person held to service or labour in one state, under the laws thereof, escaping into another, shall, in consequence of any law or regulation therein, be discharged from such service or labor, but shall be delivered up on claim of the party to whom such service or labour may be due.").

6 U.S. Const. article I, section 9, clause 1 ("The Migration or Importation of such Persons as any of the States now existing shall think proper to admit, shall not be prohibited by the Congress prior to the Year one thousand eight hundred and eight, but a Tax or duty may be imposed on such Importation, not exceeding ten dollars for each Person.")

7 U.S. Const. article V ("[N]o Amendment which may be made prior to the Year One thousand eight hundred and eight shall in any Manner affect the first and fourth Clauses in the Ninth Section of the first Article....").

8 James Madison, 2 The Debates In The Federal Convention of 1787 Which Framed The Constitution of The United States of America, *KS needs page

number in physical book for August 22, 1787 (Gaillard Hunt & James Brown Scott eds., Prometheus Books 1987) (1902).

9   *Id.*

10   Aristotle, Politics, Book I, 1254b 16–21.

11   *Id.*

12   Marquette Law Review, *Legal Philosophers: Aristotle, Aquinas and Kant on Human Rights*, 55 Marq. L. Rev. 264, 269 (1972); *See also* Aristotle, Politics, Book I, 4–7, 1253b 23–1255b 40.

13   Marquette Law Review, *Legal Philosophers: Aristotle, Aquinas and Kant on Human Rights*, 55 Marq. L. Rev. 264, 269(1972) (citing Aristotle, Politics, "For that some should rule and others be ruled is a thing not only necessary, but expedient; from the hour of their birth, some are marked out for subjection, others for rule...").

14   *Id.*

15   *Id.* at 270.

16   *Id.* at 269 (citing M. Hamburger, Morals And The Law: The Growth of Aristotle's Legal Theory 135 (1951)).

17   *Augustine, The City of God, 19:15.*

18   *Id.*

19   *Id.*

20   *St. Thomas Aquinas, Summa Theologica, I QQ LXXV.*CII. Vol. 4 (Treatise on Man)* (1256). In particular, Aquinas poses the question "Whether in the state of innocence man would have been master over man?" and answers, "The condition of man in the state of innocence was not more exalted than the condition of the angels. But among the angels some rule over others; and so one order is called that of *Dominations.* Therefore it was not beneath the dignity of the state of innocence that one man should be subject to another." *Id.*

21   *St. Thomas Aquinas, Summa Contra Gentiles* *KS needs to get physical copy of this book for page number.

22   *St. Thomas Aquinas, Summa Theologica, II QQ LVIII.* Vol. 4 (1256).

23   Heinrich Rommen, The Natural Law: A Study In Legal And Social History And Philosophy xxiii (Thomas R. Hanley, trans.) (1936) (Indianapolis: Liberty Fund 1998).

24   Tierney, Chapter 1, note 82, at 272 (1997).

25   Paolo G. Carozza, *"They are our brothers, and Christ gave His life for them": The Catholic Tradition and the Idea of Human Rights in Latin America,* 6 Logos: A J. Catholic Thought & Culture 81, 86 (2003).

26   *Id.*

27   *Id.*

28   Lewis Hanke, All Mankind Is One: A Study of The Disputation Between Bartolome De Las Casas And Juan Gines De Sepulveda In 1550 On The Religious And Intellectual Capacity of The American Indians, 67 (1974).

29   *Id.*

30   Ángel Losada, *The Controversy between Sepulveda and Las Casas in the Junta of Vallodolid*, reprinted in Juan Friede and Benjamin Keen, Bartolomé De Las Casas In History: Toward An Understanding of His Work (De Kalb, 111.: Northern Illinois Univ., 1971), 279-309.

31   Tierney, Chapter 1, note 82, at 272-273 (footnote omitted).

32   Henry Raup Wagner, The Life And Writings of Bartolomé De Las Casas, 178–79 (1967).

33   Hanke, Chapter 15, note 28, at 82-90.

34   *Id.* at 77 (footnote omitted).

35   Carozza, Chapter 15, note 25, at 89-90.

36   *Id.* at 89.

37   HANKE, Chapter 15, note 28, at 76.

38   Carozza, Chapter 15, note 25, at 90.

39   *Id.*

40   Mary Ann Glendon, *The Forgotten Crucible: The Latin American Influence on the Universal Human Rights Idea*, 16 Harv. Hum. Rts. J.

27, 33 (2003) (citing Brian Tierney, The Idea of Natural Rights: Studies On Natural Rights, Natural Law And Church Law 1150-1625, at 276 (1997)).

Hugo Grotius, *The Rights of War And Peace (2005 ed.) 3 vols.* [1625] (II.XXII.xii) "Nor is it less unjust to go to War, and lay Claim to a Place upon the Score of making the first Discovery of it, if already inhabited, tho' the Possessor should be a wicked Man, or have false Notions of GOD, or be of a stupid Mind; because by the Right of Discovery we can pretend to those Places only which are not appropriated." *Id.*

41   Hugo Grotius, *The Rights of War And Peace (2005 ed.) 3 vols.* [1625] (II. XXII.ix).

42   *Id.* AT (II. XXVII. i.).

44   Locke, Chapter 1, note 133, at 240.

45   *Id.*

46   1 William Blackstone, Commentaries *423.

47   *Id.*

48   *Id.* (*eo instanti*, at that moment).

49   *Id.* at *421.

50   Letter from Thomas Jefferson to Thomas Cooper (September 10, 1814) *Founders Online*, National Archives, *available at* https://founders.archives.gov/documents/Jefferson/03-07-02-0471.

51   Letter from Thomas Jefferson to William Short (September 8, 1823) *Founders Online*, National Archives, *available at* https://founders.archives.gov/documents/Jefferson/98-01-02-3750.

52   Thomas Jefferson, Notes On The State of Virginia (Boston: Lilly and Wait, 1832), 170 (emphasis added).

53   *Id.*

54   *Id.* Yet, elsewhere in his same *Notes on Virginia*, Jefferson opined that blacks "are inferior to whites in the endowments both of body and mind." Jefferson, *Notes on Virginia, Query XIV, 143.*

55   A Bill concerning Slaves, June 18, 1779, in The Papers of Thomas Jefferson: Retirement Series, Volume 2, pg. 470-73.

56   Thomas Jefferson, Autobiography, January 6- July 29, 1821. Peterson, ed., *Writings*, 44.

57   *Id.*

58   Letter from Thomas Jefferson to John Holmes (April 22, 1820) *available at* https://www.loc.gov/exhibits/jefferson/159.html.

59   *Id.*

60   Lysander Spooner, *The Unconstitutionality of Slavery, 117* (1860) *available at https://oll.libertyfund.org/titles/spooner-theunconstitutionality-of-slavery-1860.*

61   *Id.*

62   *Id.*

63   *Ogden v. Saunders*, 25 U.S. 213, 332 (1827).

64   Lysander Spooner, *The Unconstitutionality of Slavery* at **68.**

65   Lysander Spooner, *No Treason: No. 1*, 7 (1867).

66   Lysander Spooner, *Natural Law; or the Science of Justice: A Treatise on Natural Law, Natural Justice, Natural Rights, Natural Liberty, and Natural Society; showing that all Legislation whatsoever is an Absurdity, a Usurpation, and a Crime.* Part First, X (1882) *available at* https://oll.libertyfund.org/titles/spooner-natural-law-or-the-scienceof-justice-1882.

67   Spooner ran a front page ad in the New York Daily Tribune announcing the creation of the company: "The Company design also (if sustained by the

public) is to thoroughly agitate the questions, and test the Constitutional right of the competition in the business of carrying letters - the ground on which they assert this right are published and for sale at the post offices in pamphlet form." Michael Billy, *Lysander Spooner and the United States Postal Monopoly*, Apr. 18, 2009 *available at* http://www.digitaljournal.com/article/271139.

68 Lysander Spooner, *The Unconstitutionality of the Laws of Congress, prohibiting Private Mails* (1844). Some things never change.

69 Christina M. Bates, *From 34 Cents to 37 Cents: The Unconstitutionality of the Postal Monopoly*, 68 Mo. L. Rev., 132 (2003).

70 *Id.* at 137.

71 *Id.*

72 *Id.* at 137-138.

73 *Id.* at 132.

74 David Reynolds, *Worse Than 'Dred Scott*,' The Wall Street Journal, Aug. 8-9, 2015.

75 *Id.*

76 *The Antelope*, 23 U.S. 66, 120-121 (1825). [77] *Id.*

78 *Id.* at 102-103.

79 *Id.* at 121-122.

80 In addition to being a Justice of the Supreme Court, Story was a great legal scholar, and in his capacity as a Professor at Harvard Law School, he authored *Commentaries on the Constitution. See* Joseph Story, Commentaries On The Constitution of The United States: With A Preliminary Review Of The Constitutional History of The Colonies And States, Before The Adoption of The Constitution (Hillard, Gray & Co. 1833).

81 Christopher L.M. Eisgruber, *Justice Story, Slavery, and the Natural Law Foundations of American Constitutionalism*, 55 U. Chi. L. Rev. 273, 318 (1988).

82 *United States v. La Jeune Eugenie*, 26 F. Cas. 832, 846 (C.C.D. Mass. 1822) (No. 15,551).

83 *Id.*

84 *Id.* In comparison, Justice Story was willing to enforce the Fugitive Slave Law of 1793 in *Prigg v. Pennsylvania*, despite his view, articulated here, that slavery was unjust. 41 U.S. 539 (1842).

85 *United States v. La Jeune Eugenie*, 26 F. Cas. 832, 845-848 (C.C.D. Mass. 1822) (No. 15,551).

86 *Id.* at 846.

87   *The Amistad*, 40 U.S. 518, 524 (1841).

88   Article 9 of this treaty holds that "all ships and merchandises of what nature soever, which shall be rescued out of the hands of pirates or robbers on the high seas, ... shall be restored, entire, to the true proprietor."

89   Argument of John Quincy Adams Before the Supreme Court of the United States in the case of the United States, Appellants, vs. Cinque, and others, Africans, captured in the schooner *Amistad*, by Lieut. Gedney, Delivered on the 24th of February and 1st of March 1841, page 10 *available at* https://avalon.law.yale.edu/19th_century/amistad_002.asp

90   *Id.* at 9.

91   *Id.* at 82.

92   *Id.* at 126.

93   *The Amistad*, 40 U.S. 518, 553 (1841).

94   *Id.*

95   *Id.*

96   *Dred Scott v. Sandford*, Chapter 11, note 73. It is not the province of the court to decide upon the justice or injustice, the policy or impolicy, of these laws. The decision of that question belonged to the political or law-making power; to those who formed the sovereignty and framed the Constitution. The duty of the court is, to interpret the instrument they have framed, with the best lights we can obtain on the subject, and to administer it as we find it, according to its true intent and meaning when it was adopted.

     Id. at 405.

97   Roberta Alexander, *Dred Scott: The Decision that Sparked a Civil War*, 34 N. Ky. L. Rev. 643, 644 (2007). Notwithstanding this federal sounding name, this was a Missouri state trial court. Dred Scott sued under an 1824 Missouri law, which read: " [i]t shall be lawful for any person held in slavery to petition the circuit court, or the judge thereof in vacation, praying that such person may be permitted to sue as a poor person, and stating the ground upon which his or her calm to freedom is founded." An Act To Enable Persons Held In Slavery To Sue For Their Freedom (Dec. 30, 1824), Mo. Rev. Stat. 404-406 (1825).

98   *Dred Scott v. Sandford*, Chapter 11, note 73, at 394.

99   Roberta Alexander, *Dred Scott: The Decision that Sparked a Civil War*, 34 N. Ky. L. Rev. 651-652 (2007).

100 For even further discussion, *see* Andrew P. Napolitano, Dred Scott's Revenge: A Legal History of Race And Freedom In America, 57-67 (2009) (arguing that because *Dred Scott v. Sandford* constitutionalized the status of blacks in the United States as nonpersons presaged the maltreatment of blacks by all levels of government in the following 150 years).

101 Taney wrote:

> [The Declaration of Independence] then proceeds to say: "We hold these truths to be self-evident: that all men are created equal; that they are endowed by their Creator with certain unalienable rights; that among them is life, liberty, and the pursuit of happiness; that to secure these rights, Governments are instituted, deriving their just powers from the consent of the governed."

> The general words above quoted would seem to embrace the whole human family, and if they were used in a similar instrument at this day would be so understood. But it is too clear for dispute, that the enslaved African race were not intended to be included, and formed no part of the people who framed and adopted this declaration; for if the language, as understood in that day, would embrace them, the conduct of the distinguished men who framed the Declaration of Independence would have been utterly and flagrantly inconsistent with the principles they asserted; and instead of the sympathy of mankind, to which they so confidently appealed, they would have deserved and received universal rebuke and reprobation. *Dred Scott v. Sandford*, Chapter 11, note 73, at 410.

102 In fact, the Supreme Court had rejected such a focus on original public understanding in 1825 in the case *Bank of United States v. Halstead. Bank of United States v. Halstead*, 23 U.S. 51 (1825). The Supreme Court, in *Halstead*, analyzed the All Writs Act (AWA), a section of the Judiciary Act of 1789 that permitted Courts to issue various writs, and in doing so, relied on the common law to reason through the issue. It held that the AWA "doubtless embraces writs sanctioned by the principles and usages of the common law." *Halstead* at 56. With respect to writs of execution, it "would be too limited a construction … to restrict [them] to such only as were authorized by the common law" since "[i]t was well known to Congress, that there were in use in the State Courts, writs of execution, other than such as were comfortable to the usages of the common law." *Id.* at 56. Justice Thompson believed "it is reasonable to conclude, that such were intended to be included under the general description of writs agreeable to the principles and usages of law" and that if Congress had "intended to restrict the power to common law writs" it probably would have imposed such limitations. *Id.* Justice Thompson, and through him, the Supreme Court, placed tremendous confidence in the ability of the Congress to legislate. Justice Thompson takes a tremendous step away from what would later be called a strict constructionist approach by eschewing any notion of the original public understanding of a writ of execution by attributing to Congress the prescience and foresight to write what he believes to be a flexible statute. He wrote: To limit the operation of an execution now, to that which it would have had in the year 1789, would open a door to many and great inconveniencies, which Congress seems to have foreseen, and to have guarded against, by giving ample powers to the Courts, so to mould [sic] their process, as to meet

whatever changes might take place. *Id.* at 62. Justice Thompson appears to find the notion that the meaning of the words of a statute are frozen in time would "open a door to many and great inconveniences," and, accordingly, holds that the AWA allows the Courts great range in the issuance of writs. *Id.* at 645. This holding, however, is unsurprising since a contrary holding would have greatly restricted the powers of the courts to operate. As was later expressed by the Court, "[t]he result of [the Delegation Doctrine], as practically expounded or applied in the case of the *Bank of the United States v. Halstead*, is, that the courts may, by their rules, not only alter the forms, but the effect and operation of the process, whether mesne or final, and the modes of proceeding under it; so that it may reach property not liable, in 1789, by the state laws to be taken in execution, or may exempt property, which was not then exempted, but has been exempted by subsequent state laws." *Beers v. Haughton*, 34 U.S. 329, 360 (1835). *Beers* involved an inquiry into an Ohio law in 1828, at the time of the passage an act on May 19, 1828, of which § 3 focusses on freezing the "writs of execution and other final process issued on judgments and decrees" in courts—other than those of equity—unless or until the respective state legislatures adopt new rules. Act of May 19, 1828 quoted in 4 Stat. 278-81 (Richard Peters ed., 1846) (to further regulate processes in the courts of the United States). See also *Fink v. O'Neil*, 106 U.S. 272, 278-279 (1882) for a discussion of *Beers* and the 1828 Process Act.

CHAPTER 16

1   Robert Nozick, Anarchy, State, And Utopia, ix, (Basic Books 2013) (1974).

A position also advanced by Robert Nozick in posing the initial question of his book, *Anarchy, State, and Utopia*, "[i]f the state did not exist would it be necessary to invent it?" *Id.* at 3; *id.* at chs. 1-2. However, Nozick relies on an account of invisible hand explanations to underlie his account (in the absence of a social compact per Locke), *id.* at 18-22, whereas your author relies on a cognitivist account of human nature and the ability to see non-instrumental reasons to realize the benefits of Natural Laws, such as self-ownership.

2   In a 1990 Preface to a revised edition of the book, Rawls points to his original preface in which explained that he "wanted to work out a conception of justice that provides a reasonably systematic alternative to utilitarianism, which[,]" he goes on to claim, "in one form or another has long dominated the Anglo-Saxon tradition of political thought." John Rawls, A Theory of Justice Revised Edition, xi (1990) (1999) [hereinafter Atoj]. In 1990, Rawls still maintained "that utilitarianism [could not] provide a satisfactory account of the basic rights and liberties of citizens as free and equal persons, a requirement of absolutely first importance for an account of democratic institutions." *Id.* at XII. He explained that he had "attempted to […]

generalize and carry to a higher order of abstraction the traditional theory of the social contract as represented by Locke, Rousseau, and Kant." *Id.* at xviii.

3   Douglas Martin, *John Rawls, Theorist on Justice, Is Dead at 82*, N.Y. Times (Nov. 26, 2002).

4   *Id.*

5   "Justice is the first virtue of social institutions, as truth is of systems of thought." Atoj at 3.

6   Rawls argues "laws and institutions no matter how efficient and well arranged must be reformed or abolished if they are unjust." *Id.*

7   Rawls theorized:

"Each person possesses an inviolability founded on justice that even the welfare of society as a whole cannot override. For this reason justice denies that the loss of freedom for some is made right by a greater good shared by others. It does not allow that the sacrifices imposed on a few are outweighed by the larger sum of advantages enjoyed by many." *Id.*

8   "The only thing that permits us to acquiesce in an erroneous theory is the lack of a better one; analogously, an injustice is tolerable only when it is necessary to avoid an even greater injustice." *Id.* at 4.

9   *Id.* at 5. "Men disagree about which principles should define the basic terms of their association. Yet we may still say, despite this disagreement, that they each have a conception of justice. That is, they understand the need for, and they are prepared to affirm, a characteristic set of principles for assigning basic rights and duties and for determining what they take to be the proper distribution of the benefits and burdens of social cooperation." *Id.*

10   *Id.* at 6.

11   *Id.* at 6-7.

12   *Id.* at 7.

13   *Id.* at 11.

14   *Id.* at 10-12.

15   *Id.* at 266.

16   *Id.* at 266.

17   *Id.* at 273 (footnote omitted).

18   *Id.*

19   *Id.* at 274-275.

20   *Id.* at 275.

21   *Professor Robert Nozick*, The Telegraph, Jan. 28, 2002.

22   "The fundamental question of political philosophy, one that precedes questions about how the state should be organized, is whether there should be any state at all." Nozick, Chapter 16, note 1, at 4.

23   *Id.* at 5.

24   *Id.*

25   *Id.* at 7

26   Lee J. Strang, *Originalism and Legitimacy*, 11 Kan. J. L. & Pub. Pol'y 657, 666 (2002) *signaling* Robert Nozick, Anarchy, State, And Utopia at ix (Basic Books, Inc. 1974).

27   Nozick, Chapter 16, note 1, at 149.

28   *Id.*

29   Nozick used the metaphor of children wanting pie to criticize Rawls:

The term "distributive justice" is not a neutral one. Hearing the term "distribution," most people presume that some thing or mechanism uses some principle or criterion to give out a supply of things. Into this process of distributing shares some error may have crept. So it is an open question, at least, whether redistribution should take place; whether we should do again what has already been done once, though poorly. However, we are not in the position of children who have been given portions of pie by someone who now makes last minute adjustments to rectify careless cutting.

Id. However, Nozick later praised Rawls:

A Theory of Justice is a powerful, deep, subtle, wide-ranging, systematic work in political and moral philosophy which has not seen its like since the writings of John Stuart Mill, if then. It is a fountain of illuminating ideas, integrated together into a lovely whole. Political philosophers now must either work within Rawls' theory or explain why not. The considerations and distinctions we have developed are illuminated by, and help illuminate, Rawls' masterful presentation of an alternative conception. Even those who remain unconvinced after wrestling with Rawls' systematic vision will learn much from closely studying it. I do not speak only of the Millian sharpening of one's views in combating (what one takes to be) error. It is impossible to read Rawls' book without incorporating much, perhaps transmuted, into one's own deepened view. And it is impossible to finish his book without a new and inspiring vision of what a moral theory may attempt to do and unite; of how beautiful a whole theory can be.

Id. at 183 (footnote omitted).

30   *Id.* at 149.

31   *Id.* at 151.

32   Letter from Thomas Jefferson to Thomas Earle (Sept. 24, 1823) *available at* https://founders.archives.gov/documents/Jefferson/98-0102-3770.

33   *Id.*

34   "[T]he first foundations of the social compact would be broken up were we definitively to refuse to its members the protection of their persons and property, while in their lawful pursuits." Letter from Thomas Jefferson to James Maury (Apr. 25, 1812) *available at* https://founders. archives.gov /documents/Jefferson/03-04-02-0551.

35   The unattributed quote of Blackstone is from *Commentaries on the Laws of England* (Oxford: Clarendon Press, 1765-1769), II:2. Blackstone had written, "The right of property; or that sole and despotic dominion which one man claims and exercises over the external things of the world, in total exclusion of the right of any other individual in the universe."

36   Madison, "Property," in Papers of James Madison, 14:266 (March 29, 1792).

37   Nozick, Chapter 16, note 1, at 185.

38   *Id.*

39   *Id.*

40   *See, e.g.*, Randy Barnett, Restoring The Lost Constitution (2004), at ch. 1; Joseph Raz, Between Authority And Interpretation: On The Theory of Law And Practical Reason 334 (Oxford University Press 2009).

41   Raz, Chapter 16, note 41, at 334.

42   Full disclosure, your author has lauded this work publicly and intends to continue to do so.

43   "[C]onsent must be real, not fictional—unanimous, not majoritarian. Anything less than *unanimous consent* simply cannot bind nonconsenting persons." Barnett, Restoring The Lost Constitution, Chapter 16, note 41, at 11 (emphasis added).

44   *Id.* at 21.

45   Tacit consent theories nearly all basically argue that those born into a society governed by certain rules and customs expresses their tacit consent to those rules and customs by staying within that jurisdiction.

46   Barnett, Restoring The Lost Constitution, Chapter 16, note 41, at 15.

47   *Id.* at 16.

48   *Id.*

49   *Id.*

50   *Id.* at 17.

51   *Id.* at 19.

52   *Id.*

53 *Id.* at 20.

54 *Id.* at 21.

55 *Id.* at 11 (quoting Edmund S. Morgan, Inventing The People: The Rise of Popular Sovereignty In England And America 13-14 (1988)).

57 Barnett, Restoring The Lost Constitution, Chapter 16, note 41, at 22-23; *see also* Raz, Chapter 16, note 41, at 334 ("Not only is it a mistake to identify constitutions with rules of recognition, but the rules of recognition do not play the legitimating role that constitutions can play."). Raz also notes that constitutional amendment is an entirely different form of entrenchment than that which rules of recognition have. *Id.* at 333.

58 Barnett, Chapter 16, note 41, at 23.

59 *Id.* at 29.

60 *Id.*

61 *Id.* at 20.

62 *See* RAZ, Chapter 16, note 41, at 333-38. For a full comprehensive discussion of the hypothetical consent theory's weaknesses, *see, generally* Joseph Raz, *Government by Consent, in* Joseph Raz, Ethics In The Public Domain: Essays In The Morality of Law And Politics (Oxford University Press 1995).

63 RAZ, Chapter 16, note 41, at 334.

64 *Id.* at 335.

65 *Id.* at 337.

66 *Id.* at 337-38.

67 In recounting a secular foundation for NLT is of note to also mention Baruch Spinoza (1632-1677), born in Amsterdam the same year as John Locke. Spinoza was an excellent student in his congregation's Talmud Torah school, but was ultimately excommunicated from his Sephardic community for his belief that the Law was not given by God. In his masterpiece, *Ethics*, he discussed in depth the "state of nature" as well as the nature of a political society, and contradicted the right of every individual to do whatever he can to preserve himself (i.e., the state of nature) with the rights he gives up under a "social contract" or state of Reason:

Whatever every person, whenever he is considered as solely under the dominion of Nature, believes to be to his advantage, whether under the guidance of sound reason or under passion's sway, he may by sovereign natural right seek and get for himself by any means, by force, deceit, entreaty, or in any other way he best can, and he may consequently regard as his enemy anyone who tries to hinder him from getting what he wants.

Steven Nadler, Spinoza: A Life, 281-282 (Cambridge Univ. Press 1999). Moreover, Spinoza showed "that our happiness and well-being lie not in a life enslaved to the passions and to the transitory goods we ordinarily pursue; nor in the related unreflective attachment to the superstitions that pass as religion, but rather in the life of reason." Id. at 227.

68   Randy Barnett, The Structure of Liberty: Justice And The Rule of Law 17-23 (2d ed., Oxford University Press 2014).

69   Barnett, Chapter 16, note 41, at 44.

70   *Id.* (emphasis added).

71   *Id.*

72   Nozick gives a rosy view of how these associations would operate, benignly and by freezing out anyone who engages in private retaliation. NOZICK, Chapter 16, note 1, at 12-15. He believes that the two agencies will develop the equivalent of jurisdictional borders, a common federal-type appeals system to lower the costs of enforcement will develop, or a monopoly will arise. *Id.* at 11. He overlooks the other possibilities that are much darker, like the imperialism, royalism, a feudalistic defense system, warlord governance, and popular subjugation to these powerful firms that lack even a pretense of moral constraints. Moreover, as Barnett notes, consent, such as that given to a defense firm, can justify larger deprivations of liberty than necessity, such as the imposition of feudal-like codes. Barnett, Chapter 16, note 41, at 45.

73   This necessarily rejects government based on totalitarianism or despotism as mechanism of collective decision-making for protection liberty. Robert Post, *Religion and Freedom of Speech: Portraits of Muhammad* 14 Constellations 72-90 (2007) (discussing the aims and nature of democracy as a decision-making method). Republicanism and democracy are examples of acceptable mechanisms. Moreover, readers should not confuse the normative account of the subjugation of *some* minimal natural liberty with the subjugation of one's entire will to a collective decision-making method.

74   Randy Barnett, *Necessary and Proper*, 44 UCLA L. Rev. 745, 748 (1997).

75   *Id.* at 748-756.

76   *Id.* at 764.

77   Randy Barnett, *The Original Meaning of the Necessary and Proper Clause*, 6 U. Penn. J. of Const. L. 13-14 (2003).

78   David Stout, *Murray N. Rothbard, Economist And Free-Market Exponent*, N. Y. Times, Jan. 11, 1995.

79   Rothbard's Ethics, Chapter 1, note 133, at 43. In fact, the word "property" appears nearly 600 times in the 1998 volume *after* the table to contents and introduction by Hans-Hermann Hoppe. Since the substantive part of the work is only 273 pages, property appears, on average more than twice per page. In contrast, "government" and its iterations only appear 245 times.

80   *Id.* at 45.

81   *Id.*

82   *Id.* at 56.

83   *Id.* at 60 (emphasis in original). "The simplest case, of course, is property in persons. The fundamental axiom of libertarian theory is that each person must be a self-owner, and that no one has the right to interfere with such self-ownership." *Id.*

84   *Id.* at 51 (footnote omitted) (emphasis in original).

85   *Id.* at 60 (emphasis in original).

86   Murray N. Rothbard, Egalitarianism As A Revolt Against Nature And Other Essays, x (Ludwig von Mises Institute 2000) (1974) [hereinafter Rothbard's Egalitarianism].

87   *Id.* (footnote omitted).

88   *Id.*

89   *Id.* (footnote omitted).

90   Hobbes, Chapter 1, note 110, at 84.

91   Pinker, Chapter 1, note 118, at 35.

92   Hobbes, Chapter 1, note 110, at 122-123.

93   Rothbard's Ethics, Chapter 1, note 133, at 79 (emphasis in original). Likewise, "[i]t is not the proper business of law to make people be truthful or to keep their promises." *Id.*

94   *Id.* at 79-80.

95   Rothbard wrote:

Violent defense then must be confined to violent invasion— either actually, implicitly, or by direct and overt threat. But given this principle, how far does the right of violent defense go? For one thing, it would clearly be grotesque and criminally invasive to shoot a man across the street because his angry look seemed to you to portend an invasion. The danger must be immediate and overt, we might say, "clear and present"—a criterion that properly applies not to restrictions on freedom of speech (never permissible, if we regard such freedom as a subset of the rights of person and property) but to the right to take coercive action against a supposedly imminent invader.

Id. at 80, (footnote omitted). He questions whether a shopkeeper has the right to kill a child for stealing a piece of bubble gum. *Id.* Rothbard argued that such an action would "[suffer] from a grotesque lack of proportion" since "concentrating on the storekeeper's right to his bubble gum, it totally ignores another highly precious property-right: every man's—including the [thief's]—right to self-ownership." *Id.*

96 *Id.* (emphasis in original).

97 *Id.* (footnote omitted).

98 *Id.* at 83.

99 Rothbard was a supporter of the right to bear arms. "It should further be clear from our discussion of defense that every man has the absolute right to bear arms—whether for self-defense or any other licit purpose. The crime comes not from bearing arms, but from using them for purposes of threatened or actual invasion." *Id.* at 81.

100 For his part, Rothbard seemed generally to agree with the concepts of Natural Law theory and valued its importance for and benefits to those societies that adopted its tenets. In Rothbard's Ethics, he argued that:

[i]t [was] not the intention of [*The Ethics of Liberty*] to expound or defend at length the philosophy of natural law, or to elaborate a natural-law ethic for the personal morality of man. The intention is to set forth a social ethic of liberty, i.e., to elaborate that subset of the natural law that develops the concept of natural rights, and that deals with the proper sphere of "politics," i.e., with violence and non-violence as modes of interpersonal relations. In short, to set forth a political philosophy of liberty.

Id. at 25.

101 *Id.* at 41 (emphasis in original).

102 *Id.* (emphasis in original).

103 Rothbard made clear a point he considered vital:

[I]f we are trying to set up an ethic for man (in our case, the subset of ethics dealing with violence), then to be a valid ethic the theory must hold true for all men, whatever their location in time or place. This is one of the notable attributes of natural law—its applicability to all men, regardless of time or place. Thus, ethical natural law takes its place alongside physical or "scientific" natural laws. But the society of liberty is the only society that can apply the same basic rule to every man regardless of time or place.

Id. at 42-43.

104 Professor Barnett is a former prosecutor and today argues occasionally before federal courts including: the U.S. Supreme Court – on which one can only hope and pray he one day will sit.

CHAPTER 17

1 Jennifer Senior, *In Conversation: Antonin Scalia*, N. Y. Mag., Oct. 4, 2013.

2   For instance, the word *corn* referred to grain in the sixteenth and seventeenth centuries, but could also refer to seeds or smaller fruits like grapes during the medieval period through the late nineteenth century, but also maize or "Indian corn" in the early seventeenth century. *Corn, The Oxford English Dictionary, available at* www.oed.com/view/Entry/41586 (last visited Nov. 30, 2018).

3   Paul Brest, *The Original Understanding*, 60 B. U. L. Rev. 204, 204 (1980).

4   *Id.*

5   *Id.* at 205.

6   *Id.* at 206 (quoting Oliver Wendell Holmes, *The Theory of Interpretation*, 12 Harv. L. Rev. 417, 419 (1899)).

7   "[T]he intentionalist interprets a provision by ascertaining the intentions of those who adopted it. The text of the provision is often a useful guide to the adopters' intentions, but the text does not enjoy a favored status over other sources." Brest, Chapter 17, note 3, at 209 (footnote omitted).

8   "Excessive bail shall not be required, nor excessive fines imposed, nor cruel and unusual punishments inflicted." U.S. CONST. amend. VIII.

9   He also ridiculed my fidelity to the Natural Law Tradition. "You're a freak for the natural law!" he proclaimed when I suggested he would have dissented with Justice Louis Brandeis in *Olmstead v. United States*. My argument in support of the right to be left alone, he contended, was for Congress to accept or reject, not the courts.

10 Barnett, Restoring The Lost Constitution, Chapter 16, note 41, at 237.

11 *Id.* at 239.

12 *Id.* at 239.

13 "Madison himself used the Ninth Amendment to check an expansive construction of the delegated powers during the debate of the constitutionality of the national bank. Near the end of his speech in which he argued that the powers to incorporate a bank and grant it a monopoly were beyond those granted to Congress under the Necessary and Proper Clause, he observed: "The *latitude of interpretation* required by the bill is condemned by the rule furnished by the constitution itself." *Id.* at 242 (citing 2 Annals of Cong. 1896-1897) (statement of Rep. Madison) (emphasis added by Barnett).

14 *Id.* at 242. 15 *Id.* at 243. 16 *Id.* at 244.

CHAPTER 18

1   *Brown v. Allen*, 344 U.S. 443, 540 (1953) (Jackson, J. concurring in the result) (emphasis added).

2   Thus far, we have already discussed the following cases which either embrace or reject NLT: *Paxton's Case, Hancock's Case, The Boston Massacre Trial,*

Robin v. Hardaway, Chisholm v. Georgia, Penhallow v. Doane's Administrators, Calder v. Bull, Marbury v. Madison, ExParte Bollman, Fletcher v. Peck, Dartmouth College v. Woodward. Ogden v. Saunders, Gibbons v. Ogden, United States v. La Jeune Eugenie, McCulloch v. Maryland, Dred Scott v. Sandford, Plessy v. Ferguson, Lochner v. New York, Wickard v. Filburn, Korematsu v. United States, Shelley v. Kramer, Brown v. Board of Education, Griswold v. Connecticut, Loving v. Virginia, Bowers v. Hardwick, Lawrence v. Texas, Gonzales v. Raich and Kelo v. New London.

3   *Wilkinson v. Leland,* 27 U.S. 627 (1829).

4   John V. Orth, *Taking From A and Giving to B: Substantive Due Process and the Case of the Shifting Paradigm,* 14 Constitutional Commentary 337, 339 (1997).

5   *Id.*

6   *Id.*

7   *Wilkinson v. Leland,* 27 U.S. 627, 657 (1829) (Story, J.) (emphasis added).

8   *Harris v. Hardeman,* 55 U.S. 334 (1852). The Court recognized:

[I]n a variety of decisions, in which it has been settled, that a judgment depending upon proceedings *in personam* can have no force as to one on whom there has been no service of process, actual or constructive; who has had no day in court, and no notice of any proceeding against him.

Id. at 339 (italics in original).

9   *Id.*

10   *Harris v. Hardeman,* 55 U.S. 334, 339 (1852) (quoting *Borden v. Fitch,* 15 Johns. 121, 142 (1818) (Thompson, C. J.))

11   *Cummings v. Missouri,* 71 U.S. 277 (1867).

12   Writing for the Court, Justice Field noted:

We admit the propositions of the counsel of Missouri, that the States which existed previous to the adoption of the Federal Constitution possessed originally all the attributes of sovereignty; that they still retain those attributes, except as they have been surrendered by the formation of the Constitution, and the amendments thereto; that the new States, upon their admission into the Union, became invested with equal rights, and were thereafter subject only to similar restrictions, and that among the rights reserved to the States is the right of each State to determine the qualifications for office, and the conditions upon which its citizens may exercise their various callings and pursuits within its jurisdiction.

Id. at 318-319.

13   Justice Field wrote:

The deprivation of any rights, civil or political, previously enjoyed, may be punishment, the circumstances attending and the causes of the deprivation determining this fact. Disqualification from office many be punishment, as in cases of conviction upon impeachment. Disqualification from the pursuits of a lawful avocation, or from positions of trust, or from the privilege of appearing in the courts, or acting as an executor, administrator, or guardian, may also, and often has been, imposed as punishment.

Id. at 320.

14   *Id.* at 321-322. U.S. CONST. amend. XIV. ("No State shall make or enforce any law which shall abridge the privileges or immunities of citizens of the United States; nor shall any State deprive any person of life, liberty, or property, without due process of law; nor deny to any person within its jurisdiction the equal protection of the laws.")

15   *The Slaughter-House Cases*, 83 U.S. 36 (1872).

16   *Corfield v. Coryell*, 6 F. Cas. 546 (C.C.E.D. Pa. 1823).

17   *The Slaughter-House Cases*, at 76, (quoting *Corfield v. Coryell*, 6 F. Cas. 546, 551-552 (C.C.E.D. Pa. 1823)).

18   *The Slaughter-House Cases* at 76 invoking *Ward v. State*, 79 U.S. 418 (1870):

Attempt will not be made to define the words 'privileges and immunities,' or to specify the rights which they are intended to secure and protect, beyond what may be necessary to the decision of the case before the court. Beyond doubt those words are words of very comprehensive meaning, but it will be sufficient to say that the clause plainly and unmistakably secures and protects the right of a citizen of one State to pass into any other State of the Union for the purpose of engaging in lawful commerce, trade, or business without molestation; to acquire personal property; to take and hold real estate; to maintain actions in the courts of the State; and to be exempt from any higher taxes or excises than are imposed by the State upon its own citizens.

Id. at 430 (footnote omitted).

19   *The Slaughter-House Cases* at 76 (1872).

20   *Id.* at 105 (Field, J. *dissenting*).

21   *Id.*

22   *Id.* at 106 (emphasis added).

23   *Id.* at 115-116 (Bradley, J. *dissenting*).

24   *Butchers' Union Slaughter-House & Live-Stock Landing Co. v. Crescent City Live-Stock Landing & Slaughter-House Co.*, 111 U.S. 746 (1884).

25   *Id.* at 746-747.

26 *Id.* at 756-757.

27 *Monongahela Nav. Co. v. U.S.*, 148 U.S. 312 (1893).

28 *Id.* at 324.

29 *Id.* at 324-325.

30 Here, we see that the term "natural equity" is used as yet another secular phrase for the Natural Law.

31 *Monongahela Nav. Co.* at 325.

32 *Chicago, B. & Q.R. Co. v. City of Chicago*, 166 U.S. 226 (1897).

33 *Id.* at 230.

34 *Id.*

35 *Id.* at 236 (1897) (citations omitted) (emphasis added).

36 U.S. CONST. amend. V.

CHAPTER 19

1 Letter from Thomas Jefferson to Pierre Samuel Du Pont de Nemours, (Apr. 24, 1816) (footnotes omitted) *reprinted in* 11 Jefferson, Chapter 2, note 11, at 522.

2 *Lochner v. New York*, 198 U.S. 45 (1905).

3 The Dictionary of Modern Legal Usage contains an entry related to the *Lochner* case. Lochnerize, [verb]; Lochnerization, [noun]. These terms derive from the case *Lochner v. New York*, 198 U.S. 45 (1905). *Lochnerize* = to scrutinize and invalidate economic regulations under the guise of enforcing the due-process clause. The term carries no small degree of opprobrium. "*Lochnerizing* has become so much an epithet that the very use of the label may obscure attempts at understanding." Laurence Tribe, *American Constitutional Law* 435 (1978)." Bryan A. Garner, A Dictionary of Modern Legal Usage 536 (2 ed., Oxford Univ. Press 1991) (1987).

4 *Lochner v. New York*, 198 U.S. 45 (1905).

5 Courts used natural rights theory "not as a source of novel constitutional norms, 'but as confirmation of rights they thought were embedded' in the Anglo-American tradition.'" David E. Bernstein, Rehabilitating Lochner: Defending Individual Rights Against Progressive Reform 17 (University of Chicago Press 2011).

6 *See Id.* at 107-124 (discussing "Lochner in Modern Times"); *see also* Book Note, *Rehabilitating Lochner: Defending Individual Rights Against Progressive Reform. by David E. Bernstein. Chicago, Ill.: University Of Chicago Press. 2011. Pp. Viii, 194. $34.99*, 125 Harv. L. Rev. 1120, 1121-23 (2012) (reviewing Bernstein).

7   *See* Bernstein, Chapter 19, note 5, at 4-5.

8   *Adair v. United States*, 208 U.S. 161 (1908).

9   Section 10 of the Erdman Act of 1898 provided:

That any employer subject to the provisions of this Act and any officer, agent, or receiver of such employer who shall require any employee, or any person seeking employment, as a condition of such employment, to enter into an agreement, either written or verbal, not to become or remain a member of any labor corporation, association, or organization; or shall threaten any employee with loss of employment, or shall unjustly discriminate against any employee because of his membership in such a labor corporation, association, or organization; or who shall require any employee or any person seeking employment, as a condition of such employment, to enter into a contract whereby such employee or applicant for employment shall agree to contribute to any fund for charitable, social, or beneficial purposes; to release such employer from legal liability for any personal injury by reason of any benefit received from such fund beyond the proportion of the benefit arising from the employer's contribution to such fund; or who shall, after having discharged an employee, attempt or conspire to prevent such employee from obtaining employment, or who shall, after the quitting of an employee, attempt or conspire to prevent such employee from obtaining employment, is hereby declared to be guilty of a misdemeanor, and, upon conviction thereof in any court of the United States of competent jurisdiction in the district in which such offense was committed, shall be punished for each offense by a fine of not less than one hundred dollars and not more than one thousand dollars.

Erdman Act of 1898, ch 370, § 10, 30 Stat. 424 (Jun 1, 1898).

10   *Adair* at 170-171.

11   *Id.* at 171.

12   Erdman Act of 1898, ch 370, § 10, 30 Stat. 424 (Jun 1, 1898).

13   *Adair* at 174 (quoting *Lochner v. New York*, 198 U.S. 45, 56 (1905)).

14   Erdman Act of 1898, ch 370, § 10, 30 Stat. 424 (Jun 1, 1898).

15   *Adair* at 172. Justice Harlan also reminded readers that

This court has said that 'in every well-ordered society, charged with the duty of conserving the safety of its members, the rights of the individual in respect of his liberty may, at times, under the pressure of great dangers, be subjected to such restraint, to be enforced by reasonable regulations, as the safety of the general public may demand.'

Id. (citing *Jacobson v. Massachusetts*, 197 U.S. 11, 29 (1905)).

16   The Court noted that:

Adair's right—and that right inhered in his personal liberty, and was also a right of property—to serve his employer as best he could, so long as he did nothing that was reasonably forbidden by law as injurious to the public interests. It was the right of the defendant to prescribe the terms upon which the services of Coppage would be accepted, and it was the right of Coppage to become or not, as he chose, an employee of the railroad company upon the terms offered to him. Mr. Cooley, in his treatise on Torts, p. 278, well says: 'It is a part of every man's civil rights that he be left at liberty to refuse business relations with any person whomsoever, whether the refusal rests upon reason, or is the result of whim, caprice, prejudice, or malice. With his reasons neither the public nor third persons have any legal concern. It is also his right to have business relations with anyone with whom he can make contracts, and, if he is wrongfully deprived of this right by others, he is entitled to redress.'

Adair at 172-173.

17 *Id.* at 174 (1908) (emphasis added).

18 *Twining v. State of N.J.*, 211 U.S. 78 (1908).

19 *Id.* at 82.

20 *Id.*

21 *Id.* at 106 (emphasis added). Justice Moody continues:

The power of the people of the states to make and alter their laws at pleasure is the greatest security for liberty and justice, this court has said in *Hurtado v. California*, 110 U. S. 516, 527, 28 L. ed. 232, 235, 4 Sup. Ct. Rep. 111, 292. We are not invested with the jurisdiction to pass upon the expediency, wisdom, or justice of the laws of the states as declared by their courts, but only to determine their conformity with the Federal Constitution and the paramount laws enacted pursuant to it. Under the guise of interpreting the Constitution we must take care that we do not import into the discussion our own personal views of what would be wise, just, and fitting rules of government to be adopted by a free people, and confound them with constitutional limitations.

Id. at 106-107.

22 *Id.* at 114. The Supreme Court would reinforce this mistake in 1947 in *Adamson v. California*, 332 U.S. 46 (1947) before recognizing its error and applying the Fifth Amendment's right against self-incrimination to the states through its incorporation in the Fourteenth Amendment. *Malloy v. Hogan*, 378 U.S. 1 (1964).

23 Justice Harlan wrote:

The court, in its consideration of the relative rights of the United States and of the several states, holds, in this case, that, without violating the

Constitution of the United States, a state can compel a person accused of crime to testify against himself. In my judgment, immunity from self-incrimination is protected against hostile state action, not only by that clause in the 14th Amendment declaring that 'no state shall make or enforce any law which shall abridge the privileges or immunities of citizens of the United States,' but by the clause, in the same Amendment, 'nor shall any state deprive any person of life, liberty, or property, without due process of law.' No argument is needed to support the proposition that, whether manifested by statute or by the final judgment of a court, state action, if liable to the objection that it abridges the privileges or immunities of national citizenship, must also be regarded as wanting in the due process of law enjoined by the 14th Amendment, when such state action substantially affects life, liberty, or property.

Twining at 117 (Harlan, J. *dissenting*).

24   *Id.* at 118-119 (emphasis added).

25   He noted:

It is indisputably established that, despite differences in forms of government, the people in the colonies were a unit as to certain leading principles, among which was the principle that the people were entitled to 'enjoy the rights and privileges of British-born subjects and the benefit of the common laws of England' (1 Story, Const. § 163), and that (to use the words of the Continental Congress of 1774) 'by immigration to the colonies, the people by no means forfeited, surrendered, or lost any of those rights, but that they were then, and their descendants are now, entitled to the exercise and enjoyment of them as their local and other circumstances enable them to exercise and enjoy.' *Id.*

26   Justice Harlan recalled:

[Justice Miller], delivering the opinion in [*Davidson v. New Orleans*, 96 U.S. 97 (1878)], said: "The prohibition against depriving the citizen or subject of his life, liberty, or property without due process of law, is not new in the constitutional history of the English race. It is not new in the constitutional history of this country, and it was not new in the Constitution of the United States when it became a part of the Fourteenth Amendment, in the year 1866." After observing that the equivalent of the phrase "due process of law," according to Lord Coke, is found in the words "law of the land," in the Great Charter, in connection with the guarantees of the rights of the subject against the oppression of the crown, the court said: "In the series of amendments to the Constitution of the United States, proposed and adopted immediately after the organization of the government, which were dictated by the jealousy of the States as further limitations upon the power of the Federal Government, it is found in the Fifth, *in connection with other guarantees of personal rights of the same character." Among these guarantees* this court distinctly said was protection against being twice tried for the same offense, and protection "*against the accused being compelled, in a criminal case, to testify against himself.*" Again, said the court: "It is easy to see that when the great barons of England wrung from King John, at the point of the sword, the concession that neither their lives nor their property should be disposed of by the crown, except as provided by the law of the land, they meant by 'law of the land' the ancient and customary laws of the English people, or laws enacted by the Parliament of which those barons were a controlling element. It was not in their minds, therefore, to protect themselves against the enactment of laws by the Parliament of England."

Id. at 125-126 (citing *Davidson v. New Orleans*, 96 U.S. 97, 101, 102 (1878)) (emphasis in original).

27   *Twining* at 126 (Harlan, J. *dissenting*).

28   *Id.*

29   *Id.* at 126-127 (emphasis added).

30   *Coppage v. State of Kansas*, 236 U.S. 1, 9 (1915).

31   *Id.* at 7.

32   Justice Mahlon Pitney, speaking for the court, wrote:

Under constitutional freedom of contract, whatever either party has the right to treat as sufficient ground for terminating the employment, where there is no stipulation on the subject, he has the right to provide against by insisting that a stipulation respecting it shall be a *sine qua non* of the inception of the employment, or of its continuance if it be terminable at will. It follows that this case cannot be distinguished from *Adair v. United States*.

Id.

33   *Id.*

34   *Id.* at 11-12.

35   *Id.* at 13.

36   *Id.*

37   *Id.* at 14.

38   *Id.*

39   The Court finally found that:

Upon both principle and authority, therefore, we are constrained to hold that the Kansas act of March 13, 1903, as construed and applied so as to punish with fine or imprisonment an employer or his agent for merely prescribing, as a condition upon which one may secure employment under or remain in the service of such employer, that the employee shall enter into an agreement not to become or remain a member of any labor organization while so employed, is repugnant to the 'due process' clause of the 14th Amendment, and therefore vo*id.*

Id. at 26.

40   *Rochin v. California*, 342 U.S. 165, 166 (1952).

41   *Id.* at 171.

42   *Id.* at 166.

43   *Id.*

44   *Id.*

45   *Id.*

46   *Id.*

47   *Id.*

48   *Id.*

49   *Id.* at 166-167.

50   *Id.* at 168.

51   In contemplating the limitations imposed on Congress and state legislatures by Article 1, sec 8, cl 1 of the Constitution with reference to the prohibition on bills of attainder, ex post facto laws, and of the Thirteenth and Fourteenth Amendments, the Court recognized:

These limitations, in the main, concern not restrictions upon the powers of the States to define crime, except in the restricted area where federal authority has pre-empted the field, but restrictions upon the manner in which the States may enforce their penal codes. Accordingly, in reviewing a State criminal conviction under a claim of right guaranteed by the Due Process Clause of the Fourteenth Amendment, from which is derived the most far reaching and most frequent federal basis of challenging State criminal justice, 'we must be deeply mindful of the responsibilities of the States for the enforcement of criminal laws, and exercise with due humility our merely negative function in subjecting convictions from state courts to the very narrow scrutiny which the Due Process Clause of the Fourteenth Amendment authorizes.'

Rochin at 168 (1952) (quoting *Malinksi v. People of the State of New York,* 324 U.S. 401, 412, 418 (1945)).

52   *Id.* at 169 (quoting *Malinksi* at 416-417).

53   *Id.* (quoting *Malinksi* at 416-417).

54   *Id.*

55 *Id.* (quoting *Snyder v. Commonwealth of Massachusetts*, 291 U.S. 97, 105 (1934) and *Palko v. State of Connecticut*, 302 U.S. 319, 325 (1937) (footnote omitted)).

56 *Id.* at 169-170 (emphasis added) (footnotes omitted).

57 *Id.* at 170 (emphasis added).

58 *Id.* at 170-171 (emphasis added) (footnote omitted).

59 *Id.* at 171 (footnote omitted).

60 *Id.*

61 *Id.*

62 *Id.*

63 *Id.* at 171-172 (emphasis added).

64 *Palmer v. Thompson*, 403 U.S. 217 (1971).

65 *Id.* at 227.

66 "My conclusion is that the Ninth Amendment has a bearing on the present problem." *Id.* at 233 (Douglas, J., *dissenting*).

67 *Id.* Included in those non-enumerated rights, according to Justice Douglass, included the right travel (*United States v. Guest*, 383 U.S. 745, 758 (1966)), and the right to marry (*Loving* at 12, *Palmer v. Thompson* at 233 (Douglas, J., *dissenting*)).

68 *Palmer v. Thompson* at 233. For instance, "the Fourth Amendment speaks of the 'right of the people to be secure in their persons, houses, papers, and effects' and protects it by well-known procedural devices." *Id.*

69 *Id.* signaling *Griswold v. Connecticut*, 381 U.S. 479 (1965).

70 *Palmer v. Thompson* at 233-234 (Douglas, J., *dissenting*).

71 *Id.* at 234.

72 *Id.*

73 *Id.* (citing *West Virginia State Board of Education v. Barnette*, 319 U.S. 624, 638 (1943)).

74 *Id.* at 234-235 (citing *Lucas v. Forty-Fourth Colorado General Assembly*, 377 U.S. 713, 736-737 (1964)).

75 *Id.* at 237-238 (Douglas, J., *dissenting*) (footnotes omitted) (citing to "40 TUL. L. REV. 487, 490-492 (1966); [Norman] Redlich, *Are There 'Certain Rights ... Retained by the People?*,' 37 N. Y. U. L. REV. 787, 810812 (1962); [Charles L.] Black, [Jr.],] *The Unfinished Business of the Warren Court*, 46 WASH. L. REV. 3, 37-45 (1970); [Luis] Kutner, *The Neglected Ninth Amendment: The 'Other Rights' Retained by the People*, 51 MARQ. L. REV. 121, 134-137 (1968)[.]")

76   *Id.* at 239 (Douglas, J., *dissenting*) (emphasis added) (footnote omitted).

77   *Obergefell v. Hodges*, 135 S.Ct. 2584 (2015).

78   *Id.* at 2593.

79   *Id.* at 2597.

80   *Id.*

81   "The identification and protection of fundamental rights is an enduring part of the judicial duty to interpret the Constitution." *Id.* at 2598.

82   *Id.* (citing *Poe v. Ullman*, 367 U.S. 497, 542 (1961) (Harlan, J., *dissenting*)).

83   *Obergefell* at 2598 (citations omitted).

84   *Id.*

85   *Id.* at 2589.

86   *Id.*

87   *Id.* at 2599.

88   *Id.*

89   *Id.*

90   According to Murray Rothbard, "…in the Thomistic tradition, natural law is ethical as well as physical law; and the instrument by which man apprehends such law is his *reason* – not faith, or intuition or grace, revelation, or anything else." Rothbard, Chapter 1, note 133, at 6 (citing John Wild, Natural Law and Modern Ethical Theory," *Ethics* (October 1952), who proclaimed: Realistic [natural law] ethics is now often dismissed as theological and authoritarian in character. But this is a misunderstanding. Its ablest representatives, from Plato and Aristotle to Grotius, have defended it on the basis of empirical evidence alone without any appeal to supernatural authority.

CHAPTER 20

1   Henry Hazlitt, The Foundations of Morality 267-268 (The Foundation for Economic Education, Inc. 2010) (1964).

2   He was nominated on December 2, 1902, confirmed by the U.S. Senate by voice vote on December 4, and sworn in as an associate justice on December 8 at age 61 after sitting on the bench in Massachusetts for 11 days shy of 20 years. Gary J. Aichele, Oliver Wendell Holmes, Jr. Soldier, Scholar, Judge 132 (1989).

3   Catherine Drinker Bowen, Yankee From Olympus Justice Holmes And His Family, 410 (Little, Brown & Co. 1945) (1944). Bowen reports that Holmes's voice began to falter and became barely audible as he delivered the majority opinion in *Dunn v. United States*, 284 U.S. 390 (1932). *Id.* After Holmes finished the opinion, "[a]t the noon recess, [he] left the Courtroom with the

other justices, ate his box lunch, and returned to the Bench. When the Court rose at four-thirty, he got his hat and coat, walked over to the Clerk's desk. 'I won't be down tomorrow,' he sa*id*." *Id.* Bowen reports: "[t[hat night, Holmes wrote his resignation to the president … *The time has come and I bow to the inevitable. I have nothing but kindness to remember from you and my brethren. My last word should be one of grateful thanks*." *Id.* (emphasis in original). He served with John Marshall Harlan, Louis Brandeis, and Harlan Fiske Stone, and was succeeded on the bench by Benjamin Cardozo. Of the justices we have discussed in some detail, only Chief Justice Marshall, Hugo Black, John Marshall Harlan, Joseph Story, and Antonin Scalia served longer.

4   After Fort Sumter fell in 1861 and President Lincoln appealed to the state militias for soldiers to staff an army, Holmes "signed up for duty in the Boston unit of the Massachusetts Volunteer Militia, the New England Guards or Fourth Battalion." Susan Mary Grant, Oliver Wendell Holmes, Jr. Civil War Soldier, Supreme Court Justice, 41-42 (2016).

5   While lawyers and students will recall Holmes for his more famous opinions, few know the extent to which he commanded the respect of his fellow justices. Justice Felix Frankfurter declared Holmes "was essentially the philosopher who turned to law." Felix Frankfurter, Mr. Justice Holmes And The Supreme Court 24 (1938). And, "though [Holmes] did not bring to the Court the experience of great affairs, not even [Chief Justice John Marshall] exceeded him in judicial statesmanship," Frankfurter maintained. "Other judges have been guided by the wisdom distilled from an active life; Mr. Justice Holmes was led by the divination of the philosopher and the imagination of the poet." *Id.* at 24-25.

6   Holmes, *The Path of the Law*, Chapter 12, note 37.

7   *Id.* at 459.

8   *Id.*

9   *Id.*

10   He wrote:

I take it for granted that no hearer of mine will misinterpret what I have to say as the language of cynicism. The law is the witness and external deposit of our moral life. Its history is the history of the moral development of the race. The practice of it, in spite of popular jests, tends to make good citizens and good men. When I emphasize the difference between law and morals I do so with reference to a single end, that of learning and understanding the law. For that purpose you must definitely master its specific marks, and it is for that that I ask you for the moment to imagine yourselves indifferent to other and greater things.

I do not say that there is not a wider point of view from which the distinction between law and morals becomes of secondary or no importance, as all mathematical distinctions vanish in presence of the infinite. But I do say that

> that distinction is of the first importance for the object which we are here to consider, — a right study and mastery of the law as a business with well understood limits, a body of dogma enclosed within definite lines. I have just shown the practical reason for saying so. When I emphasize the difference between law and morals I do so with reference to a single end, that of learning and understanding the law. For that purpose you must definitely master its specific marks, and it is for that that I ask you for the moment to imagine yourselves indifferent to other and greater things. *Id.*

11   *Id.*

12   "We must beware of the pitfall of antiquarianism, and must remember that for our purposes our only interest in the past is for the light it throws upon the present." *Id.* at 474.

13   *Id.* at 459.

14   *Id.* at 460.

> For instance, when we speak of the rights of man in a moral sense, we mean to mark the limits of interference with individual freedom which we think are prescribed by conscience, or by our ideal, however reached. Yet it is certain that many laws have been enforced in the past, and it is likely that some are enforced now, which are condemned by the most enlightened opinion of the time, or which at all events pass the limit of interference as many consciences would draw it. Manifestly, therefore, nothing but confusion of thought can result from assuming that the rights of man in a moral sense are equally rights in the sense of the Constitution and the law.
>
> *Id.*

15   *Id.* at 474. "Every effort to reduce a case to a rule is an effort of jurisprudence, although the name as used in English is confined to the broadest rules and most fundamental conceptions." *Id.*

16   *Id.* at 465.

17   *Id.*

18   *Id.*

19   *Id.*

20   *Id.* at 41 (emphasis in original).

21   Holmes, *The Path of the Law*, Chapter 12, note 37, at 469.

22   Robert P. George, *Natural Law*, 31 Harv. J. L. & Pub. Pol'y 171, 171 (2008).

23   Robert P. George, *Holmes on Natural Law*, 4 Vill. L. Rev. 1, 2 (2003) (emphasis in original).

24   *Id.*

25   *Id.* (emphasis in original).

26 *Id.* He added:

They are ethically neutral facts-about the world-like the fact that sharks kill and eat seals, or that a hurricane struck southern Florida, or that AIDS is ravaging sub-Saharan Africa. We may, according to our own "value system," deplore Hitler's values; indeed, we may, in light of our own subjective values, be willing to fight and die to frustrate Hitler's ends. But, according to the perspective adopted by Holmes, our ultimate values are, from the point of view of rational inquiry, neither more nor less rational than, say, Hitler's. Our values, too, are mere facts about the world. All that rational inquiry can do is to record them as facts, and, perhaps, explore possible psychological and sociological causes of their existence.

Id. at 2-3.

27 *Id.* at 3.

28 *Id.*

29 *Id.* at 5 (footnotes omitted). George explained:

Natural law, on Aquinas's understanding of the matter, is the body of principles, including moral norms, providing practical reasons, that is to say, reasons for action and restraint. Some positive laws such as those prohibiting murder, rape, theft and other grave injustices, are derived from the natural law by a process akin to the deduction of demonstrable conclusions from general premises in mathematics and the sciences. Other positive laws, however, cannot be derived from the natural law in so direct and straightforward a fashion. Where law is required to solve a coordination problem, it is often the case that a variety of possible solutions, each having its own advantages and disadvantages, are rationally available as options.

Id. at 5-6 (footnotes omitted).

30 *See, e.g.* Gerard Verschuuren, Matters of Life & Death: A Guide To The Moral Questions of Our Time 31 (2018) ("Just as science needs geniuses like Newton and Einstein to discover laws no one else has seen before them, so morality needs 'geniuses' such as prophets and saints to uncover moral laws to which others are blind.").

31 Pinker, Chapter 1, note 118, at 622 (footnote omitted) (emphasis in original).

32 Robert P. George, *Holmes on Natural Law*, 4 Vill. L. Rev. 1, 8 (2003).

33 *Id.* at 9.

34 *Id.* (footnote omitted) (emphasis in original).

35 Robert P. George, *Natural Law*, 31 Harv. J. L. & Pub. Pol'y 171, 172 (2008).

36 *Id.* (footnote omitted).

37   *Id.*

38   *Id.*

39   *Id.* at 173.

40   *Id.* at 176 (footnote omitted).

41   *Id.* at 178.

42   George questioned:

Now, if I am correct in affirming that human reason can identify human rights as genuine grounds of obligation to others, rights which people possess as a matter of natural law (what have been termed "natural rights"), how can we explain or understand widespread failures to recognize and respect human rights and other moral principles?

Id. at 180.

43   Robert P. George, *Natural Law*, 31 Harv. J. L. & Pub. Pol'y, 171, 180 (2008).

44   *Id.*

45   "A conscientious judgment may nevertheless be erroneous." *Id.*

46   Albert Alschuler, Law Without Values, The Life, Work And Legacy of Justice Holmes 27-29(2000).

47   *Buck v. Bell*, 274 U.S. 200, 206 (1927) (Holmes, J.).

48   *Id.* at 205.

49   *Id.* at 207. To be fair to Holmes, he wrote the opinion of the Court in which he was joined by Chief Justice William Howard Taft, and Justices Willis Van Devanter, James McReynolds, Louis Brandeis, George Sutherland, Pierce Butler, Edward Terry Stanford, and Harlan Fiske Stone. Alschuler noted that:

One discovers many familiar names on the list of twentiethcentury English and American eugenists, including H. G. Wells, Theodore Roosevelt, Beatrice and Sidney Webb, Margaret Sanger, Havelock Ellis, George Bernard Shaw, and Harold Laski.

Alschuler, Chapter 20, note 46, at 29 (footnote omitted).

50   *Id.* at 28 (footnote omitted).

51   *Adamson v. California*, 332 U.S. 46 (1947).

52   *Id.* at 48.

53   *Id.* at 50.

54   *Id.* at 58-59.

55   *Id.* at 69 (Black, J., *dissenting*) (citation omitted) (footnote omitted).

56   *Id.* at 90.

57   *Id.* (footnote omitted).

58 *Griswold v. Connecticut*, 381 U.S. 479, 484 (1965).

59 *Id.* at 511-512 (Black, J., joined by Stewart, J., *dissenting*) (footnotes omitted).

60 at 512. He did, however, add:

While I completely subscribe to the holding of [*Marbury v. Madison…*], and subsequent cases, that our Court has constitutional power to strike down statutes, state or federal, that violate commands of the Federal Constitution, I do not believe that we are granted power by the Due Process Clause or any other constitutional provision or provisions to measure constitutionality by our belief that legislation is arbitrary, capricious or unreasonable, or accomplishes no justifiable purpose, or is offensive to our own notions of 'civilized standards of conduct.'

Id. at 513 (footnote and citation omitted).

61 *Id.* at 518-519 (footnotes omitted).

62 *Id.* at 522 (footnotes omitted) (emphasis added).

63 *Id.* (footnotes omitted).

64 *Id.* at 525 (footnotes omitted).

65 *Id.* at 525-526 (emphasis added) (footnotes omitted).

66 Adam Liptak, *Antonin Scalia, Justice on the Supreme Court, Dies at 79*, N. Y. Times, Feb. 13, 2016.

67 Robert Barnes, *Supreme Court Justice Antonin Scalia dies at 79*, Wash. Post., Feb. 13, 2016.

68 Liptak, Chapter 20, note 66, (emphasis added).

69 Such as when he blistered in front of an audience of thousands at the Brooklyn Academy of Music in 2014 when I needled him about the original public understanding of "cruel and unusual punishment" within the Eighth Amendment. It was during this same event that Nino, with a wry smile, accused me of being "a *freak* for the Natural Law." I could hardly imagine a higher compliment.

70 Barnes, note Chapter 20, note 67.

71 Scalia wrote:

Wow. Do you really want human judges setting aside positive law because they believe it contradicts natural law? Again, bear in mind that these judges are not angels-- and are not even Thomas Aquinas. Do you not think that the five-justice majority that last term disregarded -- "struck down"-- numerous state laws providing that marriage was between a man and a woman, do you not think those judges believed that that is what natural law required? Do you really want judges -- fallible

judges--- going about enforcing their vision of natural law, contrary to
the dictates of democratically enacted positive law? Lord, no.

Antonin Scalia, Scalia Speaks: Reflections On Law, Faith, And Life Well
Lived 248 (2017).

72 *Id.* at 248-249.

73 *Lawrence v. Texas*, 539 U.S. 558, 586 (2003) (Scalia J., joined by Roberts,
C.J., and Thomas, J., *dissenting*) (citation omitted).

74 *Id.*

75 *Id.*

76 *Id.* (citing *Washington v. Glucksberg*, 521 U.S. 721 (1997)).

77 *Lawrence v. Texas* at 594 (Scalia J., joined by Roberts, C.J., and Thomas, J.,
dissenting) (citing *Bowers v. Hardwick*, 478 U.S. 186, 192 (1986)).

78 *Id.* at 597 (2003) (Scalia J., joined by Roberts, C.J., and Thomas, J.,
dissenting) (emphasis in original) (citations omitted).

79 *Id.* at 598.

80 *Kerry v. Din*, 135 S. Ct. 2128, 2131 (2015).

81 *Id.* at 2133.

82 *Id.* (citing *Reno v. Flores*, 507 U.S. 292, 301-302 (1993)).

83 *Id.* at 2133-2134 (emphasis added).

84 *Arizona v. Hicks*, 480 U.S. 321, 321 (1987).

85 *Id.*

86 *Id.*

87 *Id.*

88 *Id.* at 323.

89 *Id.* at 321.

90 A warrant that allows an officer to search for a life-sized statue of George
Washington, for instance, would not permit an officer to search a kitchen
cabinet for the piece but would allow an officer to take investigative
recognition of a corpse propped up in a rocking chair.

91 *Arizona v. Hicks* at 323.

92 *Id.* at 326.

93 *Id.*

94 *Id.* at 329 (emphasis added).

95 *Id.*

96 Ludwig Von Mises, Liberty & Property 34 (Ludwig von Mises Institute,
2009) (1958).

CHAPTER 21

1 Letter from Thomas Jefferson to Issac H. Tiffany, Monticello (April 4, 1819) *reprinted in* 7 Works of Thomas Jefferson X (H. A. Washington ed., 1884).

2 A. Scott Loveless, *The Forgotten Founding Document: Considering the Ends of the Law*, 27 Byu J. Pub. L. 365, 369 (2013). A. Scott Loveless, JD, PhD, is a retired faculty member and former Executive Director of the World Family Policy Center at the J. Reuben Clark Law School, Brigham Young University, Provo, Utah. He has served as a consulting attorney in natural resources law and works in the Office of the Solicitor of the U.S. Department of the Interior. This paper was presented at the *Symposium on Whether the Legalization of Same-Sex Marriage Is Constitutionally Required* at the J. Reuben Clark Law School at Brigham Young University, Provo, Utah, on November 2, 2012.

3 The Declaration of Independence para. 2 (U.S. 1776).

4 Loveless, Chapter 21, note 2, at 370.

5 Thomas Jefferson, *A Summary View of the Rights of British America* (1774) (emphasis added).

6 Loveless, Chapter 21, note 2, at 376.

7 *Id.*

8 *Id.*

9 *Id.* at 374.

10 Zuckert, *Do Natural Rights Derive From Natural Law?*, Chapter 1, note 2, at 711.

11 St. Thomas Aquinas, Summa Theologica I-II, q. 94, art. 2.

12 Zuckert, *Do Natural Rights Derive From Natural Law?*, Chapter 1, note 2, at 711.

13 Heinrich Rommen, The Natural Law, A Study In Legal And Social History And Philosophy, 221-223 (1936).

14 St. Thomas Aquinas, Summa Theologica I-II, q. 96, art. 2 (emphasis added).

15 *See* Joshua Foa Dienstag, *Between History and Nature: Social Contract Theory in Locke and the Founders*, 58 J. Pol. 985, 986 (1996) ("Lockean theory was actually understood in considerable detail, at least by certain important revolutionary figures.")

16 Letter from Thomas Jefferson to Benjamin Rush, *in* 11 The Works of Thomas Jefferson 168 (Paul Leicester Ford, ed. 1905).

17 John Locke, Two Treatises of Government 102 (Ian Shapiro ed., Yale University Press 2003) (1689).

18   Thomas Jefferson, *Notes on the State of Virginia* in *Jefferson, Writings* 285 (Library of America ed. 1984). Jefferson continued by explaining, "it does me no injury for my neighbour to say there are twenty gods, or no God. It neither picks my pocket nor breaks my leg." *Id.* Jefferson knew that "freedom of belief and 'free argument and debate' were essential human rights, but, when those 'principles break out into overt acts against peace and good order,' it is the 'rightful purpose[] of civil government, for its officers to interfere.'" Marci A. Hamilton, *Religious Institutions, the No-Harm Doctrine, and the Public Good*, 2004 B.Y.U. L. Rev. 1099, 1153 (2004) (citing Thomas Jefferson, *An Act for Establishing Religious Freedom*, 1785, in 12 Statutes at Large: Being a Collection of All the Laws of Virginia 84, 85 (photo. reprint 1969) (William Waller Hening ed., Richmond 1823)).

19   Zuckert, *Do Natural Rights Derive From Natural Law?*, Chapter 1, note 2, at 725.

20   Matthew K. Suess, *Punishment in the State of Nature: John Locke and Criminal Punishment in the United States of America*, 7 Wash. U. Jurisprudence Rev. 367, 377-379 (2015) ("The theoretical foundation for punishment in the state of nature, and therefore punishment in civil society, is that by transgressing the law of nature, the offender has put himself outside the protections of the community.")

21   John Locke, Two Treatises of Government 103 (Ian Shapiro ed., Yale University Press 2003) (1689).

22   David C. Snyder, *Locke on Natural Law and Property Rights*, 16 Canadian J. Phil. 723, 732 (1986).

23   John Locke, *A Second Letter Concerning Toleration*, *in* The Works of John Locke 281 (2d ed. 1722). Since his work, several thinkers, notably H.L.A. Hart, Joel Feinberg, and Gerald Dworkin, have effectively argued against the second prong of this principle—that one's own good is never sufficient cause to do harm to (interfere with the liberty of) another. *See Generally*, H.L.A. Hart, Law, Liberty, And Morality 31-33 (Stanford University Press 1963); Fitzjames Stephens, Liberty, Equality, And Fraternity 24-32 (Holt & Williams, New York 1873).

24   A. John Simmons, *Locke and the Right to Punish*, 20 Phil. & Pub. Aff. 311, 314 (1991).

25   John Locke, Two Treatises of Government 402-03 (Peter Laslett ed., Cambridge University Press 1965) (1689) (emphasis omitted).

26   John Stuart Mill, On Liberty 13 (Liberal Arts Press 1956) (1859).

27   *Id.* at 149.

28   *Id.*

29   *Id.*

30 *Id.* at 89. For example, Mill provides the following scenario: "No person ought to be punished simply for being drunk; but a soldier or a policeman should be punished for being drunk on duty." *Id.*

31 *Id.* at 149.

32 *Id.*

33 *Baskin v. Bogan*, 766 F.3d 648, 669 (7th Cir. 2014) (Posner, J.). In contrast, to explain nontemporal harm, Judge Posner writes that Mill used an example of the English people's revulsion against polygamy in Utah (4000 miles away), which, despite its offensiveness, was not a proper political concern of England, as it was improbable that the Mormonite doctrine of polygamy in Utah could have adverse effects in England. *See Id.*

34 John Stuart Mill, On Liberty 29 (Liberal Arts Press 1956) (1859).

35 *Id.* at Chapter IV, Of the Limits to the Authority of Society over the Individual.

36 *Id.* at Chapter 1, Introductory. *See also* John Lawrence Hill, *The Father of Modern Constitutional Liberalism*, 27 WM. & MARY BILL RTS. J. 431, 460–61 (2018) ("Each of Mill's three zones of liberty provided a template for, and undoubtedly spurred, the liberal jurisprudence of the Supreme Court in the last half of the twentieth century.... The second sphere remained an impetus for Justice Brandeis' "right to be let alone" and ultimately the template for the constitutional "right to privacy.").

37 *Id.* at Chapter 1, Introductory.

38 *See Id.* at 68.

39 David A. J. Richards, *Liberalism, Public Morality, and Constitutional Law: Prolegomenon to a Theory of the Constitutional Right to Privacy*, 51 Law And Contemporary Problems 123-150, 141 (Winter 1988).

40 John Stuart Mill, On Liberty 13 (Hackett Publishing 1978) (1859).

41 *Id.*

42 Joel Feinberg, Offense To Others ix (1984).

43 Joel Feinberg, Harm To Others 15 (1984).

44 *Id.*

45 Richard Warner, *Liberalism and the Criminal Law*, 1 S. Cal. Interdisc. L.J. 39 (1992).

46 Joel Feinberg, Harm To Others 14-15 (1984).

47 *Id.* at 15.

48 *Id.* at 34-36.

49 *Id.* at 35.

50 *Id.*

51   *Id.* at 115-117.

52   Donald L. Beschle, *Lawrence Beyond Gay Rights: Taking the Rationality Requirement for Justifying Criminal Statutes Seriously*, 53 Drake L. Rev. 231, 259 (2005).

53   Joel Feinberg, Offense To Others 6 (1984).

54   Beschle, Chapter 21, note 52, at 260.

55   Discussed in Chapter 13. It is worth noting here, that I would not make the same extension that Feinberg does.

56   Joel Feinberg, Offense To Others 3 (1984).

57   Joel Feinberg, Harm To Self 4 (1984).

58   Mitchell F. Park, *Defining One's Own Concept of Existence and the Meaning of the Universe: The Presumption of Liberty in Lawrence v. Texas*, 2006 B.Y.U. L. Rev. 837, 79 (2006) (citing Feinberg, Harm To Self at 12).

59   Beschle, Chapter 21, note 52, at 260.

60   *Id.*

61   Thaddeus Mason Pope, *Balancing Public Health Against Individual Liberty: The Ethics of Smoking Regulations*, 61 U. Pitt. L. Rev. 419, 428–29 (2000).

62   Cristina de Maglie, *Punishing Mere Immorality? Skeptical Thoughts from A Comparative Perspective*, 23 Berkeley J. Crim. L. 323, 327 (2018) (citing Feinberg, Harm To Others at 4).

63   Rothbard's Egalitarianism, Chapter 16, note 86, at 116.

64   Rothbard, Chapter 1, note 133, at xlviii.

65   *Id.* at 51.

66   Murray N. Rothbard, Law, Property Rights, And Air Pollution, Cato Journal 2, No. 1 (Spring 1982): pp. 55-99, 61.

67   *Id.* at 60.

68   *Id.*

69   *Id.* at 63.

70   S. R. Sankaran, *Police Reforms: Need to Review Power to Arrest*, 35 Econ. & Pol. Wkly. 4082, 4083 (2000).

71   Ronald Bayer, *Heroin Decriminalization and the Ideology of Tolerance: A Critical View*, 12 L. & Soc. Rev. 301, 312 (1978).

72   John Lawrence Hill, *The Constitutional Status of Morals Legislation*, 98 KY. L.J. 1, 3-4 (2010).

73   *Poe v. Ullman*, 367 U.S. 497, 545 (1961) (II. Harlan, J., dissenting).

74   *Mugler v. Kansas*, 123 U.S. 623 (1887).

75   *Osborn v. United States*, 385 U.S. 323, 352 n.15 (1966) (Douglas, J., dissenting) (quoting Kelley, *The Uncertain Renaissance of the Ninth Amendment*, 33 U. Chi. L. Rev. 814, 835 (1966)).

76   The Ninth Amendment was "intended to preserve the underlying theory…that individual rights exist independently of government, and to negate the…argument that the enumeration of certain rights would imply the forfeiture of all others." *Osborn v. United States*, 385 U.S. 323, 352 n.15 (1966) (Douglas, J., dissenting) (quoting Kelley, *The Uncertain Renaissance of the Ninth Amendment*, 33 U. Chi. L. Rev. 814, 835 (1966)). All persons "[own] a residue of individual rights and liberties which have never been, and which are never to be surrendered to the State, but which are still to be recognized, protected and secured." *Colorado Anti-Discrimination Com. v. Case*, 151 Colo. 235, 245, 380 P.2d 34, 40 (1962) (quoting Bennett B. Patterson, The Forgotten Ninth Amendment. A Call For Legislative And Judicial Recognition of Rights Under Social Conditions of Today (The Bobbs Merrill Company, Inc. 1955). These rights "define a private domain within which persons have a right to do as they wish, provided their conduct does not encroach upon the rightful domains of others…[and] as long as their actions remain within this rightful domain, other persons – including the government – should not interfere." Randy E. Barnett, *A Ninth Amendment for Today's Constitution*, 26 Val. U.L. Rev. 419, 425 (1991).

77   *See* Randy E. Barnett, *A Ninth Amendment for Today's Constitution*, 26 Val. U.L. Rev. 419, 425 (1991).

78   Letter from Thomas Jefferson to Francis W. Gilmer Monticello (June 7. 16, 1816).

79   *Mugler v. Kansas*, 123 U.S. 623, 661 (1887).

80   *Watson v. Thompson*, 321 F. Supp. 394, 401 (E.D. Tex. 1971) (5th Cir. 1972) (Justice, J.).

CHAPTER 22

1   Murray N. Rothbard, *What's Wrong with Conservatism*, LewRockwell.com, originally published in Modern Age, 5, 2 (Spring 1961), pp. 217-220.

2   Edward Gibbon published his six-volume set *The History of the Decline and Fall of the Roman Empire* between 1776 and 1789. Gibbon's works were some of the most borrowed library books by the members of the First Congress when it met in New York in 1789. Bordewich, Chapter 7, note 2, at 112.

3   U.S. Const. amend. IX.

4   While Gerald Dworkin may quibble that it is actually three separate principles. Gerald Dworkin, *Paternalism*, in Joel Feinberg, et al., Philosophy of Law 451 (9th ed. 2014). I do not believe it to be so as neither of these can

stand on their own, nor do I believe that any two can be derived from a single third.

5   Gerald Dworkin in Paternalism 19 (Rolf Sartorius ed., 1 ed. 1984).

6   *See, e.g.,* Dworkin in Joel Feinberg, et al., Chapter 22, note 4, at 457.

7   While absolute necessity may absolve a person of facing *criminal* consequences for such behavior, it would not necessarily permit them to escape the civil consequences of such an action in which the original owner may seek damages or some other form of restitution to restore them to state in which they were *before* the property was taken.

8   Dworkin in Joel Feinberg, et al., Chapter 22, note 4, at 457 (emphasis in original).

9   Self-ownership, of course, is a truism—except, according to Rothbard, in children until they reach a certain age. Rothbard's Egalitarianism, Chapter 16, note 86, at 149. Absent Rothbard's declaration, anyone can reasonably derive the self-ownership beginning with the Cartesian *"cogito, ergo sum"* [I think, therefore I am] through the derivative use of the power of the mind to control the body and necessity of self-ownership as extending from the notion of self or ego.

10 This at some level and in a clearer manner incorporates the legal concept woven into any scheme of appeal based on right and as ancient as St. Thomas—*lex iniustia est non lex* [an unjust law is no law], or, as Locke expresses it, the arbitrary exercise of powers is unjustifiable (and unconstitutional in the American order).

11 Joel Feinberg, *The Nature and Value of Rights*, in Joel Feinberg, et al, Chapter 22, note 4, at 410-415.

BIBLIOGRAPHY

Adams, Charles Francis, Coolidfge, T. Jefferson, Green, Samuel A., and Upham, William P., "November Meeting, 1902. Diary of John Quincy Adams; Some Extracts from an Autobiography." *Proceedings of the Massachusetts Historical Society*, volume 16. Massachusetts Historical Society. 1902.

Adams, Henry. *History of The United States During The Administration of Thomas Jefferson*. Earl N. Harbert ed., 1986.

Adams, John. *Diary and Autobiography of John Adams, vol. 3, Diary, 1782–1804; Autobiography, Part One to October 1776*. Cambridge, MA: Harvard University Press, 1961.

Adams, John, "Letter from John Adams to Abigail Adams (Jul. 3, 1776)." Reprinted in *Adams Family Correspondence*.

Adams, John, "Notes of Debates in the Continental Congress." *Diary of John Adams*. L. H. Butterfield ed., 1962.

Adams, John. *The Works of John Adams*. Boston: Little, Brown. 1854.

Adams, John. *The Works of John Adams Vol. 4: Novanglus, Thoughts on Government, Defence of the Constitution*. Charles Francis Adams ed., Charles C. Little and James Brown. 1851.

Adams, John, "To the Inhabitants of the Colony of Massachusetts-Bay, 23 January 1775." *Papers of John Adams*, vol. 2, December 1773–April 1775. Cambridge, MA: Harvard University Press, 1977.

Adams, Samuel, "The Rights of the Colonists." *The Report of the Committee of Correspondence to the Boston Town Meeting*. 1772.

Alexander, John K. *Samuel Adams: America's Revolutionary Politician*. Rowman & Littlefield. 2004.

Alexander, Roberta, "Dred Scott: The Decision that Sparked a Civil War." *Northern Kentucky Law Review*. 2007.

Alschuler, Albert. Law Without Values, *The Life, Work And Legacy of Justice Holmes*. University of Chicago Press, 2000.

Antieau, Chester James, "Natural Rights And The Founding Fathers-The Virginians." *Wash. & Lee L. Rev.* Vol. 17. 1960.

Aptheker, Herbert. *The American Revolution 1763-1783: A History of the American People, An Interpretation*. New York: International Publishers. 1960.

Aquinas, St. Thomas, "Quaestiones Disputatae De Veritate XVII." *St. Thomas Aquinas Philosophical Texts*. 1952.

Aquinas, St. Thomas. *Summa Theologica*, I-II Q. 94.

Areli, Yehoshua. *Individualism And Nationalism In American Ideology.* Cambridge, Mass; Harvard University Press, 1964.

Aristotle. *On Rhetoric: A Theory of Civic Discourse.*

Aristotle. *Politics*, Book 1.

Augustine, *On The Free Choice of The Will, on Grace and Free Choice, and Other Writings,* Peter King ed., trans., 2010.

Bailyn, Bernard. *Faces of The Revolution: Personalities & Themes In The Struggle For American Independence.* 1990.

Barnes, Robert, "Supreme Court Justice Antonin Scalia dies at 79." Wash. Post. 2016.

Barnett, Randy E., "A Ninth Amendment for Today's Constitution." *Valparaiso University Law Review.* Vol. 26. 1991.

Barnett Randy E., & Kates, Don B., "Under Fire: The New Consensus on the Second Amendment." *Emory Law Journal.* Vol. 45. 1996.

Barnett, Randy, "Necessary and Proper." *UCLA Law Review*, 1997.

Barnett, Randy. E. *Restoring The Lost Constitution: The Presumption of Liberty.* Princeton University Press, 2004.

Barnett, Randy E., *Rights Retained By The People: The History And Meaning of The Ninth Amendment.* 1989.

Barnett, Randy E., "The Ninth Amendment: It Means What It Says," *Tex. L. Rev.* 2006.

Barnett, Randy E., "The Original Meaning of the Commerce Clause." *University of Chicago Law Review.* Volume 68. 2001.

Barnett, Randy, "The Original Meaning of the Necessary and Proper Clause." *University of Pennsylvania Journal of Constitutional Law*, 2003.

Barnett, Randy E., "The Relevance of the Framer's Intent." *Harvard Journal of Law and Public Policy.* 1996.

Barnett, Randy. *The Structure of Liberty: Justice And The Rule of Law*, 2nd ed.,. Oxford University Press, 2014.

Bates, Christina M., "From 34 Cents to 37 Cents: The Unconstitutionality of the Postal Monopoly." *Missouri Law Review,* 2003.

Bayer, Ronald, "Heroin Decriminalization and the Ideology of Tolerance: A Critical View." *Law & Society Review.* Vol. 12. 1978.

Bayne, David C., "The Supreme Court and the Natural Law." DePaul Law. Review. 1952.

Beard, Charles. *An Economic Interpretation of The Constitution of The United States.* Dover Publications. 2004.

Beeman, Richard. *Plain, Honest Men: The Making of The American Constitution.* 2009.

Bell, Tom W., "The Third Amendment: Forgotten but Not Gone." *WM. & Mary Bill RTS. J.* Vol.2. 1993.

Benkler, Yochai, "The U.S. Supreme Court needs to keep up with our cellphones- and the NSA." *The Guardian,* 2014.

Bentham, Jeremy. *A Comment on the Commentaries and a Fragment on Government.* Univ. of London Athlone Press, 1977.

Bentham, Jeremy. *An Introduction To The Principles of Morals And Legislation.* 1776.

Bernstein, David E. *Rehabilitating Lochner: Defending Individual Rights Against Progressive Reform.* University of Chicago Press, 2011.

Beschle, Donald L., "Lawrence Beyond Gay Rights: Taking the Rationality Requirement for Justifying Criminal Statutes Seriously." *Drake Law Review.* 2005.

Billy, Michael. *Lysander Spooner and the United States Postal Monopoly.* digitaljournal.com, 2009.

Blackstone, William. *The Oxford Edition of Blackstone's: Commentaries on the Laws of England: Book I, II, III, and IV.* Oxford University Press. 2016.

Bordewich, Fergus. *The First Congress How James Madison, George Washington, And A Group of Extraordinary Men Invented Government.* Simon & Schuster Paperbacks. 2017.

Boston, William Emmons. *The Trial of The British Soldiers of The 29th Regiment of Foot,* 1863.

Bowen, Catherine Drinker. *The Lion And The Throne: The Life And Times of Sir Edward Coke (1522-1634.* Little Brown & Co., Reissue ed. 1990

Bowen, Catherine Drinker. *The Miracle At Philadelphia.* Back Bay Books. 1986.

Bowen, Catherine Drinker. *Yankee From Olympus Justice Holmes And His Family.* Little, Brown & Co. 1945.

Bradburn, Douglas. *The Citizenship Revolution: Politics and The Creation of The American Union, 1774-1804,* 2009.

Brest, Paul, "The Original Understanding." *Boston University Law Review.* Vol.60. 1980.

Brett, Annabel, "Natural Right and Civil Community: The Civil Philosophy of Hugo Grotius." *The Historical Journal.* Cambridge University Press. 2002.

Brust, Steven J., "Retrieving a Catholic Tradition of Subjective Natural Rights from the Law Scholastic Francisco Suarez, S.J." *Ave Maria Law Review.* Vol. 10. 2002.

Campbell, Jud, "Natural Rights and the First Amendment." *Yale Law Journal.* 2017.

Cane, Peter, "Taking Law Seriously: Starting Points of the Hart/Devlin Debate." *The Journal of Ethics.* Volume 10. 2006.

Carozza, Paolo G., "They are our brothers, and Christ gave His life for them": The Catholic Tradition and the Idea of Human Rights in Latin America." *Notre Dame Law School.* 2003.

Chesney, Robert M., "Democratic-Republican Societies, Subversion, and the Limits of Legitimate Political Dissent in the Early Republic." *N.C. L. Rev.* 1525, 1533. 2004.

Chroust, Anton-Hermann, "Hugo Grotius and the Scholastic Natural Law Tradition." *New Scholasticism.* 1943.

Chroust, Anton-Hermann, "The Fundamental Ideas in St. Augustine's Philosophy of Law," *American Journal of Jurisprudence*: Vol. 18. 1973.

Chroust, Anton-Hermann, "The Philosophy of Law of St. Thomas Aquinas: His Fundamental Ideas and Some of His Historical Precursors." *The American Journal of Jurisprudence*, 1974.

Churchill, Robert. *To Shake Their Guns In The Tyrant's Face: Libertarian Political Violence And The Origins of The Militia Movement.* The University of Michigan Press. 2012.

Clancy, Thomas K., "The Framers' Intent: John Adams, His Era, and the Fourth Amendment." *Indian Law Journal.* 2011.

Coakley, Robert W. & Conn, Stetson. *The War of The American Revolution Narrative, Chronology, And Bibliography.* 1975.

Cogan, Neil H. *The Complete Bill of Rights: The Drafts, Debates, Sources, And Origins.*1997.

Cooley, Thomas M. *Commentaries on the Laws of England.* Chicago: Callaghan And Company, 1884.

Cooley, Thomas. *The General Principles of Constitutional Law In The United States of America,* 1st ed. American Foundation Publication, 1880.

Corwin, Edwin S., "The "Higher Law" Background of American Constitutional Law." *Harvard Law Review.* Volume 42. 1928.

Corwin, Edwin S. *The Natural Law and Constitutional Law.* 1949.

Crowe, M.B. "The "Impious Hypothesis": A Paradox in Hugo Grotius?" *Tijdschrift Voor Filosofie. 1976.*

Cullen, Charles T., "New Light on John Marshall's Legal Education and Admission to the Bar." *The American Journal of Legal History.* Vol.16. Oxford University Press. 1972.

De Bracton, Henry. *On The Laws and Customs of England,* George E. Woodbine ed., Samuel S. Thorne trans. 1968 (c. 1235)

de Littleton, Thomas. *Lyttleton, His Treatise of Tenures, in French and English. a New Edition, Printed from the Most Ancient Copies, and Collated with the Various Readings.* 1970.

de Maglie, Cristina, "Punishing Mere Immorality? Skeptical Thoughts from A Comparative Perspective." *Berkeley Journal of Criminal Law.* 2018.

Devlin, Patrick. *The Enforcement of Morals,* 7th ed. Oxford: Oxford University Press, 1970.

Dickerson, Oliver M. *The Navigation Acts and the American Revolution.* University of Pennsylvania Press. 1951.

Dienstag, Joshua Foa, "Between History and Nature: Social Contract Theory in Locke and the Founders." *The Journal of Politics.* Volume 58. 1996.

Drahozal, Christopher R., "On Tariffs v. Subsidies in Interstate Trade: A Legal and Economic Analysis." *Wash. Univ. L. Rev.* Volume 74. 1996.

Dworkin, Ronald M., "Lord Devlin and the Enforcement of Morals." *Yale Law Journal,* 1966.

Eisgruber, Christopher L.M., "Justice Story, Slavery, and the Natural Law Foundations of American Constitutionalism." *University of Chicago Law Review.* 1988.

Elliot, Jonathan, "Elliot's Debates." *Journals of the Continental Congress.*

Elliot, Jonathan, "The Debates in The Several State Conventions on The Adoption of The Federal Constitution as Recommended by The General Convention at Philadelphia in 1781." *Journal of The federal Convention*. 1996.

Ellis, Joseph J. *American Creation Triumphs And Tragedies At The Founding of The American Republic.* 2007.

Ely, James. *The Guardian of Every Other Right: A Constitutional History of Property Rights.* Oxford University Press, 2008.

Feldman, Noah. *The Three Lives of James Madison Genius, Partisan, President.* 2017.

Feinberg, Joel. *Harm To Others: The Moral Limits of The Criminal law.* Oxford University Press, 1984.

Finnis, John, "Natural Law and Legal Reasoning." *Clev. St. L. Rev.* 1990.

Finnis, John. *Natural Law and Natural Rights*, 2nd ed.

Frank, Jerome. *Law And The Modern Mind.* New York: Brentano's Inc.,1930.

Freedman, Eric M., "Milestones in Habeas Corpus: Part I Just Because John Marshall Said It, Doesn't Make It So: Ex Parte Bollman and the Illusory Prohibition on the Federal Writ of Habeas Corpus for State Prisoners in the Judiciary Act of 1789." *Alabama Law Review*. Volume 51. 2000.

Friede, Juan, and Keen, Benjamin. B*artolomé De Las Casas In History: Toward An Understanding of His Work*. Northern Illinois University Press, 1971.

Friedman, Barry, & Lakier, Genevieve, "To Regulate," Not "To Prohibit": Limiting the Commerce Power." *The Supreme Court Review.* 2012.

Fuller, Lon L., "Positivism and Fidelity to Law—A Reply to Professor Hart." *Harvard Law Review.* Volume 71. 1958.

Fuller, Lon L., "The Case of the Speluncean Explorers." *Harvard Law Review.* Volume 62. 1949.

Fuller, Lon. L. *The Morality of Law.*

Garner, Bryan A. *A Dictionary of Modern Legal Usage*, 2 ed. Oxford Univ. Press, 1991.

George, Robert P., "Holmes on Natural Law." *Villanova Law Review.* Volume 4. 2003.

George, Robert P., "Natural Law." *Harvard Journal of Law and Public Policy.* Volume 31. 2008.

George, Robert P., "The 1993 St. Ives Lecture - Natural Law and Civil Rights: From Jefferson's "Letter to Henry Lee" to Martin Luther King's "Letter From Birmingham Jail,"" *Catholic University Law Review.* 1994.

Gerry, Elbridge. *Letter to the State Legislature of Massachusetts.* 1787.

Gewirth, Alan. *The Ontological Basis of Natural Law: A Critique and An Alternative, American Journal of Jurisprudence*: Vol. 29: Iss. 1, Article 5. 1984.

Gierke, Otto. *Natural Law and the Theory of Society 1500 to 1800.* Cambridge University Press, 1950.

Glendon, Mary Ann, "The Forgotten Crucible: The Latin American Influence on the Universal Human Rights Idea." *Harvard Human Rights Journal.* Vol. 16.

Gray, David, and Citron, Danielle, "The Right to Quantitative Privacy."
Minnesota Law Review. 2013.

Grey, Thomas C., "Origins of the Unwritten Constitution: Revolutionary
Thought." *Stanford Law Review*. 1987.

Grotius, Hugo. *De Jure Belli Et Pacis Libri Tres*. 1625.

Grotius, Hugo. *The Law of War and Peace*.1625.

Haakonssen, Knud, "Natural Law And Moral Philosophy, From Grotius to The
Scottish Enlightenment." *Mind*. Vol. 109. Oxford University Press. 2000.

Haines, Charles Grove, "The American Doctrine of Judicial Supremacy."
University of Pennsylvania Law Review and American Law Register, Vol.1.
The University of Pennsylvania Law Review. 1933.

Hale's, Sir Matthew. *Historia Placitorum Coronae. The History of the Pleas of
the Crown*. Oxford University. 1800.

Hall, Mark David. *The Political And Legal Philosophy of James Wilson 1742-
1798*. Univ of Missouri Pr. 1997.

Hamburger, M., "Morals And The Law: The Growth of Aristotle's Legal Theory."
Harvard Law review. 1951.

Hamilton, Alexander, & Madison, James. *The Pacificus-Helvidius Debates of
1793-1794*. Morton J. Frisch, ed. 2007.

Hamilton, Alexander. *The Farmer Refuted*. 1775.

Hamilton, Marci A. "Religious Institutions, the No-Harm Doctrine, and the Public
Good." *Brigham Young University Law Review*. 2004.

Hammelmann, H.A., "Committee on Homosexual Offences and Prostitution."
The Modern Law Review. Volume 21. 1958.

Handler, Alan B., "Judicial Jurisprudence." *New Jersey Law Journal*. 2000.

Han, Tomislav. *The Transformation of Aristotelian Political Epistemology in
Eighteenth-Century American Constitutional Discourse*. 2003.

Hart, H.L.A., "Positivism and the Separation of Law and Morals." *Harvard Law
Review*. Volume 71. 1958.

Hart, H. L. A. *The Concept of Law*. Oxford University Press.

Hart, H. L. A. *The Morality of Criminal Law*. 1965.

Haskins, C. H., "The Yazoo Land Companies." *The American Historical
Association*. 1891.

Hazlitt, Henry. *The Foundations of Morality*. The Foundation for Economic
Education, Inc., 2010.

Helmholz, Richard H., "Natural Law and Human rights in English Law: From
Bracton to Blackstone." *Ave Maria Law Review*.

Helmholz, R. H. *Natural Law in Court: A History of Legal Theory in Practice*.
Harvard University Press, 2015.

Hill, John Lawrence, "The Constitutional Status of Morals Legislation." *Kentucky
Law Journal*. Vol. 98. 2010.

Holmes, Oliver Wendell, "The Path of the Law." *Harvard Law Review*.

Holmes, Oliver Wendell, "The Theory of Interpretation." *Harvard Law Review*.
Volume 12. 1899.

Hume, David. *A Treatise On Human Nature*. Clarendon Press, Oxford, 1888.

Hume, David. *The History of England From The Invasion of Julius Caesar to The Revolution In 1688*, Vol. 6. Indianapolis: Liberty Fund. 1983

Hutchinson, Thomas. *The History of The Province of Massachusetts Bay, From 1749 to 1774*. 1828.

Jefferson, Thomas, "Letter from Thomas Jefferson to Noah Webster, Jr." *18 Papers of Thomas Jefferson.* 1971.

Jefferson, Thomas. *A Summary View of the Rights of British America*. 1774.

Jefferson, Thomas. *7 Works of Thomas Jefferson.*

Jefferson, Thomas. *Letter from Thomas Jefferson to Issac H. Tiffany, Monticello.* 1819.

Jensen, Merrill, and Kaminski, John P. *The Documentary History of the Ratification of the Constitution of the United States, Constitutional Documents and Records, 1776-1787*. University of Wisconsin Press. 1976.

Kainz, Howard P. *Natural Law: An Introduction and Reexamination. Open Coyrt Publishing Company,* 2004.

Kelly, Brent P., & Schlesinger, Arthur M., *James Madison: Father of The Constitution*. 2000.

Kelley, James F., "The Uncertain Renaissance of the Ninth Amendment." *University of Chicago Law Review. Rev.* Vol. 33. 1966.

Kidd, Thomas S. *God of Liberty: A Religious History of The American Revolution.* Basic Books, 2010.

Kolakowski, Leszek. *Is God Happy? On Natural law*, 250 (2013).

Kroger, John, "The Philosophical Foundations of Roman Law: Aristotle, The Stoics, and Roman Theories of Natural Law." 2004.

Labunksi, Richard. *James Madison And The Struggle For The Bill of Rights.* 2006.

Lash, Kurt T., "Rejecting Conventional Wisdom: Federalist Ambivalence in the Framing and Implementation of Article V." *American Journal of Legal History*, Volume 38, Issue 2, April 1994.

Lash, Kurt T., "The Lost Original Meaning of the Ninth Amendment." *Tex. L. Rev.* 2004.

Lasson, Nelson B. *The History And Development of The Fourth Amendment To The United States*. 1970.

Lisska, Anthony J. *Aquinas's Theory of Natural Law An Analytic Reconstruction.* 1996.

Lee, Daniel, "Popular Liberty, Princely Government, and the Roman Law in Hugo Grotius's "De Jure Belli Ac Pacis." *Grotius and Law*. 2011.

Lewis Hanke, "All Mankind Is One: A Study of The Disputation Between Bartolome De Las Casas And Juan Gines De Sepulveda In 1550 On The Religious And Intellectual Capacity of The American Indians." *Northern Illinois University Press.* 1974.

Liptak, Adam, "Antonin Scalia, Justice on the Supreme Court, Dies at 79." New York Times. 2016.

Locke, John, "A Second Letter Concerning Toleration." in *The Works of John Locke*. 2nd ed. 1722.

Locke, John. *Two Treatises On Government*. George Routledge and Sons. 1884.

Long, Roderick T., "Aristotle's Concept of Freedom." *The Review of Metaphysics. 1996.*

Lovejoy, David S., "Rights Imply Equality: The Case against Admiralty Jurisdiction in America, 1764–1776." *The William and Mary Quarterly.* 1959.

Loveless, A. Scott, "The Forgotten Founding Document: Considering the Ends of the Law." Brigham Young University Journal of Public Law. Volume. 27. 2013.

Lynch, Joseph M., "Fletcher v. Peck: The Nature of the Contacts Clause." Seton Hall L. Rev. Vol. 13. 1982.

Lynd, Staughton, "Abraham Yates' History of the Movement for the U.S. Constitution." *The William and Mary Quarterly.* Vol. 20. Omohundro Institute of Early American History and Culture. 1963.

Machan, Tibor R. *Liberty and Democracy*, 1st ed. 2002.

Maclin, Tracey, "The Central Meaning of the Fourth Amendment." *WM. & Mary L. Rev.* Vol. 35. 1993.

Madison, James, "A Candid State of Parties." *Nat'l Gazette.* 1792.

Madison, James. *James Madison to George Washington,* (Mar. 19, 1789). *reprinted in* 5 Writings of James Madison 1787-1790 329 (Gaillard Hunt ed., 1904).

Madison, James. *The Debates In The Federal Convention of 1787 Which Framed The Constitution of The United States of America.* New York: Oxford University Press, 1920.

Maier, Pauline. *From Resistance To Revolution: Colonial Radicals And The Development of American Opposition To Britain, 1765-1776.* Norton Paperback. 1991.

Maier, Pauline. *Ratification The People Debate The Constitution, 1787-1788.* 2010.

Maitland, Frederic William, and Pollock, Sir Frederick. *The History of English Law before the Time of Edward I: In Two Volumes.*

Marcus, Maeva. *The Documentary History of the Supreme Court of the United States, 1789-1800.* Columbia University Press. 2004.

Marquette Law Review, "Legal Philosophers: Aristotle, Aquinas and Kant on Human Rights." *Marquette Law Review.* 1972.

Martin, Douglas, "John Rawls, Theorist on Justice, Is Dead at 82." *New York Times,* 2002.

Martin, Douglas, "Mildred Loving, Who Battled Ban on Mix-Race Marriage, Dies at 68." *N. Y. Times,* 2008.

McConnell, Donald R, "Nature in Natural Law." *Liberty University Law Review*: Vol. 2: Iss. 3, Article 8. 2008.

McCutcheon, J. Paul, "Morality and the Criminal Law: Reflections on Hart-Devlin." *Crim. L. Q.,* 2002.

McDougall, Walter A. *Freedom Just Around The Corner A New American History 1585-1812.* 2004.

Mendelson, Wallace, "New Light on Fletcher v. Peck and Gibbons v. Ogden." *The Yale Law Journal.* Volume 58. 1949.

Meese III, Edwin, "Law of the Constitution." *Tulane Law Review.* 1987.

Mill, John Stuart. *A System of Logic.* 1843.

Mill, John Stuart. *August Comte And Positivism.* 1865.

Mill, John Stuart. *Considerations on Representative Government.* 1861.

Mill, John Stuart. *Essays on Some Unsettled Questions of Political Economy.* 1844.

Mill, John Stuart. *On Liberty*, 2ed, 1863.

Mill, John Stuart. *The Principles of Political Economy: With Some of Their Applications to Social Philosophy.* 1848.

Mill, John Stuart. *The Subjection of Women.* 1869.

Mill, John Stuart. *Three Essays on Religion.* 1874.

Mill, John Stuart. *Utilitarianism.* 1863.

Milton, John. *Areopagitica: A Speech to The Parliament of England For The Liberty of Unlicensed Printing.* T. Holt White, Esq. ed., 1819.

Minton, Clarence E., "The Natural Law Philosophy of the Founding Fathers." *U. Of Notre Dame Natural L. Inst. Proc.* 1949.

Morgan, Edmund S., *Inventing The People: The Rise of Popular Sovereignty In England And America.* W W Norton & Co. 1988.

Morgan, Edmund S., & Morgan, Helen S. *The Stamp Act Crisis.* 1995.

Morgenthau, Hans J., "Positivism, Functionalism, and International Law." *American Journal of International Law.* 1940.

Mullet, Charles F., "Classical Influences on the American Revolution." *Classical J.* 1939.

Nadler, Steven. *Spinoza: A Life.* Cambridge Univ. Press, 1999.

Napolitano, Andrew P., "Health-Care Reform and the Constitution: Why hasn't the Commerce Clause been read to allow interstate insurance sales?" *The Wall Street Journal.* 2009.

Napolitano, Andrew P., "Suicide Pact: The Radical Expansion of Presidential Powers And The Lethal Threat To American Liberty." *The Independent Review.* Volume 20. 2015.

Napolitano, Andrew P. *The Constitution In Exile.* 2006.

Nelson, Grant S., and Pushaw Jr., Robert J., "Rethinking the Commerce Clause: Applying First Principles to Uphold Federal Commercial Regulations but Preserve State Control over Social Issues." *Iowa Law Review.* 1999.

Nemeth, Charles P. *Aquinas in The Courtroom: Lawyers, Judges, and Judicial Conduct.* 2001.

Natelson, Robert G., "The Founders Interpret the Constitution: The Division of Federal and State Powers." *Federalist Society Review*, Volume 19. 2018.

Nozick, Robert. *Anarchy, State, And Utopia.* Basic Books, 2013.

Nussbaum, Martha C. *Capabilities and Human Rights.* 1997.

O. Brooks, Richard & Murphy, James Bernard. *Aristotle and Modern Law.* 2003.

Oppenheimer, David Benjamin, "Martin Luther King, Walker v. City of Birmingham, and the Letter from a Birmingham Jail." *UC Davis Law Review.* 1993.

Otis, James. "Rights of British Colonies Asserted and Proved." (*Pamphlet*) 1763.

Pace, Eric, "Harry S. Ashmore, 81, Whose Editorials Supported Integration in Arkansas, Dies." *N. Y. Times.* 1998.

Paine, Thomas. *The Writings of Thomas Paine.* Vol. 1. Collected and Edited by Moncure Daniel Conway. New York: G.P. Putnam's Sons, 1894.

Park, Mitchell F., "Defining One's Own Concept of Existence and the Meaning of the Universe: The Presumption of Liberty in Lawrence v. Texas." *Brigham Young University Law Review.* 2006.

Paul, Joel Richard. *Without Precedent: Chief Justice John Marshall and His Times.* 2018.

Pinker, Steven. *The Better Angels of Our Nature Why Violence Has Declined.* Penguin Books. 2012

Pope, Thaddeus Mason, "Balancing Public Health Against Individual Liberty: The Ethics of Smoking Regulations." *University of Pittsburgh Law Review.* 2000.

Post, Robert, "Religion and Freedom of Speech: Portraits of Muhammad." *Constitutional Secularism in an Age of Religious Revival.* Oxford University Press, 2014.

Pound, Roscoe, "Grotius in the Science of Law." *The American Journal of International Law, Vol.19.* Cambridge University Press. 1925.

Pound, Roscoe. *The Development of Constitutional Guarantees of Liberty.* New Haven: Yale University Press. 1957.

Preston, Jr., Wilbur D., "The Due Process Clause as a Limitation on the Reach of State Legislation: An Historical and Analytical Examination of Substantive Due Process." *University of Baltimore Law Review.* Volume 8. 1978.

Price, Polly J., "Natural Law and Birthright Citizenship in Calvin's Case (1603)." *Yale J. of L. & Human.* 1997.

Priel, Dan, "Jurisprudence Between Science and the Humanities." *Washington University Jurisprudence Review.* Volume 4, Issue 2. 2012

Priel, Dan, "Toward Classic Legal Positivism." *Virginia Law Review.* Volume 101. 2015.

Qunicy, Jr., Josiah. *Reports of Cases Argued and Adjudged in the Superior Court of Judicature of the Province of Massachusetts Bay Between 1761 and 1772.* Little, Brown & Co. 1865.

Rapp, Hans, "Grotius and Hume on Natural Religion and Natural Law." *Archiv Für Rechts-Und Sozialphilosophie.*

Rawls, John. *A Theory of Justice,* Revised 2nd Edition. Harvard University Press, 1999.

Raz, Joseph. *Ethics In The Public Domain: Essays In The Morality of Law And Politics.* Oxford University Press, 1995.

Read, James H., "Our Complicated System: James Madison on Power and Liberty." Pol. Theory, Volume 23. Sage Publications, Inc. 1995.

Reynolds, David, "Worse Than 'Dred Scott.'" *The Wall Street Journal*, 2015.

Richards, David A. J., "Liberalism, Public Morality, and Constitutional Law: Prolegomenon to a Theory of the Constitutional Right to Privacy." *Law And Contemporary Problems*. Vol 51. 1988.

Richards, Peter Judson, "Hugo Grotius, Hosti Humani Generis, and the Natural Law in Time Of War," *Liberty University Law Review*: Vol. 2: Iss. 3, Article 11. 2008.

Ristroph, Alice, "Sovereignty and Subversion." *101 Virginia Law Review*. 2015.

Roelofsen, C.G., "Grotius and International Law an Introduction to Some Themes in the Field of the Grotian Studies." *Grotius Reader*.

Rommen, Heinrich. *The Natural Law: A Study In Legal And Social History And Philosophy*. Indianapolis: Liberty Fund, 1998.

Ronald J. Rychlak, *Natural Law from a Birmingham Jail*. 2011.

Rothbard, Murray N. *Conceived In Liberty*. Ludwig Von Mises Institute, 2011.

Rothbard, Murray N. *Egalitarianism As A Revolt Against Nature And Other Essays*. Ludwig von Mises Institute, 2000.

Rothbard, Murray N., "Law, Property Rights, And Air Pollution." *Cato Journal*. Volume 2. 1982.

Russell, Bertrand. *The History of Western Philosophy*. Simon & Schuster Touchstone, 1967.

Sankaran, S. R., "Police Reforms: Need to Review Power to Arrest." *Economic & Political Weekly*. Vol. 35. 2000.

Scalia, Antonin. *Scalia Speaks: Reflections On Law, Faith, And Life Well Lived*. Crown Forum, 2017.

Schauer, Frederick and Wise, Virginia J., "Legal Positivism as Legal Information." *Cornell L. Rev.*1997.

Schauer, Frederick, "Positivism before Hart." *The Canadian Journal of Law & Jurisprudence*. 2011.

Schauer, Frederick, "The Path-Dependence of Legal Positivism." *Virginia Law Review*. 2015.

Schwartz, David S., "Misreading McCulloch v. Maryland." *University of Pennsylvania Journal of Constitutional Law*. Volume 18. 2015.

Sebok, Anthony J., "Misunderstanding Positivism." *Mich. L. Rev.* 1995.

Senior, Jennifer, "In Conversation: Antonin Scalia." *New York Magazine*, 2013.

Shelfer, Lochlan F., "Special Juries in the Supreme Court." *Yale Law Journal*. (2013).

Sidney, Algernon. *Discourses Concerning Government*. Indianapolis: Liberty Fund. 1996.

Simmons, A. John, "Locke and the Right to Punish." *Philosophy & Public Affairs*. Vol 20. 1991.

Slack, Charles. *Liberty's First Crisis: Adams, Jefferson And The Misfits Who Saved Free Speech*. Atlantic Monthly Press. 2015.

Smelser, Marshall. "George Washington and the Alien and Sedition Acts." *The American Historical Review*. Vol.59. 1954.

Smith, Adam. *An Inquiry Into The Nature And Causes of The Wealth of Nations*. David Buchanan ed.,. 1814.

Smith, Jean Edward. *John Marshall: Definer of A Nation*. Holt Paperbacks. 1998.

Spooner, Lysander. *Natural Law; or the Science of Justice: A Treatise on Natural Law, Natural Justice, Natural Rights, Natural Liberty, and Natural Society; showing that all Legislation whatsoever is an Absurdity, a Usurpation, and a Crime. Part First*. Boston: A Williams & Co., 1882.

Spooner, Lysander. *The Unconstitutionality of the Laws of Congress, prohibiting Private Mails*. American Letter Mail Company. 1844.

Stinneford, John F., "The Original Meaning of Unusual: The Eighth Amendment as a Bar to Cruel Innovation." *Nw. U. L. Rev.* Vol.102. 2008.

Stoner, Jr., James R. *Common Law and Liberal Theory: Coke, Hobbes and the Origins of American Constitutionalism*. 1992.

Stolzenberg, Nomi Maya, "Bentham's Theory of Fictions--A "Curious Double Language." *Cardozo Studies in Law and Literature*. Vol. 11. Taylor & Francis, Ltd. 1999.

Story, Joseph. *Commentaries On The Constitution of The United States: With A Preliminary Review Of The Constitutional History of The Colonies And States, Before The Adoption of The Constitution*. Hillard, Gray & Co. 1833.

Stout, David, "Murray N. Rothbard, Economist And Free-Market Exponent." New York Times, 1995.

Strang, Lee J. "Originalism and Legitimacy." *Kansas Journal of Law & Public Policy*, 2002.

Strass, David R., "Why the Supreme Court Justices Should Ride Circuit Again." *Minn. L. Rev.* 2007.

Straumann, Benjamin. "Is Modern Liberty Ancient? Roman Remedies and Natural Rights in Hugo Grotius's Early Works on Natural Law." *L. & Hist. Rev.* 2009.

Strauss, Leo. *Natural Right And History*. The University of Chicago Press, 1953.

Suárez, Francisco. *Tractatus De Legibus Et Legislatore Deo*. Book. I. Carolo Berton ed., Paris, Ludovicum Vivès 1856.

Suárez, Francisco. *Tractatus Secundus: De Voluntario Et Involuntario in Genere, Deque Actibus Voluntariis in Speciali*, Bk. I.

Suess, Matthew K., "Punishment in the State of Nature: John Locke and Criminal Punishment in the United States of America." Wash. U. Jurisprudence Rev. Volume 7. 2015.

Snyder, David C., "Locke on Natural Law and Property Rights." *Canadian Journal of Philosophy*. Volume 16. 1986.

Taylor, Alan. *American Revolutions: A Continental History 1750-1804*. W.W. Norton & Company. 2016.

Tierney, Brian, "Historical Roots of Modern Rights: Before and Locke and After," *Ave Maria L. Rev.* 2005.

Tierney, Brian. *The Idea of Natural Rights: Studies On Natural Rights, Natural Law And Church Law, 1150-1625*. Scholars Press for Emory University, 1997.

Tomlinson, Brett, "The Continental Congress at Nassau Hall." *Princeton Alumni Weekly*. Oct. 1983.

Trethewey, Richard J., "The Economic Burden of the Sugar Act." *The American Economist*, Vol. 13. 1969.

Tribe, Laurence. *American Constitutional Law*. 1978.

Tribe, Laurence H., "Lawrence v. Texas: The "Fundamental Right" That Dare Not Speak Its Name." *Harvard Law Review*. 2004.

Turner, Lynn W., "The Impeachment of John Pickering." The American Historical Review. Volume 54. 1949.

Vermeulen, B. P. and Van Der Wal, G. A., "Grotius, Aquinas and Hobbes Grotian Natural Law between Lex Aeterna and Natural Rights." *Grotiana*. 1995.

Verschuuren, Gerard. *Matters of Life & Death: A Guide To The Moral Questions of Our Time*. Angelico Press, 2018.

Von Mises, Ludwig. *Liberty & Property*. Ludwig von Mises Institute. 2009.

Warner, Richard, "Liberalism and the Criminal Law." *Southern California Interdisciplinary Law Journal*. 1992.

Wagner, Henry Raup, "The Life And Writings of Bartolomé De Las Casas." *Hispanic American Historical Review*. 1968.

Washington, George, "Proclamation of Neutrality." *12 Papers of George Washington*. Worthington Chauncy Ford ed., 1891.

Wharton, Francis. *State Trials of The United States During The Administrations of Washington And Adams With References Historical And Professional, And Preliminary Notes On The Politics of The Times*. 1849.

Wilson, James, and Mckean, Thomas. *Commentaries on the Constitution of the United States of America With that Constitution*.

Wilson, James. *Considerations on Nature and Extent of the Legislative Authority of the British Parliament*. 1774.

Wilson, James. *Speech to Public Meeting in Philadelphia*. Oct. 6, 1787.

Wood, Gordon S. *Empire On Liberty: A History of The Early Republic, 1789-1815*. 2009.

Wood, Gordon S. *The American Revolution: A History*. Modern Library Paperback Ed., 2002.

Yoo, John, "George Washington and the Executive Power." *U. St. Thomas J.L. & Pub. Pol'y*.Vol.5. 2010.

Zuckert, Michael P., "Do Natural Rights Derive From Natural Law?" *Harv. J. L. & Pub. Pol'y*. 1997.

Zuckert, Michael P. *Natural Rights And The New Republicanism*. Princeton University Press. 1994.

Zuckert, Michael. *The Fullness of Being: Thomas Aquinas and the Modern Critique of Natural Law*, 2007.

INDEX

www.ingramcontent.com/pod-product-compliance
Lightning Source LLC
Chambersburg PA
CBHW050238270326
41914CB00041BA/2036/J